Functional Discourse Gramr

Functional Discourse Grammar

A typologically-based theory of language structure

KEES HENGEVELD AND
J. LACHLAN MACKENZIE

OXFORD
UNIVERSITY PRESS

OXFORD
UNIVERSITY PRESS

Great Clarendon Street, Oxford OX2 6DP

Oxford University Press is a department of the University of Oxford.
It furthers the University's objective of excellence in research, scholarship,
and education by publishing worldwide in

Oxford New York

Auckland Cape Town Dar es Salaam Hong Kong Karachi
Kuala Lumpur Madrid Melbourne Mexico City Nairobi
New Delhi Shanghai Taipei Toronto

With offices in

Argentina Austria Brazil Chile Czech Republic France Greece
Guatemala Hungary Italy Japan Poland Portugal Singapore
South Korea Switzerland Thailand Turkey Ukraine Vietnam

Oxford is a registered trade mark of Oxford University Press
in the UK and in certain other countries

Published in the United States
by Oxford University Press Inc., New York

British Library Cataloguing in Publication Data
Data available

Library of Congress Cataloging in Publication Data
Data available

Typeset by SPI Publisher Services, Pondicherry, India
Printed in Great Britain
by
CPI Antony Rowe, Chippenham, Wiltshire

ISBN 978–0–19–927810–7 (Hbk.)
ISBN 978–0–19–927811–4 (Pbk.)

1 3 5 7 9 10 8 6 4 2

Contents

Preface

At the Ninth International Conference on Functional Grammar (ICFG9), held in Madrid in September 2000, Kees Hengeveld proposed the idea of a Functional Discourse Grammar. At the time it was conceived of as a revised version of Functional Grammar (FG; Dik 1997a, 1997b), a theory of the organization of natural languages developed by the late Simon C. Dik and his colleagues from 1978 onwards, the year in which the first book bearing the title *Functional Grammar* appeared (Dik 1978). The addition of the word Discourse in the denomination of the model was meant to reflect the awareness that the impact of discourse features on linguistic form should be given greater prominence in the theory. A number of the features of FDG as presented in this book were already present in Hengeveld's (2000) presentation, notably: the distinction between an interpersonal, a representational, and a morphosyntactic level of analysis, all of them with hierarchical layering; the actional status of ascription and reference; the top-down operation of the model; the interaction of the grammatical component with the conceptual and contextual components; and the analysis of reflexive language use.

The ideas were taken up in lively discussion in the years following that conference, not least at ICFG10 in Amsterdam (The Netherlands), ICFG11 in Gijón (Spain), and ICFG12 in São João do Rio Preto (Brazil). This led to such collections as Mackenzie and Gómez-González (2004, 2005), de Groot and Hengeveld (2005), and García Velasco and Rijkhoff (2008), in which a range of scholars from various countries contributed to the development of a new architecture of the theory, with a strong desire to retain the best of FG while increasing the scope and ambition of the model.

Just like FG, FDG seeks to reconcile the patent fact that languages are structured complexes with the equally patent fact that they are adapted to function as instruments of communication between human beings. FDG has also inherited from its precursor the desire to achieve maximum typological neutrality: the theory is designed to be equally applicable to languages of all types, and indeed this book presents and analyses data from a very wide range of languages, resorting to exemplifying from more familiar languages only where the comprehensibility of the presentation makes this advisable.

However, FDG diverges from FG in so many ways that by now it should be considered a theory in its own right, and it has been recognized as such, as evidenced by encyclopaedia entries such as Hengeveld and Mackenzie (2006, fc.) and special issues of journals on FDG (van Staden and Keizer fc.; Hengeveld and Wanders fc.; Hattnher and Hengeveld 2007). FDG represents a significant advance on FG in separating out the Interpersonal Level and the Representational Level and investigating the full complexity of the former as well as the complex interaction between the two in determining linguistic form. It also differs from its predecessor in regarding the Morphosyntactic Level and the Phonological Level as more than mere expressions of the other Levels, but as having their own principles of organization; these are fully elaborated for the first time in this book. And finally, it differs crucially from FG in being a top-down rather than a bottom-up model. All in all, then, FDG has outgrown its intellectual origins and now offers an autonomous and balanced account of the systematic impact of pragmatic, semantic, morphosyntactic, and phonological phenomena on linguistic form.

The present book began life during a joint sabbatical of both authors in Amsterdam in 2004. It then continued to grow in the form of e-mail correspondence, with drafts being sent back and forth between Amsterdam and Lisbon when other commitments permitted. In the last phase Mackenzie was awarded a Visitor's Scholarship from the Netherlands Organization for Scientific Research (NWO) for the first months of 2007 under project number B30-664, when he was able to work together with Hengeveld on a daily basis in Amsterdam again. Mackenzie also wishes to acknowledge support received in the early days from the Spanish Ministry of Education, the European Regional Development Fund and the Xunta de Galicia under project number BFF2002-02441 (PGIDIT03PXIC20403PN), and Hengeveld is grateful for support provided by the Amsterdam Center for Language and Communication and the Department of Theoretical Linguistics of the University of Amsterdam.

We also wish to recognize the contribution of innumerable colleagues and students who over the past years have contributed their ideas, encouragement, and criticism to our enterprise of developing FDG. We were fortunate enough to be given the opportunity to present FDG at conferences, in postgraduate courses, and in guest lectures at many different places, and though we cannot name all those who contributed with their questions, remarks, and criticisms (for there have been so many), we would like to thank in general terms our audiences at ICFG10 (Amsterdam, The Netherlands, 2002), International Conference on Role and Reference Grammar (Logroño, Spain, 2002), LOT Winter School (Amsterdam, The Netherlands, 2003), Journées de Linguistique Fonctionelle (Agadir, Morocco, 2003), ACLC/ILLC-Colloquium (Amsterdam, The Netherlands, 2003), Københavns Universitet (Copenhagen, Denmark, 2003), Århus Universitet (Århus, Denmark, 2003), Örebro Universitet and Södertörn Högskola (Stockholm, Sweden, 2003), Universidad de Castilla La Mancha (Cuenca, Spain, 2003), Workshop on Grammar and Discourse (Ghent, Belgium, 2003), Universidade Estadual Paulista (São José do Rio Preto, Brazil, 2003, 2004), SIL International Training Programme (High Wycombe, UK, 2004), ESSE-7 (Zaragoza, Spain), 52° Seminário do GEL (Campinas, Brazil, 2004), ICFG11 (Gijón, Spain, 2004), ICFG12 (São José do Rio Preto, Brazil, 2006), Universidade Federal de Goiás (Goiânia, Brazil, 2006), TWIST Student Conference (Leiden, 2007), Workshop on the Representational Level in Functional Discourse Grammar (Zaandijk, 2007), Università degli Studi del Molise (Campobasso, Italy, 2007), Universidade Federal do Rio de Janeiro (Rio de Janeiro, Brazil, 2007), Universidade Federal Fluminense (Niterói, Brazil, 2007), Moulay Ismail University (Meknès, Morocco, 2007) and Universiteit van Amsterdam (Amsterdam, The Netherlands, 2007). Portions of this book were furthermore discussed at various occasions within the context of the Functional Grammar Colloquium at the University of Amsterdam, and these discussions have led to considerable improvements of the relevant parts. To all colleagues and students who participated in these events, our deepest gratitude.

We are grateful to John Davey of Oxford University Press for his constant support, his interest, and his advice.

Finally, we would like to give our special thanks to Inge Genee, Daniel García Velasco, and Gerry Wanders, who read the entire pre-final manuscript and generously gave us their detailed and invaluable comments. We hope they will find their highly appreciated feedback reflected in the current book.

Kees Hengeveld
Amsterdam

J. Lachlan Mackenzie
Lisbon

List of tables and figures

Tables

Figures

Abbreviations and symbols

Abbreviations used in glosses

1	first person	ASSV	associative
2	second person	ATTR	attributive
3	third person	AUG	augmentative
A	actor	AUX	auxiliary
ABIL	ability	AV	actor voice
ABL	ablative	AVOL	avolitional
ABS	absolutive	BEN	benefactive
ACC	accusative	CAUS	causative
ACQ	acquired	CERT	certain
ACTNR	action nominalizer	CL	class
ADH	adhortative	CLF	classifier
ADJR	adjectivalizer	CNTRL	control
ADMON	admonitive	COLL	collective
ADVR	adverbializer	COMM	commissive
AFF	affected	COMP	complementizer
AG	agent	COMPL	completive
AGR	agreement	COMPV	comparative
ALL	allative	COND	conditional
ANAPH	anaphoric	CONJ	conjunction
ANIM	animate	CONN	connective
ANR	agent nominalizer	CONT	continuative
ANT	anterior	CONTG	contingent
AOR	aorist	CONTR	contrastive
APPL	applicative	COP	copula
APPROX	approximative	CORR	correlative
ART	article	CV	conveyance voice
ASP	aspect	CVB	converb
ASS	assertive	DAT	dative

DECL	declarative	FOC	focus
DEF	definite	FUT	future
DEICT	deictic	GEN	genitive
DEM	demonstrative	GENR	general tense
DEP	dependent	GER	gerund
DET	determiner	HAB	habitual
DETRANS	detransitivizer	HEST	hesternal (happening yesterday)
DIM	diminutive		
DIR	direction	HOD	hodiernal (happening today)
DISHORT	dishortative		
DISP	dispensative	HON	honorific
DISTR	distributive	HORT	hortative
DOX	doxastic	HUM	human
DRCT	direct	IMM	immediate
DS	different subject	IMP	imperative
DU	dual	IMPF	imperfect
DUB	dubitative	IMPR	imprecative
DUM	dummy	INABIL	inability
DUR	durative	INAN	inanimate
DYN	dynamic	INCH	inchoative
EMPH	emphasis	INCL	inclusive
ERG	ergative	IND	indicative mood
ERGR	ergativizer	INDF	indefinite
ESS	essive	INDFTNS	indefinite tense
EX	existential	INDEP	independent
EX.PREV	previously existing	INESS	inessive
EXACT	exact ascription	INF	infinitive
EXCL	exclusive	INFER	inferential
EXCLAM	exclamative	INGR	ingressive
EXCT	exactly	INS	instrument
F	feminine	INT	intentive
FACT	factual	INTENS	intensifier
FAM	familiar	INTER	interrogative
FIN	finite	INTERP	interpellative

INTR	intransitive	NONPERC	non-perceived
INTR.ABIL	intrinsic ability	NONPST	non-past
INV	inverse	NONSBJ	non-subject
IRR	irrealis	NONTOP	non-topic
IRRAT	irrational	NONVIS	non-visual sensory evidence
ITER	iterative		
ITIVE	itive	NUCL	nucleus
LD	locative direction	OBJ	object
LK	linker	OBJP	objective paradigm
LOC	locative	OBJRESP	object of respect
LOCNR	locative nominalizer	OBJV	objective
LOG	logophoric	OBL	oblique
LV	locative voice	OBLG	obligation
M	male, masculine	OBV	obviative
MANN	manner	OPT	optative
MANN.NR	manner nominalizer	PART	particle
MIR	mirative	PARTV	partitive
MIT	mitigation	PASS	passive
MS	male speaker	PAUS	pause
N	neuter	PC	paucal
NARR	narrative	PERC	perceived
NEG	negative, negation	PERM	permanent
NEWTOP	new topic	PFV	perfective
NF	non-feminine	PL	plural
NFACT	non-factual	PLUP	pluperfect
NH	non-human	PM	predicate marker
NML	nominal	POL	polite
NMLZ	nominalizer	POS	positive
NOM	nominative	POSS	possessive
NON.A/S	non-nominative	POST	posterior
NON.INTER	non-interrogative	POT	potential
NONATTR	non-attributive	POTV	potentive voice
NONF	non-finite	PRED	predicate
NONFUT	non-future	PREP	preposition

PRES	presentative	RLS	realis
PRESUP	presupposed	S	argument of intransitive verb
PRF	perfect		
PRIV	privative	SBJ	subject
PROC	procrastinative	SBJV	subjunctive mood
PROF	profession	SEQ	sequence
PROG	progressive	SG	singular
PROH	prohibitive	SGLTV	singulative
PRONE	prone (to negative characteristic)	SIM	simultaneous
		SIT	situational
PROPR	proprietive	SPEC	specific
PROX	proximate	SRDIR	superdirective
PRS	present tense	SS	same subject
PST	past tense	STAT	stative
PTCP	participle	SUB	subordinator
PUNCT	punctual	SUBDIR	subdirective
Q	question marker	SUBESS	subessive
QUOT	quotative	SUBL	sublative
REALNR	realis nominalizer	SUBS	subsequent
REASNR	reason nominalizer	SUPPL	supplicative
REC	recipient	TAM	tense-aspect-mood
RECPST	recent past	TMPNR	temporal nominalizer
RED	reduplication		
REFL	reflexive	TNS	tense
REFR	referential	TOP	topic
REINF	reinforcement	TR	transitivity marker
REL	relativizer	U	undergoer
RELR	relator	UV	undergoer voice
REM	remote	VAL	validator
REP	reportative	VFIN	finite verb
REPV	repetitive	VIS	visible
RES	resultative	VIS.EVID	visual evidence
REV	reversative	VOC	vocative
		VOL	volitive

Abbreviations used in representations

General

⊂	is entailed by

Interpersonal Level

◆	lexeme
[±A]	± involving the addressee
[±S]	± involving the speaker
± for	± formal
± id	± identifiable
± s	± specific
A	addressee
A_1	discourse act
ADMON	admonitive
approx	approximative
Aside	aside
C_1	communicated content
COMM	commissive
Conc	concession
Cor	corrective
DECL	declarative
DISHORT	dishortative
DISP	dispensative
emph	emphasis
exact	exact ascription
Expl	explanation
F_1	illocution
Feedb	feedback
Foc	focus
H	head
h	higher social status
HORT	hortative
ILL	variable for an illocution
IMP	imperative illocution
IMPR	imprecative
INTER	interrogative
INTERP	interpellative
M_1	move
MIR	mirative
mit	mitigation
Motiv	motivation
OPT	optative
Orient	orientation
P_1	speech-act participant
PROH	prohibitive
R_1	subact of reference
rep	reportative
S	speaker
SA	subact
SUPPL	supplicative
T_1	subact of ascription
V_1	any interpersonal variable
Y/N	yes-no
Π	operator
$Π^M$	operator on a move (etc.)
Σ	modifier
$Σ^M$	modifier of a move (etc.)
Φ	function
$Φ^M$	function of a move (etc.)

Representational Level

◆	lexeme
∀	universal quantifying operator
∃	existential quantifying operator
∅	zero
1	singular
2	dual
3	trial
A	actor
Abl	ablative
ant	anterior
C	comitative
$^c f_1$	contingent property
Circ	circumstance
Cons	consequence
$^c x_1$	collective individual
$^d e_1$	dynamic state-of-affairs
distr	distributive
e_1	state-of-affairs
ep_1	episode
Ess	essive
f_1	property
h	head
hab	habitual
infer	inferential
Ins	instrument
In	inessive
L	locative
l_1	location
m	plural, more than one
m_1	manner

magn	magnitude
$^m x_1$	mass individual
p_1	propositional content
past	past
pc	paucal
perc	perception
$^p f_1$	permanent property
post	posterior
pres	present
prog	progressive
prox	proximal
q_1	quantity
r_1	reason
Ref	reference
rem	remote
$^s e_1$	stative state-of-affairs
sim	simultaneous
$^s x_1$	set individual
t_1	time
Temp	temporal
U	undergoer
v_1	any representational variable
x_1	individual
π	operator
σ	modifier
σ^f	modifier of property
σ^l	modifier of location
σ^m	modifier of manner
σ^t	modifier of a time
Φ	function
Φ^p	function of a propositional content (etc.)

Morphosyntactic Level

Aff_1	affix
Adp_1	adpositional phrase
$Advp_1$	adverb phrase
$Advw_1$	adverbial word
Ap_1	adjective phrase
As_1	adjectival stem
Aw_1	adjectival word
Cl_1	clause
$^{bal}Cl_1$	balanced clause
$^{dep}Cl_1$	dependent clause
$^{der}Cl_1$	deranked clause
Gw_1	grammatical word
Le_1	linguistic expression
Np_1	noun phrase
Nr_1	nominal root
Ns_1	nominal stem
Nw_1	nominal word
P^2	second position
P^{2+N}	position situated N places after the second position
P^{centre}	position of clause with respect to pre- and postclausal positions
P^F	final position
P^{F-N}	position situated N places before the final position
P^I	initial position
P^{I+N}	position situated N places after the initial position
P^M	medial position

P^{M+N}	position situated N places after the medial position
P^{M-N}	position situated N places before the medial position
P^{post}	postclausal position
P^{pre}	preclausal position
Vp_1	verb phrase
Vr_1	verbal root
Vs_1	verbal stem
Vw_1	verbal word
$^fVw_1$	finite verb(al word)
Xm_1	morpheme (of type x)
Xp_1	phrase (of type x)
Xr_1	root (of type x)
Xs_1	stem (of type x)
Xw_1	word (of type x)

Phonological Level

CAP	characteristic accent position
f	falling
F	foot
h	high
IP_1	intonational phrase
l	low
m	mid
PP_1	phonological phrase
PW_1	phonological word
r	rising
s	stressed
S_1	syllable
U_1	utterance

Parts-of-speech

A	adjective
Ad	adposition
Adv	adverb
Cont	contentive
DAdv	degree adverb
Det	determiner
Intj	interjection
MAdv	manner adverb
N	noun
Num	numeral
Pro	pronoun
V	verb

Grammatical models

FDG	Functional Discourse Grammar
FG	Functional Grammar
RRG	Role and Reference Grammar
SFG	Systemic-Functional Grammar

1

Introduction

1.1 Functional Discourse Grammar

This introduction provides a general overview of Functional Discourse Grammar (FDG) as part of a wider theory of verbal interaction. It starts out by describing various distinguishing features of the FDG model in Section 1.2. Section 1.3 goes on to present the architecture of FDG, introducing notions that will be expanded and justified in the remaining chapters of the book and explaining in general terms how the grammar can be implemented in linguistic analysis. The following Section (1.4) discusses the relation of FDG to linguistic functionalism, the relevance of FDG for language typology and various methodological prerequisites. The penultimate section, 1.5, sets out various notational conventions to be observed in the following chapters, which are briefly previewed in Section 1.6.

1.2 Basic properties

1.2.1 Introduction

There are a number of distinguishing features that set off Functional Discourse Grammar from other structural-functional theories of language (Butler 2003). These features, which are discussed in the following sections, are the following: FDG has a top-down organization (1.2.2); FDG takes the Discourse Act as the basic unit of analysis (1.2.3); FDG includes morphosyntactic and phonological representations as part of its underlying structure, alongside representations of the pragmatic and semantic properties of Discourse Acts (1.2.4); and, as the Grammatical Component of the theory of verbal interaction, FDG systematically links up with a Conceptual, a Contextual, and an Output Component (1.2.5).

1.2.2 Top-down organization

FDG starts with the speaker's intention and then works down to articulation. This is motivated by the assumption that a model of grammar will be more effective the more its organization resembles language processing in the individual. Psycholinguistic studies (e.g. Levelt 1989) clearly show that language production is a top-down process, which starts with intentions and ends with the articulation of the actual linguistic expression. The implementation of FDG reflects this process and is accordingly organized in a top-down fashion. This does not mean that FDG is a model of the speaker: FDG is a theory about grammar, but one that tries to reflect psycholinguistic evidence in its basic architecture (cf. 1.2.5 below).

Two major operations have to be distinguished in the top-down construction of utterances: FORMULATION and ENCODING. Formulation concerns the rules that determine what constitute valid underlying pragmatic and semantic representations in a language. Encoding concerns the rules that convert these pragmatic and semantic representations into morphosyntactic and phonological ones. The operation of Formulation involves three interlinked processes: the selection of appropriate frames for the Interpersonal and Representational Levels; the insertion of appropriate lexemes into these frames; and the application of operators symbolizing the grammatical distinctions required in the language under analysis. Encoding also involves three processes: the selection of appropriate templates for the Morphosyntactic and Phonological Levels; the insertion of free and bound grammatical morphemes; and the application of operators that play a role in the process of articulating the output of the grammar. Details will emerge from the relevant chapters.

Our presentation, in progressing from formulation to encoding and within encoding from morphosyntax to phonology, clearly mimics the sequence found in production. Despite this seductive analogy between the architecture of FDG and the processes of speech production, it is important to emphasize, as pointed out by Hengeveld (2004b: 366–7), that FDG is a 'model of encoded intentions and conceptualizations' rather than, as is Levelt's 'blueprint for the speaker' (1989: 8 ff.), a model of language production. FDG aims to understand how linguistic units are structured in terms of the world they describe and the communicative intentions with which they are produced, and models this in a dynamic implementation (Bakker and Siewierska 2004) of the grammar, i.e. the sequence of steps that the analyst must take in understanding and laying bare the nature of a particular phenomenon. This is how our discourse in this book is to be understood, for example where we remark that some operation precedes another one, or that two units are available simultaneously.

Note that, although the presentation of the FDG model will focus on the generation of utterances, the model could in principle be turned on its head to account for the parsing of utterances. It is clear that listeners analyse phonetic input into phonological representations, which are subsequently grouped into morphosyntactic constituents, from which meaningful representations are then constructed.

The top-down organization of the model is a precondition for a grammatical theory that aims at describing discourse units rather than clauses. In a discourse-oriented model the clause is just one of the options that the speaker can use to contribute to the ongoing discourse, for which reason formulation has to precede encoding. This is the topic of the next section.

1.2.3 Discourse grammar

There are many grammatical phenomena that can only be interpreted in terms of units larger than the individual clause. Examples of these are narrative constructions, the use of discourse particles, anaphorical chains, and tail-head linkage. By way of example, consider the following instance of tail-head linkage in Tidore (van Staden 2000: 275):

(1)   ...turus jafa cahi   saloi   ena=ge   turus
       ...then Jafa carry.on.the.back basket   3.NH=there then
       ena=ge   paka   *ine.*   *Ine*   una   oka koi...
       3.NH=there ascend go.upwards go.upwards 3.SG.M pick banana
       '...then Jafa carried the basket upwards and picked the bananas...'
       "...then Jafa carried the basket and went upwards. Went upwards he picked the bananas..."

In many Indo-Pacific languages there are several grammatical phenomena that are a faithful and direct reflection of discourse organization. In Foley's (1986: 176) words: 'A text is a coherent linking of clauses and sentences, and this coherence is achieved by rules of the language which state how clauses and sentences can be joined'. Example (1) illustrates one of these linking devices. Episodes within stories are in Tidore often realized as single linguistic expressions containing strings of clauses. The linguistic expressions are linked to each other by means of tail-head linkage: the last verb of the one linguistic expression is repeated as the first verb of the next linguistic expression, as illustrated in (1).

The crucial point here is that, as stated in the quotation from Foley (1986), phenomena such as tail-head linkage are governed by rules of the language and thus form part of the grammatical system as it applies to narratives. Grammatical phenomena like these thus clearly show the need for a grammatical model that allows for the treatment of units larger than the individual clause and of the relations that obtain between and within these units.

As argued in Mackenzie (1998b), the need for a discourse-oriented grammar also becomes apparent when units smaller than a clause are considered. The following examples illustrate what he treats as holophrases of various types:

(2)   (What are you eating?) A donut.

(3)   Congratulations!

(4)   Oh John!

The answer in (2), the exclamation in (3), and the vocative expression in (4) all take a non-clausal form. Yet in the appropriate circumstances they all count as full and complete contributions to the discourse. In fact, any further elaboration of (2), for example, would lead to a relatively less natural exchange. These utterances are accordingly not interpreted as reduced clauses, but as being non-clausal right from the start. The model should thus find a way of dealing with non-clausal utterances which recognizes the fact that they constitute fully grammatical discourse units.

The conclusion that FDG draws from the facts discussed in the preceding sections is that the basic unit of discourse is not the clause but the Discourse Act. Discourse Acts combine into larger discourse structures, such as Moves. These larger structures account for the units larger than the individual clause discussed above. On the other hand, Discourse Acts may be manifested in language as clauses, but also as fully grammatical clause fragments, phrases or words. The latter point is a crucial one: it requires the grammatical model to be capable of mapping the unit of Discourse Act onto morphosyntactic units of various kinds. This mapping procedure in turn requires a top-down approach.

Moves and Discourse Acts are notoriously difficult to define. Anticipating a more extensive discussion in Chapter 2, we here use the definitions offered in Kroon (1995: 65–6; see also Hannay and Kroon 2005), who following Sinclair and Coulthard (1975) defines a Move as 'the minimal free unit of discourse that is able to enter into an exchange structure' and a Discourse Act as 'the smallest identifiable unit of communicative behaviour'. Note that a Move consists of a single central Discourse Act, which may be supported by one or more Subsidiary Discourse Acts.

1.2.4 Levels of representation

The organization of Moves and Discourse Acts is dealt with at one level of the grammar, the Interpersonal Level. This is one of four levels of organization distinguished in FDG: two levels for formulation (the Interpersonal and Representational Levels, for pragmatic and semantic analysis respectively) and two for encoding (the Morphosyntactic and Phonological Levels). One of the reasons for having these four levels of linguistic organization is that anaphoric reference is possible to any of them. This means that these levels should be available as potential antecedents in underlying representations. Consider the following examples:

Interpersonal Level

(5)   A   Get out of here!
        B   Don't talk to me like *that*!

Representational Level

(6)   A   There are lots of traffic lights in this town.
        B   I didn't notice *that*.

Morphosyntactic Level

(7)   A   I had *chuletas de cordero* last night.
        B   Is *that* how you say 'lamb chops' in Spanish?

Phonological Level

(8)   A   I had /tʃuˈletasdekorˈdero/ last night.
        B   Shouldn't *that* be '/tʃuˈletasdeθorˈdero /'?

In (5B) the anaphoric element *that* refers back to the communicative strategy chosen by A, which is indicative of the presence of an Interpersonal Level in the underlying representation of (5A). In (6B) *that* refers back to the situation in the external world that is described within (6A). This purely semantic reference shows that the underlying structure of (6A) contains a Representational Level of organization.

The anaphoric references in (7B) and (8B) are different since they are metalinguistic in nature. They are instances of 'reflexive language' (Lucy 1993) or 'messages about the code' (Jakobson 1971). In (7B) *that* does not refer to the entity described by *chuletas de cordero* but to the phrase 'chuletas de cordero' as such. This phrase is a morphosyntactic unit, hence the conclusion must be that this phrase is present in underlying structure and can therefore function as an antecedent for anaphoric reference. A similar line of reasoning can be set up for the anaphoric reference in (8B), the only difference being that here the antecedent is a phonological rather than a morphosyntactic unit.

From these facts it may be concluded that the underlying representation of an utterance contains four levels of organization: an Interpersonal Level (pragmatics), a Representational Level (semantics), a Morphosyntactic Level (morphosyntax), and a Phonological Level (phonology). Note that all these levels are purely linguistic in nature. This holds for the Interpersonal Level and the Representational Level too: these levels describe language in terms of its functions and meanings, but only in so far as these functions and meanings are encoded in the grammar of a language. Thus the Interpersonal Level

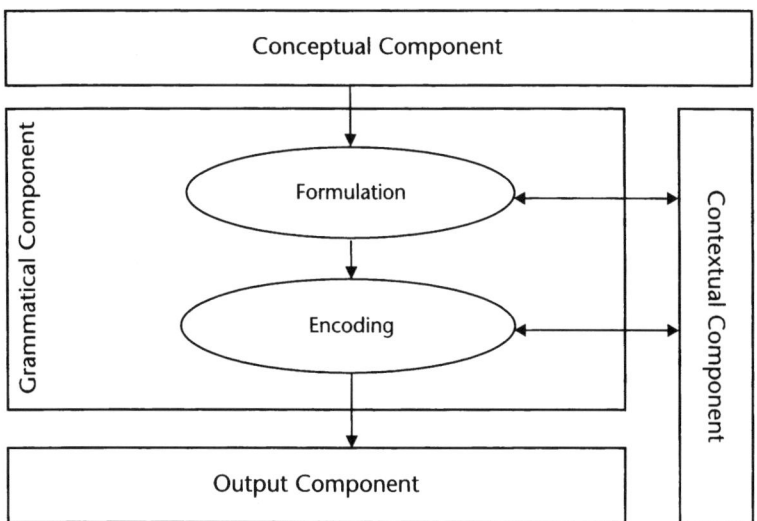

FIGURE 1. FDG as part of a wider theory of verbal interaction

represents a linguistic unit in terms of its communicative function, and the Representational Level in terms of its semantic category.

1.2.5 Conceptual Component, Contextual Component, and Output Component

FDG as the Grammatical Component in a wider theory of verbal interaction is linked to a Conceptual Component, an Output Component, and a Contextual Component within an overall model of verbal interaction. These non-grammatical components interact in various ways with the Grammatical Component. The Conceptual Component (1.2.5.1) is responsible for the development of both a communicative intention relevant for the current speech event and the associated conceptualizations with respect to relevant extra-linguistic events. The Output Component (1.2.5.2) generates acoustic, signed, or orthographic expressions on the basis of information provided by the Grammatical Component. The Contextual Component (1.2.5.3) contains a description of the content and form of preceding discourse and of the actual perceivable setting in which the speech event takes place and of the social relationships between Participants. The relationships among the Components are sketched in Figure 1.

This general design of a wider theory of verbal interaction is again inspired by the extensive research into the processes of speech production embodied in Levelt (1989). His model distinguishes three fundamental modules: the Conceptualizer, the Formulator, and the Articulator. Very roughly, these correspond to our Conceptual Component, Grammatical Component, and Output

Component respectively. The distinction within the Grammatical Component between formulating and encoding also owes much to Levelt's own use of these terms, although for him encoding is an aspect of formulation (1989: 11–12).

1.2.5.1 The Conceptual Component

The Conceptual Component is the driving force behind the Grammatical Component as a whole. It is here that is represented the ideational and inter-active material presupposed by each piece of discourse under analysis and the various communicative Moves and Discourse Acts that it contains. The Conceptual Component does not include every aspect of cognition that is potentially relevant for linguistic analysis, but only those that affect the imme-diate communicative intention. Harder (2004: 202) gives various pertinent examples, for example that given in (9):

(9)   Speaker does his/her duty towards Addressee by conveying relevant bad news ('**John is ill**'), mitigated by showing sympathy.

This will be expressed in Spanish as (10), an example drawn from Hengeveld (2004a) and also discussed by Harder (2004):

(10)   Me   tem-o   que   Juan está   enfermo.
        1.SG fear-1.SG.PRS COMP   Juan COP.3.SG.PRS.IND ill
        'I am afraid that Juan is ill.'

There are two vital linguistic facts about (10) that must be captured in the Grammatical Component. Firstly, there is the presence of the indicative mood in the embedded clause, as opposed to the subjunctive mood in (11), which expresses a quite different communicative intention, namely the Speaker's expression of his fear that Juan may be ill:

(11)   (Me) tem-o   que   Juan esté   enfermo.
        1.SG fear-1.SG.PRS COMP   Juan COP.3.SG.PRS.SBJV ill
        'I fear that Juan may be ill.'

Secondly, we note the obligatory status of the reflexive pronoun *me* in (10) as against its optionality in (11). Without entering here into the actual analy-sis (but see Hengeveld 2004a: 15), we may observe that the communicative intention behind (10) is represented rather informally in (9) in language and not in abstract conceptual structures, which we will not go into in this book. See, on the many rivalling proposals for conceptual representation, Pederson and Nuyts (1997) and, for the necessity of distinguishing between semantic (-pragmatic) and conceptual representations, Levinson (1997).

Slobin (1996) stresses how thinking for speaking is language-specific and involves 'picking those characteristics of objects and events that (i) fit some conceptualization of the event, and (ii) are readily encodable in the language' (1996: 76). Examples he gives (1996: 72) of 'picking characteristics' are the witnessed/non-witnessed opposition in Turkish or the perfective/imperfective distinction in Spanish. For FDG, however, thinking for speaking is not part of the Conceptual Component. Rather, the selection of the language-specific distinctions of the type discussed by Slobin is a task of the Grammatical Component, specifically the operation of Formulation, which has the task of translating conceptual configurations into the semantic and pragmatic distinctions available within a specific language.

In the informal representation of the language user's intention shown in (9), the material in normal print corresponds to the pragmatic, interpersonal side of the interaction, while the material in bold print lines up with its semantic, representational side. This distinction corresponds well with Butler's (2008b: 10) proposal that the Conceptual Component should distinguish a 'conceptual component proper' and an 'affective/interactional component', an opposition which he tentatively links to neurophysiological notions and the chemistry of brain processes. In turn, this distinction correlates nicely with the two aspects of formulation to be distinguished within the Grammatical Component: the formulation of the Interpersonal Level and that of the Representational Level, dealt with in Chapters 2 and 3 respectively.

1.2.5.2 The Output Component

Let us now turn briefly to the Output Component, which—again to adopt the language of dynamic implementation—converts the final structures of the Grammatical Component into output. This output will in the case of speech (the kind of discourse that will primarily be considered in this book) be acoustic in nature and consist of articulatory gestures of the respiratory, laryngeal, and supralaryngeal structures of the human anatomy. With signed languages, which have been shown to have all the grammatical levels required for the description of spoken languages (including a phonological level, cf. Uyechi 1996), the output will consist of manual and other bodily gestures; and with written languages, the Output Component will oversee the motor control required for the production of orthographic expressions. Its function in speech may be seen as translating the digital (i.e. categorical, opposition-based) information in the grammar into analogue (i.e. continuously variable) form: thus an utterance boundary in the grammar will yield *inter alia* a pause of so many milliseconds in the Output Component; or a syllable with a 'falling' operator will effect a decline in the fundamental frequency of the corresponding segment of the output. The Output Component will accordingly also be the location for long-term settings, such as the tempo at which an individual's speech, signing, or writing is carried out: *allegro* forms attributable to fast speech, or less accurate signing due to high tempo, or indeed 'sloppier' handwriting due to rapid use of the pen or keyboard are the kind of phenomenon to be treated here.

The distinction between the analogue nature of the Output Component and the digital nature of the grammar gives us an opportunity to emphasize an important characteristic of FDG. The analysis of linguistic data does not always lead to clear-cut results. Criteria used to distinguish between word classes, for example, do not always give unequivocal classifications when applied to the forms found in a particular language; and the data drawn from corpus analysis will often show statistical (>0% and <100%) rather than categorical (0% or 100%) distributions. This has led a number of current grammatical approaches to promote the notion of gradience, the position that boundaries between categories are fluid and that categorization should be based upon prototypes rather than on inviolable criteria (for discussion, cf. Aarts 2007); gradience would then be taken to apply within grammar.

In particular, this notion of gradience has been extended to the distinction between lexical and grammatical phenomena. From a diachronic viewpoint, it is undeniable that grammatical phenomena derive overwhelmingly and uni-directionally from lexical units, an observation that has been developed and deepened in the substantial literature on grammaticalization. As a corollary of this process, individual phenomena may find themselves somewhere on a scale between the initiation and the completion of a historical change and thus sharing properties of both the initial and final stages thereof. From a synchronic viewpoint, however, FDG postulates a sharp distinction between the lexical and the grammatical, a distinction that is integral to the way in which items will be represented in our analyses (but see Anstey 2006: 61–70 for a critical examination of this standpoint). The lexical–grammatical distinction will return extensively in Chapters 2 and 3, where it correlates strongly with the opposition between modifiers and operators.

1.2.5.3 The Contextual Component

Functional Discourse Grammar is so called because it seeks to understand the structure of utterances in their discourse context, though it is in no sense a discourse-analytical model. The intention developed by the speaker does not arise in a vacuum, but in a multifaceted communicative context. For some FDG-related suggestions as to the many aspects of the sociocultural situat-edness of verbal interaction, see Connolly (2004). With the last of the non-grammatical components to be introduced in this chapter, the Contextual Component, FDG as presented here makes no effort to offer anything like a complete description of the overall discourse context. Rather, this Com-ponent contains two types of information, both of them limited in scope. Firstly, it houses the immediate information received from the Grammatical

Component concerning a particular utterance which is relevant to the form that subsequent utterances may take. Secondly, it contains longer-term information about the ongoing interaction that is relevant to the distinctions that are required in the language being used, and which influence formulation and encoding in that language. The influence on formulation and encoding of both kinds of information, immediate and longer-term, is symbolized by the arrows from the Contextual Component to the Grammatical Component in Figure 1. Just as with the Conceptual Component, we will not go into the internal constitution of the Contextual Component in this book.

As examples of long-term settings within the Contextual Component, we may consider the sex of the speech-act participants as well as the social relation between them. These are both relevant for Spanish, as shown in example (12):

(12) ¡Qué pálid-a   est-ás!
      what pale-F.SG COP-IND.PRS.2.SG.FAM
      'How pale you look!'

Here the choice of the forms *pálida* (rather than *pálido* 'pale-M.SG') and *estás* (rather than *está* 'COP-IND.PRS.2.SG.POL') reflects specifications in the Contextual Component, i.e. the sex of the Addressee and the formality of the relation between Speaker and Addressee respectively. For an account of the grammatical properties of the corresponding utterance in English, as in the translation of (12), no such specification is required.

FDG adopts what Butler (2008a) refers to as a 'conservative stance' on the Contextual Component. Many of the matters that he himself includes in such a Component, like the factors that would induce selection of the informal lexeme *kid* rather than *child* in English to designate a child, would not find their way into an FDG Contextual Component. There are so many aspects of the context of interaction that could be argued to have an incidental impact upon a speaker's linguistic choices that modelling them within our theory would deprive it of much of its power. In an informal context, after all, a child may indeed be evoked by means of *kid*, but nothing prevents the choice of *child*. For this reason, factors relating to matters of genre, register, style, etc. will be included only where these can be shown to have a systematic effect upon grammatical choices in formulation (as in example (12) above); on the difficulties inherent in any attempt to include such factors in grammatical description, see Falster Jakobsen (2005).

Further examples of the type of phenomena which call upon the Contextual Component are reflexives, anaphora, and instances of narrative chaining, all of which we will deal with at the respective stage of the presentation. In languages with logophoric pronouns, for example, the Contextual Component will have to keep track of the status of (typically human) entities as belonging to a particular embedded discourse domain or not. In such languages a systematic formal opposition is made between the two readings of *He said that he was ill,* according as the second instance of *he* identifies the creator of the embedded domain (i.e. the referent of the first instance of *he*; this is indicated by the logophoric form) or some other male individual, indicated by the non-logophoric form (see 2.8.3.2.4 for discussion). Similarly, according as a language permits reflexive pronouns to apply across larger or smaller stretches of discourse, the Contextual Component will be adjusted to make particular possible antecedents available.

Note that the short-term information in the Contextual Component must be continually kept up to date. Anaphoric chains depend upon the availability in the Contextual Component of valid antecedents. As the discourse progresses, so some of these cease to be available while others arise as potential antecedents. The Contextual Component will be responsive to the requirements of the particular language in this respect. This also applies to narrative chaining, where the positioning of a State-of-Affairs within an Episode must be specified with regard to previous or later States-of-Affairs. Where the anaphora or narrative chaining works forwards in time (cataphora), the Contextual Component will create an empty position constraining the formulator to supply the awaited information.

As seen in Figure 1, the input to the Contextual Component does not only come from the result of formulation but also from the result of encoding, in other words the Morphosyntactic and Phonological Levels within the Grammatical Component. This is because, as we saw in 1.2.4, anaphoric reference is possible not only to pragmatic and semantic constructs but also to sections of the actual morphosyntactic structure of clauses and phonological structure of utterances. In the following chapters, we will detail various ways in which there is interaction between the Contextual Component and the various Levels of the Grammatical Component.

In 1.2.5 we classified the Conceptual, Output, and Contextual Components as non-grammatical. Our discussion of the three non-grammatical Components has shown, however, that they are certainly not non-linguistic. Indeed, all three will differ from language to language, according to the impact that each has on linguistic form. The decision whether to include a particular phenomenon in the grammar or in one of the flanking Components will be taken language-specifically and will be determined by considerations of systematicity. If, for example, every single utterance in a language ends in a lengthened syllable, this should be shown as a systematic aspect of the grammar; if there is a statistical tendency to utterance-final syllable-lengthening, this is something to put into the Output Component. If a language expresses all commands as a question about ability (*Can you open the window?* etc.), then this is a grammatical fact about that language. If the Speaker may express commands either directly by means of an Imperative Illocution or indirectly as a question about ability, the circumstances determining that choice are a matter for the Conceptual Component while the alternative formulations are a matter for the grammar.

We have now seen in general terms how FDG operates as a top-down grammar of the Discourse Act, recognizes four Levels of description and interacts with Conceptual, Output, and Contextual Components. In the following section, we will consider the architecture of FDG in greater depth.

1.3 The architecture of FDG

1.3.1 Overall organization

The general architecture of FDG and the Components that flank the Grammatical Component may now be represented as in Figure 2, in which the Grammatical Component is presented in the centre, the Conceptual Component at the top, the Output Component at the bottom, and the Contextual Component to the right. Note that this figure fleshes out Figure 1.

Within the various Components, circles contain operations, boxes contain the primitives used in operations, and rectangles contain the levels of representation produced by operations. In line with the top-down organization of FDG, we start our discussion of Figure 2 at the top.

As mentioned in 1.2.5.1, in the prelinguistic Conceptual Component a communicative intention (e.g. issuing a warning) and the corresponding mental representations (e.g. of the event causing danger) are relevant. Through the operation of Formulation these conceptual representations are translated into pragmatic and semantic representations at the Interpersonal and the Representational Levels, respectively.

The rules used in Formulation are language-specific, i.e. FDG does not presuppose the existence of universal pragmatic and semantic notions. As a result, similar conceptual representations may receive different pragmatic and semantic representations in different languages. To give just one example: warnings are in some languages encoded as a distinct type of speech act, whereas in others they receive the same treatment as orders. This type of crosslinguistic variation may be expected to be governed by typological hierarchies, just like morphosyntactic and phonological variation.

Formulation rules make use of a set of primitives that contains frames, lexemes, and operators (see 1.3.3.2). The configurations at the Interpersonal and the Representational Levels are translated into a morphosyntactic structure at the Morphosyntactic Level through the operation of Morphosyntactic Encoding. The Morphosyntactic Encoding rules draw on a set of primitives

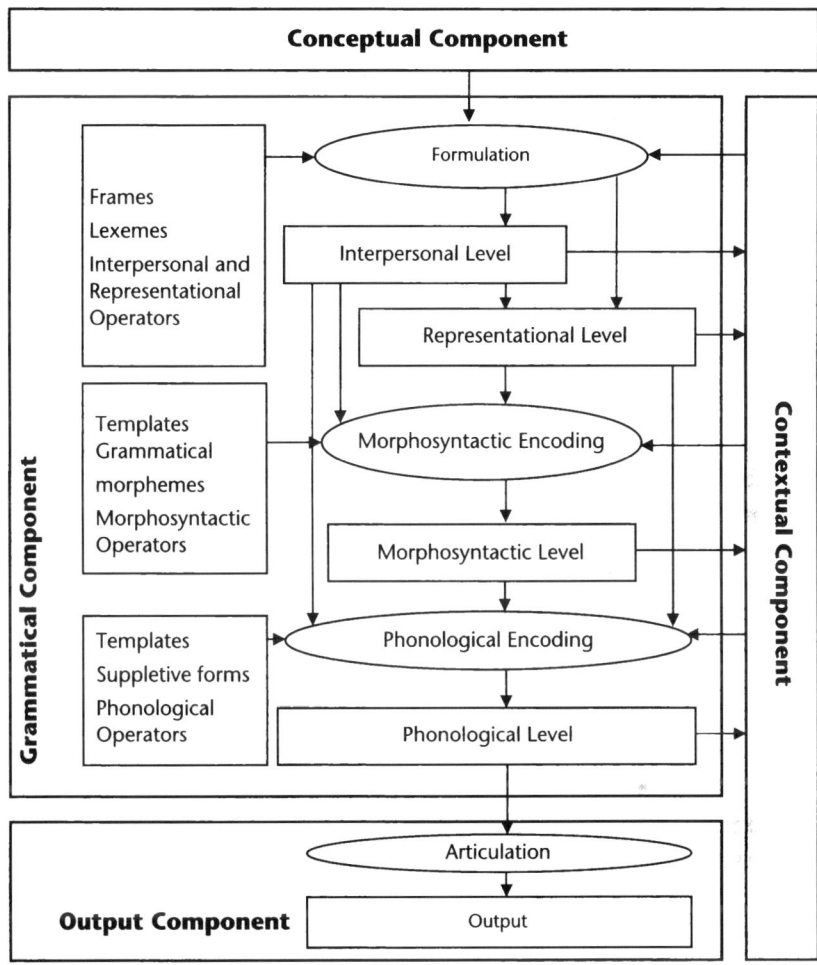

FIGURE 2. General layout of FDG

containing Morphosyntactic Templates, Grammatical Morphemes, and Morphosyntactic Operators (see 1.3.3.3). Similarly, the structures at the Interpersonal, Representational, and Morphosyntactic Levels are translated into a phonological structure at the Phonological Level. The phonological encoding rules draw on a set of primitives containing Phonological Templates, Suppletive forms, and Phonological Operators (see 1.3.3.4).

By organizing the Grammatical Component in this way, FDG takes the functional approach to language to its logical extreme: within the top-down organization of the grammar, pragmatics governs semantics, pragmatics and semantics govern morphosyntax, and pragmatics, semantics, and morphosyntax govern phonology.

The Phonological Level of representation is the input to the operation of Articulation, which, in the case of an acoustic (as opposed to written or signed) Output Component, contains the phonetic rules necessary for arriving at an adequate utterance. Articulation takes place outside the grammar proper.

The various levels of representation within the grammar feed into the Contextual Component, thus enabling subsequent reference to the various kinds of entity relevant at each of these levels once they are introduced into the discourse. The Contextual Component feeds into the operations of formulation and encoding, so that the availability of antecedents, visible referents, and speech-act participants (and possibly bystanders; cf. Rijkhoff 1995) may influence the composition of (subsequent) Discourse Acts. Note that the representation of these feeding relations in Figure 2 is a simplification when looked at from the perspective of the language user. In order to create a contextual specification, the Addressee has to reconstruct all the levels of representation within the grammar on the basis of the actual output of that grammar, i.e. the phonetic utterance. Since in this book we restrict ourselves to the perspective of language production and concentrate on the Grammatical Component, we abstract away from this complication by provisionally assuming direct feeding relationships between the Grammatical Component and the Contextual Component.

1.3.2 Levels and Layers

1.3.2.1 Introduction

Each of the levels of representation distinguished within the Grammatical Component in Figure 2 is structured in its own way. What all the levels have in common is that they have a hierarchically ordered layered organization and are displayed as a layered structure. In its maximal form the general structure of layers within levels is as follows:

(13) $(\pi v_1: [\text{head } (v_1)_\Phi]: [\sigma (v_1)_\Phi])_\Phi$

Here v_1 represents the variable of the relevant layer, which is restricted by a (possibly complex) head that takes the variable as its argument, and may be further restricted by a modifier σ that takes the variable as its argument. The layer may be specified by an operator π and carry a function Φ. Heads and modifiers represent lexical strategies, while operators and functions represent grammatical strategies. The difference between operators and functions is that the latter are relational, holding between the entire unit and other units at the same layer, while the former are not, applying only to the unit itself.

Of course, not all relations between units are hierarchical. In those cases in which units together form a non-hierarchical (equipollent) configuration,

$$(M_1: [(A_1: [(F_1) (P_1)_S (P_2)_A (C_1: [(T_1)_{\{\Phi\}} \dots (T_{1+N})_{\{\Phi\}} (R_1)_{\{\Phi\}} \dots (R_{1+N})_{\{\Phi\}}] (C_1)_{\{\Phi\}})] (A_1) \dots (A_{1+N})_{\{\Phi\}}] (M_1))$$

FIGURE 3. The Interpersonal Level

they are enclosed between square brackets, as exemplified in (13), where the relationship between a head and its argument and a modifier and its argument is indicated by square brackets.

The levels differ in the sense that at each level a linguistic expression is analysed in terms of the distinctions relevant to that level. It should be stressed again that the representations at all levels are purely linguistic in nature, so that only those distinctions are provided that are actually reflected in the grammar of the language involved.

1.3.2.2 The Interpersonal Level

At the Interpersonal Level the hierarchical structure given in Figure 3 applies.

As indicated in 1.2.3, we recognize as a unit of analysis at the Interpersonal Level the Move (M), which may contain one or more (N) Discourse Acts (A). Each Discourse Act contains an Illocution (F), which specifies a relation between speech-act Participants (P, the Speaker S, and the Addressee A) and (except in the case of Expressives, 2.5.2.4.2) the Communicated Content (C). The Communicated Content contains a varying number of Ascriptive (T) and Referential (R) Subacts. Note that the latter two units are operative at the same layer, i.e. there is no hierarchical relation between them; in such cases of equipollence, square brackets are applied. In general, then, at the Interpersonal Level units are analysed in terms of their communicative function.

1.3.2.3 The Representational Level

At the Representational Level the relevant layers are those presented in Figure 4.

At this level of analysis linguistic units are described in terms of the semantic category they designate (see Hengeveld 1989, 2004a; Mackenzie 2004c). These categories are of different types, such as Propositional Contents (p), which may contain one or more (n) episodes (ep) (see Gómez Soliño 1995), which may contain one or more descriptions of States-of-Affairs (e); the latter, in turn, are characterized by one or more Properties (f_1), which may contain descriptions of Individuals (x_1) and further Properties (f_2). Further classes of semantic category are presented in Chapter 3. Note that, as is indicated by the

$$(p_1: [(ep_1: [(e_1: [(f_1: [(f_2)^n (x_1)_\Phi \dots (x_{1+n})_\Phi] (f_1)) \dots (f_{1+n}) (e_1)_\Phi]) \dots (e_{1+n})_{\{\Phi\}} (ep_1)) \dots (ep_{1+n})_{\{\Phi\}}] (p_1))$$

FIGURE 4. The Representational Level

square brackets, the Individuals and further Properties in Figure 4 belong to the same layer, i.e. there is no hierarchical relation between them.

The nature of a semantic category is not indicative of the way the linguistic unit describing that category is used within a Discourse Act. Semantic categories, as the name indicates, are categories, not functions. The functional analysis is given at the Interpersonal Level. Thus, the same Property (f) may be either ascribed (T) or referred to (R). The following examples illustrate this point (note that the formal difference between *tall* and *tallness* is accounted for at the Morphosyntactic Level as arising from coercion, cf. 4.6.1):

(14) a. The teacher is *tall*.
          (Ascription of Property: T/f)
      b. *Tallness* impresses the teacher.
          (Reference to Property: R/f)

Similarly, an Individual may be ascribed or referred to:

(15) a. Sheila is *my best friend*.
          (Ascription of Individual entity: T/x)
      b. *My best friend* visited me last night.
          (Reference to Individual: R/x)

A more elaborate representation of (14a–b) is given in (16a–b):

(16) a. $(C_I$: $[(T_I)$
          $(p_i$: $(ep_i$: $(e_i$: $[(f_i$: $[(f_j$: tall $(f_i))$
          (R_I) $]$ $(C_I))$
          $(x_i$: teacher $(x_i))_\Phi$ $]$ $(f_i))$ $(e_i)_\Phi])$ $(ep_i))$ $(p_i))$

      b. $(C_I$: $[(T_I)$ (R_I)
          $(p_i$: $(ep_i$: $(e_i$: $[(f_i$: $[(f_j$: impress $(f_j))$ $(f_k$: tallness $(f_k))_\Phi$
          (R_I) $]$ $(C_I))$
          $(x_i$: teacher$_N$ $(x_i))_\Phi$ $]$ $(f_i))$ $(e_i)_\Phi])$ (ep_i) $(p_i))$

Examples like these show that, though there are regular correspondences between the Interpersonal Level and the Representational Level, the two are basically independent of each other, allowing for a wide variety of interactions between them.

1.3.2.4 The Morphosyntactic Level

Figure 5 shows the general maximal template for morphosyntactic frames at the layer of the linguistic expression, where each unit may occur more than once.

At this level a linguistic unit is analysed in terms of its syntactic constituents, with, from the highest to the lowest layers: Linguistic Expressions (Le), Clauses

$$(\text{Le}_1: [(\text{Xw}_1)\,(\text{Xp}_1)\,(\text{Cl}_1: [(\text{Xw}_2)\,(\text{Xp}_2: [(\text{Xw}_3)\,(\text{Xp}_3)\,(\text{Cl}_3)]\,(\text{Xp}_2))_{\{\Phi\}}(\text{Cl}_2)_{\{\Phi\}}]\,(\text{Cl}_1))]\,(\text{Le}_1))$$

FIGURE 5. The Morphosyntactic Level

(Cl), Phrases of several types (Xp), and Words of several types (Xw). Within Words we furthermore distinguish Morphemes of several types (Xm), not shown in Figure 5. As is to be explained in 1.4.4, the notion 'sentence' is not applied in FDG.

There is no necessary one-to-one mapping between semantic and pragmatic units on the one hand and morphosyntactic units on the other. As argued earlier, Discourse Acts may be expressed as Clauses, Phrases, or Words. To give another example: semantic predications consisting of a unit designating a Property and two units designating Individuals may be realized in one language as a Clause with three constituents and in others as a single Word. Consider the following examples, from English and Southern Tiwa (Allen *et al.* 1984: 293; the gloss 1.SG.SBJ>PL.OBJ in (18) should be read as 'first person singular subject acting on plural object').

(17)   I made shirts.

(18)   Te-shut-pe-ban
       1.SG.SBJ>PL.OBJ-shirt-make-PST
       'I made (the) shirts.'

The English Clause in (17) can be subdivided into three syntactic constituents corresponding to the three semantic units mentioned earlier: a unit designating a Property (*made*) and two units designating Individuals (*I, shirts*). The same semantic configuration is expressed in Southern Tiwa as a single syntactic constituent, as shown in (18). The Actor argument is expressed by means of a prefix on the Verb and does not have to be expressed independently. The Undergoer argument is incorporated into the Verb. The fact that the Undergoer is cross-referenced on the verb shows that it is really an argument of that Verb. Assuming a similar underlying semantic representation for (17)–(18), these examples thus clearly demonstrate that there are many possible mappings between the Representational and the Morphosyntactic Levels.

1.3.2.5 The Phonological Level

The Phonological Level is equally language-specific, and contains both the segmental and the suprasegmental phonological representation of an Utterance, which is the largest phonological unit considered in FDG. Figure 6 shows the phonological template for an Utterance, with a number of simplifications for purposes of exposition. Again, every unit may occur more than once.

$$(\text{U}_1\text{: }[(\text{IP}_1\text{: }[(\text{PP}_1\text{: }[(\text{PW}_1)]\ (\text{PP}_1))]\ (\text{IP}_1))]\ (\text{U}_1))$$

FIGURE 6. The Phonological Level

At this level the linguistic expression is analysed in terms of the phonological units it contains, such as the Utterance (U), the Intonational Phrase (IP), the Phonological Phrase (PP), and the Phonological Word (PW).

Again, there is no necessary one-to-one mapping between pragmatic, semantic, and morphosyntactic units on the one hand, and phonological units on the other. Thus, in some languages subordinate clauses are set off from the main clause by means of a break between two Intonational Phrases, whereas in others they form a single Intonational Phrase with the main clause. To give another and perhaps more pervasive example: Phonological Words at the Phonological Level are not necessarily in a one-to-one relationship with constituent boundaries at the Morphosyntactic Level, as can be illustrated with the following example from Dutch, as pronounced in certain varieties in the Netherlands:

(19)   Ik wou   dat   hij kwam.
       I   want.PST COMP he come.PST
       'I wish he would come.'

An alignment of the morphosyntactic analysis with the phonological analysis would be as follows (the symbol '–' is used to indicate the beginning and the end of a fragment that is not further analysed in detail, see 1.5 below):

(20) $(\text{Cl}_i\text{: }[\quad\quad (\text{Np}_i\text{: }-\text{ik}-(\text{Np}_i))\ (\text{Vp}_i\text{: }-\text{wou}-(\text{Vp}_i))$
       $(\text{U}_i\text{: }\quad [\text{IP}_i\text{: }[\quad(\text{PP}_i\text{: }(\text{PW}_i\text{: }-\text{kʋɑu}-(\text{PW}_i))\ (\text{PP}_i))$
       $(\text{Cl}_j\text{: }[\quad(\text{Gw}_i\text{: }-\text{dat}-(\text{Gw}_i))\quad(\text{Np}_j\text{: }-\text{hij}-(\text{Np}_j))$
       $(\text{PP}_j\text{: }[\quad(\text{PW}_j\text{: }-\text{dɑti}-(\text{PW}_j))$
       $(\text{Vp}_j\text{: }-\text{kwam}-(\text{Vp}_j))\ ]\quad(\text{Cl}_j))]\quad\quad(\text{Cl}_i))$
       $(\text{PW}_k\text{: }-\text{kʋɑm}-(\text{PW}_k))\ ]\ (\text{PP}_j))\ ]\ (\text{IP}_i))]\ (\text{U}_i))$

This example shows that the first Phonological Phrase (PP_i) corresponds to the first two syntactic constituents of the main clause, while the second corresponds to the embedded clause. Within the second Phonological Phrase there are two Phonological Words (PW_j) and (PW_k), one corresponding to the first two syntactic constituents of the embedded clause, the second corresponding to the single remaining syntactic constituent.

1.3.3 Primitives

1.3.3.1 Introduction

The various operations creating the levels just discussed make use of sets of primitives which serve as the building blocks for their respective levels of application. The rules that constitute the operations within the grammar (formulating and encoding) combine these primitives in order to produce the various levels of representation.

1.3.3.2 Primitives used in Formulation

The operation of formulation has to produce two different levels of representation: the Interpersonal Level and the Representational Level. For each of these levels, similar (although distinct) primitives are relevant. These will be presented in brief here: full detail will be given in Chapters 2 and 3.

First of all, the set of primitives contains Frames which define the possible combinations of elements at the Interpersonal Level and at the Representational Level for a certain language. Despite their language-specific nature, the inventory of frames is expected to be partly predictable in terms of crosslinguistically valid typological hierarchies. Relevant distinctions captured by frames at the Interpersonal Level include, for example, the expressive or communicative nature of Discourse Acts, the encoded configurations of information structure, and the rhetorical functions of Discourse Acts. At the Representational Level frames capture such matters as quantitative and qualitative valency, the combinations of semantic categories allowed, and possible modification structures.

Secondly, this set of primitives contains Lexemes; these are given in phonemic form, although for ease of exposition we shall generally simply use orthographic form. Within the set of Lexemes a distinction is made between those that function at the Interpersonal Level (e.g. interjections, proper names, illocutionary adverbs, performative expressions, etc.) and those that function at the Representational Level. Lexemes are independent units that have to be associated with the aforementioned frames (see García Velasco and Hengeveld 2002 for discussion of this issue). In the implementation of the grammar the frames are selected first, and only after that are lexemes inserted. This reflects the choice the Speaker often has in describing one and the same entity through a variety of lexemes with different connotations and/or denotations. It also provides a natural framework for understanding the phenomenon of coercion, through which lexemes that are strongly associated with a particular frame can be forced for expressive purposes into a frame that is usually coupled with lexemes of another meaning class.

Thirdly, this set of primitives contains interpersonal and representational operators, which represent grammatical expressions in terms of their pragmatic or semantic content respectively. The classification of these operators will be addressed extensively in Chapters 2 and 3. Here we just give a number of examples. At the Interpersonal Level, mitigation is an operator at the illocutionary layer, reportative is an operator at the layer of the Communicated Content, approximation ('sort-of') is an operator at the layer of the Ascriptive Subact, and identifiability operates at the layer of the Referential Subact. At the Representational Level, examples are subjective modality at the layer of the Propositional Content, tense at the layer of the State-of-Affairs, number at the layer of the Individual, and phasal aspect at the Property layer.

1.3.3.3 Primitives used in Morphosyntactic Encoding

The Morphosyntactic Level is organized on the basis of morphosyntactic templates for Linguistic Expressions, Clauses, Phrases, and Words which are stored as part of the set of primitives relevant for the operation of Morphosyntactic Encoding. The inventory of templates has to be specified for each language individually, although again the expectation is that crosslinguistically valid generalizations will make this inventory largely predictable on the basis of a limited number of parameters.

The second set of primitives relevant at the Morphosyntactic Level consists of grammatical morphemes, which are unmodifiable elements such as Auxiliaries, Particles, and Affixes. These grammatical morphemes have to be introduced at the Morphosyntactic Level, since they occupy slots in the morphosyntactic configuration, which is determined at this level. To give an example at the clause layer: in Dutch the main verb normally occurs in second position in a Clause, but when an auxiliary verb is present, this Auxiliary occupies the second position and the main verb occurs in final position, as illustrated in (21) and (22):

(21) Karel won   de   wedstrijd.
      Karel win.PST.SG DEF game
      'Karel won the game.'

(22) Karel heeft   de   wedstrijd gewonnen.
      Karel have.PRS.3.SG DEF game   win.PTCP
      'Karel has won the game.'

Examples like these clearly show that it is impossible to determine the order of constituents without taking grammatical morphemes into account. Similar examples can be given at the Phrase and the Word layers.

Often, various semantic distinctions map onto a single grammatical morpheme. For instance, the accusative case in a certain language may be triggered by the semantic function Undergoer, but also by various types of Modifier, or it may be lexically triggered by certain verbs or adpositions. The other way around, a single semantic category may map onto various morphosyntactic categories, as when the form of the accusative expressing the Undergoer argument is dependent on the noun class of the head of that Undergoer argument.

Grammatical morphemes are introduced in their phonemic form when they are regular and predictable. They are introduced by means of a Morphosyntactic Operator, the third set of primitives at the Morphosyntactic Level, in those cases in which their final form is not fully predictable and has to be selected from a suppletive paradigm. Morphosyntactic Operators can thus be considered to be placeholders for actual forms or sets of forms. In assigning names to Morphosyntactic Operators we will generally use labels similar to the ones used in glosses, so as to enhance readability. It is important to realize, however, that these names could just as well be represented by numerical codes, like *581*, since they trigger forms, and at this level no longer represent meanings.

1.3.3.4 Primitives used in Phonological Encoding

The Phonological Level is organized on the basis of phonological templates for Utterances, Intonational Phrases, Phonological Phrases, Phonological Words, Feet, and Syllables, which are stored as part of the set of primitives relevant for the operation of Phonological Encoding. The inventory of templates has to be specified for each language individually, and certain languages may lack entire layers altogether (for example, Vietnamese has been claimed to lack the layer Phonological Word, cf. 5.6), although again the expectation is that crosslinguistically valid generalizations will make this inventory largely predictable on the basis of a limited number of parameters.

The second set of primitives consists of the suppletive forms that correspond to the Morphosyntactic Operators introduced in the previous section and to unpredictable forms from the paradigms of lexemes. Suppletive forms are introduced at the Phonological Level, since in many languages the form of a morpheme may be affected by the morphosyntactic configuration in which it occurs. Bakker (2005: 3) cites the following example of this phenomenon from Yagua (Payne 1990: 30):

(23) a. Sa-juuy   Anita.
         3.SG.SBJ-fall Anita
         'Anita fell.'

b.   Anita Ø-juuy.
     Anita 3.SG.SBJ-fall
     'Anita fell.'

In Yagua, the subject-agreement prefix on the verb is *sa-* when the Subject term occurs in postverbal position (23a), but it is Ø- when the Subject occurs in preverbal position (23b). This means that in this language the form of the third singular subject marker 3.SG.SBJ can only be determined after the constituent order of the Clause is established.

A third set of primitives potentially relevant at the Phonological Level consists of Phonological Operators. These anticipate aspects of the articulatory, signed, or orthographic output that are not a direct reflection of an Interpersonal, Representational, or Morphosyntactic Operator. A good example of a phenomenon for which such Phonological Operators are necessary is intonation. The Phonological Level will distinguish such operators as r(ising) and f(alling) or h(igh) and l(ow), typically applying these to the syllable layer. Depending on the language type, some or all syllables will be marked by such an operator; in tone languages, each syllable will be in principle be marked with an operator (5.7). The 'digital' information given by these Phonological Operators provides instructions to the Output Component which then will perform phonologically insignificant but phonetically necessary operations to ensure a smooth 'analogue' intonation contour.

1.3.3.5 Generalizations

There are certain correspondences across the three sets of primitives. Within each set there is a subset of units with a structuring function: the frames used in Formulation and the Templates in Morphosyntactic and Phonological Encoding all serve the purpose of providing an overall organizing structure for their respective levels. Within each set of primitives there is furthermore a subset of units in phonemic form: the Lexemes used in Formulation, the Grammatical Morphemes used in Morphosyntactic Encoding, and the Suppletive Forms used in Phonological Encoding all contribute to the cumulative segmental specification of the underlying representations. Finally, within each set of primitives there is a subset of operators: Interpersonal and Representational Operators are relevant to the operation of Formulation, Morphosyntactic and Phonological Operators to the operation of Encoding.

1.3.4 Levels and primitives

For a simple illustration of how a single constituent gets different representations at each level, using different sets of primitives, consider the example in

(24). The constituent *these bananas* is represented in four different ways within FDG, as provisionally indicated in (25).

(24)   (I like) these bananas.

(25)   a.   IL   (+id R_I)
      b.   RL   (prox m x_i: [(f_i: /bə'nɑ:nə/$_N$(f_i)) (x_i)$_Φ$])
      c.   ML   (Np_i: [(Gw_i: this-pl(Gw_i)) (Nw_i: /bə'nɑ:nə/-pl (Nw_i))] (Np_i))
      d.   PL   (PP_i: [(PW_i: /ði:z/ (PW_i)) (PW_j: /bə'nɑ:nəz/ (PW_j))] (PP_i))

At the Interpersonal Level (IL, 25a), the constituent is characterized as having a referential function (R). The referent is furthermore assumed by the Speaker to be identifiable (+id) by the Addressee. At the Representational Level (RL, 25b) the constituent is characterized as designating more than one (m) Individual (x) with a Property (f) and in terms of the location of its referent (prox). The Property (f) is specified by the Nominal (N) Lexeme /bə'nɑ:nə/. At the Morphosyntactic Level (25c) the constituent is characterized as being a Noun Phrase (Np), which consists of a Grammatical Word (Gw) and a Nominal Word (Nw). At this level a Morphosyntactic Operator is introduced, for convenience here shown as 'this', which acts as a placeholder in the appropriate syntactic position. The Representational Operator m is converted into the Morphosyntactic Operator Pl(ural), which occurs twice, since it has to be expressed on each of the two Words making up the Noun Phrase. At the Phonological Level (25d) the appropriate plural forms of the Words are introduced, in the case of the noun by adding the appropriate form of the plural suffix, in the case of the determiner by selecting the appropriate suppletive form corresponding to the combination of Morphosyntactic Operators. The Phonological Level in this case consists of one Phonological Phrase (PP) containing two Phonological Words (PW).

1.3.5 Implementation

1.3.5.1 Introduction

The various levels of organization are related to each other through rules of Formulation and Encoding, in a dynamic implementation of the grammar (cf. Bakker 2001, 2005). Two principles are crucial in this implementation, and these are discussed in the following sections.

1.3.5.2 Depth first

The depth-first principle was proposed in Bakker (1999) in the context of FG and is adopted in FDG, but with a somewhat different interpretation. In defining its role within the grammar, recall that a basic assumption in FDG is that a grammatical model will be more efficient the more it resembles language production in the individual. There is a consensus in the psycholinguistic literature that language production is incremental, in the sense that prelinguistic conceptualizations arise gradually through time (in microseconds, it should be said) and that material is sent ahead for encoding before the entire communicative intention has been fully developed (Levelt 1989: 24–7; see also Mackenzie 2000, 2004b and Harder 2007). In accordance with this, information from a certain level is sent down to a lower level as soon as the necessary input information for that lower level is complete. The grammar would slow down considerably if first the Interpersonal Level had to be fully specified, and second the Representational Level had to be filled in completely, so that only then could the morphosyntactic configuration be determined, which after that would be mapped onto a phonological configuration. This is not how language production in the individual works, and it would therefore, given the basic assumption mentioned above, not lead to a very efficient model of grammar either. (Fortescue 2004: 169 warns of the dangers of 'hybrid models', oriented partly to pattern and partly to process: our model is a pattern model that is inspired by process without seeking to model the latter.)

As an example, consider the effect of specifying an illocutionary value at the Interpersonal Level (cf. Risselada 1993: 78–86). As soon as an Imperative (IMP) frame has been selected for the Discourse Act, there are potentially important consequences at all subsequent levels of representation: (i) at the Representational Level, the State-of-Affairs frame will have to designate a controlled State-of-Affairs, and the first argument will have to include the Addressee; (ii) at the Morphosyntactic Level, in some languages a specific constituent order is used, or there may be special imperative auxiliaries or morphological markers; (iii) at the Phonological Level, there may be specific prosodic patterns that are used with Imperatives (cf. 5.4). All this means that the selection of an Imperative frame at the Interpersonal Level may trigger a whole range of specifications at subsequent levels, both in terms of formulation and of encoding, irrespective of the specification of further elements at the Interpersonal and lower levels.

Note, however, that evidence is also available that there is also a role in language production for processes which involve looking ahead to a unit-final element: cf. Hannay and Martínez-Caro (2008) for the notion of working up to a clause-final position in syntax, Fortescue (2007: 340–1) for morphological processes that involve 'backtracking' from a word-final position, and again Levelt (1989: 401–5) for look-ahead in phonology. In our modelling of morphosyntax, too, based as it is on observations about the patterning of linguistic units, we will see that counting forwards from an initial position and backwards from a final position are both called for. In all these ways, and others, we may observe a general analogy between production processes and the sequence of steps involved in a pass through the model of FDG.

1.3.5.3 Maximal depth

The principle of maximal depth states that only those levels of representation that are relevant for the build-up of (a certain aspect of) an utterance are used in the production of that (aspect of the) utterance. This principle, too, is meant to speed up the implementation of the grammar. It avoids the vacuous specification of levels of representation that are irrelevant to the production of the utterance at hand.

Following up on the example in the previous section, this means that in a certain language there may be a direct connection, circumventing the Representational Level, between the Interpersonal Level and the Morphosyntactic Level in those cases in which the Imperative frame has to be mapped onto a specific clausal template. Similarly, there may be a direct connection, circumventing the Representational Level and the Morphosyntactic Level, between the Interpersonal and Phonological Levels when the Imperative frame is mapped onto a specific prosodic pattern. In this way, superfluous steps in passing on information within the top-down procedure are avoided. Looking at this from a bottom-up perspective, it means that the expression of underlying structures is potentially based on information from all higher levels, not just from the next one up.

Having seen something of the architecture of FDG and of its implementation in the analysis of various phenomena, let us now place it in its broader context.

1.4 FDG in its broader context

1.4.1 Introduction

Functional Discourse Grammar is so called because it adheres to the principles of linguistic functionalism and takes the Discourse Act as its basic unit of analysis. As we have seen, it is a grammatical model that constitutes one component of an overall theory of verbal interaction and aims to be equally valid for all types of language. As a result the notions of functionalism, language typology, language modelling, and Discourse Act all play a central role in FDG. Accordingly, Section 1.4.2 will deal with functionalism, contrasting it with formalism and indicating how FDG is to be located with respect to these two major schools of linguistic thought and to two closely related theories. Section 1.4.3 will turn to linguistic typology, and consider both the influence of typology upon the theory of FDG and the role it could play in typological work. Section 1.4.4, finally, will present FDG as a form-oriented function-to-form model, showing how it relates to psycholinguistic work on speech production and giving some indications on how a practising linguist can work with FDG. In all three sections, the Discourse Act will play a central role.

1.4.2 Functionalism

FDG occupies a position halfway between radically functional and radically formal approaches to grammatical analysis. Functionalism refers here to an approach to linguistic analysis that is based on the belief that the properties of linguistic utterances are adapted to those communicative aims which the language user, in interaction with other language users, seeks to achieve by using those utterances (Dik 1986). Radical functionalism is an extreme form of this standpoint, denying the cognitive reality of linguistic structure and seeing linguistic form as an ephemeral manifestation of the language user's attempt to achieve his/her communicative purposes. Radical functionalists tend to support a usage-based linguistics, one which typically involves the detailed examination of corpus data and the extraction of inductive generalizations which typically pertain only to the language under examination. Patterns discerned in these data are seen as emergent rather than as reflecting any kind of structure. A major statement of this position is Hopper (1987: 142), who takes a view of structure as 'always provisional, always negotiable, and in fact as epiphenomenal'.

Formalism, by contrast, is strongly committed to the existence of mental structure, the foundations of which are typically regarded as innate. The deeper properties of linguistic phenomena cannot from this perspective be understood directly from data. Rather, the utterances in an actual text or transcript of speech reflect (quite imperfectly, it is generally believed) an underlying system that is governed by rules that predict the form taken by idealized linguistic units. Radical formalism is in our terms an extreme manifestation of this standpoint, one that limits linguistic study to the investigation of this covert system, totally independent of the uses to which it is put. For a critique of both radical positions and a plea for the recognition of both flexibility (i.e. variability) and rigidity (i.e. the requirement for rules) in the make-up of language, see Givón (2002: ch. 2).

The position taken by FDG lies between these extremes. FDG, like formalist models, seeks to describe the knowledge that underlies a language user's potential to communicate in his/her language in an explicit and highly formalized way. The language user is seen as having knowledge both of units (e.g. lexemes, auxiliaries, syntactic constituents, phonemes) and of the ways in which these units may be combined (into Discourse Acts, Propositions,

Clauses, and Intonational Phrases). This knowledge displays a large degree of stability, such that it can be compared across languages, revealing universal trends in linguistic structure, as studied in language typology. However, FDG takes the position that this knowledge of units and their combination is instrumental in interpersonal communication and has arisen as a result of historical processes: forms that have served Speakers well through the ages have sedimented into the repertory now available to language users and are well-adapted to their purposes. The forms that are at language users' disposal are variable across languages, but do not vary without limits. Rather, the limits on variation are set by the range of communicative purposes displayed by all language users and by the cognitive constraints they are subject to. FDG thus offers not only an inventory of forms but also seeks to clarify how these are combined in verbal interaction.

The two sides of the dualist position taken by FDG, i.e. its orientation to both form and function, may perhaps be compared to different ways of analysing the bicycle (here disregarding the fact that, while a bicycle is an artefact purposefully invented to satisfy certain needs, language has evolved naturally). One aspect of an FDG-style analysis of a bicycle would be to give a complete and descriptively adequate account of this phenomenon, i.e. one that accurately covers all necessary properties for an object to count as a bicycle: a frame with certain geometrical and engineering properties, a handlebar, pedals, a chain, etc., and of course two wheels (with their various characteristics). The account would make a distinction between allowable variation (for instance in the overall size of the bicycle or in the relative size of the wheels) and impermissible variation (without pedals and chain, the object is a child's scooter rather than a bicycle; with fewer or more than two wheels it is not a well-formed bicycle, but a monocycle or tricycle, for example). A description of other non-criterial properties of a bicycle, such as a bell or lights, would be added for completeness. These, then, would be elements of the formalist side of the FDG account.

What is missing from this description is any indication of how the bicycle is used for human purposes (transportation, diversion, competition, etc.). In principle, such a function-free description is possible, but is less enlightening: it offers no answer to the question why bicycles have been designed to have two wheels, just as the formalist account offers no answer to the question why languages have evolved to have the properties that they do have. What is more, it fails to show how the variation in the weight and structure of bicycles depends upon the uses to which they are put: a bicycle designed to carry shopping will not be suitable for racing and vice versa. Similarly, the formalist account does not clarify how linguistic structures co-vary with the purposes to which they are put in communication.

The both-function-and-form approach (such as FDG adopts within linguistics) offers an understanding of why the unmarked form of the cycle is the bicycle. The monocycle offers the advantages of small size and light weight and of consequently being extremely manoeuvrable in traffic; on the other hand, it is relatively dysfunctional in being highly unstable (for the untrained user), in being largely limited to even surfaces and in not offering the possibility of transporting goods. The tricycle is highly stable, can be used in a range of environments and for the transportation of goods; however, it is relatively heavy, obstructive, and difficult to manoeuvre. In this light, the bicycle emerges as a perfect compromise, being of moderate weight, fairly stable (in use), appropriate for flat and inclined surfaces, and offering reasonable facilities for transportation.

This example typifies the FDG approach to linguistic forms. FDG recognizes that the forms taken by utterances are variable but that the variation is limited by the (communicative rather than transportational!) needs of users. Let us give a couple of linguistic examples that will be developed in later chapters. There is a strong tendency for the principal units of verbal interaction (Discourse Acts) to contain one element with the pragmatic function Focus (for details, see 2.7.2.2). Only under rather special circumstances will it contain more than one Focus (as in such multiple wh questions as *Who gave what to whom?*). In a sense it might indeed seem more efficient to cram many Foci into one Discourse Act, and some languages, such as English, do not forbid this from happening, although others do. Why there should be a preference for one-Focus Discourse Acts is something to be explained in terms of human communicative practices. Similarly, the units describing States-of-Affairs will across languages tend to contain one or two essential participants (arguments) (for details, cf. Chapter 3); certain languages also permit predications with three or more arguments, and certain languages permit predications without any arguments. Again, the question arises why this should be (as with the two wheels of the bicycle). Whereas a formalist description confines itself to a mere observation of this regularity, the approach taken by FDG calls for an explanation in terms of human cognition and communication.

FDG shares with the formalist approach, but not with certain more radical functionalist approaches, that it is concerned with the criterial properties of the language under description. Just as the laws of a country may require that a bicycle be provided with a bell and lights, so social conventions may require linguistic utterances to display certain properties. To the extent that these are not criterial to the functioning of language, these properties fall outside the scope of an FDG. Thus FDG will not concern itself directly with the impact of *genre* distinctions on linguistic form: the distinction between the style of an official letter and that of an informal e-mail, for example, falls outside the scope of FDG, since this concerns norms of communication rather than properties of the language system. However, where norms do impinge upon the system, e.g. through the introduction of systematic oppositions that reflect interpersonal relations (honorific morphology, pronouns of intimacy and distance), these must be accounted for.

The above will have made clear that FDG is what Butler (2003) refers to as a *structural-functional grammar*, a term which nicely captures its intermediary status. While accepting that grammar is shaped by use, FDG holds 'that in synchronic terms the grammar of a language is indeed a system, which must be described and correlated with function in discourse' (Butler 2003: 30). This standpoint brings FDG into a close relation with two other structural-functional approaches, Systemic-Functional Grammar (SFG; Halliday and Matthiessen 2004) and Role and Reference Grammar (RRG; Van Valin and LaPolla 1997, Van Valin 2005). Although there is no room here for a detailed comparison (but see Butler 2003 for an exhaustive comparison of FG, SFG, and RRG, and Gonzálvez García and Butler 2006 for a mapping in multi-dimensional space of these three approaches and eight others), we may venture the hypothesis that FDG occupies a position intermediate between SFG, which stands closer to radical functionalism, for example in embracing the study of *genre*, and RRG, which stands closer to radical formalism, for example in seeing itself as first and foremost a theory of syntax (Van Valin 2001: 172). A brief consideration of the differences among the three approaches may help to clarify the aims and ambitions of FDG.

A characteristic feature of work in SFG is its orientation to the use of language in social contexts; as explained above, FDG limits itself to systematic grammatical reflections of social meanings. SFG furthermore takes 'the text rather than the sentence' (Halliday 1994: 4505) to be the object of linguistic description. This does not apply to FDG, which is not a 'discourse grammar' in the sense of a grammar of discourse (if such an entity is attainable at all) deriving from text-linguistic analysis. Rather, FDG wishes to understand those systematic properties of the Discourse Act (the *minimal* unit of communication) that require reference to its being situated within an interactive Move by the language user. FDG also differs from SFG in concentrating on the individual-psychological rather than the social dimension of the language user, although the two aspects are of course closely connected in that social interaction is mediated through individual psychologies. A final difference is one of emphasis: whereas FDG has a strong typological orientation, seeking to provide a general theory of linguistic resources, SFG is more centrally concerned with the description of individual languages, only recently having devoted some attention to implications of particular language descriptions for crosslinguistic generalization (cf. Caffarel and Matthiessen 2004). What emerges is a picture of SFG as an approach that shares FDG's general aims but is less oriented to cognition and more to the analysis of texts in their social context: indeed many followers of Halliday prefer the contraction SFL, Systemic-Functional Linguistics, dropping the reference to Grammar.

Nevertheless, a comparison of FDG with its predecessor, FG, does suggest a certain rapprochement with SFG, especially with respect to the work of Fawcett (2000, 2007). In giving equal emphasis to the Interpersonal Level and the Representational Level, FDG shares Halliday and Matthiessen's (2004: 29) concern with the omnipresent dual functionality of language as 'making sense of our experience, and acting out social relationships'. As for the textual metafunction, which Halliday and Matthiessen (2004: 30) see as an 'enabling or facilitating function' reflecting our ability to 'build up sequences of discourse, organizing the discourse flow and creating cohesion and continuity', FDG proposes that grammatically relevant textual relations will be accounted for within each of the levels: at the Representational Level, States-of-Affairs may be grouped into Episodes, and at the Interpersonal Level, Discourse Acts are grouped into Moves. Indeed both the terms 'interpersonal' and 'move' are inspired by SFG-oriented work.

Role and Reference Grammar (RRG), on the other hand, positions itself closer to the formalist end of the spectrum in taking the syntactic unit of the clause as its object of attention, whereas to FDG, being oriented to the Discourse Act, the clause is merely one possible syntactic form. In RRG, the clause receives a single representation, both syntactic and semantic, with information structure being overlaid upon it where relevant. Although FDG recognizes the need for all three types of structure, these are not collapsed into one representation but pertain to three levels of analysis. Apart from a range of technical differences, the central distinction between RRG and FDG is that the former's point of departure is the predicate as a syntactico-semantic unit, whereas the latter sees itself as providing an analysis of the Discourse Act as an interactional unit, with predicates being introduced into the emerging structure where called for.

Whatever the differences of emphasis and execution, FG (as FDG's predecessor) incorporates various aspects of RRG, while proponents of RRG underline the close relationship between their theory and FG. In particular, Van Valin and LaPolla stress that both share a strong typological orientation (1997: 14), that both assume that levels of analysis are structured by means of layering (1997: 46), and that various FG analyses, such as Rijkhoff's layered view of the Np, have been important to RRG proposals (1997: 640). The close relationship between RRG and FG also emerges from Butler's (2003) assessment, and his more recent work on the comparison of models (Gonzálvez García and Butler 2006) shows this to apply equally to FDG. The RRG view of semantic functions (cf. Van Valin 2004), for example, has been very influential on the proposals made here for the treatment of semantic functions (cf. Chapter 3).

Finally, brief mention should be made of a model that displays various similarities to our own, Autolexical Syntax as developed by Sadock (1991). In that theory, the lexicon plays a central role, forging connections between autonomous representations of semantics, syntax, and morphology. Although his theory is unlike ours in separating morphology and syntax and in lacking interpersonal and phonological levels of analysis, it shares our rejection of a derivational model, our commitment to multiple orthogonal representations of linguistic phenomena, and our interest in mismatches between the levels. Where Sadock's model goes further than ours, as presented in the present book, is in presenting and indeed concentrating on the interface conditions between the various levels he proposes; we recognize the importance of such interfaces, but for reasons of space will not enter into a discussion of them in this book.

For all the fruitful overlaps with other approaches, the central point is that FDG sees itself primarily as a grammar of the Discourse Act. Its goal is to describe and, as far as possible, explain the formal properties (syntactic, morphological, and phonological) of Discourse Acts from a functionalist perspective. These formal properties reflect in various ways the dual purposes of the language communicator: to interact successfully and to impart propositional information. The former is modelled at the Interpersonal Level of the grammar, the latter at the Representational. Together these 'formulating' levels form the input to the 'encoding' levels (the Morphosyntactic Level and the Phonological Level) which yield corresponding structures. The nature of these levels will be dealt with in detail in Chapters 2 to 5.

1.4.3 Typology

Linguistic typology, the study of the principles underlying variation across the languages of the world, is an essential source of inspiration for FDG. Linguistic typology is oriented to laying bare limitations on variation, otherwise known as linguistic 'universals', by formulating statements that purport to be true of all languages. Since data is not currently (and is unlikely ever to be) available about all languages, typologists typically, although not exclusively, work with a principled sample of languages (cf. Rijkhoff *et al.* 1993). Even so, the problems arise that the amount of information available in descriptive grammars varies enormously from language to language and that the methodology inevitably compares languages that are used in very different social circumstances, some of them moreover having a written form while others do not. However, even with these difficulties, it has been possible to elaborate a large body of universals, each of which stands in need of explanation. FDG is a theory that is capable of providing a framework for the enunciation and comparison of universals and of offering lines of explanation.

A universal, despite its name, very rarely takes the form of a statement such as 'All languages are . . . / have . . . '. Rather, they make implicational statements that apply within the grammars of all languages, of the form A ⊂ B, to be understood as saying that property A *stands higher in the hierarchy than* B, in other words, if a language has property B it will also have property A. This permits of languages with neither A nor B, both A and B, or A only, but excludes languages with B but without A. The universal A ⊂ B could thus be formulated as a negative statement that 'No language with B will lack A'. Such implication statements may be rendered more complex: where A ⊂ B and B ⊂ C, then A ⊂ B ⊂ C. Where there are multiple implications of this sort, we speak of an implicational hierarchy. The more complex an implicational hierarchy, the more language types are excluded: where n is the number of properties in the hierarchy, the number excluded (m) can be calculated as follows: $m = 2^n - (n + 1)$. For this reason, typologists attempt to strengthen their claims by formulating maximally complex hierarchies. Very often, implicational hierarchies do not apply to all languages in the sample; then it is necessary to formulate statistical implicational hierarchies, which indicate the percentage of the sample for which the hierarchy is true.

The hierarchies apply in principle to all domains of linguistic organization (see van Lier 2005 on their applicability in various areas). In FDG, as mentioned above, a strict division is made between four levels of analysis within the grammar; within each, the options available are subject to being organized into implicational hierarchies. At the Phonological Level, the inventory of phonemes can, at least to some extent, be treated in this manner: the nearly absolute universal /n/ ⊂ /m/ ⊂ /ŋ/ indicates that languages pattern systematically in their inventory of (at least these) nasal phonemes. At the level of morphosyntax, we find universals that apply to the relative distance between affixes and stems: Hengeveld (1989) shows that morphological distinctions pertaining to a range of verbal categories are ordered in terms of relative distance from the stem. The hierarchy in (26):

(26)   qualitative aspect/agentive modality ⊂ tense/realis-irrealis/quantitative aspect/negation ⊂ evidentiality ⊂ illocution ⊂ mitigation-reinforcement

is here to be understood as meaning that morphology with the leftmost meaning has greater proximity to the stem than morphology with the next meaning along, etc.; languages with deviant orderings of morphology are excluded by the hypothesis expressed in this hierarchy. In an FDG framework, two observations should be made about this hierarchy. Firstly, it applies not only to morphology but also to the syntax of auxiliary verbs, as for example in English *They should* (evidentiality) *have* (tense) *begun to* (qualitative aspect) *work*, and indeed FDG treats morphology and syntax at one level, the Morphosyntactic Level. Secondly, the hierarchy also reflects the organization of the grammar into levels: the first three meanings are accounted for at separate layers within the Representational Level, and the last two (the most peripheral) at separate layers of the Interpersonal Level. As we shall see (2.7, 3.3), FDG distinguishes two types of 'evidentiality', reportativity (a category of the Interpersonal Level) and evidentiality proper (a category of the Representational Level).

There are also typological hierarchies that apply more purely to semantics. Here the hierarchies indicate, not as in phonology the presence or absence of categories and the implications derivable from those, but rather the degree to which the forms of the language in question enforce semantic distinctions. The classical example in the area of semantics is the hierarchy of colour distinctions developed by Berlin and Kay (1969) and refined in the intervening decades (for quite a radical revision, see Kay et al. 1997). Their original observations, as they relate to semantic distinctions available in languages, may be represented as the semantic hierarchy (27) (these semantic distinctions are said by Berlin and Kay to correlate with physiological properties of the human perception system; this has however been challenged by Saunders and van Brakel 1997):

(27)   black and white $\subset$ red $\{\subset$ green $\subset$ yellow$\}$ or $\{\subset$ yellow $\subset$ green$\}$ $\subset$ blue
         $\subset$ brown $\subset$ purple and pink and orange and grey

However, this hierarchy is not purely semantic but also morphological in that multimorphemic words for colours (e.g. 'sky colour' for blue) are excluded.

We find a similar combination of semantic and morphosyntactic considerations in Hengeveld (1992)'s discovery of hierarchical relations in the way the languages in his sample express the semantics of non-verbal predication. In the area of non-verbal predication, the following implicational hierarchy is proposed:

(28)   Locative $\subset$ Property $\subset$ Status $\subset$ Possessive

A prediction made by this hierarchy is that, if there is conflation in expression, languages will show the same form for constructions adjacent on this hierarchy. In Turkish, for example, all four types of predication are expressed in the same manner (i.e. total conflation), whereas Babungo uses one strategy for Locative and one other for the remaining three meanings. Spanish introduces a further complication, using one form (*estar*) for Locative and contingent Properties, but another for inherent Properties and all remaining constructions in the hierarchy. These observations, concerning semantic distinctions, clearly pertain to the Representational Level of FDG. Hengeveld (1992) points out that distinctions in this area are also sensitive to the communicative status of the construction as [± presentative], with regard to Locative and Possessive. In FDG, the last-mentioned generalization relates to the Interpersonal Level, where it is understood in terms of the informational status of Subacts (see 2.7.2), with [+ presentative] applying where one Subact is concurrently Topic and Focus. Thus Turkish uses a special strategy for [+ presentative] constructions that involves the introduction of a copula, cf. (29), whereas the formal distinctions in Babungo are indifferent to the presence or absence of presentativeness, cf. (30):

(29) Bahçe-de   köpek var.
      garden-LOC dog   COP
      'There's a dog in the garden.' (Hengeveld 1992: 118)

(30) Zŭ wī   lùu shɔ.
      wife POSS.3.SG COP there
      'He has a wife.'
      "His wife is there."

Implicational hierarchies also apply more generally to the Interpersonal Level. As will be reported in greater detail in 2.5.2.3, Hengeveld *et al.* (2007) have found that the crosslinguistic comparison of the formal marking of illocutionary distinctions in various languages of Brazil reveals a set of interlocking hierarchies. For example, the presence of a content Interrogative (like English *wh*-questions) in a language predicts the presence of a polar Interrogative (like English yes/no-questions), but not vice versa.

The question now arises as to the status of these hierarchies. Although they can be distinguished at each of the levels of analysis in FDG, they do not in themselves form part of the description of individual languages. Rather, they are derived from such descriptions, so that their theoretical status is that of generalizations that permit empirically falsifiable predictions. In other words, they are hypotheses about possible and impossible language systems, since each hierarchy, as mentioned above, excludes certain combinations of values. In addition, they allow linguistic constructions to be categorized in terms of markedness: those that are most restricted in their occurrence, i.e. those that are rightmost in the representation of the hierarchy, are said to be marked. Markedness can manifest itself in various ways: lesser frequency in use, longer forms (i.e. a greater number of phonemes), more syncretism, less suppletion, etc.

The use of hierarchies has manifested its value in intralinguistic studies, too. It is to be expected that linguistic forms, in extending their meanings diachronically, will gradually move from unmarked to more marked items on the hierarchy. For instance, the extension of the meaning of English *will* from Desiderative to Future to Evidential can be seen as following the first three stages of the above-mentioned hierarchy (cf. Goossens 1987). In language acquisition and language attrition, as well, the expectation is that the order in which semantic distinctions are gained or lost respectively as formally marked categories will follow relevant hierarchies (cf. Boland 2006 and Keijzer 2007 respectively for evidence in this regard). Quantitative studies of individual languages, too, such as that of Pérez Quintero (2002) on subordination in English, may be expected to reflect the hierarchies in that more marked, hierarchically lower, categories will be statistically less prevalent than unmarked, hierarchically higher categories. These are thus examples of various ways in which FDG can impact the study of individual languages while remaining under the general inspiration of language typology.

The hierarchies that emerge from crosslinguistic and intralinguistic investigations are more than mere descriptive generalizations, however. The hypothesis must be that the hierarchies, although deriving from distinctions made within linguistic systems, reflect aspects of the cognition that drives linguistic communication. The assumption is that the crosslinguistically most widespread distinctions, i.e. those leftmost on the hierarchies, are those with the greatest degree of communicative salience and/or cognitive or physical simplicity. In phonology, for example, from the presence of implosive consonants in a phoneme inventory we can predict the presence of explosive consonants, but not vice versa:

(31) explosive $\subset$ implosive

This is generally felt to reflect the greater articulatory complexity of implosives (superimposing an ingressive airstream on the basically egressive airstream of speech). In morphosyntax, we find that languages that have Subject assignment differ systematically with respect to the semantic functions of the units that can undergo Subject assignment, roughly according to the following hierarchy (the semantic functions Locative, Undergoer, and Actor will be explained in 3.6.2 and the details of Subject assignment in 4.4.3):

(32) Actor $\subset$ Undergoer $\subset$ Locative

In other words, a language permitting Subject assignment to a unit with a Locative function will also permit Subject to be assigned to Undergoer, but the reverse implication does not hold; examples of such languages are, respectively, English, which does permit Locative Subjects of the recipient type, and French, which does not. The validity of the hierarchy may be understood in terms of the anthropocentricity of language: if Subject assignment is a matter of perspective-taking, speakers as active human beings will most naturally take the vantage point of an Actor; seeing a State-of-Affairs from the viewpoint of an Undergoer, and then of a Locative requires ever greater cognitive effort.

In pragmatics, a prominent distinction, to which we shall return in 2.8.3.2, concerns the identifiability of referents. In FDG we distinguish between identifiability for the Speaker and identifiability for the Addressee; the former is equivalent to specificity and the latter to definiteness. In the typological and Optimality Theory literature (cf. Comrie 1989; Aissen 2003) it has been observed that the pragmatic notion of definiteness and the semantic notion of animacy interact in determining case-marking in ways that can best be captured using hierarchies. Thus Aissen (2003: 437) proposes the following hierarchy for definiteness:

(33)   Personal pronoun ⊂ Proper name ⊂ Definite NP ⊂ Indefinite specific NP ⊂ Non-specific NP

Although FDG does not recognize Np at the Interpersonal Level (but at the Morphosyntactic Level), the Aissen hierarchy comprises various notions that are central to distinctions made at the FDG Interpersonal Level. In FDG terms, we might break the hierarchy down into two as follows, on the assumptions (to be supported in Chapters 2 and 3) that personal pronouns are to be shown as units with an identifiable/specific operator and an abstract head; proper names as units with an identifiable/specific operator and a lexical head; and the remaining categories as all requiring insertion of a lexical head at the Representational Level:

(34)   a.   [+id, +s] ⊂ [−id, +s] ⊂ [−id, −s]
        b.   Interpersonal abstract ⊂ Interpersonal lexical ⊂ Representational lexical

FDG derives much of its inspiration from typological work. At the same time, it can provide a coherent model for the kind of language description that feeds into typological investigations. The application of a framework such as FDG, with its multilayered mode of description, to a wide range of languages will permit more reliable comparisons of language systems. Current typological and language-comparative work tends to eschew particular grammatical models, and indeed Dryer (2006) has recognized that most of this activity is based upon what he calls, following Dixon (1997), 'basic linguistic theory'. By this is simply meant 'traditional grammar, modified in various ways by other theoretical traditions over the years' (Dryer 2006: 212). For Dryer, the functional factors identified by grammarians serve only retroactively to explain instances of language change; he denies that the user of a linguistic system has any access to such factors. In his view, knowing a grammar involves no more than knowing a set of brute facts: the language user is unable to draw the kinds of generalization achieved by typologists. While this is clearly correct, it leaves a number of phenomena unaccounted for. If, as we have suggested, language systems do not vary without limit and the differences between them as well as the changes they undergo can be described and circumscribed in terms of implicational hierarchies, those hierarchies must be tapping into matters of general cognitive relevance. Similarly, if—as has often been found—there is a correlation between hierarchical position and frequency in use, this again suggests that the hierarchies are reflecting cognitive preferences. If FDG sees the hierarchies distilled from applications of its principles to various languages as having explanatory relevance, that is because they together define a space within which linguistic activity is constrained to operate.

1.4.4 Language modelling

The predecessor of FDG, Functional Grammar (FG), proclaimed itself to be a quasi-productive model of the natural language user (Dik 1997a: 1; for detailed presentations of FG see Siewierska 1991 and García Velasco 2003). This was to be interpreted as meaning that the various steps in the grammar should be understood as having a loose parallelism with the temporal sequence of actions conducted by a language user in producing language. Thus the formulation of a communicative intention was seen as being carried out in anticipation of the Addressee's interpretation of the linguistic unit. Encoding was then a matter of linguistic choices judged by the Speaker to be likely to have the desired communicative effect upon the Addressee. For FG, the primary linguistic choice was that of the lexical items. These brought with them various frames, which were fitted together into an underlying predication. This procedure was made fully explicit in the computer model of FG (Dik 1992), which similarly generated linguistic expressions by building upwards from a lexical frame. To the basically semantic underlying predication were added operators and functions which further specified the meaning until every formal property of the linguistic unit could be accounted for.

FDG is like FG in emphasizing the parallels with language production (cf. 1.2.2). However, FDG differs sharply from FG in its architecture, taking not the minimal unit (the lexical predicate) but the Discourse Act as the essential constituent of the entire communicative event initiated by the Speaker as its point of departure. FG was justifiably criticized for treating communicative notions like Topic and Focus (pragmatic functions) as appendages to a semantically complete representation: terms inherited a semantic function from the predicate frame into which they were inserted, e.g. Agent; they could then be adorned with a syntactic function, e.g. Subject; and, finally, to this AgentSubject could be appended the pragmatic function Topic. This suggested a primacy of semantics and syntax over pragmatics that ran counter to the principles of functionalism. FDG reverses this by giving pride of place to the Discourse Act.

In FDG's view, each desire to communicate linguistically involves the appearance of a corresponding intention, which is modelled as taking place in the Conceptual Component. This is the impulse that drives the 'motor' of the grammar. The intention involves a decision to expend linguistic energy, to perform one or more acts in pursuance of the Speaker's desire to influence the thinking and action of the Addressee. These acts typically do not occur in isolation, but form part of a longer-term strategy, and as such are known as Discourse Acts. The grammatical form taken by Discourse Acts (which is the ultimate object of FDG) is often influenced by the presence of preceding and following Discourse Acts. For this reason, Discourse Acts are modelled as combining into Moves where there is grammatical justification for doing so. Moreover, the form of each Move may be influenced by preceding and following Moves. Detailed justification for this approach and the hierarchical structure that follows from it will be given in Chapter 2. Every unit analysed in FDG will thus involve the Discourse Act.

This entails a significant difference between FDG and most other models of grammar. Most grammars see themselves as offering accounts of the clause or the sentence, i.e. syntactic units; although there are countless in-depth studies of smaller syntactic units (the noun phrase or the adpositional phrase, for example), and certain so-called text grammars have sought to extend the range of grammatical study to larger units, this is typically done against the background of the clause as the essential unit of analysis. In practice, this was also true of FG. However, FG did purport from the earliest days to take the linguistic expression (Dik 1978: 15) as its object of analysis, foreshadowing FDG's orientation to units both larger and smaller than the clause. Note in particular that the sentence, as a 'discourse unit whose composition and complexity is subject to cultural variation and rhetorical fashion' (Miller and Weinert 1998: 42), plays very little part in FDG. Although easy to recognize in standardized written languages, it has no straightforward counterpart in oral languages or even in the oral use of languages that do have written forms. As such, it will not be treated within FDG.

What kind of a language model is FDG? It is a fundamental characteristic of functionalist grammars that they seek to relate language form to language function. Those approaches that have attempted to detect the functions underlying the formal distinctions made in language, such as FG, may for this reason be classified as 'form-to-function': they seek to account for formal properties of syntactic units in terms of their functions in communication. FDG, however, takes a rather more complex position, what we might call a *form-oriented 'function-to-form'* approach. It is form-oriented in providing, for each language analysed, an account of only those interpersonal and representational phenomena which are reflected in morphosyntactic or phonological form. It is 'function-to-form' in positing a range of functions flowing from the Speaker's communicative intentions, for example a language-specific set of Illocutions. More specifically, as shown above, communicative intentions are translated in the process of formulation into one or two rather complex functional representations, and these in turn provide the input to the section of the grammar that deals with the formal aspects of utterances, known as encoding.

Formulation involves the strategic arrangement of the communicative intention, which itself is a dynamic, strategic entity, into a temporal sequence of (in principle, discrete) Discourse Acts that may themselves form part of a temporal sequence of larger Moves. As will become clear in Chapter 2, formulation may be restricted to this process, but this usually applies only in the case of relatively simple or ritualized Discourse Acts; in such cases we shall say that only the Interpersonal Level is involved. However, formulation will typically also bring into play the Representational Level, which displays the semantics of the content communicated through the Discourse Acts; Chapter 3 enters into the full detail of this aspect of the formulation process. Formulation is thus distributed over two levels, and deals with the conversion of conceptual material into the functional categories made available by the language system being used by the speaker.

In a simple function-to-form approach, there would be no need for the formulation levels. Then one could progress directly from cognitive intentions to encoding, say in the manner of a phrasebook that tells its users how to ask for a beer or complain about cockroaches in their hotel bedroom without giving them any knowledge of the language. It is because of the obvious inadequacy of a direct linking of cognition to expression, which does no justice to the speaker's knowledge of the formulating potential of his/her language, that FDG adopts a form-oriented function-to-form approach. How does this approach work in practice? What it entails is that, for each language examined, the grammarian will consider all its formal properties (variation in constituent order, the repertory of morphological elements, the distribution of particles, the impact of intonation contours, etc.). Then a determination is made which of these grammatical characteristics regularly reflect distinct communicative intentions, for example the desire to indicate the source of one's observations about reality. If the language possesses a set of forms which reveal this aspect of communicative activity, that is a *prima facie* indication that formulation will make available a semantic category of evidential distinctions; further grammatical analysis will uncover the precise location of the units to which these distinctions apply. More generally, those formal distinctions that pertain to constitutive elements of the communicative intention will be seen as encoding the results of formulation of the Interpersonal and Representational Levels.

In addition, languages will display characteristics that cannot be brought into correspondence with distinct communicative intentions (cf. Moutaouakil 2004). These will be regarded as 'a-functional' and will be accounted for as autonomous characteristics of the Morphosyntactic Level and/or the Phonological Level. For example, the languages of the world divide fairly evenly into those with a syntactic head – modifier arrangement and those with a modifier – head arrangement (in FG terms, Postfield and Prefield languages; cf. Dik 1997a: 397). These arrangements are fairly stable, but have been shown to reverse gradually over millennia (with various mixed structures arising in the interim). The very fact that no preference has arisen for one arrangement over the other strongly suggests that it is a-functional. Neither appears, to use a genetic metaphor, to be better adapted than the other. The Postfield/Prefield distinction will therefore not be derived from deeper communicative motivations, but will be regarded as an autonomous setting at the Morphosyntactic Level, relating to a preference for using unit-initial or unit-final positions as basic. Several alternative constituent orders within a language, however, will be seen as flowing from communicatively motivated distinctions, in keeping with the long tradition of such observations and explanations within functionalist grammar.

A crucial aspect of the FDG methodology is that the process of formulation as reflected at the Interpersonal and Representational Levels will not, for any one language, make distinctions that are not reflected in the language in question: thus in a language in which evidentiality is not reflected morphosyntactically (or phonologically), it will simply not be indicated as an operator at formulation. Although the theory of FDG makes evidentiality operators available as an 'etic' option (since there are demonstrably languages in which relevant distinctions are made), for each language it has to be determined whether they are pertinent, whether they are 'emic': and similarly for every other category introduced in this book. In keeping with the discussion of implicational hierarchies above, none of the distinctions made in FDG inherently carries a claim to universality. In the discussion of parts-of-speech, for example, in 3.7, it will be seen that these, too, are subject to a hierarchy such that the theory allows for languages which make no distinctions in this respect at all.

A further crucial aspect of the FDG methodology, inherited from its predecessor FG, is that it constrains potential analyses of linguistic phenomena to those that do not involve the postulation of transformations and filters

(Dik 1997a: 18–24). These two restrictions ensure that no underlying structures arise that are later discarded. This is warranted from a psycholinguistic point of view, since in this way underlying structures are 'recoverable from their outward manifestations' (Dik 1997a: 23). Furthermore, by applying these constraints there is a limit on possible hypotheses concerning the analysis of a linguistic phenomenon, which strongly enhances the testability of these hypotheses.

1.4.5 On using FDG

It may be useful to conclude this section with some reflection on the uses to which FDG can be put by practising linguists of various kinds. Our principal hope is that FDG will offer a structured framework within which it will be possible to enunciate and test linguistic hypotheses. Because FDG provides an overall perspective on linguistic phenomena, comprising four levels of analysis, and being integrated into a four-component model of the natural language user, it will be possible to articulate those phenomena more clearly and with greater sensitivity to their place in the overall scheme of linguistic things. As Jackendoff (2002: 18), in presenting an encompassing framework for language study, rightly emphasizes, 'Any adequate theory must begin with the fact that even the simplest sentences contain ... rich ... structure' and 'If one wishes to join the conversation about the nature of language, one must recognize and acknowledge this complexity'.

As we stated above, FDG seeks to bring order to this complexity by providing formalizations of its claims. The purpose of these formalizations is to provide a rigorous framework in which linguistic claims can be enunciated, and then tested, substantiated, or disproved, and then submitted to further refinement or sophistication. At the same time, it provides a structure for the observation of linguistic phenomena, and in this way is involved in the entire cycle of research, from observation to prediction, to the testing of prediction through further observation, which leads to new predictions, and so on. A clear example of this cycle pertains to the notion of layering within FDG: the principle of layered structure was first developed in FG (cf. Hengeveld 1989, inspired by Foley and Van Valin 1984) for what is now roughly speaking the Representational Level, and only later with the emergence of FDG was the hypothesis formulated that a similar degree of layering might be found at the Interpersonal Level (Hengeveld 2004a and references cited there); this in turn engendered the expectation that notions established for the Representational Level such as operator and modifier could be equally relevant for the Interpersonal Level (Hengeveld 2004b); and later, this led to the proposal that the FDG notion of layering could also link up with the already generally accepted hierarchical organization of morphosyntax and phonology (as in this book). In short, the parallelisms between the levels themselves have arisen from the cycle of observation and prediction, and provide the basis for new cycles.

Although FDG provides precise representations for its claims, the formalisms it uses should not be confused with the formal languages employed by truth-conditional semanticists and in radical formalism. Ultimately, while every effort is made to keep them mutually consistent, clear and usable, the representations are but a means to the end of insightful analysis of linguistic phenomena.

As is implicit in what has just been said, one form of work within FDG will engender proposals for the development and improvement of the theoretical apparatus. Of particular interest for the further advancement of FDG will be future studies on the interface issue, the question of how best to connect the four concurrent representations that characterize the current model. It is to be expected that mismatches across the various levels will be of particular importance in this enterprise.

As for research primarily oriented to using rather than reforming the model, we may differentiate various emphases. FDG seeks to provide a framework for typological and language-contrastive and language-contact work that is neutral with respect to any specific language type. At the same time, it can be employed for the description of individual languages (but always with a view to the implications for other languages), as well as the growth and decline of languages in contexts of acquisition and attrition. FDG lends itself to the investigation of the crosslinguistic distribution of interpersonal, representational, morphosyntactic, and phonological categories, but also to the detailed examination of individual phenomena within a single language. For various FDG treatments of phenomena in single languages, see the articles in van Staden and Keizer (fc.), Hengeveld and Wanders (fc.) and Hattnher and Hengeveld (2007).

As we emphasized above, FDG, despite its name, is not a functionally oriented Discourse Grammar (in the sense of an account of discourse relations). Rather, it is an account of the inner structure of Discourse Acts that is sensitive to the impact of their use in discourse upon their form. From this viewpoint, there is little to be gained from an application of FDG as a tool for the inductive examination of texts or segments from the transcription of speech. As Butler (2004) points out, the proper relation between functionalist theories and corpora is for the former to provide hypotheses which can be tested against data; for a fine FDG example, see Anstey (2006). The description of data in corpora need be no more exhaustive than is necessary for the analytical task at hand. As we will show in the next section, FDG provides for the possibility of formally simplifying non-essential aspects of its representations with a view to focusing on the essential questions.

1.5 Notational conventions

As the formalisms for the various levels are further elaborated in the following chapters, they will become increasingly detailed and complex. Such detail is necessary for the model to achieve precision and predictive power. In order to enhance readability, we apply a number of special conventions within the formalisms.

The first concerns the use of different typefaces for variables at the different levels of analysis, tacitly applied in the preceding text: capitals at the Interpersonal Level (e.g. 'M' for Move), lower case at the Representational Level (e.g. 'ep' for episode), title case at the Morphosyntactic Level (e.g. 'Np' for Noun Phrase), and small capitals at the Phonological Level (e.g. 'PP' for Phonological Phrase). At all levels operators are given in lower case and functions in title case.

Secondly, in many cases not all details are necessary for the analysis of the phenomenon at hand. For these situations we use a special symbol '–' to indicate the beginning and the end of a fragment that is not further analysed in detail. Thus, if we are just interested in the nature of the relation between Discourse Acts within a Move, the analysis of (35) may be as in (36):

(35)   Watch out, because there is a bull in the field.

(36) $(M_I: [(A_I: -\text{watch out}- (A_I)) (A_J: -\text{there is a bull in the field}- (A_J))_{Expl}]$
        $(M_I))$

in which it is indicated that A_J is grammatically encoded as an explanation of A_I, but no further claims are made as to the internal structure of the Discourse Acts.

Similarly, at the Representational Level, if one is interested in the semantic functions of arguments irrespective of their internal complexity, (37) may be represented as in (38):

(37)   My neighbour bought a book about bullfighting.

(38) $(f_i: [(f_j: \text{buy} (f_j)) (x_i: -\text{my neighbour}- (x_i))_A (x_j: -\text{a book about}$
        $\text{bullfighting}- (x_j))_U] (f_i))$

in which it is indicated that x_i is the Actor and x_j the Undergoer in the buying State-of-Affairs, but no details are given about the internal structure of these two descriptions of Individuals.

In a similar way morphosyntactic representations may be simplified if, for example, one is interested in Phrases rather than in Words; and phonological representations may be simplified if, for example, one wants to concentrate on Phonological Phrases rather than on Phonological Words. An example of the former is given in (20a) above, in which (Np$_i$: (Nw$_i$: ik$_{Pro}$ (Nw$_i$)) (Np$_i$)) is reduced to (Np$_i$: –ik– (Np$_i$)), and so on. An analogous reduction of (20b) would yield the following phonological representation:

(39)   (U$_i$: [(IP$_i$: [(PP$_i$: –kuɑu– (PP$_i$)) (PP$_j$: –dɑtikuɑm– (PP$_j$))] (IP$_i$))] (U$_i$))

Another important convention applied within FDG formalizations concerns the use of subscripts for variables. In presenting general frames and templates we use numerical subscripts, indicating that the variable is uninstantiated. In representations of actual examples we use alphabetical subscripts, indicating that the variable is instantiated. Thus, the general frames underlying (36) and (38) are (40) and (41) respectively:

(40)   (M$_1$: [(A$_1$) (A$_2$)$_{Expl}$] (M$_1$))

(41)   (f$_1$: [(f$_2$) (x$_1$)$_A$ (x$_2$)$_U$] (f$_1$))

Square brackets are used to keep elements together that are in a non-hierarchical relationship with respect to one another, but together are hierarchically subordinate to a higher layer, as in (40), where the two Discourse Acts are non-hierarchically related, but together within the scope of the (M$_1$)-variable, or as in (41), where three semantic categories are in a non-hierarchical relation, but all three within the scope of the (f$_1$)-variable. Finally, curly brackets are used in cases in which it is desirable to explicitly indicate the optionality of elements.

In running text, words are capitalized when they are used as technical terms as applied within the FDG framework. Thus, we use capitals for analytical units such as Move, Propositional Content, Verb Phrase, and Phonological Word, but also for operators and functions such as Past, Undergoer, Subject, etc., even though the latter are not capitalized in representations.

One aspect of our glossing conventions requires brief comment. When giving examples from languages other than English, we supply a morphemic gloss according to the principles of the Leipzig Glossing Rules, <http://www.eva.mpg.de/lingua/files/morpheme.html>; the glosses listed as an appendix to those rules have been used, supplemented by many more, as required by the data examined (see the list of Abbreviations and Symbols preceding this chapter). The morphemic gloss is followed by a idiomatic translation of the example into English between single quotation marks. In addition, but only where this aids the understanding of the example, we also provide a more literal translation between double quotation marks. For a case in point, see (1) in this chapter.

1.6 Structure of the book

This book offers a complete overview of Functional Discourse Grammar, understood as the Grammatical Component of the full theory of verbal interaction set out in Figure 2 above. The next four chapters deal at length with the four levels of analysis, beginning with the two formulation levels and moving on to the two encoding levels. Accordingly, Chapter 2 deals with the Interpersonal Level and Chapter 3 with the Representational Level. The overall structure of these two chapters is, as far as this is possible, the same: the aim is to bring out the default relations that hold between the inner workings of each level. Chapter 4 presents the Morphosyntactic Level, working down from the highest to the lowest layers of analysis, and the same technique applies in Chapter 5, devoted to the Phonological Level.

The data examined in the following chapters have been drawn from a variety of sources. The principal source has been a wide range of grammatical descriptions of the languages of the world; our intellectual debt to the authors of those descriptions is enormous. Alongside consultation of our own intuitions about languages we know well, we have also had recourse to the Internet as a source of data. For aesthetic reasons, and also in the knowledge that URLs can change or disappear overnight, we have in such cases simply used the indication 'Internet'.

Since this book is primarily oriented to the presentation of a theory rather than the analysis of data (although we hope to persuade the reader that the theory promises interesting analyses), the linguistic examples are cited above all to illustrate the potential of FDG. Our analyses of particular phenomena should therefore be taken as indicative rather than as representing any claim to a definitive FDG statement (if such were even possible) about the phenomena in question.

2

The Interpersonal Level

2.1 Introduction

This chapter is concerned with the Interpersonal Level of FDG. As the name suggests, this is the level that deals with all the formal aspects of a linguistic unit that reflect its role in the interaction between the Speaker and the Addressee. Each participant in an interaction does so with a particular purpose in mind. In some cases, that purpose may be very prominent (as in a job interview); in others, the purpose may be merely to sustain social relationships (as in phatic communion). The purposiveness of interaction entails that each speaker will employ a strategy to attain his/her communicative goals. This strategy—of which the speaker may or may not be fully conscious—will have to take account of the fact that language production unfolds in time, and that not all goals can be attained immediately. In most instances of communication, a number of steps will be needed before the final goal is achieved. En route, the speaker may have to deal with misunderstandings, interruptions, and irrelevancies, and possibly the rejection of his/her purposes. Achieving one's communicative purposes thus involves the input of energy, yielding a series of actions governed by the overall strategy; and these actions take place in the knowledge that the Addressee also has his/her own purposes and strategies.

The properties of interactions that follow from their strategic, purposive nature are studied in a range of disciplines that fall under the general headings of rhetoric and pragmatics. Rhetoric is fundamentally concerned with the ways in which components of a discourse are ordered towards the achievement of the speaker's communicative strategy, and also with the formal properties of utterances that influence the Addressee to accept the Speaker's purposes. For that reason, those formal aspects of linguistic units that reflect the overall structuring of discourse will be accounted for in FDG in terms of rhetorical functions. Pragmatics will here be understood as studying how speakers mould their messages in view of their expectations of the Addressee's current state of mind. This influences, for instance, which parts of a linguistic unit will be presented as particularly salient, which are chosen as the Speaker's point of departure, and which are taken to be shared by Speaker and Addressee. The influence of these considerations upon the structure of linguistic units will be examined under the rubric of pragmatic functions.

The units to which these functions are assigned together form a hierarchical structure within the Interpersonal Level. The highest node in this structure represents the particular segment of discourse under analysis, with various intermediary layers leading down to components of the individual linguistic unit. Each of the elements of this hierarchical structure represents (or describes) an action, which may itself be internally complex, consisting of distinguishable smaller actions, just as the action of running consists of distinguishable movements by the arms and legs, and within those, distinct movements of the right and left limbs. At the layers of the Move and the Discourse Act the hierarchy crucially also represents the sequence or time course of the actions, which is essential to the realization of the Speaker's strategy. The positioning of a Subsidiary Discourse Act before or after a Nuclear Discourse Act to which it is attached, determines whether it is understood as an Orientation (as in the first element of *Football, I don't really like it*) or as a Clarification (as in the last element of *I don't really like it, football*). The sequencing of linguistic actions thus reflects the order of their strategic organization by the Speaker.

The Speaker's communicative decisions are not modelled within the grammar as such, but in the Conceptual Component of the wider theory of verbal interaction described in 1.2.5. It is this component that triggers the functioning of the grammar as a whole, starting with the Interpersonal and Representational Levels. The Conceptual Component thus contains the Speaker's communicative intention and the strategies that s/he wishes to deploy in order to achieve that intention. There will thus be a certain mapping between the content of the Conceptual Component and the contents of the Interpersonal and Representational Levels. However, whereas the contents of the Conceptual Component are in principle unconstrained by language, the frames made available within the grammar restrict the number of expressive choices available to the Speaker. To give one simple example: a Speaker will feel several grades of nuance in the formality of his/her relationship to the Addressee, but in a language such as French must choose between the *tu* (informal) and *vous* (formal) forms of pronouns and verbs.

At the same time, the possible discrepancies between the Conceptual Component and the initial levels of the grammar allow the Speaker to indicate his/her intention indirectly. The intention to have the Addressee close a window may be expressed directly by means of a mitigated Imperative Illocution (*Please close the window*), or indirectly by means of a Declarative Illocution (e.g. *There's a draught in here*). What the grammar will contain in the former case is an indication of the Imperative Illocution. In the latter case, however, there will be merely an indication of the Declarative Illocution, since there is no direct linguistic reflection of the Speaker's intention. The Addressee's task is to find the communicative relevance of this Declarative Illocution, and (if the social relations between Speaker and Addressee are appropriate) to act upon it by closing the offending window. The FDG position on indirect speech acts is thus that the grammar represents communicative intentions only to the extent that they are encoded in the message. Similarly, a Speaker may indicate displeasure with someone by praising him/her ironically (*She IS a fine friend!*). But only where the language offers a systematic means of displaying irony, for example by means of a recognizable intonation contour (Chapter 5) or a grammatical particle (Chapter 4), will this be reflected at the Interpersonal Level as an aspect of the grammar.

2.2 The organization of the Interpersonal Level

The Interpersonal Level contains descriptions of all and only those properties of linguistic units that reflect, and indeed influence, their use in verbal interaction. It is modelled in FDG as a hierarchical structure that indicates the part-whole relations among units of discourse. The hierarchical structure shows how Moves are composed of Discourse Acts, how Discourse Acts themselves are built up from component elements, and also how one of those component elements of Discourse Acts, the Communicated Content, itself contains Subacts. The sections of this chapter will follow the hierarchical structure downwards from the largest to the smallest units. Section 2.3 will deal with the Move, and 2.4 with the Discourse Act; the following sections will deal with the components of the Discourse Act, namely the Illocution (2.5), the Participants (2.6), and the Communicated Content (2.7) respectively; 2.8, on the Subact, deals with the components of the Communicated Content. A final section, 2.9, demonstrates the gradual build-up of the Interpersonal Level in a dynamic implementation.

There is strong parallelism among the structures at the various hierarchical layers within the Interpersonal Level (and exactly the same formula applies to the structures at the Representational Level, see 3.2.3):

  (i) each layer and each component of each layer is symbolized by an indexed variable (V);
  (ii) each variable can be expanded by a lexical item or by a complex representation of a lower layer, to be known as the head (H);
  (iii) each head can be further modified by one or more modifiers (Σ), again either drawn from the lexicon, or internally complex;

(iv) each variable can be specified by one or more operators (π), which will be expressed by grammatical or phonological rather than lexical means;

(v) the units at each layer may have a function (Φ), rhetorical or pragmatic.

The resultant structure of each layer is as follows:

(1) $(\pi V_1: H (V_1): \Sigma^N (V_1))_\Phi$

Note that only the variable is obligatory, i.e. the minimum structure is (V_1). In each of the following sections, we shall consider which heads H, modifiers Σ, operators π, and, where relevant, functions Φ are available for each of the units symbolized by a variable. In this way, we shall determine the inventory of frames that must be assumed for each kind of unit.

Applying the structure in (1) to the various layers that will be discussed in this chapter, we arrive at the overall organization of the Interpersonal Level in (2).

(2)

$(\pi M_1:$ [Move
     $(\pi A_1:$ [Discourse Act
         $(\pi F_1: ILL (F_1): \Sigma (F_1))$ Illocution
         $(\pi P_1:\ldots(P_1): \Sigma (P_1))_\Phi$ Speaker
         $(\pi P_2:\ldots(P_2): \Sigma (P_2))_\Phi$ Addressee
         $(\pi C_1:$ [Communicated Content
             $(\pi T_1: [\ldots] (T_1): \Sigma (T_1))_\Phi$ Subact of Ascription
             $(\pi R_1: [\ldots] (R_1): \Sigma (R_1))_\Phi$ Subact of Reference
         $] (C_1): \Sigma (C_1))_\Phi$ Communicated Content
     $] (A_1): \Sigma (A_1))_\Phi$ Discourse Act
$] (M_1): \Sigma (M_1))$ Move

In cases of multiple Discourse Acts within a Move, the linear ordering of the Discourse Acts reflects their temporal succession. Within the individual Discourse Act, where units no longer have a rhetorical function but only a pragmatic function, the linear ordering of elements in the structure is arbitrary. Note that in the case of multiple Discourse Acts within the Move, overlaps at the Morphosyntactic Level are possible such that the expression of one Discourse Act, once started, may be interrupted by another Discourse Act before being completed later, as in the case of certain centre-embedded non-restrictive relative clauses, cf. (3):

(3)   The game (beginning of A_I), which began at 7.30 (A_J), ended in a draw (end of A_I).

The description of (3) at the Interpersonal Level will show the Discourse Acts ordered as (A$_I$) before (A$_J$), since (A$_J$) starts later. The coreference between the Referential Subacts in (A$_I$) and (A$_J$) triggers the formation and positioning of the non-restrictive relative clause at the Morphosyntactic Level.

2.3 The Move

2.3.1 Introduction

FDG assumes that the largest unit of interaction relevant to grammatical analysis is the Move (M). In terms of its interpersonal status, a Move may be defined as an autonomous contribution to an ongoing interaction (cf. Kroon's 1995: 66 definition of the Move as a 'minimal free unit of discourse'). More specifically, what is characteristic of a Move is that it either is, or opens up the possibility of, a reaction. In other words, a Move has a perlocutionary effect. Whereas a Discourse Act (cf. 2.4) may provoke a backchannel (i.e. a response that encourages the Speaker to continue), only a Move can provoke a reaction from the interlocutor (an answer to a question, an objection to a point of argument, etc.), and that reaction must itself take the form of a Move. Since Moves may consist of a single Discourse Act, it is not always easy to distinguish between the two. A Move may be grammatically relevant because it corresponds to a single grammatically identifiable unit of discourse, or because it serves as the domain for certain grammatical processes, such as reflexivization (4.4.9).

The alternation of Moves is clearest in conversation. There, a Move will often correspond with a Speaker's turn. Thus in a simple conversation like the following, each turn corresponds exactly to a Move:

(4)   A: What is the capital of Latvia?
     B: Riga.

Note that the correspondence between Moves and turns is not perfect, since a Speaker may elect to use a turn to perform two or more Moves, as in B's turn in (5):

(5)   A: What is the capital of Latvia?
     B: Riga. Why do you ask?
     A: I'm doing my homework.

The completeness of a Move in the spoken language will typically be indicated intonationally; the Phonological Level (Chapter 5) will in those cases be sensitive to the extent of each Move as indicated at the Interpersonal Level, for example clearly distinguishing the two Moves in B's turn in (5). Let us consider the following example from everyday life.

A customer's order in a butcher's shop may be quite complex in terms of turns, but will still amount to one Move. After each turn, the customer gives the butcher time to fetch or prepare the item ordered in that turn. Accordingly, the naming of each item will show a non-terminal contour, only the last turn having an intonation that indicates closure of the Move. Consider the following dialogue, in which both the Customer and the Butcher perform three Moves each (Cn and Bn respectively):

(6)   Customer: Good morning. (Move C1)
      Butcher: Good morning. (Move B1) What will it be today? (Move B2)
      Customer: 100 grams of ham ↗
                Butcher places ready-sliced ham on counter.
                200 grams of roast beef ↗
                Butcher places ready-sliced roast beef on counter.
                And four meatballs ↘ (Move C2)
                Butcher places four meatballs on counter.
      Butcher: Here you are. (Move B3)
      Customer: Thank you. (Move C3)

After the initial exchange of greetings (Moves C1 and B1), the Butcher utters Move (B2), to which the Customer responds with a complex Move consisting of three Discourse Acts. To make life easier for the butcher, s/he breaks the Move up into its component Discourse Acts; the completion of the Move is signalled by the falling intonation on the last Discourse Act. Note that the butcher might also have accompanied the various actions with a backchannel (e.g. *yes*), but that only the final *Thank you* constitutes a separate Move.

The completeness of a Move in the written language will typically be reflected in the strategic division of the text recognized as the paragraph. In an argumentative genre, the introductory statement of the paragraph, the units (typically sentences) developing that statement and its conclusion will each typically be Discourse Acts within that Move. In narrative genres a Move will tend to correspond rather well with an Episode (see 3.4). Yet whereas the Episode is an objectively established set of connected States-of-Affairs, the Move remains above all a strategic unit that derives from the Speaker's communicative intentions. Consider in this respect the following translated narrative fragment from a Dutch television talk show (Redeker 2006):

(7)   a.   but we had a seamstress
      b.   *and* we were calling her Mietje.
      c.   But I think we were calling everyone Mietje back then
      d.   you know, I don't know why,
      e.   but anyway,

   f.   so that was also a Mietje.

   g.   *And* uh- she was from Belgium.

   h.   *And* there were- she was a Belgian refugee,

   i.   'cause during during the war, during the First World War

   j.   all those refugees were coming from Belgium,

   k.   *and* they were coming to Zealand

   l.   *and* they were looking for work there.

   m.   *And* so SHE was our seamstress, (...)

The main episode introducing the seamstress Mietje is here interrupted twice by interruptions (shown through indentation) which comment on the main storyline. The narrator apparently realizes the need to provide certain types of background information for the addressee to be able to properly understand this part of the story. These interruptions are strategically determined and therefore correspond to separate Moves at the Interpersonal Level. Note that the interruptions are accompanied by 'push' (*but*, *'cause*) and 'pop' (*so*) markers (Polanyi & Scha 1983) indicating digression from and return to the main storyline respectively.

The complexity of a Move in discourse may vary from silence (for example, where the Reaction to an Initiation is a shrug unaccompanied by any linguistic sign) to a lengthy stretch of discourse. Where linguistic material is present, it will always take the form of one or more Discourse Acts. The general frame for a Move with linguistic content may therefore be symbolized as follows:

(8) $(\pi\, M_1: [(A_1) \ldots (A_{1+N})_{\{\Phi\}}]\, (M_1): \Sigma\, (M_I))$, where $n \geq 0$

Moves may have functions, and these may impinge on their expression, but we will refrain from discussing and representing these functions. The reason for this is that Moves constitute the highest layer of the Interpersonal Level that we consider here, and their functions can only be sensibly studied in relation to the longer stretches of discourse in which they figure.

2.3.2 Heads

The head of each Move will be one or more Discourse Acts. Discourse Acts have been defined by Kroon (1995: 65) as 'the smallest identifiable units of communicative behaviour. In contrast to the higher order units called Moves, they do not necessarily further the communication in terms of approaching a conversational goal'. Their own internal characteristics will be further discussed in 2.4 below. Of interest here is the possibility of the head of the Move consisting of several Discourse Acts. In such cases, the relationship between these Discourse Acts may be one of two kinds: equipollence and dependence.

Equipollence holds between two Discourse Acts to which the Speaker gives equal communicative status. Consider the following dialogue:

(9)   A: What happened yesterday in the Scottish Premier League?
      B: Celtic won. And Rangers lost.

A's Initiation Move provokes B's Reaction Move, which in turn consists of two Discourse Acts, each with its own intonation contour (although less distinctly so than in the case of a turn consisting of more than one Move), and each with the same communicative status. The analysis will be as in (10):

(10) $(M_I: [(A_I : -Celtic\ won- (A_I)) (A_J: -Rangers\ lost- (A_J))] (M_I))$

In actual practice, it can be hard to determine whether two equipollent units, as in (9B), are two Discourse Acts or two Moves. As a criterion for determining the Discourse Act status of each of these units, we can apply the test of adding modifiers such as *briefly*, indicating a stylistic property of the Discourse Act. As we shall see in 2.4.3 below, adverbials of this type function as modifiers at the layer of the Discourse Act. The proposed analysis of (9B) as in (10) is thus supported by the possibility of adding *briefly* to the second unit:

(11)   Celtic initially went two goals behind and seemed to be in big trouble but thanks to a fantastic hattrick from their new signing ended up winning. And, briefly, Rangers lost.

Compare (12), in which there is only one Discourse Act:

(12)   Briefly, Celtic won and Rangers lost.

Inasmuch as (11) will typically be pronounced as several Intonational Phrases, and (12) as one, we see that Discourse Acts often correspond to one intonation unit, a point to be pursued in 2.4 and 5.4 below.

Dependence holds between Discourse Acts to which the Speaker gives unequal communicative status. Dependence is shown in underlying representation through the presence of a rhetorical function on the Subsidiary Discourse Act. A Subsidiary Discourse Act may have various rhetorical functions, such as Motivation, Concession, Orientation, and Correction.

Consider a Move such as (13):

(13)   Watch out, because there will be trick questions in the exam.

Here, the Speaker's strategy is oriented to warning the Addressee. This strategy is implemented by uttering two (intonationally distinct) Discourse Acts in succession, one with an Imperative Illocution and one with a Declarative Illocution (cf. 2.5 below). The presence of the conjunction *because* indicates that the second Discourse Act is intended to be understood as subsidiary to the first, specifically as indicating the Speaker's Motivation for uttering the Imperative Illocution. A Move such as (13) will therefore be analysed as in (14), with the function Motivation showing the dependency of (A_J):

(14) $(M_I: [(A_I: -watch out- (A_I)) (A_J: -there will be trick questions in the exam- (A_J))_{Motiv}] (M_I))$

Compare (15), in which the dependency is in the other direction:

(15) There will be trick questions in the exam, so watch out.

(15) contains the marker *so*, which indicates the Nucleus status of the Discourse Act in which it occurs, and will accordingly be analysed as follows:

(16) $(M_I: [(A_I: -there will be trick questions in the exam- (A_I))_{Motiv}(A_J: watch out (A_J))] (M_I))$

Notice that (14) and (16) indicate the order in which the Discourse Acts are uttered within the Move and that the realization of the Rhetorical Functions is dependent upon the relative positioning of the Discourse Act with the function Motivation with respect to the Nucleus. If the Motivation precedes the Nucleus, realization by *because* is impossible; and marking of the Nucleus by *so* is possible only if it follows the Motivation:

(17) *Because there will be trick questions in the exam, watch out.

(18) *So watch out, there will be trick questions in the exam.

Subsidiary Discourse Acts are often, as in (13), expressed in ways that are reminiscent of the expression of clause Modifiers at the Representational Level, here by a clause introduced by the subordinator *because*. However, we may observe that there are conjunctions/subordinators that are specialized for the expression of Subsidiary Discourse Acts, such as, in the realm of Motivation, English *for*, French *car*, Dutch *want*, and German *denn* (cf. also Jadir 2005).

Another dependency relation is that between Nucleus and Concession, as in (19), to be analysed as in (20):

(19) The work was fairly easy, although (I concede that) it took me longer than expected.

(20) $(M_I: [(A_I: -the work was fairly easy- (A_I))(A_J: -it took me longer than expected- (A_J))_{Conc}] (M_I))$

The Concession relation holds not only between units of the Representational Level but also, as is evidenced here by the possibility of inserting the performative predicate *concede* in (19), between two Discourse Acts (cf. Crevels 2000:

32–3). Note that the order of Discourse Acts is again of importance here, as with *because* and *so* above. In (21), for example, the relationship does not hold between two Discourse Acts, but between two Propositional Contents at the Representational Level:

(21) Although (*I concede that) the work took longer than expected it was easy.

This is shown by the difficulty of adding *I concede that* to the first clause in (21). Returning to Subsidiary Discourse Acts of Concession, note the possibility of marking the Nucleus with *but*, as in:

(22) The work (admittedly) took longer than expected, but it was easy.

The subsidiary status of the first Discourse Act in (22) is supported by the possibility of adding the modifier *admittedly*, which engenders the expectation of an upcoming Nucleus:

(23) $(M_I: [(A_I: –the work took longer than expected– (A_I))_{Conc} (A_J: it was easy (A_J))] (M_I))$

Other Subsidiary Discourse Acts do not relate two entire Discourse Acts, but rather relate one Discourse Act to some constituent part of the Nuclear Discourse Act. This applies for example to the phenomena referred to in FG as Theme and Tail (Dik 1997a: 389–405), as in (24a–b), respectively:

(24) a. My brother, I promise not to betray him.
      b. I promise not to betray him, my brother.

As with the *because* and *although* clauses discussed above, the relative ordering of the elements is vital to an understanding of their functioning. That *my brother* in (24a) is a Discourse Act is clear from the fact that it is encoded as a separate Intonational Phrase and that it can have its own Illocution (cf. *My brother? I promise not to betray him*). Constructions such as (24a) arise from the Speaker's desire, within one Move, to perform the Discourse Act of introducing a referent into the discourse before moving on to a new Discourse Act which is relevant to that referent. The Communicated Content of the Discourse Act constituted by *my brother* in (24a) will contain only a Subact of Reference. The function of the Discourse Act will be that of Orientation, as it serves to orient the Addressee to the Speaker's communicative intentions:

(25) $(M_I: [(A_I: –my brother– (A_I))_{Orient} (A_J: –I promise not to betray him– (A_J))] (M_I))$

The Orientation function is clearly not relevant to the 'Tail' in (24b), which occurs after the Nuclear Discourse Act has been completed. It appears to result from the Speaker's self-monitoring, and indeed Geluykens (1987) found that Tails are typical of unplanned spoken interaction. This is supported by the observation that they can also occur in mid-Discourse Act, to correct or clarify a Subact of Reference or Ascription that the Speaker suspects may not be communicatively adequate:

(26)   I'd like to give your mother—your sister (I mean)—her book back.

(27)   Can you drive—(I mean) ride—my bike home?

Nevertheless, since the Speaker is clearly carrying out a Discourse Act of self-correction, instructing the Addressee to replace some element in his/her cognitive representation, we shall represent a Tail as a Discourse Act in its own right and regard it as following the Discourse Act an element of which it corrects. Example (24b) will thus be represented as in (28):

(28) $(M_I: [(A_I: -I$ promise not to betray him– $(A_I))$ $(A_J: -my$ brother– $(A_J))_{Cor}]$ $(M_I))$

Note that the Corrective function may be signalled by markers such as *I mean* in (26) and (27).

Frequent use of the Orientational or Corrective strategy in a language may lead to the emergence of a pattern at the Morphosyntactic Level with a preclausal and postclausal position that come to be used for elements that do not represent Subsidiary Acts but pertain to the Nuclear Discourse Act itself. In 4.4.1 these positions will be identified as the preclausal position P^{pre} and the postclausal position P^{post}, both to be interpreted with respect to the clausal position P^{centre}. Let us consider an example. The *if*-clause in (29) is given by Dik (1997b: 132) as an instance of an Orientation. However, in this sentence the relation between the *if*-clause and the apodosis holds between two Propositional Contents at the Representational Level, since the Speaker makes going to the movies dependent upon another State-of-Affairs:

(29)   If you don't stop crying, then we won't go to the movies.

At the Interpersonal Level, (29) contains a single Discourse Act, with a Declarative Illocution, which is contained in a Move with the strategic status of a warning. The placement of *if you don't stop crying* in P^{pre}, as evidenced by the comma and the presence of *then* in the initial position of the main clause, is therefore to be understood as an application of the autonomous $[P^{pre}, P^{centre}]$ structure at the Morphosyntactic Level. Note, in support of this analysis, that (29) could be reported as (30), but not as (31):

(30)   She warned me that if I didn't stop crying, then we wouldn't go to the movies.

(31)   *If I didn't stop crying, she warned me that we wouldn't go to the
       movies.

Something similar can be said about the following example from Imbabura
Quechua (Cole 1982: 55), which Dik (1997b: 88) analyses as containing an
example of an Orientation in the form of an internally headed relative clause:

(32)   Ñuka chay punlla-pi chaya-shka-ka   sumaj-mi   ka-rka.
       I   that day-on   arrive-NMLZ-TOP beautiful-VAL be-PST
       'The day on which I arrived was beautiful.'

Dik reanalyses the topic suffix -*ka* as a marker of Orientation and paraphrases
the example as 'Given my arriving on that day, it was beautiful.' However
one may wish to analyse the semantics of the construction, it is clear that the
example contains only one Discourse Act. In FDG, we therefore would analyse
ñuka chay punllapi chayashkaka as the Topic of the Communicated Content
of that one Discourse Act. The application of the [P^{pre}, P^{centre}] structure will
again be attributed to the Morphosyntactic Level.

As Reesink has shown for Usan (Reesink 1987) with respect to units marked
by the particle *eng*, the sequence of an Orientation Discourse Act and a
Nuclear Discourse Act within a Move can come in time to be reinterpreted
as a single Discourse Act, with the Orientation Discourse Act becoming the
Topic of the Communicated Content of that Discourse Act. Both possibilities
can be understood from the perspective of on-line language processing: in
producing an Orientation Discourse Act, the Speaker awards him/herself time
to formulate and encode the following Nuclear Discourse Act; in marking a
Subact with typically given information (cf. *ñuka chay punllapi chayashkaka* in
(32)) as Topic, the Speaker similarly postpones the identification of the Focus
of that Discourse Act.

This section will close with a consideration of non-restrictive relative
clauses, which manifest yet another kind of dependence between Discourse
Acts. Our claim will be that such constructions involve a dependence between
two Nuclear Discourse Acts; the attachment of the non-restrictive relative
clause to its antecedent will take place at the Morphosyntactic Level, which
necessarily contains a template for restrictive relative clauses. Restrictive relative clauses arise at the Representational Level as secondary restrictors within
entity descriptions headed by a noun; non-restrictive relative clauses partially
imitate their structure, but have a radically different origin in the grammar
(see Hannay and Vester 1987).

Non-restrictive relative clauses, as observed by Dik (1997b: 41–2), admit
illocutionary Modifiers; as such, and given the fact that they characteristically
have an independent intonation contour, they must be analysed as Discourse
Acts in their own right, which explains why they can accept adverbials with

the function of the modifier of an Illocution such as *frankly*. Consider the italicized portion of (33):

(33)   The students, *who, frankly, had worked hard*, passed the exam.

Their illocutionary status is also independent of that of the host Discourse Act, as we see in (34), in which the relative clause has a Declarative Illocution and the host clause an Interrogative Illocution, or in the Spanish example in (35), in which the non-restrictive relative clause has an Optative Illocution:

(34)   Did the students, who after all had worked very hard, pass the exam?

(35)   Tu   madre, que descans-e   en paz,
       your mother REL rest-SBJV.PRS.3.SG in peace
       quer-ía   que te   cri-aras   fuerte.
       want-PST.IMPF.3.SG COMP 2.SG grow-PST.SBJV.2.SG strong
       'Your mother—may she rest in peace—wanted you to grow up strong.'
       (Internet)

Nevertheless, as observed by Dik (1997b: 43), there is a difference between (34) and (36), namely that the content of the relative clause in (34) is dependent upon that of the host clause, while the relation between the Discourse Acts in (36) is one of equipollence:

(36)   Did the students pass the exam? They after all had worked very hard.

Let us propose that the characteristic function of a non-restrictive relative clause is that of providing background information with respect to an Individual introduced in the main clause. We will capture this through the rhetorical function *Aside*. A further requirement is of course that each of the Communicated Contents of (A_1) and (A_2) should contain a Referential Subact R evoking the same entity description at the Representational Level.

    Example (36) will thus be analysed using the Interpersonal Frame in (37), but (34) and (35) using the one in (38):

(37) $[(A_1: [...] (A_1)) (A_2: [...] (A_2))]$

(38) $[(A_1: [...(R_1)...] (A_1)) (A_2: [...(R_2)...] (A_2))_{Aside}]$

where an additional condition is that R_1 and R_2 refer to the same entity at the Representational Level. It is this particular combination of dependency and coreference that triggers the appropriate Morphosyntactic Template at the Morphosyntactic Level.

2.3.3 Modifiers

Moves can be modified lexically, i.e. by elements from the lexicon that specify the Move's role in the ongoing discourse. These modifiers appear in position Σ in (39):

(39) $(M_1: [\dots] (M_1): \Sigma (M_1))$

Thus, to sum up a narrative monologue, expressions such as *to cut a long story short* introduce a Move that rounds off the story, as in:

(40)   To cut a long story short, I'm still considering it, but I doubt very much I'll get there. (Internet)

which may be represented as in (41) (cf. example (23) above):

(41) $(M_I: [(A_I: -I'm \text{ still considering it} - (A_I))_{Conc} (A_J: -I \text{ doubt very much}$ I'll get there $- (A_J))] (M_I): -\text{to cut a long story short} - (M_I))$

Note that the Move contains two Discourse Acts, and that the modifier has scope over both of them.

2.3.4 Operators

Moves can also be modified grammatically, in which case the grammatical element is represented by an operator in the π-position in (42):

(42) $(\pi M_1: [\dots] (M_1))$

A grammatical element that can modify a Move is English *however*. The reason to consider this a grammatical particle rather than a lexical element is that it can itself in no way be modified:

(43)   *very/exactly/etc. however

An example of the use of *however* in contrasting two Moves with each other is given in (44):

(44)   The Federal Trade Commission's ('FTC') recent promulgation of the amended Telemarketing Sales Rule ('TSR') has served to cement regulatory compliance as the number one issue for companies that engage in telemarketing. The triple threat posed by the FTC's new 'national' Do Not Call list, the Caller ID transmission rules, and the three percent abandonment rate for predictive dialers promises to further complicate an already confusing array of state and federal telemarketing regulations.

However, another issue, one that has been lurking in the background since the advent of the first Do Not Call list law in 1989, is also gradually moving to the front burner for major corporations that oversee complex telemarketing operations. Today, with the majority of states having passed DNC registry laws and the FTC federal list looming on the horizon, the importance of reviewing the issue of liability for Do Not Call violations in the outsourced call center scenario cannot be understated.

> Be it under federal or state law, when it comes to enforcement of Do Not
> Call rules, there is no distinction made between the seller of the goods
> or services in question and the outsourced call center hired to provide
> telemarketing services. (Internet)

This use of *however* can be captured by applying a Move operator Contr(ast).
Another example in English of a Move operator is *in_sum*, used with the same
function as the Move modifier in the previous section.

In actual practice, it may be difficult to distinguish between Move operators
and Discourse Act operators, since often the same item may be used for both
purposes. Consider the following example:

(45)   Celtic won; however, Rangers lost.

Assuming that (45) is a single Move (answering (9A) above), we see that
however here has scope over the second Discourse Act only, and therefore
qualifies as an operator of that Discourse Act, but not of the whole Move.
The distinction lies in the scope of the operator: only if it ranges over all
the Discourse Acts within the Move, as it does in (44), will it qualify as a
Move operator. Generally speaking, Move operators are typically constrained
at the Morphosyntactic Level to appear either Move-initially or towards the
beginning of the Move.

2.3.5 Frames

The conclusion of this section is that the set of primitives makes available the
following frames at the layer of the Move:

(46) $(\pi \, M_1: [(A_1) \dots (A_{1+n})_{\{\Phi\}}] \, (M_1))$
      where $n \geq 0$
      Position π is occupied by operators such as Contr(ast) and Sum(mary)
      Position Σ is occupied by a reduced set of lexical expressions

2.4 The Discourse Act

2.4.1 Introduction

Discourse Acts have been defined by Kroon (1995: 65) as 'the smallest identifiable units of communicative behaviour. In contrast to the higher-order units
called Moves they do not necessarily further the communication in terms of
approaching a conversational goal'.

It is important to emphasize that, just as there is no formal equivalent
of the Move, so there is also no one-to-one correspondence between the
Discourse Act and any linguistic unit. Everything else being equal, a Speaker

need not express more of his/her communicative intention than is required to understand it. In many cases a fragment of a clause (a single Np or Adp) may be enough. FDG will in such cases not take the position that fragmentary utterances are linguistically reduced forms of fuller, clausal expressions. Rather, at the Interpersonal Level, the representation of a Discourse Act will show only those components that have actually been deployed by the Speaker; this directly reflects the actional nature of the Interpersonal Level.

Let us consider an example from Newmeyer (2003: 689) in this light:

(47) a. A: Who does John$_i$ want to shave?
      b. B: Himself$_i$.
      c. B: *Him$_i$.

(48) a. John$_i$ wants to shave himself$_i$.
      b. *John$_i$ wants to shave him$_i$.

Newmeyer takes this sort of data to argue against a grammatical approach such as FDG in which form is linked to use, since in his view the choice of pronoun in (47b–c) is determined by the same rules as those that regulate the choice of pronoun in (48a–b). In FDG, by contrast, the interpersonal representation of the sole Discourse Act that makes up B's Move in (47b) will contain an indication of a Declarative Illocution and a Communicated Content containing only one Referential Subact. The ungrammaticality of (47c) is dealt with at the Representational Level, at which the full semantics of B's utterance is given. It is thus at the Interpersonal Level that the Speaker's strategic choice of how much semantic content to express is located; in the case of (47b), the Speaker produces a Move with a single Discourse Act, which in turn comprises a single Subact of Reference (cf. 2.8.3 below). The choices available to a Speaker are of course partly determined by the information that is contextually available. This information is contained in FDG's Contextual Component.

The opposite situation obtains when languages show special chaining strategies to express units larger than a single predication or Propositional Content in individual Discourse Acts. An example of such a strategy is shown in (49)–(51) for Turkish (Kornfilt 1997: 110; Ersen-Rasch 1980: 107):

(49) Hasan iş-e   gid-ip   ev-e   dön-dü-Ø.
      Hasan work-DAT   go-NARR   house-DAT   return-PST-3
      'Hasan went to work and returned home.'

(50) Reçete-yi   al-ıp   eczane-ye   gid-eyim.
      prescription-ACC   take-NARR   chemist's-DAT   go-ADH.1.SG
      'Let me take the prescription and go to the chemist's.'

(51)   Televizyon-u teyze-m-ler-e   götür-üp bırak-ınız.
       tv.set-ACC   aunt-1.SG.POSS-PL-DAT take-NARR leave-IMP.2.PL
       'Take the TV set to my aunt's family and leave it there.'

Turkish has a narrative converb in -*Ip*, sensitive to vowel harmony, which is used to signal that the verb form carrying this ending is to be interpreted as if it were carrying the same inflectional endings as the next finite verb. In (49) the narrative verb form is to be interpreted as a Declarative verb form with a third person subject, in (50) as an adhortative verb form with a first person singular subject, and in (51) as an imperative verb form with a second person plural subject. Since in each example the illocutionary value for the various subclauses has to be identical, we can conclude that they form a single Discourse Act at the Interpersonal Level, while constituting a unit larger than a description of a single State-of-Affairs at the Representational Level. This unit will be identified as an Episode in Chapter 3.

In languages like English the articulation of discourse into Discourse Acts has repercussions at the Phonological Level, where each Discourse Act generally corresponds to an Intonational Phrase, irrespective of the morphosyntactic counterpart of that Intonational Phrase. Other languages provide morphological evidence that the marking of the illocutionary value of a Discourse Act is independent of the syntactic unit. In Jamul Tiipay, for example, the interrogative clitic =*aa* can be attached either to a clause or to a noun phrase (Miller 2001: 195–6):

(52)   Me-mcheyuy-pe-ch   aayip=aa
       2-relatives.PL-DEM-SBJ arrive.PL=Q
       'Did your relatives come over?'

(53)   Maap   me-suum-pe-ch=aa
       your+ABS 2-younger.brother-DEM-SBJ=Q
       'What about your younger brother?'

Similarly, in Turkish, we find that the interrogative particle *mI* can occur, with vowel harmony with the immediately preceding vowel, attached to a structural unit of any type: a clause, as in (54a); an adverb, as in (54b); or an interjection, as in (54c) (Kornfilt 1997: 5; Lewis 1967: 105):

(54)   a.   Ahmet sinema-ya git-ti mi?
            Ahmet cinema-DAT go-PST INTER
            'Did Ahmet go to the movies?'

       b.   Bugün mü?
            today INTER
            'Today?'

    c. Tamam mı?

       OK   INTER

       'OK?'

The basic frame for a Discourse Act, with variations to be discussed in this section, will be as follows:

(55) $(\pi A_1: [(F_1) (P_1)_S (P_2)_A (C_1)_\Phi] (A_1): \Sigma (A_1))$

The head of the Discourse Act consists of, maximally, four different types of unit: (i) the Illocution (F_1), (ii)–(iii) the speech-act Participants $(P_1)_S$ and $(P_2)_A$, and (iv) the Communicated Content (C_1). The Illocution (F_1) is the core of the Discourse Act and can be subdivided into two types, Expressive and Communicative. Illocutions will be discussed at length in 2.5; $(P_1)_S$ and $(P_2)_A$ will be dealt with in 2.6; (C_1) is the subject matter of 2.7.

    Within the remainder of this section on Discourse Acts we first discuss possible Heads in 2.4.2, modifiers Σ of the Discourse Act in 2.4.3, and operators π on the Discourse Act in 2.4.4. A summary of frames available for Discourse Acts is given in 2.4.5.

2.4.2 Heads

The complex head of an Act contains at least two positions: that for the Illocution (F_1) and that for the Speaker $(P_1)_S$. In the representation of so-called Expressive Discourse Acts, which give direct expression to the Speaker's feelings rather than communicating some content to an Addressee, the head does not contain positions for either an Addressee or for a Communicated Content. An example of this is (56), represented in (57):

(56) Ouch!

(57) $(A_1: [(F_1: Ouch_{Int} (F_1)) (P_1)_S] (A_1))$

As we will argue in 2.5.2.4.2, *ouch* is the direct expression of the illocutionary value in cases like (56).

    All other Discourse Acts are Communicative Discourse Acts. In contrast to Expressive Discourse Acts they are other-related, in the sense of requiring the attention of the Addressee, so that the position $(P_2)_A$ will be present in the head of the Discourse Act. Within Communicative Discourse Acts we may distinguish an Interactive subclass, to which the structure in (58) will be applied:

(58) $(A_1: [(F_1: \blacklozenge (F_1)) (P_1)_S (P_2)_A] (A_1))$

In this structure the symbol $\blacklozenge$ stands for a lexical filler of the illocutionary slot (F_1). An example is (59):

(59)   Congratulations!

We will argue in 2.5.2.4.3 that *congratulations* indeed occupies the F-slot rather than the C-slot.

In Interactives the C-slot may potentially be filled, as in (60):

(60)   Congratulations *on winning the race*!

In these cases the representation will be as in (61), which differs from (58) in the presence of a Communicated Content:

(61) $(A_1: [(F_1: \blacklozenge (F_I)) (P_1)_S (P_2)_A (C_1)_\Phi] (A_1))$

A second subclass of Communicative Discourse Acts consists of Contentive Discourse Acts, characterized by the fact that they always have a Communicated Content. In this type of Discourse Act (F_1) may be expanded by either an abstract Illocution (ILL) or by a lexical ($\blacklozenge$) performative expression. Communicative Discourse Acts will therefore be represented as in (62):

(62) $(A_1: [(F_1: ILL/\blacklozenge (F_I)) (P_1)_S (P_2)_A (C_1)_\Phi)] (A_1))$

To summarize, the following complex heads are used in Discourse Acts:

(63)

$(A_1: [(F_1: \blacklozenge (F_I)) (P_1)_S] (A_1))$	Expressive Discourse Acts
$(A_1: [(F_1: \blacklozenge (F_I)) (P_1)_S (P_2)_A \{(C_1)_\Phi\}] (A_1))$	Communicative—Interactive
$(A_1: [(F_1: ILL/\blacklozenge (F_I)) (P_1)_S (P_2)_A (C_1)_\Phi] (A_1))$	Communicative—Contentive
$(A_1: [(F_1: \blacklozenge (F_I)) (P_1)_S (P_2)_A (C_1)_\Phi] (A_1))$	Performative
$(A_1: [(F_1: ILL (F_I)) (P_1)_S (P_2)_A (C_1)_\Phi] (A_1))$	Abstract

2.4.3 Modifiers

Discourse Acts may be modified by a lexical element which takes the form of a restrictor (Σ) on the Discourse Act:

(64) $(\pi A_1: [(F_1) (P_1)_S (P_2)_A (C_1)_\Phi] (A_1): \Sigma (A_1))$

Modifiers of Discourse Acts allow the Speaker to comment on that Discourse Act. The modifier may indicate the stylistic properties of the Discourse Act (e.g. *briefly*), or the status of the Discourse Act within the Move (e.g. *in addition*).

Another type of modifier is concerned with emphasizing the Discourse Act, as when words like *dammit* are integrated into a construction expressing Discourse Acts of various types, such as:

(65)   Answer me *dammit*!

(66)   I want to go home *dammit*.

(67)   Did you do it or not *dammit?*

(68)   Let's go *dammit.*

The emphasizing element *dammit* occurs with Discourse Acts with all kinds of Illocutions, such as Imperatives (65), Declaratives (66), Interrogatives (67), and Hortatives (68), which shows that it operates at a higher level than the Illocution itself, that of the Discourse Act.

Modifiers of these types are introduced directly into the Interpersonal Level in the position Σ in (64). Their status as modifiers is typically reflected in their having a relatively peripheral position in the expression of the Discourse Act. Modifiers are typically not allowed in Expressives and Interactives.

2.4.4 Operators

The representation of the Discourse Act contains a position for operators, π in (64). One such operator is that for Irony. Irony will be understood here as involving a strategic choice to (i) formulate at the Representational Level a Propositional Content that is at variance with the Speaker's actual beliefs and (ii) to indicate this to the Addressee. The latter aspect of Irony involves the Interpersonal Level, since it concerns the Speaker's attempt to regulate the interaction (and specifically not to be misunderstood as really meaning the Propositional Content as uttered). In English, for example, an Ironic intention can be signalled by a special intonation contour (see e.g. Bryant and Fox Tree 2002), characterized by being rather flat, with stress on a non-Focal element. An example is (69), in which the Speaker indicates by means of these techniques that s/he is not having fun:

(69)   This IS fun.

The presence of an Iron(ic) operator will cause the Phonological Level to shift the accent placement and engender the desired intonation contour (for details see 5.5). That Iron(ic) has a Discourse Act in its scope, and not an entire Move, is clear from examples like the following, in which only the first of the two Discourse Acts in the Move has the Ironic intention and intonation:

(70)   This IS fun, don't you think?

Lexical marking of Irony is found in spoken or informal written Dutch, in which the Subsidiary Discourse Act *maar niet heus* (literally 'but not really') indicates that the previous Discourse Act is to be understood as Ironic; the following examples are not untypical:

(71)   a.   Dat was dus wel   fijn,   maar niet heus.
            that was so   rather good but   not really
            'So that was rather good ... not.' (Internet)

b. Hoe romantisch, maar niet heus.
   how romantic   but   not really
   'How romantic ... not.' (Internet)

c. Alternatieve houtsoorten   waren niet voorhanden
   alternative   kinds.of.wood were   not available
   (maar niet heus).
   (but not really)
   'There were no other kinds of wood available (... not).' (Internet)

As is shown by these examples, *maar niet heus*, and its equivalent for some users of English *not* (cf. the Linguist List discussion summarized at <http://linguistlist.org/issues/2/2-877.html>) occurs as a Subsidiary Discourse Act after an Ironic Nuclear Discourse Act. In (71c) we see a Discourse Act containing a negated predication, a fact that indicates the frozen nature of this formula, since *niet heus niet voorhanden* 'not really not available' is not well-formed. In certain users' speech, this formula can be integrated into the Ironic Discourse Act, so that the following has the intonation typical of a single Discourse Act:

(72) Geweldig interessant maar niet heus.
      terribly   interesting but   not really
      'How TERRibly interesting!'

For such language-users, *maar niet heus* has attained the status of an invariable particle and therefore can be seen as an expression of an Ironic operator.

   Another example of an operator upon a Discourse Act is the Emphatic operator. Consider the following utterances:

(73) a. She has grown!
      b. Did you say you were pregnant?!
      c. Hurry up!

We shall regard such utterances as Emphatic Discourse Acts with varying illocutionary values (cf. Moutaouakil's 2005 analysis of exclamation as an operator at the Interpersonal Level rather than an Illocution). Across the languages of the world, they are associated with an intonation contour involving relatively extreme pitch movements (see Chapter 5) of the type generally reflected in writing by the application of an exclamation mark. The Emphatic operator is also relevant at other layers within the Interpersonal Level.

   Emphasis is thus the result of the Speaker's intensification of a Discourse Act. This applies irrespective of the nature of the Illocution (F_1), and hence can apply equally to Declarative (73a), Interrogative (73b), or Imperative (73c)

Illocutions. This is also visible in the following examples from Spanish, in which emphasis is expressed segmentally through the particle *que*:

(74) a. ¡Que   no   me   gusta   nada   esa
          EXCLAM NEG 1.SG.DAT please.PRS.IND.3.SG nothing that
          película!
          movie
          'I don't like that movie at all!'

      b. ¿¡Que   si   vienes   mañana!?
          EXCLAM whether come.PRS.IND.2SG tomorrow
          'Are you coming tomorrow?!'

      c. ¡Que   no   te   marches   mañana!
          EXCLAM not 2.SG.REFL leave.PRS.SBJV.2.SG tomorrow
          'Don't you leave tomorrow!'

Further proof for not considering Emphatic an Illocution comes from Tauya. MacDonald (1990: 214) points out that what she initially calls the 'exclamatory mood' of Tauya, marked by the suffix –ʔae, actually consists of the Declarative suffix –ʔa and the exclamatory suffix –e, as in (75) (MacDonald 1990: 214):

(75) Fofe-a-ʔa-e.
      come-3.SG-DECL-EXCLAM
      'He's coming!'

This suffix is also used in warnings and greetings (MacDonald 1990: 164–5):

(76) a. Oʔo-e.
          fire-EXCLAM
          'Fire!'

      b. ʔʷeisa-e
          night-EXCLAM
          'Good night!'

The analysis of Emphatic Discourse Acts will thus involve a structure of the following kind at the Interpersonal Level:

(77) (emph A_1: [(F_1: ILL (F_1)) (P_1)$_S$ (P_2)$_A$ (C_1)$_\Phi$] (A_1))

Note that in 2.5 below we will distinguish intensified Discourse Acts of the type represented in (77) from Discourse Acts with a Mirative Illocution, which are used for the expression of surprise.

Opposite in effect to Emphatic is Mitigative, as exemplified by the Mandarin Chinese particle *a/ya* (cf. Li and Thompson 1981: 313–17). Note that, as with

Emph, Mit can apply to Discourse Acts with all types of Illocution, Declarative (78), Interrogative (79), and Imperative (80):

(78) Wǒ bìng   méi zuò-cuò   a.
      1.SG on.the.contrary NEG do-wrong MIT
      'On the contrary, I didn't do wrong.'

(79) Nǐ ziǎng bu ziǎng tā   a.
      2.SG think NEG think 3.SG MIT
      'Don't you miss her/him?'

(80) Chī-fàn a.
      Eat-food MIT
      'Eat, OK?!'

2.4.5 Frames

The conclusion of this section is that the set of primitives makes available the following frames at the layer of the Discourse Act:

(81) $(\pi A_1: [(F_1: \blacklozenge (F_I)) (P_1)_S] (A_1): \Sigma (A_1))$
      $(\pi A_1: [(F_1: \blacklozenge (F_I)) (P_1)_S (P_2)_A [(C_1)_\Psi]] (A_1) : \Sigma (A_1))$
      $(\pi A_1: [(F_1: \text{ILL}/\blacklozenge (F_I)) (P_1)_S (P_2)_A (C_1)_\Phi] (A_1) : \Sigma (A_1))$

The position π may be occupied by one of the operators Iron(ic), Emph(atic), or Mit(igative)

The position Σ may be occupied by members of a specialized set of invariable forms

We shall now progress to an examination of the various components of the Discourse Act.

2.5 Illocution

2.5.1 Introduction

The Illocution of a Discourse Act captures the lexical and formal properties of that Discourse Act that can be attributed to its conventionalized interpersonal use in achieving a communicative intention. Communicative intentions include such Discourse Act types as calling for attention, asserting, ordering, questioning, warning, requesting, etc., which may map onto Illocutions such as Vocative, Declarative, Imperative, etc. There is no one-to-one relation between a specific communicative intention and an Illocution, as languages may differ significantly in the extent to which they make use of linguistic means to differentiate between communicative intentions. Since every

Discourse Act contains an Illocution, the presence of illocutionary indicators is an important diagnostic for the Discourse Act status of a linguistic unit.

The general frame for Illocutions has the following structure:

(82) $(\pi \ F_1: \blacklozenge/ILL \ (F_1): \Sigma \ (F_1))$

The head of the Illocution, which is simplex and can be either lexical or abstract, is discussed in detail in 2.5.2. Illocutions may be modified by lexical material which bears upon the illocutionary predicate, be it abstract or concrete. These modifiers, discussed in 2.5.3, occupy the Σ-slot in (82). When the Illocution is modified by grammatical means, this is captured by operators occupying the π-slot in (82). These operators are presented in 2.5.4. An overview of available frames at the level of the Illocution is given in 2.5.5.

2.5.2 Heads

2.5.2.1 Introduction

As briefly indicated in 2.4.2, the slot for the Illocution of a Discourse Act may be filled by (i) explicit performative verbs, (ii) abstract Illocutions, or (iii) members of a limited set of interjections and related expressions that by themselves constitute a Communicative or Expressive Discourse Act. We will discuss these three categories one by one.

2.5.2.2 Performative verbs

The familiar distinction between explicit and implicit performatives will be reflected in FDG in the choice between a verbal and an abstract expansion of the F-variable. In the following Discourse Acts, the F-variable is specified by means of the verbs *promise* and *inform* respectively:

(83)   a.   I promise to do the washing-up.
          b.   I am hereby informing you that I wish to resign.

to be analysed as

(84) $(A_1: [(F_1: \blacklozenge \ (F_1)) \ (P_1)_S \ (P_2)_A \ (C_1)_\Phi] \ (A_1))_\Phi$

The possible occupants of the position $\blacklozenge$ are drawn from a set of verbs known as 'performative verbs', i.e. *promise* and *inform* respectively in (83).

The necessarily Present-tense form of the verb will be assigned by default at the Morphosyntactic Level in response to the utterance time; both utterance time and utterance location are registered in the Contextual Component, also being required for the appropriate use and understanding of deictic expressions. Against this view it may be objected that the *ing*-form in (83b) is an expression that originates in an aspectual operator from the Representational

Level. It should be observed, however, that the *ing*-form in this particular use has a reinforcing effect rather than an aspectual meaning. This reinforcing effect is captured by an emphatic operator at the Interpersonal Level (see 2.5.4) rather than at the Representational Level. Thus, the fact that this special communicative value of the *ing*-form arises in the context of performative formulas actually supports our analysis of its interpersonal status in (83b).

With a lexical performative predicate filling the slot for the Illocution of the utterance, the Speaker and the Addressee be both can made explicit, which means that the (P_1) and (P_2) positions are filled:

(85)   I promise you-guys that I'll come back.
        $(A_I: [(F_I: promise_V (F_I)) (1 P_I)_S (m P_J)_A (C_I: -I'll come back- (C_I))_\Phi] (A_I))_\Phi$

Here the Speaker is characterized as being singular (1) and the Addressee as plural (m). Potential fillers of P-positions are discussed in 2.6.

2.5.2.3 Abstract Illocutions

Illocutionary Discourse Acts without a lexical specification of the Illocution are 'implicit performatives' and involve the choice of a ready-made Illocution, where Illocution, often also called 'sentence type', is defined as 'a coincidence of grammatical structure and conventional conversational use' (Sadock and Zwicky 1985: 155). Each language makes available a set of illocutionary primitives which differ in which 'abstract predicate' (for example Declarative or Interrogative) occupies the position ILL in (86):

(86) $(A_1: [(F_1: ILL (F_1)) (P_1)_S (P_2)_A (C_1)_\Phi] (A_1))_\Phi$

The distinction between explicit and implicit performatives is thus that the former involve the introduction of a lexical predicate into the Interpersonal Level, whereas the latter involve the introduction of an abstract predicate. In both cases we consider the indicator of the Illocution, ♦ in (84) and ILL in (86), to be predicates, observing that the relation between the units that make up a Discourse Act is comparable to that of a predicate and three arguments, namely the two Participants in the Discourse Act and the Communicated Content. With an abstract predicate, the two Participants generally remain implicit.

In keeping with the principles of FDG, no more abstract illocutionary primitives will be posited for each language than are justified by the grammatical distinctions present in the language. These distinctions may be morphosyntactic or phonological. The following list contains a range of illocutionary categories and their conventional conversational uses, from which the languages of the world make a selection. We illustrate this list here with examples of the segmental expression of the illocutionary category involved (see also Hengeveld 2004c):

DECLarative: the Speaker informs the Addressee of the Propositional Content evoked by the Communicated Content. Example (87) (MacDonald 1990: 209), as are (88)–(91), is from Tauya:

(87) Ya-ni   tei-mene-amu-ʔa.
      1.SG-ERG catch-STAT-1.SG.FUT-DECL
      'I will have it.'

INTERrogative: the Speaker requests the Addressee's response to the Propositional Content evoked by the Communicated Content, as in the following example (MacDonald 1990: 210):

(88) Nen-ni   sen-yau-i-*nae*?
      3.PL-ERG 1.PL-see-3.PL-INTER
      'Did they see us?'

IMPERative: the Speaker directs the Addressee to carry out the action evoked by the Communicated Content, as illustrated in (89) (MacDonald 1990: 212):

(89) Ni-a-*e*!
      eat-2.SG.FUT-IMP
      'Eat!'

PROHibitive: the Speaker forbids the Addressee to carry out the action evoked by the Communicated Content. An example is given in (90) (MacDonald 1990: 213):

(90) Yate-ʔatene!
      go-PROH.SG
      'Don't go!'

OPTative: the Speaker indicates to the Addressee his/her wish that the positive situation evoked by the Communicated Content should come about, as in (91) (MacDonald 1990: 213):

(91) ʔei   mene-ʔe-*no*.
      there stay-3.SG.FUT-OPT
      'Let her be there!'

IMPRecative: the Speaker indicates to the Addressee his/her wish that the negative situation evoked by the Communicated Content should come about, as in the following example from Turkish (Lewis 1967: 115):

(92)   Geber-*esi*!
       die.like.a.dog-IMPR.3.SG
       'May he die like a dog!'

HORTative: the Speaker encourages himself or an Addressee together with himself to carry out the action evoked by the Communicated Content, as in example (93) from Desano (Miller 1999: 73):

(93)   Guʔa-rã   wa-rã.
       bath-ANIM.PL go-HORT
       'Let's go bathe!'

DISHORTative: the Speaker discourages himself or an Addressee together with himself from carrying out the action evoked by the Communicated Content, as in the following example from Kamaiurá (Seki 2000: 333):

(94)   T=a-ha-ume=n.
       HORT=1.SG-go-NEG.HORT=HORT
       'Let me not go.'

ADMONitive: the Speaker advises the Addressee to realize the situation evoked by the Communicated Content, as in the following example from Mandarin Chinese (Li and Thompson 1981: 311):

(95)   Xiǎoxīn *ou*!
       careful ADMON
       'Be careful!'

COMMissive: the Speaker commits him/herself to future realization of a situation evoked by the Communicated Content in which both Speaker and Addressee are involved, as in (96) from Jamul Tiipay (Miller 2001: 191):

(96)   Xiikay ny-iny-*ma*.
       some   1/2-give-COMM
       'I'll give you some.'

SUPPLicative: the Speaker asks permission of the Addressee to realize the situation evoked by the Communicated Content. The following example from Tucano (Ramirez 1997: 147) illustrates this Illocution:

(97)   Apê-*ma*.
       play-SUPPL
       'Let me play!'

MIRative: the Speaker expresses his surprise about the Propositional Content evoked by the Communicated Content, as in example (98) from Kamaiurá (Seki 2000: 156):

(98) H-ajme-ma'e   te'   an   *pa.*
      3SG-have.sharpness.NMLZ FOC PROX MIR.MS
      'Wow, how sharp is this (knife)!'

Of these 12, English grammar will contain six. The Declarative Illocution is characterized by intonation and a clausal constituent order in which the clause-initial position P^I is not occupied by a verb (99); the Interrogative Illocution by intonation and placement of a Q-word or the finite verb in P^I (100); the Imperative Illocution by intonation and placement of a verb in P^I (101); the Optative Illocution by the placement of the invariable *let* (without the sense of the homophonous Imperative use of the permissive verb *let*) or the modal *may* in P^I (102); the Hortative Illocution by the placement of the invariable particle *Let's* in P^I (103a), with the subject position generally not filled, although many examples are found in current usage (103b); and the Mirative by the presence of a question word in the absence of inversion (104):

(99)   Mary left the club.

(100) a. Who left the club?
       b. Did she leave the club?

(101) Leave the club!

(102) a. Let her leave the club!
       b. May she leave the club!

(103) a. Let's leave the club.
       b. Let's you and me leave the club.

(104) How beautifully she sang!

The other Illocutions are not realized grammatically in English, and therefore will not occur as primitives in the analysis of that language: the Prohibitive and the Admonitive correspond to a combination of the Imperative Illocution with particular choices at the Representational Level, while the Imprecative and the Commissive will typically involve lexical verbs.

Note that we treat the MIRative Illocution as different from the Emphatic Discourse Act operator discussed in 2.4.4. One reason for this is that the Emphatic operator combines with a range of Illocutions, and thus represents a more general communicative strategy than Illocution itself. Another reason is that Miratives cannot be interpreted as a subtype of Declarative, since the communicative intention behind a Mirative Discourse Act is not to pass on a Communicated Content, as in Declarative Discourse Acts, but pass on surprise about a Communicated Content typically presupposed to be known to the Addressee. This explains the fact that Miratives show a tendency to holophrastic expression, i.e. as Communicated Contents with only one Sub-act. In (105) and (106) respectively, we see a Communicated Content containing just a Subact of Reference and a Subact of Ascription:

(105) What a fine day!
$(A_1: [(F_1: MIR (F_1)) (P_1)_S (P_2)_A (C_1: [(R_1)] (C_1))_\Phi] (A_1))$

(106) How silly!
$(A_1: [(F_1: MIR (F_1)) (P_1)_S (P_2)_A (C_1: [(T_1)] (C_1))_\Phi] (A_1))$

A pervasive feature of Miratives is their approximation to the form of Interrogative Illocutions, compare Mirative (107) with Interrogative (108):

(107) How beautifully she sang!

(108) How beautifully did she sing?

(107) differs above all from (108) in having its elements ordered at the Morphosyntactic Level by the template that is also associated with DECL Illocutions, rather than the one associated with INTER Illocutions. (107) thus shares one expression feature with the INTER Illocution (the introduction of the Q-word *how*) and one feature with the DECL Illocution (the application of the DECL template). In Marathi, the assimilation goes further, with only the intonation distinguishing Interrogative and Mirative Illocutions (Pandharipande 1997: 15, 265):

(109) Tyāne   kittī   ãmbe   khālle?
       3.SG.AG how.many mango.3.PL.M eat-PST.3.PL.M
       'How many mangoes did he eat?'

(110) Tyāne   kittī   ãmbe   aṇle!
       3.SG.AG how.many mango.3.PL.M bring-PST.3.PL.M
       'How many mangoes he brought!'

From a typological perspective, it is expected that the presence versus absence of certain Illocutions is not random, but can be described systematically along a limited number of parameters. For a subset of the Illocutions discussed above, Hengeveld *et al.* (2007) show that the formally encoded Illocutions of a sample of the native languages of Brazil are distributed according to the configuration of implicational hierarchies shown in Figure 7.

All languages in the sample used by Hengeveld *et al.* (2007) have a Declarative, a Polar Interrogative, and an Imperative Illocution, but in one language, Sanuma, the distinction between Declarative and Polar Interrogatives may remain unexpressed. Using the term Propositional Illocutions to cover both Informing and Questioning Illocutions, i.e. those that have to do with the exchange of information, they speculate that the most basic opposition in

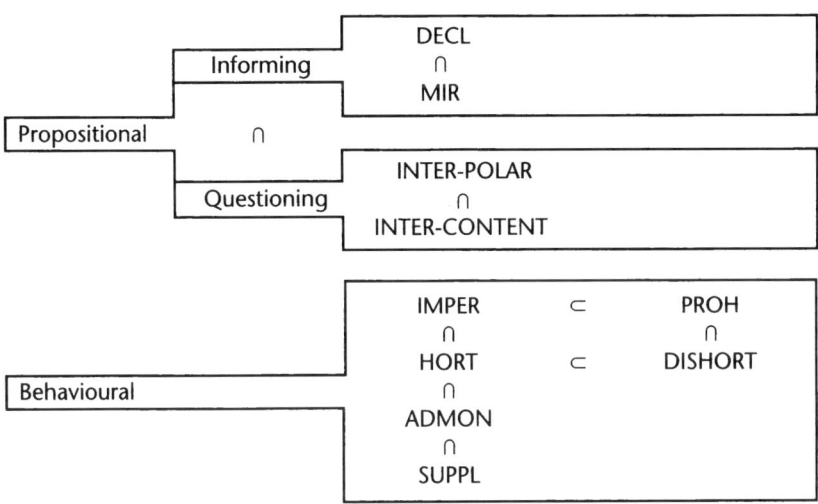

FIGURE 7. Implicational relations between Illocutions

languages is the one between Propositional and Behavioural Illocutions, i.e. those that have to do with influencing behaviour, the next step being a split within Propositional between Informing and Questioning.

While Polar Interrogatives are available in all languages of the sample, Content Interrogatives are not, so that the presence of a Content Interrogative predicts the presence of a Polar Interrogative. Consider the Kwaza examples (111)–(113) (van der Voort 2004: 297, 240, 241):

(111)   o'ja-da-tsy-'re.
        leave-1.SG-POT-Q
        'Am I going to leave?'

(112)   'peDro jere'xwa dilɛ-'wã   wa'dy-re.
        Pedro jaguar   someone-ANIM.OBJ give-Q
        'To whom did Pedro give a dog?'

(113)   dilɛ-'wã-here   aw're-da-tara-tsɛ.
        someone-ANIM.OBJ-INT   marry-1.SG-PROC-DECL
        'I'm going to marry someone.'

In Kwaza, both polar questions (111) and content questions (112) occur in the interrogative mood. What at first sight may seem to be a question word in (112) is also used as an indefinite pronoun, as can be seen in the Declarative sentence in (113). Thus, no formal distinction is made in Kwaza between polar and content questions. A content question is simply a polar question containing an indefinite pronoun. This ties in nicely with the way in which question words are treated in FDG, as will be shown in 2.8.3.4 below.

As furthermore shown in Figure 7, the presence of behavioural Illocutions can be predicted in a two-dimensional implicational grid, one parameter concerning the Actor and/or Beneficiary of the requested behaviour, the other its negative or positive value. Two logically possible negative Illocutions were not attested in Hengeveld *et al.*'s (2007) sample: the negative counterparts of the Admonitive and the Supplicative.

2.5.2.4 Interjections and related expressions

2.5.2.4.1 *Introduction*   The head of the slot for Illocution may also be occupied by interjections and related expressions, within both Expressive and Interactive act frames as discussed in 2.4.2 and repeated here:

(114) $(A_1: [(F_1: \blacklozenge (F_I)) (P_1)_S] (A_1))$ Expressives

(115) $(A_1: [(F_1: \blacklozenge (F_I)) (P_1)_S (P_2)_A \{(C_1)_\Phi\}] (A_1))$ Interactives

We discuss Expressives in 2.5.2.4.2 and Interactives in 2.5.2.4.3. Vocatives constitute a special class of Interactives, and are treated separately in 2.5.2.4.4.

2.5.2.4.2 *Expressives*   The meanings of Expressives tend to recur across different languages. Thus we very regularly find expressions for Ekman *et al.*'s (1972) six basic emotions anger (*damn*), disgust (*yuck*), fear (*help*), joy (*wow*), sadness (*aw*) and surprise (*well, well*). These are ways for Speakers to give vent to their reactions to elements of the ongoing communicative situation. One could easily imagine them being produced in solitude, as when one hits one's thumb with a hammer. They are close to instinctive cries like sighs, screams, gasps, etc. In FDG, however, only those utterances will be considered as Expressives that have language-specific form. This is apparent, for example, in expressions of pain, which, although barely voluntary, differ formally from one language to another:

(116)   English   *ow, ouch*
        French   *aïe*
        Kannada   *ayyo:*
        Evenki   *enu*
        Hungarian *jaj*

Further evidence for the lexical status of such expressive forms is their availability for word formation processes: thus from Hungarian *jaj* one can form frequentative *jaj-gat* 'say ouch repeatedly' (Kenesei *et al.* 1998: 455) by applying the frequentative affix *-gat* (1998: 360).

Because they do not assume an Addressee and have no Communicated Content, Expressives can be represented as in (114). A specific instance of this is (117):

(117) $(A_I: [(F_I: yuck_{Intj}(F_I)) (P_I)_S] (A_I))$

2.5.2.4.3 *Interactives*   Like Expressives, Interactives are generally expressed through lexical elements and are available for a restricted set of recurrent situations. An example is (118):

(118)   Congratulations!

They differ from Expressives in being clearly directed to the Addressee. Generally speaking, forms such as *Congratulations*, *Thank you*, etc. are invariable. The Speaker has no possibility of 'singularizing' the apparently plural *Congratulations* into *Congratulation*. This suggests that, like Expressives, Interactives are sent directly from the Interpersonal to the Phonological Level.

However, certain languages show limited variability conditioned by contextual circumstances. Thus the choice between the greetings *Good morning*, *Good afternoon*, and *Good evening* in English is dependent upon the time of day; otherwise they are communicatively entirely equivalent. The divisions of the day differ from culture to culture: in the Spanish of Spain, for example, roughly speaking *Buenos dias* is used till 14h, after which *Buenas tardes* applies until 21h, when *Buenas noches* becomes applicable; in the Spanish used in California, however, these terms are applied in keeping with the corresponding English expressions *Good morning*, *Good afternoon*, and *Good evening*.

The form of Interactives may also be dependent upon the identity of Speaker and Addressee. In Portuguese, the expression of gratitude is *obrigado* for a male Speaker but *obrigada* for a female Speaker (no matter whether s/he is expressing the gratitude of one or more Participants), although there is a tendency, discouraged by many feminists, to generalize the first form. And in Dutch, the social relation between the Speaker and the Addressee determines the choice between the familiar *dank je* for an Interactive of gratitude and the formal *dank u*, with the alternative form *bedankt* being neutral as to this distinction. It is this kind of data that justifies the presence of the positions for the two Participants in the Discourse Act frame for Interactives, which act as anchors for the information about the Participants available in the Contextual Component, e.g. in an FDG of Portuguese:

(119)   a. $(A_I: [(F_I: obrigada (F_I)) (P_I)_S (P_J)_A)] (A_I))$ [where P_I is female]
         b. $(A_I: [(F_I: obrigado (F_I)) (P_I)_S (P_J)_A)] (A_I))$ [where P_I is male]

Many Interactives can be expanded with a Communicated Content. Example (118) above, for example, could be expanded as follows:

(120)   Congratulations on winning the race!

A requirement with Interactives is that the C contains presupposed information. This requirement is exploited in the familiar sign (121):

(121)   Thank you for not smoking.

in which the reader is enjoined not to smoke by having his/her non-smoking presented as a shared presupposition. Those instances that have a frame including a (C_I) will require recourse to the Representational Level and the Morphosyntactic Level for the formulation and encoding of that segment of the Discourse Act. The (F_I) segment, however, is sent directly to the Phonological Component, as explained above.

It has been observed that Interactives may display phonological peculiarities that mark them off as being different from other forms. Thus in Babungo (Schaub 1985: 386), where word forms generally commence with a consonant, such Interjections have initial vowels. Interactives, being frequent in communication, are also often subject to phonological reduction. Examples in contemporary languages include the Dutch greeting *Dag* (from the now almost archaic *Goeden dag*, lit. 'good day') or the comparable Australian English *G'day*.

Historically, Interactives come from the lexicalization of what will have been regularly formed expressions. Thus *Goodbye* derives historically from *God be with you*, with a full finite (subjunctive) predication, etc. Interactives, it appears, may develop into Expressives: thus in Dutch we find *Goeie morgen* (lit. 'Good morning'), pronounced with an extreme intonation contour, being used to express surprise: the fact that it can be used at any time of day suggests progress towards further arbitrariness.

The representation of Interactives may thus be illustrated as follows:

(122)   (A_I: [(F_I: Sorry$_{Intj}$ (F_I)) (P_I)$_S$ (P_J)$_A$] (A_I))

(123)   (A_I: [(F_I: Congratulations$_{Intj}$ (F_I)) (P_I)$_S$ (P_J)$_A$ (C_I: –on winning the race– (C_I))$_\Phi$] (A_I))

2.5.2.4.4 *Vocatives*   Vocatives constitute a special class of Interactives. At the beginning of a segment of discourse, these Discourse Acts serve to gain the Addressee's attention; in the course of a discourse, the use of a Vocative signals the Speaker's continuing orientation to the Addressee.

Vocatives in their simplest form come close to greetings, which involve invariable Interactives of the type discussed above. Thus (124) will be analysed as in (125), in parallel with Interactives such as *congratulations*:

(124)   Hey!

(125)   (A_I: [(F_I: hey (F_I)) (P_I)$_S$ (P_J)$_A$] (A_I))

Certain languages may have specialized Vocatives for particular situations: in Dutch, at least traditionally, one calls for service in an apparently abandoned shop by means of the interjection *Volk!* (lit. 'People!').

Given their orientation towards the Addressee, the $(P_2)_A$ slot is often lexically filled in Vocatives, minimally with a 2nd person pronoun, as in (126), to be analysed as (127):

(126)   Hey you!

(127) $(A_I: [(F_I: hey (F_I)) (P_I)_S (P_J: you (P_J))_A] (A_I))$

The description of the Addressee may also take the form of a proper name, as in (128), to be analysed as (129):

(128)   Hey Bert!

(129) $(A_I: [(F_I: hey (F_I)) (P_I)_S (P_J: Bert (P_J))_A] (A_I))$

Whereas the form *Hey* or its archaic/formal equivalent *O* is invariable in English, its form is in other languages subject to variation according to the characteristics of $(P_2)_A$ and possibly also the relationship between $(P_1)_S$ and $(P_2)_A$. In Marathi (Pandharipande 1997: 332), there is a complex system in which 'the choice of vocative particles is determined by conditions of appropriateness according to the sex, age and social status of the Addressee relative to that of the Speaker'. In Punjabi (Bhatia 1993: 39), the particle *óé* is used for calling a male, and *nii* for calling a female; if one wishes to add rudeness, these are substituted by *saalaa* 'lit. brother-in-law' and *saalii* 'lit. sister-in-law' respectively. Kashmiri (Wali and Koul 1997: 41–2) similarly distinguishes between polite and impolite Vocatives, and between masculine and feminine forms; but it also has distinct forms for singular and plural, and within the polite class, has a class of honorific vocative particles.

Languages differ as to whether they require a lexical element in the position held by *Hey* in e.g. (128) or whether the position is filled by an abstract predicate. English, for example, allows Vocatives without any explicit marking, so that (130) will be analysed as (131), where INTERP is an abstract predicate of Interpellation:

(130)   Bert!

(131) $(A_I: [(F_I: INTERP (F_I)) (P_I)_S (P_J: Bert (P_J))_A] (A_I))$

Other languages require marking of the Interpellative Illocution, as for example Kashmiri (see above), or Scottish Gaelic:

(132)   A   Sheumais!
        INTERP   James.VOC
        'James!'

Note that there is no Subact of Reference involved in this type of Vocative. In calling for James's attention in (132), the Speaker is not referring to him. None of the operators characteristic of reference, such as definiteness, can be applied. In European Portuguese, in which proper names used referentially are marked by the definite article, no such article appears in Vocative uses:

(133) Vi   o   João.
       see.PST.1.SG DEF.SG John
       'I saw John.'

(134) João, o   que est-ás   a   fazer?
       John DEF.SG what be-2.SG.PRS PROG do.INF
       'John, what are you doing?'

The form corresponding to the Addressee may be marked for its Vocative function. In Fijian (Schütz 1985: 355–6) we find the preposition i, which Schütz speculates may be related to the accusative preposition i (1985: 357, n. 15). In other languages, the $(P_2)_A$ maps onto a Vocative case at the Morphosyntactic Level: in Marathi (Pandhardipande 1997), for example, the noun in question appears in the oblique form, additionally followed by the suffix -no in the plural, e.g. from $b\bar{a}l$ 'child':

(135) baḷ-ãn-no
       child-PL.OBL-VOC
       'o children'

Like other Interactives, Vocatives may be expanded with a Communicated Content containing a description of the Addressee. Where this is the case, the description is indicated at the Representational Level, and may then of course contain all distinctions that pertain to that level. Consider the following example from Standard Moroccan Arabic (Moutaouakil 1989: 146):

(136) Yā/ʔa   man yantaẓiru   Zayd-an   ʔinnahu   wasala.
       INTERP REL await.PRS   Zayd-ACC   DEM.3.SG   arrive.PST
       'You who are waiting for Zayd, he has arrived.'

Here the (C) corresponds to a predication at the Representational Level ('you are waiting for Zayd'). Note that the form of the interpellative particle $y\bar{a}$ or $\textit{ʔa}$ is determined at the Morphosyntactic Level, being dependent upon the morphosyntactic environment. Where the relativizer $l\text{-}la\underline{d}\bar{\imath}$ is applied, the Interpellative takes the form $\textit{ʔayyuhā}$ (Moutaouakil 1989: 146):

(137) ʔayyuhā l-ladī yantaẓiru Zayd-an   ʔinnahu   wasala.
       INTERP   REL   await.PRS Zayd-ACC DEM.3.SG arrive.PST
       'You who are waiting for Zayd, he has arrived.'

Let us summarize this section by considering the epistolary salutation (138) as a Vocative Discourse Act:

(138)   Dear John

It will be clear that *dear* here lacks any representational meaning, since even an angry letter to John in which it is clear that John is far from being 'dear' to the writer may begin with this word. Rather it is an interpellative particle standardized for this communicative context. In other languages, but not in English, the form of the Interpellative varies with the social relation between writer and reader: in Dutch, for example and by way of a rough approximation, *geacht(e)* 'lit. respected' is used for communication with authorities, *beste* 'lit. best' for colleagues and *lief/lieve* 'lit. dear, sweet' for close friends and relatives. Note that the choice between *geacht* and *geachte* is dependent upon the association of this word with a gendered noun (neuter and common respectively) at the Morphosyntactic Level. To return to *John* in (138), this will be shown as the $(P_2)_A$ of the Discourse Act. It will thus be analysed as (139):

(139) $(A_I: [(F_I: dear (F_I)) (P_I)_S (P_J: John (P_J))_A] (A_I))$

This will bypass the Representational Level and pass to the Morphosyntactic Level (in English only for the ordering of the two component words) and from there to the Phonological Level (or more precisely Graphological Level, since this is written language).

2.5.3 Modifiers

Illocutions may be modified by lexical material which bears upon the illocutionary predicate, be it abstract or lexical. Modifiers are restrictive, and will accordingly be represented as restrictors upon the illocutionary predicate. Let us consider an example of the modification of a lexical illocutionary predicate:

(140)   I promise you sincerely that this is not a trick.

Here *sincerely* is a lexical modification, not of the Discourse Act as a whole, but of the Illocution; it is a sincere promise that is being made:

(141) $(A_I: [(F_I: promise (F_I): sincerely (F_I)) (P_I)_S (P_J)_A (C_I)_\Phi] (A_I))$

The same analysis, but now with an abstract predicate, is appropriate for (142):

(142)   Sincerely, this is not a trick

(143) $(A_I: [(F_I: DECL (F_I): sincerely (F_I)) (P_I)_S (P_J)_A (C_I)_\Phi] (A_I))$

Modifiers of the abstract predicate INTER can either be Speaker-related or Addressee-related, in the latter case anticipating the DECL Illocution in the

Response Move. Thus (144) can mean either 'I ask you frankly why you did it' or 'I ask you to tell me frankly why you did it'.

(144)   Frankly, why did you do it?

(145)   (A$_I$: [(F$_I$: INTER (F$_I$): frankly (F$_I$)) (P$_I$)$_S$ (P$_J$)$_A$ (C$_I$)$_Φ$] (A$_I$))

The position occupied by *frankly* in (145) can be occupied by 'a family of expressions', as Dik (1997a: 305) observes, such as *in all frankness, if I can speak frankly*, etc. To the extent that these are restrictive, they can be included among the lexical items available for this type of frame. However, where the relationship is non-restrictive, their analysis as modifiers is excluded. Rather, there is a relationship between two Discourse Acts, each with its own Illocution, as in (146):

(146)   Please tidy your sister's room, although why am I asking you?

(147)   (M$_I$: [(A$_I$: [(F$_I$: IMP (F$_I$)) etc.] (A$_I$)) (A$_J$: [(F$_J$: INTER (F$_J$)) etc.] (A$_J$))$_{Conc}$] (M$_I$))

It will be clear that the status of illocutionary modifiers is very similar to that of Manner Modifiers at the Representational Level (see 3.6.3); after all, they indicate the manner in which the Illocution is being carried out, and languages with manner adverbs typically use these in the modifier position under discussion here. It is noticeable that the possible ambiguity that may arise between interpersonal and representational uses of these adverbs can be avoided by adding some indication of the illocutionary status of the former, as in Dutch, where *gezegd* is iconic of the illocutionary status of the preceding modifier:

(148)   Eerlijk gezegd werkt   hij niet.
        Honest   said   work-PRS.3.SG he NEG
        'To be honest, he isn't working.'

(149)   Eerlijk werkt   hij niet.
        Honest   work-PRS.3SG he NEG
        'He doesn't work honestly.'

Explicit performative Discourse Acts in English can be accompanied by the adverb *hereby* (cf. (83b) above). This adverb, which is interpreted as 'by means of this Discourse Act', has pronominal status, and will be analysed accordingly.

(150)   I hereby state that I wish to resign.

(151)   (A$_I$: [(F$_I$: [state$_V$] (F$_I$)): (A$_I$)$_{Means}$ (F$_I$)) (P$_I$)$_S$ (P$_J$)$_A$ (C$_I$)$_Φ$] (A$_I$))

For some additional puzzles about illocutionary modifiers, now with regard to Latin, see Pinkster (2004).

2.5.4 Operators

The illocutionary variable F can take an operator. This operator accounts for grammatical emphasis and mitigation of a specific Illocution. Just as the Discourse Act as a whole can be emphasized and mitigated, in which case these operations combine with any Illocution (see 2.4.5), so also the force of specific Illocutions can be affected. Thus Vismans (1994: 62) has shown that Imperatives in Dutch can be emphasized by the particle *dan*:

(152)   Doe je   werk dan!
        Do   your work EMPH
        'Go on, do your work.'

Dan is not available for emphasizing other types of Illocution (Vismans 1994: 5). Dutch also has mitigating particles, such as *maar*, which is restricted to DECL and IMPER Illocutions:

(153)   a. Je   moet maar gaan fietsen. (DECL)
            you must MIT go   cycle
            'You should go for a bike ride, you know.'

        b. Ga maar fietsen. (IMP)
            Go MIT   cycle
            'Why not go for a bike ride?'

        c. *Kun je   maar gaan fietsen? (INTER)
            Can you MIT   go   cycle
            'Could you go for a bike ride?'

A language expressing the emphatic operator morphologically is Evenki, suffixing *–r'e:*, *–k'e:* or *–e:* to a verb stem as in (154) (Nedjalkov 1997: 325):

(154)   enu-k'e:
        be.ill-EMPH
        'It hurts!'

These suffixes are limited in their application to Discourse Acts expressing displeasure: *kandar'e:* 'I am sick and tired!'; *ngokk'e:* 'it smells bad!', etc.

2.5.5 Frames

In sum, the following frames may be distinguished for Illocutions:

(155) $(\pi\ F_1: \blacklozenge\ (F_1): \Sigma\ (F_1))$
        $(\pi\ F_1: \text{ILL}\ (F_1): \Sigma\ (F_1))$

        The head position may be occupied by an abstract illocutionary predicate, a lexical performative verb, or a prefabricated interjection with a specific illocutionary value;

The modifier position may be occupied by expressions specifying the manner of the speech act;

The operator position may be occupied by an emphatic or mitigating operator.

2.6 The Participants

2.6.1 Introduction

The two Participants in the interaction, (P_1) and (P_2), alternate as Speaker and Addressee. Speaker and Addressee are therefore functions, akin to the semantic functions Agent and Recipient respectively. With abstract Illocutions, where there is no lexical illocutionary predicate, there is generally a corresponding non-expression of the Participants. Nevertheless, even in these cases there are good reasons for requiring that at least one Participant should be represented. Firstly, the distinction between self-related and other-related Illocutions (i.e. between Expressives and all other types of Discourse Act) is correlated with the absence or presence respectively of a Participant in the Addressee function. Secondly, the understanding of references to first and second person in the Communicated Content is handled through co-reference with the two Participants in the Illocution.

The general frame for Participants has the following structure:

(156) $(\pi \, P_1: \emptyset/\blacklozenge \, (P_1): \Sigma \, (P_1))$

The head of the Participant slot may be $\emptyset$ or lexical. The latter case is discussed in 2.6.2. Lexically headed Participant slots may contain lexical modifiers Σ, discussed in 2.6.3, and operators π, dealt with in 2.6.4. An overview of available frames at the layer of the Illocution is given in 2.6.5.

2.6.2 Heads

Examples of headed Addressee expressions have already been given in passing in our discussion of Vocatives in 2.5.2.4.4. A head for the Speaker slot is called for in examples such as the following (Levinson 1983: 260):

(157)   The company hereby undertakes to replace any can of Doggo-Meat that fails to please, with no questions asked.

The representation of (157) will be shown as follows:

(158) $(A_I: [(F_I: undertake_V \, (F_I): (A_I)_{Means} \, (F_I)) \, (P_I: company_N \, (P_I))_S \, (P_J)_A$
$(C_I: -the \, company \, replaces \, any \, can \, of \, Doggo\text{-}Meat \, that \, fails \, to \, please,$
$with \, no \, questions \, asked- \, (C_I))_\Phi] \, (A_I))$

Note that the Addressee in (157) remains unspecified, and this is reflected in the lack of a head in the Addressee slot in (158).

The Addressee may be specified lexically as well, as in the following example from Japanese (Hinds 1986: 257):

(159)   Iroiro-to suwan san ni shitsumon shimasu.
        various   Swan Ms to question   do
        'I'd like to ask you a variety of questions, Ms Swan.'
        "I'd like to ask Ms Swan a variety of questions."

It follows that the first and second person pronouns, where explicit, must also reflect a head. The representation of (160) must therefore be as in (161):

(160)   I request you to complete this form.

(161)   (A$_I$: [(F$_I$: request$_V$ (F$_I$)) (P$_I$: I$_{Pro}$ (P$_I$))$_S$ (P$_J$: you$_{Pro}$ (P$_J$))$_A$ (C$_I$: –you complete this form– (C$_I$))$_\Phi$] (A$_I$))

2.6.3 Modifiers

A modifier is possible where there is restrictive specification of the head. The Speaker will then be indicating a facet of him/herself or of the Addressee that is relevant to the Illocution, or will be selecting a particular Addressee. Consider such expressions as *I Caesar* or *you there*:

(162)   (P$_1$: you$_{Pro}$ (P$_1$): there$_{Adv}$ (P$_1$))

2.6.4 Operators

Many of the grammatical operations upon the expression of Participants in an Illocution will be represented by operators. The Participants in the speech event are also represented in the Contextual Component, where all their grammatically relevant properties are listed. These can be copied as operators onto the appropriate Participant, Speaker or Addressee, in each Discourse Act. For example, we find operators for number, relating to both Participants. Among the operators to be distinguished here are:

(163)   1   singular
        2   dual
        3   trial
        pc   paucal
        m   plural

Changing first the informal representations of pronouns above to a system of abstract features (see de Groot and Limburg 1986), the representation of (164), which assumes a number of co-Participants in the Illocution, will be as in (165):

(164)   (In a petition:) *We* declare that we have no confidence in the management.

(165) $(A_I: [(F_I: declare_V (F_I)) (m P_I: [+S] (P_I))_S (P_J)_A (C_I: -we have no confidence in the management- (C_I))_\Phi] (A_I))$

It is the application of the plural operator m to the abstract representation that here yields *we*, in the sense of 'group containing the Speaker'.

In Hortative Illocutions, where the sense is 'I hereby encourage you to join me in C', the inclusive form of 'we', in languages that make that distinction, is appropriate. In Kwaza (van der Voort 2004: 235) there is a distinction between inclusive and exclusive first person plural pronouns (*txa'na* and *tsi'tsɛ* respectively). In this language, the form of the Hortative affix, as *-ni* or *-ja* respectively, is dependent upon the number of the Addressee (van der Voort 2004: 311–12); where the Addressee is paucal (2 or 3), the latter is chosen, otherwise it is the former.

(166)   Txa'na   ja-'ja.
        we.INCL eat-HORT.PC
        'Let us eat . . . and not give the food to the others.'

This shows the necessity of marking the number, in Kwaza, on the (P_2), here with the paucal operator pc:

(167) $(A_I: [(F_I: HORT (F_I)) (1 P_I)_S (pc P_J)_A (C_I: -txa'na ja- (C_I))] (A_I))$

The grammatical properties of Participants can have consequences at both the Interpersonal and the Representational Levels. The relevant information is available to the language user in the Contextual Component and can be distributed to these locations through the Formulator as required.

The distinctions are relevant at the Interpersonal Level when they are applied strategically by the Speaker, for example in languages that employ morphological or other distinctions to indicate a Speaker's degree of formality to an Addressee. An example is (168), from Spanish, in which the form of the verb (*están* rather than *estáis*) betrays that the Speaker is attributing higher (h) social status to the Addressee than to him/herself; this strategic property needs to be represented at the Interpersonal Level (IL). However, the number and gender of the Addressee (plural 'm' and feminine 'f') are non-strategic properties, and will be copied from the Contextual Component to the Representational Level (RL):

(168)   ¿Están   despiertas?
        2.PL.COP.PROG.POL awake.PL.F
        'Are you awake?'

(169)   IL: $(A_I: [(F_I: INTER (F_I)) (P_I)_S (hP_J)_A (C_I:[(T_I) (R_I)] (C_I))_\Phi] (A_I))$
        RL: $(p_i: (ep_i: (e_i: [(f_i: [(f_j: despiert- (f_j)) {}^f(m x_i)_\Phi] (f_i)) (e_i)_\Phi]) (ep_i))$
        $(p_i))$

Similarly, in Japanese several forms are available for insertion into head position. Hinds (1986: 257) lists 6 forms to evoke the Speaker and 5 for the Addressee, the distinctions pertaining to 'sex of referent, social status of referent, and degree of politeness'. This would again be captured by operators sensitive to the information on speech-act participants available in the Contextual Component.

2.6.5 Frames

In sum, the following frames are available for Participants in the Discourse Act:

(170) $(\pi P_1: \emptyset (P_1))$
       $(\pi P_1: \blacklozenge (P_1): \Sigma (P_1))$

The head position may be empty, or filled by self-descriptions or forms of address;
The modifier position may be occupied by expressions specifying the identity of the Participant;
The operator position may be occupied by indications of number and status.

2.7 The Communicated Content

2.7.1 Introduction

Whereas the Illocution indicates the conventionalized conversational use of a Discourse Act, and the Participants represent the essential Speaker-Addressee dyad, the Communicated Content contains the totality of what the Speaker wishes to evoke in his/her communication with the Addressee. In actional terms it corresponds to what Searle (1969) calls the 'representational act' and corresponds to the choices the Speaker makes in order to evoke a picture of the external world s/he wants to talk about. The Communicated Content is thus the unit within which the mapping to the Representational Level takes place. In Discourse Acts in which such a mapping is absent, as in Expressives and certain Interactives, there is correspondingly no Communicated Content.

In most situations, the Communicated Content of a Declarative Discourse Act will either be entirely new for the Addressee or a composite of new and familiar information. At times, however, the information may already be familiar to the Addressee; the Speaker's purpose is to remind the Addressee or for some strategic reason to state the obvious. The German lexical modifier *bekanntermassen* functions to signal this status, as in (171):

(171) Von   anderen kann man *bekanntermaßen* oftmals lernen.
       From others can   one as.is.well-known often   learn
       'As is well known, one can often learn from other people.'

In Lillooet the enclitic =qa?, which attaches to the clause-initial element, similarly indicates presupposition, as in (172) (van Eijk 1997: 204):

(172)   Níɬ=qa?   s-kxi?úɬ
        'because'=PRESUP NMLZ-Kci76lh
        ti=um'ən-c-ás=a
        DET=give-1.SG.OBJ-3.S.SBJV=REINF
        'Well, it is Kci76lh who gave it to me, as you should know.'

Bekanntermaßen in (171) will be analysed as a modifier (cf. 2.7.3) and =qa? in (172) as an operator (cf. 2.7.4).

Each Communicated Content contains one or more Subacts, so called because they are hierarchically subordinate to Discourse Acts, and yet each is a form of communicative action by the Speaker. The Communicated Content will be represented as follows:

(173) $(\pi C_1: [\ldots (T_1)^N (R_1)^N \ldots] (C_1): \Sigma (C_1))$
        where $N \geq \varnothing$, but a minimum of 1 Subact is required

2.7.2 Heads

2.7.2.1 Introduction

The Subacts contained by the Communicated Content come in exactly two types. A Subact of Ascription (T_1) is an attempt by the Speaker to evoke a Property. Despite the word 'ascription', it need not be the case that the Speaker is actually ascribing a Property to a referent: in uttering *It is raining*, for example, the Speaker is merely evoking a meteorological Property without evoking any referent; raining is not being 'ascribed to', but simply 'ascribed'. A Subact of Reference (R_1) is an attempt by the Speaker to evoke a referent, i.e. a null, singleton, or multiple set of entities or qualities.

The number of Subacts in a Communicated Content is minimally one. There is no maximum: the number of Subacts will tend to be affected by the type of communicative event, with informal speech being typically characterized by rather simple Cs, and formal written prose permitting more complex combinations.

Subacts carry pragmatic functions, and heads of Communicated Contents can be formulated in terms of configurations of these pragmatic functions. These configurations have been called 'message modes' (Hannay 1991) or 'pragmatic articulations' (Smit fc.) in the FG literature. We will use the term 'content frames' in what follows. Before turning to these complex heads in 2.7.2.6 we discuss the individual pragmatic functions that Subacts may carry.

2.7.2.2 Focus (vs Background)

The Focus function signals the Speaker's strategic selection of new information, e.g. in order to fill a gap in the Addressee's information, or to correct the Addressee's information. The Focus function is assigned only in those cases in which this is linguistically relevant, i.e. when languages use linguistic means to indicate that some part of a Linguistic Expression constitutes the relevant new information. The information not assigned the Focus function constitutes the Background. The linguistic marking of Background rather than new information seems to be very rare. In Smit (fc.) Focus is defined as an update instruction to the Addressee.

The Focus function may be assigned to a Referential Subact (174), an Ascriptive Subact (175), several Subacts (176), or the Communicated Content as a whole (177). In these examples the focal status of constituents is manifested in prosodic differences, to be discussed in Chapter 5.

(174)   I saw *a heron*. $(C_I: [(T_I) (R_I) (R_J)_{Foc}] (C_I))$

(175)   The wind *is blowing*. $(C_I: [(T_I)_{Foc} (R_I)] (C_I))$

(176)   *Peter* had bought *a book* for Mary. $(C_I: [(T_I) (R_I)_{Foc} (R_J)_{Foc} (R_K)] (C_I))$

(177)   *A train arrived*. $(C_I: [(T_I) (R_I)]_{Foc} (C_I))$

All-new sentences like (177) are known as thetic statements (Sasse 1987; Cornish 2004). The other cases are instances of categorical statements, characterized by the presence of both a Topic (see below) and a Focus.

Generally speaking, categorical statements have one Focus, as in (174)–(175). Focus assignment is, as Dik (1997a: 328–30) points out, often rather like filling out a form. Forms typically ask us to provide one piece of information per question. However, in some languages questions such as (178) are possible (cf. Siewierska 1991: 223 for an example from Polish), with (179) as a possible answer:

(178)   Who recommended whom to whom?

(179)   Professor Brown recommended Nora to the personnel manager.

In (179) *Professor Brown, Nora* and *the personnel manager* are all in Focus. Thus this sentence is a further example of a single Communicated Content with several Foci.

The status of multiple questions like (179) is crosslinguistically variable. Whereas there are no restrictions on their occurrence in Malayalam (Asher and Kumari 1997: 21), they are possible in Finnish only as 'checking questions', i.e. in metacommunicative use (Sulkala and Karjalainen 1992: 15): *Who (did you say) recommended whom to whom?*. They are possible but rare in Babungo

(Schaub 1985: 16–17), 'hypothetically possible, but never used' in Koromfe (Rennison 1997: 27) and quite impossible in Ndyuka (Huttar and Huttar 1994: 36) and in Evenki (Nedjalkov 1997: 12). They would appear also to be restricted to those languages or constructions that mark Focus through intonation or through the use of special forms (e.g. Q-words or negative words). Where Focus is indicated by other means, we would not expect multiple Foci per Communicated Content. Thus we may conclude that the assignment of one Focus to each Communicated Content is merely a typological preference, not a universal restriction.

The assignment of Focus, of whatever type, to an element of the Interpersonal Level is dependent upon the presence of one or more types of 'special treatment' (Dik 1997a: 313) of the expression of that element. Dik distinguishes:

   (i) adaptation of the form
   (ii) the presence of a Focus marker (e.g. a particle) [-FOC] (F →Bech)
   (iii) unusual position in the sequence of constituents
   (iv) a special Focus construction
   (v) a special prosodic contour (e.g. tonic accentuation)

An example of adaptation of form is to be found in Tariana (Aikhenvald 2003: 139), in which (to simplify a little) the suffix -nhe/-ne is applied to Subjects in Focus. This case marker is thus a marker of pragmatic and syntactic function concurrently. This marking can be overridden by the assignment of the reportative marker (cf. Aikhenvald 2003: 303):

(180)   Mepuku-nuku   katu-pida   dhe.
        net-TOP.NONSBJ piraiba-PRS.REP   3.SG.NONF.enter
        'A piraiba fish entered our net, I'm told.'

The Present Reportative evidential marking here signals that *katu* is in Focus.

Other languages have markers that are specialized in marking Focus. A case in point is Wambon (de Vries 1985: 172), which marks Focus by means of -*nde*:

(181)   A.   Jakhove kenonop-nde takhim-gende?
             3.PL   what-FOC   buy-3.PL.PRS.FINAL
             'What do they buy?'

        B.   Ndu-nde   takhim-gende.
             Sago-FOC buy-3.PL.PRS.FINAL
             'They buy sago.'

A third way of marking Focus is by assigning a special syntactic position to the Focus element. Thus in Aghem (182) (Watters 1979: 144), for example, the immediately postverbal position is reserved for Focus; in Hungarian (183) (Kenesei *et al.* 1998: 166), by contrast, it is the immediately preverbal position that is occupied by the Focus.

(182)   A   mɔ̀   ñíŋ éná?.
        DUM REM.PST run Inah
        'It was Inah that ran.'

(183)   A   vendégek tegnap   érkeztek a   szálloda-ba.
        the guests   yesterday arrived the   hotel-LOC
        'It was yesterday that the guests arrived at the hotel.'

Many languages indicate the Focus by employing a special Focus construction. Where this construction takes the form of a cleft construction, this strategy involves the Representational Level as well, since the semantic material is organized in a particular way. In particular, the content is divided into two segments, one of which is in Focus. These two segments are equated with each other. The Communicated Content thus takes on the form of two Referential Subacts and the corresponding individuals are equated with each other at the Representational Level:

(184) $(C_1: [(R_1)_{Foc}(R_2)] (C_1))$

This structure leads to such constructions as (185a–c), cf. Dik (1997b: 291–312) for discussion:

(185)   a. It was tomatoes that I bought.
        b. What I bought were tomatoes.
        c. Tomatoes were what I bought.

As observed by Dik, it appears to be possible in some languages to Focus upon a predicate by means of such a construction. A construction that comes close to this in English is (186) (Dik 1997b: 314):

(186)   What he does for a living is teach.

However, note that we cannot regard *teach* here as an Ascriptive Subact, since it is equated with the Referential Subact *What he does for a living*.

Focus assignment, finally, is strongly associated in many languages with intonational prominence (cf. 5.5), and typically with pitch movement on the characteristic accent position (CAP) of the major lexical item in the Focused element. However, as was already pointed out by Dik (1997a: 461), 'there is no one-to-one relation between Focus and accent distribution'; his position appears to be that phonological prominence is applied above all where structural clues (e.g. the Focus constructions discussed above) are unavailable. This matter will receive more detailed treatment in Chapter 5.

2.7.2.3 Topic (vs Comment)

Another dimension of the organization of information structure is the Topic-Comment dichotomy. The Topic function, where relevant in languages, is not complementary to Focus, but part of this second dimension. Indeed, as we will show below, in certain circumstances a constituent can be simultaneously Focus (along the Focus-Background dimension) and Topic (along the Topic-Comment dimension). Topic function will be assigned to a Subact which has a special function within the Discourse Act, that of signalling how the Communicated Content relates to the gradually constructed record in the Contextual Component. The information not assigned the Topic function constitutes the Comment. The linguistic marking of the Comment rather than the topical information seems to be very rare. In Smit (fc.) Topic is defined as the linguistic reflection of a 'retrieve' instruction to the Addressee.

In (187), for example, from Dutch, the antecedent of the Topic *dat* is located in the Contextual Component:

(187)   Dat   heb   ik   nooit   gezegd.
        That   have   I   never   said
        'I never said that.'

The assignment of Topic function makes it explicit that the other Subacts will in some way further develop the information in the Contextual Component. This definition predisposes the assignment of Topic to Given information, but this is no more than a default correlation. Dik (1997a: 324) stresses that Topics can also contain information that can be 'legitimately inferred' from the Contextual Component (his SubTopics) or information that is no longer active in the episodic memory (his Resumed Topics; Dik 1997a: 327–8), but the link with the Contextual Component is primary.

Given the basic function of Topics of relating the Communicated Content to existing information in the Contextual Component, a Communicated Content will generally not consist of just a Topic. Where there is more than one Subact, however, there is the possibility of assigning Topic to one of the Subacts. Again, as with Focus assignment, this is done only where this function has some repercussions on the linguistic realization of the Discourse Act. Thus Mackenzie and Keizer (1991) argued that English (on this basis) lacks a Topic function, since no formal features exist in that language which justify the assumption of Topic function. In Dutch, on the other hand, the expression of a Referential Subact can occur in clause-initial position as a result of the assignment of Topic function, as was shown in (187), in which the clause-initial positioning of the anaphor *dat* 'that' can be ascribed to its being the Topic of the ongoing Discourse Act. In English (188), by contrast, clause-initial *that* is necessarily accented and is used for the expression of Contrast, with (implied) comparison with other possibilities:

(188)   That I never said.

An essential characteristic of the Topic function is that it is assigned to a Subact within the Communicated Content. It should therefore be distinguished from Theme or Tail, analysed above as a dependent Discourse Act of Orientation and Correction (2.3.2; see further below). Consider the following example from Persian (Mahootian 1997: 124):

(189)   Doxtar-i ke   hæmkelasi-m-e   be-heš telefon-zæd-æm
        girl-DEM that classmate-1.SG-COP.3.SG to-3.SG telephone-hit-1.SG
        'The girl who is my classmate, I called her.'

(190)   Be mæhin bilit-o   dad-æm
        to Mahin ticket-OBJ give.PST-1.SG
        'I gave the ticket to Mahin.'

In (189) there is a double reference to 'the girl' by means of *doxtar-i* and *be-heš*, whereas in (190) there is initial positioning of the phrase *be mæhin* but no corresponding pronoun *be-heš*. The *prima facie* analysis of (189) will therefore be as a succession of Discourse Acts, *doxtar-i ke hæmkelasi-m-e* and *be-heš telefon-zæd-æm*, with the first dependent upon the second, whereas (190) will be analysed as a single Discourse Act, with Topic *be mæhin*.

Persian has another strategy for topicalization, suffixation with *-ra/-ro/-o*, also used to indicate a definite Undergoer; this suffixation is never obligatory. If the head of the topicalized phrase is an adverb, the suffixation may or may not be accompanied by clause-initial placement (Mahootian 1997: 121–2):

(191)   a.   Kæmal emšæb-o   inja mi-mun-e
             Kamal tonight-TOP here DUR-stay-3.SG
             'Kamal is staying here tonight.'

        b.   Emšæb-o   Kæmal inja mi-mun-e
             tonight-TOP Kamal here DUR-stay-3.SG
             'Kamal is staying here tonight.'

However, if the head is a noun, suffixation entails placement in initial position (perhaps to avoid misinterpretation as the marker of a definite Undergoer), as in the case of the Recipient argument *golaro* in (192):

(192)   Gol-a-ro   mæhin ab   dad
        flower-PL-TOP Mahin water gave
        'Mahin watered the flowers.'

The preceding examples exemplify several other points about the assignment of the Topic function. Firstly, observe that Topic can be assigned to Subacts that serve to indicate the setting of the State-of-Affairs being evoked, as in (191). The Contextual Component contains information about spatial and temporal coordinates, and these can also be selected for Topic status. Secondly, pragmatic functions tend to take priority over semantic functions at the Morphosyntactic Level; whereas a Recipient not morphosyntactically marked for Topic is indicated by the preposition *be* (cf. (190)), a Recipient that is marked for Topic is not simultaneously marked for its semantic function (cf. *golaro* in (192)). Thirdly, it is instructive that there is homonymy in Persian between the marker of definiteness on Undergoers and the marker of Topic: Topic correlates strongly not only with Givenness, but also with expected identifiability for the Addressee, i.e. definiteness.

The positioning of a Topical element at the beginning of a clause can also apply to an element of a clause embedded within that clause. Consider the following example, also from Persian (Mahootian 1997: 126):

(193)   Mæšrub goft-æm   (ke)   næ-xor.
        alcohol say.PST-1.SG COMP NEG-eat
        'Alcohol I told you not to drink.'

At the Representational Level, *mæšrub* will be analysed as an argument of the verb *xor*, at the Morphosyntactic Level; however, the corresponding noun phrase will appear as a constituent of the higher clause. This raising effect (cf. 4.4.8.5) is treated in FDG as triggered by the pragmatic function of this constituent at the Interpersonal Level, which here too overrules the Representational Level.

Multiple Topics are possible in certain languages. Thus in Turkish, in which Topic can be expressed by initial placement, we find (194), from Kornfilt (1997: 205), in which both *kitab-ı* and *Ali-ye* are Topic, as is evident from their placement in front of the subject constituent *Hasan*:

(194)   Kitab-ı   Ali-ye Hasan dün   ver-di
        book-ACC Ali-DAT Hasan yesterday give-PST
        'Hasan gave Ali the book yesterday.'

In this example *dün* has Focus function, expressed through placement in the preverbal position. This brings us to the following representation of (194):

(195)   (C$_I$: [(T$_I$) (R$_I$: Hasan (R$_I$)) (R$_J$)$_{Top}$ (R$_K$: Ali (R$_K$))$_{Top}$ (R$_L$)$_{Foc}$] (C$_I$))

Not all languages make use of the function Topic, as was mentioned above for English. Others can be described as clearly topic-prominent. Mandarin Chinese clauses, for example (Chao 1968), are based upon the principle of the succession of Topic and Comment (with the latter containing the Focus of the Communicated Content). Consider (196) from van den Berg (1989: 38):

(196) Wǒmen chī miàn.
      we   eat noodles
      'We are eating noodles.'

In the context provided, *wǒmen*, being placed first, is Topic, and the rest is Comment. Within the Comment *miàn* is Focus. In Modern Standard Chinese a Topic may be followed by a pause marker *a* which van den Berg (1989: 42) interprets as giving the Speaker time to formulate his/her utterance. Van den Berg (1989: 41) gives an example with two Topics:

(197) Wǒmen a   jīntiān a   chī miàn.
      We   PAUS today PAUS eat noodles
      'We ... ah ... today ... ah ... are eating noodles.'

Topic assignment is not restricted to Referential Subacts. Ascriptive Subacts may also form (part of) the point of departure for a statement, as in the following Spanish example, uttered in the context of a question about the amount of rainfall:

(198) Llov-er no   lluev-e.
      rain-INF NEG rain-PRS.3.SG.IND
      'It doesn't rain here.'
      "Raining it doesn't rain."

The topical Ascriptive Subact is realized through an infinitival copy of the main verb in initial position. In the equivalent Dutch construction a dummy verb is used instead in the finite position:

(199) Regen-en doet   het hier niet.
      rain-INF do.3.SG.PRS it here not
      'It doesn't rain here.'
      "Raining it doesn't do here."

We will return in 4.4.6. to the syntactic analysis of this type of construction.

As mentioned in 2.3.2 there is a close connection between Orientations (as Subsidiary Discourse Acts) and Topics. An example of a sequence of a Subsidiary Discourse Act and a Nuclear Discourse Act can be found in Finnish, from Sulkala and Karjalainen (1992: 189):

(200) Tuo tyttö, hänessä   on   jota-kin   tuttua
      that girl   3.SG.INESS COP which.PARTV-too familiar-PARTV
      'That girl, there is something familiar about her.'

The Dependent Discourse Act *tuo tyttö* presents a Referential Subact, with the Np in the neutral nominative case; the Nuclear Discourse Act contains a Topic *hänessä*, in clause-initial position, and marked for the Inessive case. This formulation is pragmatically convenient for the Speaker and Addressee, but is dissonant with the unified conceptualization 'There is something familiar about that girl'. There is therefore some pressure upon Speakers (especially in the written language where there are fewer time restrictions) to express such States-of-Affairs within a single Discourse Act, in which the initially realized Referential Subact is treated as the Topic. This leads to the integration of Orientations discussed by Dik (1997b: 403–4) as a recurrent diachronic process.

2.7.2.4 Contrast (vs Overlap)

A final information-structural function to be discussed here is Contrast, which signals the Speaker's desire to bring out the particular differences between two or more Communicated Contents or between a Communicated Content and contextually available information. The counterpart of Contrast would be Overlap, signalling the Speaker's desire to bring out the particular similarities between two or more Communicated Contents or between a Communicated Content and contextually available information. The marking of Overlap rather than Contrast, however, seems to be non-existent.

Contrast is often treated as a special type of Focus, but we treat it as an independent function here, since Contrast may combine with both Focal and Topical constituents. For an example of the latter, consider the following example from Wambon (de Vries 1985: 174):

(201) A: Nombone ndu-ngup ande-ngup?
            this   sago-and banana-and
            'What about this sago and bananas?'

       B: Wembane ndu-nde   takhima-tbo,
            Wemba   sago-CONTR buy-3SG.PST.FINAL
            'Wemba bought the sago,
            Karolule ande-nde   takhima-tbo.
            Karolus banana-CONTR buy-3.SG.PST.FINAL
            Karolus bought the bananas.'

Here the elements carrying the Contrast marker are clearly not new; rather they provide the pieces of knowledge from the Contextual Component that form the points of departure of the two statements in (201b).

Another example of this is given in (202):

(202) John and Bill came to see me. *John* was *nice*, but *Bill* was *rather boring*.

Of this example Dik (1997a: 326) claims that *John, nice, Bill* and *rather boring* are all subject to Focus assignment (cf. also Siewierska 1991: 178), and indeed it is possible to pronounce (202) with pitch movement on each of these (cf. 5.4). However, where *John* and *Bill* are treated in this way, this is just because the Speaker wishes also to signal the differences between the two Communicated Contents *John was nice* and *Bill was rather boring*, not because s/he wishes to update A's knowledge with new or correcting information. Thus *John* and *Bill* should be treated here as Contrastive Topics, not as Contrastive Foci.

The fact that Contrast has often been interpreted as a special type of Focus is probably related to the fact that Focus and Contrast often make use of the same expression format. This is the case of the morphological marker *–nde* in Wambon, which is used as a Focus marker in example (181) and as a Contrast marker in (201). It is also the case of pitch movement in English. The explanation for this overlap is that both Focus and Contrast (and Emphasis, see below) involve saliency. There are, however, also many languages in which the marking of Focus and Contrast is clearly distinct. Thus, Kham (Watters 2002: 183) has a specialized marker for Contrast:

(203)   Ao   po:-lə   te   tam   ja:h-si-u   li-zya.
        this place-in CONTR wheat put-DETRANS-NML be-CONT
        'In this place, as opposed to others, wheat has been sown.'

In Tuvaluan (Besnier 2000: 244–5), 'the case marker *a* can mark option- ally any noun phrase in the absolute case or otherwise not marked for case. ... However, when it is optional ..., *a* marks contrastiveness', as in (204):

(204)   Maaua   e   olo atu,   a   tino   koo   seeai.
        we.DU.EXCL NONPST go DEICT CONTR person INCH NEG
        'We came along, but there was no one left.'

In Bulgarian (Stanchev 1997), a constituent with Contrast function is placed in preverbal position, but before any clitics:

(205)   Az   kola-ta   *vchera*   ya   prodadox,   a   ne   dnes.
        1.SG car-DEF   yesterday 3.SG.ACC   sell.PST.1.SG and NEG today
        'It was yesterday that I sold the car, and not today.'

A constituent with Focus function, on the other hand, is preferably placed in clause-final position (although Contrastive Focus may also appear there):

(206)   Az   vchera   v   magazina kupix   *edna kniga*.
        1.SG yesterday in shop.DEF buy.PST.1.SG INDF book
        I yesterday bought a book in the shop.'

Focus may also appear in clause-initial position, but then with intonational prominence, cf. (207) in answer to *Ti kakvo kupi na pazara?* 'What did you buy at the market?':

(207) *Domati*   kupix.
       tomato.PL buy.PST.1.SG
       'I bought tomatoes.'

In Stanchev's (1997) analysis, Bulgarian is a language in which the placement of constituents (with respect to the main verb) is very strongly influenced by their pragmatic functions.

Of related interest here is the claim by Dik (1997a: 330) that Focus can be assigned to restrictors and operators from the Representational Level. In principle, in English pragmatically induced pitch movement is applied to the last CAP syllable of the Focused element, here informally shown as capitalization:

(208)   I like the green CAR.

(209)   I am rePAINTing it.

However, in the context of another Participant's having said that s/he preferred the red car, the Speaker is likely to shift the stress to the word indicating the concept when expressing Contrast as in (210); similarly, in answer to the question *Are you painting the house?* the Speaker is likely to say (211):

(210)   I like the GREEN car.

(211)   I am REpainting it.

Dik claims that in (210) (Contrastive) Focus is assigned to the restrictor in the representation of *the green car* and in (211) to 'part of the predicate'. We interpret these examples as cases of Contrast assignment rather than as cases of Focus assignment. Note that what the Speaker of (210) likes remains 'the green car' and what the Speaker of (211) is doing remains 'repainting' the house. What the data in (210)–(211) show is that the assignment of stress at the Phonological Level is sensitive not only to Contrast assignment to these constituents, but also to the information in the Contextual Component. The presence of 'the red car' and 'painting' in the Contextual Component justifies the switch of stress to the marked position.

There are languages in which this local expression of Contrast is not permitted. For instance, in Kham, which was shown to have a specialized marker for Contrast in (203), this marker can only occur at the phrasal layer (Watters 2002: 184):

(212)   a.   mol-o   ka:h-ye   te
             black-NMLZ dog-ERG   CONTR

b. *mol-o   te   ka:h-ye
    black-NMLZ CONTR dog-ERG
    'the black dog'

2.7.2.5 Combinations of pragmatic functions

We have treated information-structural functions in the preceding paragraphs as pertaining to three different parameters: Focus (versus Background), Topic (versus Comment), and Contrast (versus Overlap). In each case it is the first value for which we normally find linguistic manifestations. These three values, Focus, Topic, and Contrast, may in principle be combined with each other, so that we would expect configurations like the following to be linguistically relevant as well:

— Focus/Contrast
— Topic/Contrast
— Focus/Topic
— Focus/Topic/Contrast

As indicated earlier, Contrast is assumed to be a subtype of Focus in many approaches, so that the combination Focus/Contrast is not a surprising one. In English this combination is typically expressed through a cleft sentence, as in:

(213)   It was the zoo that they went to, not the museum.

The combination Topic/Contrast was illustrated above for Wambon and English in (201) and (202) respectively. These languages use the same means for expressing this combination of values as they do for Focus. A more salient example of how the combination Topic/Contrast may manifest itself comes from Korean, a language that has a marker that is exclusively used for Contrastive Topics (see Lee 1999). Consider the following example (Pultr 1960: 224):

(214)   Na-nɯn   morɯ-mnida
        1.SG-CONTR.TOP not.know-HON
        'I don't know (but others maybe do)'

The combination Focus/Topic is relevant for the analysis of presentative constructions, which serve the purpose of introducing a new topic into the discourse. The following example is from Saisiyat (Hsieh and Huang 2006: 100):

(215)   Hiza= hayza' ila koSa'en ka   SaiSiyat.
        there EX   PFV PAUS   NOM Saisiyat
        'Once there were Saisiyats.'

In this language the nominative particle *ka* is used with a postverbal subject in presentative constructions. In non-presentative constructions the subject is preverbal and the nominative particle is absent (Hsieh and Huang 2006: 99):

(216)   Takem kas'oehaz   ila.
        frog   A.FOC.move.out PFV
        'The frog moved out.'

Another example is the following French construction, adapted from Dik (1997a: 317):

(217)   Il est   arrivé   trois trains.
        it AUX.PRS.3.SG arrive. PTCP.SG.M three trains
        'There arrived three trains.'

This presentative construction is characterized by the dummy subject *il*, the postverbal position of the single argument, and the absence of agreement of the verb, all of which are in contrast with features of the non-presentative construction illustrated in (218):

(218)   Les trois trains sont   arrivés.
        the three trains AUX.PRS.3.PL arrive.PTCP.PL.M
        'The three trains arrived.'

Finally, a constituent that is focal and topical may be presented contrastively, as in:

(219)   There is BEER without alcohol, not whisky.

where the combination of the functions Top and Foc leads to the choice of the presentative construction type, while the function Contr is reflected in stress assignment.

Thus, by separating the three dimensions of information structuring, the aforementioned constructions come out naturally as the expression of combinations of information-structuring functions.

2.7.2.6 Content frames

We are now ready to look at the possible combinations of Subacts with pragmatic functions that may fill the head position of the Communicated Content. We will call such combinations *content frames*, which are non-hierarchically organized combinations of Subacts, to distinguish them from *interpersonal frames*, which take care of the hierarchical organization of the Interpersonal Level. Content frames constitute the FDG formalization of Hannay's (1991) idea of message modes. A few examples based on the distribution of Topic and Focus are the following (observe that SA here stands for any Subact):

(220) Thetic
$[(SA)^N]_{FOC}$

(221) Categorical
$[(SA)_{TOP} (SA)^N (SA)_{FOC}]$

(222) Presentative
$[(SA)^N (SA)_{TOPFOC}]$

Note that the inventory of frames is language-specific. Thus, in Topic-oriented languages a categorical content frame could take the form in (223), while in a Focus-oriented language it could take the form in (224):

(223) Categorical—Topic-oriented
$[(SA)^N (SA)_{TOP}]$

(224) Categorical—Focus-oriented
$[(SA)^N (SA)_{FOC}]$

Tidore is a strongly Topic-oriented language, as is shown by the following examples (van Staden 2000: 273):

(225) turus una=ge,   mina mo-sango   una
then 3.SG.M=there 3.SG.F 3.SG.F.A-answer 3.SG.M
'Then she answered him.'
"Then he, she answered him."

(226) tagi nde,   fangato koliho rea
go 3.NH.here 1.SG.M.A go.back not.anymore
'I won't come back anymore.'
"Given this going, I won't come back anymore."

The Topics in these examples are marked in three different ways: (i) they occur in first position, (ii) they are followed by a locative enclitic or particle, (iii) they are set off intonationally from the main clause. Both referential (225) and ascriptive (226) Subacts may be treated in this way. Thus, specifying the units in the basic content frame in (223) we arrive at the formalizations in (227) and (228) for (225) and (226) respectively:

(227) $[(T_I) (R_I) (R_J)_{TOP}]$

(228) $[(T_I)_{TOP} (R_I)]$

Kisi is a strongly Focus-oriented language, as illustrated by examples (229) and (230) from Childs (1995: 270–1):

(229) Màálóŋ ó có   cùùcúúwó ní.
rice   he AUX sow   FOC
'It's rice he is sowing.'

(230)   Pùέŋndáŋ yá púέŋ ní.
        forgetting I   forget FOC
        'It's forgetting that I did.'

Focus is marked in two ways in Kisi: (i) the Focused constituent occurs in first position, and (ii) a Focus particle occurs in clause-final position. This operation can be applied to both referential (229) and ascriptive (230) Subacts. Using the basic content frame in (224), (229), and (230) may be represented as in (231)–(232) respectively:

(231) $[(T_I) (R_I) (R_I)_{FOC}]$

(232) $[(T_I)_{FOC} (R_I)]$

As a final example, consider the following Turkish example (Kornfilt 1997: 205), discussed before as (194), in which both *kitab-ı* and *Ali-ye* are Topic, as reflected in their placement in clause-initial position, preceding the Subject constituent *Hasan* that would occupy that position otherwise, and *dün* is Focus, as shown by its preverbal position, which is the Focus position in Turkish:

(233)   Kitab-ı   Ali-ye   Hasan dün   ver-di
        book-ACC Ali-DAT Hasan yesterday give-PST
        'Hasan gave Ali the book yesterday.'

For this example a content frame containing multiple Topics and a single Focus is needed, as given in (234):

(234) $[(T_1) (R_1) (R_2)_{Top} (R_3)_{Top} (R_4)_{Foc}]$

2.7.3 Modifiers

As with all other units, the Communicated Content can be modified by lexical material. Potential modifiers at this layer include emphatic ones. This type of modifier is pervasive at the Interpersonal Level, in the sense that it applies to all kinds of actional units. At the layer of the Communicated Content this means that the entire content of an utterance is emphasized, as in the following examples:

(235)   I *really* don't like you.

(236)   Do you *really* want to hurt me?

These are different from emphatic modifiers of the Discourse Act, in the sense that they do not express irritation, anger, and the like, but intensify the content of the Discourse Act. They furthermore have a more limited distribution, in the sense that they are incompatible with certain Illocutions. Another difference is that their expression is not peripheral, but internal. And lastly, they can combine with Discourse Act modifiers, as in:

(237)   I *really* don't like you *dammit!*

Other modifiers of C express the Speaker's subjective attitude towards the Communicated Content. Examples are items such as *(un)fortunately* and *luckily*. Such content-oriented evaluations are speaker-bound and therefore pertain at the Interpersonal Level.

Yet another class of modifiers serve to indicate that the Speaker is passing on a Communicated Content expressed or implied by others. Whereas modifiers of Propositional Contents at the Representational Level indicate an attitude to what is being communicated (an assessment of the likelihood or obviousness of what is being said, see 3.3.3), modifiers of Communicated Contents merely indicate that the Speaker is relaying the views of others. English adverbials with this function include *reportedly, purportedly*, etc. We already mentioned the German *bekanntermassen* in 2.7.1. In South American Spanish, we find *dizque* (historically 's/he says that') in a similar function:

(238)   Lo   hizo   *dizque*   para ayud-ar.
        3.SG.N do.PST.3.SG reportedly to   help-INF
        'Reportedly he did it to help.'

Whereas these adverbials do not indicate the source of the report, other modifiers of the Communicated Content such as *according to reliable sources, in Bill's words*, etc. are more specific about whose voice is being transmitted.

To some extent, this analysis is also appropriate for indications of whose voice is being relayed in direct quotation. At the Representational Level we would wish to regard the quoted speech in (239a) as an argument of *say*, a position supported by the correspondence with (239b). In the context of a Speaker narrating a dialogue between Bill and Mary as in (240), however, there are reasons to believe that the clauses *Bill said* and *Mary said* are to be seen as modifiers of the relayed Communicated Content rather than as being part of the head:

(239)   a.   Bill said, 'The weather is getting worse.'
        b.   Bill said that the weather was getting worse.

(240)   < ... > 'I'm not leaving yet,' Bill said. 'But we'll be late,' Mary said. 'That's not so important,' Bill said < ... >

Notice that *Bill said* in (240), but not so readily in (239a), can appear in the inverted order *said Bill*, and the very order of presentation (Communicated

Content and then source) suggests a head + modifier relation. The modifier status of such clauses unsurprisingly leads to their becoming formally less flexible: consider how the past tense of the Middle English verb *quethan* 'say' has survived in the invariable (mock-)archaic Modern English *quoth*. We shall analyse (240), therefore, as consisting of a series of Moves, each consisting of one Discourse Act, the Communicated Content of which is the part within quotation marks, each with a modifier indicating the source of that Content (cf. Gonçalves 2003). The Speaker of (240) is, as it were, acting the parts of Bill and Mary alternately.

2.7.4 Operators

The relayed status of a Communicated Content is often indicated grammatically. Thus in Shipibo (Faust 1973) we find the suffix *-ronqui* in this reportative function:

(241)   Cai-ronqui reocoocainyantanque.
        going-REP   he.turned.over
        'Reportedly, while he was going (in the boat), he turned over.'

Such a suffix will be represented as a Rep(ortative) operator on the C-variable.

In a tale told in Sliammon (Watanabe 2003: 548–92), we note that once the Speaker starts telling the story, almost every Communicated Content contains the clitic k'^wa attached to the end of the first constituent; this clitic is missing again in the Speaker's final Discourse Acts, which provide the 'moral' of the story. The story, which was also recorded by Boas (1888), is part of the lore of the Sliammon people; the Speaker is relaying that story rather than telling it. This explains the recurrent use of the reportative marker. Interestingly, where the characters in the story use direct speech, there is no reportative marker in their words. In the context of the story, they are speaking for themselves, not relaying the words and thoughts of someone else.

In Lithuanian (Gronemeyer 1997), the active-participial form of the verb is used to indicate reportative status, i.e. that 'the speaker does not vouch for the validity of the claim, but merely relates what someone else has claimed'. One of her examples is (242):

(242)   Kadaise čia   buv-ę   didel-i   mišk-ai.
        long.ago here be-A.PTCP.NOM.PL large-NOM.PL   forest-NOM.PL
        'Long ago there were large forests here, it is said.'

'The finite copula is strictly excluded under the reportative interpretation' (Gronemeyer 1997: 100). The copula insertion rule will thus be blocked in Lithuanian under the influence of the operator Rep(ortative).

There is a natural association of the reportative with the third person: a Speaker does not usually communicate what others say about him/herself.

The marked application of the reportative construction in Lithuanian to the first person, for example, engenders an interpretation of detachment and non-deliberateness (Gronemeyer 1997).

(243) Aš   pa-reš-ęs   nauj-ą   knyg-ą.
       1.SG.NOM PFV-write-A.PTCP.NOM.SG.M new-ACC book-ACC
       'It seems I've written a new book!'

Curnow (2002) gives examples of applications of the Reportative from Wintu and Tucano in which the Speaker is drunk or is being born respectively: in both cases, the Speaker is unaware of the State-of-Affairs and can only report others' say-so.

A special property of truly reportative markers, which sets it off from other evidential categories, is that they often combine with a whole range of Illocutions, as shown in the following examples from Kham (Watters 2002: 297, 298):

(244) kā: ma-zyo-ke-o   di.
       food NEG-eat-PFV-3.SG REP
       'He didn't eat (or so it's said).'

(245) ba-n-ke   di.
       go-2SG-IMP REP
       'Go (you're told)!'

(246) karao di.
       why   REP
       'Why (someone wants to know)?'

Watters clearly shows that adding a reportative marker to an utterance is not the same as quoting that utterance in direct speech, since the shifters in the original utterance orient themselves towards the current Speaker. Compare (247) and (248) from Watters (2002: 298):

(247) 'ŋa-za   rəi-d-y-ā-ke'   həi   d-ī:-zya-o.
       my-child bring-SS-BEN-1.SG-IMP thus say-2.SG-IMPF-3.SG
       'She says to you: "Bring my child to me".'

(248) o-za   rəi-d-i:-ke   di.
       her-child bring-SS-BEN.3.SG-IMP REP
       'Bring her child to her (you're told)!'

From these facts we may conclude that in utterances containing a truly reportative modality it is the current Speaker who executes the Discourse Act, although on behalf of another speaker.

Spanish uses a special construction type for relayed speech as well. Compare the following examples:

(249) ¡Que venga-s   a   come-r!
       REP   come.PRS.SUBJ-2.SG to eat-INF
       'Come and eat! (I'm ordering you on behalf of someone else.)'

(250) Que si vienes   mañana.
       REP if come.PRS.IND-2.SG tomorrow
       'Will you come tomorrow? (I'm asking you on behalf of someone else).'

The sentence-initial particle *que*, identical in form to a subordinator, is used here to indicate that the current Speaker is relaying information on behalf of someone else. Note that, as indicated in 2.4.4, these constructions can also be used for the expression of Emphatic Discourse Acts, but in that case they combine with a different prosodic pattern.

Another operator is the grammatical counterpart of the emphatic modifier discussed in the previous section. Grammaticalized expressions of Emphasis at the layer of the Communicated Content often find their origin in cleft-like constructions. In Scottish Gaelic, a construction is used that is also used for the clefting on non-Nps:

(251) 'S ann a dh'fheumas tu   rud   beag de dh'eòlas   ciùil
       CLEFT   must/need 2.SG thing little of knowledge music.GEN
       'It's just that you must have some knowledge of music.'

Similarly, in Mandarin Chinese we find the original cleft pattern for emphatic constructions (Li and Thompson 1981: 591):

(252) Wǒ shì gěn nǐ kāiwánxiào de.
       1.SG COP with you joke   NMLZ
       'I'm just joking with you.'

To the extent that these constructions are grammaticalized, they are captured by an Emph(atic) operator at the C-layer.

2.7.5 Frames

To summarize, then, the Communicated Content has the following structure:

(253) $(\pi\ C_1: [(T)_{\Phi}^N\ (R)_{\Phi}^N]_{\Phi}\ (C_1): \Sigma\ (C_1))$

Among the possible occupants of the operator position π are the Reportative and the Emphatic operators. The head of the Communicated Content is occupied by a Content Frame, consisting of a range of juxtaposed Subacts of Ascription (T) and reference (R). Pragmatic functions can be assigned to these Subacts, or to the Content Frame as a whole. Finally, there is a position for lexical modifiers, to indicate the source of the C, the Speaker's subjective attitude towards C, or lexical elements emphasizing C.

2.8 Subacts

2.8.1 Introduction

It is a fundamental belief of speech-act theory that reference should be analysed as actional. This position was also taken by Dik (1978: 55), who wrote that 'referring should be regarded as a pragmatic, cooperative action of a Speaker within a pattern of verbal interaction between that Speaker and some Addressee'. By using the word 'pragmatic', Dik sought to link referring to what he saw as the primary function of communication, 'to effect changes in the pragmatic information' of that Addressee (Dik 1978: 128). The pragmatic information consists of all the information (long-term, situational and immediate) that communicators bring to bear upon their interaction.

   FDG endorses this position, but also considers that ascription is actional in the same way. Just as referring involves an attempt by the Speaker to influence the Addressee's 'pragmatic information', so does ascribing. In exactly the same way as with referring, the choice of lexical material, and the amount offered, derive from the Speaker's estimate of how best to influence the Addressee (cf. Mackenzie 1987b). Accordingly, we shall regard both ascription and reference as actional, as the two aspects of the more global action of evocation. We shall say that a Speaker evokes a Communicated Content by carrying out a number ($n \geq 1$) of Subacts of Ascription and Reference. The Interpersonal Level thus distinguishes three actional layers:

   (i) the Move, the execution of an Initiation or Response in interaction;
   (ii) the Discourse Act, the execution of an illocutionary or non-illocutionary Discourse Act;
   (iii) the Evocation, the execution of a set of Subacts which make up the Communicated Content.

In certain languages, the (T) or (R) status of elements of the Communicated Content is marked explicitly. In Samoan (Mosel and Hovdhaugen 1992: 52, 56), an ascriptive element is typically placed in clause-initial position; placement of a referential element in clause-initial position entails the addition of the presentative particle 'o, as illustrated in (255). The basic order is illustrated in (254):

(254) 'Ua o tamaiti i   Apia.
       PRF go children LD   Apia
       'The children have gone to Apia.'

(255) 'O le maile sa fasi e le teine.
       PRES ART dog PST hit ERG ART girl
       'The dog was hit by the girl.'

In Tagalog (Himmelmann fc.), another ascription-initial language, it is the
ascriptive element (T) rather than the preposed constituent that is obligatorily
marked in cases of inversion. Example (257) shows the use of the predicate
marker (PM) *ay*, which is absent when the predicate is in initial position (256):

(256) Ma-saráp   ang pag-kain.
       STAT-satisfaction SPEC GER-eating
       'The food was good.'

(257) Silá mag-iná   *ay* na-tulog   na.
       3.PL REC-mother PM RLS.STAT-sleep now
       'The mother and her daughter fell asleep.'

We find the marker –*mi* or –*mali* indicating referential status in Sabanê
(Antunes 2004: 113–15). In Modern Standard Fijian it would appear that the
referential status is indicated by the particle *na*, as in (258). This particle is
absent when a noun is being used non-referentially, as in (259), where the lack
of a transitivity marker on the verb indicates the presence of incorporation
(Crowley 1985: 136–7, cited in Rijkhoff 2002: 95):

(258) Au ŋunu-va na   wai.
       I   drink-TR PART water
       'I am drinking the water.'

(259) Au ŋunu wai.
       I   drink water
       'I drink water.'

In Boumaa Fijian (Dixon 1988: 115), *a* (the corresponding particle) is omitted when a noun is used predicatively, i.e. in the expression of an Ascriptive Subact; cf. (260), from Dixon (1988: 67), which cannot mean 'I want a
horse':

(260) Au via   ose.
       I   want horse
       'I want to be a horse.'

2.8.2 Ascription

2.8.2.1 Introduction

The Subact of Ascription is the Speaker's attempt to ascribe a semantic category. As mentioned in 2.7.1, we will not say that the Speaker ascribes a Property

to some referent, since we will allow for Communicated Contents with only an Ascriptive Subact. For example, in (261), represented in (262), the Property 'rain' is ascribed, but is not ascribed to any referent, since no Referential Subact corresponds to *it*:

(261)   It is raining.

(262) $(C_1: (T_1) (C_1))$

Note that the Interpersonal Level merely records the presence of the Subact. The lexical item *rain* will be supplied at the Representational Level.

It is not the case that every predicate at the Representational Level will correspond to an Ascriptive Subact at the Interpersonal Level. Consider instances of gapping, as in (263):

(263)   Peter has a blue car and Mike a red car.

At the Representational Level, the second clause in (263) will be shown as containing a semantic variable for the Property *have* coreferential with the lexically realized property in the first clause. At the Interpersonal Level, however, there is no corresponding Ascriptive Subact. The absence of an Ascriptive Subact will signal to the Morphosyntactic Level to implement 'gapping'. In this way, the Interpersonal Level shows what the Speaker *does*, while the Representational Level shows what s/he *means*.

Ascriptive Subacts may occur within Referential Subacts. Consider the noun phrase *a blue car* in (263). The noun phrase as a whole will be shown as a Referential Subact at the Interpersonal Level, but it clearly contains two Subacts of Ascription: the Property 'car' is evoked, as well as the Property 'blue'. The relationship between these Properties, namely that 'blue' restricts the applicability of the Property 'car', will be displayed at the Representational Level. At the Interpersonal Level, all that will be shown is that the Referential Subact is carried out by means of two Ascriptive Subacts:

(264)   a blue car

IL: $(R_I: [(T_I) \qquad (T_J) \qquad] (R_I))$
RL: $(x_i: (f_i: car (f_i) (x_i): (f_j: blue (f_j)) (x_i))$

Among the advantages of this representation are that Contrast can be assigned to (T_I), (T_J) or (R_I), according to the context of use:

(265)   a.   Peter has a blue (car)$_{Contr}$ and Mike a blue (motorbike)$_{Contr}$.
        b.   Peter has a (blue)$_{Contr}$ car and Mike a (red)$_{Contr}$ car.
        c.   Peter has (a blue car)$_{Contr}$ and Mike (a red motorbike)$_{Contr}$.

This will lead to the following representations:

(266) a. $(R_I: [(T_I)_{Contr} (T_J)] (R_I))$
       b. $(R_I: [(T_I) (T_J)_{Contr}] (R_I))$
       c. $(R_I: [(T_I) (T_J)] (R_I))_{Contr}$

2.8.2.2 Heads

The head of an Ascriptive Subact is in principle empty. In (267), for example, the Ascriptive Subact expressed as the verb *loves* will appear at the
Interpersonal Level simply as (T_I), since ascription is carried out through
the selection of a lexical item at the Representational Level, where it will be
displayed in the scope of an (f) variable.

(267) Peter loves Mary.
       $(C_I: [(T_I) (R_I: Peter (R_I)) (R_J: Mary (R_J))] (C_I))$

There are exceptional cases in which the Ascriptive Subact can perhaps be
considered to occur with a lexical head. This is the case when a Speaker can't
find the right lexical filler for a semantic unit at the Representational Level or
doesn't want to disclose the information associated with that unit. Consider
the following example from Turkish (Barış Kabak, p.c.). The context is one
in which the Addressee, who is handing in documents, is told that there is a
document that should be certified before it can be accepted:

(268) Tamam, o   zaman on-lar-ı   bırak-ın   burda,
       OK   DEM time   DEM-PL-ACC leave-IMP.PL here
       diploma-nız-ı=da   Pazartesi şey   et-tir-ip
       diploma-2.PL.POSS-ACC=TOP   Monday   thingummy do-CAUS-NARR
       öyle   getir-in.
       like.that bring-IMP.PL
       'OK, then leave the others here, and have your diploma "thingum-
       mied" (certified) on Monday and bring it like that.'

We interpret this as a strategy by means of which the Speaker indicates
incapacity or unwillingness to evoke the relevant Property, as indicated in
(269):

(269) $(T_I: şey (T_I))$

Note that the support verb *et-* is introduced at the Morphosyntactic Level
through a general verb support rule. Note further that the same element *şey*
may also be used whenever the Speaker doesn't remember or doesn't want
to use a lexeme describing an individual or object, equivalent to the English
noun *thingummy*, in which case it is used as the head of an ascriptive phrase
realizing a referential phrase, as indicated in (270):

(270) $(R_I: (T_I: şey (T_I)) (R_I))$

2.8.2.3 Modifiers

Several interpersonal modifiers that were shown to be relevant at the layer of the Communicated Content (cf. 2.7.3) show up at the layer of the Ascriptive Subact as well. Consider the following examples (cf. van de Velde 2007 for cases like 271):

(271)   an *allegedly* defamatory article

(272)   a *fortunately* slim publication

(273)   a *really* nice example

In the last example *really* indicates emphatic commitment on the part of the Speaker, and in this sense it differs from regular degree adverbs like *very*. This difference manifests itself in the fact that the two can be combined, but only in the order reflecting the appropriate scope relations, as shown in:

(274)   a.   a *really very* nice example
         b.   *a *very really* nice example

In examples (271)–(274) the scope of the modifiers is restricted to an Ascriptive Subact (T) that occurs within the context of a Referential Subact. This can be represented as in (275):

(275) $(R_I: [(T_I) (T_J: [ ] (T_J): allegedly/fortunately/really (T_J))] (R_I))$

More specific to an Ascriptive Subact is the possibility of modification by an indication on the Speaker's part that the Subact only approximates to his/her actual communicative intentions. This involves introducing a hedge to this effect. Examples are the fixed expressions *as it were* and *so to speak*, as in (276)–(277):

(276)   Leonard is my mentor *as it were*.

(277)   Leonard is my mentor *so to speak*.

The italicized expressions indicate that the Speaker is not fully willing to ascribe the Property 'my mentor' to Leonard, but that *my mentor* is close to what s/he wants to say about Leonard.

A rather comparable situation is when the Speaker indicates that s/he considers the ascription actually to be inappropriate, as in:

(278)   The *so-called* buffet is actually really limited choice. (Internet)

All these modifiers can be represented as occupying the modifier slot of the Ascriptive Subact.

2.8.2.4 Operators

Where approximative expressions of the type discussed in the previous section become grammaticalized, they will be analysed as operators. This analysis suggests itself for English *sort-of*, which for many language-users has become phonologically reduced to 'sorda' (cf. Keizer 2007: ch. 7). Note that this form serves to indicate the approximative status of Subacts of Ascription, irrespective of the part-of-speech of the lexical item that the Speaker finds to be less than fully precise:

(279)   Her shirt was *sort-of* blue.

(280)   We are *sort-of* improving.

(281)   I felt *sort-of* outside.

(282)   My *sort-of* friend has started a rock band.

Note that the grammaticalized status of this marker is substantiated by the fact that agreement in (283) is with *friends*, not with *sort*:

(283)   My *sort-of* friends have started a rock band.

Such markers will be analysed as expressing the operator Approx:

(284)   (approx T_1)

The opposite of approximation obtains when languages apply grammatical strategies to indicate that the property that is ascribed covers exactly what the Speaker means. Leti has such a marker, in the form of an enclitic indicating exactness of ascription. Compare the following examples (van Engelenhoven 2004: 160):

(285)   a.   vuar=lalavn=e
             big=mountain=EXACT
         b.   vuar=lalavn
             big=mountain

In van Engelenhoven's words, (285a) 'designates a referent which is considered definitely to be a big mountain by the speaker', while (285b) 'need not necessarily refer to a big mountain, but may very well designate that in fact the referent is something else but only looks like a big mountain'. Markers such as the one illustrated in (285a) will be triggered by an Exact operator applying to Ascriptive Subacts.

Another operator, one that, as we have seen, applies at the A and C layers as well, is Emphasis. Kham has a special emphatic particle that works at the layer of Subacts. In (286) it is applied to an Ascriptive Subact:

(286)   Ma-che:-də zə   ge-li-ke.
        NEG-fear-NF EMPH 1.PL-COP-PFV
        'We remained (totally) unafraid.'

This marker would be captured by an Emphatic operator, as in (287):

(287)   (emph T_1)

2.8.2.5 Frames

To summarize, then, the Ascriptive Subact displays the following structure:

(288) $(\pi\, T_1\colon H\,(T_1)\colon \Sigma\,(T_1))$

Among the possible occupants of the operator position π are the approximative and the emphatic operators. The head of the Ascriptive Subact is normally empty, but may also be occupied by evasive dummy lexemes. There is a position for lexical modifiers which may be of an attitudinal, an emphatic, or a reportative nature.

2.8.3 Reference

2.8.3.1 Introduction

Whereas Subacts of Ascription involve the evocation of a Property, Speakers perform Subacts of Reference in order to evoke an entity. That entity will be of a particular semantic category, may have a certain cardinality, etc.: these distinctions, to the extent that they are relevant for the language under analysis, are made at the Representational Level. At the Interpersonal Level, the distinctions that are made reflect the status of reference as an interpersonal activity.

   Thus many languages distinguish between 'referent construction' and 'referent identification'. In the former case, the Speaker wishes the Addressee to introduce the referent into his/her mental model; in the latter, the Addressee is asked to identify (in the sense of re-identify) a referent that is already available to him/her (cf. Dik 1997a: 130). We shall refer to this distinction in terms of the opposition between identifiable and non-identifiable. Another relevant distinction is between specific and non-specific reference: here the issue is whether the referent is identifiable for the Speaker or not, respectively. We shall see that this distinction is crucial for the understanding of question-word (Q-word) questions.

   A further distinction that is frequently made in this context is that between generic and non-generic reference (see Dik 1997a: 176–8 for such a position). The FDG stance will be that genericity is not an operator upon a Referential Subact. The reason is that the construction as a whole has a generic value.

Within such a construction, the individual Referential Subacts may involve non-identifiability, as in (289a), in which the Addressee is asked to construe the concept 'dog', or identifiability, as in (289b), in which the Addressee has to retrieve the concept 'dog':

(289)   a.   A dog is man's best friend.
        b.   The dog is man's best friend.

We will therefore, instead, treat genericity as an operator at the Representational Level (see Chapter 3).

Although the part-of-speech 'noun' is closely associated with Reference, not every occurrence of a noun involves a Subact of Reference. A test of referentiality will be whether or not a Speaker can refer back anaphorically to a Referential Subact. Consider the following examples:

(290)   I have lost *my dog*. *He* has a curly tail.

(291)   I want to have *a cat*. *It* doesn't have to be beautiful.

(292)   I didn't buy *an umbrella*. They didn't have *one* in the shop.

(293)   I went to *my work*. *It* was boring, as usual.

(294)   I went *in the bus*. But *it* broke down.

(295)   I went to *work* by *bus*. **It* (the work) was boring. **It* (the bus) broke down.

In (295) the nouns *work* and *bus* do not express Referential Subacts. However, note that the phrases *to work* and *by bus* do express Referential Subacts: both, for example, can be questioned, another test for referentiality:

(296)   How did you go to work? By bus.

(297)   Where did you go? To work.

Taken together, these observations strongly suggest that *in the bus* in (294) involves two Referential Subacts: the Speaker both refers to the Location expressed by the entire phrase *in the bus* ((R$_I$), questionable by *where*) and to the entity *the bus* ((R$_J$), questionable by *what*).

Where a noun is incorporated, and cannot be questioned or referred back to, it will not be associated with a Referential Subact. Thus in (298), there will be no (R$_I$) corresponding to *shoulder*:

(298)   Players are allowed to shoulder-charge their opponent.

But not all incorporation involves loss of referential status. Smit (2005) shows, following Mithun-Williams (1984), that certain instances of noun incorporation involve the expression of a Referential Subact, with the incorporated element either foregrounded (as Focus) or backgrounded (as Topic). Thus he shows that in Mohawk, incorporation serves to foreground an otherwise peripheral Individual, and the examination of a text from Gunwinggu (Smit 2005: 116) shows how incorporation is used in that language for Topics, with clear reference back to an earlier, Focused, non-incorporated Referential Subact. These analyses can be reflected at the Interpersonal Level by assigning the appropriate pragmatic functions to Referential Subacts.

2.8.3.2 Heads

2.8.3.2.1 *Introduction*   The head of a Referential Subact may consist of:

(i) one or more Ascriptive Subacts (and possibly one or more Referential Subacts)
(ii) a proper name or dummy lexeme
(iii) an abstract combination of features for Speaker and Addressee

2.8.3.2.2 *Subacts within Subacts*   The first possibility, with Ascriptive Subacts within the Referential Subact, is found in such Nps as in (299):

(299) a. the house $(+id\ R_I: [(T_I)]\ (R_I))$
       b. the red house $(+id\ R_I: [(T_I)\ (T_J)]\ (R_I))$

Note that the head is not predicated of the Referential Subact, but merely indicates how the Subact is supported by Ascriptive Subacts. The relationship between the Ascriptive Subacts is not specified at this layer; the fact that in English *red* restricts *house* is indicated at the Representational Level. In languages in which the relationship between Subacts of this type is not restrictive, but appositional or juxtapositional, the looser relationship pertaining at the Interpersonal Level is decisive for the ultimate structure. One such language is Yimas (Foley 1991), in which 'a noun and a modifier affixed with an agreement suffix are simply noun phrases in apposition to each other < ... > [t]he linking between them is done at the semantic level' (1991: 190–1). Cf. (300):

(300) imprampat yua-ra   ya-n-ampa-wat.
       basket.CL.PL good-CL.PL CL.PL.OBJ-3.SG-weave-HAB
       'She weaves good baskets, lit. She weaves baskets, good ones.'

In FDG we will interpret *imprampat yua-ra* as two Referential Subacts (each containing an Ascriptive Subact) correlated with a single entity at the Representational Level.

Referential Subacts may contain further Referential Subacts, for example in possessive constructions like the italicized Noun Phrase in (301a):

(301) a. *Joan's father's car* is not working again.
       b. So *she* can't get to school.
       c. So *he* can't get to work.
       d. So *it* will have to be repaired.

The data in (301b–d) show that one can refer back to *Joan*, *father* or *car*. Correspondingly, the appropriate representation at the Interpersonal Level will involve recursion:

(302)   (+id R_I: [(T_I) (+id R_J: [(T_J) (+id R_K: Joan (R_K))] (R_J))] (R_I))

She in (301b) refers back to the referent of (R_K), *he* in (301c) to the referent of (R_J), and *it* in (301d) to the referent of (R_I). Again, the status of *Joan's father* as restrictor of *car* and of *Joan* as argument of the relational predicate *father* will be shown at the Representational Level.

Referential anaphora, which in the preceding text has been used as a criterion for identifying Referential Subacts, works as follows. It involves both a Subact of Reference with its own index (the Speaker is doing something new), but also, at the Representational Level, coindexing (the thing referred to is the same). Example (303) is represented in (304) at the Interpersonal and Representational Levels to show this:

(303)   I have bought a new car. It is an automatic.

(304)

(T_I)	(R_I: [+S] (R_I))	(R_J: [(T_J)		(T_K)	] (R_J))
(e_i: –[(f_i: buy (f_i)) (x_i)$_A$		(x_j: (f_j: car (f_j)) (x_j): (f_k: new (f_k))		(x_j))$_U$]– (e_i))	
(T_L)		(R_K)			
(e_j: –[(x_k: (f_l: automatic (f_l))(x_k)) (x_j)]– (e_j))					

At the Interpersonal Level in (304) *it* has its own index (R_K); at the Representational Level, however, it has the same index (x_j) as *a new car*.

Consider now (305):

(305)   I have bought a new car. The old one kept breaking down.

Here the structure is similar to the one in as in (304), but (R_K) is expanded by an Ascriptive Subact, with its own index, corresponding to *old*. The coindexing holds at the Representational Level, but now between between the f-layer unit *car* and the head position in the noun phrase *the old one*. This is shown in (306):

(306)

$$(T_I) \qquad (R_I: [+S] (R_I)) \quad (R_J: [\ (T_J) \qquad\qquad (T_K) \qquad] (R_J))$$
$$(e_i: -[\ (f_i: buy \ (f_i)) \ (x_i)_A \qquad (x_j: \quad (f_j: car \ (f_j)) \ (x_j): (f_k: new \ (f_k)) \ (x_j))_U]- (e_i))$$
$$(T_L) \qquad\qquad (R_K:[\ (T_M) \quad (T_N) \qquad\quad (R_K))$$
$$(e_j: -[\ (f_l: break\_down \ (f_l)) \qquad (x_k: \quad (f_j) \ (x_k): (f_m: old \ (f_m)) \ (x_k))_U]- (e_j))$$

At the Interpersonal Level *one* has its own index (T_M), at the Representational Level it has the same index (f_j) as *car*.

Consider, finally, (307):

(307)   I talked to the boss yesterday. The bastard won't give me a raise.

Again, the structure will be basically the same as in (304), with coindexing of *the boss* and *the bastard* at the Representational Level. At the Interpersonal Level, the two Referential Subacts are each expanded by an Ascriptive Subact.

2.8.3.2.3 *Proper names*   It was observed in 2.5.2.4 above that proper names can be used in Interpellatives. In such use, they have no referential status, but occupy a Participant slot. Their non-referential status in this use shows up in the fact that they cannot be referred back to. Proper names, however, also occur in Referential Subacts, when the Speaker wishes to make unique reference to an Individual, Location, or Time. Although many proper names are historically derived from semantic material (e.g. *Baker, Dances with Wolves, Le Havre*), they have no semantic content and as such they will be assigned to the Interpersonal rather than the Representational Level. Thus in (308), *John* will be shown at the Interpersonal Level as in (309):

(308)   John was at the party.

(309) $(+id \ R_1: John \ (R_1))$

Note that the name is marked by the operator '+id' as identifiable. As noted in 2.5.2.4, this is reflected in certain languages through the use of a definiteness marker. Much play has been made of the possibility of such forms as (310) (e.g. Dik 1997a: 141), which suggest that proper names can behave grammatically like ordinary nouns:

(310)   There were three Johns at the party.

and after conversion they can in some cases even be used predicatively, as in the following example from Clark and Clark (1979) discussed in García Velasco (fc.):

(311)   My sister Houdini'd her way out of the locked closet.

We shall regard such examples as metonyms. Thus, the underlying cognitive representation of (310) would be 'three persons called John' and of (311) 'act in a way typical of a person called Houdini': in these uses 'John' and 'Houdini' will thus appear, unusually, at the Representational Level (see 3.14 for further discussion).

Returning to the normal use of proper names, the position at the Representational Level corresponding to the proper name will remain lexically empty, but may contain semantic information retrieved from the Contextual Component, for example on gender. This will ensure that an adjective will show appropriate agreement with a male or female name, for example, from French:

(312)   Marie est   belle.
         Marie be.PRS.3.SG beautiful.F
         'Marie is beautiful.'

Note, finally, that in many languages a special 'thingummy' form exists for proper names not known to the speaker, such as English *Whatchacallum*. This is the referential equivalent of the generalized ascriptive lexemes discussed in 2.8.2.2.

2.8.3.2.4 *Abstract features*   Personal pronouns and affixes fall into two classes: (i) those that refer to, or include reference to, the speech-act participants (first and second person); (ii) those that refer, anaphorically, cataphorically, logophorically or deictically, to non-speech-act participants (third person and logophoric).

Those in class (i) are essentially similar to proper names, and may be regarded as grammatical substitutes for naming oneself and naming one's Addressee. However, the pronominal systems of the world's languages permit a range of combinations of Speaker and Addressee that can best be reflected in the interplay of abstract features (cf. Dik 1997a: 152–3, following de Groot and Limburg 1986). Thus at least the following combinations are permitted, where [$\pm$S] means 'involving the Speaker or not' and [$\pm$A] means 'involving the Addressee or not' :

(313)   IL   RL
        First person singular   (+id R_1: [+S, −A] (R_1))   ($1x_1$)
        First person plural exclusive   (+id R_1: [+S, −A] (R_1))   (mx_1)
        Second person singular   (+id R_1: [−S, +A] (R_1))   ($1x_1$)
        Second person plural   (+id R_1: [−S, +A] (R_1))   (mx_1)
        First person plural inclusive   (+id R_1: [+S, +A] (R_1))   (mx_1)

Further refinements are possible at both levels. Thus the degree of politeness accorded to the Addressee may also affect the form of the pronoun/affix; this will be shown by a further operator at the Interpersonal Level. The familiar *tu/vous* distinction in French will be displayed as follows, using an operator [±h(igh)]:

(314)   IL   RL
    tu   (+id −h R$_1$: [−S, +A] (R$_1$))   (1x$_1$)
    vous (+id +h R$_1$: [−S, +A] (R$_1$))   (1x$_1$)
    vous (+id R$_1$: [−S, +A] (R$_1$))   (mx$_1$)

Similarly, at the Representational Level, distinctions may be made to account for the sex of Speaker and/or Addressee and further refinements of number (dual, trial, etc.).

The close relation between personal pronouns and proper names emerges in European Portuguese, where the Addressee's proper name appears in the [−S, +A] position in formal use (Cunha and Cintra 2001: 295):

(315) O Manuel já   leu   este livro?
       DEF Manuel already read.PST.3.SG this book
       'Have you read this book, Manuel?'

Furthermore, across languages coordinations of personal pronouns and proper names are possible, corresponding to a plural at the Representational Level. If the language displays agreement, this will be established at the Morphosyntactic Level with reference to the Person Hierarchy, which places first person higher than second person, and second person higher than third. Compare (316) from European Portuguese (Cunha and Cintra 2001: 287), which also shows a preference for placement of first person first where a negative characteristic is being predicated, and (317) from French:

(316) Eu e   Augusto fomos   os   culpados do   acidente.
       1.SG and Augusto be.PST.1.PL DEF responsible of.the accident
       'Augusto and I were responsible for the accident'

(317) Toi et   Jacques, quand allez-vous   vous mari-er?
       2.SG and Jacques when go.2.PL-2.PL 2.PL marry-INF
       'When are you and Jacques getting married?'

Deictic uses of third person pronouns may be characterized as (+id R$_1$: [−S, −A] (R$_1$)). This notation will not be used, however, for the various 'phoric' uses of pronouns. For anaphoric uses, we shall assume that the Morphosyntactic Level introduces the relevant forms in response to coindexing at the Representational Level. Consider the analysis of anaphoric *he* in (318):

(318)   I met Leila's fiancé (R$_I$, x$_i$) yesterday. He (R$_J$, x$_i$) looks very handsome.

What triggers the pronominal form at the Morphosyntactic Level is the presence of a Referential Subact, the counterpart of which is coindexed at the Representational Level to a previously occurring entity description. In processing terms, the occurrence of *he* here induces the Addressee to look for a plausible referent in the Contextual Component with which coindexing can be established. There may not, as is familiar, always be a textual antecedent for each anaphor. In such cases, the Addressee will derive a likely coreferent for the pronoun from the information present in the Contextual Component. Consider an example such as (319):

(319)   I met our new neighbours yesterday. She is an advertising executive.

Here the Addressee finds a plausible referent by making the assumption that one of the new neighbours is a female (cf. Cornish 2002 for further discussion and exemplification).

Logophoric pronouns (see 4.4.9) differ from anaphoric pronouns in not applying across Discourse Acts. Rather, in the languages in which they occur, they most commonly apply within a single Communicated Content. In Fongbe (Lefebvre and Brousseau 2002: 78–82), the logophoric pronoun *émì* occurs only in what will be analysed at the Representational Level as either an episodical or a propositional argument of one of a closed set of verbs. *Émì* is coreferential with the subject of that verb, which may be second or third person, but not first person. Thus the Fongbe equivalent of (320):

(320)   You remember that you hid Asiba's goat.

has the logophoric pronoun in the position of *you* in the embedded clause:

(321)   Mí   flín   ɖɔ̀   émì hwlá Àsibá sín   gbɔ́.
        2.PL remember COMP LOG hide Asiba GEN goat
        'You remember that you hid Asiba's goat.'

Cataphoric pronouns differ in processing terms from anaphoric and logophoric pronouns in that the coreference works forwards within its domain of operation. The domain of operation of cataphora is generally the Discourse Act, as in (322a), where the cataphoric relationship obtains between the descriptions of two States-of-Affairs within a single Discourse Act. Where the two predications are in an equipollent relationship, cataphora is not permitted in English, cf. (322b); and where the cataphor is in the main predication, it is again disallowed, cf. (322c–d):

(322)   a.   After he$_i$ took a shower, Brian$_i$ went to the movies.
        b.   *He$_i$ took a shower and Brian$_i$ went to the movies.
        c.   Brian$_i$ took a shower and he$_i$ went to the movies.
        d.   *He$_i$ took a shower before Brian$_i$ went to the movies.

Cataphora can be represented in the same way as anaphora, through coindex-ing.

Note finally that not all anaphora involves Referential Subacts. In the Dutch example (323), *het* refers anaphorically to the Ascriptive Subact expressed as *intelligent* (cf. Dik 1997b: 217):

(323)   Jan is   intelligent maar Piet is   het   niet.
         Jan be.PRS.3.SG intelligent but   Piet be.PRS.3.SG 3.SG.N NEG
         'Jan is intelligent, but Piet is not.'

The Discourse Acts in (323) will be analysed as (324), with the predicates corresponding to (T$_I$) and (T$_J$) being coindexed at the Representational Level:

(324)   ([A$_1$:... [(T$_I$) (R$_I$: Jan (R$_I$))]...(A$_1$)] [A$_J$:... [(T$_J$) (R$_J$: Piet (R$_J$))]...
         (A$_2$)]

To summarize, then, the head of the Referential Subact may consist of a complex of further Subacts, either ascriptive or referential. Alternatively, it may contain a proper name or values for the features [±S, ±A]. Finally, it may be empty, as in anaphoric, logophoric, and cataphoric reference.

2.8.3.3 Modifiers

Modification within the Referential Subact is limited to the expression of the subjective attitude of the Speaker towards the entity designated within the Referential Subact. Consider first the use of the adjectives *poor*, *old*, and *little* in such examples as the following (cf. Butler 2008a):

(325)   a.   No one was paying attention to the poor fellow.
         b.   No one was paying attention to poor me.

(326)   a.   I feel sorry for old Bill.
         b.   Don't forget to send a letter to little old me.

These adjectives are not to be understood as restricting the application of their heads, as would be the case if they were analysed at the Representational Level. In (325), poverty is not at issue, nor need Bill in (326a) be aged, nor I be small in (326b). Rather, these are modifiers at the Interpersonal Level, indicating the Speaker's subjective attitude with respect to the referent being evoked. Structural evidence for this is found in the possibility of applying these adjectives to proper names, as in (326a), or to personal pronouns, as in (326b), which as we have seen are introduced at the Interpersonal Level.

2.8.3.4 Operators

The principal operators applying to the R-variable are concerned with the identifiability of the referent, as assessed by the Speaker. As mentioned in 2.8.3.1, we will distinguish between two aspects of identifiability. The first concerns the Speaker's assumptions about the identifiability of the referent for the Addressee: this will be reflected in the operators {+id, −id} for identifiable and non-identifiable respectively. The second concerns the Speaker's indication of the identifiability of the referent for him/herself: this will be reflected in the operators {+s, −s} for specific and non-specific respectively.

The combination of operators {+id, +s} applies in all cases in which the referent is assumed identifiable for both speech-act participants, as in (327):

(327)   a.   *She's* looking well today.
        b.   Did *the teacher* give you homework?

The combination {−id, +s} is appropriate for such cases as (328)–(329):

(328)   *Someone* helped me with the crossword puzzle.

(329)   I have *a certain problem* with this text.

Here the Speaker knows the identity of the referent, but does not assume that the Addressee does. *Certain* in (329) must be seen as a co-expression of the combination of operators.

The operators {−id, −s} combine where the referent is identifiable to neither Speaker nor Addressee, as in (330):

(330)   I am looking for *someone to help me.*

(331)   Do you know *anything about physics?*

Note that *certain* cannot occur in such contexts:

(332)   *I am looking for a certain person to help me.

The fourth combination is also found, i.e. {+id, −s}. This is appropriate in those contexts in which the referent is assumed identifiable for the Addressee but not for the Speaker. This combination is naturally associated with the Interrogative Illocution, and the FDG analysis of Content Interrogatives will assume that the questioned item will be marked as {+id, −s}. (333) will therefore be analysed as (334) at the Interpersonal Level, where the {+id, −s}-marked Referential Subact (R_I) will be realized as the Q-word under the influence of the INTER Illocution:

(333)   Who stole my bike?

(334) $(A_I: [(F_I: INTER (F_I)) (P_I)_S (P_J)_A (C_I: [(T_I) (+id-s R_I) (+id+s R_J)]$
       $(C_I))_\Phi] (A_I))$

With a Declarative Illocution, the {+id, −s} combination corresponds to a number of forms in which the identifiability to the Addressee is visible in their etymology. Consider the following example from Spanish:

(335) Cualquier   día   puede   ocurrir   un   accidente.
       which-*quier* day can.PRS.3.SG happen   INDF accident
       'An accident can happen any day.'

The morpheme -*quier* is historically derived from *quiera*, the second/third person present subjunctive of *querer* 'want': the implication is that the Addressee can identify a day, and on that day an accident will happen. Observe that one could also in English say *An accident can happen any day you like*, in which the context makes it clear that *like*, like *quier(a)*, is undergoing grammaticalization in this use. For further examples of etymologies that imply reference to the Addressee, see Haspelmath (1997: 134).

The attribution of one set of operators to the analysis of what are traditionally known as interrogative and indefinite pronouns fits with the formal properties of languages such as Bininj Gun-Wok (Evans 2003: 273), in which there is 'triple polysemy between interrogative, indefinite pronoun and negative pronoun uses' (lumped together by Evans as 'ignoratives'). In Bininj Gun-Wok, it is the illocution, the intonation, the syntactic positioning of the pronoun and/or the presence of irrealis inflection that indicate the intended interpretation of the ignorative. Thus *njale* is variously glossed as 'what', 'something', or 'nothing'. In FDG, the negative reading will be attributable to a negative operator at the Representational Level, but all three readings will appear as $(+id -s R_1)$ at the Interpersonal Level.

Referential Subacts share with Ascriptive Subacts the availability of an operator for emphasis. The Emphatic operator is assigned to Subacts to which the Speaker wishes to draw especial attention. Consider the following examples from English (inspired by Hannay 1991: 143):

(336) Did you get a day off?
       a. A day off? The boss gave me a whole week.
       b. A day off? A whole week the boss gave me.

The constituent *a whole week* in (336b) is given special emphasis by placing it in clause-initial position. Note that the information status of the constituent is the same in both (336a) and (336b).

The emphatic particle *zə* in Kham, illustrated in (286) where it applies to an Ascriptive Subact, may be combined with a Referential Subact as well, as in the following example (Watters 2002: 185):

(337) ŋa-mi:-ye   zə   ŋa-r̄i:h-ke.
       1.SG-eye-INS EMPH   1.SG-see-PFV
       'I saw it with my own eyes.'

These grammatical expressions of emphasis will be captured by an operator at the R-layer:

(338) (emph R$_1$)

2.8.3.5 Frames

To summarize, then, the Referential Subact has the following structure:

(339) $(\pi R_1: H (R_1): \Sigma (R_1))$

The operator position π is used for operators that have to do with the identifiability of the entity designated by the Referential Subact, and with emphasis. The head of the Referential Subact can be filled by one or more Ascriptive Subacts, proper names, or abstract features representing deictic pronouns. There is a position for lexical modifiers which are attitudinal in nature.

2.9 Building up the Interpersonal Level

In the construction of the underlying structure of the Interpersonal Level, use is made of frames, lexemes, and primary operators. Frames come in three types: Interpersonal frames, Discourse Act frames, and Content frames. The difference between them is that interpersonal frames capture the overall hierarchical organization of the Interpersonal Level, while Discourse Act frames and content frames capture the non-hierarchical internal configurations of Discourse Acts and Communicated Contents respectively. There are a limited number of interpersonal lexemes. These capture the lexical fillers of the illocutionary slot (F), the Participant slots (P), the proper names potentially filling the slots for Referential Subacts (R), the dummy predicates filling the slots for Ascriptive Subacts (T), and the various classes of interpersonal modifiers. We have also introduced two types of abstract lexemes: abstract illocutionary predicates that may fill the (F) slot, and abstract representations of deictic pronouns that may fill the (R) slot. The third type of primitive is the primary operator. The inventories have been discussed above at the relevant places, and some of these will show up in the following example.

In keeping with the general architecture of FDG, the process of building up the structure of the Interpersonal Level proceeds in a top-down fashion, i.e. starts with the larger units and then fills these larger units with smaller ones. We will start at the layer of the Move in what follows, using the Move in (340), discussed briefly in 2.3.3. Note that here the contrast between *won* and *lost* is indicated intonationally. For a more precise representation, see the discussion in 5.4.

(340)   Celtic $\nearrow$ won. However, Rangers $\searrow$ lost.

This is an instance of a Move consisting of two Nuclear Discourse Acts. Since a Move consists of at least one Discourse Act, we may use the general frame in (341), in which N is 0 or higher in value, thus allowing for Moves consisting of 1 to N Discourse Acts:

(341) $(\pi M_I: [(A_1) (A)^N] (M_I): \Sigma (M_I))$

The subscript of the Move changes from a numerical to an alphabetical value to indicate that the variable is now instantiated.

We may now fill the Discourse Act positions which constitute the head of Move (M_I) with the appropriate Discourse Act frames. As we indicated in 2.4.2, these differ from one another in the absence or presence of a Communicated Content, and the absence of presence of an Addressee. For each Discourse Act in (341) the frame in (342) would be selected:

(342) $(\pi A_1: [(F_1) (P_1)_S (P_2)_A (C_1)_\Phi] (A_1): \Sigma (A_I))$

Insertion of this frame into the Discourse Act slots in (341) leads to (343):

(343) $(\pi M_I: [$
$(\pi A_I: [(F_1) (P_1)_S (P_2)_A (C_1)_\Phi] (A_I): \Sigma (A_I))$
$(\pi A_J: [(F_1) (P_1)_S (P_2)_A (C_1)_\Phi] (A_J): \Sigma (A_J))$
$] (M_I): \Sigma (M_I))$

Now that the head slot of the Move has been filled, it is time to specify operators and modifiers of the Move, respectively, but these are absent in the case of (340), so that the result is as in (344):

(344) $(M_I: [$
$(\pi A_I: [(F_1) (P_1)_S (P_2)_A (C_1)_\Phi] (A_I): \Sigma (A_I))$
$(\pi A_J: [(F_1) (P_1)_S (P_2)_A (C_1)_\Phi] (A_J): \Sigma (A_J))$
$] (M_I))$

In the next step, the Speaker fills in the various units of the head position of the Discourse Act frames one by one. We ignore further operator and modifier positions for these units, since they are irrelevant for the example at hand. For the head position of the two C-positions a categorical frame of the type given in (345) is selected:

(345) $[(T_1)_{FOC} (R_1)_{TOP}]$

In interaction with the Contextual Component, the Contrast function has to be added to the Focal Ascriptive Subact. The result after filling in the first Discourse Act position is then as in (346). Note that there are no operators and modifiers at the layer of this Discourse Act:

(346) $(M_I: [$

$(A_I: [$

$(F_I: DECL (F_1))$
$(P_I)_S$
$(P_J)_A$
$(C_I: [(T_1)_{FOC/CONTR} (R_1)_{TOP}] (C_I))_\Phi$
$] (A_I))$
$(\pi A_J: [(F_1) (P_1)_S (P_2)_A (C_1)_\Phi] (A_J): \Sigma (A_J))$
$] (M_I))$

Working further down within the first Discourse Act, we have to specify the Subacts. Since the Referential Subact is realized by means of a proper name, this name has to be inserted at the Interpersonal Level. The lexical realization of the Ascriptive Subact, on the other hand, takes place at the Representational Level. This is shown here by instantiation of the variable:

(347) $(M_I: [$

$(A_I: [$

$(F_I: DECL (F_1))$
$(P_I)_S$
$(P_J)_A$
$(C_I: [(T_I)_{FOC/CONTR} (R_I: Celtic (R_I))_{TOP}] (C_I))_\Phi$
$] (A_I))$
$(\pi A_J: [(F_1) (P_1)_S (P_2)_A (C_1)_\Phi] (A_J): \Sigma (A_J))$
$] (M_I))$

The same steps apply to the instantiation of the second Discourse Act:

(348)   (M$_I$: [

(A$_I$: [

(F$_I$: DECL (F$_I$))
(P$_I$)$_S$
(P$_J$)$_A$
(C$_I$: [(T$_I$)$_{FOC/CONTR}$ (R$_I$: Celtic (R$_I$))$_{TOP}$] (C$_I$))$_\Phi$

] (A$_I$))
(A$_J$: [

(F$_I$: DECL (F$_I$))
(P$_I$)$_S$
(P$_J$)$_A$
(C$_J$: [(T$_J$)$_{FOC/CONTR}$ (R$_J$: Rangers (R$_J$))$_{TOP}$] (C$_J$))$_\Phi$

] (A$_J$): Σ (A$_J$))

] (M$_I$))

After thus filling the head position of the second Discourse Act as well, the Contr(ast) operator that triggers *however* (see 4.3.4), which is relevant at the layer of this second Discourse Act, may be assigned its position, leading to the full interpersonal representation in (349):

(349)   (M$_I$: [

(A$_I$: [

(F$_I$: DECL (F$_I$))
(P$_I$)$_S$
(P$_J$)$_A$
(C$_I$: [(T$_I$)$_{FOC/CONTR}$ (R$_I$: Celtic (R$_I$))$_{TOP}$] (C$_I$))$_\Phi$

] (A$_I$))
(contr A$_J$: [

(F$_I$: DECL (F$_I$))
(P$_I$)$_S$
(P$_J$)$_A$
(C$_J$: [(T$_J$)$_{FOC/CONTR}$ (R$_J$: Rangers (R$_J$))$_{TOP}$] (C$_J$))$_\Phi$

] (A$_J$))

] (M$_I$))

Note that the construction of the Interpersonal Level actually goes hand in hand with the construction of the Representational Level, in the sense that the Representational Level responds to 'calls' from the Interpersonal Level. We will briefly go into the interaction between these levels at the end of Chapter 3, after discussing the details of the Representational Level.

3

The Representational Level

3.1 Introduction: semantics in FDG

The Representational Level deals with the semantic aspects of a linguistic unit. The term 'semantics' is used here in a very restricted way, in two different senses.

(i) The term 'semantics' is limited to the ways in which language relates to the extra-linguistic world it describes. In this sense our use of the term 'semantics' resembles Bühler's (1934) 'Darstellung' or Halliday's (1985) 'ideation'. As a result, many of the linguistic elements that have been dealt with in the previous chapter can be said not to have any semantics attached to them in this restricted use of the term. Consider the following examples:

(1) A: I insist that Sheila is ill.
    B: a. That's not true. (She isn't.)
       b. *That's not true. (You don't.)

The performatively used speech-act verb in (1A) has the function of indicating the illocutionary value of the utterance in a particular communicative setting, and not that of describing what an individual is doing at a particular moment in time. This is evident from the fact that the subsequent rejection affects the clause embedded under the performative formula only, and not the performative formula itself. In non-performative uses the speech-act verb behaves differently:

(2) A: Peter insisted that Sheila is ill.
    B: a. That's not true. (She isn't.)
       b. That's not true. (He didn't.)

The problem that (1) raises for truth-conditional semantics has become known as the performadox (Boër and Lycan 1980; see also Levinson 1983: 257), and applies not only to lexical expressions of Illocution, such as the performative verb in (1), but also to grammatical illocutionary force indicating devices, and to all kinds of modifiers at the Interpersonal Level that were discussed in the previous chapter. Compare (3) with (4):

(3)   A: Frankly/Briefly/Finally, Sheila is ill.
      B: a. No. (She isn't.)
           b. *No. (You are not being frank.)
           c. *No. (That isn't brief.)
           d. *No. (That isn't final.)

(4)   A: Peter told me frankly that Sheila is ill.
      B: a. That's not true. (She isn't.)
           b. That's not true. (He didn't tell you.)
           c. That's not true. (He was not being frank.)

What the interpersonal elements in (3) have in common is that they do not establish a relation with the external world, but function internally to the speech situation. For this same reason they may not be reported (unless in a literal direct speech or free indirect speech report) in the intended readings:

(5)   a.   *Peter told me that frankly Sheila is ill.
      b.   *Peter told me that briefly Sheila is ill.
      c.   *Peter told me that finally Sheila is ill.

The impossibility or possibility respectively of elements occurring in an indirect speech report may therefore be used as a diagnostic for their interpersonal or representational status.

   (ii) The term 'semantics' is restricted to the meanings of lexical units (lexical semantics) and complex units (compositional semantics) in isolation from the ways these are used in communication. The use that is made of linguistic units is dealt with at the Interpersonal Level, in terms of Discourse Acts and Subacts that specify the functions of linguistic units. The relevance of this distinction can be demonstrated by considering the notion of reference. Consider the following sentence:

(6)   I saw a lion.

There are two ways in which the expression *a lion* can be considered a referring expression: (i) the Speaker refers to an animal of the lion-class by using this expression; (ii) the expression refers to an animal of the lion-class. In the first case we are taking an interpersonal, actional view, in the second a representational, semantic one. To distinguish between these two uses of the notion of reference we will continue to use the term reference for the first interpretation and designation for the second one. Once this distinction is made, it is easy to see that an expression that designates a lion is not necessarily used to refer to a lion, as in:

(7)   This animal is a lion.

In (7) the expression denoting a lion is used ascriptively rather than referentially: the designation does not change, but the function does. Using the
variables for Ascriptive and Referential Subacts introduced in the previous
chapter, and aligning these on top of the relevant units, this may be indicated
as follows:

R

(8)   In the zoo I saw a lion.

T

(9)   This animal is   a lion.

In what follows we will indicate the interpersonal status of semantic units in
this way whenever relevant.

The key term that we introduced in the previous chapter to describe the
nature of interpersonal units was evocation, and the one we are introducing
here to describe the nature of representational units is designation. The first
is Speaker-bound and pragmatic, the second not bound to the Speaker and
semantic.

3.2 The organization of the Representational Level

3.2.1 Semantic categories

3.2.1.1 Introduction

Given that units at the Representational Level are characterized by the fact
that they designate, the differences between units at this level may be made
in terms of the ontological category designated. To the extent that ontological
categories are reflected in the grammar we will call them 'semantic categories',
each of which is provided with its own variable, parallel to the pragmatic
categories discussed in Chapter 2.

It is evident that not all meaning oppositions in languages can be seen
as the reflection of semantic categories in this sense of the term. The question is therefore how one determines which semantic categories are relevant
for the description of a language. We want to exclude purely lexical oppositions, the expression of operators, and the expression of functions. To start
with the first, although the existence of lexical classes and subclasses is one way
in which semantic categories manifest themselves, the fact that there are separate words for e.g. 'horse' and 'cow' in a language does not mean that we want
to distinguish between a 'horse' class and a 'cow' class of Individuals in that
language; the fact that a language has a past and a present tense does not mean
that a distinction has to be made between a 'past' class and a 'present' class of
States-of-Affairs; and the fact that a language has a conditional conjunction
is by itself insufficient to decide that that language has a 'Condition' class of

third-order entities. This leaves us with distributional criteria, i.e. with criteria that have to do with semantically based morphosyntactic configurations that are allowed in a language, and it is this type of criterion that we will use in what follows, in line with our form-oriented function-to-form approach (see 1.4.4) to grammar.

3.2.1.2 Four basic semantic categories

There are a number of basic semantic categories which we assume to be relevant for the analysis of any language. For the classification of these basic semantic categories we take as our starting point the threefold classification of entity types presented in Lyons (1977: 442–7). Lyons distinguishes three different orders of entities. An Individual is a first-order entity. It can be located in space and can be evaluated in terms of its existence. A State-of-Affairs is a second-order entity. It can be located in space and time and can be evaluated in terms of its reality. A Propositional Content is a third-order entity. Being a mental construct, it can be located neither in space nor in time. It can be evaluated in terms of its truth. To these three basic semantic categories we may add a fourth, lower-order category Property, which cannot be characterized in terms of the parameters of space and time. Properties (see Hengeveld 1992; Keizer 1992; Dik 1997a) have no independent existence and can only be evaluated in terms of their applicability, either to other types of entity or to the situation they describe in general. Thus, the Property 'green' applies to first-order entities, the Property 'hit' to two first-order entities, the Property 'recent' to second-order entities, and the Property 'undeniable' to third-order entities.

Table 1 lists the basic semantic categories.

Various phenomena in the grammars of individual languages can be understood in terms of the entity types designated. Consider the examples in Table 2 of nominalization strategies in English. These examples show that, although there are exceptions, there is a clear relation between the nature of the nominalization process on the one hand and the semantic category designated on the other.

TABLE 1. Semantic categories

Description	Variable	Example
Individual	x	*chair*
Property	f	*colour*
State-of-affairs	e	*meeting*
Propositional Content	p	*idea*

TABLE 2. Derived nominal expression of basic semantic categories

Entity type	Examples
x	*writ-er, employ-er, sing-er*
	inhabit-ant, contest-ant
f	*mean-ness, kind-ness, false-ness*
	elastic-ity, rapid-ity, san-ity
e	*explora-tion, deci-sion, deple-tion*
	break-age, cover-age
p	*hope-Ø, wish-Ø, belief-Ø*

3.2.1.3 Location and Time

In defining the basic semantic categories presented in the preceding section, the way they manifest themselves in the spatial and temporal dimensions turned out to be especially relevant. The concepts of space and time, however, cannot be reduced to any of the semantic types they define, but rather specify dimensions of those semantic categories, and therefore constitute independent semantic categories. This point has been argued in Mackenzie (1992) for Location and Olbertz (1998) for Time.

The relevance of distinguishing these semantic categories may again be illustrated by looking at nominalizations: languages may possess specialized means to form nominal expressions designating Locations and Times. Examples of locative nominalizations are the following, from Kolyma Yukaghir ((10) Maslova 2003: 131) and Basque ((11) Saltarelli 1988: 257):

(10) orp-uj-$_V$ → orp-uj-be-$_N$
      climb.ITER   climb-ITER-LOCNR
                     'mountain pass'

(11) oilo-$_N$ → oilo-tegi-$_N$
      hen   → hen-LOCNR
                     'hen-house'

Temporal nominalizations are less widespread, but are attested in for example Rukai ((12) Mantauran dialect, Formosan Language Digital Archive) and Supyire ((13) Carlson 1994: 113):

(12) lo kal-akəcəl-aə   alaka-i
      if TMPNR-STAT.NONF.cold-TMPNR because-3.SG.GEN
      o-kaoθ-inamə   koloto.
      DYN.FIN-not.exist-1.PL.EXCL.OBJ blanket
      'In the winter, we did not have any blanket.'

(13)   U   tèè-kwuu-ní   ɲyɛ   à   mɔ   mɛ́.
      his   TEMPNR-die-DEF.CL   NEG   PRF   be.long.time   NEG
      'The time of his death was not long ago.'

There are other phenomena that demonstrate the relevance of distinguishing Location and Time as separate entity types. Consider the following examples, adapted from Mackenzie and Hannay (1982: 48–9):

(14)   The place that I met Sheila was in the park.

(15)   The time that I met Sheila was around three o'clock.

In these constructions the designations of the noun phrases *the place that I met Sheila* and *the time that I met Sheila* are stated to be identical to the designations of the Preposition Phrases *in the park* and *around three o'clock*, respectively, which can only mean that the bare noun phrases have a locational and temporal value similar to that of the Preposition Phrases.

3.2.1.4 Episodes

For many languages the grammar is also sensitive to a semantic category that is actually a combination of lower-layer semantic categories: the Episode. Episodes are thematically coherent combinations of States-of-Affairs that are characterized by unity or continuity of Time (t), Location (l), and Individuals (x). Some of the grammatical phenomena that are sensitive to the category of Episodes are illustrated in the following example, in which the section enclosed in square brackets corresponds to an Episode:

(16)   The two Dyaks, paddling in silence up the dark river, proceeded for nearly three hours before they drew in to the bank and dragged the sampan up into the bushes. Then they set out upon a narrow trail into the jungle. It so *happened* that *after travelling for several miles* [they inadvertently took another path than that followed by the party under Barunda's uncle, so that they passed the latter without being aware of it, going nearly half a mile to the right of where the trailers camped a short distance from the bivouac of Ninaka]. (Internet)

The verb *happen* may be used to introduce a new Episode in a story. Its complement in that case describes the series of States-of-Affairs that constitute the Episode in connected clauses, here the series [*they inadvertently...Ninaka*]. The temporal clause introduced by *after* serves to link this Episode to the previous one, here [*Then they set out upon a narrow trail into the jungle.*].

More details on Episodes will be provided in 3.4.

3.2.1.5 Further semantic categories

Straightforward distributional criteria that were used in the preceding sections to identify semantic categories are the existence of lexical classes and nominalization patterns. Distinct nominalization patterns systematically create designational classes that are treated differentially in the morphological system of the language under consideration. Examples of nominalizations reflecting the semantic categories were given earlier in Table 2. In some languages further types of nominalization are possible. Chichewa (Bresnan 1995) has a distinct strategy for forming manner nominalizations:

(17) yend-ets   →   ka-yend-ets-edwe
      go-CAUS   CL-go-CAUS-MANN.NR
      'drive/flying'   'manner of driving/flying'

The same goes for Supyire (Carlson 1994: 114):

(18) Pyìi-bíí   sàhà   ɲyɛ na   byíí   pi   taɲjáà
      children-DEF not.yet be   PROG raise.IMPF their yesterday
      byí-ŋká-ni   na mɛ́.
      raise-MANN.NR-DEF.CL   on NEG
      'Children are no longer raised the way they were raised in the past.'

It may therefore be argued that there is a semantic category *m* ('manner') in these languages.

   Sundanese exhibits a process of reason nominalization (Robins 1959: 351, cited in Comrie and Thompson 1985: 357):

(19) dataŋ → paŋ-dataŋ
      arrive   REASNR-arrive
               'reason for arrival'

Supyire similarly exhibits reason nominalizations, as in (20) (Carlson 1994: 548):

(20) Sànyi   kà-wyiiní   li
      death.announcement.DEF REASNR-announce.DEF(CL.SG) it(CL.SG)
      ɲyɛ pùcèribílá   à ǹdìré   ye?
      COP female.clan.member.DEF to which.EMPH(CL.SG) Q
      'What is the reason for announcing the decease to the female clan members?'

Thus, we may assume the existence of a semantic category *r* ('Reason') in these languages.

   Another type of distributional argument has been illustrated earlier with reference to Location and Time. English has a special type of pseudo-cleft construction with a limited distribution that is described in Mackenzie and Hannay (1982). Consider the following examples:

(21) The way that I approached the lion was cautiously/with great caution.

(22) The place that I met Sheila was in the park.

(23) The time that I met Sheila was at three o'clock.

(24) The reason that I married her was because she would make me happy.

(25) The rate that I examined the students was at three an hour.

In all these examples the semantic category designated by a noun phrase is presented as identical to the semantic category designated by a prepositional and/or adverb phrase, expressing Manner, Location, Time, Reason, and Quantity. The first four of these have surfaced earlier as relevant semantic categories. This again suggests that these may have a special status in terms of the grammatical organization of languages. We should add a category q (for 'Quantity') to cover (25).

A final example of distributional differences concerns the possibility of pronominal reference through distinct pronominal forms to various semantic classes. It is remarkable that languages, not counting all kinds of first-order question words, often have specialized basic question words for Manner (*how*), Location (*where*), Time (*when*), Quantity (*how_many*), and Reason (*why*) at their disposal, particularly in the absence of special basic question words for e.g. condition ('*whif*'), concession ('*whalthough*'), or addition ('*whapart*'). Instead compound expressions have to be used, such as *under what conditions*, *in spite of what*, and *apart from what*. For a typological study of the distribution of question words across languages see Mackenzie (fc.b).

3.2.1.6 Intermediate summary

Table 3 gives an overview of all the semantic categories distinguished in the preceding sections. We should stress once again that we do not assume all of these categories to be relevant for all languages. They are only relevant if there are grammatical phenomena in the language that are sensitive to the semantic categories involved.

3.2.2 Subclasses of semantic categories

In many cases individual languages exhibit features that indicate that a semantic category is relevant in itself for the grammar of a language, but that there are other grammatical processes that are only relevant to subclasses of that semantic category. A simple example of this is the distinction between set,

TABLE 3. Semantic categories 2

Description	Variable	Example
Property	f	*colour*
Individual	x	*chair*
State-of-affairs	e	*meeting*
Propositional Content	p	*idea*
Location	l	*top*
Time	t	*week*
Episode	ep	*incident*
Manner	m	*way*
Reason	r	*reason*
Quantity	q	*litre*

mass, and collective expressions: these all designate Individuals, but ones that have distinct properties. Where a language systematically distinguishes between count, mass, and collective expressions, we can say that an ontological distinction is reflected in the grammatical system, and we can account for this through the use of subclassifications of entity type variables, indicated by superscripts preceding those variables, as in:

(26) $(^{m}x_1)$ mass   Ø   water   *is*   scarce here.

(27) $(^{s}x_1)$ set   *The* man   *is*   doing his job.

(28) $(^{c}x_1)$ collective *The* police *are* doing their job.

On the basis of article selection and verb agreement three types of first-order entity type descriptions may be distinguished in English.

This kind of distinction is not universal. Thus, Samoan 'does not distinguish morphosyntactically between mass and individual nouns. Samoan nouns translating English mass nouns, e.g. *vai* "water" can form the nucleus of both singular and plural noun phrases' (Mosel and Hovdhaugen 1992: 94), as shown in the following example (Mosel and Hovdhaugen 1992: 269):

(29) ..., aua   ua mafai   ona   maua Ø   suavai magalo mo
      ..., because PRF possible CONJ get   SPEC.PL water fresh   for
      le   taumafa.
      ART food
      '..., because it is possible to get fresh water (lit. "waters") for the food.'

As a result, further subclassification of the variable for first-order entities does not seem to be necessary for Samoan.

Note that the fact that a language distinguishes systematically between expression types based on the distinction between subclasses of entity types does not automatically mean that it also has special classes of lexemes for those expressions. For instance, in many classifier languages such distinctions are relevant at the phrasal layer, but not at the lexical layer. Consider the following Yucatec Maya examples (Lucy 1992: 74, cited in Rijkhoff 2003: 28):

(30)   'un-tz'íit há'as
      one-CLF   banana
      'a one-dimensional banana (i.e. the fruit)'

(31)   'un-kúuch há'as
      one-CLF   banana
      'a load of banana (i.e. the bunch)'

These examples show that the distinction between count and collective first-order expressions is made through grammatical classifiers, not through lexical choices.

As regards zero-order entities, languages may, for instance, make a systematic distinction between contingent and permanent Properties:

(32) $(^c f_1)$ contingent Property

(33) $(^P f_1)$ permanent Property

This is for instance the case in Spanish, a language in which two different copulas are used with adjectival predicates to express this distinction:

(34)   La   chica   es   guapa.
      the girl   COP.PRS.3.SG pretty
      'The girl is pretty.'

(35)   La   chica   está   guapa.
      the girl   COP.PRS.3.SG pretty
      'The girl looks pretty.'

Note that, again, the opposition is not made at the lexical level, since the adjectival predicates in (34) and (35) are identical, but at the phrasal level.

Similarly, languages may systematically distinguish between stative and dynamic States-of-Affairs, and hence make a distinction between subclasses of second-order entities, as in:

(36) $(^d e_1)$ event

(37) $(^s e_1)$ state

A language in which this parameter of dynamicity is clearly reflected in the morphological system is Abkhaz. In this language dynamic and static stems enter into different tense systems. Consider the following examples (Spruit 1986: 95, 98):

(38) Də-z-ba-wá-yt'.
      3.SG.M-1.SG-see-PROG/SIT-DECL
      'I see him.'

(39) Yə-s-taxə̀-w-p'.
      3.SG.IRRAT-1.SG-want-PRS-DECL
      'I want it.'

The suffix -wá 'progressive/situational' in (38) is one of the 'Tense A' suffixes, which only combine with dynamic stems. The suffix -w 'present' in (39) is one of the 'Tense B' suffixes, which only combine with non-dynamic verbs or with a dynamic verb + Tense A suffix (Spruit 1986: 116–17). The suffix -p' 'Declarative' in (39) is furthermore only used with the present tense of non-dynamic verbs.

One could object here that the differences illustrated in (38)–(39) are purely lexical in nature, and therefore do not require the positing of two subclasses of second-order entities. However, in Abkhaz many lexemes occur in both stative and dynamic configurations. In these cases dynamicity or stativity is signalled exclusively by the tense suffixes used, as in (Spruit 1986: 95, 96):

(40) D-t'ʷa-wá-yt'.
      3.SG.M-sit-PROG/SIT-DECL
      'He sits down.'

(41) D-t'ʷá-w-p'.
      3.SG.M-sit-PRS-DECL
      'He is sitting.'

This means that dynamicity and stativity should be seen as properties of the semantic frame for States-of-Affairs, not of lexemes inserted into this frame.

3.2.3 The structure of representational layers

In building up the underlying structure of the Representational Level, use is made of representational frames, which have a layered, hierarchical structure, and are constructed in a stepwise manner, starting with the hierarchically highest layer and ending with the lowest ones. The nature of the highest layer to be selected is determined in part by the requirements of the Interpersonal

Level. Thus, for instance, the selection of an Imperative Illocution at the Interpersonal Level requires the specification of the requested State-of-Affairs at the Representational Level.

In the specification of this underlying structure, use is made of the general structure for layers that was introduced in the preceding chapter, and which we repeat here for convenience, now with the appropriate lower-case symbols:

(42) $(\pi \, v_1: [h \, (v_1)_\phi]: [\sigma \, (v_1)_\phi])$

in which v = variable, h = head, σ = modifier, π = operator, and ϕ = function. Square brackets again enclose semantic categories that are in a non-hierarchical relationship, such as the head and the variable of which it is predicated, and the modifier and the variable of which it is predicated. See Smit and van Staden (2007) for this way of organizing the Representional Level.

At the heart of the basic standard configuration used at the Representational Level is the description of a State-of-Affairs with a complex head:

(43) $(\pi \, e_1: [(f_1: [(f_2) \, (x_1)_\phi \, (l_1)_\phi \, (t_1)_\phi \ldots] \, (f_1)) \, (e_1)_\phi]: [\sigma \, (e_1)_\phi])$

What this formalism shows is that States-of-Affairs (e) are characterized by a complex Property (f_1) (see Hengeveld and van Lier 2008), which we will call a Configurational Property, since it is a combination of semantic units that are not in a hierarchical relationship with respect to each other, including, again, Properties (f_2), Individuals (x), Locations (l), Times (t), etc. The possible combinations of these semantic units of like rank will be specified later in this chapter in terms of predication frames. Properties headed by a lexical head are called Lexical Properties, and their lexical head is indicated by the symbol ◆.

Within a predication frame there is a nucleus and there are dependents. The dependency of the latter is shown by the presence of a (semantic) function. Since the potential combinations of semantic units are language-dependent and may include many different sets of semantic units, we may generalize over the structure in (43) in the following way:

(44) $(\pi \, e_1: [(f_1: [(v_1) \, (v)_\phi{}^n] \, (f_1)) \, (e_1)_\phi]: [\sigma \, (e_1)_\phi])$

where v is a variable ranging over variables.

Using the general structure for layers in (42), including heads, modifiers, operators, and functions, for each of the units in (43), we arrive at (45).

(45) $(\pi\, e_1$:   State-of-Affairs

$\quad\quad\quad [(\pi\, f_1$: [Configurational Property

$\quad\quad\quad\quad\quad (\pi\, f_2$: $\blacklozenge\, (f_2)$: $[\sigma\, (f_2)_\phi])$ Lexical Property

$\quad\quad\quad\quad\quad (\pi\, x_1$:   Individual

$\quad\quad\quad\quad\quad\quad [(\pi\, f_3$: $\blacklozenge\, (f_3)$: $\sigma\, (f_3)_\phi)$ Lexical Property

$\quad\quad\quad\quad\quad (x_1)_\phi]$: $[\sigma\, (x_1)_\phi])_\phi$ Individual

$\quad\quad\quad\quad\quad (\pi\, l_1$:   Location

$\quad\quad\quad\quad\quad\quad [(\pi\, f_4$: $\blacklozenge\, (f_4)$: $\sigma\, (f_4)_\phi)$ Lexical Property

$\quad\quad\quad\quad\quad (l_1)_\phi]$: $[\sigma\, (l_1)_\phi])_\phi$ Location

$\quad\quad\quad\quad\quad (\pi\, t_1$: [Time

$\quad\quad\quad\quad\quad\quad (\pi\, f_5$: $\blacklozenge\, (f_5)$: $\sigma\, (f_5)_\phi)$ Lexical Property

$\quad\quad\quad\quad\quad (t_1)_\phi]$: $[\sigma\, (t_1)_\phi])_\phi$ Time

$\quad\quad\quad]\, (f_1$): $[\sigma\, (f_1)_\phi])$ Configurational Property

$\quad\quad (e_1)_\phi]$: $[\sigma\, (e_1)_\phi])$ State-of-Affairs

It is clear from this representation that (f)-units show up at many places in the semantic structure. Apart from the fact that they may form independent units in the constitution of predication frames (f_2), they are used to specify the Properties of States-of-Affairs (f_1), Individuals (f_3), Locations (f_4), Times (f_5), etc. Consider the representation in (46):

(46) $(e_i$:

$\quad\quad\quad [(f_i$:   [

$\quad\quad\quad\quad\quad (f_j$:   go $(f_j))$

$\quad\quad\quad\quad\quad (x_i$: $[(f_k$: man $(f_k))$ $(x_i)_\phi])_\phi$

$\quad\quad\quad\quad\quad (l_i$: $[(f_l$: countryside $(f_l))$ $(l_i)_\phi])_\phi$

$\quad\quad\quad]\, (f_i))$

$\quad\quad (e_i)_\phi])$

'The man went to the countryside.'

Here the State-of-Affairs (e_i) is characterized by the Configurational Property (f_i), the Individual (x_i) by the Lexical Property (f_k), and the Location (l_i) by the lexical Property (f_l). The Property (f_j) is an independent semantic constituent of the predication frame contained in (f_i), and specifies a relation between (x_i) and (l_i). In a horizontal formalization, which is the one we will use later on in this chapter, this structure would be as in (47):

(47) $(e_i$: $[(f_i$: $[(f_j$: go $(f_j))\, (x_i$: $[(f_k$: man $(f_k))\, (x_i)_\phi])_\phi\, (l_i$: $[(f_l$: countryside $(f_l))$ $(l_i)_\phi])_\phi]\, (f_i))\, (e_i)_\phi])$

'The man went to the countryside.'

Note that positions within the predication frame as well as modifier positions may in principle be filled by any semantic unit, so that there is full recursivity within the semantic structure. Consider for instance the following representation:

(48) (e$_i$:   [(f$_i$:   [
                     (f$_j$:   cause   (f$_j$))
                     (e$_j$:   [(f$_k$: rainfall (f$_k$))   (e$_i$)$_\phi$])$_\phi$
                     (e$_k$:   [(f$_l$: accident (f$_l$))   (e$_k$)$_\phi$])$_\phi$
                 ] (f$_i$))
      (e$_i$)$_\phi$]:   [(t$_i$:
                     [(f$_m$:   yesterday   (f$_m$))
                 (t$_i$)$_\phi$])$_\phi$
      (e$_i$)$_\phi$])
'Yesterday the rainfall caused an accident.'

Here the (f$_j$) specifies a causal relation between the States-of-Affairs (e$_j$) and (e$_k$), which thus occur as semantic constituents within the predication frame specifying the higher State-of-Affairs (e$_i$). The modifier-slot of (e$_i$) is occupied by (t$_i$), providing it with a temporal specification.

The horizontal formulation of (48) would be as in (49):

(49) (e$_i$: [(f$_i$: [(f$_j$: cause (f$_j$)) (e$_j$: [(f$_k$: rainfall (f$_k$)) (e$_i$)$_\phi$])$_\phi$ (e$_k$: [(f$_l$: accident (f$_l$)) (e$_k$)$_\phi$])$_\phi$ (f$_i$))(e$_i$)$_\phi$]: [(t$_i$: [(f$_m$: yesterday (f$_m$)) (t$_i$)$_\phi$])$_\phi$ (e$_i$)$_\phi$])
'Yesterday the rainfall caused an accident.'

For another example of recursivity, consider (50):

(50) (e$_i$:   [(f$_i$:   [
                     (f$_j$:   saw   (f$_j$))
                     (x$_i$:   [(f$_k$: man (f$_k$))   (x$_i$)$_\phi$])
                     (e$_j$:   [(f$_l$:   [
                                  (f$_m$:   depart   (f$_m$))
                                  (x$_j$:   [(f$_n$: woman (f$_n$))   (x$_j$)$_\phi$])$_\phi$
                                  (l$_i$:   [(f$_o$: building (f$_o$))   (l$_i$)$_\phi$])$_\phi$
                              ] (f$_l$))
                     (e$_j$)$_\phi$])$_\phi$
                 ] (f$_i$))
      (e$_i$)$_\phi$])
'The man saw the woman depart from the building.'

In this example the predication frame (f$_i$) of the State-of-Affairs (e$_i$) contains slots for a Property (f$_j$), an Individual (x$_i$) and a second State-of-Affairs (e$_j$). This State-of-Affairs in turn contains a predication frame (f$_l$) which contains slots for a Property (f$_m$), an Individual (x$_j$), and a Location (l$_i$). It will be clear from this example that recursivity at the Representational Level may trigger embedded constructions at the Morphosyntactic Level. The horizontal representation of (50) is given in (51):

(51) $(e_i: [(f_i: [(f_j: saw (f_j)) (x_i: [(f_k: man (f_k)) (x_i)_\Phi])_\Phi (e_j: [(f_l: [(f_m: depart (f_m)) (x_j: [(f_n: woman (f_n)) (x_j)_\Phi])_\Phi (l_i: [(f_o: building (f_o)) (l_i)_\Phi])_\Phi] (f_l)) (e_j)_\Phi])_\Phi] (f_i)) (e_i)_\Phi])$

States-of-affairs (e) enter into higher layers of organization: they may form thematically coherent sets that we have called Episodes (ep) earlier; and these in turn may constitute the extension of Propositional Contents, i.e. Propositional Contents are mental constructs about sets of States-of-Affairs (cf. Lyons 1989: 171). These higher layers are represented as follows:

(52)

$(\pi p_1:$	Propositional Content
$(\pi ep_1:$	Episode
$(\pi e_1:$	State-of-Affairs
$[(\pi f_1:$ [	Configurational Property
$(\pi v_1: \blacklozenge (v_1): [\sigma (v_1)_\Phi])$	any semantic category
...	...
$(\pi v_{1+n}: \blacklozenge (v_{1+n}): [\sigma (v_{1+n})_\Phi])_\Phi$	any semantic category
$] (f_1):$ $[\sigma (f_1)_\Phi])$	Configurational Property
$(e_1)_\Phi]: [\sigma (e_1)_\Phi])$	State-of-Affairs
$(ep_1): [\sigma (ep_1)_\Phi])$	Episode
$(p_1): [\sigma (p_1)_\Phi])$	Propositional Content

This representation shows that Episodes are hierarchically superior to States-of-Affairs, and Propositional Contents hierarchically superior to Episodes. That this is the correct hierarchical arrangement can be demonstrated by means of some examples.

As we argued earlier, the verb *happen* may be used to introduce an Episode. Since Episodes do not contain a Propositional Content layer according to (52), it then follows that the description of an Episode may not contain modifiers specifying a propositional attitude, since these specify the attitude of the Speaker with respect to a Propositional Content and therefore belong to the p-layer (see 5.4.3). Example (53) shows that this prediction is correct:

(53) It so *happened* [that (*probably*) they inadvertently took another path than that followed by the party under Barunda's uncle, so that they passed the latter without being aware of it, going nearly half a mile to the right of where the trailers camped a short distance from the bivouac of Ninaka].

The adverb *probably* cannot be added to the complement in the intended reading, which is the one in which it has scope over the Episode as a whole.

We may contrast this with a situation in which the same set of clauses is embedded as an argument of the verb *believe*. Unlike *happen*, the complement of *believe* denotes a Propositional Content. In this case the addition of *probably* with wide scope is perfectly acceptable:

(54) I *believe* that *probably* they inadvertently took another path than that followed by the party under Barunda's uncle, so that they passed the latter without being aware of it, going nearly half a mile to the right of where the trailers camped a short distance from the bivouac of Ninaka.

In the preceding we have concentrated on layers with complex, configurational heads. Apart from these, we distinguish lexical heads, empty heads, and absent heads. The following examples illustrate the differences between these for the layer of the Individual:

(55) The man cleaned the windows and Ø painted the door.   absent

(56) Mary wants a goodlooking man but I prefer an *honest one*.   empty

(57) The *man* painted the door.   lexical

(58) The *landlord's brother* painted the door.   configurational

In (55) ellipsis is indicative of an anaphoric relation with the preceding description *the man*, as represented by the coindexed variable for Individuals (x_i) in (59). In this case the head is simply absent, the variable by itself accounting for the designation. In (56) *one* has an anaphoric relation with the Property *man* mentioned earlier in the same sentence, represented by the co-indexed variable for Properties (f_i) in (60). In this case there is a head position within the x-layer, but it is filled with a Property variable, not with lexical material. In (57) the head position is occupied by a lexeme, represented as (f_i) in (61). And in (58) the Individual designated by the noun phrase has the Configurational Property *brother of the landlord*, (f_i) in (62).

(59) (x_i) absent

(60) $(x_i: [(f_i) (x_i)_\phi]: [(f_j: \text{honest } (f_j)) (x_i)_\phi])$ empty

(61) $(x_i: [(f_i: \text{man } (f_i)) (x_i)_\phi])$ lexical

(62) $(x_i: [(f_i: [(f_j: \text{brother } (f_j)) (x_j: [(f_k: \text{landlord } (f_k)) (x_j)_\phi])_\phi] (f_i)) (x_i)_\phi])$ configurational

In what follows we discuss the various layers that make up the Representational Level one by one, in each case starting with a general characterization, and then discussing the heads, modifiers, and operators relevant to that layer. We start with the highest units and work down to the lower ones.

3.3 Propositional contents

3.3.1 Introduction

Propositional Contents are mental constructs that do not exist in space or time but rather exist in the minds of those entertaining them. The linguistic relevance of the semantic category of Propositional Contents was illustrated initially in 3.2, where Propositional Contents were argued to behave differently in nominalization. Propositional contents may be factual, as when they are pieces of knowledge or reasonable belief about the actual world, or non-factual, as when they are hopes or wishes with respect to an imaginary world.

Given their nature, Propositional Contents are characterized by the fact that they may be qualified in terms of propositional attitudes (certainty, doubt, disbelief) and/or in terms of their source or origin (shared common knowledge, sensory evidence, inference). Lexical expressions of these modal and evidential categories are discussed in 3.3.3, grammatical expressions in 3.3.4.

Propositional Contents (p) are not identical to Communicated Contents (C), which were discussed in the previous chapter. Communicated Contents constitute the message contents of Discourse Acts, and are not necessarily propositional in nature, as amply illustrated in the previous chapter. Thus, though the Communicated Content of an act may (and actually often does) correspond to a Propositional Content, it is not identical to it. A major difference between Communicated Contents and Propositional Contents is that Communicated Contents are Speaker-bound, whereas Propositional Contents are not, at least not necessarily. This means that Propositional Contents can be attributed without problems to persons other than the Speaker:

(63)   Jenny believed that *her mother would visit her.*

(64)   Jenny's major reason for not coming was that *her mother would visit her.*

(65)   Jenny hoped that *her mother would visit her.*

(66)   Jenny went home because *her mother would visit her.*

(67)   Jenny went home so that *her mother could visit her.*

In all these examples the embedded Propositional Content is attributed to the Individual *Jenny* introduced in the main clause. The propositional nature of the parts in italics in examples (63)–(67) shows up in the fact that they may contain elements expressing a propositional attitude. The following examples, derived from a web search, parallel (63)–(67) and all contain the adverb *maybe* indicating the propositional attitude of an Individual in the main clause:

(68)   He believes that *maybe* the effect of the PeptoBismol® is due to its color.

(69)   The reason [they gave] is that *maybe* the money had come from business which was believed to be linked to the organized crime in Bulgaria.

(70)   Unable to collect from the responsible party, the original card-holder, the credit grantor hopes that *maybe* the authorized user will pay to keep their credit record clean.

(71)   Yeah, glad to be canadian our judges know whats what and they see clearly that the CRIA and RIAA are really just whining millionairs that are upset because *maybe* their CD sales have dropped over the past years.

(72)   I'm so in love with Jesus that I would spend 3 hours today to write this to you so that *maybe* one day you and I could meet in heaven as brother and sister and talk about the days on earth where we followed Jesus in love.

Recall that it is characteristic of Communicated Contents that they can be qualified in terms of their reported nature: a Speaker may relay a Communicated Content obtained from someone else within his own Discourse Act. This is not true of the examples above: the addition of an adverb (e.g. *reportedly*) or the specification of a source (e.g. *according to John*) is impossible or awkward. The general frame for Propositional Contents with a configurational head is as follows:

(73) $(\pi\, p_1\colon [(ep_1)\ldots(ep_{1+n})_{\{\phi\}}]\, (p_1)\colon [\sigma\, (p_1)_\phi])$

This structure should be read as follows: a Propositional Content with a configurational head consists minimally of one nuclear Episode (ep_1), but may contain more than one additional Episode (ep_{1+N}), which may ({}) be provided with a semantic function (ϕ). A Propositional Content may furthermore contain modifiers (σ, see 3.3.3) and operators (π, see 3.3.4).

3.3.2 Heads

Heads of Propositional Contents can be of the four general types, which we will discuss in the order indicated earlier.

(i) Absent head

Consider the following example:

(74)   John thinks Sheila is ill but *that* isn't true.

The verb *think* takes an argument designating a Propositional Content *Sheila is ill*, to which anaphoric reference is made in the second clause in (74).

Anaphoric reference is achieved through simple co-indexation of the propositional variable, leading to the representation of *that* in (75):

(75) (p_i)

(ii) Empty head

For an example of an empty-headed description of a Propositional Content consider (76):

(76)   There's an idea—a stupid *one*—that only rich people have nannies. (Internet)

Here the element *one* refers anaphorically to the head of the preceding noun phrase *idea*, as represented in (77):

(77) $(p_i: [(f_i) (p_i)_\phi]: [(f_j: stupid (f_j)) (p_i)_\phi])$

(iii) Lexical head

For Propositional Contents there are two types of lexical heads, represented in (78) and (79):

(78) $(p_1: \blacklozenge (p_1))$

(79) $(p_1: [(f_1: \blacklozenge (f_1)) (p_1)_\phi])$

The representation in (78) is of a rather exceptional type: it is used for single words that may be used as the full Propositional Content of a message, in particular the words for *yes* and *no*. The representation in (79) is used for the description of Propositional Contents though a single lexeme, often by means of nouns in languages that have them. We will treat these two types in this order. Consider first the following examples:

(80)   A: Was Peter attacked by a dog?
         B: a. Yes.
              b. No.

As suggested in Vet (1986), in answers to yes-no questions, the words *yes* and *no* substitute for full Propositional Contents. In a way they are pro-Propositional Contents. So in (80Ba) *yes* substitutes for *Peter was attacked by a dog*. One might say that Speaker B assigns a positive truth value to the Propositional Content contained in Speaker A's question. The words *yes* and *no* may be represented as in (81) and (82) in their use illustrated in (80):

(81) $(p_i: yes(p_i))$

(82) $(p_i: no(p_i))$

Note that such a Propositional Content counts as a complete filler for a Communicated Content at the Interpersonal Level. They may also be used within questions:

(83)   A: Peter was attacked by a dog.
       B: Yes?

(84)   A: Peter was not attacked by a dog.
       B: No?

It is furthermore important to note that the basic Propositional Contents in (81)–(82) may enter into an equipollent relationship with other ps, as in the following examples:

(85)   A: Was Peter attacked by a dog?
       B: a.   Yes, apparently he was.
            b.   No, probably not.

Several languages have no words for *yes* and *no* in this sense and repeat part of the content of a question in their answers. An example of such a language is Scottish Gaelic:

(86)   A: An tàinig   Seumas?
            Q   come.PST.DEP Seumas
            'Did Seumas come?'

       B: a.   Thàinig.
                 Come.PST.INDEP
                 'He came.'

            b.   Cha   tàinig.
                 DECL.NEG come.PST.DEP
                 'He didn't come.'

Note that the utterances Ba and Bb are only grammatical as answers to questions, so that their formation is dependent on information from the Interpersonal Level.

A strong argument in favour of the fact that *yes* and *no* are propositional in nature, is that in some languages they may occur as the argument of a predicate expressing a propositional attitude, as for instance in Portuguese:

(87)   Ach-o   que   sim/não.
       find-1.SG.PRS.IND COMP yes/no
       'I think so/I don't think so.'
       "I think that yes/no."

The analysis presented in (81)–(82) of *yes* and *no* in reaction to a statement or a question cannot be transferred to their use in reaction to an Imperative. Consider the following examples:

(88) A: Go home!
      B: a. No!
          b. *Yes!
          c. Okay!

The use of *no* in (88Ba) does not assign a negative truth value to the Propositional Content contained in Speaker A's order (in fact, Imperative Discourse Acts do not evocate a Propositional Content but just a State-of-Affairs). Rather, it functions as a rejection of the preceding order. In this use it is not in opposition with *yes* but with *okay*, as (88Bb–c) show.

A similar set of examples, but now illustrating two different positive and negative reactions to yes/no questions and orders is the following, from Wari' (Everett and Kern 1997: 33, 39):

(89) A: Com ta'   tamara' ma?
          sing 1.SG.RLS.FUT song   2.SG.RLS.NONFUT
          'Will you sing a song?'
          "Do you (say), 'I will sing a song'?"

      B: a. 'E'e'.
             yes
             'Yes.'

          b. 'Om.
             NEG.EX
             'No.'

(90) A: Mo   tota-Ø   ra   'e'   Xijam
          run.SG garden-1.SG 2.SG.RLS.FUT EMPH Xijam
          'Go make a garden, Xijam.'

      B: a. Ma.
             okay
             'Okay.'

          b. Noc   'ina-in.
             dislike 1.SG.RLS.NONFUT-3.N
             'I don't want to.'
             "I dislike it."

Whereas in the context of yes/no questions Wari' has the possibility of answering with words equivalent to 'yes' and 'no', in reaction to orders consent is expressed by a different particle, while dissent is expressed 'via semantically appropriate negative constructions' (Everett and Kern 1997: 38).

The difference between the two kinds of 'yes' and 'no' may be represented as in (91)–(92):

(91) $(p_1: \text{-no-} (p_1)), (p_1: \text{-yes-} (p_1))$

(92) $(A_1: \text{-no-} (A_1)), (A_1: \text{-okay-} (A_1))$

The reason that the second use, represented in (92), is to be considered a lexically realized Discourse Act rather than a Move is that the negative or positive response can be further motivated by additional Discourse Acts, as illustrated in (93):

(93)   A: Go home!
       B: Okay, if that's what you want!

The idea of having a positive response as a specific type of Discourse Act can be stretched a bit further if we consider examples like the following:

(94)   A: I'm really pissed off that you lied to me.
       B: Okay, fair enough, but...

(95)   A: So you are not going to pay the bill?
       B: Okay, let me get this straight...

Here the positive response is given in reaction to a Declarative Discourse Act (94) and an Interrogative one (95).

We may now argue, following Sadock and Zwicky (1985: 190), that in those languages in which 'yes' in reply to a negative question actually has to be interpreted as 'no', a famous case being Japanese *hai*, the word for 'yes' is not a propositional 'yes' but actional 'yes'. The following example is from Tuyuca (Barnes 1994: 339):

(96)   A: Atí-ri-gari.
            come-NEG-Q
            'Is he not coming?'

       B: ĩhĩ
            uh-huh
            'Yes (he is not coming).'

A last difference between propositional and actional 'yes' and 'no' is that in languages in which propositional 'yes' and 'no' can occur as the complement of a propositional attitude verb, this does not hold for actional yes and no. Compare (87) with the following Portuguese example, which is ungrammatical in the intended reading:

(97)   *Ach-o   que   tá_bem.
       find-1.SG.PRS.IND COMP okay
       "I think that okay."

A second type of lexical instantiation of a Propositional Content occurs when a description of a Propositional Content is realized by means of lexical heads that may be further modified. Examples are the following:

(98)   That is *a crazy idea.*

(99)   *The hope that he is entertaining* is unjustified.

Phrases like these are not regularly used as the realization of C, but rather as instantiations of T, as in (98), or of R, as in (99). Their basic underlying structure is as follows:

(100) $(\pi \, p_1: [(f_1: \blacklozenge (f_1)) (p_1)_\phi]: [\sigma (p_1)_\phi])$

That is, a lexical element that describes a Property (f_1) occupies the head slot of a unit designating a Propositional Content (p). The modifier slot σ may be filled with units designating various semantic categories such as the Property *crazy* in (98), the State-of-Affairs *he entertains it* in (99), and others. The modifier slot thus makes use of semantic categories other than Propositional Contents, in a recursive application of frames. The internal structure of the lower-layer semantic categories that are used as modifiers in (98)–(99) is described in later sections.

(iv) Configurational head

The configurational head of a Propositional Content designates one or more Episodes (ep). This is illustrated in (101) for two Episodes that are not in a dependency relation:

(101)   [He went to London to visit his brother] and [she will go to Paris to take care of her mother].

The representation of (101) is given in (102):

(102) $(p_i: [(ep_i: -he went to London to visit his brother- (ep_i)) (ep_j: -she will go to Paris to take care of her mother- (ep_j))] (p_i))$

The Episode status of the coordinated parts of the Propositional Content (p_i) in (101) can be deduced from the tense marking. Episodes can be set off from other semantic categories by the fact that they can be specified for their absolute location in time (see 3.4.4). Both units in (101) have their own absolute temporal specification, past in the first unit and future in the second, which means that both units are Episodes. At the same time both Episodes fall within the scope of a single propositional modifier. This is illustrated in (103):

(103)   Probably he went to London to visit his brother and she will go to Paris
         to take care of her mother.

These properties follow from the more detailed representation of (103),
including operators and modifiers, in (104):

(104)   (p_i: [(past ep_i: –he went to London to visit his brother– (ep_i)) (fut
         ep_j: –she will go to Paris to take care of her mother– (ep_j))] (p_i): (f_i:
         probably (f_i)) ($p_i)_\phi$)

There may also be a dependency relation between Episodes within the head
position of a Propositional Content, relation, as in (105):

(105)   He went to London to visit his brother because she will go to Paris to
         take care of her mother.

The two Episodes in (105) may fall under the scope of a single propositional
modifier again:

(106)   Probably he went to London to visit his brother because she will go to
         Paris to take care of her mother.

This leads us to the following representation:

(107)   (p_i: [(ep_i) (ep_j)$_{Reason}$] (p_i))

In sum, we find the following heads for Propositional Contents:

(108)   (p_1)   absent head

(109)   (π p_1: (f_1) ($p_1)_\phi$: σ ($p_1)_\phi$)   empty head

(110)   (π p_1: $\blacklozenge$ ($p_1)_\phi$: σ ($p_1)_\phi$)   lexical head (pro-Propositional Content)

(111)   (π p_1: (f_1: $\blacklozenge$ (f_1)) ($p_1)_\phi$: σ ($p_1)_\phi$)   lexical head

(112)   (π p_1: [(ep_1)...($ep_{1+N})_{\{\phi\}}$] (p_1): σ ($p_1)_\phi$)   configurational head

3.3.3 Modifiers

As has been mentioned and illustrated in passing, modifiers of Propositional
Contents are concerned with the specification of propositional attitudes.
These attitudes may concern the kind and degree of commitment of a rational
being to the Propositional Content, or a specification of the (non-verbal)
source of the Propositional Content. Examples are the following:

(113)   Probably/evidently/hopefully/undoubtedly Sheila is ill.

Modifiers like these may be represented as Property-designating expressions
modifying the Propositional Content, as in:

(114)   (π p_1: [...] (p_1): [(f_1: $\blacklozenge$ (f_1)) ($p_1)_\phi$])

As argued in 2.7.3, within the category of evidential modality there is a major split between those modalities that are strictly reportative in nature, and those that are not. We use the term 'reportative' for the former and 'evidential' for the latter. Reportative modality was classified in 2.7.3 as a category modifying the Communicated Content: a Speaker may relay a Communicated Content obtained from someone else within his own Discourse Act. The following type of example shows that a reportative modality may combine with an evidential one, i.e. a Speaker may relay a Communicated Content that contains a Propositional Content with an evidential qualification:

(115) *Allegedly* the area stimulated for the upper plexus would *presumably* include C7. (Internet)

Thus, the combined underlying structure of (115) is as in (116):

(116) $(C_I: [\dots \dots \dots \dots \dots \dots \dots \dots \dots \dots]$ $(C_i)_\Phi:$ allegedly $(C_i)_\Phi)$
$(p_i: [\dots] (p_i)_\Phi:$ presumably $(p_i)_\Phi)$

The hierarchical ordering (with respect to the predicate) is nicely reflected in this example, and the reverse order is actually excluded:

(117) **Presumably* the area stimulated for the upper plexus would *allegedly* include C7.

Similarly, adverbs expressing the degree of commitment of the Speaker with respect to the Propositional Content fall within the scope of reportative modifiers, as in the following examples:

(118) A lobster dinner at Legal Sea Foods, where, over red Bordeaux, he *reportedly* muses that *maybe* he could eventually have his own CNN show. To which Monica is said to have replied, 'Yeah, you'll have plenty of time when I fire you.' (Internet)

(119) Even some of C.'s friends *reportedly* are suggesting *maybe* he ought to cut back. (Internet)

Similarly, while the adverb *apparently* could mean both 'someone told me' and 'I infer from what I perceive/know', in the following sentence it can only have the former meaning:

(120) If anyone knows or has any contact with C., I would be very grateful if they could get in touch. *Apparently* he is *probably* living in lanarkshire.

Again, the inverse would be impossible:

(121) **He *maybe* muses that *reportedly* he could eventually have his own CNN show.

(122)   *Even some of C.'s friends *maybe* are suggesting *reportedly* he ought to cut back.

(123)   *Probably* he is *apparently* living in Lanarkshire.

We will show the relevance of these facts for grammatical systems of evidentiality in the next section.

The pro-Propositional Contents *yes* and *no* can be (marginally) modified just like full Propositional Contents, as illustrated in (124):

(124)   a.   *Probably* yes.
         b.   *Possibly* no/not.

Propositions headed by a lexical f-category can be modified by all kinds of other semantic categories, as illustrated earlier with the following examples:

(125)   That is *a crazy idea*.

(126)   *The hope that he is entertaining* is unjustified.

3.3.4 Operators

The operator categories relevant at the layer of the Propositional Content can likewise be subdivided into distinctions concerned with the degree and type of commitment with respect to a Propositional Content (subjective epistemic modality) and distinctions concerned with the source of the Propositional Content (evidential modality).

The most important subdistinctions to be made within the category of subjective epistemic modality are doxastic, dubitative, and hypothetical. A doxastic modality permits the Speaker to indicate that s/he believes that the Propositional Content s/he is presenting is true. Since this is the usual assumption underlying assertions, this modality type is rarely expressed by grammatical means. The following example from Hidatsa (Matthews 1965) is therefore rather exceptional, since the sentence final particle *c* 'doxastic' indicates that the Speaker has reasonable grounds to believe that the Propositional Content he is presenting is true:

(127)   Wío   i   hírawe ki   ksa   c.
         woman 3.SG sleep   INGR ITER   DOX
         'The woman fell asleep again and again.'

The much more frequently marked dubitative modality allows the Speaker to indicate that s/he has some doubts about the truth of the Propositional Content s/he is presenting, as in the following Mapuche example (Smeets 1989: 431):

(128)   Amu-y   chi.
        go-DECL.3 DUB
        'Maybe he went away.'

A hypothetical modality presents the Propositional Content as a hypothesis. In the following English examples this modality type is expressed by the particle *if*, which at the same time functions as a conjunction:

(129)   a.   If he comes, (I'll leave)
       b.   If he came, (I would leave)

Note, incidentally, that the distinction between realis and irrealis conditions, as illustrated in (129), is not a subdivision that obtains at the layer of proposition-oriented modality, but at the layer of event-oriented modality. Thus, in (129) the Speaker indicates absence of commitment to the Propositional Content introduced by *if*, and within that Propositional Content s/he characterizes a State-of-Affairs as real (129a) or unreal (129b) within the hypothesized world. We will come back to the Realis/Irrealis opposition in 3.5.4.3 below, when discussing event-oriented modalities.

A wide variety of other subjective modalities may be found. Consider the following examples from Pawnee (Parks 1976: 162):

(130)   Ti-ku-itka-is-ta.
        IND-1.SG.OBJ-sleep-PFV-INT
        'I want to sleep.'
        "It is going to sleep on me."

and Musqueam (Suttles 2004: 382):

(131)   pə́qʷ   cən ceʔ m̓ə.
        go.broke I   FUT CERT
        'I'll certainly go broke.'

In Pawnee (130) a special formation, in which the verb is inflected passively (hence the first singular object marker) is provided with 'perfect intentive aspect' suffixes, expresses volitive proposition-oriented modality. The formation is restricted to the first person. Note that the indicative mood morpheme *ti-* shows that this sentence cannot be interpreted as having Optative Illocution, i.e. it is not a wish, but an assertion concerning the Speaker's wishes. Musqueam (131) has a certainty marker.

In addition to subjective modality, there is a class of evidential operators. Evidentiality is relevant at different levels and layers. At the layer of the Propositional Content evidential modality concerns the specification of how the Speaker has arrived at a certain piece of knowledge as contained in the Propositional Content. S/he may have arrived at this knowledge through inference on the basis of sensory evidence, on the basis of inference derived from existing knowledge, or on the basis of general knowledge accumulated in the community.

A general marker (*č'a*) for inference or conjecture is found in Sliammon (Watanabe 2003: 517):

(132) Č'a=qəy' šə=ɬəx, na-t-əm=k'ʷa.
       INFER=die DET=bad say-TR.CNTRL-PASS=REP
       ' "That no good one must have died", they said.'

Markers of sensory evidence may be subdivided according to the particular sensory mode through which the information was acquired (Palmer 1986: 67; Willett 1988: 57). For instance, Maricopa (Gordon 1986, cited in Willett 1988) distinguishes between visual sensory evidence (133) and non-visual sensory evidence (134):

(133) Lima-ʔyuu.
       dance-VIS.EVID
       'He danced (I saw it).'

(134) Mashvar-ʔa.
       2SG.sing-NONVIS
       'You sang (I heard it).'

The fact that subjective modality and evidential modality occur in the same operator slot is reflected in the fact that often they constitute a single paradigm together, as shown in the following Pawnee examples (Parks 1976, cited in Bybee 1985):

(135) Tir-ra-kuːtik-Ø kuːruks.
       INF-ABS-kill-PFV bear
       'He must have killed a bear.'

(136) Kur-ra-u-Ø   piːta a ku capat.
       DUB-ABS-COP-PFV man or INDF woman
       'It was either a man or a woman.'

As these examples show, the inferential prefix in (135) and the dubitative prefix in (136) occupy the same slot, and are therefore mutually exclusive.

We have treated markers of reportativity, i.e. markers indicating that the Speaker is relaying information from another speaker, as pertaining to the Interpersonal Level, where they are operators on the Communicated Content, as discussed in 2.7.4. This means that two classes of elements that in the literature are treated as belonging to the same general class of evidentiality are actually two different categories. Evidence for this position comes from the fact that in several languages reportative and evidential markers may occur in one and the same sentence. Consider the following example from Sliammon (Watanabe 2003: 528, 517):

(137) Kʷ'a=t'aʔt'ᶿ-m qy'=ta.
       REP=bleed-DET die=VIS.EVID
       'He bled and he died.'

In (137) the reportative maker *k'ʷa* combines with the visual evidence marker *ta*, expressing a situation in which the Communicated Content relayed by the current Speaker contained a Propositional Content for which the original speaker had visual evidence.

A similar combination of markers is found in Eastern Pomo (McLendon 2003: 111–12, cited in Aikhenvald 2004):

(138) Ka·lél=xa=khí   ma·ʔóral   q'á·-ne-·e.
       simply=they.say=3.PL.AG daughter.in.law leave-INFER-REP
       'He must have simply left his daughter-in-law there, they say.'

and in Tsafiki (Barbacoan; Dickinson 2002: 7, cited in Aikhenvald 2004):

(139) Manuel ano   fi-nu-ti-e.
       Manuel food eat-PERC-REP-DECL
       'It is said Manuel must have eaten.'

We thus have clear indications that evidentiality is not a unified category. In fact, we will show in the next section that alongside C-evidentiality (reportativity) and p-evidentiality (evidence for Propositional Content), there is a third type of evidentiality that is relevant at the layer of the State-of-Affairs.

A final evidential category that is relevant at this Layer is genericity. In many languages this category is expressed through special construction types rather than through specific morphological markers. We consider this to be an evidential subcategory, since it characterizes a Propositional Content as being part of the body of common knowledge available within a certain community.

3.3.5 Frames

To summarize, the set of primitives for the Representational Level provides the following frames for the layer of the Propositional Content:

(140) $(p_1: \blacklozenge (p_1))$

(141) $(p_1: [(f_1) (p_1)_\phi])$

(142) $(\pi\, p_1: [(ep_1) \dots (ep_{1+N})_{(\phi)}]: [\sigma\, (p_1)_\phi])$

Heads of Propositional Contents may be special words such as 'yes' and 'no' (140), Lexical Properties (141) or (combinations of) Episodes (142).

The operator position in (142) may be filled by an operator expressing a propositional attitude.

The modifier position in (142) may likewise be filled by the lexical expression of a propositional attitude.

3.4 Episodes

3.4.1 Introduction

By an Episode we mean one or more States-of-Affairs that are thematically coherent, in the sense that they show unity or continuity of Time (t), Location (l), and Individuals (x). The general frame for Episodes with a configurational head is as follows:

(143) $(\pi\ ep_1: [(e_1)\dots(e_{1+N})_{\{\phi\}}]\ (ep_1): [\sigma\ (ep_1)_\phi])$

This structure should be read as follows: an Episode consists minimally of one nuclear State-of-Affairs (e_1), but may contain more than one additional State-of-Affairs (e_{1+N}), which may ({}) be provided with a semantic function (ϕ). An Episode may furthermore contain modifiers (σ, see 3.4.3) and operators (π, see 3.4.4).

In various languages the semantic category of Episodes is very manifestly present in the grammatical system. Consider the following example from Tauya (MacDonald 1990: 218):

(144)   Nono Ø-imai-te-*pa*   mai   mene-a-*te*   pai aʔate-*pa* nono
        child 3.SG-carry-get-SS come.up stay-3.SG-DS pig hit-SS   child
        wi   nen-fe-*pa* yene   wawi wi   nen-fe-*pa* mene-*pa* pai
        show 3.PL-TR-SS sacred flute show 3.PL-TR-SS stay-SS   pig
        aʔate-ti tefe-*pa* ʔeʔeri-*pa* toto-i-ʔa.
        hit-CONJ put-SS   dance-SS cut-3.PL-IND
        'She carried the child and came up and stayed; and they hit [=killed] the pigs and showed them to the children, and they showed them the sacred flutes and stayed, and they hit [=killed] the pigs and put them, and they danced and cut [the pigs].'

All of the verb forms in (144) except for the last one are medial. Via the use of same- or different-subject forms maintenance and change of perspective are established. In this way, long chains of clauses may be formed which together constitute Episodes within a larger narrative. The phenomenon is somewhat similar to the use of non-finite narrative verb forms, as in the following English example, adapted from Givón (1995, see also Wanders in prep.):

(145)   Coming out, stopping to check the mailbox, taking a look at the driveway and pausing to adjust his hat, he walked to his car.

The relevance of Episodes is not only visible in their internal constitution, as in (144)–(145), but also through the ways they are connected to each other. The following example from Tidore (van Staden 2000: 414), which we discussed earlier in 1.2.3, illustrates the phenomenon of tail-head linkage:

(146)   Turus jafa cahi   saloi ena=ge   turus paka
         then   Jafa carry.on.the.back basket 3.NH=there then ascend
         ine.   Ine   una   oka koi   ena=ge.   Oka
         go.upwards go.upwards 3.SG.M pick banana 3.NH=there pick
         koi   ngge   kam-kam tora   oma saloi
         banana 3.NH=there RED-fill   go.downwards LOC basket
         ngge   ma-doya.
         3.NH=there 3.NH.POSS-inside
         'Then Jafa, carrying the basket, went up; he picked the bananas and filled the basket with them.'
         "Then Jafa carried the basket and went upwards. Went upwards he picked the bananas. Picked the bananas and filled (downwards) the inside of the basket."

Tidore manifests the verb-chaining strategies that were illustrated for Tauya in (144). These verb chains can be seen as expressing Episodes, in the sense that they contain semantically coherent sets of States-of-Affairs. Verb chains are linked to each other by repeating the last verb or verb complex of a chain as the first verb or verb complex of the next chain, thus creating coherence between Episodes.

. A quite similar phenomenon may be found in many languages in genres such as cooking recipes, where the various major steps to be taken in preparing a dish may be said to constitute the Episodes of the recipe. The following Spanish recipe shows how every new step is clearly demarcated by the result of the previous one:

(147)   En una olla coloca el agua, el ajo, cebolla, pimentón, ají dulce, la espinaca y los vegetales picados en trozos, cuando comience a hervir, añada las hierbas aromáticas... Una vez blandos los vegetales puedes retirar, si los deseas, los trozos de ajo, pimentón, ají y cebolla, retira las hierbas y comienza a licuar poco a poco las verduras con el caldo. Una vez que tenga consistencia de crema, añade la margarina, la leche, licua bien y lleva nuevamente a la olla.

'Put water, garlic, onion, sweet pepper, chilli pepper, spinach and the vegetables cut into pieces in a pan, when it starts to boil, add the herbs. *Once* the vegetables are cooked you can take out, if you wish, the pieces of garlic, sweet pepper, chilli pepper and onion, take out the herbs and start to blend the vegetables with the broth little by little. *Once* it becomes thick, add the margarine, the milk, blend well, and put it in the pan again.' (Internet)

Finally, the transition from one Episode to the other may be indicated by particles, as in the following example from Koryak (Chukchi-Kamchatkan, Bógoras 1917: 43–5):

(148) Enñaᵋ'an Amamqu'tinu   vañvolai'ke. Amamqu'tinak Kilu'
       thus   Eme'mqut's.people lived   by.Eme'mqut Kilu'
       gama'talen, ui'ña akmi'ñika gi'linat. *Vaᵋ'yuk*   Ama'mqut
       was.married no   childless they.were afterwards Eme'mqut
       notaitiñ   ga'lqalin, va'am-e_he'ti ga'lilin,   *vaᵋ'yuk*
       to.the.country went   river.up.stream he.followed afterwards
       ganyininiña'linau' i'nalka   oya'mtiwilu, ya'nya.eᵋ'en ña'witqatu,
       appeared.to.him numerous people partly   women
       li'gan mimtelhiyalai'ke,   qla'wulu ampalto'lu,
       even resplendent.with.light men   all.in.jackets.of.broadcloth
       ña'wisqatu ammani'ssalu. Ama'mqut avi'ut   gala'lin,
       women   all.in.calico Eme'mqut in.haste came,
       gaqalei'pilin, gañvo'len vinya'tik kaña'tilaᵋk.   Avi'ut
       fell.in.love   began   to.help fishing.with.dragnets in.haste
       Yu'qyaña'ut   gama'talen. Ña'nyeu qa_i'n Yuqyamtilaᵋ'nu.
       Bumblebee.Woman he.married those   indeed Bumblebee.Men
       I'nalka   kmi'ñu gaitoi'vilenau.   *Vaᵋ'yuk*   Kilu'
       numerous children she.brought.forth.them afterwards Kilu'
       ña'nyen gapkawñivo'len yayisqa'nñik. Ga'lqalin va'amik
       that.one could.not   sleep   she.went to.the.river
       e_he'ti,   *vaᵋ'yuk*   galapit_oñvo'len, a'nke gagetañvo'lenau
       upstream afterwards she.looked.around there she.saw
       kaña'tilu.   Ama'mqut a'nke o'maka kaña'tiykin.
       the.fishing.people Eme'mqut there together is.fishing
       Gayoᵋ'olen   Kilu'nak. Amamqu'tinin ña'witqat
       she.visited.them by.Kilu' Eme'mqut's   woman
       ga_añ_isqu'lin, ya'qam ai'kipa   gapi'wyalin.
       she.trampled.her only   with.fly.eggs she.scattered.herself.around.
       Yuqya'nu   ganaᵋ'linau, imiñ kaña'tilu yuqya'nu
       bumblebees they.became also fishermen bumblebees

gana$^{\varepsilon}$'linau. Ama'mqut niyaqñivo'ykin.   Gayai'tilen.   Aččo'č.
became   Eme'mqut what.had.he.to.do he.went.home that's.all

'Eme'mqut lived with his people. He married Kilu', but they were
childless. *One time* Eme'mqut went into the open country. He followed
a river upstream. *Then* he saw numerous people. Some of them were
women. Their bodies were resplendent with the reflection of light. All
the men wore jackets of broadcloth, all the women wore calico over-
coats. Eme'mqut hurried to them. He fell in love, and began to help
those people. They were fishing with dragnets. Very soon he married
a Bumblebee-Woman. Those people were Bumblebee people. His new
wife brought forth numerous children.

   Then Kilu' became restless, and could not sleep. She came to the
river, and followed it up-stream. *Then* she looked around, and saw
those fishermen. Eme'mqut was there with them pulling in the nets.
Kilu' approached them. She trampled to death Eme'mqut's new wife,
who scattered around a large quantity of fly-eggs. All the eggs became
Bumblebees. The fishermen also turned to Bumblebees. Eme'mqut
could do nothing, so he went home. That is all.'

After the introduction of the main Individuals in the first line, the story
consists of two main Episodes. One starts with Eme'mqut's moving up the
river, the second one with Kilu's moving up the river. Within each Episode
there is a change of scene, when first Eme'mqut and then Kilu' arrive at the
village of the Bumblebee people.

   Each of the two main Episodes and each of the two changes of scene are
introduced by the first linguistic element that is of interest here: the word
va$^{\varepsilon}$'yuk. This particle-like element is glossed as 'afterwards', but translated
in various ways as 'one time' or 'then', and so does not necessarily imply
temporal sequencing. This element introduces thematically coherent parts of
the narrative discourse, i.e. Episodes.

3.4.2 Heads

Heads of Episodes can be of the four general types.

(i) Absent head

Episodes can be designated through noun phrases headed by lexical items such
as *end* in (149). In the case of elision of such a noun phrase, the Episode is
designated by just a coreferential variable, in which case the head is absent, as
indicated in (150):

(149)   We went to see a movie last night. The end was rather tragic but ∅ also
         disappointing.

(150) (ep$_i$)

(ii) Empty head

We may use the same context to construe an empty-headed Episode description. (151) is represented in (152):

(151) We went to see a movie last night. The end was a rather tragic *one*.

(152) (ep$_i$: [(f$_i$) (ep$_i$)$_\phi$]: [(f$_j$: tragic (f$_j$)) (ep$_i$)$_\phi$])

(iii) Lexical head

The noun *end* used in the previous examples illustrates a lexical head of Episodes:

(153) We went to see a movie last night. The *end* was rather tragic.

(154) (π ep$_i$: (f$_i$: end (f$_i$)) (ep$_i$)$_\phi$)

(iv) Configurational head

By far the most interesting group of heads for the episodical layer are the configurational ones. The heads of the examples (144) and (145) given earlier consist of States-of-Affairs which are simply juxtaposed, with no specific semantic relation being specified between them. Another example is (155), which may be represented as in (156):

(155) He will go to London and she to Paris.

(156) (ep$_i$: [(e$_i$: –he goes to London– (e$_i$)) (e$_j$: –she goes to Paris– (e$_j$))] (ep$_i$))

The e-status of the component parts of the Episode in (155) can be deduced from a number of facts. States-of-Affairs can be set off from other types of entity by the fact that they can be specified for their relative location in time. Accordingly, each of the units in (155) can be provided with its own relative temporal modifier, as in:

(157) He will go to London before lunch and she to Paris after dinner.

At the same time, the two States-of-Affairs fall within the scope of a single episodical absolute temporal modifier:

(158) Tomorrow he will go to London before lunch and she to Paris after dinner.

In the example in (159), with the boundaries of the individual States-of-Affairs included, one of the States-of-Affairs is explicitly presented as the consequence of another by means of the conjunction *so that*:

(159) It so *happened* that (ep$_i$: [(e$_i$: they inadvertently took another path than that followed by the party under Barunda's uncle (e$_i$)), *so that* (e$_j$: they passed the latter without being aware of it (e$_j$)), (e$_k$: going nearly half a mile to the right of where the trailers camped a short distance from the bivouac of Ninaka (e$_k$))] (ep$_i$)).

In this case there is a dependency relation that may be formalized as follows:

(160)   (ep$_i$: [(e$_i$) (e$_j$)$_{Cons}$ (e$_k$)] (ep$_i$))

In sum, the heads available for Episodes are the following:

(161)   (ep$_1$)   absent head

(162)   (π ep$_1$: [(f$_i$) (ep$_1$)$_\phi$])   empty head

(163)   (π ep$_1$: [(f$_1$: $\blacklozenge$ (f$_1$)) (ep$_1$)$_\phi$])   lexical head

(164)   (π ep$_1$: [(e$_1$)…(e$_{1+N)\{\phi\}}$] (ep$_1$))   configurational head

3.4.3 Modifiers

In an elaborated version of one of our earlier examples of episodical structure there is a temporal modifier introduced by *after*:

(165)   (ep$_i$: [–The two Dyaks, paddling in silence up the dark river, proceeded for nearly three hours before they drew in to the bank and dragged the sampan up into the bushes.–] (ep$_i$))
(ep$_j$: [–Then they set out upon a narrow trail into the jungle.–] (ep$_j$))
After travelling for several miles
(ep$_k$: [–they inadvertently took another path than that followed by the party under Barunda's uncle, so that they passed the latter without being aware of it, going nearly half a mile to the right of where the trailers camped a short distance from the bivouac of Ninaka–] (ep$_k$)).

Although not an example of tail-head linkage in the grammatical sense of that term, the clause introduced by *after* does serve to locate the entire Episode (ep$_k$) temporally with respect to the preceding Episode (ep$_j$). For this reason, it may be represented as a modifier of (ep$_k$), as in the following representation:

(166)   (ep$_k$: [(e$_i$) (e$_j$)$_{Cons}$ (e$_k$)$_{Sim}$] (ep$_k$): [(t$_i$: –after travelling several miles– (t$_i$))$_L$ (ep$_k$)$_\phi$])

The fact that this type of temporal modifier locates the Episode as a whole in time is more transparent in cases in which the chronological order of Episodes is interrupted. Consider the following example:

(167) It so happened that, *before going to Ubuntu Village*, (ep$_i$: [I had attended a small meeting of a free-market group, the Sustainable Development Network, which has the heretical view that blacks ought to be as rich as whites, that capitalism and science will improve the well-being of people, plants and animals, and, most shocking of all, that this is a good thing. There I heard three small farmers, one from the Philippines, one from India and one from KwaZulu Natal (a Zulu called Buthelezi). They all told the same story.] (ep$_i$)) [The story follows] (Internet)

In the Episode preceding (ep$_i$) in (167), the author describes his visit to Ubuntu Village. The temporal clause *before going to Ubuntu Village* situates the entire Episode (ep$_i$) as preceding the previous Episode in time. This may be represented as in (168):

(168) (ep$_i$: [–I had attended...same story–] (ep$_i$): (t$_i$: –before going to Ubuntu Village– (t$_i$))$_{Loc}$ (ep$_i$))

Individual States-of-Affairs may also be located in time with respect to one another. Compare (167) to the following example:

(169) I will have to write this down *before I go to bed*.

Here the temporal clause does not serve the purpose of situating one Episode with respect to another, but delimits the temporal extension of the main clause State-of-Affairs, as indicated in (170):

(170) (e$_i$: (f$_i$: [–I have to write this down–] (f$_i$)) (e$_i$)$_\phi$: [(t$_i$: –before I go to bed– (t$_i$))$_L$ (e$_i$)$_\phi$])

We will return in 3.5 below to the temporal localization of States-of-Affairs.

3.4.4 Operators

Similarly, just as Episodes may be located in time through temporal modifiers, they may be located in time through temporal operators. Consider the following example again:

(171) Coming out, stopping to check the mailbox, taking a look at the driveway and pausing to adjust his hat, he walked to his car.

In this example, only the last verb of the string is finite, encoding the absolute temporal location of the entire series of States-of-Affairs. The other verb forms are non-finite, the verb ending indicating simultaneity. We may interpret this as an indication that absolute temporal location is a property of Episodes, while relative temporal location is a property of States-of-Affairs, as indicated in the following representation:

(172)   (past ep$_i$: [(sim e$_i$), (sim e$_j$), (sim e$_k$), (sim e$_l$), (sim e$_m$)] (ep$_i$))

Note that simultaneity should be interpreted as occurring in the same absolute time zone, and not as 'occurring at the same moment in time'. The States-of-Affairs in (172) are interpreted as subsequent to each other because their order of presentation follows the chronological order of States-of-Affairs, not because the verb form as such expresses subsequence.

In the preceding we have argued that absolute tense is an operator at the layer of the Episode, while relative tense is an operator on States-of-Affairs. In support of this idea there are data from languages which have special narrative constructions, in which absolute tense is marked within one State-of-Affairs, usually the first, and relative tense is marked within all other State-of-Affairs. The following example is from Swahili (Ashton 1944: 133). In this case the relative verb forms indicate chronological subsequence rather than simultaneity:

(173)   Ni-li-kwenda soko-ni,   ni-ka-nunua   ndizi   sita,
        1.SG-PST-go   market-LOC 1.SG-SUBS-buy banana   six,
        ni-ka-la   tatu, ni-ka-mpa   mwenz-angu   tatu.
        1.SG-SUBS-eat three 1.SG-SUBS-give companion-1.SG.POSS three
        'I went to the market, and bought six bananas; I ate three and three I gave to my companion.'

After indicating that the first State-of-Affairs in the series occurred in the past by using the prefix *li-*, the remaining States-of-Affairs within the Episode can be marked as having taken place subsequent to the last-mentioned State-of-Affairs by means of the prefix *ka-*.

Many languages lack an absolute tense system, but for those that have one it seems that the minimal system of absolute tense oppositions is a two-way system comprising a past/non-past opposition. Finnish exhibits such a system (Sulkala and Karjalainen 1992: 299):

(174)   Istu-i-n   keittiö-ssä.
        sit-PST-1.SG kitchen-INESS
        'I sat in the kitchen.'

(175)   Istu-Ø-n   keittiö-ssä.
        sit-NONPST-1.SG kitchen-INESS
        'I am sitting in the kitchen/I'll sit in the kitchen.'

(176)   Osta-Ø-n   huomen-na auto-n
        buy-NONPST-1.SG morrow-ESS car-ACC
        'I'll buy a car tomorrow.'

As example (176) illustrates, in order to make explicit reference to the future, a temporal adverb with future meaning has to be added to a construction containing the non-past tense marker. Note that even in many ternary systems the encoding of future reference is optional.

It has been claimed in the literature that there are also binary tense systems exhibiting a non-future/future opposition, but most of these systems seem to be modal rather than temporal in nature, exhibiting a realis/irrealis opposition. We return to such systems in our discussion of event-oriented modality in 3.5.4.3.

Many languages make more subtle distinctions in either the past, the future, or both, as regards the remoteness in time of the State-of-Affairs described. Thus Garo makes a distinction between a non-imminent future (177) and an imminent future (178) (Burling 2004: 122–3):

(177)   Ang-na i-ko   nang-noa.
        I-DAT   DEM-ACC need-FUT
        'I will need this.'

(178)   Cha-·ja-ni   gimin   okri-najok.
        eat-NEG-GEN because hungry-IMM.FUT
        'Because of not eating, I will soon be hungry.'

Amele distinguishes a past tense for States-of-Affairs that happened earlier on the same day, another for States-of-Affairs that happened the day before, and yet another for States-of-Affairs that happened earlier than yesterday. Dahl (1985) coined the terms 'hodiernal past' and 'hesternal past' for the first two, respectively. These three tenses are illustrated in (179)–(181) below for Amele (Roberts 1987: 227–8):

(179)   Ija hu-g-a.
        I   come-1.SG-HOD.PST
        'I came (today).'

(180)   Ija hu-g-an.
        I   come-1.SG-HEST.PST
        'I came (yesterday).'

(181)   Ija ho-om.
        I   come.1.SG-REM.PST
        'I came.'

3.4.5 Frames

In sum, the set of primitives for the Representational Level provides the following frames for the layer of the Episode:

(182) $(ep_1: [(f_1) (ep_1)_\phi])$

(183) $(\pi\ ep_1: [(e_1) \ldots (e_{1+N})_{(\phi)}]: [\sigma\ (ep_1)_\phi])$

Heads of Episodes may be Lexical Properties (182) or (combinations of) States-of-Affairs (183).

The operator position in (183) may be filled by an operator expressing absolute tense.

The modifier position in (183) may likewise be filled by lexical absolute temporal expressions.

3.5 States-of-Affairs

3.5.1 Introduction

States-of-Affairs are entities that can be located in relative time and can be evaluated in terms of their reality status. States-of-Affairs can thus be said to '(not) occur', '(not) happen', or '(not) be the case' at some point or interval in time. States-of-Affairs are distinguishable by this temporal feature from Individuals on the one hand and Propositional Contents on the other. Compare the following examples:

(184)   *The chair was at six o'clock.

(185)   The meeting was at six o'clock.

(186)   *The idea was at six o'clock.

The general frame for States-of-Affairs with a configurational head is as follows:

(187) $(e_1: [[(f_1: [\ldots] (f_1)) \ldots (f_{1+N}: [\ldots] (f_{1+N}))_{(\phi)^n}] (e_1)_\phi])$

3.5.2 Heads

(i) Absent heads

Units designating a State-of-Affairs may consist of just a variable in cases of anaphoric reference. Some languages have special forms for anaphoric reference to an antecedent that does not designate a concrete object. Thus, Spanish has masculine and feminine personal pronouns which are used for anaphoric reference to a concrete object designated by a masculine or feminine noun. Antecedents of the (f), (e), (ep), and (p) type trigger the use of a special neuter pronoun, insensitive to the masculine/feminine distinction. Consider the following example:

(188)   María vio   salir   a   la   mujer   y   Paco
        Maria see.PST.PFV.IND.3.SG leave ANIM.U DEF woman and Paco
        lo   vio   también.
        3.SG.N see.PST.PFV.IND.3.SG too.
        'Maria saw the woman leave and Paco saw *it* too.'

The anaphoric pronoun *lo* in (188) refers back to the embedded State-of-Affairs of the woman's leaving, which means it has the underlying representation in (189), where co-indexation triggers the anaphoric expression, and the nature of the variable ensures that the appropriate pronoun is selected:

(189) (e_i)

(ii) Empty heads

Empty heads occur in such constructions as the following:

(190)   I went to an interesting lecture but she went to a boring *one*.

In the underlying representation of (190) the presence of a co-indexed Property variable indicates the empty head position, triggering the dummy expression *one* in English.

(191) $(e_i: (f_i) (e_i): (f_j: boring (f_j)) (e_i))$

(iii) Lexical heads

Descriptions of States-of-Affairs may also take lexical heads, as in the following examples:

(192) $(e_i: (f_i: meeting (f_i)) (e_i))$

(193) $(e_i: (f_i: wedding (f_i)) (e_i))$

(194) $(e_i: (f_i: war (f_i)) (e_i))$

In some languages this type of noun phrase triggers certain grammatical processes that are different from the ones triggered by first-order noun phrases. Spanish is again a case in point:

(195)   La   mesa está   en la   sala   15.
        DEF table COP.IND.PRS.3.SG in DEF room 15
        'The table is in room 15.'

(196)   La   reunión es   en la   sala   15.
        DEF meeting COP.IND.PRS.3.SG in DEF room 15
        'The meeting is in room 15.'

Spanish has two copulas, *estar* and *ser*. One of the situations in which the two are used contrastively is illustrated in (195)–(196). In locative constructions with an Individual as its argument the copula *estar* is used (195), while in those in which a State-of-Affairs occurs as the argument the copula *ser* is used (196).

A somewhat different manifestation of this phenomenon is found in Abkhaz (Spruit 1986: 97; p.c.). Consider the following examples:

(197) Də-psə̀-w-pʼ.
       3.SG.SBJ-dead-PRS-DECL
       'He is dead.'

(198) Á-mc-h°a-ra   Ø-gaza-rá-w-pʼ.
       ART-lie-tell-INF 3.SG-stupid-NMLZ-PRS-DECL
       'To tell lies is stupid.'
       "To tell lies is a stupidity."

In (197) the Property 'dead' is predicated of an argument designating an Individual. In (198), by contrast, the argument is a State-of-Affairs. In the latter case the adjective cannot be predicated directly of the argument, but has to be nominalized first, yielding a classifying instead of a Property-assigning construction.

(iv) Configurational heads

As we have shown in preceding sections, in many cases a slot that can be occupied by a lexical head can also be occupied by a configurational head. This is particularly relevant in the case of States-of-Affairs. Configurational heads of States-of-Affairs will be called predication frames in what follows, and their internal structure will be the topic of 3.6.2. They are character-ized as units of the f-type in view of the existence of pairs such as the following:

(199) The man saw *the game*.

(200) The man saw *his team beat the opposition*.

The verb *see*, when used to describe direct perception, takes a State-of-Affairs (e) as its second argument. This argument can be expressed lexically, as in (199), or configurationally, as in (200). The parallelism between these two situations is shown in the following representations of this argument:

(201) $(e_i: (f_i:$ game $(f_i)) (e_i)_\emptyset)$

(202) $(e_i: (f_i: [(f_j: beat (f_j)) (x_i: -team- (x_i))_A (x_j: -opposition- (x_j))_U] (f_i))$
        $(e_i)_\emptyset)$

In both cases the variable for States-of-Affairs is restricted by the Property (f_i), which in (201) is realized by means of a lexeme and in (202) by means of a predication frame, consisting itself of a unit denoting the (lexical) Property (f_j) and two units denoting the Individuals (x_i) and (x_j).

   A configurational head of a State-of-Affairs takes the following general format:

(203) $(e_1: [[(f_1: [\ldots] (f_1)) \ldots (f_{1+N}: [\ldots] (f_{1+N}))_{\{\phi\}}{}^n] (e_1)_\phi])$

In cases like (202) only the (f_1) position is filled. If more than one slot is filled the relation between the units may be one of equipollence or dependency. A typical example of an equipollence relation between the Configurational Properties in the head position is that of core serialization. Consider the following example from Neger-Hollands (Jansen *et al.* 1978):

(204)   Fan   som   fligi   gi   mi.
        catch   some   flies   give   me.
        'Catch some flies for me!'
        "Catch some flies give me."

In the absence of ditransitive predication frames, Neger-Hollands uses secondary verbs in serial verb constructions to introduce additional Individuals. Since the two verbs in the construction do not share the full set of arguments, this is a case of 'core serialization' in Foley and Olson's (1985) terms, i.e. the two predicates relate to two different subsets of the arguments within the clause. This may be represented as in (205), where coindexation shows the coreference relations. Note that for both verbs the Actor argument is understood to be the Addressee.

(205) $(e_i: [[$
            $(f_i: [(f_j: fan (f_j)) (x_i) (x_j: fligi (x_j))] (f_i))$
            $(f_k: [(f_l: gi (f_l)) (x_i) (x_k)] (f_k))]$
        $(e_i)_\phi])$

The construction as a whole describes a single State-of-Affairs (e_i), which is evident from the fact that the complex State-of-Affairs necessarily has a single temporal interpretation. This restriction can be illustrated by means of the following examples from Numbami (Bradshaw 1993):

(206)   a.   E   i-ma   teteu   i-ndomoni   aiya.
        3.SG RLS.3.SG-come village RLS.3.SG-seek 2.SG
        'He came to the village to look for you.'
        "He came to the village looked for you."

        b.   *E   i-ma   teteu   ni-ndomoni   aiya.
        3.SG RLS.3.SG-come village IRR.3.SG-seek 2.SG
        'He came to the village will look for you.'

In these examples, the realis is used for the non-future and the irrealis for the future. Verbs are marked either both for realis, as in (206a), or both for irrealis, as in (206b), but a core serialization never contains a combination of the two. Within our approach this can be explained as a result of the fact that temporal specification is an operator on a State-of-Affairs, not on the Properties characterizing that State-of-Affairs. Thus, it is the full set of Configurational Properties characterizing a State-of-Affairs that falls under the scope of a single operator.

An example of a dependency relation between the configurational f-units making up the head of a State-of-Affairs is given in (207):

(207)   Sliding down a rope, he left the tree house.

In constructions expressing the means by which a State-of-Affairs is carried out, such as *sliding down a rope* in (207), there is a necessary overlap in arguments of the two predicates, and the means-expression cannot be specified independently for its temporal orientation. The following examples are ungrammatical ((208b) only under the intended reading):

(208)   a.   *She sliding down a rope, he left the tree house.
        b.   *Having slid down a rope, he left the tree house.

An example such as (207) may be represented as in (209):

(209) $(e_i: [[\quad (f_i: [(f_j: leave (f_j)) (x_i) (x_j: house (x_j))] (f_i))$
        $(f_k: [(f_l: slide (f_l)) (x_i) (x_k: rope (x_k))] (f_k))_{Means}]$
        $(e_i)_\phi])$

Summarizing, we found the following heads for States-of-Affairs:

(210) (e_1) absent head

(211) $(\pi e_1: [(f_1) (e_1)_\phi]: [\sigma (e_1)_\phi])$ empty head

(212) $(\pi e_1: [(f_1: \blacklozenge (f_1)) (e_1)_\phi]: [\sigma (e_1)_\phi])$ lexical head

(213) $(e_1: [[(f_1: [\ldots] (f_1)) \ldots (f_{1+N}: [\ldots] (f_{1+N}))_{\{\phi\}^n}] (e_1)_\phi]: [\sigma (e_1)_\phi])$

                                                          configurational head

3.5.3 Modifiers

States-of-affairs may be further qualified as regards the properties of their occurrence. The major modifications concern: relative time of occurrence, place of occurrence, frequency of occurrence, reality status, physical setting, cognitive setting. The following examples illustrate:

(214) Sheila works *in London.*   (Location)

(215) Sheila went out *before dinner.*   (Relative Time)

(216) Sheila goes to London *frequently.*   (Frequency)

(217) Sheila is *actually* a guy.   (Reality)

(218) Sheila fell ill *because of the heavy rainfall.*   (Cause)

(219) Sheila stayed home *so that she could watch television.*   (Purpose)

All these modifiers have in common that they occupy the modifier slot (σ) in the following configuration:

(220) $(\pi\, e_1: [(f_1: [\ldots] (f_1)) (e_1)_\Phi]: [\sigma\, (e_1)_\Phi])$

But there are differences as to the semantic category of the modifiers: Location (l) in (214), Time (t) in (215), Property (f) in (216)–(217), State-of-Affairs (e) in (218), and Propositional Content (p) in (219).

That these modifiers act at the layer of the State-of-Affairs description and not at the layer of the Episode can be demonstrated by the fact that they occur within the scope of episodical absolute temporal expressions like *last year, last week, yesterday,* etc.:

(221) Last year Sheila worked in London.

(222) Yesterday Sheila went out before dinner.

(223) Last year Sheila went to London frequently.

(224) In the past Sheila was actually a guy.

(225) Last week Sheila fell ill because of the heavy rainfall.

(226) Yesterday Sheila stayed home so that she could watch television.

As mentioned in 3.4.4, temporal modification of States-of-Affairs is different from temporal modification of Episodes, in the sense that absolute location in time is a property of Episodes, while relative location in time is a property of States-of-Affairs. This explains why the two can be combined, as in (222).

Certain types of Manner expressions, depictives, and secondary predications also belong to the class of modifiers of States-of-Affairs. These will, however, be discussed in 3.6.3, where they will be presented in contrast with similar modifiers at the Property layer.

State of affairs descriptions with a lexical or an empty head may be modified by all kinds of modifiers typical of referential phrases, as in:

(227)   the meeting that I attended

(228)   the interesting meeting

(229)   yesterday's meeting

3.5.4 Operators

Most modifier categories at the layer of the State-of-Affairs description have a grammatical counterpart in the form of an operator category. The following classes of operators may be distinguished: Event Location, Relative Tense, Event-oriented Modality, Event Perception, Polarity, and Event Quantification. We will illustrate these one by one.

3.5.4.1 Event Location

Location is less commonly expressed by means of operators, and has therefore for a long time not been recognized in the FG-literature as an operator category. In recent work, however, de Groot (2000) has noticed the existence of an operator category Absentive in several European languages. These languages have a special periphrastic construction type indicating that the subject is away from a reference point that either coincides with the location of the Speaker or with a previously established reference point. Consider the following opposition in Dutch:

(230)   Jan is   viss-en.
        Jan COP.PRS.3.SG fish-INF
        'Jan is away fishing.'

(231)   Jan is   aan het viss-en.
        Jan COP.PRS.3.SG at   DEF fish-INF
        'Jan is fishing.'

Sentence (230) can only be used when the subject is out of sight, while the progressive periphrasis in (231) can be used whether the subject is within or out of sight.

The phenomenon is certainly not restricted to European languages. Consider the following examples from Tübatulabal (Voegelin 1935: 119–20):

(232)   A'a'c-īmı'n.
        bath.PFV-PROX
        'He bathed here.'

(233) A'a'c-ĭkı'n.
       bath.PFV-REM
       'He bathed there.'

In Tübatulabal it is possible to indicate through special verb inflections whether a State-of-Affairs took/takes place at the place where the current Speaker is (232) or at any other place away from the current Speaker's current location (233).

Categories like these are captured by e-operators, since they specify the location where the State-of-Affairs as a whole takes place. In this respect they differ from directional operators, which modify the internal structure of the State-of-Affairs and are therefore treated as f-operators, to be discussed in 3.7.4.

3.5.4.2 Relative Tense

As we indicated earlier, absolute time reference is a property of Episodes, while relative tense is characteristic of States-of-Affairs (for a related view, see Harder 1996). Some languages have a system of relative tense only, and have to specify the absolute location in time through lexical means when needed. An example of a language with a relative tense system is Hausa, which has markers of anteriority, simultaneity, and posteriority. Consider the following examples taken from the Hausa online grammar:

(234) Jiya   da 3:00 sun   shiga.
       yesterday at 3:00 3.PL.ANT   enter
       'Yesterday at three they had entered.'

(235) Gobe   da 3:00 sun   shiga.
       tomorrow   at 3:00 3.PL.ANT   enter
       'Tomorrow at three they will have entered.'

In (234) and (235) the same temporal specification of anteriority is used. It is the lexical specification of the absolute temporal location of the Episode with respect to which the anteriority is interpreted.

Other languages do have an absolute tense system, but use relative tense markers in subordinate clauses. Such a language is Imbabura Quechua. Consider the following examples (Cole 1982: 143, see also Comrie 1985: 61):

(236) Marya Agatu-pi   kawsa-j-ta   kri-rka-ni.
       María Agato-LOC   live-SIM-ACC   believe-PST-1
       'I believed that María lived in Agato.'

(237) Marya Agatu-pi   kawsa-shka-ta   kri-rka-ni.
       María Agato-LOC   live-ANT-ACC   believe-PST-1
       'I believed that María had lived in Agato.'

(238) Marya Agatu-pi   kawsa-na-ta   kri-rka-ni.
       María Agato-LOC live-POST-ACC believe-PST-1
       'I believed that María would/will live in Agato.'

The suffix -*j* in (236) indicates that the State-of-Affairs described in the subordinate clause is simultaneous with the one in the main clause, the suffix -*shka* in (237) with the one that it is anterior to it, and the suffix -*na* in (238) with the one that it is posterior to it.

3.5.4.3 Event-oriented modality

Event-oriented modalities describe the existence of possibilities, general obligations, and the like, without the Speaker taking responsibility for these judgements. This is best illustrated by means of the following sentence, which contains both a proposition-oriented and an event-oriented modal expression (Lyons 1977: 808):

(239) Certainly he may have forgotten.

Through the epistemic proposition-oriented modal adverb *certainly* the speaker commits him/herself to the truth of the Propositional Content *he may have forgotten*, which itself contains the epistemic event-oriented modal verb *may* that describes the existence of the possibility of the occurrence of the State-of-Affairs *he has forgotten*. Although the two epistemic judgements contained in (239) are non-harmonic (Lyons 1977; Coates 1983; Bybee *et al.* 1994), no contradiction arises, since the two judgements pertain to different layers: the Speaker expresses his/her certainty about the existence of an objective, logical possibility. For this reason epistemic proposition-oriented modality has been called 'subjective' and event-oriented modality 'objective' (Lyons 1977: 797–804; cf. also Halliday 1970; Coates 1983).

For a further illustration of this distinction, consider the following example from Ngiyambaa (Donaldson 1980: 256):

(240) Gali:-ŋinda-gila ŋiyanu   baluy-aga.
       water-PRIV-DUB 1.PL.NOM die-IRR
       'We'll probably die for lack of water.'

Ngiyambaa has both an irrealis marker and a special marker for dubitative modality. Both may occur in a single sentence, as illustrated in (240), which may be paraphrased as 'I guess (DUB) the unrealized (IRR) State-of-Affairs of our dying for lack of water will take place'. Thus, the dubitative gives the Speaker's subjective assessment of a Propositional Content containing an objective specification of the unrealized status of a State-of-Affairs. Event-oriented modalities are not only epistemic in nature, but may be facultative, deontic, or volitive as well.

Epistemic event-oriented modality characterizes States-of-Affairs in terms of the (im)possibility of their occurrence in view of what is known about the world. Although many different shades of meaning could be defined within this domain, grammatical encoding of this type of modality is generally restricted to a realis versus irrealis opposition. An example of this type of opposition may be found in Mapuche (Smeets 1989: 307):

(241) Trür   amu-a-y-u   üyüw.
       together   go-IRR-DECL-1.DU.SBJ   over.there
       'Together we will go over there.'

(242) Trür   amu-∅-y-u   üyüw.
       together   go-RLS-DECL-1.DU.SBJ   over.there
       'Together we went over there.'

In spite of the translation the Mapuche irrealis cannot be interpreted as a future tense morpheme, since it has a whole range of additional shades of modal meaning, including probability.

The opposition between realis and irrealis is sometimes further obscured by the fact that the realis domain is occupied by certain tenses, as a result of which the modal category irrealis stands in opposition to the temporal categories past and present. This is, for instance, the case in Ngiyambaa, where there is 'a three-way tense system, involving two contrasts, one of actuality (actualis versus irrealis) and, within the actualis category, one of time (past versus present)' (Donaldson 1980: 160). Again, the category of irrealis cannot be interpreted as a simple future tense, since it is also used for stating probabilities, as in:

(243) Yuruŋ-gu ŋidjal-aga.
       rain-ERG rain-IRR
       'It may rain.' or 'It will rain.'

In order to avoid such ambiguities some languages make a distinction between a 'certain future' and an 'uncertain future', where the latter might perhaps better be interpreted as an irrealis form, as in the following examples from Garo (Burling 1961: 27f.):

(244) Aŋa re'-aŋ-gen.
       1.SG move-DIR-FUT
       'I will go.'

(245) Re'-ba-nabadoŋa.
       move-DIR-IRR
       'He may come.'

Facultative event-oriented modality characterizes States-of-Affairs in terms of the physical or circumstantial enabling conditions on their occurrence (Bybee *et al.* 1994; Olbertz 1998). This type of modality is often referred to as root modality (Coates 1983). An example is (246):

(246)   It can take three hours to get there.

In contrast to facultative participant-oriented modality, to be discussed below, the possibility of the occurrence of the State-of-Affairs does not depend on the intrinsic capacities of a participant, but follows from the circumstances in which the State-of-Affairs takes place. This sense can most easily be detected in impersonal constructions such as (246).

Deontic event-oriented modality characterizes States-of-Affairs in terms of what is obligatory or permitted within some system of moral or legal conventions (cf. Allwood *et al.* 1977: 111). In contrast to deontic participant-oriented modality, the obligations expressed by means of deontic event-oriented modality do not rest upon a particular participant, but represent general rules of conduct. This sense of general applicability can most clearly be identified in impersonal expressions such as the Turkish modal periphrases (van Schaaik 1985) illustrated in (247) and (248):

(247)   Bura-da   ayakkabı-lar-ı   çıkar-mak   var.
        DEM-LOC shoes-PL-POSS take.off-INF EX
        'One has to take off one's shoes here.' (lit. 'There is taking off of shoes here.')

(248)   Avuç aç-mak   yok.
        hand open-INF EX.NEG
        'Begging prohibited.' (lit. 'There isn't begging.')

Volitive event-oriented modality characterizes States-of-Affairs in terms of what is generally desirable or undesirable. This category seems hardly ever to be encoded by specialized markers, but rather to group with deontic modality. An exception to this, however, is the Tauya avolitional, which '[...] implies that the action or state specified by the verb would be undesirable' (MacDonald 1990: 202f.):

(249)   Tepau-fe-ʔate-e-ʔa.
        break-TR-AVOL-1-DECL
        'It would be bad if I broke it.'

3.5.4.4 Event perception

In 3.3.4 we discussed inferential evidentials, among which there is a class of elements indicating that a conclusion has been arrived at on the basis of sensory evidence. Closely related to this latter class is Event Perception, a category that signals whether or not a State-of-Affairs was witnessed by the Speaker. To illustrate the difference between the two, consider the following examples:

(250)   Sheila saw Peter leave.

(251)   Sheila saw that Peter had left.

The difference between these two sentences is that in (251) the complement clause describes the conclusion that Sheila arrived at on the basis of perceptual evidence (for example, the absence of Peter's car), while in (250) the complement clause describes the State-of-Affairs that was directly perceived by Sheila. Dik and Hengeveld (1991) formalize the difference between these two constructions by analysing the complement in (251) as belonging to the p-category, and the one in (250) as belonging to the e-category. A range of differences between the two constructions can be accounted for in this way.

The same distinction obtains with respect to the grammatical expression of perceptual evidentiality: parallel to (251) there is a category that obtains at the layer of the Propositional Content and signals inference on the basis of perceptual evidence; and parallel to (250) there is a category that obtains at the layer of the State-of-Affairs and signals direct perception or its absence. Tariana has evidential markers for both direct perception and inference on the basis of perceptual evidence. Compare the following examples (Aikhenvald 2003: 294, 300):

(252)   Waha ikasu-nuku   hi̵-nuku   alia-naka.
         we   now-TOP.NON.A/S DEM.ANIM-TOP.NON.A/S EX-VIS.PRS
         'Here we are right now (talking).'

(253)   Pi-tedua-ɾu-nuku   pathesedape   mawári
         2.SG-cousin-F-TOP.NON.A/S   day.before.yesterday snake
         di-hña-nikha-niki.
         3.SG.NON.F-eat-INFER.RECPST-COMPL
         'The snake ate up your cousin the day before yesterday.'

Tariana has portmanteau morphemes simultaneously expressing tense and evidentiality. The visual evidential in (252) is used when the Speaker sees or is looking at the State-of-Affairs described. The inferential evidential in (253) is used when the Speaker observed the evidence, not the State-of-Affairs itself, and on the basis of that evidence arrives at a conclusion. Thus, the person uttering (253), the mother of the person addressed, has seen the remains of her niece, but did not witness the actual killing.

A similar distinction obtains in Turkish (Lewis 1967: 122). This language uses a special realis suffix indicating that the Speaker personally witnessed the

State-of-Affairs described, as in (254). In all other cases another realis suffix is used (255).

(254) Kar   yağ-dı-Ø.
       snow   rain-RLS.PERC-3
       'Snow has fallen.'

(255) Kar   yağ-mış-Ø.
       snow   rain-RLS.NONPERC-3
       'Snow has fallen.'

3.5.4.5 Polarity

Another category that is relevant at the e-layer is polarity. We exclude Prohibitives, which pertain to the Interpersonal Level, and concentrate on the simple negation of the occurrence of a State-of-Affairs. In polarity systems, the negative value is generally marked, and the positive value is not. The same is true of Tidore, which uses a sentence-final particle to express negation, and no marking for positive polarity (van Staden 2000: 232):

(256) Una=ge   kolano ua.
       3.SG.M=there king   NEG
       'He is not a king.'

Apart from a basic positive-negative polarity opposition, there are a number of more specific values that can be assigned to this category. Although generally not considered as such, several phasal aspectual particles can be seen as expressing certain types of polarity, as suggested in van Baar (1997: 50–1), who presents the following classification of polar elements:

(257) a. pos   Ø   neg   not
       b. ^{neg}pos   already   neg^{pos} not yet
       c. pos^{neg} still ^{pos}neg   no longer

Except for the first and the last item in this series, the values represented are binary and have to be read in the following way: the basic value is presented in normal typeface, and the contrasting preceding or following situation is presented in superscript. Thus, the value of *not yet* can be interpreted as 'negative anticipating a positive State-of-Affairs' and *already* as 'positive following a negative State-of-Affairs', etc.

A language presenting various types of evidence for this analysis is Tidore. The first piece of evidence concerns question formation. In forming alternative questions, the three pairs of positive/negative elements presented in (257) behave in a parallel fashion (van Staden 2000: 150):

(258) Ngon wako bolo ua?
       2.SG return or   not
       'Are you coming home?'

(259) Oyo rai   bolo yang?
       eat already or   not.yet
       'Have you eaten yet?'

(260) Coma moju bolo rewa?
       add still or   no.longer
       'Will you have some more?'

Furthermore, all three negative elements in (258)–(260) participate in a Focus construction with double negation, while the three positive elements do not (van Staden 2000: 236, 237):

(261) Una   kama wo-tagi   se   mina ua.
       3.SG.M NEG 3.SG.M.A-go OBL 3.SG.F NEG
       'He does not go with her.'

(262) Kama mansia dofu yang.
       NEG people many not.yet
       'There are not yet many people.'

(263) Ona   kama bicara se   nyanyi se   megarona nde
       3.PL NEG talk   and sing   and whatever 3.NH.there
       rewa.
       not.anymore
       'They did not speak, or sing, or whatever anymore.'

3.5.4.6 Event quantification

A last category of operators relevant at the e-layer concerns the specification of the frequency of occurrence of a State-of-Affairs. West Greenlandic is a language that is particularly rich in this domain. Consider the following examples (Fortescue 1984: 279–84):

(264) Quli-nut innar-tar-put.
       ten-ALL   go.to.bed-HAB-IND.3.PL
       'They habitually go to bed at ten o'clock.'

(265) Qimmi-t qilut-tar-put.
       dog-PL   bark-HAB-IND.3.PL
       'Dogs bark.'

(266) Saniqquti-qattaar-puq.
       go.past-ITER-IND.3.SG
       'He went past several times.'

(267) Api-qqip-puq.
       snow-REPV-IND.3.SG
       'It snowed again.'

The habitual morpheme -tar is used to characterize a State-of-Affairs as a
habit (264) but is also used in generic statements (265). The iterative morpheme -qattaar indicates the recurrent occurrence of a State-of-Affairs (266),
and repetitive -qqip expresses that a State-of-Affairs is identical to a previous
occurrence (267).

   The examples given so far all quantify over time intervals, which is under-
standable in view of the fact that States-of-Affairs are temporal units. In some
cases, tense and event quantification are encoded in a single *portmanteau*
morpheme, as for instance in English *used to* or in the habitual past in Amele
(Roberts 1987: 228):

(268) Ija ho-l-ig.
       I   come-HAB.PST-1.SG
       'I used to come.'

In a similar way, event quantification may interact with event location, as in
the case of distributive aspect. Consider the following example from Tarma
Quechua (Adelaar 1977: 142):

(269) Xa:bam išgi-ĉa-ru-ṅ.
       frost   fall-DISTR-PFV-3
       'It has frozen a little in several places.'

The distributive marker in (269) indicates that the State-of-Affairs described
in the sentence took place at various places at the same time, which means that
the quantification here concerns the spatial rather than the temporal regions.

3.5.5 Frames

In sum, the set of primitives for the Representational Level provides the following frames for the layer of the State-of-Affairs:

(270) $(e_1: [(f_1) (e_1)_\Phi])$

(271) $(e_1: [[(f_1: [\dots] (f_1)) \dots (f_{1+N}: [\dots] (f_{1+N}))_{\{\Phi 1\}^n}] (e_1)_\Phi]: [\sigma (e_1)_\Phi])$

       Heads of States-of-Affairs may be Lexical Properties (270) or (combi-
       nations of) Configurational Properties (271).

The operator position in (271) may be filled by operators expressing event location, relative tense, event-oriented modality, event perception, polarity, and event quantification.

The modifier position in (271) may be filled by lexical expressions specifying the relative time of occurrence, the place of occurrence, the frequency of occurrence, the reality status, the physical setting, or the cognitive setting of the State-of-Affairs.

3.6 Configurational Properties

3.6.1 Introduction

As we indicated in 3.2.3, Properties (f) play a crucial role in the construction of semantic representations. Configurational Properties constitute the inventory of predication frames relevant to a language, and non-Configurational Property layers host the lexemes of a language. Given this crucial role of Properties at the Representational Level, we will distribute our discussion of them across two main sections. In this section we dedicate ourselves to Configurational Properties only, while in 3.7 we will discuss Property units with a lexical head. The need to recognize Configurational Properties as a layer was first recognized by Vet (1990) and Cuvalay-Haak (1997) as a 'situational concept' and a 'core predication' respectively.

In the most common type of simple State-of-Affairs the subcomponents are a Property (f) as it manifests itself in time and the Individuals (x) for which this Property holds (see Hengeveld 2004d). Zero-order and first-order entities thus enter into the constitution of second-order entities, as in:

(272)   Sheila (x) is ill (f).

But this is just one of the many possible configurations. Consider the following example:

(273)   The heavy rainfall (e) caused (f) a lot of damage (e).

The State-of-Affairs described in (273) as a whole consists of a Property (f) which establishes a relation between yet two other States-of-Affairs. In our formalism this means that the State-of-Affairs variable (e) is restricted by a predication frame of the form given in (274). Note that in this representation we indicate, through vertical alignment, in what interpersonal function a certain semantic category is used. This is necessary, since many restrictions on the combination of semantic categories are dependent on the specific function in which these semantic categories are used, thus showing that formulation is a coordinated process taking into account both the Interpersonal and Representational Levels.

(274)   T   R   R

$(f_1: [(f_2)\ (e_1)_\phi\ (e_2)_\phi]\ (f_1))$

The general format that can be used for Configurational Properties is as follows (where v is a variable over variables):

(275) $(\pi\ f_1: [(v_1)\ (v)_{\phi^n}]\ (f_1): [\sigma\ (f_1)_\phi])$

Languages may differ markedly from one another in the nature and number of predication frames that are allowed both with respect to their quantitative valency (n), and with respect to their qualitative valency. The differences in qualitative valency concern both the semantic categories (v) that may be combined, and the semantic functions (φ) that these may carry. These issues will be addressed in 3.6.2. Modifiers (σ) and operators (π) of Configurational Properties are discussed in 3.6.3. and 3.6.4.

3.6.2 Heads

3.6.2.1 Quantitative restrictions

The combinatorial possibilities of semantic categories are not universally given and have to be determined for each individual language. First of all there are quantitative restrictions that have to do with the minimal and maximal number of units that make up a predication frame. As regards the minimal number of units, there is a noteworthy split between languages that allow the ascriptive use of zero-order expressions with zero valency, and others in which the minimal valency is one. Consider the following examples from Spanish:

(276)   Est-á   llov-iendo.
        AUX-3.SG.PRS rain-PROG
        'It is raining.'
        "Is raining."

(277)   Est-á   nev-ando.
        AUX-3.SG.PRS snow-PROG
        'It is snowing.'
        "Is snowing."

and Turkish:

(278)   Yağmur yağ-ıyor-Ø.
        rain   rain-PROG-3
        'It is raining.'
        "Rain is raining."

(279) Kar yağ-ıyor-Ø.
      snow rain-PROG-3
      'It is snowing.'
      "Snow is raining."

These examples show that for Spanish we may assume a zero-place predication frame for event-descriptions, whereas for Turkish we may not.

This example also serves to illustrate another important distinction. Consider the English equivalents of (276)–(279):

(280) It is raining/snowing.

In the absence of a semantic referential argument, English requires the insertion of a dummy subject in zero-place constructions. Since this is a semantically empty element, we may say that from a semantic perspective English allows zero-place predications, like Spanish, but that, unlike Spanish, it requires the insertion of an element in the subject slot at the Morphosyntactic Level.

Now consider the opposite situation: some languages allow constructions in which the existence, presence, or availablity of an entity may be asserted by simply presenting that entity through a first-order entity description, as shown in the following example from Tagalog (Schachter and Otanes 1972):

(281) Marami-ng pera.
      lot-LK   money
      'There is a lot of money.'
      "A lot of money."

The example from Tagalog contains just a referential phrase, which is evident from the fact that in (281) the linker *-ng* is used, which systematically joins head and modifier within Noun Phrases.

In other languages the existence itself has to be ascribed to that entity through a separate lexical expression, as illustrated in the following examples from Yagaria (Renck 1975):

(282) Sole' yale bei-d-a-e.
      plenty people sit-PST-3.PL-IND
      'There were many people.'
      "Many people sat."

(283) Yo' bogo-ko' hano-d-i-e.
      house one-LOC exist-PST-3.SG-IND
      'There's only one house.'
      "One house exists."

In Yagaria existence is expressed by lexical verbs. The lexical nature of these verbs may be derived from the fact that different verbs are used for animate (282) and inanimate (283) subjects. This means that for Tagalog we may assume the existence of a predication frame that contains just the description of a first-order entity, whereas for Yagaria existentials pattern with regular one-place predication frames. Again we may contrast this semantic distinction with a similar syntactic one. Consider the following example:

(284)   There is a lot of money.

In the absence of a semantic ascriptive predicate, English uses the dummy element *there*, itself supported by the dummy verb *to be*. Since these are semantically empty elements, we may say that from a semantic perspective English allows predicate-less predications, like Tagalog, but that, unlike Tagalog, it requires the insertion of an element in the predicate slot at the Morphosyntactic Level.

Apart from the minimal valency, there may be restrictions on the maximum valency that a language allows in combination with a single predicate. In many serializing languages the maximum valency of a verb is two, and serialization is required to expand that valency indirectly, as in the following example from Mandarin Chinese (Li and Thompson 1981: 366):

(285)   Wŏ gěi nǐ dào chá.
        1   give you pour tea
        'I'll pour you some tea.'
        "I pour tea give you."

As we indicated in 3.5.2, cases of core serialization like this one make use of two (two-place) predication frames, together constituting the head of a State-of-Affairs.

3.6.2.2 Qualitative restrictions: semantic categories

The qualitative restrictions on frames for States-of-Affairs concern the semantic categories of the component units and the way the relations between these component units are expressed, in terms of their semantic functions. In this section we will deal with the former. For a first illustration consider the following Dutch examples:

(286)   Hij is   in Frankrijk.
        he COP.3.SG.PRS in France
        'He is in France.'

(287)   *Het boek is   op de   tafel.
        the book COP.3.SG.PRS on DEF table
        'The book is on the table.'

(288) Het boek ligt op de tafel.
     the book lie.3.SG.PRS on DEF table
     'The book is lying on the table.'

The ascriptive use of a Locative phrase in Dutch is allowed when the phrase involved designates a spatial region rather than an object. Thus *in Frankrijk* 'in France' in (286) can be used ascriptively, but *op de tafel* 'on the table' in (287) cannot. In order to ascribe this Location to the subject, a lexical predicate, such as *lig-* 'lie' in (288) has to be used. As argued earlier, the difference between spatial regions and objects can be captured through the use of distinct variables: 'l' for spatial regions and 'x' for objects. The sentences in (286) and (288) may thus be said to make use of the predication frames in (289)–(290):

$$T \qquad\qquad\qquad\qquad\qquad R$$
(289) $(f_i: [(f_j: (l_i: \text{Frankrijk } (l_i))_{Loc} \quad (f_j)) \quad (x_i)_\phi] (f_i))$

$$T \qquad\qquad\quad R \qquad\qquad\qquad R$$
(290) $(f_i: [(f_j: \text{lig-} (f_j)) \quad (x_i: \text{boek-} (x_i))_\emptyset \quad (x_j: \text{tafel-} (x_j))_{Loc}] (f_i))$

Now compare this with the situation in Turkish (Kornfilt 1997: 242) and in English:

(291) Kitap masa-da-Ø-Ø.
     book table-LOC-PRS-3
     'The book is on the table.'

(292) The book is on the table.

Both Turkish and English allow the ascriptive use of a Locative phrase designating an object rather than a spatial region, i.e. both of the following predication frames are available to the formulators within the grammars of these languages:

$$T \qquad\qquad\quad R$$
(293) $(f_1: [(f_2 : (l_1)_{Loc} (f_2)) \quad (x_1)_\emptyset] (f_1))$

$$T \qquad\qquad\quad R$$
(294) $(f_1: [(f_2 : (x_1)_{Loc} (f_2)) \quad (x_2)_\emptyset] (f_1))$

The difference is that in Turkish under certain circumstances no support verb is required, whereas English under all circumstances requires copula support, which applies at the level of morphosyntactic encoding.

    This is not the place to give an exhaustive listing of all possible predication frames, but we will list below a range of possible predication frames for English together with an illustrative example. Note that we restrict ourselves here to considerations of quantitative valency and of the nature of the semantic categories involved. After that we will turn to the semantic functions of the component units within predication frames.

3.6.2.2.1 *Zero-place Property*   Zero-place Properties, illustrated and discussed above, are actually not configurational at all, and we are just presenting them here for the sake of completeness and contrast. They are lexically headed and ascribe a Property directly to the main State-of-Affairs, as in the following example:

(295)   T
   $(f_1: rain (f_1))$
   'It rained.'

3.6.2.2.2 *One-place Property*   For one-place Properties we do need predication frames of the general type given in (296). The semantic category of the argument may vary, leading to variants such as those illustrated in (297)–(300).

(296)   T R
   $(f_1: [(f_2) \quad (v_1)_\phi] (f_1))$

(297) $(f_1: [(f_2) \quad (x_1)_\phi] (f_1))$
   'The boy is swimming.'

(298) $(f_1: [(f_2) \quad (f_3)_\phi] (f_1))$
   'That colour is ugly.'

(299) $(f_1: [(f_2) \quad (e_1)_\phi] (f_1))$
   'It was a pity that she had to leave.'

(300) $(f_1: [(f_2) \quad (p_1)_\phi] (f_1))$
   'Her hope faded away.'

A full representation of a State-of-Affairs with, for instance, the predication frame given in (297) would be as follows:

(301)   T   R
   $(e_i: [(f_i: [\quad (f_j: swim (f_j)) \quad (x_i: [(f_k: boy (f_k)) (x_i)_\phi]_\phi] (f_i)) (e_i)_\phi])$
   'The boy is swimming.'

The dependency relation between the units is shown through the presence of a function marker on the dependent unit (x_i) and its absence on (f_j). The ascriptive function of (f_j) imposes restrictions on the lexical items that it can take (see 3.6.2) and will trigger its expression as the main predicate at the Morphosyntactic Level. The referential function of (x_i) also imposes restrictions on the lexical items it can host, and will trigger its expression as a Noun Phrase.

The representation in (301) incidentally also shows that predication frames are not only used to build descriptions of States-of-Affairs, but also those of other semantic categories, such as Individuals. Thus, (x_i) in (301) is expanded by means of a one-place predication frame. We will return to this issue in 3.8.2.

A special class of one-place Properties concerns those exemplified in (302)–(304):

(302)   That woman is an *aunt of my friend*.

(303)   The man is *inside the house*.

(304)   That girl is *fond of chocolate*.

The predication frames for the italicized parts of these expressions have the general structure of (305):

(305) $(f_1: [(f_2) (v_1)_\phi] (f_1))$

A specific property of this type of frame is that it cannot itself serve as the basis for a main predication. In order to form such a predication, a further predication frame has to be formed on the basis of (305) to create yet another one-place Property recursively, with the result given in (306):

(306) $(f_1: [(f_2: [(f_3) (v_1)_\phi] (f_2)) (v_2)_\phi] (f_1))$

This leads to the representation in (307) of example (304):

(307) $(f_i: [(f_j: [(f_k: fond (f_k)) (x_i: -chocolate- (x_i))_\phi] (f_j)) (x_j: girl (x_j))_\phi]$
$(f_i))$

with markers T T R R above.

This structure should be read as follows: the predication frame at the highest layer indicates that the Individual (x_j) 'that girl' has the Configurational Property (f_j) 'fond of chocolate'; to create this Configurational Property (f_j) the lower-layer predication frame indicates that the Property (f_k) 'fond' exists relative to the Individual (x_i) 'chocolate'. In this configuration (x_i) thus constitutes an inner argument, and (x_j) an outer argument. For another example consider the representation in (308) of example (303):

(308) $(f_i: [(l_i: [(f_j: inside (f_j)) (x_i: -house- (x_i))_\phi] (l_i)) (x_j: man (x_j))_\phi] (f_i))$

with markers T T R R above.

which should be read in this way: the Individual (x_j) 'the man' is ascribed the complex Location (l_i) 'inside the house'; this Location itself is evoked by indicating that the Property (f_j) exists relative to the Individual (x_i) 'the house'.

As we will show below, the distinction between inner arguments and outer arguments that we make in these cases is reflected in the assignment of semantic functions.

3.6.2.2.3 *Two-place Property* Two place Properties receive the general treatment presented in (309). Some more specific instantiations are given in (310)–(315), in which the nature of the semantic categories designated varies:

(309)
$$\text{T} \quad \text{R} \quad \text{R}$$
$$(f_1: [(f_2) \quad (v_1)_\phi \ (v_2)_\phi \ ] (f_1))$$

(310) $(f_1: [(f_2) \quad (x_1)_\phi \ (x_2)_\phi \ ] (f_1))$
'She kicked him.'

(311) $(f_1: [(f_2) \quad (x_1)_\phi \ (l_1)_\phi \ ] (f_1))$
'Charles lives in Antwerp.'

(312) $(f_1: [(f_2) \quad (x_1)_\phi \ (e_1)_\phi \ ] (f_1))$
'He saw his neighbour walk down the street.'

(313) $(f_1: [(f_2) \quad (x_1)_\phi \ (p_1)_\phi \ ] (f_1))$
'He didn't believe that she was ill.'

(314) $(f_1: [(f_2) \quad (e_1)_\phi \ (e_2)_\phi \ ] (f_1))$
'The heavy rainfall caused a lot of problems.'

(315) $(f_1: [(f_2) \quad (e_1)_\phi \ (t_1)_\phi \ ] (f_1))$
'The meeting lasted three hours.'

A full representation of a State-of-Affairs based on (315) would be as in (316):

$$\text{T} \qquad \text{R} \qquad\qquad \text{R}$$
(316) $(e_i: [(f_i: [(f_j: \text{last} (f_j)) \ (e_j: -\text{meeting}- (e_j))_\phi \ (3 \ t_i: -\text{hour}- (t_i))_\phi \ ] (f_i))$
$(e_i)_\phi])$
'The meeting lasted three hours.'

3.6.2.2.4 *Three-place Property* Three-place Properties, for languages that have them, are represented according to the general predication frame in (317). More specific instantiations are given in (318)–(321):

(317)
$$\text{T} \quad \text{R} \quad \text{R} \quad \text{R}$$
$$(f_1: [(f_2) \quad (v_1)_\phi \quad (v_2)_\phi \quad (v_3)_\phi \ ] (f_1))$$

(318) $(f_1: [(f_2) \quad (x_1)_\phi \quad (x_2)_\phi \quad (l_3)_\phi \ ] (f_1))$
'Sheila put the book on a shelf.'

(319) $(f_1: [(f_2) \quad (x_1)_\phi \quad (x_2)_\phi \quad (e_1)_\phi \ ] (f_1))$
'The woman forced the man to leave.'

(320) $(f_1: [(f_2)$ $(e_i)_\phi$ $(x_i)_\phi$ $(e_2)_\phi] (f_1))$
'His strange behaviour reminded me of his illness.'

(321) $(f_1: [(f_2)$ $(x_i)_\phi$ $(x_2)_\phi$ $(p_i)_\phi] (f_1))$
'John told me that he had forced Mary to leave.'

Examples such as (319) and (321) show embedding, which is the result of the recursive application of semantic representations containing predication frames. Consider the representation of (319) in (322):

(322) $(e_i: [(f_i:$ $[$

           $(f_j: \text{force} (f_j))$

           $(x_i: [-\text{woman}- (x_i)_\phi])_\phi$

           $(x_j: [-\text{man}- (x_i)_\phi])_\phi$

           $(e_j:$ $[(f_k:$ $[$

                  $(f_l: \text{leave} (f_l))$

                  $(x_j)_\phi]$

              $(f_k)) (e_j)_\phi])]$

      $(f_i)) (e_i)_\phi])$

'The woman forced the man to leave.'

Here the main State-of-Affairs (e_i) is based on a three-place predication frame (f_i). The third argument position is occupied again by the description of a State-of-Affairs (e_j) based on a one-place predication frame (f_k). Note the coreference relation between the second argument (x_j) of the main predication frame and the first of the embedded predication frame.

3.6.2.2.5 *Four-place Property*   Four-place predication frames seem to be rare crosslinguistically. The best examples that come to mind are derived causative constructions in languages which have three-place predication frames and extend these to four-place frames by applying the causative derivation, as illustrated for Turkish in (351) (Kornfilt 1997: 332):

(323)   Ben   Hasan-a   sürahi-yi   dolab-a   koy-dur-du-m
       I   Hasan-DAT pitcher-ACC cupboard-DAT put-CAUS-PST-1.SG
'I made Hasan put the pitcher into the cupboard.'

Such constructions are based on the general predication frame given in (324):

(324)   T   R   R   R   R
     $(f_1: [(f_2)$ $(v_i)_\phi$ $(v_2)_\phi$ $(v_3)_\phi$ $(v_4)_\phi] (f_1))$

with the subtype in (325) for example (323):

(325)   T   R   R   R   R
     $(f_1: [(f_2)$ $(x_i)_\phi$ $(x_2)_\phi$ $(x_3)_\phi$ $(x_4)_\phi] (f_1))$

3.6.2.2.6 *Relational Property*   A special type of predication frame is needed for what may be called Relational Properties. In these, a phrase marked with a relator such as an adposition or a case marker is used ascriptively, as in the following examples:

(326)   This play is *by Shakespeare*.

(327)   Mary is *in London*.

(328)   This tea is *from Sri Lanka*.

The parts in italics in these examples correspond to Ascriptive Subacts. They are not arguments of the verb *to be*, which we treat as a support verb that is introduced at the Morphosyntactic Level. Evidence for this view comes from languages that can express constructions like the ones in (326)–(328) without the intervention of a copula. The following example of a locative relational Property is from Ket (Castrén 1858: 103):

(329)   Xus-kei-di.
        tent-LOC-1.SG
        'I am in the tent.'

And example (330), from Imbabura Quechua (Cole 1982: 115), illustrates a possessive relational Property:

(330)   Chay wasi   ñuka-paj-mi.
        DEM house 1-POSS-FOC
        'That house is mine.'
        "That house is of me."

Note that expressions such as *by Shakespeare* in (326) as a whole designate a Property, while at the same time containing a referential expression, *Shakespeare*. This example may therefore be continued as in (331):

(331)   This play is by Shakespeare. He was a great dramatist.

To account for this double nature of the construction we may represent the relational Property itself in the following way:

(332)   T R_1
        $(f_1: (v_1)_\phi (f_1))$

This representation can be read in the following way: a Property (f_1), used ascriptively (T), is realized through reference to a semantic category (v_1) with the semantic function ϕ. *Xuskei* 'in the tent' in (329) can then be represented as:

(333)   T R_1
    $(f_i: (x_i: -xus- (x_i))_L (f_1))$

to be paraphrased as: 'a Property f_i, such that 'in the tent' of f_i'.

Incorporating such a Property expression into a general predication frame, we obtain (334). A number of more specific instantiations are given in (335)–(338):

          T   R   R

(334) $(f_1: [(f_2: (v_1)_\phi (f_2)) (v_2)_\phi] (f_1))$

(335) $(f_1: [(f_2: (x_1)_\phi (f_2)) (x_2)_\phi] (f_1))$
      'The play is by Shakespeare.'

(336) $(f_1: [(f_2: (t_1)_\phi (f_2)) (e_1)_\phi] (f_1))$
      'The meeting is at six o'clock.'

(337) $(f_1: [(f_2: (l_1)_\phi (f_2)) (e_1)_\phi] (f_1))$
      'The meeting is in room 106.'

(338) $(f_1: [(f_2: (e_1)_\phi (f_2)) (e_2)_\phi] (f_1))$
      'It is because she left him that he started drinking.'

3.6.2.2.7 Classification   The next set of predication frames have to do with the expression of class membership, as illustrated in the following examples:

(339)   That man is *a painter*.

(340)   A cat is *an animal*.

Again, many languages would not need a copula in this construction type, which means we can interpret the part in italics as corresponding to the Ascriptive Subact. An example is (341) from Turkish (Gerjan van Schaaik, p.c.):

(341)   O   adam çok iyi   bir   doktor.
       DEM man   very good INDF doctor
       'That man is a very good doctor.'

The predication frame needed for this type of construction is different from the one used for one-place Properties above. In classifying constructions, the ascriptive part is phrasal, not lexical. Compare the following constructions from Dutch:

(342)   Jan is   schilder.
       John COP.PRS.3.SG painter
       'John is a painter.'
       "John is painter."

(343)   Jan   is   een   schilder.
        John COP.PRS.3.SG INDF painter
        'John is a painter.'

The Ascriptive Subact *schilder* 'painter' in (342) is a bare noun, while *een schilder* 'a painter' in (343) is a noun phrase. The translations show that the distinction cannot generally be made in English, as in many other languages. The difference between the two constructions is not only reflected in the absence versus presence of the indefinite article *een*, it can also be demonstrated by differences in the syntactic behaviour of the two constructions. First of all, the bare noun in (342) does not take a plural form when used with a plural subject, cf. (344), while the noun phrase in (343) does, as shown in (345):

(344)   Jan   en   Piet zijn   schilder.
        John and Pete COP.PRS.3.PL painter
        'John and Pete are painters.'
        "John and Pete are painter."

(345)   Jan   en   Piet zijn   schilder-s.
        John and Pete COP.PRS.3.PL painter-PL
        'John and Pete are painters.'

Secondly, the bare noun cannot be modified, cf. (346), but the noun phrase can, as shown in (347):

(346)   *Jan is   erg   goede schilder.
        John COP.PRS.3.SG very good   painter
        'John is a very good painter.'
        "John is very good painter."

(347)   Jan   is   een   erg   goede schilder.
        John COP.PRS.3.SG INDF very good   painter
        'John is a very good painter.'

To account for these differences, the predication frame for classification will be as in (348). Some specific instantiations are given in (349)–(351):

(348)   T   R
        $(f_1: [(v_1) (v_2)_\phi] (f_1))$
        (where (v_1) and (v_2) are of the same semantic category)

(349) $(f_1: [(x_1) (x_2)_\phi] (f_1))$
        'John is a teacher.'

(350) $(f_1: [(f_2) (f_3)_\phi] (f_1))$
        'Yellow is a nice colour.'

(351) $(f_1: [(t_2)   (t_3)_\Phi] (f_1))$
'Now is not a good moment.'

The ascriptive nature of the predicative noun phrases is evident from the fact that they can only be referred to anaphorically by means of elements that are used for predicates:

(352)   a.   John is a teacher. *That's* what he is.
        b.   John went swimming. *That's* what he did.

(353)   a.   John is a teacher, and *so* is Peter.
        b.   John went swimming, and *so* did Peter.

3.6.2.2.8 *Identification*   The classifying constructions just illustrated differ from identificational constructions like the following:

(354)   My teacher is Peter.

Identificational constructions differ from classificational ones in that the noun phrase following the copula is not used ascriptively, as follows from (355)–(356), which are ungrammatical under the intended readings:

(355)   *My teacher is Peter, and *so* is my brother.

(356)   *My teacher is Peter. *That's* what he is.

This means that neither of the two noun phrases in (354) is used ascriptively. Nor can the verb *to be* be considered to be the manifestation of an Ascriptive Subact, since there are languages that can express the same type of construction without the intervention of a copula. The following example is from Hixkaryana (Derbyshire 1979: 132):

(357)   Romuru mosoni.
        1.SG.son   DEM.PROX
        'This is my son.'

Thus, we may conclude that the identificational predication frame is related to two Referential Subacts at the Interpersonal Level, as indicated in the general frame given in (358), illustrated in (359)–(363):

(358)   R   R
        $(f_1: [(v_1) (v_1)] (f_1))$
        (where both instances of (v_1) and (v_2) are of the same semantic category)

(359) $(f_1: [(x_1) (x_1)] (f_1))$
        'John is my best friend.'

(360) $(f_1: [(f_2)   (f_2)] (f_1))$
'Yellow is my favourite colour.'

(361) $(f_1: [(p_1)   (p_1)] (f_1))$
'The reason that I'm here is that I have no other place to go to.'

(362) $(f_1: [(l_1)   (l_1)] (f_1))$
'The place that I met Sheila was in the park.'

(363) $(f_1: [(m_1)   (m_1)] (f_1))$
'The way he approached the lion was cautiously.'

3.6.2.2.9 *Existence*   We discussed existential constructions above to illustrate the typological differences between languages as regards their availability in the language. The general existential frame proposed there is repeated in (364). Some illustrations are (365)–(367):

(364)   R
        $(f_1: [(v_1)] (f_1))$

(365) $(f_1: [(x_1)] (f_1))$
'There are lions.'

(366) $(f_1: [(e_1)] (f_1))$
'There are courses that help you become more assertive.'

(367) $(f_1: [(t_1)] (f_1))$
'There are periods of my life I wouldn't want to do all over again.'

3.6.2.3 Semantic functions of arguments

3.6.2.3.1 *Introduction*   In the preceding overview of possible predication frames, we have left semantic functions out of consideration. In this section, we enrich these frames with semantic functions. We shall first consider the semantic functions associated with the arguments of Properties, moving on to those associated with classifications, identifications, and predications of existence. It is important to recall that FDG does not assume *a priori* that underlying semantic representations are identical across languages, but that they have to be determined for each language individually, based on the grammatically relevant distinctions that are made within that language. This applies with particular force to the repertory of semantic functions found in individual languages.

    A semantic function specifies a relation between a nucleus and a dependent. In representing this relation we attach semantic functions to the dependent, as in (368):

(368) $(f_1: [(f_2) (x_1)_A (x_2)_U (x_3)_L] (f_1))$

This does not mean we interpret these functions as being more relevant to dependents than to nuclei. It is just a convention to give a unilinear representation that includes the various relations between the nucleus and each of its dependents. A far more appropriate representation of this situation would be the one in Figure 8.

We will assume the representation in Figure 8 to be the one intended by the conventional representation in (368).

Semantic functions are grammatical reflexes of the cognitive awareness that the participants in a State-of-Affairs (i) play different roles in that State-of-Affairs (in which case the State-of-Affairs is treated in grammar as a Property); (ii) play the same role in the State-of-Affairs (in which case the State-of-Affairs is treated as a classification or identification); (iii) cannot be seen as playing a role in a State-of-Affairs (in which case that State-of-Affairs is presented in a predication of existence). We will consider each of these possibilities in turn.

3.6.2.3.2 *Semantic functions in Property-designating frames*   The notion of participants playing distinct roles is clearest in dynamic two-place Properties concerning external reality, where a distinction can be made between a participant playing a more active role, the Actor, and another, the Undergoer, playing a more passive role (see Foley and Van Valin 1984 for this terminology). Thus in (369):

(369)   Beckham kicked the defender.

Beckham is identifiable as having the semantic function Actor and *the defender* the semantic function Undergoer, and in English this is reflected in their grammar: when combined with the active form of the verb, the Actor is attributed Subject function and the Undergoer appears in immediately postverbal position. The prototypical Actor is volitionally involved in the State-of-Affairs and

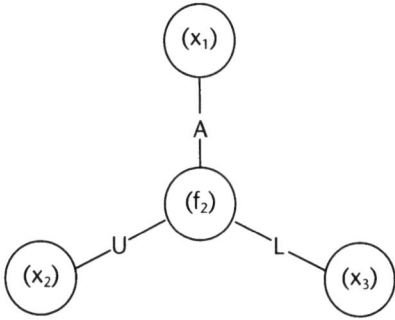

FIGURE 8. The representation of semantic functions

the prototypical Undergoer is non-volitionally affected by the State-of-Affairs, but that in the grammar of English these are mere prototypes can be seen in the possibility of overriding these expectations by adding further lexical material but without affecting the essential grammar of the clause, as in:

(370)   Beckham unintentionally kicked the defender.

(371)   The defender wanted Beckham to kick him so that he would get a red card.

As Foley (2005) has shown, Actors and Undergoers are associated with other, less prototypical, semantic Properties, and languages differ in the extent to which they allow non-prototypical actors to group with the Actor in terms of their grammatical behaviour.

English, for example, allows the Actor function to be assigned to volitional agents but also to non-volitional forces, i.e. to non-sentient causes:

(372)   Caesar destroyed the city.

(373)   The storm destroyed the city.

The storm may not be volitionally involved in the destruction, but it is not affected by the State-of-Affairs either and therefore is associated with the Actor rather than the Undergoer function. The assumption here is that while there is a cognitive awareness of a difference in roles, this difference is reduced in the representational grammar of English to the opposition between Actor and Undergoer.

The distinction between Actor and Undergoer is, as was mentioned, characteristic of dynamic States-of-Affairs, i.e. those that designate a change of state, for example with verbs such as *kick* and *destroy*. Not all States-of-Affairs are dynamic, and FDG makes a fundamental distinction between dynamic and non-dynamic States-of-Affairs. The former require the input of energy, whereas the latter do not. Examples of non-dynamic States-of-Affairs are verbs such as *lie* (as used in (374)) or adjectives such as *ugly*. An important characteristic of non-dynamic states is the absence of an Actor: however, an Undergoer, in the sense of an entity that 'undergoes' a Property, is present. In two-place Properties it is accompanied by an entity with the semantic function Locative, a function typically attributed to a participant with the semantic category Location, as in (374), where *Easter Island* has the function Undergoer and *in the Pacific Ocean* Locative.

(374)   Easter Island lies in the Pacific Ocean.

The application of the semantic function Undergoer is justified by the fact that the entity undergoes localization, without any volitional involvement.

A Locative function is also found in dynamic States-of-Affairs, where alongside the Actor–Undergoer opposition already discussed, we also find Actor–Locative and Undergoer–Locative oppositions. Thus in (375):

(375)   The president waved to the crowd.

we find a volitionally involved Actor (*the president*), no Undergoer, but a Locative (*to the crowd*). In dynamic States-of-Affairs, locative roles cover a range of spatial distinctions, namely Ablative (indicating the source of movement), Perlative (indicating the path of movement), Allative (indicating the end point of movement, and covering further distinctions such as Recipient, Beneficiary, and spatial Goal), and Approach (indicating a point towards which there is movement). (375) could thus be analysed as Actor (*the president*)–Allative (*to the crowd*).

The fact that a dynamic State-of-Affairs need not contain an Actor (although conversely a non-dynamic State-of-Affairs cannot contain one) is clear from examples like (376):

(376)   The apple fell from the twig through the branches to the ground.

Here the apple is not volitionally involved in the dynamic State-of-Affairs and thus qualifies as an Undergoer. The Locative specification in (376) is a complex one, consisting of three components, which trace the apple's 'journey' from its initial to its final positions: Ablative (*from the twig*), Perlative (*through the branches*), and Goal (*to the ground*).

In three-place dynamic Properties, the cognitive awareness of difference is necessarily divided over the three semantic functions, allowing only the constellation Actor–Undergoer–Locative. Consider the following examples:

(377)   The committee gave the prize to the youngest candidate.

(378)   The wind blew the leaves into the kitchen.

In (377), there is a straightforward association of Actor with *the committee*, Undergoer with *the prize*, and Recipient, a more specific instantiation of Locative, with *the youngest candidate*. In (378), the non-volitionally affected participant (Undergoer) is clearly *the leaves*, which given the constellation Actor–Undergoer–Locative qualifies *the wind*, despite its non-volitional character, as Actor, and *into the kitchen* emerges as Goal. Since Actor is debarred from non-dynamic States-of-Affairs, we accordingly do not encounter three-place non-dynamic States-of-Affairs.

The notions developed for two-place States-of-Affairs transfer to the description of one-place States-of-Affairs. As is well known, dynamic one-place States-of-Affairs are classified as either 'unergative' or 'unaccusative': the former corresponds to the presence of a sole Actor argument, the latter to that of a sole Undergoer argument, as in (379) and (380) respectively:

(379)   The students are working.

(380)   The bomb exploded.

In (379), *the students* are volitionally involved in the State-of-Affairs, while that is not the case for *the bomb* in (380). Since something happens to the bomb, it is non-volitionally affected and therefore counts as an Undergoer. Although the distinction between Actor and Undergoer is neutralized in the English clauses above (through Subject assignment), it becomes apparent in Dutch, in which the perfect in unergative clauses is formed with the auxiliary *hebben* and in unaccusative clauses with the auxiliary *zijn*:

(381)   De   studenten hebben   gewerkt.
         DEF   student.PL AUX-PL.PRS   work.PTCP
         'The students worked.'

(382)   De   bom   is   ontploft.
         DEF   bomb   AUX-3.SG.PRS   explode.PTCP
         'The bomb exploded.'

The sole argument of a dynamic one-place State-of-Affairs can also bear the semantic function Locative, in the more specific sense of Recipient. Consider the following examples from Icelandic (Barðdal 2001):

(383)   Honum   sárnaði.
         3.SG.M.DAT became.hurt
         'He became hurt.'

(384)   Honum   stendur.
         3.SG.M.DAT stands
         'He has an erection.'

Thus A, U, and L may all occur as the sole argument in a dynamic one-place predication frame.

As for non-dynamic one-place States-of-Affairs, the single participant is never volitionally involved and therefore receives the role Undergoer or Locative. This can best be illustrated by the following examples from a language in which agreement on the verb is sensitive to semantic functions only, not to the grammatical relation of Subject (see 4.4.3.4). Consider the following examples from Chickasaw (Munro and Gordon 1982, cited in Bickel fc.):

(385)   Malili-li.
         run-1.SG.A
         'I ran.'

TABLE 4. Basic semantic functions

Dynamic States-of-Affairs			Non-dynamic States-of-Affairs		
Quantitative valency	Semantic functions	Examples	Quantitative valency	Semantic functions	Examples
1	A	(379), (381), (385)	1	–	
	U	(380), (382)		U	(386)
	L	(383), (384)		L	(387)
2	A + U	(372)–(373)	2	–	
	A + L	(375)		–	
	U + L	(376)		U + L	(374)
3	A + U + L	(377)–(378)	3	–	

(386) Sa-chokma.
       1.SG.U-good
       'I'm good.'

(387) An-takho'bi.
       1.SG.LOC-lazy
       'I'm lazy.'

As these examples show, agreement on the verb distinguishes between Actors (385), Undergoers (386), and Locatives (of the Recipient type, 387). The latter two examples are non-dynamic, but differ in the fact that in (386) the single argument is in a state, while (387) could be paraphrased as 'it lazies to me', presenting the single argument as experiencing the laziness as the result of an internal process.

The basic system that emerges from the preceding is shown in Table 4 (for further detail, see Hengeveld and Heesakkers, n.d.).

A(ctor), U(ndergoer), and L(ocative) are general indications of (groups of) semantic functions which we hypothesize to be of universal relevance. But individual languages may display further refinements within each of these categories and thus expand the repertory of semantic functions which their predication frames attribute to arguments.

Thus in Tagalog a grammatical distinction is made between those Actors which control the dynamic State-of-Affairs and those which do not. Whereas, as we saw above, this is expressible in English through the possible addition of *inadvertently* or *by mistake*, the distinction between controlling Actor and non-controlling Actor is reflected in Tagalog in the choice between the dynamic and the potentive voices of the verb (Himmelmann 2004):

(388) Ang iták ay i-p<in>utol   ko   ng saging.
       SPEC bolo PM CV-cut<RLS.U> 1.SG.POSS GEN banana
       'I cut bananas with the bolo.'

(389)   Na-i-luto   ko   na.
        RLS.POTV-CV-cook 1.SG.POSS now
        'I happen to have cooked it already (by mistake).'

Tagalog also distinguishes grammatically among three kinds of Undergoer, again with reflections in the verb voice chosen. There is a distinction between affected Undergoer (390, with Undergoer voice), non-affected Undergoer (391, with Locative voice), and Undergoer in movement (392, with the Conveyance voice) (Himmelmann fc.; Himmelmann 2004):

(390)   Patay-ín natin   itó-ng   dalawa-ng Hapón.
        dead-UV 1.PL.INCL.POSS PROX-LK two-LK   Japan
        'Let's kill two Japanese!'

(391)   Buks-án mo   áng pintó.
        open-LV 2.SG.POSS SPEC door
        'Open the door.'

(392)   I-b<in>alik   nilá   ang bata.
        CV-return<RLS.U> 3.PL.POSS SPEC child
        'They returned the child.'

Finally, English recognizes at least three different dynamic semantic functions within the role Locative, reflected in example (376) in differential prepositional marking: *from* for ablative, *through* for perlative, and *to* for allative. Similarly, non-dynamic location (essive) is generally marked by yet another preposition, *at*. Tariana, by contrast, encodes ablative, essive, and allative in the same manner (Aikhenvald 2003: 148):

(393)   Na-pidana   uni-*se*.
        3.PL.go-REM.PST.REP water-LOC
        'They went into water.'

(394)   Nawiki pa:-putʃita-*se* nehpani-pidana.
        people one-CL-LOC   3.PL.work-REM.PST.REP
        'People were working on a clearing.'

(395)   Hĩ   wyaka-*se* ka-nu-karu   dhuma-naka
        DEM.ANIM far-LOC   REL-come-PST.REL.F 3.SG.F.hear-PRS.VIS
        waku-nuku.
        1.PL.speech-TOP
        'She who came from far away understands our speech.'

In FDG this means that the Tariana formulator makes use of a single predication frame for these constructions with the semantic function Locative, while the English formulator makes use of three different ones, with Essive, Ablative, and Allative.

The three major semantic functions and the associated distinctions within them have so far concerned States-of-Affairs that concern external reality. Let us now return to internal reality, the domain of psychological processes and states, or experiences. Experiences typically involve two participants, an experiencer and the phenomenon being experienced. It has been observed that experiences tend not to have their own grammar, but that their grammar is modelled upon those of non-experiences. Since neither the experiencer nor the phenomenon is volitionally involved, we might expect that the grammar of experience will be restricted to the roles Undergoer and Locative, and indeed this is regularly found.

In Spanish (396), for example, the experiencer of *gustar* 'please', used in non-dynamic States-of-Affairs, is marked as a Recipient (with the preposition *a* or the dative case of a clitic pronoun), in keeping with the analysis, and the phenomenon appears as an Undergoer. In Portuguese (397), however, with the etymologically related verb *gostar* 'like', it is with the experiencer that the Undergoer role is associated and the phenomenon appears as an Ablative, indicating the source of the pleasure with the preposition *de* 'from':

(396) Me   gust-an   las   fresa-s.
       1.SG.REC please-3.PL.PRS   DEF.PL   strawberry-PL
       'I like strawberries.'

(397) Eu   gost-o   de   morango-s.
       1.SG.NOM like-1.SG.PRS   from   strawberry-PL
       'I like strawberries.'

Thus the same constellation of Undergoer–Locative is linked differentially to the experiencer and the phenomenon. Note that the construction type illustrated in (397) is allowed in some colloquial varieties of Spanish too.

In other languages, the Undergoer role is associated strongly or exclusively with the experiencer. Consider Imbabura Quechua, in which the Undergoer marking (the accusative case) is found on the experiencer, too (Cole 1982: 103, 108):

(398) tayta-ka   ruwana-*ta*   awa-rka-mi.
       father-TOP   poncho-ACC   weave-PST-VAL
       'Father wove a poncho.'

(399) Juzi-*ta*   rupa-n.
       José-ACC   be.hot-3
       'José is hot.'

In (399), *José* is a true Undergoer in being non-volitionally affected by the State-of-Affairs.

Another example is German, where with a verb such as *frieren* 'be cold', occurring in a one-place non-dynamic State-of-Affairs, the experiencer is associated with the only possible role, cf. Table 4 above, the Undergoer. Where the verb is impersonal, as in (400) and (401), the Undergoer appears in the accusative case, which is associated with the Undergoer in two-place States-of-Affairs; where a personal form of the verb is chosen, as in (402), the nominative case appears, reflecting the assignment of Subject to the Undergoer:

(400)   Mich   friert.
        1SG.ACC   be.cold-3.SG

(401)   Es   friert   mich.
        3.SG.N   be.cold-3.SG 1.SG.ACC

(402)   Ich   frier-e.
        1.SG.NOM be.cold-1.SG
        'I am cold.'

In English, however, experiences, both dynamic and non-dynamic, tend to be moulded on the Actor–Undergoer model: the experiencer or the phenomenon being experienced can be attributed to either of the roles:

(403)   Snakes <Actor: phenomenon> frighten many people <Undergoer: experiencer>.

(404)   Many people <Actor: experiencer> fear snakes <Undergoer: phenomenon>.

In (403), *many people* are affected by the feeling caused by snakes: this makes the attribution of the Actor and Undergoer roles very natural. In (404), although *many people* is not active, it is the association of the Actor role with humanity (or sentience, Foley 2005) which motivates the attribution of experiencer to the Actor and the equally counter-intuitive attribution of phenomenon to Undergoer—counter-intuitive because the snakes are not affected in any way. But the analysis of *many people* as an Actor in (404) is justified by the fact that the grammar treats it as though it were like any other Actor, i.e. in allowing it to appear as a *by*-phrase in the passive equivalent:

(405)   Snakes are feared by many people.

A last semantic function to be discussed concerns the one carried by the 'internal argument' of the one-place Properties identified in 3.6.2.3.2, such as the one illustrated in (406):

(406)   the father of the boy, the boy's father

In these cases *the boy* is an argument of *father*. The semantic relationship is a general one, and can be paraphrased as 'someone is father with reference to/considered in relation to the boy'. Mackenzie (1983: 38) proposes the label Reference (Ref) for this semantic function. The underlying representation of (406) would thus be as in (407):

(407) $(x_i: [(f_i: [(f_j: father (f_j)) (x_j: -boy- (x_j))_{Ref}] (f_i)) (x_i)_\phi])$

This frame is particularly manifest in languages with special constructions for relational nouns, covering inalienable possession, kinship relations, locative expressions, and the like. The following example is from Kamaiurá (Seki 2000: 56):

(408)   kunu'um-a r-up
        boy-NUCL   RELR-father
        'the boy's father'

In this example the Ref argument is expressed in the nuclear case, while the relationality is marked on the relational noun itself.

In the predication frames discussed so far, Actor, Undergoer, Locative, and Reference (or their more specific subcategories) are semantic functions indicating the role of semantic units that are referential and arguments of an ascriptively used predicate: in (409), for example, the semantic units marked at the Representational Level as A, U, and L all correspond to Referential Subacts at the Interpersonal Level:

(409)   Mary (A) submitted her poetry (U) to the competition (L).

We now move to relational Properties, instances where the Ascriptive Subact at the Interpersonal Level corresponds to a semantic unit which itself bears one of the semantic functions distinguished in the preceding section or some other, more abstract, semantic function. All the instances are non-dynamic and in each case the ascriptively used semantic unit takes an Undergoer argument. Here are some examples that we discussed earlier with the Actor and Locative functions, and the more abstract Cause function, which in English is realized as *because*:

          T   R   R
(410) $(f_1: [(f_2: (x_1)_A   (f_2)) (x_2)_U] (f_1))$
        'The play is by Shakespeare.'

(411) $(f_1: [(f_2: (x_1)_L   (f_2)) (e_1)_U] (f_1))$
        'The meeting is at six o'clock.'

(412) $(f_1: [(f_2: (x_1)_L \quad (f_2)) \ (e_1)_U] (f_1))$
'The meeting is in room 106.'

(413) $(f_1: [(f_2: (e_1)_{Cause} \quad (f_2)) \ (e_2)_U] (f_1))$
'It is because she left him that he started drinking.'

3.6.2.3.3 *Semantic functions in frames for classificational, identificational, and existential constructions*   The next type of predication frame to be considered covers instances of classification and identification, as found in such examples as (414) and (415) respectively:

(414)   John is a teacher.

(415)   John is the teacher.

Recall that, in classification, there is at the Interpersonal Level a relation between an ascriptive and a Referential Subact, while at the Representational Level, the frame consists of two ontologically identical semantic units. The relation is one of classification, and the units are identical for the simple reason that an Individual can be classified only as an Individual, and not—except perhaps metaphorically—as a State-of-Affairs or a Property:

(416)   John is a teacher (x_1)

(417)   *John is an explosion (e_1).

(418)   *John is a high temperature (f_1).

The entity classified undergoes classification, and as such bears the semantic function Undergoer. The other semantic unit indicates the Property assigned to the Undergoer and as such bears no semantic function.

Consequently, we may specify the semantic functions in the basic predication frame for classification as follows, where v is a variable over variables:

(419)   T   R
      $(f_1: [(v_1) \ (v_2)_U] (f_1))$

As with the relational Properties discussed above, the copula *be* is inserted at the Morphosyntactic Level.

Not all languages have a classifying construction. In Scottish Gaelic, for example, apart from a rather archaic classifying construction (see Adger and Ramchand 2003), the meaning of classification is carried by one of two relational Property constructions, one for temporary and one for permanent classification, with in each case the Undergoer being assigned a Locative Property:

(420)   Tha   mi   nam   thidsear.
        COP.PRS 1.SG in.1.SG.POSS teacher
        'I am (working as) a teacher.'
        "I am in my teacher."

(421) 'S   e   tidsear a   tha   annam.
COP.PRS 3.SG teacher REL COP.PRS in.1.SG
'I am a teacher.'
"A teacher is in me."

These constructions can be represented as based on the predication frame in (422):

(422)   T   R
$(f_1: [(f_2: (x_1)_L(f_2)) (x_2)_U] (f_1))$

In Abkhaz (Hewitt 1979: 46), the meaning of classification is also associated with a different type of construction, namely a two-place Property 'exist as':

(423) Wəy rc'ay°ə-s   də-q'o-Ø-w-p'.
DEM teacher-ADVR 3.SG.SBJ-EX.PREV-COP-PRS-DECL
'He is a teacher.'
"That one is (there) as a teacher."

based on the predication frame for two-place Properties in (424):

(424)   T   R   R
$(f_1: [(f_2) (x_1)_U (x_2)_{Circ}] (f_1))$

In many languages constructions with identificational meaning are closely related in form to classificational constructions, but quite distinct in meaning and use, as in (425):

(425)   R   R
$(f_1: [(x_1) (x_1)] (f_1))$

In such identification constructions, the two semantic units represent alternative ways of viewing the same entity. There is no relation of property assignment, and hence neither of the semantic units contracts a semantic function. Consider the following example from Hixkaryana (Derbyshire 1979: 36) and its analysis:

(426) Rowtī   mokro.
my.brother that.one
'That is my brother.'

(427) R_1 R_2
$(f_i: [(x_i: (f_j: rowtī (f_j)) (x_i)) (x_i: (f_k: mokro (f_k)) (x_i))] (f_i))$

What happens here is that at the Interpersonal Level there are two Referential Subacts, R_1 and R_2, which both refer to the same entity (x_i); at the Representational Level there are simply two coindexed units of the same type.

Certain languages lack an identificational construction. Hengeveld and Mackenzie (2005: 17–18) argue that in such Abkhaz examples as the following (Hewitt 1979: 46; Spruit 1986: 124):

(428) Wəy Zaìra Ø-l-a-w-p'.
       DEM Zaira 3.SG.NH.SBJ-3.SG.F.OBJ-identical-PRS-DECL
       'That's Zaira.'
       "That is identical to Zaira."

the verb –al–ak^w is a two-place lexical stem meaning 'be identical to', so that in this language the identificational meaning (just like the classificational meaning) is to be analysed as involving a two-place Property. In Scottish Gaelic either a copular or a locative construction is used, only the former one being an identificational construction:

(429) Is   e-san   mo bhràthair.
       COP 3.SG-EMPH   my brother

(430) 'S   e   mo bhràthair a   tha ann.
       COP 3.SG my brother   REL COP in.3.SG
       'He is my brother.'

The second construction is becoming dominant, suggesting a disappearance of the identificational construction from the language.

The final type of construction to be included is the existential frame, which at the Interpersonal Level is characterized by a C containing only a single Referential Subact. The analysis at the Representational Level contains only a corresponding semantic unit, without a semantic function, since it is not the argument of any predicate:

(431)   R
       $(f_1: [(v_1)] (f_1))$

The expression of the existential construction differs from language to language: frequently they are signalled by a special particle (Tagalog *may*) or by an impersonal form of a verb (Portuguese *haver*). If the existential clause also has a Location, that will regarded as a modifier of the (e_1) and not as an argument, since it displays the mobility (and the omissibility) typical of the former:

(432)   R   T
       $(e_i: [(f_i: [(x_i: [-lion- (x_i)_\phi])] (f_i)) (e_i)_\phi]: [(l_i: Africa (l_i))_L (e_i)_\phi])$
       'There are lions in Africa.'

3.6.2.4 Inventory of predication frames

Updating the frames listed earlier with the semantic functions of their component parts, we come to the following typology of predication frames, from which languages will make a selection, as well as potentially adding further analogous frames:

1. zero-place Property

   T

   $(f_1: [(f_2)] (f_1))$

2. one-place Property

   T   R

   $(f_1: [(f_2)   (v_1)_A]   (f_1))$
   $(f_1: [(f_2)   (v_1)_U]   (f_1))$
   $(f_1: [(f_2)   (v_1)_L]   (f_1))$
   $(f_1: [(f_2)   (v_1)_{Ref}]   (f_1))$

3. two-place Property

   T   R   R

   $(f_1: [(f_2)   (v_1)_A   (v_2)_U] (f_1))$
   $(f_1: [(f_2)   (v_1)_A   (v_2)_L] (f_1))$
   $(f_1: [(f_2)   (v_1)_U   (v_2)_L] (f_1))$

4. three-place Property

   T   R   R   R

   $(f_1: [(f_2)   (v_1)_A   (v_2)_U   (v_3)_L] (f_1))$

5. four-place Property

   T   R   R   R   R

   $(f_1: [(f_2)   (v_1)_A   (v_2)_U   (v_3)_L   (v_4)_{OTHER}] (f_1))$

6. relational Property

   T   R   R

   $(f_1: [(f_2:   (v_1)_{A/U/OTHER} (f_2))   (v_2)_U] (f_1))$

7. classification

   T   R

   $(f_1: [(v_1)   (v_2)_U] (f_1))$

8. identification

   C   R   R

   $(f_1: [(v_1)   (v_2)] (f_1))$

9. existence

   R

   $(f_1: [(v_1)] (f_1))$

3.6.3 Modifiers

The preceding typology of frames for Properties abstracts from the possibility of adding modifiers at the (f) layer. These modifiers permit the introduction of lexical expressions which introduce further participants into the State-of-Affairs; these further participants are cognitively present in the Conceptual Component, but the available set of frames offers no place for them as arguments. In English, an example of a modifier at this layer is a Beneficiary, naming a person or institution for whose benefit (or sometimes against whose interests) the State-of-Affairs is effected. The modifier status of the Beneficiary (in bold) is apparent from examples like (433), in which all three positions associated with the predicate *give* are already exhausted, with *you* (A), *Mary* (L), and *these flowers* (U):

(433)   Will you give Mary these flowers *for me*?
$$(f_i: [(f_j: give (f_j)) (x_i)_A (m \ prox \ x_j: flower (x_j))_U(x_k)_L] (f_i): (x_l)_{Ben} (f_i))$$

At the Morphosyntactic Level, the semantic function Beneficiary is typically indicated by the preposition *for*, but under certain circumstances it may also be treated there as an Object:

(434)   I bought her a new coat. (= I bought a new coat for her.)

The Beneficiary is regarded as a modifier at the (f_1) layer above all because it represents a participant in the State-of-Affairs for which the grammar offers no room as an argument. A similar motivation lies behind regarding Comitative (C) and Instrument (Ins) as modifiers at this layer:

(435)   John went to Paris with Mary
$$(f_i: [(f_j: go (f_j)) (x_i)_A (x_j: Paris (x_j))_L] (f_i): (x_k)_C (f_i))$$

(436)   John cut the meat with a knife
$$(f_i: [(f_j: cut (f_j)) (x_i))_A (x_j: meat (x_j))_U] (f_i): (x_k: knife (x_k))_{Ins} (f_i))$$

Apart from additional participants, the modifiers of Configurational Properties may also designate certain types of Manner. Manner is relevant to various layers, but with differences in behaviour. As observed by Himmelmann and Schulze-Berndt (2006), drawing on Geuder (2000), the attachment points of Manner adverbials can vary considerably. Consider the following examples and their analyses:

(437)   John walked slowly.
$$(f_i: [(f_j: walk (f_j)): [(m_i: -slow- (m_i)) (f_j)_\Phi]) (x_i)_A] (f_i))$$

In this case, the Manner expression modifies only the predicate *walk*: it is the walking that was slow, but this by itself does not make John a slow person.

The usual interpretation of (438), however, is different:

(438)   John stupidly answered the question.
$(e_i: [(f_i: [(f_j: answer (f_j)) (x_i)_A (p_i: -question- (p_i))_U] (f_i)) (e_i)_\phi]:$
$[(f_k: stupid (f_k)) (e_i)_\phi])$

John's answer may have been very intelligent, but it was stupid of him to answer the question at all (rather than insist on remaining silent). Here it is therefore the State-of-Affairs which is characterized as stupid, as reflected in the fact that the manner expression occupies the position of the e-modifier.

Different again are examples like (439):

(439)   John angrily left the room.
$(e_i: [(f_i: [(f_j: leave (f_j)) (x_i)_A (l_i: -room- (l_i))_U] (f_i): [(m_i: -angry- (m_i))$
$(f_i)_\phi]) (e_i)_\phi])$

which cannot be paraphrased as *It was angry of John to leave the room* and in which the Manner expression does not modify merely the 'leaving': there is no question of John performing an 'angry leaving'. Rather, (439) is understood as meaning that the Configurational Property that is the head of the State-of-Affairs had the Property of being 'angry'—perhaps John slammed the door or kicked at the cat!

In certain languages where there is no morphological distinction between adjectives and adverbs, e.g. in German as discussed by Himmelmann and Schulze-Berndt (2006: 2), there is no formal distinction between (439) and (440):

(440)   John left the room angry.

where the adjective *angry* clearly applies only to John and is understood as a secondary predication or 'depictive' or 'participant-oriented adjunct' in Himmelmann and Schulze-Berndt's terms. In FDG, (440) will be analysed at the Representational Level as (441).

(441) $(e_i: [(f_i: [(f_j: leave_V (f_j)) (x_i)_A (l_i: room_N (l_i))_U] (f_i)) (e_i)_\phi]: [(f_k:$
$[(f_l: angry_A (f_l)) (x_i)_U] (f_k)) (e_i)_\phi])$

Here the State-of-Affairs variable (e_i) is restricted by two predication frames. *Angry* is the predicate of the second one. Note that this is thus not a Manner expression, but a secondary predication, with a coindexed participant (here x_i) occurring in both the primary and the secondary predications.

Thus, of the various examples discussed here, only (439) contains a modifier of a Configurational Property. The modifier in (437) applies at the layer of a lexically headed Property (see 3.7), and those in (438) and (440) at the layer of the State-of-Affairs.

A final modifier category at this layer concerns those elements that quantify the internal temporal constituency of a State-of-Affairs. The most prominent member of this category is Duration, which resembles Event Quantification in that it quantifies, but differs from it in that it does not quantify over States-of-Affairs, but rather defines the internal temporal extension of a single State-of-Affairs. Examples are the following:

(442)   He has lived here *for ten years*.

(443)   He waited *for three hours*.

3.6.4 Operators

The operator categories at the layer of Configurational Properties characterizing States-of-Affairs belong to three different categories: Aspect, Participant-oriented modality, and Quantification. We will discuss these one by one.

3.6.4.1 Aspect

Aspectual distinctions specify the internal temporal constituency of a State-of-Affairs, and therefore operate at the layer of the Configurational Property characterizing that State-of-Affairs. Aspect is different from relative tense in that it does not have a situating function: an aspectually characterized State-of-Affairs still can be located at any point in time. In FDG this is reflected in the fact that relative tense is a higher operator than aspect, the latter being part of the Configurational Property characterizing a State-of-Affairs.

Following Dik (1997a), we make a distinction at this layer between the Perfective–Imperfective opposition on the one hand, and a series of Phasal Aspect distinctions on the other. To start with the latter, these indicate the relation between the temporal reference point and a phase within the development of a State-of-Affairs. Consider the following examples from Welsh (Awbery 1976, cited in Dik 1997a with his informal gloss):

(444)   Mae ef ar weld   y   ddrama.
        is   he on seeing the play
        'He is about to see the play.'

(445)   Mae 'r dyn yn gweld y   ci.
        is   the man in seeing the dog
        'The man is seeing the dog.'

(446)   Mae 'r dyn wedi gweld y   ci.
        is   the man after seeing the dog
        'The man has seen the dog.'

In (444) the State-of-Affairs is characterized as being about to happen at the reference point (Prospective Aspect), in (445) as happening at the reference point (Progressive Aspect), and in (446) as having happened before the reference point (Resultative Aspect). In each case the aspectual specification relates the Configurational Property to a temporal reference point. Other possibilities in the domain of Phasal Aspect are the Ingressive and Egressive Aspects.

The Perfective–Imperfective opposition indicates whether a State-of-Affairs is presented as a single whole (Perfective), or as viewed from within (Imperfective). The combination of the two helps to show how different States-of-Affairs relate to one another in their temporal development. Consider the following Italian example:

(447) Gianni leggeva   quando entrai.
       Gianni read.PST.IMPF when   enter.PST.PFV
       'Gianni was reading when I came in.'

This combination of aspect indicates that the State-of-Affairs of entering was rounded off within the time span of the State-of-Affairs of reading.

The need to treat aspectual distinctions as operators on Configurational Properties of States-of-Affairs is manifested, among other things, in their interaction with the Aktionsart of predication frames. Thus, a stative predication frame like *someone know someone* becomes dynamic when combined with ingressive aspect, as in *someone get to know someone*, as is evident from the tests in (448)–(449):

(448) *John knew his colleagues quickly.   (−Dynamic)

(449) John got to know his colleagues quickly. (+Dynamic)

Similarly, the application of a Prospective, Progressive, or Resultative operator to a dynamic predication frame in English turns it into a non-dynamic one with respect to higher processes. Consider the following examples (see Steedman 1977):

(450) What he did was run. (+Dynamic)

(451) *What he did was going to run/be running/have run. (−Dynamic)

The perfective/imperfective distinction may affect the momentaneousness of an SoA, as in (452), where the imperfective value of the progressive cancels the momentaneousness of *reach* (see Comrie 1976: 43):

(452) a. The soldiers reached the summit.   (+Momentaneous)
       b. The soldiers were reaching the summit. (−Momentaneous)

This feature-changing property of many aspectual categories indicates that they can be analysed as operating internally within the State-of-Affairs.

3.6.4.2 Participant-oriented modality

This type of modality affects the relational part of the utterance as expressed by a predicate and its arguments and concerns the relation between a participant in a State-of-Affairs and the potential realization of that State-of-Affairs (cf. Foley and Van Valin 1984: 215). Participant-oriented modalities are better known from the literature as agent-oriented modalities. Although widely used, this term is not too felicitous in that it suggests that only controlling participants in dynamic States-of-Affairs may be subject to this type of modalization. That this is not the case is apparent from such examples as:

(453)   John wants to be young again.

The term participant-oriented modality is neutral as to the State-of-Affairs type in which this class of modal expressions occurs. Three main subcategories of participant-oriented modality may be distinguished on the basis of the domain of evaluation they are concerned with: Facultative, Deontic, and Volitive.

Facultative participant-oriented modality describes the ability of a participant to engage in the State-of-Affairs type designated by the predicate. In some languages a distinction is made between intrinsic ('be able to') and acquired ('know how to') ability, as shown in the following examples from Mapuche, which has separate auxiliaries for these two types of ability (Smeets 1989: 219):

(454)   Pepí   kuθaw-la-n.
        INTR.ABIL work-NEG-DECL.1.SG
        'I am not able to work.'

(455)   Kim   tuku-fi-n.
        ACQ.ABIL put.at-OBJ-DECL.1.SG
        'I know how to put it.'

Spanish makes the same distinction. Intrinsic ability is expressed by the modal verb *poder* 'be able to', acquired ability by the verb *saber* 'know (how to)' in its modal use.

Inability may also acquire the status of a separate category, as in the Turkish Impotential (457), which may be compared with its Potential (456), used for ability (Lewis 1967: 151):

(456)   Gel-ebil-di-Ø.
        come-ABIL-PST-3
        'He was able to come.'

(457)   Gel-eme-di-Ø.
        come-INABIL-PST-3
        'He was unable to come.'

Deontic participant-oriented modalities describe a participant's being under the obligation or having permission to engage in the State-of-Affairs type designated by the predicate. Obligation seems to be encoded by grammatical means more often than permission. The following example is from Imbabura Quechua (Cole 1982: 151):

(458)   Miku-na ka-rka-ni.
        eat-OBLG COP-PST-1
        'I must eat.'
        "I am to eat."

Volitive participant-oriented modality describes a participant's desire to engage in the State-of-Affairs type designated by the predicate. The following example is from Guajajara (Bendor-Samuel 1972: 95):

(459)   Za-hem   rəm.
        1.PL.INCL-leave VOL
        'We want to leave.'

The difference between event-oriented modality (3.5.4.3) and participant-oriented modality is that event-oriented modality characterizes States-of-Affairs as generally desirable, obligatory, etc., while with participant-oriented modality the desire originates from a specific participant, the obligation rests on a specific participant, etc. Given that they operate at different layers, the two may be combined, as in:

(460)   You have to be able to swim (to participate in this course.)

Here a general obligation concerning the abilities of a participant is specified. The scope differences are reflected in the following underlying representation of the relevant layers of (460):

(461)   (obl e_i: (abil [(f_i: [(f_j: swim (f_j)) (x_i)$_A$] (f_i)) ($e_i)_\phi$]))

Alongside event-oriented and participant-oriented modality, we have recognized a category of propositional modality, which deals with propositional attitudes and inferences. The following example from Turkish (Lewis 1967: 151), containing all three types of modality, illustrates the differences between them:

(462)   Anlı-y-abil-ecek-miş-im.
        understand-Ø-ABIL-IRR-INFER-1.SG
        'I gather that I will be able to understand.'

In this example the ability suffix -abıl (preceded by an obligatory intervocalic -y-) expresses a participant-oriented modality. The first singular subject is said to have the capacity of engaging in the relation expressed by the predicate. The irrealis suffix -ecek expresses an event-oriented modality. The State-of-Affairs described by the sentence is characterized as non-actual, which is in this case, but not necessarily, reflected in the translation by means of a future tense. The inferential suffix -miş expresses a proposition-oriented modality. It signals that the Speaker does not fully commit him/herself to the Propositional Content of his assertion.

3.6.4.3 Quantification

As the grammatical counterpart of the Duration modifiers in 3.6.3, some languages have grammatical means to express the internal temporal extension of a State-of-Affairs. The following example is from West Greenlandic (Fortescue 1984: 282):

(463)   Ukisi-uar-puq.
        stare-CONT-3.SG.IND
        'He stares continuously.'

The equivalent nature of modifier and operators of duration shows up in the fact that in West Greenlandic continuous aspect does not have to be expressed when a lexical expression of duration is present. This is illustrated in (464) (Fortescue 1984: 242):

(464)   Nalunaaqutta-p akunnir-a   naa-llugu
        clock-REL   space.between-POSS.3.SG complete-SIM
        qia-vuq.
        cry-3.SG.IND
        'He cried for a whole hour.'

Here the duration is described in a simultaneity clause and not marked on the main verb qia 'cry' itself.

3.6.5 Frames

In sum, the set of primitives for the Representational Level provides the following frame for the layer of the Configurational Property:

(465) $(\pi \, f_1: [(v_i) \dots (v_{1+N})_{(\phi)}] \, (f_1): [\sigma \, (f_1)_\phi])$

Heads of Configurational Properties are combinations of semantic categories of a wide range of quantitative and qualitative valencies.
The operator position in (465) may be filled by operators expressing aspect, participant-oriented modality, and/or quantity.

The modifier position in (465) may be filled by lexical expressions specifying additional participants, manner, and/or duration.

3.7 Lexical Properties

3.7.1 Introduction

Having discussed Configurational Properties in 3.6, we will now turn our attention to Lexical Properties (henceforth simply 'Properties'). As has become evident in earlier sections and will be reaffirmed in later ones, semantic categories may in general, among other strategies, be designated by Lexical Property expressions, either in head or in modifier position. To illustrate this once more, let us start with the following three Property expressions:

(466) $(f_i: \text{man} (f_i))$

(467) $(f_j: \text{intelligent} (f_j))$

(468) $(f_k: \text{high} (f_k))$

The latter two are used in the formation of (469):

(469) $(f_j: \text{intelligent} (f_j): [(f_k: \text{high} (f_k)) (f_j)_\Phi])$
        'highly intelligent'

in which (f_k) is used as a Property of a Property. (467) and (468) may then in turn be used to characterize an Individual, as in (470):

(470) $(x_i: [(f_i: \text{man} (f_i)) (x_i)_\Phi]: [(f_j: \text{intelligent} (f_j): [(f_k: \text{high} (f_k)) (f_j)_\Phi]) (x_i)_\Phi])$

This simple example clearly shows the importance of Properties in building up semantic representations of other semantic categories through their application in predication frames at different levels of semantic organization.

The kind of Property slot that classes of lexical items, parts-of-speech, may or may not occupy depends not only on the position that slot occupies within the underlying semantic representation, but also on the interpersonal function with which that slot is used. A large part of 3.7.2 on the heads of Properties will be dedicated to the issue of the distribution of parts-of-speech. 3.7.3 then looks at the possible modifiers of Properties, and 3.7.4 goes on to discuss operators of Properties.

3.7.2 Heads

3.7.2.1 Introduction

Before turning to the issue of parts-of-speech, we will first indicate in 3.7.2.2 what kinds of lexical head may be distinguished as regards their complexity.

Particularly relevant in this respect is the issue of compounding. After that we will define parts-of-speech in terms of the distinctions made at the Interpersonal Level and the Representational Level in 3.7.2.3.

3.7.2.2 Simple and compositional heads

Simple heads have been exemplified throughout this and in the previous section. Simple lexical heads may be dropped, leading to empty-headed constructions, as in the following Spanish example:

(471) un-a   casa   antigu-a y   un-a   modern-a
       INDF-F.SG house(F) old-F.SG and INDF-F.SG modern-F.SG
       'an old house and a modern one'

The noun phrases in (471) may be represented as in (472):

(472) $(x_i: (f_i: casa (f_i)) (x_i): (f_j: antigu- (f_j)) (x_i)) \& (x_j: (f_i) (x_j): (f_k: modern- (f_k)) (x_j))$

Note that coindexation of the variables (f_i) for the heads in (472) makes the Property *casa* available in the second noun phrase. The presence of the empty head shows up in the agreement of the adjective *moderna* with the understood feminine head *casa*.

Heads are complex when two or more lexical elements together express a single concept, as in the case of composition (for an earlier treatment of compounding in FG, as applied to Turkish, see van Schaaik 1992). Endocentric and exocentric compounds may be represented in the following way:

(473) $(f_1: (f_2: \blacklozenge (f_2): (f_3: \blacklozenge (f_3)) (f_2)) (f_1))$ Endocentric

(474) $(f_1: (f_2: \blacklozenge (f_2)) (f_3: \blacklozenge (f_3)) (f_1))$ Exocentric

In (473) (f_3) is a modifier of (f_2), with the result that the head of (f_2) is the head of the compound. In (474) (f_2) and (f_3) together constitute the head of (f_1). Examples from Dutch are given in (475) and (476) respectively:

(475) was-machine
       washing-machine
       'washing machine'
       $(f_i: (f_j: machine (f_j): (f_k: was (f_k)) (f_j)) (f_i))$

(476) zoet-zuur
       sweet-sour
       'sweet and sour'
       $(f_i: (f_j: zoet (f_j)) (f_k: zuur (f_k)) (f_i))$

This treatment of compounding also applies to nuclear serialization. In 3.6 we dealt with core serialization as a combination of two or more Configurational Properties of States-of-Affairs. Nuclear serialization concerns the combination of two Lexical Properties to form a compound Property expression. The following example from Nêlêmwa (Bril 2004: 15) is particularly telling in this respect:

(477)   Hla   diya hââhuux-e   mwa   eli.
        3.PL do   be.recent-TR house DEM.ANAPH
        'They built this house recently.'

As shown in (477), Nêlêmwa uses transitivity markers. In this example the transitivity marker occurs on the second verb, which when used by itself would be intransitive. This shows that the two verbs together are treated as a transitive predicate.

The treatment of compounding suggested here does not apply to synthetic compounding. Consider the following example:

(478)   sword-swallower

As Booij (2005: 90), from whom example (478) is taken, remarks, this type of compound raises the problem that *swallower* does not occur as a word on its own. A further property is that *sword* is an argument of *swallow*. Anticipating discussion of cases like this in 3.8, we analyse this type of compound in the following way:

(479) $(x_i: [(f_i: [(f_j: swallow (f_j)) (x_i)_A (x_j: -sword- (x_j))_U] (f_i))])$

Note that we use a configurational two-place Property frame as the head of the Individual (x_i), which also figures as an Actor argument within the predication frame itself. The resulting verbal expression is then subjected to -*er* derivation in the morphosyntactic encoder.

3.7.2.3 Parts-of-speech

3.7.2.3.1 *Introduction*   The issue of parts-of-speech is one that is relevant not only at the Representational Level, but also at the Morphosyntactic Level. We correspondingly make a distinction between LEXEME CLASSES at the Representational Level, and WORD CLASSES at the Morphosyntactic Level. This distinction is necessary since there is no one-to-one relation between lexeme class and word class. We can illustrate this by repeating example (479) with the lexeme class indications:

(480) $(x_i: (f_i: [(f_j: swallow_V (f_j)) (x_i)_A (x_j: -sword_N- (x_j))_U] (f_i)) (x_i))$

This underlying semantic representation has two lexical elements, of the lexeme classes verb and noun. The output after processing by the morphosyntactic encoder will be of the word class noun (Nw), with the following structure:

(481) $(Nw_i: [(Ns_i: sword (Ns_i)) (Vs_i: swallow (Vs_i)) (Aff_i: er (Aff_i))] (Nw_i))$

Similarly, consider the following representation:

$$T$$
(482) $(f_i: dance_V (f_i): (f_j: beautiful_A (f_j)) (f_i))$
'dance beautifully'

In this underlying semantic representation the modifier of the verb *dance* is given as an adjectival lexeme. At the Morphosyntactic Level, this will be expressed as an Adverbial Word. There are thus several morphosyntactic processes that can be interpreted as means to adapt the class of a lexeme in such a way that the resulting word can be used appropriately in the grammatical environment in which it occurs. In this section we will concentrate on lexeme classes, leaving the discussion of word classes for Chapter 4.

The architecture we have developed so far allows us to come to a precise characterization of the functions of lexeme classes in terms of their distribution across slots in the underlying Interpersonal and Representational configurations. We will first consider the potential functions of lexemes in 3.7.2.3.2, then consider how lexeme classes can be defined in terms of these functions in 3.7.2.3.3, and after that go into the question of lexical derivation in 3.7.2.3.4.

3.7.2.3.2 *Functions of lexemes*   In defining the function of a lexeme we use two main parameters: (i) its status as a head or as a modifier; and (ii) the Subact status of this category at the Interpersonal Level. Further subdivisions may then be sensitive to the nature of the semantic category designated.

Let us start with the combination of parameters (i) and (ii), limiting ourselves to independent Referential and Ascriptive Subacts, i.e. those that are not embedded within other Subacts. Cross-classifying this parameter with the distinction between heads and modifiers at the Representational Level, we arrive at four possible functional slots, which are represented in (483)–(486) (see Hengeveld and van Lier 2008). Recall that the symbol ◆ represents a lexical head:

$$T \qquad\qquad T$$
(483) $(f_1: \quad ◆ \quad (f_1): [\sigma \qquad\qquad (f_1)_\phi])$

$$T \qquad\qquad T$$
(484) $(f_1: \quad ◆ \quad (f_1): [(f_2: ◆ (f_2)) \quad (f_1)_\phi])$

$$\text{(485)} \quad \begin{matrix} R & T & & T \\ (v_1: & [(f_1: \blacklozenge (f_2)) & (v_1)_\phi]: & [\sigma & (v_1)_\phi]) \end{matrix}$$

$$\text{(486)} \quad \begin{matrix} R & T & & T \\ (v_1: & [(f_1: \blacklozenge (f_2)) & (v_1)_\phi]: & [(f_2: \blacklozenge (f_2)) & (v_1)_\phi]) \end{matrix}$$

A close look at these representations shows that all lexical elements are the heads of representational layers of the f-type. This is another way of saying that lexical items designate properties. Only when used as the main predicate of a clause does this f-unit correspond directly to an independent Ascriptive Subact. In all other cases it corresponds to an Ascriptive Subact within higher Ascriptive or higher Referential Subacts. Thus, limiting ourselves first to these higher Subacts, the functions of the lexical items ($\blacklozenge$) in (483)–(486) may be defined as in (487)–(490):

(487) head of an f-unit that is used as an independent Ascriptive Subact (483)

(488) head of an f-unit that is a modifier of an f-unit that is used as an independent Ascriptive Subact (484)

(489) head of an f-unit that is the head of a representational unit that is used as a Referential Subact (485)

(490) head of an f-unit that is a modifier of an f-unit that is the head of a representational unit that is used as a Referential Subact (486)

These definitions are precise yet cumbersome, so (491)–(494) will be our shorthand versions:

(491) head within an independent Ascriptive Subact (483)

(492) modifier within an independent Ascriptive Subact (484)

(493) head within a Referential Subact (485)

(494) modifier within a Referential Subact (486)

where the notions head and modifier refer to the use of the Lexical Property at the Representational Level, not at the Interpersonal Level.

These functions find their lexical counterparts in example (495), which may be represented as in (496):

(495) The tall girl sings well.

(496) (e$_i$: [(f$_i$: [T   T

(f$_j$:   sing$_V$ (f$_j$):   [(f$_k$: well (f$_k$)) (f$_j$)$_\phi$])

R   T   T

(x$_i$:   [(f$_l$: girl (f$_l$))   (x$_i$)$_\phi$]:   [(f$_m$: tall (f$_m$)) (x$_i$)$_\phi$])]

(f$_i$)) (e$_i$)$_\phi$])

None of the functions identified so far is sufficient to directly define lexeme classes. Let us illustrate this for the function of head within an Ascriptive Subact. In many languages various classes of lexemes can be used in this function. Compare the following Dutch examples:

(497) Jan *werk*-t.
Jan work-PRS.3.SG
'Jan works.'

(498) Jan is   *timmerman.*
Jan COP.PRS.3.SG carpenter
'Jan is a carpenter.'
"Jan is carpenter."

(499) Jan is   *ziek.*
Jan COP.PRS.3.SG ill
'Jan is ill.'

(500) Jan is   *net-jes*
Jan COP.PRS.3.SG well.organized-ADVR
'Jan is well-organized.'

These sentences illustrate the use of a Dutch verb (497), noun (498), adjective (499), and Manner adverb (500) as the head of an independent Ascriptive Subact. The predicates in examples (497)–(500) are represented as (501)–(504):

T
(501) (f$_1$: werk$_V$ (f$_i$))

T
(502) (f$_i$: timmerman$_N$ (f$_i$))

T
(503) (f$_i$: ziek$_A$ (f$_i$))

T
(504) (f$_i$: netjes$_{Adv}$ (f$_i$))

Thus, at the Representational Level four lexeme classes may go into the same slot. At the Morphosyntactic Level, however, three of these require copula insertion, and only verbs can directly be used predicatively. We may thus define the verbal lexeme class on the basis of the fact that it can be used in the relevant function without further morphosyntactic adaptation. Similar definitions can be given for the other classes of lexemes in relation to their distinguishing functions.

The various classes of lexemes also differ to a considerable extent in the kind of element that can modify them. Consider the following examples:

(505) Jan werkt   *hard.*
       Jan work-PRS.3.SG hard
       'Jan works hard.'

(506) Jan is   *voormalig* timmerman.
       Jan COP.PRS.3.SG former   carpenter
       'Jan is a former carpenter.'
       "Jan is former carpenter."

(507) Jan is   *erg* ziek.
       J.   COP.PRS.3.SG very ill
       'Jan is very ill.'

(508) Jan is   *erg* net-jes
       J.   COP.PRS.3.SG very well.organized-ADVR
       'Jan is *very* well organized.'

In Dutch, adjectival and adverbial heads may be modified by the same degree adverbs, but verbal and nominal heads mainly take their own classes of modifiers. These may be represented as in (509)–(512):

(509) $(f_i: werk_V$ $(f_i): [(f_j: hard_{Adv}$ $(f_j))$ $(f_i)_\phi])$

(510) $(f_i: timmerman-_N$ $(f_i): [(f_j: voormalig_{Adj}$ $(f_j))$ $(f_i)_\phi])$

(511) $(f_i: ziek_{Adj}$ $(f_i): [(f_j: erg_{Adv}$ $(f_j))$ $(f_i)_\phi])$

(512) $(f_i: netjes_{Adv}$ $(f_i): [(f_j: erg_{Adv}$ $(f_j))$ $(f_i)_\phi])$

Note that in these cases the interpersonal status of the unit under consideration is irrelevant. We find the following constructions side by side:

(513) een *erg* *ziek* kind
       INDF very ill   child
       'a very sick child'

(514) Het kind is   *erg* *ziek.*
       DEF child COP.PRS.3.SG very ill
       'The child is very ill.'

In (513) *erg ziek* as a whole is a modifier within a Referential Subact, in (514) it is the head within an Ascriptive Subact.

There are further classes of modifier at higher layers of semantic organization. Consider the following representations:

$$\text{T}$$

(515) $(f_i: \quad \text{–she has been drinking– } (f_i): \quad [(f_k: \text{continuous } (f_k)))   (f_i)_\phi])$
       'She has been drinking continuously.'

$$\text{T}$$

(516) $(e_i: \quad \text{–she has been drinking– } (e_i): \quad [(f_k: \text{again } (f_k))   (e_i)_\phi])$
       'She has been drinking again.'

$$\text{T}$$

(517) $(ep_i: \text{–she has been drinking– } (ep_i): \quad [(f_k: \text{today } (f_k))   (ep_i)_\phi])$
       'She has been drinking today.'

$$\text{T}$$

(518) $(p_i: \quad \text{–she has been drinking– } (p_i): \quad [(f_k: \text{probable } (f_k))   (p_i)_\phi])$
       'She probably has been drinking.'

These configurations differ from the ones in (509)–(512) in that in the latter the modifier modifies a lexical head, while in (515)–(518) it modifies a non-lexical head. These heads are of increasing representational complexity: Configurational Property in (515), State-of-Affairs in (516), Episode in (517), and Propositional Content in (518). As we have shown throughout this chapter, each of these layers takes its own class of modifiers. The fact that these modifiers indeed constitute separate classes is evident from the fact that they may be combined with one another, as in (519):

(519) She probably has been drinking continuously again today.

The ordering of the lexical modifiers in (519) reflects their differences in scope, as we will show in 4.4.2.

The functional configurations discussed so far all concerned independent Subacts. We will now turn to Embedded Subacts, i.e. Subacts occurring within other Subacts. This notion is relevant for the analysis of lexemes occurring within predication frames with an 'internal argument', as discussed in 3.6.2.3.2. Recall that, for instance, relational adjectives receive the treatment illustrated in (520):

(520) $(f_i: [(f_j: \text{fond } (f_j)) (x_i: \text{–chocolate– } (x_i))_{Ref}] (f_i))$
       'fond of chocolate'

Here the Property (f_j) *fond* takes the internal argument (x_i) *chocolate*. This combination of elements then constitutes a Configurational Property (f_i) that may be applied recursively to an external argument in a one-place predication frame:

$$
\begin{array}{ccc}
\text{T} & \text{T} & \text{R}
\end{array}
$$

(521) $(f_k: [(f_i: [(f_j: \text{fond } (f_j)) (x_i: -\text{chocolate}- (x_i))_{Ref}] (f_i)) (x_j)_\phi] (f_k))$
'He is fond of chocolate.'

A variety of elements may go into slots such as (f_j) in (521), such as the ones in (522)–(526):

(522) (I had never heard of her) *before* we met.

(523) (I met her) *inside* the building

(524) the *aunt* of my friend the football trainer

(525) the *inside* of the building

(526) a person *fond* of chocolate

If we combine the general predication frame for these expressions with an indication of the interpersonal status of their components, we get the following picture:

$$
\begin{array}{cccc}
\text{R} & \text{T} & \text{T} & \text{R}
\end{array}
$$

(527) $(v_1: [(f_1: [(f_2: \blacklozenge (f_2)) (v_2)_\phi] (f_1)) (v_1)_\phi]: [\sigma \qquad\qquad (v_1)_\phi])$

$$
\begin{array}{c}
\text{R} \qquad\qquad\qquad\qquad\qquad\qquad\qquad \text{T} \quad \text{T} \qquad \text{R}
\end{array}
$$

(528) $(v_1: [(f_1: \blacklozenge (f_1)) \qquad\qquad (v_1)_\phi]: [(f_1: [(f_2: \blacklozenge (f_2)) (v_2)_\phi] (f_1)) (v_1)_\phi])$

$$
\begin{array}{c}
\qquad\qquad\qquad\qquad\qquad\qquad\qquad\qquad \text{T} \quad \text{T} \qquad \text{R}
\end{array}
$$

(529) $(v_1: [.................])$ $\qquad (v_1): \quad [(f_1: [(f_2: \blacklozenge (f_2)) (v_2)_\phi] (f_1)) (v_1)_\phi])$

The head of the Referential Subact in (527) hosts lexical elements such as the ones illustrated in (524)–(525). (524) is represented as (531):

$$
\begin{array}{cccc}
\text{R} & \text{T} & \text{T} & \text{R}
\end{array}
$$

(531) $(x_i: [(f_i: [(f_j: \text{aunt } (f_j)) (x_j: -\text{my friend the football trainer}- (x_j))_{Ref}] (f_i)) (x_i)_\phi])$

The modifier position in (528) hosts Configurational Properties modifying within a (lexically headed) Referential Subact. It hosts lexical elements such as the one illustrated in (526), and represented in (532):

$$\text{R} \qquad\qquad\qquad \text{T} \quad \text{T} \qquad\qquad \text{R}$$

(532) $(x_i: -\text{person}- (x_i)_\Phi: [(f_i: [(f_j: \text{fond} (f_j)) (x_j: -\text{chocolate}- (x_j))_{Ref}] (f_i))$
$(x_i)_\Phi])$
'a person fond of chocolate'

Note, again, that the uses of the lexemes given by way of illustration here are their distinguishing uses, not their sole uses. Thus, all three may be used predicatively, but then require copula support.

Finally, the modifier position characterized in (529) hosts modifiers of complex representational layers, just like the direct lexical modifiers in (515)–(518). The difference is that in (529), as in (527)–(528), the lexical elements are used indirectly, in the (f_2) position within the modifier slot. This class includes *before* and *inside* in (522)–(523). Compare the following representation of (523) with the one of a simple lexical modifier in (516):

$$\qquad\qquad\qquad \text{T} \quad \text{T} \qquad\qquad \text{R}$$

(530) $(e_i: -\text{I met her}- (e_i)): [(f_i: [(f_j: \text{inside} (f_j)) (l_i: -\text{building}- (l_i))_{Ref}] (f_i))$
$(e_i)_\Phi])$
'I met her inside the building.'

3.7.2.3.3 *Lexeme classes* Now that the principal functions of lexemes have been identified, the question arises how lexeme classes are distributed across these functions. Let us first assume that a language differentiates maximally in the sense that it has lexical elements for every single functional specification; we would then end up with a list like the following, in which preposed superscripts indicate subclasses of modifying lexemes in terms of the head they modify:

In Independent Subacts:

$$\qquad \text{T}$$
(533) $(f_1: \quad \text{Verb} \qquad\qquad (f_1): \qquad [(f_2: {}^V\text{Adverb} \qquad (f_2)) \quad (f_1)_\Phi])$

$$\qquad \text{T}$$
(534) $(f_1: \quad \text{Noun} \qquad\qquad (f_1): \qquad [(f_2: {}^N\text{Adjective} \quad (f_2)) \quad (f_1)_\Phi])$

$$\qquad \text{T}$$
(535) $(f_1: \quad \text{Adjective} \qquad (f_1): \qquad [(f_2: {}^{Adj}\text{Adverb} \quad (f_2)) \quad (f_1)_\Phi])$

$$\qquad \text{T}$$
(536) $(f_1: \quad \text{Adverb} \qquad\quad (f_1): \qquad [(f_2: {}^{Adv}\text{Adverb} \quad (f_2)) \quad (f_1)_\Phi])$

$$\qquad \text{R}$$
(537) $(v_1: \quad [(f_1: \text{Noun} (f_2)) \quad (v_1)_\Phi]: \quad [(f_2: {}^v\text{Adjective} \quad (f_2)) \quad (v_1)_\Phi])$

$$(538) \quad (f_1: \quad [\ldots\ldots\ldots] \quad (f_1): \quad \overset{T}{[((f_2: {}^f Adverb \quad (f_2)) \quad (f_1)_\Phi])}$$

$$(539) \quad (e_i: \quad [\ldots\ldots\ldots] \quad (e_i): \quad \overset{T}{[(f_1: {}^e Adverb \quad (f_1)) \quad (e_i)_\Phi])}$$

$$(540) \quad (ep_i: \quad [\ldots\ldots\ldots] \quad (ep_i): \quad \overset{T}{[(f_1: {}^{ep} Adverb \quad (f_1)) \quad (ep_i)_\Phi])}$$

$$(541) \quad (p_i: \quad [\ldots\ldots\ldots] \quad (p_i): \quad \overset{T}{[(f_1: {}^P Adverb \quad (f_1)) \quad (p_i)_\Phi])}$$

And in Embedded Subacts:

$$\begin{array}{l}
\overset{R \quad T \quad T}{} \quad \quad \quad \quad \overset{R}{} \\
(542) \quad (v_1: [(f_1: [\ (f_2: Noun(f_2)) \quad (v_2)_\Phi] \ (f_1)) \ (v_1)_\Phi]: \quad [\sigma \ (v_1)_\Phi]) \\
\overset{R \quad T}{} \quad \quad \quad \quad \quad \quad \overset{T}{} \quad \quad \quad \quad \quad \quad \quad \overset{R}{} \\
(543) \quad (v_1: [(f_1: Noun \ (f_1)) \ (v_1): \quad [(f_1: [\ (f_2: {}^f Adjective \ (f_2)) \quad (v_2)_{Ref}] \ (f_1)) \ (v_1)_\Phi]) \\
\overset{R \quad T}{} \quad \quad \quad \quad \quad \quad \quad \quad \quad \quad \overset{T}{} \quad \quad \quad \quad \quad \quad \quad \quad \overset{R}{} \\
(544) \quad (v_1: [\ldots\ldots\ldots\ldots] \quad [(f_1: [\ (f_2: Adposition \ (f_2)) \quad (v_2)_{Ref}] \ (f_1)) \ (v_1)_\Phi])
\end{array}$$

Languages do not necessarily have specialized lexeme classes for all the functions listed here. Some languages use a single class of lexemes in more than one function. Others lack lexical items for a certain function and have to resort to syntactic solutions instead. The former are called 'flexible', the latter 'rigid' in Hengeveld (1992) and Hengeveld *et al.* (2004). By way of illustration of these two situations, consider the following examples, which concern the distribution of lexemes across the functions of head and modifier within Ascriptive and Referential Acts, i.e. the functions identified in (533) and (537).

In Warao (Romero-Figeroa 1997: 49, 50, 119) the same lexical item may be used as the head within a Referential Subact (545), as a modifier within a Referential Subact (546), and as a modifier within an Ascriptive Subact (547):

(545) *yakera*
beauty
'beauty'

(546) Hiaka *yakera* auka saba tai nisa-n-a-e.
garment beauty daughter for she buy-SG-PUNCT-PST
'She bought a beautiful dress for her daughter.'

(547) Oko kuana   yaota-te   arone   *yakera* nahoro-te...
       we   hardness work-NONPST although beauty eat-NONPST
       'Although we work hard and eat well, ...'

The situation in Garo (Tibeto-Karen; Burling 1961: 27, 33) is rather different. It has classes of nouns and verbs, but no adjectives and only a limited number of manner adverbs. In order to modify a head noun within
a Referential Subact, a relative clause has to be formed on the basis of
a verbal lexeme, as illustrated in (548) and (549). In (548b), the verb *ca'*
'eat' is turned into the predicate of a relative clause by the addition of the
relativizing suffix *-gipa*. The notionally adjectival but morphologically verbal lexeme *da'r* 'big' in (549b) receives exactly the same treatment. Thus
we can say that the function of modification within Referential Subacts is
achieved in Garo by means of relative clauses, not by lexical modifiers. These
relative clauses are built on the basis of verbs that fulfil the function of
ascription within the relative clause, in the same way as they do in main
clauses.

(548) a. *Ca'*-gen-ma?
           eat-FUT-INT
           'Will you eat?'

       b. *ca'*-gipa man.de
           eat-REL man
           'the man who eats.'

(549) a. *Da'r*-an-gen.
           big-ITIVE-FUT
           'It will get big.'

       b. *da'r*-gipa man.de
           big-REL   man
           'the big man'

In a similar way, in order to modify a head verb within an Ascriptive Subact, in
most cases a manner adverbial clause has to be created on the basis of a verb,
as illustrated in (550) (Burling 1961: 29):

(550) a. Bi.a *gar-e*   kat-an-aha.
           3.SG throw-SUB run-ITIVE-PST
           'Throwing he ran away.'

       b. *Rak-e*   dok-aha.
           strong-SUB hit-PST
           'He hit hard.'

Language	head within Ascriptive Subact	head within Referential Subact	modifier within Referential Subact	modifier within Ascriptive Subact
Warao	Verb	Non-Verb		
English	Verb	Noun	Adjective	Adverb
Garo	Verb	Noun	–	–

FIGURE 9. Flexible, differentiated, and rigid languages

The subordinating morpheme -e is added to the verb gar- 'throw' in (550a) and to the notionally adjectival but morphologically verbal lexeme rak- 'strong' in (550b). These verbs constitute Ascriptive Subacts within the respective subordinate clauses, which as a whole fulfil the function of modification.

The difference between Warao and Garo is that Warao has a class of flexible lexical items that are used in several functions, whereas Garo lacks open classes of lexical items for the modifier functions, and resorts to alternative compositional strategies to compensate for the absence of a lexical solution. This difference is represented in Figure 9.

As Figure 9 shows, Warao and Garo are similar in that they have two main classes of lexemes. They are radically different, however, in the extent to which one of these classes may be used in the construction of underlying representations: the Warao class of non-verbs may be used in three functions, while the Garo class of nouns may be used as the head of a Referential Subact only.

On the basis of a comparison of fifty languages, Hengeveld et al. (2004) conclude that the differences between languages as regards their flexibility and rigidity can be described by means of the following implicational hierarchy:

(551)   head within   ⊂ head within   ⊂ modifier within   ⊂ modifier within
        Ascr. Subact   Ref. Subact   Ref. Subact   Ascr. Subact

The more to the left a function is on this hierarchy, the more likely it is that a language has a separate class of lexemes to realize that function and the more to the right, the less likely. The hierarchy is implicational, so that, for example, if a language has a separate class of lexemes to fulfil the function of modifier within a Referential Subact, i.e. adjectives, then it will also have separate classes of lexemes for the functions of head within a Referential Subact, i.e. nouns, and head within an Ascriptive Subact, i.e. verbs. Similarly, if a language has no class of adjectives, it will not have a separate class of lexemes for the function of modifier within an Ascriptive Subact, Manner adverbs.

The hierarchy in (551), combined with the distinction between flexible and rigid languages, leads to the classification of parts-of-speech systems in

PoS system	head within Ascriptive Subact	head within Referential Subact	modifier within Referential Subact	modifier within Ascriptive Subact
1	Contentive			
2	Verb	Non-Verb		
3	Verb	Noun	Modifier	
4	Verb	Noun	Adjective	Manner Adverb
5	Verb	Noun	Adjective	
6	Verb	Noun		
7	Verb			

FIGURE 10. Parts-of-speech systems

Figure 10. Figure 10 shows that languages can display three different degrees of flexibility (systems 1–3), and three different degrees of rigidity (systems 5–7). Of the languages discussed earlier Warao would be a type 2 language, English a type 4 language, and Garo a type 6 language. Note that the term 'contentive' is used for lexical elements that may appear in any of the four functions under discussion here.

What the preceding discussion shows is that in order to identify lexeme classes we first have to identify the relevant functions, and then study the way in which lexemes are distributed across these functions.

The studies we just reported on were limited in scope, in the sense that only four such functions were studied, while we distinguished many more, which may also either participate in lexical flexibility or be absent in a language. Let us just give two more examples of flexibility in other domains. First of all, it is evident that for many languages it is not useful to make a distinction between all the classes of adverbs listed in (533)–(541). They have a single class of adverbs, characterized as the lexeme class that modifies any head but a nominal one, be it simple or complex. As a second example, consider the following examples from English, as discussed in Mackenzie (1992, 2001):

(552)   The *outside* of the office needs painting.

(553)   I met him *outside* the office.

(554)   I'll wait for you *outside*.

The use of *outside* in (552) corresponds to the function identified in (542), the one in (553) to (544), and the one in (554) to (539). The basis for this flexibility is that the frames in (542) and (544) are similar in the sense that both have an internal argument, while (544) and (539) share the feature of (spatiotemporally) modifying a State-of-Affairs.

3.7.2.3.4 *Derived lexemes* In the preceding we have concentrated on basic lexemes. Processes of derivation can expand the lexeme inventory of a language. Not all of these, however, produce new lexemes. In our approach, some of them produce words rather than lexemes, as we argued in 3.7.2.3.1. The latter involve operations that adapt the form of a lexeme that has been inserted into a underlying semantic slot it was not designed to occupy, and produces the appropriate word form. For example, if a basically transitive lexeme is inserted into a one-place predication frame, it will in some languages have to be adapted so as to show its intransitive use. Other examples are participle formation to show embedding as a modifier, or nominalization to show embedding in a referential slot. These processes have aptly been called 'word-class changing inflection' (Haspelmath 2002: 230) to distinguish them from other derivational processes. As long as these processes are productive and predictable, they will be dealt with in the morphosyntactic encoder. We will go into this issue in more detail in 4.6.6.

Other derivational processes do more than just adapt a lexeme to an environment it was not designed for, but add independent aspects of meaning. The following miscellaneous examples of such derivational processes are from Turkish (Kornfilt 1997: 446),

(555)   diş-   →   diş-çi-
        tooth   tooth-PROF
                   'dentist'

Tuvaluan (Besnier 2000: 596),

(556)   konaa-   →   konaa-goofie-
        drunk   drunk-PRONE
                     'readily drunk'

Spanish,

(557)   perro-   →   perr-ito-
        dog   dog-DIM
                     'small dog'

and Evenki (Nedjalkov 1997: 303):

(558)   tev-   →   tev-lge-
        load   load-REV
                   'unload'

Such derivational processes, with a semantic import that goes beyond the adaptation of a lexeme to a slot, will be dealt with in the lexicon, as a process of extending the set of primitives, and not in the grammar, as a process of preparing lexemes for morphosyntax.

3.7.3 Modifiers

In the previous section we showed that Lexical Properties can be modified by other Lexical Properties. The lexeme class of the lexical modifier is in these cases determined by the lexical class of the head. Thus we have:

(559)   dance *beautifully*

(560)   *extremely* famous

(561)   *very* astonishingly

(562)   *former* neighbour

Especially relevant is example (562), which is an example of what Bolinger (1967) calls 'reference modification', but which we interpret as property modification. Compare (562) with (563):

(563)   *rich* neighbour

In (563) an Individual (x) is characterized as having the Properties 'neighbour' and 'rich'. (562), on the other hand, cannot be paraphrased as describing an Individual with the Properties 'neighbour' and 'former'. Rather, it is the Property (f) 'neighbour' that is restricted in its application by the Property 'former', and these together constitute a Property of an Individual. The two adjectives in (562) and (563) may be combined, as in (564):

(564)   a rich former neighbour

which may be represented as:

(565) $(x_i: [(f_i: neighbour (f_i): [(f_j: former (f_j)) (f_i)_\phi]) (x_i)_\phi]: [(f_k: rich (f_k)) (x_i)_\phi])$

What this representation shows is that only the adjective *former* modifies a Property (f_i); the adjective *rich* modifies an Individual (x_i). It also shows that *former neighbour* constitutes a Configurational Property, which is consistent with the fact that it may be referred to anaphorically as a single unit:

(566)   a rich former neighbour and a poor one

A language in which the difference between the modification of Properties and of Individuals shows up clearly is Dutch. As we showed in 3.6.2.2.6, in this language bare nouns may be used as predicates, alongside noun phrases that may be used predicatively:

(567) Jan is   timmerman.
       Jan COP.PRS.3.SG carpenter
       'Jan is a carpenter.'
       "Jan is carpenter."

(568) Jan is   een   timmerman.
       Jan COP.PRS.3.SG INDF carpenter
       'Jan is a carpenter.'

In our analysis in 3.6.2.2.6, the predicate in (567) is of the f-type, while the one in (568) is of the x-type. We thus predict that the predicate in (567) may combine with f-modifiers, but not with x-modifiers, and this is indeed the case:

(569) Jan is   *voormalig* timmerman.
       Jan COP.PRS.3.SG former   carpenter
       'Jan is a former carpenter.'
       "Jan is former carpenter."

(570) *Jan is   *rijk-e*   timmerman.
       Jan   COP.PRS.3.SG rich-AGR carpenter
       "Jan is rich carpenter."

The latter type of modification is possible, of course, with an x-type predicate:

(571) Jan is   een   *rijk-e*   timmerman.
       Jan COP.PRS.3.SG INDF rich-AGR carpenter
       'Jan is a rich carpenter.'

Finally, note that Dutch obligatorily shows Adjective-Noun agreement in the case of referent modification (571), but not necessarily in the case of property modification (569).

Since Lexical Properties may be modified by other Lexical Properties, and the resulting complex Properties may be used to characterize other entity types, it is not difficult to find examples like (572), represented in (573):

(572) a very amazingly good book

(573) $(x_i: [(f_i: book (f_i)) (x_i)_\phi]: [(f_j: good (f_j)): [(f_k: amazing (f_k)): [(f_l: very (f_l)) (f_k)_\phi]) (f_j)_\phi]) (x_i)_\phi])$

In this example the modifier of the head noun shows recursive embedding of Lexical Properties. In example (574) from Dutch both the head and the modifier of the noun phrase are each internally complex, as shown in the representation in (575):

(574) de   wereldwijd bekend-e   voormalig hacker
       DEF   worldwide famous-AGR   former   hacker
       'the world-famous former hacker'

(575) $(x_i: [(f_i: hacker_N(f_i): [(f_j: voormalig (f_j)) (f_i)_\Phi]) (x_i)_\Phi]:$
       $[(f_k: bekend (f_k): [(f_l: wereldwijd (f_l)) (f_k)_\Phi]) (x_i)_\Phi])$

Note incidentally the absence of agreement on *voormalig-* 'former' and its presence on *bekend-* 'famous' in (574).

Modifiers of Lexical Properties may themselves designate other semantic categories. This is, for instance, relevant for a class of modifiers that usually combine with movement verbs, as illustrated in (576):

(576) He went up(wards) / down(wards) / in(wards) / out(wards) /
       right(wards) / left(wards) / home(wards) / back(wards) / east(wards) /
       west(wards) / etc.

The modifiers in (576) all indicate directional orientation (see Foley and Van Valin 1984). They are different from directional arguments, which were treated in 3.6.2.3, as is evident from the fact that they can co-occur with this type of argument, as in:

(577) He went down to the station.

(578) He walked up to the church.

These modifiers are of the l-type, i.e. they designate Locations, which, incidentally, explains why we get *homewards* and not *housewards* (see below in 3.9). Thus, the verb-modifier combination in (577) may be represented as in (579):

(579) $(f_i: gov (f_i): [(l_i: (f_j: down (f_j)) (l_i)) (f_i)_\Phi])$

The close relationship of these modifiers with the verbs they modify shows up not only in the fact that they are restricted in use to movement verbs, but also that many languages encode directional meanings lexically. Thus, in Spanish (577) and (578) would be rendered as in (580) and (581):

(580) Baj-ó   a   la   estación.
       go.down-IND.PST.PFV.3.SG   ALL DEF.F.SG station(F)
       'He went down to the station.'

(581) Subi-ó   a   la   iglesia.
       go.up-IND.PST.PFV.3.SG   ALL DEF.F.SG church(F)
       'He went up to the church.'

In other languages the close relationships shows up formally as a tight relationship between verb and modifier. In German there are separable verbs of the type:

(582)   hin-gehen
        away-go
        'to go away from where the Speaker is'

(583)   her-kommen
        here-come
        'to come to where the Speaker is'

(584)   her-unter-kommen
        here-down-come
        'to come down to where the Speaker is'

3.7.4 Operators

Operators on Lexical Properties are narrow-scope operators qualifying through grammatical means the meaning of the lexical item introduced by the (f) variable. The nature of the operator depends on the nature of the lexical head. The following seem to be recurrent combinations of operators and lexical classes: Lexical Properties headed by nouns combining with nominal aspect, Lexical Properties headed by verbs combining with directionality, and Lexical Properties headed by adjectives combining with grading.

Nominal aspect (Rijkhoff 2002) concerns modifications of the *Seinsart* of a nominal Property. Rijkhoff defines *Seinsart* as the way in which a nominal Property behaves with respect to the features Shape and Homogeneity. There are important crosslinguistic differences in this domain. We will limit the discussion here to two of Rijkhoff's types, and refer to Rijkhoff (2002) for full discussion.

One type of noun is the set noun. This is a noun not intrinsically designating a singular object, but a set of objects, which may be either a singleton set or a collection. The noun by itself may therefore be interpreted as either singular or plural. A numeral co-occurring with such a noun specifies the size of the set, rather than multiplying over its members, so that the noun is not specified for plurality, as in Georgian (Fähnrich 1986: 158, cited in Rijkhoff 2002: 39):

(585)   or-i   mc̣eral-i
        two-NOM   writer-NOM
        'two writers'
        "one set of two writers"

It is typical of languages with set nouns that they display 'number discord' (Rijkhoff 2002: 105), as shown by the following Georgian examples (Harris 1981: 50–1, cited in Rijkhoff 2002: 109):

(586) Knuṭ-eb-i   gorav-en.
       kitten-PL-NOM roll-3.PL
       'The kittens are rolling.'

(587) Sam-i   knuṭ-i   gorav-s.
       three-NOM   kitten-NOM   roll-3.SG
       'Three kittens are rolling.'

Notice the singular agreement on the verb in (587), which indicates that here agreement is with the set, not with its members.

Languages with set nouns may have specific markers to indicate that the set is to be interpreted either as a singleton set or as a collective set. Rijkhoff (2002: 102–3) cites Oromo as an example. Consider the following examples (Stroomer 1987: 77):

(588) a. c'irreesa
           'doctor/doctors'

       b. c'irr-oota
           doctor-COLL
           'doctors'

       c. c'irree-ttii
           doctor-SGLTV
           'doctor'

Rijkhoff interprets the collective suffix in (588b) and the singulative suffix in (588c) not as number markers but as nominal aspect markers: they indicate whether the nominal Property should be interpreted as a collective set or as a singleton set. This distinction would then be comparable to the one in English between the nouns *police* and *policeman*. The grammatical specification of this opposition may then be captured by operators on a Lexical Property, as indicated in (589):

(589) (coll/sgltv f_i: $\blacklozenge_N$ (f_i))

Another type of nominal Property is displayed by the sort noun. While individual object nouns and set nouns have in common that they designate individual objects or sets of objects that have shape, this feature is absent with sort nouns. As a result, the noun cannot enter into direct construction with a numeral, but has to combine with a sortal classifier first in order to become countable. This is for instance the case in Nung (Saul and Freiberger Wilson 1980: 23, cited in Rijkhoff 2002: 42):

(590) slóng tú   luhc
       two   CLF child
       'two units with the property child'

Here again we may say that the classifier affects the nature of the Lexical Property by converting a general noun into, for instance, a set noun or a noun designating a singleton set, often employing more specific subdistinctions, such as the shape of the object.

Lexical directionality was discussed already in 3.7.3 and combines particularly well with verbs. Here it may suffice to show some examples in which directionality is expressed grammatically. Mokilese (Harrison 1976) is especially rich in this respect. It has suffixes relating movement to the location of the Participants in the speech event (towards the Speaker, away from the Speaker, towards the Addressee), horizontal movement (up, down), and multiple movement (reciprocal, separating, distributed). Here are some examples, one from each group:

(591) a. aluh-do   'walk towards the Speaker'
       b. aluh-da   'walk up'
       c. aluh-pene   'walk towards each other'

These may be represented in general terms as:

(592) (dir f_i: $\blacklozenge_V$ (f_i))

Mokilese also marks lative arguments on the verb, and directionality may be combined with marking of this argument, parallel to what we showed to be the case with lexical modifiers of direction and lative arguments. An example of this is (593) (Harrison 1976: 202):

(593) Ih il-la-hng   poh-n   oaroahrr-o.
       he go-DIR-ALL top.POSS shore-DEF
       'He is going towards the shore.'

In which *la* indicates direction away from the Speaker, and *hng* signals the presence of an allative argument.

Grading is the grammatical counterpart of degree modification and captures e.g. intensification strategies such as that illustrated in the following Spanish example:

(594) fácil- facil-ísim-
       easy   easy-INTENS
       'easy' 'very easy'

Grading may also take the form of narrow-scope negation, as in the following example of litotes:

(595) a not unintelligent girl

Cases like these may be represented as in (596):

(596) (neg f_i: unintelligent$_A$ (f_i))
'not unintelligent'

3.7.5 Frames

In sum, the set of primitives for the Representational Level provides the following frame for the layer of the Lexical Property:

(597) (π f_1: ◆ (f_1): [σ (f_i)$_\phi$])

> Heads of Configurational Properties are lexical items that enter into different classes depending on the function(s) they fulfil.
> The operator position in (597) may be filled by a operators expressing nominal aspect, direction, and grade.
> The modifier position in (597) may be filled by lexical expressions of property modification, manner, and degree.

3.8 Individuals

3.8.1 Introduction

Semantic units introduced by the variable (x_1) designate concrete, tangible entities of the type recognized by Lyons (1977: 442) as first-order entities. These are known in FDG as 'Individuals' (cf. Vossen 1995). They are defined as occupying a portion of space, such that no two Individuals can occupy the same place. The expressions 'Individual' and 'entity', being themselves countable nouns, abstract away from the distinction made in some languages between countable and non-countable entities ('things' and 'stuff'), as we have illustrated in the preceding section. However, all kinds of concrete phenomena are meant, irrespective of their countability properties.

The notion of *Seinsart* discussed in the previous section is relevant not only to the classification of nominal Properties, but also to the Individuals they describe. For instance, if a language can designate individual objects directly through a class of nominal Properties, then there is a direct match between a certain class of nominal Properties and a certain class of Individuals. Where it is relevant to draw distinctions among classes of Individuals with respect to their *Seinsart* the distinctions in question are marked as superscripts to the left of the (x) variable, cf. 3.2.2 above. Rijkhoff (2002) recognizes six such *Seinsarten* (general, sort, mass, singular object, set, and collective), but for exemplificatory purposes we will here distinguish, where relevant, only (^{c}x) and (^{m}x), for 'countable' and 'mass' respectively. Thus in English the applicability of the operator '1' (singular) will be dependent upon the presence of an Individual of the subclass 'countable'; and the selection of the quantity

(q) expressions *much* and *many* will be dependent upon their applying to an Individual of the subclass 'mass' and 'count' respectively:

(598) $(1^c x_i: [(f_i : tree_N (f_i)) (x_i)_\phi])$ 'a tree'

(599) $(^m x_i: [(f_i : wine_N (f_i)) (x_i)_\phi]: [(q_i: much (q_i)) (x_i)_\phi])$ 'much wine'

(600) $(m ^c x_i: [(f_i : grape_N (f_i)) (x_i)_\phi]: [(q_i: many (q_i)) (x_i)_\phi])$ 'many grapes'

3.8.2 Heads

The head of an Individual may be (i) absent, (ii) empty, (iii) lexical, or (iv) configurational.

(i) Absent heads

As we saw in Chapter 2, pronouns and personal names are introduced at the Interpersonal Level, cf. the following representation of a Referential Subact *John*:

(601) $(R_I: John (R_I))$

A semantic unit corresponding to this Subact will contain no lexical information and therefore will have no head. The unit cannot be merely omitted, however, since it partakes in the valency of its semantic environment:

(602)   John arrived.

(603)   IL: $(A_I: [(F_I: DECL (F_I)) (P_I)_S (P_J)_A (C_I: [(T_I)_{Foc} (R_I: John (R_I))] (C_I))] (A_I))$
         RL: $(past ep_i: (sim e_i: [(f_i: [(f_j: arrive (f_j)) (1x_i)_A] (f_i)) (e_i)_\phi]) (ep_i))$

The headless unit $(1x_i)$ at the Representational Level (the operator '1' is relevant for agreement in English) corresponds to the Subact $(R_I: John (R_I))$ at the Interpersonal Level. Anaphors, cataphors, deictic expressions, whether explicit or implicit (i.e. zero-realized) will be treated in the same way as elsewhere, i.e. through coindexation at the Representational Level.

    Where the head is empty, it follows that no modification is possible. And this is indeed what we find: any qualification of *John* in (604) can only be of the interpersonal type (cf. the discussion of cases like *poor John* in Chapter 2; see also Butler 2008a, Hengeveld 2008); otherwise the qualification is non-restrictive, as in (604):

(604)   John, poor guy, he has nowhere to stay.

As we saw in Chapter 2, non-restrictive modification is handled at the Interpersonal Level as involving a separate Discourse Act, as in (605), in which we recognize two Discourse Acts: that expressed as *whose train had been delayed* is linked to the Discourse Act expressed as *John finally arrived*:

(605)   John, whose train had been delayed, finally arrived.

(ii) Empty heads

Let us now turn to Individuals with empty heads. In such cases as (606), the expression *the yellow one* contains an anaphor *one* which refers back not to a referential item but to a previously mentioned semantic item; in other words, the relation is between units, specifically Properties (f_1), shown at the Representational Level:

(606)   I liked the red car, but Mary preferred the yellow one.

One will be analysed as a pluralizable pronoun, rather than as a numerator, cf. (607)–(608):

(607)   *I liked the red and the green cars, but Mary preferred the yellow two.

(608)   I liked the red and the green cars, but Mary preferred the yellow ones.

As with all pronouns, *one* will be introduced at the Morphosyntactic Level.
    Whereas absent heads cannot take modifiers, empty heads can, which permits the desired analysis of *the yellow one* in (606) above:

(609) $(1x_i: [(f_i) (x_i)_\phi]: [(f_j: yellow_A (f_j)) (x_i)_\phi])$
        where (f_i) is coindexed with $(f_i: car_N: (f_i))$ in a preceding State-of-Affairs

In other languages, (f_i), receives zero-expression, cf. Dutch:

(610)   Mij beviel de   rode auto, maar Marie had een voorkeur
        me pleased the red   car   but   Marie had a   preference
        voor de gele.
        for the yellow
        'I liked the red car but Marie preferred the yellow one.'

Nevertheless, in such languages the same style of analysis will be given in order to account for the semantic anaphora that is intended by the language user.

(iii) Lexical head

The third kind of head is the unmarked type, with lexical filling of the head, most typically by a noun:

      R   T

(611) $(x_i: [(f_i: president_N (f_i)) (x_i)_\phi])$
        'the president'

The x-variable indicates that this representational layer designates an Individual; this Individual has the lexically expressed Property f_i, which shows that designation, in contrast to the cases of empty heads, is achieved by lexical means. This structure may be further expanded, in ways to be discussed below, with operators and modifiers.

This shows an important general principle as regards the construction of representational layers in general. The lexical head in (611) is not simply a lexical item, but is part of a one-place predication frame such as the ones we introduced in 3.6.2.2.2. Thus, to the opening variable (x_i) in (611) we apply the predication frame in (612):

(612) $\quad$ T
$\quad\quad$ $[(f_i: president_N (f_i)) (x_i)_\phi]$
$\quad\quad$ 'x_i is president'

thereby predicating the property 'president' of (x_i). In (611) this predication is used in a Referential Subact, but the same predication frame might have been used in a main predication, as in:

(613)   This man is president.

(614) $\quad$ T $\quad\quad\quad\quad\quad\quad\quad\quad$ R
$\quad\quad$ $[(f_i: president_N (f_i)) (x_i: -man- (x_i))_\phi]$

These examples, and others that will appear in later sections, show that the application of predication frames is fully productive across the Representational Level.

(iv) Configurational head

Where the language user employs more than one lexical item within the head position, we find the fourth type of head, the configurational head.

In a language such as English we find many nouns designating parts of wholes, members of kinship systems, etc. that take an argument, typically with the semantic function Ref. These were discussed at some length in 3.6 and 3.7. The appropriate analysis of such examples is shown in (615):

(615) $(x_i: [(f_i: [(f_j: brother (f_j)) (x_j: [(f_k: king_N (f_k)) (x_j)_\phi])_{Ref}] (f_i)) (x_i)_\phi])$
$\quad\quad$ 'the brother of the king'

Here the head is configurational because *brother* is a relational noun. The head of (x_i) as a whole is a Configurational Property, as is clear from examples like (616), in which the Configurational Property 'brother of the king' is predicated of 'he':

(616)   He is brother of the king.

Apart from these cases in which relational nouns express a configurational property, there are languages that use verbal descriptions of States-of-Affairs to characterize an Individual. In Hupa, for example, it often happens that an Individual entity is characterized in terms of a State-of-Affairs in which it is typically involved. Consider the following example (Golla 1985: 58):

(617)   mi-de'-xo-Ø-le:n
         3.SG.POSS-horn-3.SG.OBJ-INDFTNS-plenty
         'cow' (lit. "Its horns are plenty on it")

At first sight it might seem that the expression in (618) is not a noun phrase but a clause in the indefinite tense. However, as shown in (618), the same expression may take a possessive prefix, which a clause could never take, thus clearly showing the phrasal nature of the expression (Golla 1985: 59):

(618)   whi-mi-de'-xo-Ø-le:n-'
         1.SG.POSS-3.SG.POSS-horn-3.SG.OBJ-INDFTNS-plenty-1.SG.POSS
         'my cow' (lit. 'My "its horns are plenty on it" ')

In other words, the Individual (a first-order entity) is being characterized in terms of a State-of-Affairs (a second-order entity) in which this same Individual participates. Example (617) may accordingly be represented as in (619), which shows that the same entity is referred to twice:

$$
\begin{array}{ccccc}
R & T & R & R & R
\end{array}
$$

(619) $(x_i: (indef\ e_i: [(f_i: [(f_j: le:n\ (f_j)) (x_j: -de'- (x_j): (x_k)_{POSS}\ (x_j))_U (x_i: -xo- (x_i))_L]\ (e_i)_\Phi]))$

Further support for the presence of an (e) variable in such examples is the fact that the construction used to designate an Individual may contain a spatiotemporal modifier, as in (620) (Golla 1985: 58):

(620)   q'an-ch'i-wil-chwil
         recently-3.SG.SBJ-TNS-grow.up
         'young man'
         "He has grown up recently."

The similarity between such examples and kinship nouns such as the one in (616) above is shown by such examples as (621) from Iwaidja (Pym and Larrimore 1979: 58–9, cited by Evans 2000: 123). This example contains a kinship verb which carries the expression of an operator Past. Since this is an absolute tense operating at the episodical level, the underlying representation is as in (622):

(621)   ŋabi   ŋa-buɹagbu-ɲ
         1.SG   1/3-be.older.sibling.to-PST
         'my late younger brother/sister'

$$R \qquad\qquad T \qquad\quad R \quad R$$
(622) $(x_i: (past\ ep_i: (e_i: [(f_i: [(f_j: buɹagbu (f_j)) (x_j)_U (x_i)_{Ref}] (e_i)_\phi]) (ep_i)))$

Note the coreference of the argument with the Reference function within the predication frame with the variable of the Individual description as a whole.

(623) ŋabi a-bana-maɽyarwu-n.
1.SG 1/3-FUT-be.father.to-NONPST
'my future son'
"I will be his father."

The State-of-Affairs (e_i) in (619) contains a coreferential (x_i) that is referred to in a second Referential Subact and may therefore be considered internally headed. Coreferentiality is also possible without there being a second Referential Subact, in which case the configurational head is not itself internally headed. This is the case of so-called 'headless relative' clauses in English, such as *what you read* in (624), in which an Individual (x_i) is identified through a State-of-Affairs in which it is involved, as represented in (625) (cf. Van der Auwera 1990: 151ff.):

(624) I will read what you read.

$$R \qquad\quad T \qquad\qquad R$$
(625) $(x_i: (e_i: [(f_i: [(f_j: read_V (f_j)) (x_j)_A (x_i)_U] (f_i)) (e_i)_\phi]))$

To recapitulate, then, the head of an Individual-designating unit may be:

(626) (x_1) \hspace{5cm} absent

(627) $(x_1: (f_1) (x_1))$ \hspace{4.3cm} empty

(628) $(x_1: (f_1: \blacklozenge (f_1)) (x_1))$ \hspace{3.7cm} lexical

(629) $(x_1: [(e_1/f_1: [(f_2: \blacklozenge (f_2)) \ldots] (e_1/f_1))] (x_1))$ configurational

3.8.3 Modifiers

All types of Individual-designating unit may in principle be qualified by modifiers, except for those with an absent head. We may distinguish between lexical and complex modifiers. In languages with adjectives, many are found as the head of lexical modifiers in Individual-designating units, cf. (630), since this is the position that defines adjectives, cf. 3.7.2.2:

(630) $(1x_i: [(f_i: man_N (f_i)) (x_i)_\phi])$ 'the man'

(631) $(1x_i: [(f_i: man_N (f_i)) (x_i)_\phi]: [(f_i: old_A (f_i)) (x_i)_\phi])$ 'the old man'

(632) $(1x_i: [(f_i: man_N (f_i)) (x_i)_\phi]: [(f_i: old_A (f_i)) (x_i)_\phi]: [(f_i: rich_A (f_i)) (x_i)_\phi])$
'the rich old man'

A couple of observations may be made. Firstly, where more than one modifier is present, these are 'stacked' into each other: (632) is thus to be understood as 'a man who is old such that that old man is rich'. In English the order of the modifiers, *ceteris paribus*, reflects this stacking in the sense that the most deeply stacked modifier is placed furthest from the head by the morphosyntactic rules. In French, in cases where more than one adjectival modifier is placed after the noun, distance again tends to indicate degree of stacking, but now in a mirror image to the situation in English: *une personne âgée riche* 'a person old rich' is more natural than *une personne riche âgée*. The relative positioning of modifiers (of otherwise equal complexity) is governed by semantic principles, a point which in itself provides justification for the Representational Level. As a rule, the more objective qualifications tend to appear closer to the head than more subjective ones, cf. *a beautiful old Swiss gold watch* in which the succession of modifiers reflects increasing objectivity of description (cf. Rijkhoff 2008).

Secondly, just like heads, the modifiers encountered at this layer are analysed as entering into one-place predications with the (x_1): in (631) above, for instance, the modifier involves the assignment of the Property $(f_i: \text{old}_A (f_i))$ to (x_i) in a one-place predication frame of the type $[(f_1) (x_1)_U]$. Correspondingly, these modifiers can also appear as the predicate in a full clause, cf. *The man is old, The old man is rich*, etc. This possibility is generally not available to modifiers of (f_1) discussed in 3.7.3: corresponding to *the medical student* there is no *The student is medical*.

Modifiers may be of other semantic categories as well. An example of a locative modifier and its representation is:

(633)   the man in the moon
$$(1x_i: [(f_i: \text{man}_N (f_i)) (x_i)_\Phi]: [(f_i: [(f_j: \text{in}_{Adp} (f_j)) (1l_j: (f_k: \text{moon}_N (f_k)) (l_j))_{Ref}] (f_i)) (x_i)_\Phi])$$

Some languages have specialized attributive forms to express locative and temporal modifiers. Consider the following German examples:

(634)   in all-en   *hiesig-en*   / *dort-ig-en*   Läde-n
         in all-DAT.PL here.ATTR-DAT.PL   there-ATTR-DAT.PL shop-DAT.PL
         'in all shops over here/over there'

(635)   die   *heutig-en*   Künstler
         DEF.PL.M today.ATTR-PL   artist
         'the present-day artists'

This formation is very productive, witness the existence of such diverse forms as *gestr-ig* 'yesterday-ATTR', *morg-ig* 'tomorrow-ATTR', *letzt-wöch-ig* 'last-week-ATTR', *nächst-jähr-ig* 'next-year-ATTR', *ob-ig* 'up-ATTR', *untr-ig* 'down-ATTR', *rück-wärtig-ig* 'back-wards-ATTR', *mehr-seit-ig* 'more-side-ATTR'. Turkish exhibits a similar process (Lewis 1967: 69–70):

(636) izmir'-de-ki   büro-muz   küçük, Adana'-da-ki   daha
Izmir-LOC-ATTR office-1.PL.GEN small Adana-LOC-ATTR more
büyük-tür.
big-ASSV
'Our office in Izmir is small, the one in Adana is bigger.'

(637) şimdi-ki   durum
now-ATTR situation
'the current situation'

(638) okul çağ-ın-da-ki   çocuk-lar
school age.POSS-LOC-ATTR child-PL
'children who are of school age'

A prominent type of modifier is the so-called possessive modifier. Only instances of alienable possession will be analysed as modifiers, cf. (639)–(640). This type of modifier is based on a predication frame for relational properties (see 3.6.2.2.6). Since the relationship is very often not one of prototypical possession, we follow Li and Thompson (1981) in using the semantic function Ass(ociative) rather than Poss(essor) for these cases. In cases of inalienable possession, as in (641)–(642), possessors are regarded as internal arguments and are given the semantic function Ref introduced earlier.

(639) the teacher's dog

(640) $(1x_i: [(f_i: dog_N (f_i)) (x_i)_\Phi]: [(f_j: (1x_j: [(f_k: teacher_N (f_k)) (x_j)_\Phi])_{Ass} (f_j))$
$(x_i)_\Phi])$

(641) the teacher's arm

(642) $(1x_i: [(f_i: [(f_j: arm_N (f_j)) (1x_j: [(f_k: teacher_N (f_k)) (x_j)_\Phi])_{Ref}] (x_i)_\Phi])$

Modifiers may also take the form of restrictive relative clauses or participial clauses, in which case a description of a State-of-Affairs in which an Individual is involved is used to described that Individual, as in:

(643) the man sweeping the pavement

which may be represented and paraphrased as in (644):

(644) $(1x_i: [(f_i: man_N (f_i)) (x_i)_\Phi]: (sim\ e_i: [(f_j: [(f_k: sweep_V (f_k)) (x_i)_A (1x_j:$
$(f_l: pavement_N (f_l)) (x_j))_U] (f_j)) (e_i)_\Phi]))$
'a man such that he engages in sweeping the pavement'

There are cases in which the absolute tense marking within a relative clause is independent of that of the relative clause, in which case the relative clause does not represent a State-of-Affairs but an Episode. An example is given in (645), and the relevant representation for an Individual is given in (646):

(645)   I see that man who was sweeping the pavement yesterday.

(646)   (1x$_i$: [(f$_i$: man$_N$ (f$_i$)) (x$_i$)$_\Phi$]: (past ep$_i$: (e$_i$: [(progr f$_j$: [(f$_k$: sweep$_V$ (f$_k$)) (x$_i$)$_A$ (1 x$_j$: (f$_l$: pavement$_N$ (f$_l$)) (x$_j$))$_U$] (f$_j$)) (e$_i$)$_\Phi$]) (ep$_i$): (t$_i$: yesterday$_{Adv}$ (t$_i$)) (ep$_i$)))
        'a man such that he engaged in sweeping the pavement yesterday'

At the Morphosyntactic Level, the assignment of Subject to the A argument of *sweep* and the absence of the absolute tense operator are the factors determining the form *sweeping* in the case of (643). In (645), the absolute tense operator triggers a finite clause and the finite verb phrase *was sweeping* as well as the introduction of the relative pronoun.

   In languages in which numerals are lexical rather than grammatical elements, they are treated as modifiers. In some cases they are simple modifiers, comparable to adjectives, in other cases they are complex, comparable to relative clauses. Kayardild (Evans 1995: 235) illustrates the first strategy:

(647)   dathin-a kiyarrng-a jungarra nal-da   banga-a
        that-NOM two-NOM   big.NOM head-NOM turtle-NOM
        'those two big turtle heads'

Rijkhoff (2002) notices that within Nps modifiers of quality, quantity and localization show increasing scope, which is nicely reflected in the ordering of the demonstrative, numeral, and adjective in (648), our representation of (647) in which these scope relations are shown in the relative ordering of modifiers (and operators):

(648)   (rem x$_i$: –nal_banga– (x$_i$): –jungarra– (x$_i$): –kiyarrng– (x$_i$))

The second type of numeral modifier is illustrated for Fijian (Milner 1972: 23) in (649):

(649)   e   dua na   gone
        INDFTNS one SPEC child
        'one child'
        "The child is one/There is a child."

Numerals in Fijian can be used predicatively only, which means that the Np reading and the clausal reading of (649) are not formally distinguishable out of context. For the Np reading we may assume the internally headed representation given in (650):

$$\text{(650)} \quad \overset{R}{(x_i:} \; \text{(Indef } e_i: \overset{T}{(f_i:} [\; \overset{R}{(f_j:} \text{ dua } (f_j)) \; (x_i: [-\text{gone}- (x_i)_\phi])] \; (f_i)) \; (e_i)_\phi]))$$

3.8.4 Operators

The operators that apply to the (x) variable cover the same areas of meaning as the modifiers discussed in the previous section: localization, quantification, and—to a lesser extent—qualification. In the actual expression of a noun phrase at the Morphosyntactic Level, the operators of the Representational Level are merged with those applying to, typically, Referential Subacts at the Interpersonal Level: the latter cover such interpersonal categories as identifiability (definiteness) and specificity (Brown 1985).

Operators of localization deal with distinctions among demonstratives, indicating 'the relative distance between the real-world counterpart of a referent and a certain reference point, which usually coincides with the speaker's position' (Rijkhoff 2002: 178). Although demonstratives thus reflect aspects of the speech situation, the distinctions made within the category are semantic oppositions. The category of demonstratives is in this regard comparable to that of absolute tense, one of the types of operator applied to the (ep) variable, see 3.4.4 above. The distinction between, for example, Present and Past tense is a semantic opposition that may be operative within a language and serves to localize an Episode relative to the speech situation—but these categories do not refer directly to the speech situation. So it is with demonstratives: a form like English *this*, in identifying an Individual as being close ('proximate') to the Speaker, does not refer directly to the Speaker, but enunciates a semantic distinction which is interpreted by the Addressee relative to the Speaker's location. *This pen* is thus roughly equivalent to 'the pen which is near the Speaker' where *which is near the Speaker* is a modifier and *this* is its grammatical equivalent.

Standard English has a rather simple demonstrative system, with an opposition between proximate (*this/these*) and distal (*that/those*), the actual form being chosen being dependent upon the absence or presence of the quantifying operator m (= plural). The French demonstrative (*ce/cet/cette/ces*; the form is conditioned by number, gender and the phonological properties of the following word) knows no obligatory distinctions: *cet homme* may be interpreted as 'this man' or 'that man'; optionally, an Np-final clitic *-ci* (proximate) or *-là* (distal) may be attached: *cet homme-là* 'that man'. However, other languages may display a rich system of distinctions, grammatically encoding phenomena such as degrees of distance (here, there, and yonder), visibility, shape, and height, as well as (typically in languages spoken by small communities) features of the language user's physical environment. Where such marking can be shown to be grammatical rather than lexical, the distinctions must be shown as operators.

The spatial distinctions carried by demonstrative operators are frequently carried over into other domains, so that proximal demonstratives become associated with the present time and distal with non-present time or even with attitudinal matters, proximal typically being linked to positive and distal to negative characterizations:

(651)   I think you should get to know this pretty girl I met last night.

(652)   I had dinner with that (awful) Harry Jones last night.

We will return to demonstrative operators when discussing the designation of Locations and times.

Turning now to quantifying operators, we may expect to find 'general quantifiers' such as *all, some, every, each,* and their equivalents. These operators may have restrictions as to the count/mass properties of the Individual to which they apply. Thus, in English, *some* ($\exists$) co-occurs with ($^c x_i$) and ($^m x_i$), *all* ($\forall$) with (m $^c x_i$) and ($^m x_i$) (where 'm' as an operator = plural), and *each* and *every* (distr, for distributive) only with ($1^c x_i$), where '1' = singular. Note that a negative marker such as *no* as in *no people* or *no cheese* is also seen as a quantifying operator (see Dik 1997a, Kahrel 1987), indicating the quantity zero, and accordingly is represented as $\emptyset$.

Cardinal and ordinal numbers may be analysed as operators when they are not lexical expressions. But they too often have properties that justify analysis as a lexical item. Consider the following data:

(653)   *We are all/some/every/each.

(654)   ?We are many.

(655)   ?We are few.

(656)   ?We are three.

(657)   We are third.

Whereas *all, some, every,* and *each* cannot occur in predicative position in English, the other quantifying expressions can, which suggests a lexical analysis—although the examples are marked as dubious and are typically expressed as *There are many/few/three of us.* It would appear that in English *all, some, every,* and *each* are fully grammaticalized, the remaining quantifiers and numerators less so, with ordinal numerals such as *third* being fully lexical. The classification of a quantifying element as lexical or grammatical will thus be a matter for close inspection from language to language.

Here, then, are some typical quantifying operators:

(658) Name   Symbol
       Existential   ∃
       Universal   ∀
       Distributive   distr
       Zero   ∅
       Singular   1
       Plural   m
       Numeral   {2, 3, 4, ...}

Corresponding to qualifying modifiers we must reckon with the possibility of a class of qualifying operators. Qualifying meanings in general seem to be too specific to regularly enter into processes of grammaticalization, so that qualifying operators on the (x) variable are not often found. An exception to this are cases of productive and predictable diminutive formation. The following example is from West Greenlandic (Fortescue 1984: 317), a language which has several options to express this type of meaning:

(659) qimi-iraq
       dog-DIM
       'puppy'

3.8.5 Frames

In sum, the set of primitives for the Representational Level provides the following frames for the layer of the Individual:

(660) $(\pi \; x_1: [(f_1) \; (x_{1)\phi}]: [\sigma \; (x_{1)\phi}])$

(661) $(\pi \; x_1: [(f_1: [(f_2) \; (v_{1)\phi}] \; (f_1)) \; (x_{1)\phi}]: [\sigma \; (x_{1)\phi}])$

(662) $(\pi \; x_1: (v_1: [\ldots (x_1) \ldots] \; (v_1)))$

Heads of Individuals may be Lexical Properties (660), Lexical Properties with an internal argument (661), or higher layers of organization, such as States-of-Affairs and Episodes in which the Individual is involved (662).

The operator positions in (660)–(662) may be filled by operators expressing localization and quantification.

The modifier positions in (660)–(662) may be filled by lexical expressions specifying qualities, location, quantity, and associations of the Individual.

3.9 Location

3.9.1 Introduction

Alongside Individuals, which are concrete, tangible entities, languages also recognize a class of Locations (for the background to the distinction between Individuals and Locations, see Mackenzie 1992: 254–5). In the Conceptual Component, we must assume that the conceptualization of Individuals such as 'blanket', 'rock', or 'Martin Luther King' differs in a corresponding manner from the conceptualization of Locations such as 'environment', 'north', or 'Atlanta, Georgia'. However, one and the same phenomenon in external reality may be construed mentally as either an Individual or a Location, depending upon the conceptualizer's goals. Consider the example of a house: to a prospective buyer, that house may be conceptualized above all as a location, as a place to live; to the real estate agent, in contrast, the house will be conceptualized above all as an Individual, as a commodity to be sold. Notice that this very distinction is more or less reflected linguistically in the use of the words *home* and *house*: the former is specialized to occur in designations of Locations, the latter in designations of Individuals:

(663) $(1l_i: [(f_i: home_N (f_i)) (l_i)_\phi])$ 'a home'

(664) $(1x_i: [(f_i: house_N (f_i)) (x_i)_\phi])$ 'a house'

This distinction is further reflected in the fact that *house* is a clear member of the part-of-speech Noun, while *home* displays various properties that overlap with the class of (spatial) adverbs: (i) the ability to occur as an invariable form without determiners (665); (ii) neutrality with regard to the distinction between Locative and Allative (666); (iii) compounding with the Approach morpheme *-wards* (667); (iv) the possibility of being co-ordinated with an (other) adverb:

(665)   He cycled home/down/*house.

(666)   I stayed/went home; I stayed in the house/went into the house.

(667)   She headed homewards/downwards/*housewards.

(668)   My team always wins, home and away.

Other languages have other ways of reflecting this distinction. In Finnish, for example, the word *talo* 'house' is inflected for spatial cases like any other noun: *talossa* (inessive), *talosta* (abessive), *taloon* (illative); the word *koti* 'home', however, unusually uses the essive and the partitive cases respectively for the meanings 'at home' (*kotona*) and 'from home' (*kotoa*), although the illative is used for the meaning 'to one's home' (*kotiin*); cf. Kracht (2004: 85).

More generally, the distinction between Locations and non-Locations can have clear grammatical consequences. In Hawaiian, the form taken by prepositions marking Subject, Object, and Stative Agent is sensitive to this distinction (Kracht 2004: 79–80). Interestingly, Locations and place names (toponyms) are identical in this respect.

Place names will be regarded as unique identifiers of Locations, just like personal names, and therefore inserted at the Interpersonal Level (see 2.8.3.2.3). Some support for this parallel treatment of both types of name comes from Fijian. In this language several grammatical processes are sensitive to the presence of a proper name. One of these concerns article selection. Fijian has a dedicated 'proper article' (k)o and it uses this article both for personal names and place names, as shown by the following contrastive examples (Schütz 1985: 320, 314):

(669) a. o   Mere   b. na   tagane
           PROPER.ART Mere (personal name)   COMMON.ART man

(670) a. o   Suva   b. na   koro
           PROPER.ART Suva (place name)   COMMON.ART village

Personal names and place names are accordingly treated in FDG in the same way at the Interpersonal Level. The difference between them obtains at the Representational Level, personal names being mapped onto x-units, and place names onto l-units.

Locations are identifiable in English by the fact, first noticed for toponyms by Whorf (1945: 5), that anaphoric reference to them, in the context of the semantic function Location, involves *there* or *here* rather than *in/at/to it/them*:

(671)   Ever since I saw that film about Lisbon, I wanted to live there/*in it.

(672)   Ever since I saw that film about the capital of Portugal, I wanted to live there/*in it.

(673)   As soon as I spotted the magnificent piano, I wanted to sit at it/*there.

There in (671)–(672) will accordingly be analysed as $(l_i)_L$ and *at it* in (673) as $(x_i)_L$.

3.9.2 Heads

(i) Absent heads

At the Representational Level, designations of Locations that correspond to proforms, deictics, and question words will appear as in (674)–(675), possibly with a relevant operator:

(674)   IL: $(-id -s R_i)$
        RL: (l_i)
        ML: *somewhere*

(675)   IL: $(A_I : [(F_I : INTER (F_I)) (P_I)_S (P_I)_A (C_i : [...(+id -s R_i)...] (C_i))]$
$(A_I))$
RL: (l_i)
ML: *where*

(ii) Empty heads

Under parallel circumstances to those that obtain for Individuals, a Location-designating unit may have an empty head. Consider *the old one* in (676)

(676)   Do I go to the new station or to the old one?

which will be analysed as:

(677) $(1l_i : [(f_i : station_N : (f_i)) (l_i)_\phi] : [(f_j : new_A (f_j)) (l_i)_\phi])_{All}$
$(1l_j : [(f_i) (l_j)_\phi] : [(f_k : old_A (f_k)) (l_j)_\phi])_{All}$

where the two mentions of (f_i) are coindexed.

(iii)   Lexical heads

Locations with a lexical head will be represented as follows:

(678) $(l_1 : [(f_1 : \blacklozenge (f_1)) (l_1)_\phi])$

Examples of simple Locations are those involving such English lexemes as *airport, battlefield,* and *quay,* and the most general locational lexeme of all, *place.*

(679) $(l_i : [(f_i : airport_N (f_i)) (l_i)_\phi])$

(680) $(l_i : [(f_i : place_N (f_i)) (l_i)_\phi])$

In addition, Location-identifying adverbs such as *away, aloft,* and *inside* (when used non-relationally and not as a preposition) will receive the same analysis:

(681) $(l_i : (f_i : away_{Adv} (f_i)) (l_i))$

(682) $(l_i : (f_i : inside_{Adv} (f_i)) (l_i))$

Like Location nouns, they designate a place in the sense of identifying an area of space, but make a greater appeal to the context for their interpretation. Historically, they typically arise from constructions involving Location-designating nouns, cf. *away* < prep + *way, aloft* < prep + *loft* 'air, sky', *inside* < adverb + *side.*

(iv) Configurational heads

Where a Location is defined in terms of another kind of entity, the following representation is called for:

(683) $(l_1: [(f_1: [(f_2: \blacklozenge (f_2)) (v_1)_{Ref}] (f_1) (l_1)_\phi]$

This kind of configurational Location involves a partitive relation: thus in the following examples *top* designates the highest part of what is designated by its Ref argument, and similarly for *inside* and *capital* (in the sense of 'politically most important city in a country'):

(684) $(l_i: [(f_i: [(f_j: top_N (f_j)) (x_i: [(f_k: mountain_N (f_k)) (x_i)_\phi])_{Ref})] (f_i)) (l_i)_\phi])$
        'the top of the mountain'

(685) $(l_i: [(f_i: [(f_j: inside_N (f_j)) (x_i: [(f_k: box_N (f_k)) (x_i)_\phi])_{Ref})] (f_i)) (l_i)_\phi])$
        'the inside of the box'

(686) $(l_i: [(f_i: [(f_j: capital_N (f_j)) (l_j: [f_k: country (f_k)) (l_j)_\phi])_{Ref})] (f_i)) (l_i)_\phi])$
        'the capital of the country'

In our approach to lexeme classes, presented in 3.7.2.3.3, what distinguishes lexical adverbs from lexical adpositions (as opposed to the grammatical ones that express semantic functions) is that the latter resemble the nouns in (684)–(686) in taking an argument with the semantic function Reference. Thus *inside of the box* or *inside the box* as a Preposition Phrase in English is representationally parallel to *the inside of the box*. Here are some examples of Location-designating adpositional phrases:

(687) $(l_i: [(f_i: [(f_j: above_{Adp} (f_j)) (mx_i: [(f_k: tree_N (f_k)) (x_i)_\phi])_{Ref})] (f_i)) (l_i)_\phi])$
        'above the trees'

(688) $(l_i: [(f_i: [(f_j: inside_{Adp} (f_j)) (x_i: [(f_k: box_N (f_k)) (x_i)_\phi])_{Ref})] (f_i)) (l_i)_\phi])$
        'inside the box'

The parallel between adpositional and nominal lexemes in such locational semantic units has been commented on in various contexts. It is generally agreed that adpositions originate historically, across the languages of the world, in one of two sources. The major source is from relational nouns designating a Location, typically a body part (e.g. *back, foot*, etc.), a division of a larger entity (*top, bottom, side*, etc.), or a geometrical concept (e.g. *interior, exterior*, etc.). The remaining adpositions either defy etymological analysis (Kahr 1975: 43) or can be traced to a verbal origin, often resulting from a serial verb construction.

Thus in the Kwa languages as described by Aboh (2005), there are two types of adposition: a limited number of prepositional P1s (which are etymologically deverbal and assign case) and an extended number of postpositional P2s (which are denominal and occur as the head of the adpositional phrase). Both P1 and P2 can occur in the same adpositional phrase, as in (689), from Gungbe (Aboh 2005: 624):

(689) Asíbá zé kwέ   ɖó távò lɔ́ jí.
       Asiba take money P1 table DET P2
       'Asiba put money on the table.'

In this example, *ɖó* belongs to a closed class of general locative prepositions and *jí* is one of the larger class of more specific postpositions glossed as 'top', deriving from a noun (*ò*)*jí* meaning 'above or sky' (Aboh 2005: 642).

The appropriate analysis for *ɖó távò lɔ́ jí* 'on the table' would therefore be as in (690), with the semantic function L(ocative) expressed as the grammatical preposition *ɖó*:

(690) $(l_i: (f_i: [(f_j: jí_{Adp} (f_j)) (x_i: (f_k: távò_N (f_k)) (x_i))_{Ref})] (f_i)) (l_i))_L$

Strikingly similar phenomena apply in Persian (Pantcheva 2006), where again two classes of spatial adposition must be distinguished, one grammatical and one lexical and denominal. The former class has four members: *daer* (Essive), *aez* (Ablative or Perlative), *be* (Allative), and *ta* (Approximative); the latter is much larger. Lexical adpositions take a Reference argument. For some, the Reference function may be marked by the EZAFE morpheme, for others, there is no marking; this is reminiscent of the requirement, option or prohibition of *of* as a marker of Reference in English: *out *(of), inside (of), underneath *of*. Any lexical adposition can be combined with any grammatical adposition, cf. (691):

(691) æz   ru(-ye)   miz
       from face-EZAFE   table
       'off the table'
       "from the table's face"

(692) $(l_i: [(f_i: [(f_j: ru_{Adp} (f_j)) (x_i: [(f_k: miz_N (f_k)) (x_i)_\phi])_{Ref})] (l_i)_\phi])_{Abl}$

Languages with case-marking rather than adpositions or with a combination of adpositions with case-marking will not be treated differently at the Representational Level; these are all matters dealt with at the Morphosyntactic Level (see Chapter 4).

Consider the case-marking in Avar (Kracht 2004: 81) as presented in Table 5. It is clear that the lexical forms for the five spatial meanings are those reflected directly in the essive case. Thus static position translated as 'at' may be represented as follows, where Essive has zero realization:

(693) $(l_i: [(f_i: [(f_j: -q_{Ad} (f_j)) (x_i: [(f_k: \blacklozenge (f_k)) (x_i)_\phi])_{Ref})] (f_i)) (l_i)_\phi])_{Ess}$

In the position occupied by Essive we may also have Ablative, Allative, or Perlative, realized as *-e*, *-(ss)-a*, and *-(ss)a-n* respectively.

TABLE 5. The Locatives of Avar

Spatial meaning	Essive	Ablative	Allative	Perlative
on	-da	-d-e	-da-ssa	-da-ssa-n
at	-q	-q-e	-q-a	-q-a-n
under	-χ'	- χ'-e	- χ'-a	- χ'-a-n
in	-χ	-χ-e	-χ-a	-χ-a-n
in a hollow	-∅	-∅-e	-∅-ssa	-∅-ssa-n

Locative adpositional constructions (as in English, Gungbe, and Persian) and locative agglutinative morphology of the type represented by Avar are thus analysed as involving an amalgamation at the Morphosyntactic Level of one of the subtypes of the semantic function Locative and a lexical adposition. However, in languages with spatial case-marking in which the morphology is not as agglutinative as in Avar and in which a single morpheme covers both the spatial distinctions expressed by the adpositional lexemes of Avar and the semantic function, an alternative analysis is possible. This alternative analysis postulates a larger set of semantic functions, each of which indicates a spatial distinction. In Hungarian (de Groot 1989: 16–18), the inessive case (meaning 'in') takes the form -ban, with vowel harmony variations; the elative suffix (meaning 'out of') is -ból and the illative (meaning 'into') is -ba. Although it may seem appealing to analyse these as agglutinations of -b 'in' and essive, ablative, and allative suffixes respectively, examination of other such sets (for the meanings 'on' and 'near') shows that this is not possible: -ban, -ból, and -ba must analysed as monomorphemic. The meaning 'in' cannot be associated with a lexical morpheme, and therefore must be given the more abstract analysis as a semantic function. The analyses that suggest themselves for Hungarian a medencében 'in the pool', a medencéből 'out of the pool' and a medencébe 'into the pool' are therefore as follows, with 'In' as a semantic function of interiority:

(694) $(l_1: [(f_1: (x_1:medencé (x_1))_{In} (f_1)) (l_{1)\Phi}])_{Ess}$

(695) $(l_1: [(f_1: (x_1:medencé (x_1))_{In} (f_1)) (l_{1)\Phi}])_{Abl}$

(696) $(l_1: [(f_1: (x_1:medencé (x_1))_{In} (f_1)) (l_{1)\Phi}])_{All}$

The type of analysis proposed in this section is supported by the observation that verbs tend to select for the outer semantic function (here Ess, Abl, and All) (Kracht 2004: 63). A static verb like *remain* will typically require an Essive argument, i.e. *remain in*, **remain from*, **remain into*. On the other hand, it will not have any requirements as to the inner semantic function (here In). Thus *remain in/on/near/under* are all grammatical.

Finally, we must consider configurational heads of Locations which are clausal in nature. This applies where a Location is identified in terms of a State-of-Affairs located at that Location. A straightforward example would be the italicized section of (697), which can be paraphrased as 'the place in which you hung that picture':

(697) I like *where you hung that picture*.
       (l_i: (past ep$_i$: (e_i: [(f_i: [(f_j: hang$_V$ (f_j)) (x_i)$_A$ (1 dist x$_j$: [(f_k: picture$_N$ (f_k)) (x_j)$_\Phi$])$_U$ (l_i)$_L$)] (f_i)) (e_i)$_\Phi$]) (ep$_i$)))

The structure is that of a 'headless relative clause': to the variable (l_i) is assigned the State-of-Affairs (e_i) which itself contains another occurrence of the variable (l_i). This structure here occurs as the Undergoer of the verb *like*. It can also occur as a Locative adverbial clause:

(698) *Where I live*, you cannot ski.
       (l_i: (e_i: (f_i : [(f_j: live (f_j)) (x_i)$_U$ (l_i)$_L$] (f_i)) (e_i)$_\Phi$]))

3.9.3 Modifiers

Modification of semantic units with locational designation is possible at two points. Firstly, the Location-designating lexeme itself may be modified, shown as σ^f in (699)–(700); secondly, the entire locational expression, including any argument, may be modified, shown as σ^l:

(699) (l_1: [(f_1: ♦ (f_1): σ^f (f_1)) (l_1)$_\Phi$]: [σ^l (l_1)$_\Phi$])

(700) (l_1: [(f_1: [(f_2: ♦ (f_2): σ^f (f_2)) (v_1)$_{Ref}$] (f_1)) (l_1)$_\Phi$]: [σ^l (l_1)$_\Phi$])

The class of σ^f modifiers are modifiers of Properties such as those that we discussed in 3.7.3. For contrastive reasons we will discuss those that modify locative Properties together with σ^l modifiers.

Let us consider examples of each kind of modifier, beginning with σ^f modifiers occurring in non-relational Locations, as in (699). Modifiers of the lexical item affect only that item, and therefore are used only attributively. Here are some examples:

(701) main road
       *That road is main.

(702) former shop
       *This shop is former.

The representation of these Locations will thus be as follows:

(703) (l_i: [(f_i: road$_N$ (f_i): [(f_j: main$_A$ (f_j)) (f_i)$_\Phi$]) (l_i)$_\Phi$])

(704) $(l_i: [(f_i: shop_N (f_i): [(f_j: former_A (f_j)) (f_i)_\phi]) (l_i)_\phi])$

The following examples show σ^f in configurational Locations:

(705)   the very top of the tree

(706)   the deepest inside of my soul

Again, these modifiers pertain only to the lexical item $(f_2: \blacklozenge (f_2))$ in (700), as is apparent from the impossibility of:

(707)   *The top of the tree was very.

(708)   *The inside of my soul is deepest.

Similar modifiers are also available for adpositional lexemes, as in the following examples from Portuguese:

(709)   O   museo   fica   mesmo em_frente à   estação.
        DEF museum is.located right opposite PREP.DEF station
        'The museum is situated right opposite the station.'

and Dutch:

(710)   Het fiets-pad   liep   pal   naast   de   snelweg.
        DEF cycle-path run.PST.SG right next.to DEF motorway
        'The cycle path ran right next to the motorway.'

The Portuguese intensifying modifier *mesmo* and the Dutch modifier *pal* (which is specialized in this function) indicate that the topological relations indicated by *em frente a* and *naast* respectively hold with particular geometrical precision, and thus serve to modify only those prepositions. We therefore use the following representations for (705) and (710) respectively:

(711) $(l_i: [(f_i: [(f_j: top (f_j): [(f_k: very (f_k)) (f_i)_\phi]) (x_i: [(f_l: tree (f_l)) (x_i)_\phi])_{Ref}]$ $(f_i)) (l_i)_\phi])$
        'the very top of the tree'

(712) $(l_i: [(f_i: [(f_j: naast (f_j): [(f_k: pal (f_k)) (f_i)_\phi]) (l_j: [(f_l: snelweg (f_l))$ $(l_i)_\phi])_{Ref})] (f_i)) (l_i)_\phi])$
        'pal naast de snelweg'

Non-relational spatial adverbs can also be modified in this way:

(713)   far away

(714)   right inside

with the representations:

(715) $(l_i: [(f_i: away (f_i): [(f_j: far (f_j)) (f_i)_\phi]) (l_i)_\phi])_L$

(716) $(l_i: [(f_i: inside (f_i): [(f_j: right (f_j)) (f_i)_\phi]) (l_i)_\phi])_L$

Modifiers of the σ^l type take the entire semantic unit in their scope. Here are some examples:

(717)   simple, nominal
        a dilapidated workshop
        $(l_i: [(f_i: workshop_N (f_i) (l_i)_\phi]: [(f_j: dilapidated_A (f_j)) (l_i)_\phi])$

(718)   configurational, nominal
        the unpainted side of the house
        $(l_i: [(f_i: [(f_j: side_N (f_j)) (x_i: [(f_k: house_N (f_k)) (x_i)_\phi])_{Ref}] (f_i)) (l_i)_\phi]: [(f_j: unpainted_A (f_i)) (l_i)_\phi])$

(719)   simple, adpositional
        dangerously close
        $(l_i: [(f_i: close_A (f_i)) (l_i)_\phi]: [(f_j: dangerous_A (f_j)) (l_i)_\phi])$

(720)   configurational, adpositional
        dangerously close to the spectators
        $(l_i: [(f_i: [(f_j: close_A (f_j)) (x_i: (t_k: spectator_N (f_k)) (x_i)_\phi])_{Ref}] (f_i))] (l_i): [(f_i: dangerous_A (f_i)) (l_i)_\phi])$

In the case of the Locations with nominal heads in (717) and (718), this type of modifier can be used predicatively, as shown in (721) and (722):

(721)   The workshop is dilapidated.

(722)   The side of the house is unpainted.

3.9.4 Operators

Locations, especially where the lexical element is nominal, may display much the same range of operators as Individuals (cf. 3.8.4). Thus we find operators of localization applying to Locations, to specify them further, e.g. (prox l_i) for *here* and (dist l_i) for *there*, with similar distinctions in other languages. Other languages may have many more distinctions, covering such matters as degrees of distance, visibility, and prominent features of the physical environment.

We also find operators of quantification applying to Locations, although in English there are fewer than apply to Individuals: (distr l_i) *everywhere*, ($\exists l_i$) *somewhere*, and ($\emptyset_i$) *nowhere*. Remaining operators need to be supported by the noun place$_N$: ($\forall l_i$) *all places*, ($2l_i$) *two places*, etc.; Mackenzie (1992) argues that place$_N$ has become grammaticalized in this function.

3.9.5 Frames

The set of primitives for the Representational Level makes the following frames available for Locations:

(723) $(\pi\, l_1 \colon [(f_1)\, (l_1)_\Phi] \colon [\sigma\, (l_1)_\Phi])$

(724) $(\pi\, l_1 \colon [(f_1 \colon [(f_2)\, (v_1)_\Phi]\, (f_1))\, (l_1)_\Phi] \colon [\sigma\, (l_1)_\Phi])$

(725) $(\pi\, l_1 \colon (v_1 \colon [\,\ldots (l_1)\, \ldots .]\, (v_1)))$

> Heads of Locations may be Lexical Properties (723), Lexical Properties with an internal argument (724), or higher layers of organization, such as States-of-Affairs and Episodes in which the Location plays a role (725).
> The operator positions in (723)–(725) may be filled by operators expressing localization and quantification.
> The modifier positions in (723)–(725) may be filled by lexical expressions specifying qualities and quantities of the Location.

3.10 Time

3.10.1 Introduction

Languages have specialized expressions for designating temporal categories. Some are linked for their contextual interpretation to the moment of speech (e.g. *today, next year*), others establish relative positions on the time line (*before Friday, duration*), while yet others relate to a socially established calendar (*Monday, Christmas Day*). Some temporal expressions identify a point on the time line (*moment, 12 a.m.*), others a stretch on that line (*period, April*). In FDG, all these expressions have in common that they are introduced by the variable (t):

(726) $(t_i \colon [(f_i \colon \mathrm{moment_N}\, (f_i))\, (t_i)_\Phi])$

(727) $(t_i \colon [(f_i \colon [(f_j \colon \mathrm{before_{Adp}}\, (f_j)\, (t_j \colon [(f_k \colon \mathrm{Friday_N}\, (f_k))_{Ref}]\, (t_j)_\Phi)])\, (f_i))\, (t_i)_\Phi])$

Any talk of a time line implies that time is conceptualized as involving an imaginary spatial construct (the line) on which any number of points or stretches can be placed. This metaphor is familiar from the work of Reichenbach (1947) on tense and temporal expressions. The relationships among points and stretches of time are indeed typically expressed by morphosyntactic devices that have their origins in spatial location, and this will be reflected in FDG by assigning the semantic function L(ocative) to such expressions as *on Saturday* or *until 31 December*.

3.10.2 Heads

As with Locations, the head of a Time expression may be (i) absent, (ii) empty, (iii) simple, or (iv) configurational.

(i) Absent head

At the Representational Level, designations of Times that correspond to pro-forms, deictics, and question words will appear as in (728)–(729), possibly with a relevant operator:

(728) IL: $(-\text{id} -\text{s } R_i)$
       RL: $(\forall t_i)$
       ML: *always*

(729) IL: $(A_I : [(F_I : \text{INTER} (F_I)) (P_I)_S (P_I)_A (C_i: [\ldots (+\text{id} -\text{s } R_i) \ldots] (C_i))]$
       $(A_I))$
       RL: (t_i)
       ML: *when*

(ii) Empty head

Under parallel circumstances to those that obtain for Locations, a Time-designating unit may have an empty head. Consider *next* in (730):

(730)   Will this be a cold winter or a moderate one?

which will be analysed as:

(731) $(1 \ t_i: [(f_i: \text{winter}_N (f_i)) (t_i)_\phi]: [(f_j: \text{cold}_A (f_j)) (t_i)_\phi])$
       $(1 \ t_j: [(f_i) (t_j)_\phi]: [(f_j: \text{moderate}_A (f_j)) (t_j)_\phi])$

(iii) Lexical head

Examples of Time expressions with a lexical head are *yesterday*$_{Adv}$ and *while*$_N$ as in (732) and (733) respectively:

(732) I saw him yesterday.
       $(e_i: [(f_i: [(f_j: \text{see}_V (f_j)) (x_i)_A (x_j)_U] (f_i)) (e_i)_\phi]: [(t_i: [(f_k: \text{yesterday}_{Adv} (f_k)_\phi]) (t_i)) (e_i)_\phi])$

(733) I spent a while with her.
       $(e_i: [(f_i: [(f_j: \text{spend}_V (f_j)) (x_i)_A (t_i: [(f_k: \text{while}_N (f_k)) (t_i)_\phi])_U (l_i: [(f_l: [(f_m: \text{with}_{Adp} (f_m)) (x_j)_{Ref})] (l_i)_\phi])_L] (f_i)) (e_i)_\phi])$

The general format for such expressions is thus:

(734) $(t_1: [(f_1: \blacklozenge (f_1)) (t_i)_\phi])$

(iv) Configurational head

Examples of configurational Time expressions are nouns and adpositions which require an argument, such as *duration* and *after*:

(735)   the duration of the fight

$(t_i: [(f_i: [(f_j: \text{duration}_N (f_j)) (e_i: (f_k: \text{fight}_N (f_k)) (e_i))_{Ref}] (f_i)) (t_i)_\phi])$

(736)   After the meal, (we had a brandy).

$(t_i: [(f_i: [(f_j: \text{after}_{Adp} (f_j)) (e_i: (f_k: \text{meal}_N (f_k)) (e_i))_{Ref}] (f_i)) (t_i)_\phi])$

The semantic function L(ocative) borne by *after the meal* in (736) should be more narrowly specified as Essive. Mackenzie (2001: 128–30) argues that in an example such as (737):

(737)   The war lasted from Monday for six days until Saturday.

the sequence of Time expressions exactly parallels the Ablative–Perlative–Allative sequence of spatial Locatives in (738):

(738)   John walked from his flat via the park to the station.

This parallel lies at the heart of the localist hypothesis, which analyses Time expressions as resulting from a consistent metaphorical extension from space to time (Lyons 1977: 718–19). This metaphor is reflected linguistically in the fact that in English, but also quite generally across languages, the subtypes of the Locative and Temporal functions will receive the same or similar expression, whether the unit is (l_1) or (t_1). Thus in both (737) and (738), Ablative is realized as *from*. The combination of Allative with (l_1) admittedly gives *to*, while the combination of Allative with (t_1) yields *until* or its variant *till*. Nevertheless, *to* is also possible in this meaning (cf. *from Monday to Saturday*), there is a close historical link between *to* and *till*, and semantically speaking, both share telicity. Perlative is expressed differently, appearing as *for* with Time expressions. For English Time expressions, we may recognize the following grammatical prepositions:

(739)
Essive	*at*	cf.	*at the weekend*
Ablative	*from*	cf.	*from Monday*
Perlative	*for*	cf.	*for six days*
Allative	*until, till, to*	cf.	*until Saturday*

At times the selection of the preposition is affected by the type of Time noun: thus, for essive Locatives, *on* appears with days (*on/*at Saturday*), and *in* with months and years (*in/*at January*; *in/*at 1999*), but *at* is retaining for hours (*at 2 o'clock, at midnight*).

    The Time prepositions of English not listed as grammatical will accordingly be regarded as configurational; here are some examples:

(740) (t$_i$: [(f$_i$: [(f$_j$: prior_to$_{Adp}$ (f$_j$)) (e$_i$: [(f$_k$: meal$_N$ (f$_k$)) (e$_i$)$_\Phi$])$_{Ref}$] (f$_i$))
       (t$_i$)$_\Phi$])$_{Ess}$
       'prior to the meal'

(741) (t$_i$: [(f$_i$: [(f$_j$: during$_{Adp}$ (f$_j$)) (e$_i$: [(f$_k$: match$_N$ (f$_k$)) (e$_i$)$_\Phi$])$_{Ref}$] (f$_i$))
       (t$_i$)$_\Phi$])$_{Ess}$
       'during the match'

(742) (t$_i$: [(f$_i$: [(f$_j$: before$_{Adp}$ (f$_j$)) (t$_j$: [(f$_k$: eighth_century$_N$ (f$_k$)) (t$_j$)$_\Phi$])$_{Ref}$]
       (f$_i$)) (t$_i$)$_\Phi$])$_{Abl}$
       'from before the eighth century'

(743) (t$_i$: [(f$_i$: [(f$_j$: after$_{Adp}$ (f$_j$)) (t$_j$: [(f$_k$: midnight$_N$ (f$_k$)) (t$_j$)$_\Phi$])$_{Ref}$] (f$_i$))
       (t$_i$)$_U$])$_{All}$
       'till after midnight'

As with Locations, so the configurational head of a Time expression may be
clausal in nature, again involving a headless construction. Consider (744), in
which the Speaker indicates his/her liking for a time of the year:

(744) I like *when the leaves fall from the trees*.
       (t$_i$: (e$_i$: [(f$_i$: [(f$_j$: fall$_V$ (f$_j$)) (x$_i$: [(f$_k$: leaf$_N$ (f$_k$)) (x$_i$)$_\Phi$])$_U$ (x$_j$: [(f$_l$: tree$_N$
       (f$_l$)) (x$_j$)$_\Phi$])$_{Abl}$] (f$_i$)) (e$_i$)$_\Phi$]: [(t$_i$) (e$_i$)$_\Phi$]))

As Declerck (1996) points out, the Time interpretation may yield to a simple
State-of-Affairs interpretation in examples like (745):

(745) I liked when you gave him a cookie.

in which the Speaker is understood as having liked not so much the time of
giving but the State-of-Affairs itself.
    The structure in (744), with a Locative function, is also available for the
analysis of adverbial clauses of Time such as the following:

(746) *When the news arrived*, no one was shocked.
       (1t$_i$: (e$_i$: [(f$_i$: [(f$_j$: arrive$_V$ (f$_j$)) (p$_i$: [(f$_k$: news$_N$ (f$_k$)) (p$_i$)$_\Phi$])$_U$] (f$_i$)) (e$_i$)$_\Phi$]:
       [(t$_i$)$_L$ (e$_i$)$_\Phi$])$_L$

3.10.3 Modifiers

As with Locations, so with Times too we must make a distinction between
modifiers of the Time-designating lexeme (σ^f) and modifiers of the entire
Time expression (σ^t); (747) and (748) show the placement of these modifiers
in lexical and configurational Time expressions respectively:

(747) (t$_1$: [(f$_1$: ◆ (f$_1$): [σ^f(f$_1$)$_\Phi$]) (t$_1$)$_\Phi$]: [σ^t (t$_1$)$_\Phi$])

(748) $(t_1: [(f_1: [(f_2: \blacklozenge (f_2): [\sigma^f(f_2)_\phi]) (v_1)_{Ref}] (f_1)) (t_i)_\phi]: [\sigma^t (t_i)_\phi])$

σ^f serves to narrow the meaning of the lexical item, as for example *very* in (749), while σ^t qualifies the entire head of the Time expression, as for example *exciting* in (750):

(749) the very moment
       $(1t_i: [(f_i: moment_N (f_i)): [(f_j: very_A (f_j)) (f_i)_\phi]) (t_i)_\phi])$

(750) these exciting times
       $(prox\ m\ t_i: [(f_i: time_N (f_i)) (t_i)_\phi]: [(f_j: exciting_A (f_j)) (t_i)_\phi])$

The noun *time* and a number of salient time nouns (*moment, minute, hour, day, month, year*) may be modified, like any other, by a relative clause:

(751) The time at which he arrived was fairly late.

(752) The day on which she left was unforgettable.

However, these nouns may be followed by a complete subordinate clause, shown in italics in the following examples; this is not a relative clause, since it lacks any anaphoric gap:

(753) The time *that he arrived* was fairly late.

(754) The day *she left* was unforgettable.

In this case, the clause must be seen as an argument of the noun, which thereby enters into a configurational frame of the type shown in (748) above:

(755) $(t_i: [(f_i: [(f_j: time_N (f_j)) (sim\ e_i: [(f_k: [(f_l: arrive_V (f_l)) (x_i)_A] (f_k)) (e_i)_\phi]:$
       $[(t_i) (e_i)_\phi])_{Ref}] (f_i)) (t_i)_\phi])$
       'the time that he arrived, the time he arrived'

This distinction between clauses modifying a temporal head noun and those occurring as the argument of a temporal noun shows up very neatly in Mokilese (Harrison 1976: 260):

(756) Ngoah suh-oang John anjoau-o ma ngoah in-la sidow-a.
       I   meet-ALL John time-REM REL I   go-DIR store-DEF
       'I met John when I went to the store.'
       "I met John the time at which I went to the store."

(757) Ih dupukk-oang ngoahi mwoh-n   oai japahl-do Mwoakilloa.
       he pay-ALL   I   front-POSS my return-DIR Mokil
       'He paid me before I returned to Mokil.'
       "He paid me front of my returning to Mokil."

In (756) we find the noun *anjoua* 'time' restricted by a finite relative clause, in (757) the relational noun *mwoh* 'front' with a nominalized argument. This difference may be represented as in (758)–(759):

(758) $(t_i: [(f_i: anjoua (f_i)) (t_i)_\phi]: (e_i: (f_j: [(f_k: in- (f_k)) (x_i)_A (l_i: [(f_l: sidow-(f_l)) (l_i)_\phi])_{All}] (f_j)) (e_i)_\phi]: [(t_i)_L (e_i)_\phi]))$
'the time I went to the store'

(759) $(t_i: [(f_i: [(f_j: mwoh- (f_j)) (e_i: [(f_k: [(f_l: japahl- (f_l)) (x_i)_A (l_i)_{All}] (f_k)) (e_i)_\phi])_{Ref}] (f_i)) (t_i)_\phi])$
'before I returned to Mokil'

3.10.4 Operators

As with Locations, the operators available for Time expressions are the same as those for Individuals: those of localization, as in English *this Tuesday* or *that century*, and of quantification, cf. *a moment/moments/every moment* etc. *All those moments* will thus appear as:

(760) $(\forall \text{ dist m } t_i: [(f_i: moment (f_i)) (t_i)_\phi])$

Where the head is absent we find such forms as:

(761) *always* $(\vee t_1)$
       never $(\emptyset t_1)$
       some time $(\exists t_1)$
       once $(1 t_1)$
       twice $(2 t_1)$

3.10.5 Frames

The set of primitives for the Representational Level makes the following frames available for Times:

(762) $(\pi t_1: [(f_1) (t_1)_\phi]: [\sigma (t_1)_\phi])$

(763) $(\pi t_1: [(f_1: [(f_2) (v_1)_\phi] (f_1)) (t_1)_\phi]: [\sigma (t_1)_\phi])$

(764) $(\pi t_1: (v_1: [\ldots (t_1) \ldots] (v_1)))$

Heads of Times may be Lexical Properties (762), Lexical Properties with an internal argument (763), or higher layers of organization, such as States-of-Affairs and Episodes in which the Location plays a role (764).

The operator positions in (762)–(764) may be filled by operators expressing localization and quantification.

The modifier positions in (762)–(764) may likewise be filled by lexical expressions localizing or quantifying the period of Time.

3.11 Manner

3.11.1 Introduction

Alongside Locations and Times, another notion which is frequently designated by dedicated linguistic forms is the manner in which a State-of-Affairs is
carried out. In other words, languages permit us to talk about not only 'where'
and 'when', but also 'how'. For this reason, FDG recognizes a variable (m) for
cases where a language has specialized expressions for designating Manners.

One strong piece of evidence for the existence of Manners as a linguistic
category in English is that in equative (identifying) predications, Manners can
only be equated with Manners:

(765)   *The way in which she acted* was also *how I would have handled it.*

The two italicized sections of (765) are Manner expressions and cannot be
replaced by any other kind of expression without destroying the equative
nature of the whole Clause.

Manner expressions should be distinguished from other closely related
categories. Questioning with *How?* offers an insufficient criterion, since such
questions can also elicit expressions with the semantic functions Means and
Instrument:

(766)   How did he start the engine?
        By turning the ignition switch.
        $(f_i: [(f_j: turn (f_j)) (x_i)_A (1x_j: -ignition switch- (x_j))_U] (f_i))_{Means}$

(767)   How did he cut the meat?
        With a knife.
        $(1x_j: [(f_i: knife (f_i)) (x_j)_\Phi])_{Instr}$

(768)   How did he answer the question?
        Stupidly.
        $(m_i: [(f_i: stupid (f_i)) (m_i)_\Phi])$

Another test to be considered is clefting: Means and Instruments can be the
Focus of a cleft construction, while Manner expressions modifying a Lexical
Property, as in (771), cannot:

(769)   It was by turning the ignition switch that he started the engine.

(770)   It was with a knife that he cut the meat.

(771)   *It was slowly that he walked.

Note, however, that Manner expressions that modify Configurational Properties (see 3.6.3) can be clefted, at least to judge by (772), cited by Cheng (1991:
62; see also Mackenzie 1998a: 248):

(772)   It was very angrily that John left the room.

The criterion that works best, at least in English, appears to be the possibility of paraphrasing the expression with a phrase of the form *in a...way*. This excludes expressions of Instrument and Means:

(773)   a.   with a knife   b.   *in a knife way

(774)   a.   by turning the switch   b.   *in a switch-turning way

(775)   a.   stupidly   b.   in a stupid way

Manners also need to be distinguished from Circumstances. Modifiers with the semantic function Circumstance designate States-of-Affairs that occur simultaneously with the modified State-of-Affairs (cf. Dik *et al.* 1990: 33). Thus in the following example from Spanish (Matsumoto 2003: 404):

(776)   El   globo   subi-ó   por   la   chimenea
        DEF   balloon rise-PST.PFV.3.SG.IND through DEF   chimney
        flot-ando.
        float-GER
        'The balloon floated up the chimney.'
        "The balloon rose through the chimney floating"

flotando plays the role of a Circumstance with respect to the State-of-Affairs of rising, suggesting an analysis as a secondary predication (see 3.6.3):

(777)   (e$_i$: [(f$_i$: [(f$_j$: subir (f$_j$)) (x$_i$: –globo– (x$_i$))$_U$ (l$_i$: –chimenea– (l$_i$))$_{PERL}$]
        (f$_i$)) (e$_i$)$_\phi$]: [(f$_k$: [(f$_l$: flotar (f$_l$)) (x$_i$)$_U$] (f$_k$)) (e$_i$)$_\phi$])

This kind of construction is typical of so-called 'verb-framed languages'. It has been claimed that in these languages, in contrast to 'satellite-framed languages' like English, the manner of motion is not expressed within the main verb (Talmy 1991) but separately. In our view, however, such elements as *flotando* in (776) above do not indicate a Manner, since they cannot be paraphrased in the same way as Manner modifiers: **flotandamente* ('floatingly'), **de una manera flotante* ('in a floating manner'). Rather the concept underlying (776) is formulated grammatically as a State-of-Affairs with a primary (with *subir* 'rise') and a secondary (with *flotar* 'float') predication frame, which given the fact that they fall within the scope of the same tense operator are necessarily simultaneous.

One last distinction needs to be made, between Manners and Comparisons. In English, Comparison is typically signalled by the preposition *like*, as in (778):

(778)   She sings like a nightingale.

The same preposition is used in anaphoric and cataphoric references to Manners:

(779) A: Joan talked to me cheekily.
       B: She talks to everyone like that.

(780) The argument runs like this: ...

In (779), B's answer does not compare the way Joan talks to everyone with the way she talked to A, but s/he means that Joan talks to everyone in that very same way, i.e. cheekily; analogously, what follows the colon in (780) is not similar to the argument, it *is* the argument. It would appear that we can indicate Manners indirectly by comparing: in (778) above, the manner of her singing is understood figuratively, through the simile *like a nightingale*. It is then a small step to reinterpreting *like* as a literal marker of Manner.

Having demarcated the semantic category Manner, let us now turn to the internal structure of Manner expressions.

3.11.2 Heads

(i) Absent head

At the Representational Level, designations of Manners that correspond to proforms, deictics, and question words will appear as in (781)–(782), possibly with a relevant operator. Consider the following examples from Dutch:

(781) IL: $(+\text{id} +\text{s } R_i)$
       RL: (m_i)
       ML: *zo* 'like that'

(782) IL: $(A_I : [(F_I : \text{INTER } (F_I)) (P_I)_S (P_I)_A (C_i: [\dots (+\text{id} -\text{s } R_i) \dots] (C_i))]$
       $(A_I))$
       RL: (m_i)
       ML: *hoe?* 'how?'

(ii) Empty head

Whereas empty heads are easily attested for designations of Locations and Times, comparable examples with Manner expressions are ill-formed:

(783) *I marked the exam in the old way, but he did it in the new one.

(784) *He answered a little cheekily, but she answered very.

(iii) Lexical head

If a Manner expression has a lexical head, the item in question may be of various categories. Let us consider the Manner expression *carelessly* in (785):

(785)   John drove carelessly.

This is to be interpreted as 'in a manner that is careless': (m_i) is said to have the Property 'careless', suggesting analysis as an adjective:

(786) $(m_i: [(f_i: careless_A (f_i)) (m_i)_\Phi])$

The suffixation of *-ly* is inflectional, being almost fully regular when an adjective finds itself in this environment; as such, the process is properly situated at the Morphosyntactic Level. For arguments that Spanish *-mente* is similarly attached in morphosyntax, see Torner (2005). This is thus a case of word-class-changing inflection (Haspelmath 1996) as discussed in 3.7.2.3.4.

The lexical item may also be drawn from the class of nouns, as in the Manner expression in (787):

(787)   John drove with great care.
        $(m_i: [(f_i: care_N (f_i)) (m_i)_\Phi]: [(f_1: great_A (f_i)) (m_1)_\Phi])_L$

In languages lacking manner adverbs, this may be the only resource available.

(iv) Configurational head

The general noun for Manners, comparable to *place* and *time* in the preceding sections, is *way*. Like *place* and *time*, *way* (but not apparent synonyms like *manner*, *fashion*, etc.) enters into configurational constructions:

(788)   The way (that) she drives
        $(m_i: [(f_i: [(f_j: way_N (f_j)) (sim e_i: [(f_k: [(f_l: drive_V (f_l)) (x_i)_A] (f_k))$
        $(e_i)_\Phi])_{Ref}] (f_i)) (m_i)_\Phi])$

As with Locations and Times, the configurational head of a Manner expression may represent a clause as in (789):

(789)   I admire *how you live*.
        $(m_i: (sim e_i: [(f_i: [(f_j: live_V(f_j): (m_i) (f_j)) (x_i)_\Phi] (f_i)) (e_i)_\Phi]))$

A similar analysis may also be appropriate for such nominalizations as the italicized portion of (790):

(790)   *Annette's dancing* was beautiful.

Since the nominalization in (790) means *how she danced* rather than, say, *that she danced*, Dik (1975: 117) criticized then current semantic proposals for not making explicit that it is here the manner of dancing that is being described: 'this means that this manner must be explicitly represented in semantic structure', he wrote. A possible representation that satisfies this demand is accordingly:

(791) $(m_i: (e_i: [(f_i: [(f_j: dance_V(f_j)) (x_i)_A] (f_i)) (e_i)_\Phi]) (m_i))$

3.11.3 Modifiers

As with Locations and Times, a distinction can be made between modifiers of the Manner-designating lexeme (σ^f) and modifiers of the entire Manner expression (σ^m), as shown in (792):

(792) $(m_1: [(f_1: \blacklozenge (f_1): [\sigma^f (f_1)_\phi]) (m_1)_\phi]: [\sigma^m (m_1)_\phi])$

Adverbs intensifying the degree to which a Manner applies will be analysed as σ^f, i.e. as in the representation of the Dutch example (793) given in (794):

(793)   erg   netjes
         very   neat-ADVR
         'very neatly'

(794) $(m_i: [(f_i: netjes_{MAdv} (f_i): [(fj: erg_{DAdv} (fj)) (f_i)_\phi]) (m_i)_\phi])$

Adjectives qualifying a Manner, as in *the new method*, will be placed in the σ^m position, as in (795):

(795) $(1 \ m_i: [(f_i: method_N (f_i)) (m_i)_\phi]: [(fj: new_A (fj)) (m_i)_\phi])$

As with the Time nouns *time, day, moment*, etc. discussed in 3.10.3, so the noun *way* in English can take either a regular modifier, expressed as a relative clause, as in (796), or an argument, expressed as a subordinate clause introduced by *that* (797) or zero (798):

(796)   the way in which the work was done

(797)   the way that the work was done

(798)   the way the work was done

The forms in (797) and (798) will be shown as follows:

(799) $(1 \ m_i: [(f_i: [(fj: way_N (f_j)) (sim \ e_i: [(f_k: [(f_l: do_V (f_l)) (x_i)_A (e_j: [(f_m: work_N (f_m)) (e_j)_\phi])] (f_k)) (e_i)_\phi])_{Ref}] (f_i)) (m_i)_\phi])$

3.11.4 Operators

As with Locations and Times, the operators available for Manner expressions are the same as those for Individuals. Operators of localization will apply in the analysis of the expression *like this*:

(800) $(prox \ m_i)$

Operators of quantification can also apply, as in the following representation of *various ways for the public to react*:

(801) (m m$_i$: [(f$_i$: [(f$_j$: way$_N$ (f$_j$)) (e$_i$: [(f$_k$: [(f$_l$: react$_V$ (f$_l$)) (x$_i$: [(f$_m$: public$_N$ (f$_m$)) (x$_i$)$_\Phi$])$_A$] (f$_k$)) (e$_i$)$_\Phi$])$_{Ref}$] (f$_i$)) (m$_i$)$_\Phi$]: [(q$_i$: (f$_n$: various$_A$(f$_n$)) (q$_i$)) (m$_i$)$_\Phi$])

3.11.5 Frames

The set of primitives for the Representational Level makes the following frames available for Manners:

(802) (π m$_1$: [(f$_1$) (m$_1$)$_\Phi$]: [σ (m$_1$)$_\Phi$])

(803) (π m$_1$: [(f$_1$: [(f$_2$) (v$_1$)$_\Phi$] (f$_1$)) (m$_1$)$_\Phi$]: [σ (m$_1$)$_\Phi$])

(804) (π m$_1$: (v$_1$: [... (m$_1$) ....] (v$_1$)))

> Heads of Manners may be Lexical Properties (802), Lexical Properties with an internal argument (803), or higher layers of organization, such as States-of-Affairs in which the Manner plays a role (804).
>
> The operator positions in (802)–(804) may be filled by operators expressing localization and quantification.
>
> The modifier positions in (802)–(804) may be filled by lexical expressions of degree and quality.

3.12 Quantity

3.12.1 Introduction

Languages may permit the designation of Quantities. This term is designed to cover both amounts of an uncountable phenomenon or numbers of countable phenomena. Indeed the words *amount* and *number* are typical heads of Quantity expressions; in relational use, they will occur in expressions with a configurational head. Note the use of the variable (q$_1$) in (805), as a first analysis of *a large amount of cheese*:

(805) (q$_i$: [(f$_i$: [(f$_j$: amount$_N$ (f$_j$)) (x$_i$: [(f$_k$: cheese$_N$ (f$_k$)$_\Phi$]) (x$_i$))$_{Ref}$] (f$_i$)) (q$_i$)$_\Phi$]: [(f$_l$: large$_A$(f$_l$)) (q$_i$)$_\Phi$])

Quantities arise from the hypostatization of the results of measurement (whether that be counting, estimation or comparison). They can be talked about, for example in mathematical or financial discourse, but typically an expression like *a large amount of cheese* will be used in contexts where what is being designated is cheese rather than an abstraction, as in (806):

(806) Felicity eats a large amount of cheese every day.

Where the designation is an Individual, as in (806), the appropriate representation is therefore one with an internal head:

(807)   (x_i: (q_i: [(f_i: [(f_j: amount$_N$ (f_j)) (x_i: [(f_k: cheese$_N$ (f_k)) ($x_i)_\phi$])$_{Ref}$] (f_i))
($q_i)_\phi$]: [(f_l: large$_A$(f_l)) ($q_i)_\phi$]))

This representation reflects the fact that the Undergoer of *eat* in (806) is an Individual.

Similar representations will be offered for lexical mensural classifiers. Rijkhoff (2002: 48) gives the following example from Thai (drawn from Hundius and Kölver 1983: 170):

(808)   náamtaan   săam   thûaj
sugar   three   lump
'three lumps of sugar'

(809)   (x_i: (3 q_i: [(f_i: [(f_j: thûaj$_N$ (f_j)) (x_i: [(f_k: náamtaan$_N$ (f_k)) ($x_i)_\phi$])$_{Ref}$] (f_i))
($q_i)_\phi$]))

This also points to the correct representation of instances in which the cardinal number is the head and the quantified noun its modifier. In the following example, from Scottish Gaelic, the noun *triùir* 'threesome, set of three' is used to quantify over human entities:

(810)   triùir   pheathraichean
three.HUM sister.GEN.PL
'three sisters'
"a threesome of sisters"

(811)   (x_i: (q_i: [(f_i: [(f_j: triùir$_N$ (f_j)) (mx_i: [(f_k: piuthair$_N$ (f_k)) ($x_i)_\phi$])$_{Ref}$] (f_i))
($q_i)_\phi$]))

3.12.2 Heads

(i) Absent head

Designations of Quantities that correspond to proforms, deictics, and question words will appear as in (817)–(818), possibly with a relevant operator. Consider the following examples from Dutch:

(812)   IL: (R_i)
RL: (magn q_i)
ML: *zoveel* 'so much/many, that much/many'

(813)   IL: (A_I: [(F_I : INTER (F_I)) (P_I)$_S$ (P_I)$_A$ (C_i: [... (+id −s R_i) ...] (C_i))]
(A_I))
RL: (q_i)
ML: *hoeveel?* 'How much?'

(ii) Empty head

Like with Manner expressions, empty-headed Quantity expressions seem to be limited to arguments expressing Quantities rather than objects:

(814)   *Felicity eats a large amount of cheese every day and I a small one of meat.

(815)   The road measures 40 metres and the path 20.

The latter example may be represented as in (816):

(816) $(40 \; q_i: [(f_i: metre_N \; (f_i)) \; (q_i)_\phi])$
$(20 \; q_j: [(f_i) \; (q_j)_\phi])$

(iii) Lexical head

An example of a Quantity with a lexical head has already been given in (816). Another would be the degree adverb in (817), represented in (818). Degree adverbs will be seen as indicating the Quantity of application of their head:

(817)   highly intelligent

(818) $(f_i: intelligent_A \; (f_i): [(q_i: [(f_j: high_A \; (f_j)) \; (q_i)_\phi]) \; (f_i)_\phi])$

Similarly, lexical quantifiers should also be analysed as heads of (q_1) expressions, as in (819):

(819)   frequent interruptions
$(e_i: [(f_i: interruption_N \; (f_i)) \; (e_i)_\phi]: [(q_i: [(f_j: frequent_A \; (f_j)) \; (q_i)_\phi])$
$(e_i)_\phi])$

(iv) Configurational head

Nouns such as *number, amount, volume, population* (in the sense of 'number of inhabitants'), *dose*, etc. typically occur in the frame offered by the (q_1) variable; other nouns such as *bag* (e.g. of coal) or *lump* (e.g. of sugar), which usually designate Individuals, can be used to indicate 'quanta' (cf. Lyons 1977: 434). Where these nouns occur with a Reference argument, they together form a configurational head, as in (807) above or as in (820):

(820)   the volume of traffic
$(q_i: [(f_i: [(f_j: volume_N \; (f_j)) \; (e_i: [(f_k: traffic_N \; (f_k)) \; (e_i)_\phi])_{Ref}] \; (f_i)) \; (q_i)_\phi])$

Another such noun is *rate*, a prominent meaning of which is 'frequency relative to a stretch of time', as in *his rate of success* (i.e. how frequently he is successful in any time period). This indicates that designations of frequency can be analysed as Quantities of time. Like *place, time,* and *way, rate* can also take a State-of-Affairs as its argument, as in the italicized portion of (821):

(821)   *At the rate that he works*, we'll be finished before lunch.
        (q$_i$: [(f$_i$: [(f$_j$: rate$_N$ (f$_j$)) (sim e$_i$: [(f$_k$: [(f$_l$: work$_V$ (f$_l$)) (x$_i$)$_A$] (f$_k$))
        (e$_i$)$_\phi$])$_{Ref}$] (f$_i$)) (q$_i$)$_\phi$])

The configurational head may also be expressed as a clause in (822):

(822)   It's amazing *how much he eats*.
        (q$_i$: (sim e$_i$: (f$_i$: [(f$_j$: eat$_V$ (f$_j$)) (x$_i$)$_A$ (q$_i$)$_\phi$] (f$_i$)) (e$_i$)))

Our introduction of a variable for Quantities also helps to understand so-called 'degree relatives' (see de Vries 2002: 16), such as:

(823)   (Jill spilled) the milk that there was in the can.

In expressions like (823) the noun phrase refers to the quantity of milk that was in the can, rather than to the milk itself, and may therefore be represented as in:

(824)   (q$_i$: (x$_i$: [–milk– (x$_i$)$_\phi$]): [(q$_i$) (x$_i$)$_\phi$]: (sim e$_i$: [(f$_i$: [(x$_i$) (x$_j$: [–can–
        (x$_j$)$_\phi$])$_L$] (f$_i$)) (e$_i$)$_\phi$]))

3.12.3 Modifiers

Quantities can be modified in the same way as other semantic categories, as in (825)–(826) (for (826) cf. Wiese fc.):

(825)   a generous dose of medicine
        (1 q$_i$: [(f$_i$: [(f$_j$: dose$_N$ (f$_j$)) (x$_i$: [(f$_k$: medicine$_N$ (f$_k$)) (x$_i$)$_\phi$])$_{Ref}$] (f$_i$)) (q$_i$)$_\phi$]:
        [(f$_l$: generous$_A$ (f$_l$)) (q$_i$)$_\phi$])

(826)   twelve large sacks of cement
        (12 q$_i$: [(f$_i$: [(f$_j$: sack$_N$ (f$_j$)) (x$_i$: [(f$_k$: cement$_N$ (f$_k$)) (x$_i$)$_\phi$])$_{Ref}$] (f$_i$)) (q$_i$)$_\phi$]:
        [(f$_l$: large$_A$ (f$_l$)) (q$_i$)$_\phi$]

3.12.4 Operators

Operators of localization and quantification can apply to Quantities. For the latter, consider (827) from Dutch:

(827)   drie liter melk
        three litre milk
        'three litres of milk'
        (3q$_i$: [(f$_i$: [(f$_j$: liter$_N$ (f$_j$)) (x$_i$: [(f$_k$: melk$_N$ (f$_k$)) (x$_i$)$_\phi$])$_{Ref}$] (f$_i$)) (q$_i$)$_\phi$])

Note that *liter* is not marked for plural here, unlike most nouns following a numeral in Dutch.

3.12.5 Frames

The set of primitives for the Representational Level makes the following frames available for Quantities:

(828) $(\pi\, q_1: [(f_1)\, (q_1)_\phi]: [\sigma\, (q_1)_\phi])$

(829) $(\pi\, q_1: [(f_1: [(f_2)\, (v_1)_\phi]\, (f_1))\, (q_1)_\phi]: [\sigma\, (q_1)_\phi])$

(830) $(\pi\, q_1: (v_1: [\ldots(q_1)\ldots]\, (v_1)))$

> Heads of Quantities may be Lexical Properties (828), Lexical Properties with an internal argument (829), or higher layers of organization, such as Individuals, in which the Quantity plays a role (830).
>
> The operator positions in (828)–(830) may be filled by operators expressing localization and quantification.
>
> The modifier positions in (828)–(830) may be filled by lexical expressions of degree and quantity.

3.13 Reason

3.13.1 Introduction

We showed in 3.2.1.5 that for some languages there is evidence for the existence of a semantic category Reason, which may show up in dedicated nominalization patterns, as e.g. in Yami (Rau 2002: 175):

(831) saway   i-saway
       escape   REASNR-escape
       'escape' 'reason to escape'

or the existence of a Reason question word such as English *why*. Reasons could be considered a special type of Propositional Content, as they represent the thoughts that drive a human agent to act in a certain way.

3.13.2 Heads

The usual head types can be found for Reasons as well.

(i) Absent head

Designations of Reasons that correspond to proforms, deictics, and question words will appear as in (832)–(833), possibly with a relevant operator. Consider the following examples from Dutch:

(832) IL: (R_i)
       RL: (r_i)
       ML: *daarom* 'therefore'

(833)   IL: $(A_I: [(F_I: INTER (F_I)) (P_1)_S (P_1)_A (C_i: [\ldots(+id -s R_i)\ldots] (C_i))] (A_I))$
RL: (r_i)
ML: *waarom?* 'why?'

(ii) Empty head

The head position of a Reason may remain empty, as in:

(834)   He had a good reason but she had a bad one.

to be represented as in (835):

(835) $(1 r_i: [(f_i: reason_N (f_i)) (r_i)_\phi]: [(f_j: good (f_j))(r_i)_\phi])$
$(1 r_j: [(f_i) (r_i)_\phi]: [(f_k: bad (f_k)) (r_i)_\phi])$

(iii) Lexical head

The number of possible lexical heads seems to be extremely limited, the noun *reason* itself being the prime candidate, as illustrated in the first part of (834).

(iv) Configurational head

The noun *reason* can be used as the lexical centre of a Configurational Property as well, in such constructions as the following:

(836)   his reason that he left

(837)   the reason for which he left

where the *that*-clause in (836) is a Ref-argument of *reason*, while in (837) it is a relative clause, as represented in (838) and (839) respectively:

(838) $(r_i: [(f_i: [(f_j: reason_N (f_j)) (e_i: [(f_k: [(f_l: leave (f_l)) (x_i)_A] (f_k)) (e_i)_\phi])_{Ref}]$
$(f_i)) (r_i)_\phi])$

(839) $(r_i: [(f_i: [(f_j: reason_N (f_j): (e_i: [(f_k: [(f_l: leave (f_l)) (x_i)_A] (f_k)) (e_i)_\phi]:$
$[(r_i)_{Reas}(e_i)_\phi]))$

The configurational head may also be expressed as a clause in (840):

(840)   It's unclear to me *why he left.*

in which the italicized part is the headless equivalent of *the reason for which he left* in (837). This may be represented as in (841):

(841) $(r_i: (e_i: [(f_i: [(f_j: leave_V (f_j)) (x_i)_A] (f_i)) (e_i)_\phi]: [(f_k: (r_i)_{Reas} (f_k)) (e_i)_\phi]))$

Note that in (839) and (841) the relativized element is a modifier of the e-variable, as restrictive Reason clauses are modifiers of States-of-Affairs. Thus, when the reason that is unclear in (840) is identified, the answer might be as in (842):

(842)   He left because his mother is ill.

which would be represented as in (843), with the Reason clause modifying the main State-of-Affairs, for which it provides x_i's reason:

(843)   (sim e_i: [(f_i: [(f_j: leave$_A$ (f_j)) (x_i)$_A$] (f_i)) (e_i)$_\phi$]:
        (r_i: (e_j: [(f_k: [(f_l: ill$_A$ (f_l)) (x_j: [–his mother– (x_j)$_\phi$])] (f_k)) (e_j)$_\phi$]: [(r_i)
        (e_i)$_\phi$])

3.13.3 Modifiers

As mentioned before, the propositional nature of Reasons makes them suitable to be modified by elements expressing a propositional attitude. This is true of Reason clauses, in which the modifier takes an adverbial form, and for nominal Reason phrases, in which it takes an adjectival form:

(844)   He left because apparently his mother is ill.

(845)   The apparent reason for his leaving is that his mother is ill.

3.13.4 Operators

Quantifying operators may apply to Reasons as well, as in the following example:

(846)   I have three reasons for being late:...

In this context Spanish seems to prefer to use the numeral predicatively, as in:

(847)   Las   razon-es   son   tres:...
        DEF.PL.F reason(F)-PL COP.PRS.IND.3.PL three
        'There are three reasons:...'
        "The reasons are three:..."

Given the propositional nature of Reasons, demonstratives never have a local-izing interpretation, but can only be interpreted as textual, as in:

(848)   He gave three reasons for being late. *These* (reasons) were the follow-ing: ...

3.13.5 Frames

The set of primitives for the Representational Level makes the following frames available for Reasons:

(849)   (π r_1: [(f_1) (r_1)$_\phi$]: [σ (r_1)$_\phi$])

(850)   (π r_1: [(f_1: [(f_2) (v_1)$_\phi$] (f_1)) (r_1)$_\phi$]: [σ (r_1)$_\phi$])

(851) $(\pi\, r_1\!: (v_1\!: [\ldots(r_1)\ldots] (v_1)))$

Heads of Reasons may be Lexical Properties (849), Lexical Properties with an internal argument (850), or higher layers of organization, such as Configurational Properties in which the Manner plays a role (851). The operator positions in (849)–(851) may be filled by operators expressing localization and quantification.

The modifier positions in (849)–(851) may be filled by lexical expressions indicating a propositional attitude.

3.14 Reflexive language

We have now gone through all the semantic categories that enter into the Representational Level proper. However, when we talk we do not necessarily talk only about the external world (the narrated event); we may also talk about what happens in communication itself (the speech event) and its products. Jakobson (1971) appropriately characterizes these two situations as 'message about the message' and 'message about the code'. Examples of these are the following:

(852) He said: 'You're a crook'.

(853) That's not a *tomayto*, that's a *tomahto*.

In (852) we have a message about a message: through the use of a reported speech construction a Discourse Act produced by someone else is repeated in its original form. Since this construction entails that something that is a unit at the Interpersonal Level is now being talked about, we may say that an interpersonal unit enters the Representational Level. Similarly, in (853), taken from Sweetser (1990: 140), we have a message about the code. Here it is the choice of a certain pronunciation that is being commented upon. This may be made explicit in a metalinguistic conditional, as in (854) (Sweetser 1990: 140):

(854) OK, I'll have a *tomahto*, if that's how you pronounce it.

The architecture of FDG allows us to deal with cases like these in a straightforward way. Recall from 1.3.1 that all four levels of organization (Interpersonal, Representational, Morphosyntactic, and Phonological) within the Grammatical Component feed directly into the Contextual Component of the model. Once stored there, all units may be accessed by the Formulator and be re-used in posterior messages. In this way units of the Interpersonal, the Morphosyntactic, and the Phonological Levels may end up at the Representational Level, since once they have been produced, they become entities that can be talked about metalinguistically. The term 'reflexive language' (see e.g. Lucy 1993) is particularly appropriate for the use of language to talk about language.

In principle, all interpersonal, morphosyntactic, and phonological units may thus enter the Representational Level. We will not provide an exhaustive overview here, but give a few examples which show how reflexive language may be dealt with. First consider the following example:

(855)   He said that there was some history of threats of domestic abuse in the family.

In (855) the current Speaker reports what a past speaker has said: the current Speaker thus transmits the original Communicated Content of the past speaker to the current Addressee. This may be represented as in (856):

(856) $(e_i: [(f_i: [(f_j: say_V (f_j)) (x_i)_A (C_I: (p_i: -there is some history of threats of domestic abuse in the family- (p_i)) (C_I))_U] (f_i)) (e_i)_\Phi])$

By using this representation we now predict that modifiers typical of Communicated Contents at the Interpersonal Level such as *reportedly* and *unfortunately* (see 2.7.3) may occur within the complement clause, given the availability of this modifier slot in the underlying representation. And this is indeed the case:

(857)   He said that reportedly there was some history of threats of domestic abuse in the family.

(858)   He said that unfortunately there was some history of threats of domestic abuse in the family.

These may be represented as in (859):

(859) $(e_i: [(f_i: [(f_j: say_V (f_j)) (x_i)_A (C_I: (p_i: -there is some history of threats of domestic abuse in the family- (p_i)) (C_I): reportedly/unfortunately (C_I))_U] (f_i)) (e_i)_\Phi])$

In German this type of configuration triggers the use of the subjunctive, as shown in the following example (Frankfurter Rundschau 04.06.2004):

(860)   Der Angeklagte hingegen—ein kleiner, gedrungener Mann mit T-Shirt und breiten Hosenträgern—behauptete, die 30-Jährige *habe* ihn provoziert, indem sie zu ihm gesagt *habe*: "Halt doch das Maul, du dreckiger Deutscher!" Daraufhin *habe* er ihr gesagt, sie *solle* hingehen, wo sie hergekommen *sei*. Nie und nimmer aber *habe* er den Satz mit dem Vergasen gesagt. Das *sei* ein ganz normaler Streit auf dem Flohmarkt gewesen, wo es eben rauh *zugehe*.

'The defendant, on the other hand—a short, thick-set man with a T-shirt and broad braces, claimed that the thirty-year-old *had* provoked him by *saying*: "Shut up, you bloody German!". After that he *had* said to her that she *should* go back to where she *came* from. Never *had* he said the sentence about the gassing. It *was* just a normal quarrel at the flea market, where things regularly *get* rough.'

The verb *behauptete* 'claimed' introduces the reported Communicated Content C, here realized as a series of clauses each containing a subjunctive verb form, through which it remains clear that each of these clauses forms part of the report. We can account for this in the following way:

(861) $(e_i: [(f_i: [(f_j: behaupt- (f_j)) (x_i: (f_k: Angeklagte- (f_k)) (x_i)_\Phi)_\Phi (rep\ C_I: [....] (C_I))_\Phi] (f_i)) (e_i)_\Phi])$

Interpersonal units often enter the Representational Level through complementation strategies, as illustrated here. In 4.4.8.3 we will go into this issue in more detail, when talking about the formal reflections of the various embedded interpersonal units.

An example of a phonological unit being referred to at the Representational Level consider the following representation of the part *how you pronounce it* in (862):

(862) $(m_i: (e_i: [(f_i: [(f_j: pronounce_V(f_j): (m_i) (f_j)) (x_i)_A (pw_i)_U] (f_i)) (e_i)_\Phi]))$

As indicated here the second argument of *pronounce* is of the category Phonological Word (pw), as discussed in Chapter 5.

Finally, the Morphosyntactic Level is involved in such metalinguistic statements as the following:

(863)   My brother-in-law, if that's the right word for him, hasn't been around for ages.

Here the anaphoric element *that* refers back to the nominal word (Nw) *brother-in-law*.

3.15 Building up the Representational Level

When constructing the underlying structure of the Representational Level, use is made of frames, lexemes, and primary operators. Frames come in two types: representational frames and predication frames. The difference between them is that representational frames capture the hierarchical organization of the Representational Level, while predication frames capture non-hierarchical configurations of semantic units.

As shown at various places in this chapter, in many cases a slot that can be occupied by a predication frame can also be occupied by a lexeme: both are units of the f-type, i.e. units designating Properties. Predication frames designate Properties in a configurational way, while lexemes do so in a non-configurational way. Compare the following two configurations:

(864)   The man saw *the game.*

(865)   The man saw *his team beat the opposition.*

The verb *see,* when used to describe direct perception, takes a State-of-Affairs (e) as its Undergoer argument. This argument can be expressed lexically, as in (864), or configurationally, as in (865). The parallelism between these two situations is shown in the following representations:

(866) $(e_i: [(f_i:$ game $(f_i)) (e_i)_\Phi])$

(867) $(e_i: [(f_i: [(f_j: beat (f_j)) (x_i: [-team- (x_i)_\Phi])_A (x_j: [-opposition- (x_j)_\Phi])_U]$
$(f_i)) (e_i)_\Phi])$

In both cases the variable for States-of-Affairs is restricted by the Property (f_i), which in (866) is realized by means of a lexeme and in (867) by means of a predication frame itself consisting of a unit designating a Property (f_j) and two units designating the Individuals (x_i) and (x_j).

For a second illustration of the parallelism between lexemes and predication frames, consider the following examples:

(868)   I bought flowers for *the girl.*

(869)   I bought flowers for *that boy's girlfriend.*

The Beneficiary in (868) and (869) is in both cases an Individual (x). This Individual is described lexically in (868), and configurationally in (869). Their representations in (870) and (871) are parallel, in the sense that in both cases the Property (f_i) is attributed to (x_i):

(870) $(x_i: [(f_i:$ girl $(f_i)) (x_i)_\Phi])$

(871) $(x_i: [(f_i: [(f_j: girlfriend (f_j)) (x_i: -boy- (x_i))_{Ref}] (f_i)) (x_i)_\Phi])$

We will make use of this parallelism between lexemes and predication frames below.

In keeping with the general architecture of FDG, the process of building up the structure of the Representational Level proceeds in a top-down fashion, and runs partly parallel to the build-up of the Interpersonal Level. In certain respects the Representational Level responds to calls from the Interpersonal Level: the selection of a certain Illocution may impose restrictions on what is a possible representational frame. In other respects the Representational Level calls upon the Interpersonal Level. Once a certain predication frame has been selected the various positions in this frame have to be filled through evocational Subacts within the Communicated Content.

Consider this simple example of an Imperative Discourse Act:

(872)   Take this book to the library!

Imperative Illocutions require the Communicated Content to be mapped onto a State-of-Affairs at the Representational Level. This State-of-Affairs represents the action the Speaker wants to be carried out by the Addressee. Crucially, Imperatives lack the layer of a Propositional Content, since they are not about the exchange of information. There is thus a call from the Interpersonal Level to realize a description of a State-of-Affairs:

(873) $(\pi \, e_i: [(f_1) \, (e_i)_\phi]: [\sigma \, (e_i)_\phi])$

Notice that in (873) the subscript of the e-variable is alphabetic, not numerical, indicating that (e_i) is the instantiated variable representing the State-of-Affairs the Speaker has in mind. Within the configuration there are three slots that can now be filled with further material: the operator slot (π), the Property slot (f_1), carrying the numerical subscript to indicate that it has as yet not been instantiated, and the modifier slot (σ).

In the next step, the Speaker selects a predication frame that best fits his/her conceptual needs, and inserts it into the Property slot (f_1), which now becomes instantiated, as reflected in the nature of the subscript:

(874) $(\pi \, e_i: [(\pi \, f_i: [(f_2) \, (x_1)_A \, (x_2)_U (x_3)_L] \, (f_i): [\sigma \, (f_i)_\phi]) \, (e_i)_\phi]: [\sigma \, (e_i)_\phi])$

Within the predication frame we now have four positions that can potentially be filled. In the context of an Imperative in English, however, the Actor is normally not expressed. This is reflected at the Interpersonal Level in the absence of a Referential Subact corresponding to this Actor. This position therefore does not have to be replaced by a more complex structure, though the variable will be instantiated, as the referent is recoverable from the immediate context. Each of the three remaining positions will be expanded, with the following structure as the result:

(875) $(\pi \, e_i: [(\pi \, f_i: [$
$\qquad\qquad\qquad (\pi \, f_j: \text{take} \, (f_j): [\sigma \, (f_j)_\phi])$
$\qquad\qquad\qquad (x_i)_A$
$\qquad\qquad\qquad (\pi \, x_j: [(f_3) \, (x_j)_\phi]: [\sigma \, (x_j)_\phi])_U$
$\qquad\qquad\qquad (\pi \, x_k: [(f_4) \, (x_k)_\phi]: [\sigma \, (x_k)_\phi])_L \,]$
$\qquad\qquad (f_i): [\sigma \, (f_i)_\phi])$
$\qquad\quad (e_i)_\phi]: [\sigma \, (e_i)_\phi])$

There are a number of uninstantiated f-variables left now. In this case, all of these are instantiated by lexical means:

(876) $(\pi\ e_i: [(\pi\ f_i: [$

$(\pi\ f_j:$ take $(f_j): [\sigma\ (f_j)_\Phi])$
$(x_i)_A$
$(\pi\ x_j: [(\pi\ f_k:$ book $(f_j): [\sigma\ (f_j)_\Phi])\ (x_j)_\Phi]: [\sigma\ (x_1)_\Phi])_U$
$(\pi\ x_k: [(\pi\ f_l:$ library $(f_l): [\sigma\ (f_l)_\Phi])\ (x_k)_\Phi]: [\sigma\ (x_k)_\Phi])_L\ ]$
$(f_i): [\sigma\ (f_i)_\Phi])$
$(e_i)_\Phi]: [\sigma\ (e_i)_\Phi])$

Thus, by recursive application of the insertion procedure, triggered by the non-instantiated semantic slots, we arrive at a complete semantic structure at the Representational Level.

In the preceding we have skipped an important aspect of the construction of the Representational Level: the insertion of operators and modifiers. In our top-down implementation these have to be inserted step by step for each relevant layer. The selection of operators and modifiers precedes the selection of heads, since they have scope over their head and are therefore hierarchically higher: the head is always one step down in a configuration like the following:

(877) $(\pi\ v_1: [(v_2)\ (v_1)_\Phi]: [\sigma\ (v_1)_\Phi])$

The head of (v_1) is (v_2) in (877), so that the operator and modifier of (v_1) have scope over (v_2) and therefore have to be inserted first according to our strict hierarchical principles. In Chapter 4 we will show that in morphosyntax this hierarchical superiority of operators and modifiers is reflected in their ordering with respect to the head of the layer at which they apply.

Combining the hierarchical approach to the construction of the layers making up the representational level with the hierarchical approach to the insertion of modifiers and operators before heads at each layer, the following steps can be distinguished in the creation of the underlying semantic representation of (878). Operator and modifier positions irrelevant to the analysis have been left out to save space. Stepwise additions are indicated in bold.

(878)   Take this book to the library today!

1. $(\pi\ e_i:\quad [(f_1)\ (e_i)_\Phi]: [\sigma\ (e_i)_\Phi])$
2. $(\textbf{post}\ e_i: [(f_1)\ (e_i)_\Phi]: [(\textbf{t}_i: [(f_2)\ (t_i)_\Phi])\ (e_i)_\Phi])$
3. $(\textbf{post}\ e_i: [(f_i:\ [(f_2)\ (\textbf{x}_1)_A(\textbf{x}_2)_U(\textbf{x}_3)_L]\ (f_i))]\ (e_i)_\Phi]: [(t_i: [(f_j: \textbf{today}\ (f_j))\ (t_i)_\Phi])\ (e_i)_\Phi])$
4. $(\text{post}\ e_i: [(f_i:\ [$

a $(\textbf{f}_j: \textbf{take}\ (\textbf{f}_j))$
b $(\textbf{x}_i)_A$
c $(\pi\ \textbf{x}_j: [(\textbf{f}_3)\ (\textbf{x}_j)_\Phi])_U$
d $(\textbf{x}_k: [(\textbf{f}_4)\ (\textbf{x}_k)_\Phi])_L\ ]$
$(f_i))\ (e_i)_\Phi]: [(t_i: ([f_j: today\ (f_j))\ (t_i)_\Phi])\ (e_i)_\Phi])$

5. (post e_i: (f_i: [
a   (f_j: take (f_j))
b   (x_i)$_A$
c   (**prox** x_j: [(f_3) (x_j)$_\Phi$])$_U$
d   (x_k: [(f_4) (x_k)$_\Phi$])$_L$]
            (f_i)) (e_i): (t_i: (f_j: today (f_j)) (t_i)) (e_i))

6. (post e_i: [(f_i: [
a   (f_j: take (f_j))
b   (x_i)$_A$
c   (**prox** x_j: [(**f_k: book** (f_j)) (x_j)$_\Phi$])$_U$
d   (x_k: [(**f_l: library** (f_j)) (x_k)$_\Phi$])$_L$]
            (f_i)) (e_i)$_\Phi$]: [(t_i: [(f_j: today (f_j)) (t_i)$_\Phi$]) (e_i)$_\Phi$])

4

The Morphosyntactic Level

4.1 Introduction

4.1.1 Purpose and scope of the chapter

The preceding chapters have shown in some detail how Discourse Acts and Propositional Contents are analysed at the Interpersonal Level and the Representational Level respectively. Both those levels are concerned with formulation, i.e. with the translation of conceptual intentions into the language-specific structures that underlie linguistic forms. We have seen that there can be a considerable degree of parallelism between the two levels but also that they can diverge in important respects, as might be expected, given that they differ in their functionality. In this and the next chapter, we turn to the matter of encoding, a task that is divided over the Morphosyntactic Level and the Phonological Level. The task of the Morphosyntactic Level is to take the dual input from the Interpersonal Level and the Representational Level and to merge the two into a single structural representation which will in turn be converted into a phonological construct at the next level; that finally will be input to the articulator, the Output Component of the overall model.

To some considerable extent, the Morphosyntactic Level is dependent on its input: the input structures provide information to which the Morphosyntactic Level applies its own principles of organization. It must pass on to the Phonological Level an exact coverage of that information, such that an interpreter will be able to reconstruct the input structures exactly. In other words the Morphosyntactic Level cannot add or subtract semantic or pragmatic information. The input contains lexical information that must be preserved (even if it is subject to morphological alteration) in the output. In addition the input contains a range of non-lexical information: (i) information about dependencies, e.g. modifier-head and nucleus-dependent relations; (ii) information about functions, e.g. the semantic relations between arguments and predicates or the pragmatic relations between Subsidiary and Nuclear Discourse Acts; (iii) information about operators, each applying to its own domain; and (iv) abstract information of the type that must be converted into proforms of various kinds. The Morphosyntactic Level must accordingly be set up in such a way that this information is preserved and represented correctly at the right places in syntactic and morphological structure.

The purpose of this chapter is to show how this complex task is achieved and also to indicate which tasks have to be left to the Phonological Level. It will be shown that, just like the Interpersonal Level and the Representational Level, the Morphosyntactic Level is hierarchical in its internal organization, although it will be stressed that the degree of hierarchy (or 'configurationality') differs according to the type of language being accounted for. The chapter will then go on to show how the various morphological types that have emerged from research in language typology can be handled according to the same set of principles. The remainder of the chapter will deal with each of the layers of morphosyntactic organization in turn, adopting the top-down order familiar from the preceding chapters. Each layer will be analysed with regard to the linear ordering of its constituents, to alignment (in the sense of the selection of a privileged argument, e.g. Subject), and to such issues as subordination and agreement. Within the lowest layer, that of the word, finally, we will consider such specifically morphological issues as the distinction between inflectional and derivational morphology and the rendering of proforms.

4.1.2 Relation to the Interpersonal Level and the Representational Level

The relation between the Morphosyntactic Level and the two input levels is governed by three principles, those of Iconicity, Domain Integrity, and Functional Stability. Each in its own way, these contribute to maximizing the parallelism between the structures, thereby enhancing the transparency and easy interpretability of linguistic structure.

Although language is a symbolic construct and thus could tolerate a maximally arbitrary relation between function and form, in actual languages we observe a range of phenomena that betray a certain homology of function and form. One such phenomenon is iconicity, which we will illustrate with the correspondence between the order in which Moves and Discourse Acts (at the Interpersonal Level) and Propositions and Episodes (at the Representational Level) are introduced and the order in which they are expressed. Although there is some circularity here (since the ordering of units stipulated at the formulation levels is of course dependent upon the actual sequence of forms encountered), the possibility of adding modifiers that specifically indicate the position of a unit in a sequence (*firstly, secondly*) or of operators that allude to the relative ordering of States-of-Affairs in a temporal sequence (e.g. operators for Anterior, Subsequent, or Simultaneous States-of-Affairs) suggests that there is ordering in physical and mental experience (i.e. in the Conceptual Component) that should be reflected at the higher layers of the Interpersonal Level and the Representational Level. Notice that iconicity does not apply to lower layers: the components of the configurational heads of Communicated Contents (content frames) and Configurational Properties (predication frames) are ordered by grammatical convention, not by the Conceptual Component.

Iconicity applies straightforwardly in an example such as the following:

(1)   The game began at 7.30 and it ended in a draw.

Here we have a Move consisting of two Discourse Acts which are ordered in keeping with the chronological sequence of the States-of-Affairs evoked by each Discourse Act. The Interpersonal Level will order the Discourse Acts accordingly, and this order will be directly reflected at the Morphosyntactic Level, where we will have a Linguistic Expression consisting of two coordinated clauses. However, as mentioned in 2.2, where two Discourse Acts are connected through a shared referent, the Speaker has the option of treating one as nuclear and the other as subsidiary. Let us reconsider the example discussed in 2.2:

(2)   The game (beginning of A_I), which began at 7.30 (A_J), ended in a draw (end of A_I).

to be analysed at the Interpersonal Level as:

(3) $(M_I: [(A_I: [\ldots (R_I^{v_i}) \ldots] (A_I)) (A_j: [\ldots (R_J^{v_i}) \ldots] (A_j))_{Aside}] (M_i))$

with an additional indication that at the Representational Level the referents (v_i) of the two Referential Subacts (R) are coindexed.

Here iconicity is overruled in the interests of giving greater prominence to one piece of information (the Speaker judging the result to be more important than the time of kick-off). The information sent to the Phonological Level is that the Move (M_I) consists of two Discourse Acts, one of which (A_J) is subsidiary to but also interrupts the other (A_I). The Phonological Level will treat this as an instruction to give an intonation contour to each segment of (A_I) and to (A_J), yielding three intonational phrases in all, two with a non-final contour and one with a final contour. What remains for the Morphosyntactic Level is to integrate the two Discourse Acts syntactically, which is achieved by applying a general mould for relative clauses. The details may wait until 4.5.5, but the resultant clause structure at the Morphosyntactic Level will appear basically as follows:

(4) $(Cl_i: [(Np_i: [(Gw_i) (Nw_i) (Cl_j: [(Gw_j) (Vp_i) (Adp_i)] (Cl_j))] (Np_i)) (Vp_j) (Adp_k)] (Cl_i))$

This structure is also required for restrictive relative clauses of the type italicized in (5), which—save for some details to be discussed later—are morphosyntactically identical to non-restrictive relative clauses:

(5)   The game *which began at 7.30* ended in a draw.

In (5), *which began at 7.30* will form part of the same intonation contour as the surrounding material *The game...ended in a draw*. The role of the Morphosyntactic Level is thus to assign the same structure (4) to both types of relative clause while that of the Phonological Level is to ensure that the Aside status of (A$_J$) in (3) is reflected in the prosody. This is an example of how iconic order, which remains a default preference, may be overridden by other independent communicative strategies.

Another principle that constrains the Morphosyntactic Level to reflect the organization of its input levels is domain integrity. This refers to the crosslinguistic preference for the units that belong together at the Interpersonal Level and at the Representational Level also to be juxtaposed to one another at the Morphosyntactic Level. In other words, modifiers should ideally be placed in expression next to the heads that they modify; and functions and operators should be realized by elements that are close to the morphosyntactic units to which they apply. This means that there is a preference for a one-to-one relation between the hierarchical structure of the input levels and that of the Morphosyntactic Level: the realization of one Subact of Reference, for example, should not be interrupted by that of another Subact of Reference or of a Subact of Ascription.

This principle applies as a default, i.e. the correspondence between the levels will be such as to guarantee, everything else being equal, that domain integrity will be respected. Nevertheless, many languages show instances where domain integrity is overridden by other communicative strategies. Here are some simple examples from English:

(6)   a.   Are you going to town?
         b.   Where are you going to?

(7)   I am now going to town.

(8)   The guy has arrived who's going to fix my lock.

In (6a) the integrity of the Verb Phrase (Vp) *are going* is violated by the placement of *are* in clause-initial position to signal an Interrogative Illocution. In (6b) there is in addition to non-integrity of the Vp a violation of the integrity of the Adposition Phrase (Adp) *to where* (which itself is ill-formed), given the clause-initial placement of the question-word in English. In (7) the Vp *am going* loses integrity by being interrupted by an Adverb Phrase (Advp) *now*. And in (8) the integrity of the Np *the guy who's going to fix my lock* is broken by the placement of the modifier in clause-final position. Examples (6a) and (6b) involve the clause-initial position (to be known as P^I—for Initial Position), whose special functionality frequently causes domain integrity violations, attracting elements away from their domain. Example (7) shows another common source of such violations, the placement of modifiers—where these do not occur in clause-initial or clause-final position, they may penetrate into other syntactic domains. Example (8), finally, shows the role of the clause-final position (to be known as P^F) as a placement option for bulky modifiers.

Languages differ with regard to domain integrity. Whereas the presence of Interrogative Illocution may lead to infringement of domain integrity, as we saw above for English, in other languages it may signalled by clause-initial or clause-final particles that do not violate domain integrity, or may be indicated only through prosodic contours at the Phonological Level. Many, probably the majority of, languages leave the equivalents of English wh-words *in situ*, preserving domain integrity, and many do not permit modifiers to interrupt domains, or to be postponed to a clause-final position: Japanese, for example, does not allow extraposition of relative clauses of the type shown in (8) above. On the other hand, other languages allow relatively massive violations of syntactic domain integrity, relying for example on morphological agreement and government to signal interpersonal and representational connectedness; we shall see some examples below, when discussing so-called non-configurational languages. FDG will assume that domain integrity applies even to such languages, but that it will have less resistance to other forces determining constituent order.

In morphology, it would appear that domain integrity is generally well respected across languages. The major exception is formed by infixes, which are crosslinguistically less frequent than suffixes and prefixes, both of which do respect domain integrity. Thus in Tagalog the infinitive form with Actor agreement verbs is created by placing the infix -*um*- between the first consonant of the verb stem and the following vowel: the verb *sulat* 'write' appears as *sumulat* in the active infinitive.

A third principle to be discussed here is that of functional stability, the requirement that constituents with the same specification, be it interpersonal or representational, be placed in the same position relative to other categories. In certain languages, the positioning of a constituent bearing the Focus function is determined by the position with respect to the verb. In Turkish, for example, a Focus-bearing constituent is placed in immediately preverbal position, with the tense-bearing verb position also being fixed, namely as clause-final; although this is generally backed up by prosodic means, immediately preverbal position is a sufficient indication of Focus status without further marking being required. In Dutch, there is a strong preference for a particular relative ordering of (l_1) and (t_1) modifiers where both apply to the same State-of-Affairs, namely (t_1) before (l_1):

(9) a. Ik   zag   hem vorige week in het park.
         1.SG see.PST 3.SG last   week in DEF park
         'I saw him in the park last week.'

     b. ?Ik   zag   hem in het park vorige week.
         1.SG see.PST 3.SG in DEF park last   week

     c. Vorige week zag   ik   hem in het park.
         last   week see.PST 1.SG 3.SG in DEF park

     d. ?In het park zag   ik   hem vorige week.
         in DEF park see.PST 1.SG 3.SG last   week

In morphology, the principle of functional stability is of considerable importance in the sense that in complex words the relative order of meaning-bearing
elements will strongly tend to be fixed. This is important in the analysis of
words such as the following from Turkish (Lewis 1967: 124), in which the
suffix -miş occurs twice in succession, once as a resultative and once as an
evidential marker:

(10) Gel-miş-miş-Ø.
      come-RES-NONVIS.PST-3.SG
      'He is said to have come.'

It is the position closer to the stem that marks off the first occurrence of the
suffix as 'resultative' and the position further from the stem that indicates the
evidential nature of the second occurrence.

The principle of functional stability, to the extent that languages apply it,
is translated in FDG into structural templates, which, as we shall see, apply
to each of the layers of analysis. At each, a series of slots will be introduced
which constrain elements with the same functional specification to appear in
the same relative positions.

The general relation between the Interpersonal Level and the Representational Level on the one hand and the Morphosyntactic Level on the other is
one of a mapping from the former to the latter. The effect of iconicity, domain
integrity, and functional stability is for the relations to be basically as simple
and as stable as possible. Nevertheless, as we will see in the sections from 4.2
onwards, a range of factors cause the actual mappings encountered in the
languages of the world to show considerable complexity and variety, under
the influence of competing factors of different strength.

4.1.3 Relation to Phonological Level

The output of the Morphosyntactic Level serves as input to the Phonological
Level of organization. The latter also receives input directly from the Interpersonal Level and the Representational Level, the former typically having

greater impact on its suprasegmental aspects. The hierarchically structured output of the Morphosyntactic Level maps onto a hierarchical structure at the Phonological Level. Again, much as with the mappings discussed in the previous section, there is a preference for one-to-one relations, with for example the phrase at the Morphosyntactic Level corresponding to the phonological phrase, but discrepancies are certainly possible, and will be dealt with in Chapter 5.

In previous chapters we have seen how lexemes can be introduced at the Interpersonal Level and the Representational Level. Where the phonemic form of these lexemes undergoes no further internal change (this will be dependent upon the morphological typology of the language concerned, see 4.2.3 below), these may be immediately shown as phonemic representations. This also applies to those items introduced at the Morphosyntactic Level whose phonological form is not subject to further internal processes. One of the tasks of the Phonological Level is therefore to take the phonological material introduced at the three previous levels and to integrate it into a phonological structure. Consider (11), as a clause in English:

(11)   John must try.

All three words in this sentence can be displayed in their phonological form at the Morphosyntactic Level:

(12)   (Cl$_i$: [(Np$_i$: (Nw$_i$: /dʒɒn/ (Nw$_i$)) (Np$_i$))$_{Subj}$ (Vp$_i$: [(Vw$_j$: /mʌst/ (Vw$_j$)) (Vp$_j$: (Vw$_k$: /traɪ/ (Vw$_k$)) (Vp$_j$))] (Vp$_i$))] (Cl$_i$))

This is because the element *John*, being a personal name, is introduced at the Interpersonal Level and is not subject to further morphological or phonological processes; the element *try*, as a lexical item, is introduced at the Representational Level and can already take the form /traɪ/, since its bare lexical form is identical to its final phonological representation; and the element *must*, to be classified as an auxiliary verb, is introduced at the Morphosyntactic Level, where—being invariable (**musts*, **musting*, etc.)—it can already take the form /mʌst/.

Let us, however, consider a slightly more complex example with the same basic morphosyntactic structure, now showing how it appears at the Phonological Level:

(13)   (IP$_i$: [(PP$_i$: [(pw$_i$: /hɪ/ (pw$_i$)) (pw$_j$: /kɑːnt/ (pw$_j$)) (pw$_k$: /swɪm/ (pw$_k$))] (PP$_1$))] (IP$_i$))
       'He can't swim.'

Here, as we shall see below, neither of the words *he* and *can't* receives its definitive form until the Phonological Level. The Morphosyntactic Level in such cases offers a structure anticipating the final expression, in which each of the elements does however already occupy its position in the appropriate syntactic order. The Morphosyntactic Level thus indicates relative syntactic order as well as providing the Phonological Level with the information it needs to produce the final forms in (13). The morphosyntactic structure corresponding to (13) will accordingly be as follows:

(14) $(Cl_i: [(Np_i: (Nw_i: he (Nw_i)) (Np_i))_{Subj} (Vp_i: [(Vw_i: can (Vw_i)) (Gw_i: not (Gw_i)) (Vp_j: (Vw_j: /swɪm/ (Vw_j)) (Vp_j))] (Vp_i))] (Cl_i))$

This structure displays the linear sequence of two phrases. The occupant of the first position cannot yet have its definitive form, since this is dependent upon its syntactic function (Subject), which—as the representation shows—is not assigned until this Morphosyntactic Level (see 4.4.3 below). It will be the task of the Phonological Level to produce the phonemic sequence that associates the two morphosyntactic elements 'he' and Subj. A further factor that the Phonological Level must bear in mind in English when dealing with such cases is the pragmatic function passed down from the Interpersonal Level: the presence of a Focus or Contrastive function will in this case entail the form /hiː/, while their absence is indicated by the form /hɪ/. The word position (Nw_i) is occupied in (14) by the orthographic form *he*, which must, crucially, be understood as a placeholder for the entire range of phonological forms available to express the third person singular masculine pronoun (including at least /hiː, hɪ, hɪm, ɪm, hɪz, ɪz, hɪmself, ɪmself/).

The occupant of the second position is a phrase consisting of two words and another phrase. The forms of the first word cannot have its definitive form, in the sense that when followed by negation the phonological form is /kɑːn/; if not followed by negation, as in *He can swim*, Ability would be expressed as /kæn/. The second word is inserted into the structure in response to the Negative operator at the Representational Level, but is not definitive either, since depending on the circumstances it will appear as a contracted form or not. At the Phonological Level, a clitic—a separate word at the Morphosyntactic Level with its own distribution—becomes part of the same phonological word as the element to which it attaches. The actual form required $(Pw_j: /kɑːnt/ (Pw_j))$ is brought about through a process known as lexical priority (the preference for a ready-made form over one created by the application of rules; cf. Dik 1997a: 345). The occupant of the only word slot within the embedded (Vp_j), finally, has already acquired its definitive form /swɪm/ at the Representational Level, just like /traɪ/ in the previous example. The ability operator is expressed not only as 'can' but also as a requirement that the immediately following verb should appear in its stem form; this will also apply to /mʌst/ in (12) above as an expression of Obligation.

Consider now (15):

(15)   John must have been swimming.

for which we assume the following morphosyntactic structure:

(16)   (Cl$_i$: [(Np$_i$: (Nw$_i$: /dʒɒn/ (Nw$_i$)) (Np$_i$))$_{Subj}$ (Vp$_i$: [(Vw$_j$: /mʌst/ (Vw$_j$))
        (Vw$_k$: /hæv/ (Vw$_k$)) (Vw$_l$: be-Part (Vw$_l$)) (Vp$_j$: (Vw$_m$: /swɪm-ɪŋ/
        (Vw$_m$)) (Vp$_j$))] (Vp$_i$))] (Cl$_i$))

This structure is the morphosyntactic expression of the following configuration at the Representational Level:

(17)   (infer p$_i$: (ep$_i$: (ant e$_i$: [(prog f$_i$: [(f$_j$: swim (f$_j$)) (x$_i$)$_A$] (f$_i$)) (e$_i$)$_U$]) (ep$_i$))
        (p$_i$))

in which the following operators apply to the following layers: (i) Infer(ential) to the Propositional Content (p$_i$); (ii) Ant(erior) to the State-of-Affairs (e$_i$); (iii) Prog(ressive) to the Configurational Property of the State-of-Affairs (f$_i$). Thus (iii) is within the scope of (ii) and both are within the scope of (i). These scope relations will not be reduplicated at the Morphosyntactic Level, but rather will help to determine the forms found there. As we will show below, morphosyntactic expression proceeds in a top down fashion, which in this case means that higher operators are expressed before lower ones. Thus, Inferential is realized first as the invariable form /mʌst/ plus the above-mentioned requirement that the following word within the Verb Phrase should appear in the stem form. Anterior is realized as a form of *have* (here, given the requirement imposed by Inferential, the stem form) plus the requirement that the following verb take the suffix -Part[iciple]. The verb that actually occurs is triggered by the Progressive operator, which is realized as a form of *be* (plus the suffix-Part imposed by Anterior) plus the requirement that the following verb take the suffix /-ɪŋ/. A definitive form of the verb *be* cannot be inserted here, hence the analysis with the placeholder; at the Phonological Level we will find /bɪn/ corresponding to be-Part. The verb *swim* is given in the form of a placeholder for the alternative forms {/swɪm, swæm, swʌm/}. Note, finally, that the suffix /-ɪŋ/ is already in its definitive form and can be introduced at this level. *Swimming* is here analysed as a Verb Phrase rather than a Verbal Word because of the possibility of placing it in clause-initial position, where in English only phrases or sequences of phrases may appear:

(18)   Swimming they must have been.

These few examples have served to show that the phonological representations that constitute the ultimate output of the grammar (and the input to the Output Component) are made up of elements that are introduced as soon as they attain their definitive form. As a result, FDG can show exactly to which level or levels of organization each component part of an utterance must be ascribed.

Note that in what follows we will only make a distinction between phonemic forms and placeholders in those cases in which we are explicitly discussing the division of labour between the two. Where this issue is not at stake, we will use orthographic forms for both.

4.2 The organization of the Morphosyntactic Level

4.2.1 Introduction

Having looked at the relation between the Morphosyntactic Level and the other levels of the grammar (and thereby inevitably seen something of the internal workings of the former), let us now turn to a presentation of the Morphosyntactic Level as such. We will consider the various layers that need to be assumed in the hierarchical make-up of this level. An important point here will be the claim that languages may differ in the extent to which they impose hierarchical organization upon their morphosyntactic structure. This will bring us to a hoary issue in functional linguistics, whether or not to recognize a Vp in the sense of a grouping of verb and non-subject arguments, concluding that this, too, is a matter in which languages may differ in a principled manner. The section will conclude with a discussion of the morphological typology of languages, drawing upon two dimensions of variation: the degree of semantic transparency, i.e. the extent to which there is in a language a one-to-one correspondence between units of meaning and units of form; and the degree of synthesis, i.e. the extent to which languages permit more than one lexical unit to occur within a single morphosyntactic word. We will consider the repercussions of these distinctions for FDG and end with an FDG view on another parameter of typological analysis, the difference between what have become known as head-marking and dependent-marking languages.

4.2.2 Hierarchical structure

The general schema for the Morphosyntactic Level of a Linguistic Expression consisting of at least one Clause is as follows, where each constituent unit may occur more than once:

(19) $(Le_1: [(Cl_1: [(Xw) (Xp_1: [(Xw) (Xp_2) (Cl_2)] (Xp_1))(Cl_3)] (Cl_1))] (Le_1))$
      Le = Linguistic Expression
      Cl = Clause
      Xp = Phrase (of the type x)
      Xw = Word (of the type x)

We will show below that not all Linguistic Expressions contain a Clause. In (19) we see a hierarchy of layers of analysis that shows many parallels with the hierarchical organization of the Interpersonal Level and the Representational Level. Thus the largest unit of analysis, a Linguistic Expression, is seen as consisting of Clauses; in turn, each Clause may consist of one or more Words, one or more Phrases and, as an instance of recursion, one or more Clauses; each Phrase can similarly consist of one or more Words, one or more Phrases and one or more Clauses (the two last-mentioned again involving recursion). The Word will also have its internal structure, namely as a series of morphemes (or placeholders for morphemes).

The structure given in (19) shows the possibilities allowed by the theory and is therefore highly abstract (or etic) in various ways. Firstly, the number of the items constituting any layer is unspecified, and the items are unordered and unlabelled. In the (emic) grammar of any particular language, the number of items of a particular kind to be found at each layer will be specified; the linear order of those items will be laid down; and each of the resultant positions will be labelled by means of a subscript. Secondly, as emphasized in our discussion of the Interpersonal Level in Chapter 2, FDG covers units of all degrees of morphosyntactic complexity or simplicity. Thus no more hierarchy will be assumed than is required for satisfactory analysis.

Let us briefly consider what is meant by the various morphosyntactic categories introduced by (19). Each of the categories will be discussed in depth in the following sections of this chapter.

A Linguistic Expression is any set of at least one unit; where there is more than one unit within a Linguistic Expression, they will demonstrably belong together in their morphosyntactic properties. These units may be Clauses or Phrases. Consider the following examples from Kashmiri (Wali and Koul 1997: 75):

(20)   Paga:h   yizi   jalɨd natɨ   ne:rɨ   bɨ   kunuyzon.
        tomorrow come.IMP soon   otherwise   leave-FUT 1SG alone
        'Come early tomorrow, otherwise I will go alone.'

(21) $(Le_i: [(Cl_i: [(Advp_i: (Advw_i: paga:h (Advw_i)) (Advp_i)) (Vp_i: (Vw_i: yizi (Vw_i)) (Vp_i)) (Advp_i: (Advw_j: jalɨd (Advw_j)) (Advp_i))] (Cl_i)) (Cl_j: [(Gw_i: natɨ (Gw_i)) (Vp_j: (Vw_j: ne:rɨ (Vw_j)) (Vp_j)) (Np_i: (Nw_i: bɨ (Nw_i)) (Np_i)) (Advp_j: (Advw_k: kunuyzon (Advw_k)) (Advp_j)) (Cl_j))] (Le_i))$

Here two Clauses (Cl_i) and (Cl_j) are linked paratactically within one Linguistic Expression (Le_i). Neither could be used on its own due to the use of the correlative strategy. The morphosyntactic organization corresponds to two Discourse Acts within one Move at the Interpersonal Level, with the fact that they can be understood as a conditional implication ('If you do not come early tomorrow, I will go alone.') strengthening the case for regarding (20) as forming a single unit.

The following example of a Linguistic Expression is from German:

(22) Je   kürzer   desto besser.
      CORR short.COMPV CORR good.COMPV
      'The shorter the better.'

Here we have two adjective Phrases linked by the correlative pair *je...desto*, thus illustrating a Linguistic Expression which does not contain a Clause:

(23) $(Le_i: [(Ap_i: [(Gw_i: je (Gw_i)) (Aw_i: kürzer (Aw_i))] (Ap_i)) (Ap_j: [(Gw_j: desto (Gw_j)) (Aw_j: besser (Aw_j))] (Ap_j))] (Le_i)$

(22) would be used in a context where brevity is being praised, for example in giving advice to a public speaker. Again the intimate connection between the two elements, linking relative lack of length to relative quality, strongly supports regarding (22) as one Linguistic Expression.

The Clause is a grouping of one or more Phrases characterized, to a greater or lesser extent, by a template for the ordering of those Phrases and, also to a greater or lesser extent, by morphological expressions of connectedness (notably government and agreement); in addition, the Clause operates as a domain for several morphosyntactic processes. While for each language analysed, the identification of Clauses will be dependent upon language-specific criteria, we believe that it is justified to posit the Clause as a universal category of morphosyntactic structure. Note, however, that Discourse Acts realized by single Phrases will not be regarded as minimal or reduced Clauses. This means that in particular Linguistic Expressions the Clause layer can— where there is no evidence for its presence, as in (22) above—be dispensed with, and that structures of the following kind are permitted, in addition to the structure shown in (19) above:

(24) $(Le_1: (Xp)^n (Le_1))$

Clauses are characterized, in keeping with the principle of functional stability (see 4.1.2 above), by templates that play an important role in determining the linear sequence of the Phrases and other units that make up each Clause. These templates interact with other constituent order principles to be presented in 4.4 to determine the ultimate sequence that will be passed on to the Phonological Level. Assignment of a Phrase to a position in the template will result from an often complex interplay between their morphosyntactic category (as Np, Vp, etc.) and their function. That function may be: (i) inherited from the Interpersonal Level (covering such pragmatic functions as Topic, Focus, Contrast, etc.); (ii) inherited from the Representational Level (covering such semantic functions as Actor, Undergoer, Locative, etc.); (iii) assigned at the Morphosyntactic Level (covering such syntactic functions as Subject and Object). The assignment of syntactic functions at the Morphosyntactic Level will be dealt with in 4.4.3.

For any one Clause in any one language, the template to be chosen will be drawn from the available primitives at the Morphosyntactic Level, much as with the choice of frames at the Interpersonal Level and the Representational Level. This could mean, of course, that the number of possible templates in any one language will be immense, and indeed, given the possibility of recursion, potentially infinite. For this reason we must allow for the possibility, in a dynamic implementation of our model, of one template calling upon another for the creation of ever more complex structures. Thus the template for an (Np_1) can call upon another template for a Clause to account for the occurrence of relative Clauses. There is a nursery song one of whose verses runs as follows—and further verses follow which add more complexity:

(25)   This is the cat that killed the rat that ate the malt that lay in the house that Jack built.

in which the Np *the cat…built* can be represented making use of an Np template consisting of a Nominal Word (Nw) and a Clause (Cl), with the Clause containing an Np position that may be filled again by this Np template:

(26) $(Np_i: [(Nw_i: cat (Nw_i)) (Cl_i: […(Np_j: [(Nw_j: rat (Nw_j)) (Cl_j: […(Np_k: [(Nw_k: malt (Nw_i)) (Cl_k: […(Np_l: [(Nw_l: house (Nw_l)) (Cl_l) (Np_l))…] (Cl_k))] (Np_k))…] (Cl_j))] (Np_j))…] (Cl_i))] (Np_i))$

This is how FDG reflects, at clausal layer, the notion of recursion, with a finite stock of templates permitting an unbounded number of possible configurations.

The various templates that can be observed will, where possible, be reduced to a small number of macrotemplates. These, it will be assumed, provide the skeleton of the morphosyntax of the language under examination. In a sense, the familiar SVO, SOV, etc. characterizations of languages can be seen as highly schematic macrotemplates. We will, however, transfer to the Morphosyntactic Level a formalism that showed its value in our discussion of the Representational Level (cf. 3.2.3). Just as the optional addition of States-of-Affairs may be shown as in (27), so the possibility of adding an in principle unlimited number of Adposition Phrases to a template can be shown as in (28):

(27) $[\dots(e_{1+n})\dots]$

(28) $[\dots(\text{Adpp}_{1+n})\dots]$

Thus, English (29) would satisfy the macrotemplate in (30):

(29)   I saw him in London on Thursday with his mother in a car on several different occasions.

(30) $(\text{Cl}_1\colon [(\text{Np}_1)\,(\text{Vp}_1)\,(\text{Np}_2)\,(\text{Adpp}_{1+n})]\,(\text{Cl}_1))$

Similarly, the representation of (31) would satisfy the macrotemplate (32):

(31)   John must have been swimming.

(32) $(\text{Vp}_1\colon [(\text{Vw}_{1+n})\,(\text{Vp}_2)]\,(\text{Vp}_1))$

where the actual value of n is 3, the maximum being 4, given that examples like *must have been being observed* display the maximum complexity available.

   Copula insertion (to be presented in greater detail below in 4.5.6) is one example of how the Morphosyntactic Level responds to mismatches at the Representational Level. Where, for semantic reasons, any kind of non-verb, for example a Noun or Adjective, is used as the main predicate in a predication, there is a mismatch between the definitional function of the non-verb (see 3.7.2.3) and its actual use. By inserting a verbal copula, as in English, the Morphosyntactic Level mitigates the mismatch at that level. In Hengeveld and Mackenzie (2005: 21–2) it is argued that in an example of a presentative like (33):

(33)   There is beer without alcohol.

the Communicated Content at the Interpersonal Level contains only a Referential Subact: $(C_I\colon [(R_I)_{\text{TOPFOC}}]\,(C_I))$ (cf. 2.7.2.6). If the (R_I) were to be realized as only an Np, there would be no place for marking the tense of (33). The Morphosyntactic Level resolves this by introducing the dummy copula. (For a thorough treatment of such existential constructions in FG, see Hannay 1985.)

   The analysis of adverbs like *quickly* in (34) should also be seen as a matter of resolving a mismatch:

(34)   That dog runs quickly.

Here a Manner with the adjective *quick* as its head modifies the Verb *run*, as is clear from the following analysis at the Representational Level:

(35)   (pres e$_i$: [(f$_i$: [(f$_j$: run$_V$ (f$_j$): [(m$_i$: [(f$_k$: quick$_A$ (f$_k$)) (m$_i$)$_U$]) (f$_j$)$_U$) (dist 1
       x$_i$: [(f$_l$: dog$_N$ (f$_l$)) (x$_i$)$_U$])$_A$] (f$_i$)) (e$_i$)$_U$])

The mismatch between the Verb-modifying function of the adjective and its expected Noun-modifying function is resolved at the Morphosyntactic Level by marking it with the suffix -ly. Note that not all dialects of English require this marking (dial. *The dog runs quick*), which suggests it is indeed a morphosyntactic rather than a deeper property of the English language.

A Phrase (Xp) is characterized by the fact that it is headed by a lexical item that is passed on from the Interpersonal Level or the Representational Level. There is no necessary one-to-one correspondence between the lexeme classes recognized in a language and the Phrase types and corresponding word classes recognized within that same language. A language with a highly flexible lexeme class may have a variety of Phrase types. Consider the following example from Mundari (Evans and Osada 2005: 354–5):

(36)   Buru=ko   bai-ke-d-a.
       mountain=3.PL make-COMPL-TR-PRED
       'They made the mountain.'

(37)   Saan=ko   buru-ke-d-a.
       firewood=3.PL mountain-COMPL-TR-PRED
       'They heaped up the firewood.'

The lexeme *buru* can be used as the head within a Referential Subact (36) and as the head within an Ascriptive Subact (37), and can thus be characterized as a contentive lexeme. Yet the morphosyntax of Mundari makes a clear distinction between the Phrase expressing the Ascriptive Subact and and the one expressing the Referential Subact, traditionally called 'Verb Phrase' and 'Noun Phrase'. We will use this traditional terminology, but do not commit ourselves to the view that a Verb Phrase is headed by a verbal lexeme, and a Noun Phrase by a nominal lexeme, though the result in syntax will be a Verbal Word and a Nominal Word. The Verbal Words in (36)–(37) carry suffixes for aspect, transitivity and predicativity, while the Nominal Words lack affixation (note that *ko* is a second-position clitic, not a suffix). Thus, the two instances of *buru* in (36) and (37) may be represented as in (38) and (39) respectively:

(38)   (Np$_i$: (Nw$_i$: buru$_{Cont}$ (Nw$_i$)) (Np$_i$))

(39)   (Vp$_i$: (Vw$_i$: buru$_{Cont}$ (Vw$_i$)) (Vp$_i$))

The Nominal and Verbal Word templates will then be different as regards their possibilities for suffixation.

By extension, we will apply this analysis to isolating languages, where the differences between Verb Phrases and Noun Phrases are visible not so much in different word forms but rather in different configurational properties. The following examples are from Samoan (Mosel and Hovdhaugen 1992: 80):

(40)   'Ua mālosi le   lā.
       PRF strong ART sun
       'The sun is strong.'
       "The sun strongs."

(41)   'Ua lā   le   aso.
       PRF sun ART day
       'The day is sunny.'
       "The day suns."

The lexeme lā can be used as the head within a Referential Subact (40) and as the head within an Ascriptive Subact (41), and can thus be characterized as a contentive lexeme. Yet the syntax of Samoan makes a rigid distinction between the Phrase expressing the Referential Subact and the Phrase expressing the Ascriptive Subact. In the former the contentive is preceded by an article, in the latter by a tense/aspect particle. Thus the contentive lexeme is a Nominal Word in syntax in (40) and a Verbal Word in syntax in (41).

The extent to which the Clause is divided into Phrases will differ from language to language in response to the structuring of the Interpersonal Level. The frequently mentioned distinction between configurational and non-configurational languages (cf. Hale 1983; Heath 1986; Golumbia 2004) is, as we shall see, in FDG not simply a matter of different syntactic analyses varying in degree of hierarchy. To give an example of nonconfigurationality, let us consider Blake's analysis of Kalkatungu, in which 'there are in fact no noun phrases, but...where an argument is represented by more than one word we have nominals in parallel or in apposition....Each word is a constituent of the Clause' (Blake 1983: 145; quoted by Rijkhoff 2002: 19–20). We will slightly rephrase this by saying that in Kalkatungu there are Noun Phrases, but that these do not provide a slot for modifiers. In such a language, then, Noun Phrases would have the following maximal structure:

(42) $(Np_1: (Nw_1) (Np_1))$

Consider a Clause such as the following, from Kalkatungu (Blake 1983: 145):

(43)   Cipayi icayi yaɲi   ʈukuyu yauntu.
       this.ERG bite white.man dog.ERG big.ERG
       'This big dog bit/bites the white man.'

Whereas in the configurational language English a Phrase such as *this big dog* cannot be broken up, in Kalkatungu each of the three ergative-marked elements of (43) and the two other elements can appear in any position in the Clause. Thus (43) represents only one of $5 \times 4 \times 3 \times 2 \times 1 = 120$ different word-order possibilities. The three Words *cipayi*, *ṭukuyu*, and *yauntu* share ergative marking, which allows the Addressee to understand that they belong together semantically: for this reason, they will be shown as one unit at the Representational Level, bearing the semantic function Actor. Nevertheless, there is morphosyntactically no reason to assume that such a unit corresponds to a Phrase, as it would in English. Rather the choice of word order is fully determined by other factors than connectedness at the Representational Level; word-order choices, where they are not simply arbitrary, must be determined by factors from the Interpersonal Level. Accordingly, the three Words in question will correspond to different Referential Subacts at the Interpersonal Level, evoking—without any ordering or dependency—'this one', 'a dog one', and 'a big one'. The example will therefore be analysed as follows at the various levels, with the Morphosyntactic Level quite directly reflecting the Interpersonal Level:

(44)   IL: $(C_I: [(T_I) (R_I) (R_J) (R_K) (R_L)] (C_I))$

RL: $(e_i: (f_i: [(f_j: icayi_V (f_j)) (x_i: [(f_k: ṭukuyu_N(f_k)) (x_i)_U]: [(f_l: yauntu_N (f_l)) (x_i)_U]: [(f_m: cipayi_N (f_m)) (x_i)_U])_A(x_j: [(f_n: yaɲi_N(f_n)) (x_j)_U])_U] (f_i)) (e_i)_U])$

ML: $(Cl_i: [(Np_i: (Nw_i: cipayi (Nw_i)) (Vp_i: (Vw_i: icayi (Vw_i)) (Vp_i)) (Np_j: (Nw_j: yaɲi (Nw_j)) (Np_j)) (Np_k: (Nw_k: ṭukuyu (Nw_k)) (Np_k)) (Np_l: (Nw_l: yauntu (Nw_l)) (Np_l))] (Cl_i))$

Some support for this approach to nonconfigurational languages comes, perhaps paradoxically, from Legate (2003), who argues in a formalist framework for an analysis of Warlpiri, the first language to be identified as nonconfigurational (Hale 1983), as being configurational after all. She argues, for example, that the placement of adverbials in Warlpiri is not free but follows the ordering principles enunciated for a strongly hierarchical view of Italian syntax by Cinque (1999), in an approach which closely parallels—as Cinque himself points out—the semantic layering originally used in FG and taken over in FDG. In this light, we take Legate's observations to support the notion of a hierarchically structured Representational Level for such languages. In addition, Legate argues that the syntactic units of Warlpiri are ALL moved by transformation from their underlying positions to a number of 'higher' positions characterized by pragmatic functions as Illocution Phrase, Focus Phrase, or Topic Phrase: this in turn supports the notion of the relative placement of units in such languages being sensitive to the pragmatic function of interpersonal units.

The notion of non-configurationality at the Phrase layer, in languages for which the Phrase is a relevant category, is linked to another important issue, the question whether any Phrases should be inherently grouped into a higher-order 'superphrase', a VP constituent in the sense of a syntactic grouping, in relevant Clauses, of the verb and its non-subject arguments (note that we will use the capitalized form VP to refer to such a constituent rather than Vp, which in FDG is a Phrase that may consist of just a verb or another lexical element used predicatively); this would add configurationality to such a series of Phrases in the same way as phrase structure lends configuration to a set of words. As shown in (19) above, FDG does not recognize a layer of morphosyntax between the Phrase and the Clause. At the Representational Level, there is no combination of the arguments of a predicate that would correspond to a VP, nor is there a similar grouping of the Subacts within the Communicated Content (but see Smit fc. for a different view). However, it can happen that more than one Subact has the same pragmatic function. As we will see, this can be the basis for certain languages to treat them as a syntactic grouping.

Although many syntactic approaches assume a VP, it is not universally valid across the languages of the world. The matter is discussed by Van Valin (2001: 119ff.). He argues that the presence of highly 'free' constituent order in a language (such as for example Lakhota) does not entail the non-existence of a VP. Rather he proposes that the recognition of a VP is determined by three tests: (i) is there evidence of a pro-VP in the language, like English *do so*?; (ii) is permutation possible, i.e. can the alleged constituent appear in different positions in the Clause while retaining its integrity? (iii) can the alleged VP be coordinated with another grouping of the same structure? On this basis, the grouping *catch a fish for dinner* is indeed a VP in English:

(45) a. I caught a fish for dinner and Bill *did so* too.
      b. I said I would catch a fish for dinner, and *catch a fish for dinner* I did!
      c. I caught a fish for dinner and *baked it in the oven*.

Van Valin (2001: 121) then examines the situation in Lakhota, and finds that this language yields a negative answer to all three questions.

Where, then, does the VP grouping of English come from? Note that the crucial test examples all involve the coordination of Discourse Acts; what is more, the second Discourse Acts in (45) are all dependent for their occurrence (and grammaticality) on the presence and particular type of the preceding Discourse Act. In addition, as already noted by Van Valin and LaPolla (1997: 527–8), the Illocution of the respective Discourse Acts must be the same:

(46) a. *I caught a fish for dinner and did Bill *do so too*?
      b. *You said you would catch a fish for dinner, and *catch a fish for dinner* did you?
      c. *He caught a fish for dinner and *did bake it in the oven*?

These observations are pointers to the involvement of the Interpersonal Level. Note that in (46a), the Communicated Content of the first Discourse Act will contain four Subacts, one of which will be Topic so that the others will not have a pragmatic function on that parameter (i.e. will belong by default to the Comment). In this light, *do so* in (46a) can be seen as representing a communicative unit corresponding to the group of Subacts that are Comment in the preceding utterance. In the formulation of *Bill did so too*, the Conceptual Component draws upon information registered in the Contextual Component arising from the Comment section of the immediately preceding utterance. In (46b), *catch a fish for dinner* again represents a Comment (again in the sense of a group of non-Topic Subacts), but in this case, arguably for purposes of emphasis, the Speaker draws from the Contextual Component not just the information but also the form of the Words and now deploys it as the Topic of the second Discourse Act (this supports the observation in 3.14 that the Contextual Component may on occasion store actual Word sequences). In (46c), finally, we see a variant of Discourse Act coordination in which the second Discourse Act is presented without any explicit Topic because it is shared with the preceding Discourse Act. What this discussion suggests is that VP in English is a reflection of the division of the Communicated Content of Discourse Acts into Topic and Comment, and corresponds to a grouping of non-Topics. Van Valin and LaPolla (1997: 218) come to much the same conclusion, namely that what they call 'the actual focus domain' (in FDG, the Comment) 'includes exactly what would traditionally be considered the VP'.

Nevertheless, there is evidence that the VP does have some autonomous status in the structure of the English Clause, namely the fact that Topics that are not Subject are not treated in the same way—and Subject is of course complementary to VP. Consider the following data:

(47) A: What about that fish?
      B: a. Well, I caught it for dinner and Mary baked *Ø in the oven.
          b. Well, it was caught for dinner (by me) and baked in the oven (by Mary).

In (47Ba), the fish is Topical, and yet the expression of the Comment Subacts (*I, caught, for dinner*) cannot be coordinated with those of the second Clause (*Mary, baked, in the oven*). This is only possible if, as in (47Bb), the Topic is also Subject. The conclusion may then be that Subject relates to VP in the same way as Topic to Comment: just as Comment is an epiphenomenon that does not require systematic marking, so the VP can be regarded as an epiphenomenon, namely the totality of Phrases that remain within a Clause after one of them has been assigned Subject function, discounting of course Phrases with a modifying function.

To conclude this section, then, we have seen that the morphosyntactic Component allows crosslinguistic flexibility with regard to the issue of configurationality: languages may differ in the extent to which semantically related Words are grouped into Phrases, and to which Phrases are grouped into larger units.

4.2.3 Grammatical morphemes and secondary operators

The aim of FDG is to provide an account of structure which is equally valid for all types of languages. Differences in the linear order within the Clause and within the Phrase will be dealt with in 4.4.2 and 4.5.2 respectively. Here will we focus on morphological typology and on the distinction between head-marking and dependent-marking languages.

Morphological types can be defined according to the two parameters of semantic transparency and synthesis. Along the first parameter we may distinguish isolating, agglutinating, and fusional languages. Isolating languages are semantically transparent in the sense that in the ideal type of an isolating language there is a one-to-one relation between a Word and a unit of meaning, whereas in agglutinating languages there is ideally a one-to-one relation between a morpheme and a unit of meaning. Fusional languages are semantically opaque in the sense that there is no one-to-one relation between a unit of form and a unit of meaning. Along the second parameter we may distinguish between polysynthetic and non-polysynthetic languages. Polysynthetic languages allow the presence of more than one lexical element within a single Word, while non-polysynthetic languages do not.

The two parameters are basically independent of each other: the first is primarily concerned with the status of grammatical elements in the language, whereas the second has to do with the status of lexical elements. As a result, polysynthetic languages can be either fusional or agglutinating just like non-polysynthetic languages. The only restriction in terms of combinations of the two parameters is that a polysynthetic language cannot at the same time be isolating. The types distinguished here are of course idealized: many languages exhibit features of more than one morphological type.

Examples from languages of these different types are given below: Fijian (48, Milner 1972: 42) exemplifies an isolating language, Turkish (49, van Schaaik p.c.) an agglutinating language, Spanish (50) a fusional language, and Southern Tiwa (51, Allen *et al.* 1984: 293) a polysynthetic language. The glosses clearly reveal the morphological structure of the languages involved: in (48) the gloss is a word-by-word translation, in (49) it is a morpheme-by-morpheme translation, in (50) a one-to-many translation; and in (51) the gloss reveals the presence of two lexical elements within a single word. Note that (51) is a case of syntactic incorporation (cf. Smit 2005), as the incorporated object is cross-referenced on the verb.

(48)   Mo dou kauta mada yani na cina.
     IMP 2.PC take MIT away ART lamp
     'Take the lamp away.'

(49)   Anlı-y-abil-ecek-miş-im.
     understand-CONN-ABIL-IRR-INFER-1.SG
     'I gather I will be able to understand.'

(50)   Lleg-ó.
     arrive-IND.PST.PFV.3.SG
     'He/she/it arrived.'

(51)   Te-shut-pe-ban.
     1.SG.SBJ>PL.OBJ-shirt-make-PST
     'I made (the) shirts.'

Let us now consider how each language type will be handled by FDG.

The analysis of (48) at the Interpersonal Level and the Representational Level will be as in (52):

(52)   IL: $(A_I: [(mit F_I: IMP (F_I)) (P_I)_S (P_J)_A (C_I: [(T_I) (R_I: [-S,+A] (R_I))$
           $(+s R_J)] (C_I))] (A_I))$
     RL: $(e_i: [(f_i: [(f_j: kauta (f_j): (l_i:-yani-(l_i)) (f_i)_U) (pauc x_i)_A$
           $(x_j:-cina-(x_j))_U])f_i)) (e_i)_U])$

The lexical items *kauta*, *yani*, and *cina* are available at the Representational Level and are transferred to the Morphosyntactic Level without change. The grammatical Words *mo*, *mada*, and *na* are inserted at the Morphosyntactic Level, in direct translation of the Illocution 'IMP' and the primary operators Mit and +s respectively. Finally, the combination of $(R_I: [-S,+A] (R_I))$ at the IL and (pauc x_i) at the Representational Level yields *dou* '2nd person paucal' at the Morphosyntactic Level. It is characteristic of an isolating language that the translation from the Interpersonal and Representational Levels to the Morphosyntactic Level is maximally simple and that the definitive form of morphemes is already available in formulation or is finalized at the

Morphosyntactic Level; there is thus no need for placeholders of the type discussed in 4.1.3 above. Here is the Morphosyntactic Level analysis of (48):

(53) ML: (Le$_i$: (Cl$_i$: [(Gw$_i$: mo (Gw$_i$)) (Vp$_i$: [(Gw$_j$: dou (Gw$_j$)) (Vw$_i$: kauta (Vw$_i$)) (Gw$_k$: mada (Gw$_k$)) (Advp$_i$: (Advw$_i$: yani (Advw$_i$)) (Advp$_i$))] (Vp$_i$)) (Np$_i$: [(Gw$_l$: na (Gw$_l$)) (Nw$_i$: cina (Nw$_i$))] (Np$_i$))] (Cl$_i$)) (Le$_i$))

To summarize, the characteristics of an isolating language are as follows: (i) there is a one-to-one relation between Words at the Morphosyntactic Level and units at the Representational and Interpersonal Levels; (ii) there is no need for placeholders; (iii) Words have no internal layering.

Turning now to the agglutinating language Turkish and example (49) (van Schaaik p.c.), which we repeat here for convenience as (54):

(54) Anlı-y-abıl-ecek-miş-im.
understand-CONN-ABIL-IRR-INFER-1.SG
'I gather I will be able to understand.'

we note that there is again a one-to-one correspondence between the elements of the Interpersonal and Representational Levels and the morphemes at the Morphosyntactic Level. Here are the representations of (54) at the Interpersonal and Representational Levels:

(55) IL: (A$_I$: [(F$_I$: DECL (F$_I$)) (P$_I$)$_S$ (P$_J$)$_A$ (C$_I$: [(T$_I$) (R$_I$: [+S, −A] (R$_I$))] (C$_I$))] (A$_I$))

RL: (infer p$_i$: (ep$_i$: (irr e$_i$: [(abil f$_i$ [(f$_j$: anlı$_V$ (f$_j$)) (1x$_i$)$_A$] (f$_i$)) (e$_i$)$_U$]) (ep$_i$)) (p$_i$))

In Turkish, the actual form of the morpheme is determined by the phonological process of vowel harmony. As a shorthand for the phonological representation, the vowels subject to vowel harmony are capitalized: AbIl, −EcEk, −mIş, and −Im. These four morphemes are in a one-to-one relationship with the primary operators Abil, Irr, Infer and the combination of (R$_I$: [+S, −A] (R$_I$)) at the Interpersonal Level with (1x$_i$)$_A$ at the Representational Level respectively. The connecting intervocalic glide −y− is inserted at the Phonological Level in response to the phonological environment: it will be absent from the Morphosyntactic Level. All this reflects the morphological transparency of this language. The morphosyntactic analysis of (54) will be as in (56) (for further details see 4.6.5 below on Word templates):

(56) (Le$_i$: (Cl$_i$: (Vp$_i$: (Vw$_i$: [(Vs$_i$: anlı (Vs$_i$)) (Aff$_i$: AbIl (Aff$_i$)) (Aff$_i$: EcEk (Aff$_i$)) (Aff$_i$: mIş (Aff$_i$)) (Aff$_i$: Im (Aff$_i$))] (Vw$_i$)) (Vp$_i$)) (Cl$_i$)) (Le$_i$))

To summarize, the characteristics of an agglutinating language are as follows: (i) there is a one-to-one relation between morphemes at the Morphosyntactic Level and units at the Representational and Interpersonal Levels; (ii) there is no need for placeholders; (iii) Words have internal layering.

The Spanish example (50), which we repeat here for convenience as (57), exemplifies a fusional language:

(57)   Lleg-ó.
       arrive-IND.PST.PFV.3.SG
       'He/she/it arrived.'

The bound grammatical morpheme -*ó* must be inserted at the Phonological Level, being the expression of the placeholder 'indpastpf3sg' introduced at the Morphosyntactic Level. Let us consider the Representational and Interpersonal Level representations:

(58)   IL: $(A_I: [(F_I: DECL (F_I)) (P_I)_S (P_J)_A (C_I: [(T_I) (R_I: [-S, -A]$
             $(R_I))_{Top}] (C_I))] (A_I))$
       RL: $(past ep_i (sim e_i: [(pf f_i: [(f_j: \lambda eg_V- (f_j)) (1x_i)_A] (f_i)) (e_i)_U]) (ep_i))$

Here there is a many-to-one relationship between on the one hand the presence of the Illocution DECL (cf. 4.5), the primary operators Past and Pf and the combined presence of $(R_I: [-S, -A] (R_I))$ and $(1x_i)_A$, and on the other hand the single morpheme -*ó*. This is typical of the lack of transparency of this language. This means that the Morphosyntactic Level will suffix a placeholder 'indpastpf3sg' to the verbal stem /ʎeg-/. The Phonological Level will convert this to an accent-bearing suffix -*ó*. Here is the Morphosyntactic Level analysis of (59):

(59) $(Le_i: (Cl_i: (Vp_i: (Vw_i: [(Vs_i: /\lambda eg/ (Vs_i)) (Aff_i: indpastpf3sg (Aff_i))]$
       $(Vw_i)) (Vp_i)) (Cl_i)) (Le_i))$

To summarize, the characteristics of a fusional language are as follows: (i) there is a one-to-many relation between a morpheme at the Morphosyntactic Level and multiple units at the Representational and Interpersonal Levels; (ii) placeholders are required; (iii) Words have internal layering.

Turning now to the Southern Tiwa example (51), we immediately note similarity with the agglutinating type exemplified in (49). However, a distinctive feature of this example is that two lexical items that are semantically distinct are united within the same Word. Let us consider the Interpersonal and Representational Level analyses of this example, repeated here as (60):

(60)   Te-shut-pe-ban
       1.SG.A>PL.U-shirt-make-past
       'I made (the) shirts.'

(61) IL: $(A_I: [(F_I: DECL (F_I)) (P_I)_S (P_J)_A (C_I: [(T_I) (R_I: [+S, -A] (R_I))$
            $(R_J)] (C_I))] (A_I))$

      RL: $(past ep_i: (sim e_i: [(f_i: [(f_i: pe_V (f_i)) (1x_i)_A (mx_j: (f_j: shut_N (f_j))$
            $(x_j))_U] (f_i)) (e_i)_U]) (ep_i))$

Among the morphosyntactic primitives of Southern Tiwa, there will be a Word template (62):

(62) $(Vw_1: [(Aff_1) (Ns_1) (Vs_1) (Aff_1)] (Vw_1))$

which will permit translation of the Interpersonal and Representational Level representations into the morphosyntactic representation (63):

(63) $(Le_i: (Cl_i: (Vp_i: (Vw_i: [(Aff_i: ti (Aff_i)) (Ns_i: shut (Ns_i)) (Vs_i: pe (Vs_i))$
      $(Aff_j: ban (Aff_j))] (Vw_i)) (Vp_i)) (Cl_i)) (Le_i))$

To summarize, polysynthetic languages like Southern Tiwa are characterized by: (i) a lack of isomorphism between the Interpersonal and Representational Levels on the one hand and the Morphosyntactic Level on the other hand; (ii) internal layering of Words. Depending on the fusional or agglutinating nature of the language placeholders may or may not be required.

Let us now turn to the distinction between head-marking and dependent-marking languages, which was introduced in Nichols (1986). According to this approach to language typology, entire languages, or particular constructions within them, may be classified according as head or dependents display morphosyntactic marking of the relation between them. Nichols shows that each language as a whole will tend to use one or the other type of marking and that crosslinguistically there is a certain tendency for languages to adopt head-marking rather than dependency-marking, although both types are found in sufficient measure. She criticizes grammatical theories for usually assuming dependent-marking to be basic, perhaps because the Indo-European languages most familiar to western grammarians are all dependent-marking.

In FDG terms, a careful distinction needs to be made between, on the one hand, head–modifier relations and, on the other, nucleus–dependent relations. Typical examples of the former are the relations between noun and attributive adjective, between noun and alienable possessor, and between adjective and degree adverb. For these, FDG predicts that, if one of the two members of the pair is morphosyntactically marked, it will be the modifier. This is in keeping with the correspondence between functional markedness and morphosyntactic marking: just as a modifier is functionally marked in being an optional specification of the head, so we may expect it to be the bearer of morphological marking reflecting its modifying role.

Nucleus–dependent relations are those between a predicate and its argument(s), whether that predicate be verbal, nominal, or adpositional. Here the relation is not one of an expansion of a head with an optional modifier: the arguments and the predicate are in an equipollent relationship determined by the relevant predication frame and together constitute a head. It might appear, since semantic functions are shown as subscripts on arguments, that FDG is nevertheless biased towards dependent-marking in the same way as other theories criticized by Nichols (1986). Nevertheless, as pointed out in 3.6.2.3, this is merely a representational convention: the semantic function holds BETWEEN the nucleus and the dependent and should be understood as characterizing that relation:

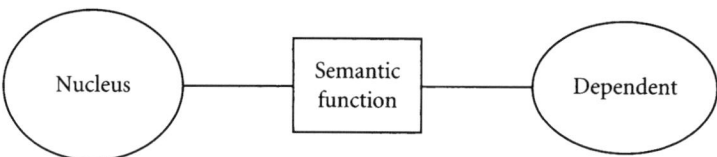

At the Morphosyntactic Level, the expression of the semantic function, which expresses the relation between nucleus and dependent, can be attributed to either.

As an example of dependent-marking, consider the following example from Chechen (Nichols 1986: 61):

(64)   Da:-s   woʕa-na urs-Ø   tü:xira.
       father-ERG son-DAT knife-NOM strike.PST
       'The father stabbed the son.'

The two arguments of the verb and the instrument modifier are all dependents of the verb as nucleus of the predication, and in this language are marked for the semantic function that links them to the nucleus. Compare now the following example of head-marking from Abkhaz (Nichols 1986: 61, Hewitt 1979: 36), in which the nucleus contains three prefixes, one for each of the semantic relations between the nucleus and its three arguments (none of which is morphologically marked):

(65)   A-xac'a   a-pħ° əs   a-š°q°'ə
       DEF-man DEF-woman DEF-book
       Ø-lə-y-te-yt'.
       3.NH.ABS-3.F.DAT-3.M.ERG-give-FIN
       'The man gave the woman the book.'

Nucleus–dependent relations also obtain between nominal and adpositional predicates and their arguments: thus in *John's brother* and *under the table*, the heads are *brother* and *under* respectively. In consistently nucleus-marking languages, as we shall call them, it is the nucleus that bears the marking of the dependency. In Jarawara (Dixon 2000: 489; 2004: 314–15), for example, the gender-marking on the head of an expression of inalienable possession (i.e. in which the possessee takes the possessor as its argument at the Representational Level) is for about 50 per cent of inalienably possessed nouns determined by the gender of the possessor. Thus *man-* 'arm' is marked as feminine if the person whose arm is being described in feminine:

(66)   Manira   man-i
       Manira   arm-F
       'Manira's arm'

With alienable possession in Jarawara, where the relationship is between head and modifier, the gender-marking on the head is determined by the inherent gender of the possessed noun.

As an example of the marking of an adpositional predicate as nucleus, consider (67), again from Abkhaz (Nichols 1986: 60, Hewitt 1979: 103):

(67)   a-jǝyas   a-q'nǝ
       DEF-river   3.NH.POSS-at
       'at the river'

FDG thus generates the expectation that where there are relations between a nucleus and its dependents, then, if there is marking of the relationship, either the nucleus or the dependent, or indeed both, may be marked. An instance of double marking (of nucleus and dependent) may be observed in Hungarian two-place verbs with a definite second argument, which are nucleus-marked for both the first and the second argument, as well as dependent-marked for the roles of these arguments (see de Groot 1989: 20–1).

FDG also generates the expectation that with head–modifier relations, the modifier rather than the head will be marked, and indeed marking of the head is rather rare. Bickel (in prep.) states that of the 157 languages he investigated, head-marking in this sense is found in only 3. An example of this rare type is Persian, in which the head is marked by the 'ezafe' marker *-e* (Mahootian 1997: 68, see also 3.9.2):

(68)   ketab-e   jaleb
       book-EZAFE   interesting
       'an interesting book'

To conclude this section, then, we may state that FDG is capable of hosting languages of all morphological types and of showing how exactly they differ from one another in how the Morphosyntactic Level interacts with the Interpersonal Level and the Representational Level. Furthermore FDG generates specific predictions as regards what is usually considered to be head-dependent marking. The way in which FDG representations are built up leads to a further subdivision of the markings of relation between head and modifiers on the one hand, and nucleus and dependents on the other.

4.3 Linguistic Expressions

A Linguistic Expression is any set of at least one unit that can be used independently; where there is more than one unit within a Linguistic Expression, they will demonstrably belong together morphosyntactically, while, crucially, one is not part of the other. The units that may combine in this way may be Clauses or Phrases, which do not only combine with themselves but also with each other. Consider the following examples from Kashmiri (Wali and Koul 1997: 138):

(69) Sɔ cha t'uːt jaːn   gevaːn   yuːt mohni oːs.
      she is   CORR much.good sing.PRS.PTCP REL   Mohan was
      'She sings as well as Mohan used to sing.'

(70) Yuth vɔstaːd t'uth tsaːṭh.
      REL   teacher   CORR   disciple
      'The disciple is as the teacher.'

These examples both illustrate mutual dependency. Given the use of correlative elements, neither of the two units in (69) and (70) could be used independently, yet neither is a constituent of the other. We will call this situation 'equiordination'.

Apart from these cases of mutual dependency of two units, Linguistic Expressions may also contain one unit that could be used independently and one that could not. Van der Auwera (1997) illustrates this by means of the following examples from Tauya (MacDonald 1990: 227) and English:

(71) Peima   fitau-fe-e-te   wate tepau-a-ʔa.
      carefully throw-PF-1/2.SG-DS NEG   break-3.SG-IND
      'I threw it carefully and it didn't break.'
      "Me having thrown it carefully, it didn't break."

(72) As for the students, they have heard the news yesterday.

The Tauya example in (71) illustrates the phenomenon of cosubordination (Olson 1981), a phenomenon that we touched upon when discussing Episodes in 3.4. Here the first Clause could not occur on its own, yet it is not a constituent of the second Clause, which could occur on its own. In (72) the Clause could be used independently, but the introductory Noun Phrase could not; yet the latter is not a constituent of the former.

TABLE 6. The constitution of a Linguistic Expression

	Mutually dependent	One-way dependent	No dependency
Clause	Equiordination (69)	Cosubordination (71)	Coordination (73)
Phrase	Equiordination (70)	Extra-clausality (72)	Listing (74)

A final situation in which two or more units form a Linguistic Expression is one in which neither is a constituent of the other, each could occur on its own, but the combination of units forms a single formal unit. The following examples illustrate this situation:

(73) Celtic won and Rangers lost.

(74) (Can I take your order?) A Big Mac, French fries, and a Coke.

The coordination of two Discourse Acts in (73) is realized morphosyntactically as an explicitly marked coordination of two Clauses. (74) is a typical example of listing. Note that we have deliberately chosen a context in which the list cannot be interpreted as an incomplete Clause.

The various examples of the constitution of a Linguistic Expression can be summarized as in Table 6.

These can be represented as follows:

(75) $(Le_1: [(^{dep}Cl_1) (^{dep}Cl_2)] (Le_1))$ Clausal Equiordination

(76) $(Le_1: [(^{dep}Cl_1) (^{dep}Cl_{n-1}) (Cl_n)] (Le_1))$ Cosubordination

(77) $(Le_1: [(Cl_1) (Cl_{n-1}) (Gw_1) (Cl_n)] (Le_1))$ Coordination·

(78) $(Le_1: [(Xp_1) (Xp_2)] (Le_1))$ Phrasal Equiordination

(79) $(Le_1: [(Xp_1) (Cl_1)] (Le_1))$ Extra-clausality

(80) $(Le_1: [(Xp_1) (Xp_{n-1}) (Gw_1) (Xp_n)] (Le_1))$ Listing

Note that the superscript used for dependent Clauses is here just shorthand for the specific templates that individual languages may require for dependent Clauses.

4.4 Clauses

4.4.1 Introduction

Ignoring the specific order in which constituents occur, a Clause in a configurational language like English has the following formula:

(81) $(Cl_1: [(Xw) (Xp)_{\{\Phi\}}(Cl)_{\{\Phi\}}] (Cl_1))$

where each constituent may occur more than once. In other words, a Clause in such a language consists of a sequenced configuration of Words (Xw), Phrases (Xp), and other (embedded) Clauses (Cl). (For a foundational FG study of positional syntax in English, see Connolly 1991.) Phrases and Clauses may carry a syntactic function (ϕ). The semantic dependency relations among these items have been specified at the Representational Level and therefore need not be reduplicated here. Since, as we have argued earlier, lexical elements are always the heads of Phrases at the Morphosyntactic Level, Words at the Clause layer can only be grammatical ones, such as conjunctions, particles, and the like. In this section we consider the internal constitution of Clauses.

The linear order of elements within the Clause will be considered from two different perspectives. As we argued earlier, the Interpersonal Level is organized on the basis of two types of frame: interpersonal frames and content frames. The former take care of the hierarchical organization of the Interpersonal Level, the latter of the non-hierarchical organization of the Subacts within the Communicated Content. Similarly, the Representational Level is organized on the basis of representational frames, taking care of the hierarchical aspects of the Representational Level, and of predication frames, taking care of the non-hierarchical organization of Configurational Properties. This may be shown as in (82)–(83):

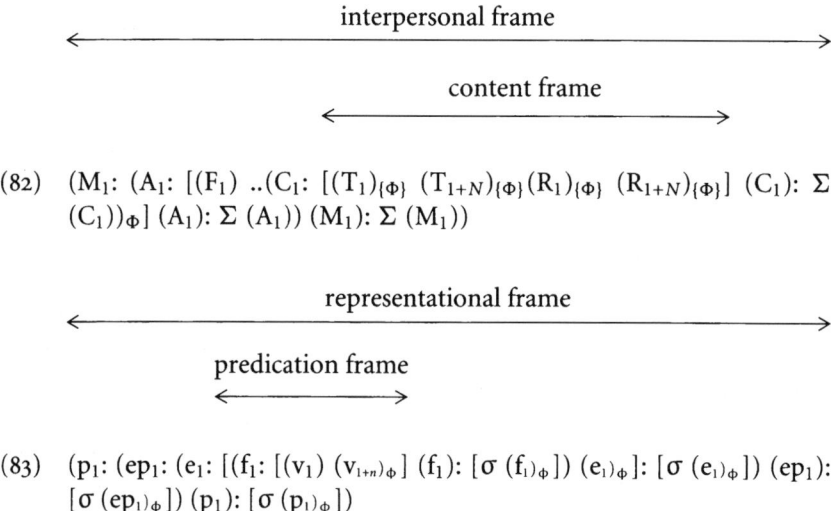

interpersonal frame

content frame

(82) $(M_1: (A_1: [(F_1) \,..(C_1: [(T_1)_{\{\Phi\}} \ (T_{1+N})_{\{\Phi\}}(R_1)_{\{\Phi\}} \ (R_{1+N})_{\{\Phi\}}] (C_1): \Sigma (C_1))_{\Phi}] (A_1): \Sigma (A_1)) (M_1): \Sigma (M_1))$

representational frame

predication frame

(83) $(p_1: (ep_1: (e_1: [(f_1: [(v_1) \ (v_{1+n})_\phi] (f_1): [\sigma \ (f_1)_\phi]) (e_1)_\phi]: [\sigma \ (e_1)_\phi]) (ep_1): [\sigma \ (ep_1)_\phi]) (p_1): [\sigma \ (p_1)_\phi])$

Given the overall and systematic top-down organization of FDG, we will assume that the ordering of elements in morphosyntax also proceeds in a top-down manner, and will therefore start in 4.4.2 with the morphosyntactic expression of the hierarchically organized parts of the Interpersonal and Representational Levels, starting with the highest layers and working down to the lowest ones until we touch upon the content and predication frames. The expression of the latter is not sensitive to hierarchical ordering, but to alignment, an issue we will discuss in 4.4.3 before discussing the actual ordering of the elements constituting content and predication frames in 4.4.4. We will thus assume that there are morphosyntactic counterparts, to be called templates, presented in 4.4.5, to hierarchical and non-hierarchical frames, though as we will see these may partly interlock.

Obligatory positions in templates for which no material is available from the Interpersonal and Representational Levels are filled with dummies, which will be treated in 4.4.4. We are then ready to treat agreement relations in 4.4.7. Since agreement may be sensitive to order, it can only be dealt with as this stage. After thus concluding the discussion of the organization of main Clauses, we will pay attention to the form and structure of subordinate Clauses in 4.4.8, and coreferential relations within and between Clauses in 4.4.9.

4.4.2 Ordering of hierarchically related units

In the top-down and hierarchical approach outlined above, we predict that the optimal way to proceed in a dynamic implementation of encoding interpersonal and representational units, excluding those that are in a configurational rather than hierarchical relationship, is as follows:

$$(84) \quad \Sigma^M/\pi^M \rightarrow \Phi^A/\Sigma^A/\pi^A \rightarrow \Sigma^F/\pi^F \rightarrow \Phi^C/\Sigma^C/\pi^C \rightarrow$$
$$\phi^{ep}/\sigma^{ep}/\pi^{ep} \rightarrow \phi^p/\sigma^p/\pi^p \rightarrow \phi^e/\sigma^e/\pi^e \rightarrow \sigma^f/\pi^f$$

That is, we start by putting functions, modifiers, and operators of Moves into the appropriate clausal (and extra-clausal, see below) positions and end with operators and modifiers of Configurational Properties of States-of-Affairs. Within each group functions are expressed before operators and modifiers, since functions are external to the unit to which they apply. Thus, we obey the principle of iconicity (see 4.1.2) when ordering hierarchically related units.

When starting out the process of placing elements in the appropriate position, three positions are immediately available: the Clause-initial position (P^I), the Clause-medial position (P^M), and the Clause-final position (P^F). The two peripheral positions (P^I and P^F) are psychologically salient (Gernsbacher 1990) and their deployment in communication has been much studied within the functional-linguistic framework (cf. Mackenzie 2000, Hannay and Martínez-Caro 2008). Some systems of constituent order can be systematically described starting from just these two positions. The Clause-medial position is less salient as it is not a uniquely identifiable position, given the varying numbers of constituents a Clause may contain. The relevance of this distinction was shown in Hengeveld *et al.* (2004).

Further clausal positions can be defined relative to these three absolute positions, such as the postinitial (P^{I+1}), penultimate (P^{F-1}), and postmedial (P^{M+1}) positions within the Clause. These can only be filled when the absolute position relative to which they are defined has been filled already. Note that, at the outset, the postinitial (P^{I+1}) and penultimate (P^{F-1}) relative positions coincide superficially with the absolute medial position (P^M), as follows:

(85) P^M
    P^I P^{I+1}
        P^{F-1} P^F

Note furthermore that some languages have an absolute second position, P^2, which we will come back to later. The combinations of Clauses with extra-clausal constituents give further opportunities to distinguish positions at the Clause margins, as illustrated in (86) and (87):

(86)   As for his ideas, I don't like them.

(87)   I don't like them, his ideas.

The positions involved here are actually not clausal positions, but positions within the Linguistic Expression (Le). For reasons of exposition we will deal with their ordering here. The relevant positions could be defined as P^I and P^F within the Linguistic Expression, the Clause itself occupying the medial position, as indicated in (88), in which the bar (|) provisionally indicates the Clause boundary, in anticipation of a more systematic treatment in 4.4.5.

(88)   Linguistic Expression: P^I | Clause | P^F
       Clause: | P^I P^M P^F |

To distinguish between P^I and P^F at the layer of the Linguistic Expression and of the Clause, we will use P^{pre} for the preclausal position, P^{centre} for the clausal position, and P^{post} for the postclausal position within the resulting expression, with the result given in (89):

(89)   Linguistic Expression: P^{pre} | P^{centre} | P^{post}
       Clause: | P^I P^M P^F |

These are the positions the encoder has to work with when starting to put elements into the appropriate positions in a top-down manner: three absolute positions, and two relative ones. Only when elements have been put into any of these positions do new relative positions become available.

As an illustration of how this affects the expression of modifiers in a top-down approach, consider the following constructed example:

(90) Finally (Σ^A), she honestly (Σ^F) reportedly (Σ^C) has been drinking again.

Example (90) contains a series of interpersonal modifiers. It is clear from the example that these are placed in a centripetal manner, i.e. starting from the outside. The relatively highest modifier has to be in the outermost non-clausal position (P^{pre}). If this modifier is not present, the next modifier down may occupy this position, as illustrated in (91):

(91) Honestly, she reportedly has been drinking again.

Interpersonal modifiers prefer this Clause-external position when it is available, i.e. not occupied by a higher modifier. When this position is not available, the next candidate goes to the P^M position, as in the case of *honestly* in (90). That this is Clause-medial position P^M and not the postinitial position P^{I+1} can be deduced from the fact that P^I has not yet been filled at this stage, so that no further positions can be defined relative to it. Once P^M is filled, new relative positions can be defined with respect to it and host other modifiers, as in the case of *reportedly* in (90). These patterns may thus be represented as in (92) and (93):

	P^{pre}		P^I	P^M	P^{M+1}	
(92)	finally$^{\Sigma A}$	|		honestly$^{\Sigma F}$	reportedly$^{\Sigma C}$	(=90)
(93)	honestly$^{\Sigma F}$	|		reportedly$^{\Sigma C}$		(=91)

Now consider the placement of representational modifiers in (94a–c):

(94) a. Probably (σ^p), she has been drinking continuously (σ^f) again (σ^e) recently (σ^{ep}).
  b. Probably (σ^p) she has been drinking continuously (σ^f) again (σ^e) recently (σ^{ep}).
  c. She probably (σ^p) has been drinking continuously (σ^f) again (σ^e) recently (σ^{ep}).

In these examples of grammatical orderings of modifiers the same principle applies. Representational modifiers prefer to stay within the main Clause, and they too are positioned within the Clause in a centripetal manner, by starting from the left and the right edges, filling in absolute positions first and thereby creating new relative positions, as shown in the following representations of (94a–c):

(95) P^{pre} | P^I P^M ... P^{F-2} P^{F-1} P^F

  a.   probably$^{\sigma P}$ | continuously$^{\sigma f}$ again$^{\sigma e}$ recently$^{\sigma ep}$ (=94a)
  b. | probably$^{\sigma P}$ continuously$^{\sigma f}$ again$^{\sigma e}$ recently$^{\sigma ep}$ (=94b)
  c. | probably$^{\sigma P}$ continuously$^{\sigma f}$ again$^{\sigma e}$ recently$^{\sigma ep}$ (=94c)

When (90) and (94) are conflated, the result is as in (96):

(96)   Finally, she honestly reportedly probably has been drinking continuously again recently.

In this unnatural, yet grammatical example it becomes clear that the placement of interpersonal modifiers precedes the placement of representational modifiers, witness the position of *probably* to the right of the series of interpersonal modifiers counting from the left edge. This is represented in (97):

      P^{pre} | P^I P^M P^{M+1} P^{M+2} ...P^{F-2}
(97)   finally$^{\Sigma A}$ | honestly$^{\Sigma F}$ reportedly$^{\Sigma C}$ probably$^{\sigma P}$ ...continuously$^{\sigma f}$
      P^{F-1} P^F

    again$^{\sigma e}$ recently$^{\sigma ep}$

As we indicated already in 3.7.2.3.2, we find a lot of evidence across languages that functions, operators, and modifiers are indeed placed centripetally. If there is morphosyntactic marking of Illocution, for example, we observe a strong tendency for Illocution markers to take either Clause-initial or Clause-final position, or both. As pointed out in 2.5.2.3, in English the nature of the occupant of the Clause-initial position is a good guide to the Illocution of the Discourse Act. Other languages have specific markers for yes-no questions, which in Polish is Clause-initial (the particle *czy*) and in Mandarin Chinese Clause-final (the particle *ma*; Li and Thompson 1981: 547ff.). In Russian, a yes-no question is signalled phonologically; an alternative is placement of *li* immediately after the Clause-initial constituent (Meyer and Mleinek 2006); in Ute (Givón 1984: 219; 277), yes-no questions are formed by adding the clitic *-a(a)* after the first Word of a Clause (even if it is part of a Phrase). In Wolof (Torrence 2005: 67) the question particle *ndax* may occur in either Clause-initial or Clause-final position. Truly Clause-medial indicators of illocutionary status are to our knowledge not found.

   Relations between Discourse Acts, as expressed by rhetorical functions, are also typically expressed by Clause-initial or Clause-final elements. Coordinators, for example, are usually found in Clause-initial position with respect to a non-initial series of coordinated Clauses; an interesting case is Scots *but*, which may be found Clause-finally, cf., from the online Dictionary of the Scots Language, s.v. *but* adv.:

(98) You can get maist things on video these days. Ye have tae look aroon but.

Adverbs acting as modifiers of Discourse Acts are similarly encountered above all in either of the extreme positions of the Clause. Thus we find *not* as an irony signaller in Clause-final position *He's cute not*, and similarly for the emphasizer *dammit*.

All these phenomena point towards a preference for phenomena that are situated higher in the hierarchy to be expressed in either initial or final position within the Clause. The position may be fixed: the interrogative particles *czy* in Polish and *ma* in Mandarin Chinese, for example, can only appear in initial and final position respectively, just as English ironic *not* can only be Clause-final. Some modifiers, however, display more freedom to appear in either initial position (where they indicate the interpersonal role of what is to follow) or in final position, often as an adjustment of what has been said to the ongoing interaction.

In languages that are predicate-initial or predicate-final, we might expect to find two possibilities. Where the languages in question are rigidly predicate-initial or predicate-final, hierarchically related units will be obliged to situate themselves at the opposite end of the sequence. An example of a strongly predicate-final language is Korean, in which it would appear that a Discourse Act modifier like *tahaynghi* 'fortunately' can only occur Clause-initially (Lee 2001: 58):

(99) Tahaynghi John-i   Mary-ka   chayk-ul ilk-key   hayessta.
     Fortunately John-NOM Mary-NOM book-ACC read-NMLZ cause.PST
     'Fortunately, John caused Mary to read a book.'

However, no language seems to be so strongly predicate-initial that it disallows hierarchically related units in initial position. Thus predicate-initial Scottish Gaelic permits the act-modifying *gu fortanach* 'fortunately' to precede the predicate:

(100) Gu_fortanach bha   caraid a'   fuireach faisg orm.
      Fortunately be.PST friend PROG dwell   near on-1.SG
      'Fortunately, there was a friend of mine living near me.'

And similarly in Tagalog we find (Nagaya 2006):

(101) Sa=kasamaang-palad bhumiagsak si=Gaga   sa=pagsusulit.
      Unfortunately   AV.failed   NOM=Gaga DAT=examination
      'Unfortunately Gaga failed the examination.'

Where the language is less strongly oriented to initial or final position of the predicate, we might expect hierarchically related units to precede or follow the verb respectively. Consider Japanese as a predicate-final language that (primarily in conversational interaction, Hinds 1986: 166) allows final placement of a modifier of the Discourse Act:

(102)   Datte, nodo ga   itai mono, hontoo-ni.
         and   throat NOM hurt thing really
         'And I have a sore throat, really.' (Hinds 1986: 167)

As for the Representational Level, the same observations hold. As we saw in 3.5.3, a modifier of an Episode may be combined with a modifier of a State-of-Affairs. In example (103):

(103)   Yesterday Sheila went out before dinner.

the Episode-modifier *yesterday* occurs in initial position and the State-of-Affairs modifier *before dinner* in final position. If both were to be combined in final position, note that *yesterday* (despite being formally simpler) prefers to occur in absolute final (i.e. a more peripheral) position:

(104)   Sheila went out before dinner yesterday.

(105)   ?Sheila went out yesterday before dinner.

Example (105), if used, could only be justified by application of Contrast to *before dinner*, i.e. if the reflection of a pragmatic function outweighs that of hierarchical structure. This situation is related to non-hierarchical aspects of order, which we will return to in 4.4.4.

4.4.3 Alignment

4.4.3.1 Introduction

We use the term alignment to refer to the way in which non-hierarchically related pragmatic and semantic units map onto morphosyntactic ones. Foley (2005: 385) refers to this as the 'mapping problem' and defines it as: 'how to align lexically specified arguments of a predicate with their formal, structural realizations'. Many theories take recourse to grammatical relations to account for alignment, assuming universality for these. In FDG grammatical relations are also recognized, and formalized as syntactic functions at the Morphosyntactic Level, but they are not assumed to be universal. Syntactic functions are relevant only in those cases in which the formal properties of linguistic units cannot be reduced to the pragmatic and the semantic categories and functions underlying them, i.e. they are relevant when there is neutralization of semantic and pragmatic distinctions (see e.g. Bakker and Siewierska 2007). In cases where there is no such neutralization, we will not assume the presence of syntactic functions in the morphosyntactic representation of a Clause (see also Falk 2006). Given the organization of FDG, we may, as a result, distinguish three basic types of alignment:

(i) interpersonal alignment: in this type of alignment the morphosyntactic organization reflects the organization of the Interpersonal Level, either in terms of the pragmatic functions (Topic, Focus, etc.) of Subacts, and/or in terms of their reference (definiteness, specificity, etc.);

(ii) representational alignment: in this type of alignment the morphosyntactic organization reflects the organization of the Representational Level, either in terms of the semantic functions (Actor, Undergoer, etc.) of semantic categories, or in terms of their designation (animacy, person, etc.);

(iii) morphosyntactic alignment: in this type of alignment the morphosyntactic organization is not a direct reflection of the organization of the Interpersonal and/or the Representational Level, but exhibits its own organization in terms of the syntactic functions (Subject, Object) of morphosyntactic constituents, and/or in terms of complexity/weight (Word, Phrase, etc.).

Given these three types of alignment we might classify languages as having an interpersonally organized grammar, a representationally organized grammar, or a morphosyntactically organized grammar. But these can just be considered as tendencies. As with the types of languages recognized in e.g. morphological typology and word-order typology, languages often exhibit mixed systems of alignment, for instance one in which referentiality (interpersonal) and animacy (representational) together produce certain alignment effects; or one in which agreement is representational in nature, but conjunction reduction is morphosyntactically determined (see Keenan 1976 on coding and behavioural properties of Subjects). Nevertheless, to show the effects of the three types of alignment, we will discuss them one by one, looking at a number of examples of relatively pure alignment of the three types.

4.4.3.2 Interpersonal alignment

An interesting example of interpersonal alignment may be found in Tagalog (cf. van der Auwera 1981). The alignment system of this language has provoked a lot of interest and conflicting analyses in the literature, but we will here follow Bickel (fc.), who argues that, in order to account for the occurrence of an Np with the preposed clitic *ang*, 'all that matters is that the NP has specific reference and that it is the most topical element in discourse' (Bickel fc.: 8). Bickel is clearly referring here to notions that we have identified in Chapter 2 as being interpersonal in nature. Consider the following examples:

(106)   bumilí   *ang=lalake*   ng=isda   sa=tindahan.
        PFV.AV.buy   SPEC.TOP=man   OBL=fish   LOC=store
        'The man bought fish at the/a store.'

(107)   binilí   ng=lalake *ang=isda*   sa=tindahan.
        PFV.UV.buy   OBL=man   SPEC.TOP=fish   LOC=store
        'The/a man bought the fish at the/a store.'

(108)   binilhan   ng=lalake ng=isda   *ang=tindahan.*
        PFV.LV.buy   OBL=man   OBL=fish   SPEC.TOP=store
        'The/a man bought fish at the store.'

Although the *ang*-marker can be said to be interpersonal in nature, it clearly interacts with the Representational Level when it comes to expressing the predicate of the sentence: the form chosen for the predicate depends on the semantic function of the representational unit which corresponds to the specific Topical Interpersonal Subact. Thus in (106) the predicate shows that the Topic is an Actor, in (107) that is an Undergoer, and in (108) that it is a Location. Since *ang*-marking masks the expression of the semantic function of the argument involved, it is only through the form chosen for the predicate that the semantic function of this argument can be retrieved. Thus, we find the following correspondences between the Interpersonal Level, the Representational Level, and the Morphosyntactic Level in (106)–(108):

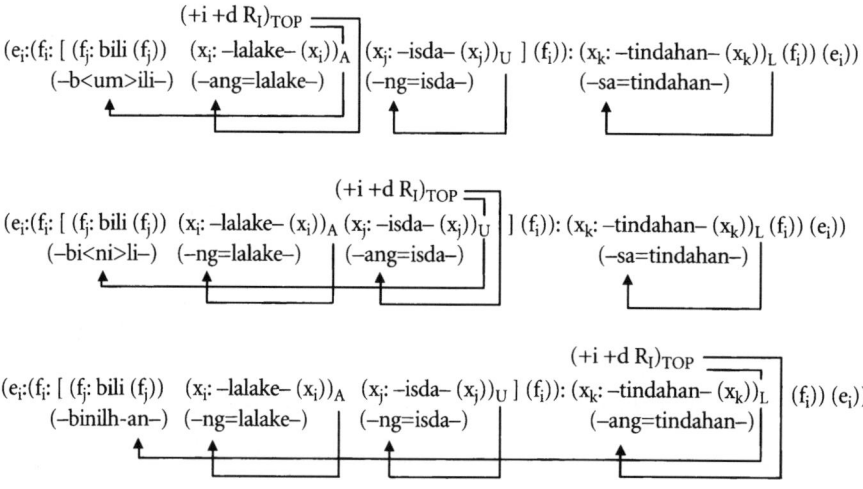

In order to account for these facts there is no need to postulate syntactic functions. The morphosyntactic encoder just has to know what the Topic is in order to mark the corresponding unit with *ang,* and what the semantic function of the *ang* Phrase is in order to select the appropriate form of the predicate. Not only coding properties but also behavioural properties can be dealt with in this way. Conjunction reduction, which applies to *ang* Phrases, can be defined in terms of the Topic notion directly.

If *ang*-marking is determined at the Interpersonal Level, we expect it to be insensitive to the argument/modifier distinction that is relevant to other types of alignment, since the argument/modifier opposition is irrelevant at the Interpersonal Level. And indeed Tagalog allows a wide range of semantic units to be expressed as the specific Topic, including modifiers of the State-of-Affairs, such as the Locative modifier in (104). Another example is the following, in which the *ang*-Phrase (here realized in a special demonstrative form) is an Instrument (Himmelmann 2005):

(109) ipang-pù-putol ko   na   lang itóng   kutsilyo.
       INS-IMPF-cut   1.SG.POSS now only PROX.LK knife
       'I will just cut it with this knife.'

The prefix *ipang-* in this example consists of the conveyance voice marker *i-* and the instrument marker *pang-*. The combination is sometimes considered to constitute a single marker of instrument topics (see Himmelmann 2005).

The fact that the marking is independent of the argument/modifier distinction also shows up in the fact that both argument and non-argument expressions with the same semantic function occur with the same type of marking on the predicate. Thus, Locative arguments and Locative modifiers acting as specific Topics will both be marked by the locative form of the predicate.

4.4.3.3 Representational alignment

4.4.3.3.1 *Introduction*   Representational alignment systems may be sensitive to the semantic function of a semantic category, or to the designation of such categories. We will discuss both types of alignment here.

4.4.3.3.2 *Semantic function*   A language in which alignment is highly sensitive to semantic functions is Acehnese. Durie (1985: 190) explicitly presents Acehnese as a subjectless language, showing that its syntax is sensitive to semantic functions rather than to grammatical relations. Arguments may have one of three semantic functions: Actor (A), Undergoer (U), and Recipient (R). Actors and Undergoers (in both cases mainly human ones) are cross-referenced on the verb through clitic pronouns. The Actor clitics precede the verb, the Undergoer clitics follow the verb. This is also true of Actors and Undergoers in one-place predication frames (Durie 1985: 55–8):

(110)   Lôn teungöh=lôn=jak.
        1   middle=1.A=go
        'I am going/walking.'

(111)   Gopnyan galak=geuh   that
        3.POL   happy=3.POL.U very
        'He is very happy.'

(112)   Gopnyan na=lôn=timbak=geuh
        3.POL   AUX=1.A=shoot=3.POL.U
        'I shot him.'

The Actor in (110) is cross-referenced on the verb through a proclitic, the Undergoer in (111) through an enclitic, and both are present to mark the Actor and Undergoer in (112).

Freestanding Actors are furthermore marked by means of the preposition *lê*, while for Recipients the preposition *keu* is available. In the absence of cross-referencing on the verb for Recipients, this is the only expression of this semantic function (Durie 1985: 182):

(113)   Keu=jih   ka=geu=jôk   buku=nyan lê=gopnyan.
        to=3.FAM   INCH=3.POL.A=give book=that   by=3.POL
        'He (polite) gave him (familiar) that book.'

Note that the inanimate Undergoer is not cross-referenced on the verb.

One further factor is that when any argument is topicalized, it occurs without its preposition. The Topic position in Acehnese is the one immediately preceding the verb. The absence of the agentive preposition *lê* in this position was illustrated in the earlier example (110). The absence of the dative preposition is shown in (114) (Durie 1985: 182):

(114)   Gopnyan ka=lôn=bi   peng.
        3.POL   INCH=1=give money
        'I have given him some money.'

The dative marking in (113) seems to contradict the analysis, given the fact that the Recipient is in preverbal position. However, it is not obligatory to have a Topic, as shown by the fact that one can be added to a sentence like (113). Compare the following examples (Durie 1985: 182):

(115)   Keu=gopnyan lôn hana=galak=lôn.
        DAT=3.POL   I   NEG.AUX=like=1
        'I don't like him.'

(116)   Gopnyan   (*lôn)   hana=galak=lôn.
        3.POL   I   NEG.AUX=like=1
        'I don't like him.'

The unmarked Recipient in (116) does not allow a following unmarked argument, while the marked Recipient in (115) does.

We may describe these facts without having recourse to grammatical relations. The organization of argument expression in Acehnese is primarily organized in terms of the semantic functions of arguments. Secondarily, in the presence of Topic assignment at the Interpersonal Level semantic functions are not expressed. Thus the interaction between the three levels may be illustrated as in the following representations of (112)–(114):

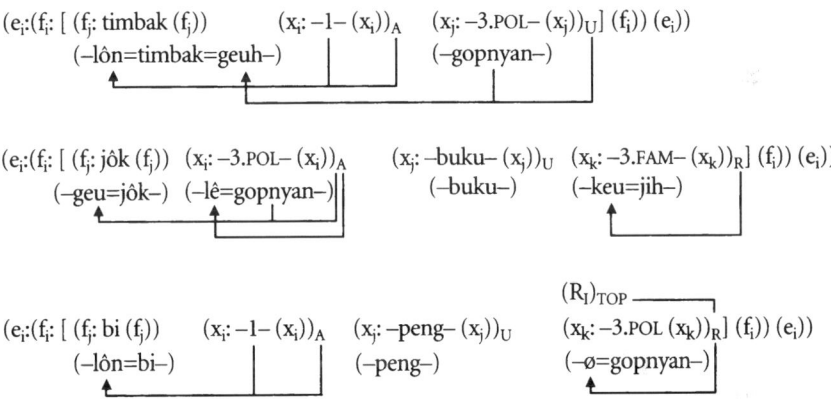

4.4.3.3.3 *Designation*   The second type of representational alignment is called hierarchical alignment, since its organization is dependent on hierarchies of animacy and person. A good example of a language exhibiting this type of alignment is Plains Cree, as described in Wolvengrey (2005). The following examples serve to illustrate some features that are crucial to this type of alignment system (Wolvengrey 2005: 423):

(117)   Ni-wîcih-â-nân-ak
        1-help-DRCT-1.PL.3.PL
        'We help them.'

(118)   Ni-wîcih-iko-nân-ak
        1-help-INV-1.PL.3.PL
        'They help us.'

In (117) and (118) the same person markers are used for first person plural (*ni-*
-nân) and third person plural (*-ak*), in exactly the same positions, regardless of

the semantic functions (Actor and Undergoer) of the participants. In order to correctly assign a semantic function to the two participants a person hierarchy has to be taken into account, which ranks second person over first person over third person. If the higher-ranking person is the Actor, the verb is inflected as being direct (DRCT), if the lower-ranking person is the Actor, the verb is inflected as being inverse (INV); see also Nedergaard Thomsen (2005) on Mapudungun. Thus, since in (117) first person ranks over third person, and the first person is the Actor, the direct construction is used, while in (118) the third person is the Actor and the inverse construction is used.

When there are two third persons one is marked as proximate (PROX) and the other as obviative (OBV). The proximate third person ranks over the obviative third person, so that the resulting person hierarchy is as in (119) (Wolvengrey 2005: 424):

(119)   2 → 1 → 3.PROX → 3.OBV

A third person is marked as proximate when it is the Topic at the Interpersonal Level, and obviative when it is not, so that (119) may be rewritten as:

(120)   2 → 1 → 3.TOP → 3.NONTOP

The result of this arrangement is that the interpretation of the semantic functions of participants may be reversed through the direct-inverse system or through the proximate-obviative system. When both are applied simultaneously, the interpretation of the semantic functions does not change, thus opening up the possibility of expressing all possible combinations of pragmatic and semantic functions, as the following examples illustrate (Wolvengrey 2005: 425):

(121)   Câniy-Ø   kî-wîcih-ê-w   Mêrî-wa.
        Johnny-PROX TNS-help-DRCT-3 Mary-OBV
        'Johnny helped Mary.'

(122)   Câniy-wa   kî-wîcih-ê-w   Mêrî-Ø.
        Johnny-OBV TNS-help-DRCT-3 Mary-PROX
        'Mary helped Johnny.'

(123)   Câniy-Ø   kî-wîcih-ikw(-w) Mêrî-wa.
        Johnny-PROX TNS-help-INV-3   Mary-OBV
        'Mary helped Johnny.'

(124)   Câniy-wa   kî-wîcih-ikw(-w) Mêrî-Ø.
        Johnny-OBV TNS-help-INV-3   Mary-PROX
        'Johnny helped Mary.'

In (121) Johnny is Topic-Actor, in (122) NonTopic-Undergoer, in (123) Topic-Undergoer, and in (124) NonTopic-Actor. Similarly, Mary is NonTopic-Undergoer in (121), Topic-Actor in (122), NonTopic-Actor in (123), and Topic-Undergoer in (124). The system may be illustrated by means of the following multilevel representation of (121) and (123):

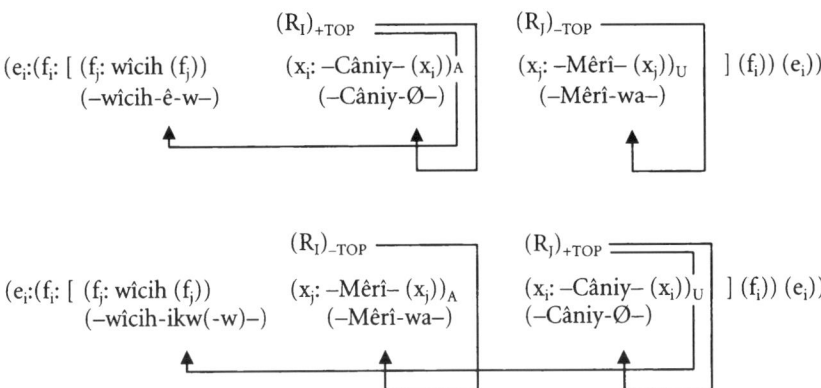

Note that in Cree the importance of notions such as animacy and person is also manifest in ditransitive constructions. In these, it is always the Recipient that is treated as the Object, being higher in animacy (Wolvengrey, p.c.). This is typical of the primative-secundative alignment type that we will discuss in 4.4.3.4.2.

Hierarchical alignment is also relevant for the analysis of languages for which the grammatical relation of Subject is relevant but the grammatical relation of Object is not. In this type of language the Undergoer argument may align in different ways depending on its place on a designational hierarchy. Thus, in Spanish the marking of an Undergoer is dependent on its humanness and specificity. Consider the following examples:

(125) Busco   una   casa.
       look.for-1.SG.PRS INDF house
       'I'm looking for a house.'

(126) Busco   una   secretaria.
       look.for-1.SG.PRS INDF secretary
       'I'm looking for a secretary.'

(127) Busco   a   una   secretaria.
       look.for-1.SG.PRS HUM.SPEC.U INDF secretary
       'I'm looking for a secretary.'

The sentence in (126) is used in the case of non-specific reference, and would for instance be appropriate in an advertisement. Sentence (127) is used in the case of specific reference and would be appropriately used by someone looking for a known person. The marker *a* is used for definite and indefinite reference as long as it is specific, and for persons and pets, but not for other animals.

4.4.3.4 Morphosyntactic alignment

4.4.3.4.1 *Introduction*   Morphosyntactic alignment may be sensitive to the syntactic functions assigned to morphosyntactic constituents, or to the complexity of these constituents. We will discuss these two situations one by one.

4.4.3.4.2 *Syntactic function*   In those cases in which the organization of morphosyntactic units cannot be reduced to the pragmatic and semantic categories and functions underlying them, syntactic functions become relevant. Consider the following examples:

(128)   The man walked.

(129)   The man fell.

The constituent *the man* is Actor in (128) and Undergoer in (129), but it is nevertheless expressed in the same way in both examples. However, in other circumstances this difference in semantic functions is relevant, as shown in the following examples:

(130)   The man saw *a dog* (U).

(131)   The dog was seen *by the man* (A).

(132)   the seeing *of the dog* (U) *by the man* (A)

This identity in form of the constituent *the man* in (128) and (129) can thus not be attributed to the semantic function of this constituent.

   The similarity in form of the constituent *the man* in (128)–(129) cannot be attributed to the pragmatic function of the constituent either, since in both cases it may be Topical, Focal, or neither. Thus (128), for example, may be an answer to any of the following questions:

(133)   What did the man do?

(134)   Who walked?

(135)   What happened?

In cases such as these, where there is neutralization of semantic and pragmatic oppositions that are otherwise relevant in the language, the neutralized

	1-place	2-place
Actor	Nominative	
Undergoer		Accusative

FIGURE 11. Nominative-Accusative alignment

behaviour of morphosyntactic constituents may be described in terms of their syntactic function, which, depending on the type of neutralization, may be either Subject or Object.

The grammatical function Subject may, as shown above, be relevant for the analysis of the expression of one-place predication frames, in the sense that languages may neutralize the distinction between Actor and Undergoer arguments in this type of frame. In languages such as English one may furthermore argue that the grammatical function of Subject is relevant even for the expression of zero-place predication frames, as it rigidly inserts a dummy subject in these constructions as well:

(136)   It is cold. (*What is cold?)

Since in this case the subject does not correspond to any underlying semantic or pragmatic unit, it can be considered a truly morphosyntactic category. The notion of Subject is equally relevant to Nominative-Accusative and to Absolutive-Ergative languages, as shown in Van Valin and LaPolla (1997), among others. The difference is that in Nominative-Accusative languages the neutralization is between the Actor/Undergoer argument of one-place predication frames and the Actor argument of two-place predication frames, while in Absolutive-Ergative languages it is between the Actor/Undergoer argument of one-place predication frames and the Undergoer argument of two-place predication frames. This is shown in Figures 11 and 12.

The relevance of the syntactic function Subject does not only follow from the neutralization facts as such, but may also be manifested by special operations leading to differential assignment of the Subject function to arguments with different semantic functions. This is, for instance, the case with passivization in Nominative-Accusative languages, when a non-Actor argument is made into the Subject:

	1-place	2-place
Actor		Ergative
Undergoer	Absolutive	

FIGURE 12. Absolutive-Ergative alignment

(137)   The man gave the book to the boy.   (A-Subject)

(138)   The book was given to the boy by the man.   (U-Subject)

(139)   The boy was given the book by the man.   (R-Subject)

In Absolutive-Ergative languages one finds anti-passivization, turning a non-Undergoer argument into the Subject of the Clause, as in the following examples from Basque (Hualde and Urbina 2003: 431):

(140)   Gutun hau   zuk   idatzia   da.   (U-Subject)
        letter this.ABS you.ERG write.PRF.DET AUX.3.SG
        'This letter has been written by you.'

(141)   Ni gutun asko   idatzia   naiz.   (A-Subject)
        I letter a.lot.ABS write.PRF.DET AUX.1.SG
        'I have written a lot of letters.'
        "I am written a lot of letters."

The same type of reasoning can be set up for the syntactic function Object. Consider the following examples from Kham (Watters 2002: 67–8, 313):

(142)   ŋa:-Ø   no:-lai   ŋa-Ø-rɨ:h-ke.
        I-NOM   he-OBJ   1.SG.SBJ-3.SG.OBJ-see-PFV
        'I saw him.'

(143)   ŋa-lai ca-o   u-cyu:-na-o-kə.
        I-OBJ good-NMLZ   DUM-look1.SG-3.SG-OPT
        'May he look favourably upon me!'

(144)   ŋa-lai bəhtanji y-ā:-ke-o.
        I-OBJ potato   give-1.SG.OBJ-PFV-3.SG.SBJ
        'He gave me a potato.'

What these examples show is that the opposition between the Undergoer in a two-place predication (142) and the Recipient in a two-place (143) or three-place predication (144) is neutralized, in the sense that they receive the same case marker and trigger the same agreement patterns on the verb. This is the only way in which these arguments can be realized in Kham and is called Primative-Secundative alignment in Haspelmath (2007). Given the neutralization involved this system has to be interpreted as involving a syntactic function Object. The system may be represented as in Figure 13.

    This is different from Directive-Indirective alignment, illustrated in the following English examples:

	2-place	3-place
Undergoer		Secundative
Recipient	Primative	

FIGURE 13. Primative-Secundative alignment

(145) He bought a book (U).

(146) He spoke to Sheila (R).

(147) He gave a book (U) to Sheila (R).

Just on the basis of these examples there would be no justification for postulating an Object function for English, since there is no neutralization involved here: Undergoers behave as Undergoers, and Recipients behave as Recipients, as shown in Figure 14.

There is, however, the possibility of assigning the Object function to the Recipient argument, with the result known as 'dative shift' shown in (148):

(148) He gave Sheila the book.

which shows neutralization of the grammatical properties of the Undergoer (in a two-place predication frame) and the Recipient (in a three-place predication frame), parallel to the situation in Kham illustrated above. This neutralization manifests itself in the order of the constituents involved and the absence of prepositional marking on the Recipient.

Many languages have special verbal derivations, usually called an applicative, to mark the shift in Object function. The following example is from Standard Indonesian (Cole and Son 2004: 341):

(149) Saya memanggang roti   untuk Eric.
      1.SG A.bake   bread for   Eric.
      'I baked bread for Eric.'

(150) Saya memanggang-kan Eric roti.
      1.SG A.bake-APPL   Eric bread
      'I baked Eric bread.'

We may thus set up the following steps showing an increasing relevance of syntactic functions. Let us start with a system with representational

	2-place	3-place
Undergoer	Directive	
Recipient	Indirective	

FIGURE 14. Directive-Indirective alignment

alignment that is completely role-based, such as that shown for Acehnese in 4.4.3.3.2, cf. Figure 15:

	1-place	2-place	3-place
A	Actor		
U	Undergoer		
R	Recipient		

FIGURE 15. Role-based alignment

In the next step, displayed in Figures 16 and 17 respectively, the syntactic function Subject becomes relevant, in either a Nominative-Accusative system or an Absolute-Ergative system, in each case with Directive-Indirective, which, as shown above, is actually role-based:

	1-place	2-place	3-place
A	Subject		
U		Undergoer	
R		Recipient	

FIGURE 16. Subjects in Nominative-Accusative/Directive-Indirective systems

	1-place	2-place	3-place
U	Subject		
A		Actor	
R		Recipient	

FIGURE 17. Subjects in Absolutive-Ergative/Directive-Indirective systems

Examples of languages exhibiting this type of alignment are English and Basque respectively. Adding the grammatical function of Object then leads to the configuration displayed in Figure 18 in a Nominative-Accusative language that has Primative-Secundative alignment, such as Kham:

	1-place	2-place	3-place
A	Subject		
R		Object	
U			Undergoer

FIGURE 18. Subjects and Objects in Nominative-Accusative/Primative-Secundative systems

	1-place	2-place	3-place
R	Subject		
U			Undergoer
A		Agent	

FIGURE 19. Subjects in Absolutive-Ergative/Primative-Secundative systems

In Absolutive-Ergative languages, however, the effect is different. If in a language the Undergoer in a two-place predication behaves like the single argument in a one-place predication (Absolutive-Ergative alignment), and the Recipient in a three-place predication behaves like the Undergoer in a two-place predication (Primative-Secundative alignment), then in fact the Subject behaviour of the single argument in a one-place predication and the Undergoer argument in a two-place predication is cumulatively extended to the Recipient argument in a three-place predication, which now takes precedence over the Undergoer in Subject behaviour, as shown in Figure 19.

The syntactic function Object is thus irrelevant in this type of system. Note that the result of the configuration in Figure 19 is that the only argument of a one-place predication, the Undergoer of a two-place predication, and the Recipient of a three-place predication all receive the same treatment, as argued convincingly in Dryer (1986: 818), who cites the following examples from Tzotzil (Aissen 1983: 277, 280):

(151)   Vinik-on.
        man-ABS.1.SG
        'I am a man.'

(152)   Mi č-a-mah-on.
        Q   ASP-ERG.2.SG-hit-ABS.1.SG
        'Are you going to hit me?'

(153)   Mi mu š-a-čon-b-on   l-a-čitome.
        Q   NEG ASP-ERG.2.SG-sell-BEN-ABS.1.SG the-your-pig
        'Won't you sell me your pigs?'

The absolutive first singular marker -on marks the single argument of the one-place predication frame in (151), the Undergoer argument of the two-place predication frame in (152), and the Recipient argument of the three-place predication frame in (153).

If a language makes use of syntactic functions, this does not mean that its grammatical organization depends in all respects on these. In Chickasaw (Munro and Gordon 1982, cited in Bickel fc.) agreement-marking on the verb shows full representational alignment, as illustrated in the following examples:

(154) a. Malili-li.   b. Chi-sso-li.
           run-1.SG.A   2.SG.U-hit-1.SG.A
           'I ran.'   'I hit you.'

(155) a. Sa-chokma.   b. Is-sa-thaana.
           1.SG.U-good   2.SG.A-1.SG.U-know
           'I'm good.'   'You know me.'

(156) a. An-takho'bi   b. Iss-am-a
           1.SG.R-lazy   2.SG.A-1.SG.L-give
           'I'm lazy.'   'You give it to me.'

The same markers are used for Actor, Undergoer, and Recipient irrespective of the valency of the frame in which they occur. The semantic functions of the arguments are sufficient to trigger the right expression here. But in its system of switch reference there is Nominative-Accusative alignment, i.e. the single argument of an intransitive predication aligns with the Actor argument of a two-place predication, as shown in the following examples:

(157) Top-at   tiwwa-li-kat   sa-hotolhko-tok.
       bed-NOM   lie-1.SG.A-SUB.SS   1.SG.U-cough-PST
       'Lying in bed, I coughed.'

(158) Alhponi' aa-sa-bashafa-kā   Bonnie-akot
       kitchen   LOC-1.SG.U-be.cut-SUB.DS Bonnie-CONTR.NOM
       sa-bashaffi-tok.
       1.SG.U-cut-PST
       'I got cut in the kitchen, and Bonnie did it.'

From the above we may derive some crosslinguistic generalizations as to the accessibility of different types of argument for the Subject or Object function. We follow Van Valin and LaPolla (1997: 317–18) in distinguishing between the accessibility hierarchies for Nominative-Accusative and Absolutive-Ergative languages, and add the Recipient.

(159) Absolutive-Ergative—Subject Assignment
       U   ⊂   A   ⊂   R

(160) Nominative-Accusative—Subject Assignment
       A   ⊂   U   ⊂   R

(161) Nominative-Accusative—Directive-Indirective—Object Assignment
                 U   ⊂   R

(162) Nominative-Accusative—Primative-Secundative—Object Assignment
                 R   ⊂   U

An important question now is how languages choose which argument becomes the Subject or Object, in those cases in which they have a choice through (anti-)passivization, dative shift, or the use of an applicative construction. After all, if these choices were determined entirely at the Interpersonal and Representational Levels we would not have to postulate syntactic functions in the first place, as argued above. The most plausible answer to this question is that the actual factors triggering the choice of Subject and Object assignment apply in the Contextual Component, outside the Grammatical Component as such. Bolkestein (1985) and Bolkestein and Risselada (1987) argue that the key factor to understanding these choices is cohesiveness, which concerns the extent to which referents have already been invoked in the preceding discourse or can be inferred from it. This type of information is stored in the Contextual Component and has to be called upon in the process of morphosyntactic encoding.

4.4.3.4.3 *Complexity*   Just as interpersonal alignment may be determined by the (referential) properties of interpersonal Subacts rather than by their function, and representational alignment may be determined by the (designational) properties of semantic categories rather than by their function, so morphosyntactic alignment may be determined by the complexity of a constituent rather than by its syntactic function. Thus, many languages have a special Clause-final, often optional position for subordinate Clauses, irrespective of the question whether that Clause is a complement Clause, a relative Clause, or an adverbial Clause. English is an example of such a language:

(163) a. That he has left is a pity.
       b. It is a pity that he has left.

(164) a. That man that you met in the train yesterday has left.
       b. The man has left that you met in the train yesterday.

(165) a. The man left because he can't stand smoke.
       b. Because he can't stand smoke the man left.

In (163a) the Subject complement Clause is in the Subject position, but it generally prefers the Clause-final position, with a dummy in the original Subject slot, as in (163b). In (164a) the relative Clause is in modifier position within the Np, but it may be extraposed, again to the Clause-final position, as in (164b). The adverbial Clause in (165) may occur both Clause-initially and Clause-finally, but other things being equal is preferably placed Clause-finally. The functions of the subordinate Clauses are different in these three cases, so it is their morphosyntactic constitution that determines the preferred placement.

As we will see later, this tendency is stronger at the Phrase layer than at the Clause layer. Consider the following examples:

(166) a. the singing detective
     b. the detective who is singing

Just as languages may have a special position for heavy constituents, so they may have a special position for light constituents such as clitics: morphosyntactic words that are phonologically dependent. The special position may be available irrespective of the categories expressed by those clitics. French, for example, has a special preverbal position that hosts not only pronominal clitics ((167)–(169), partly taken from Miller and Sag 1997), but also a negative clitic (170):

(167) a. Marie voit   Jean.
        Marie see.PRS.3.SG Jean
        'Marie sees Jean.'

     b. Marie *le*   voit.
        Marie 3.SG.U see.PRS.3.SG
        'Marie sees him.'

(168) a. Marie donne   un livre à Anne.
        Marie give.PRS.3.SG INDF book to Anne
        'Marie gives a book to Anne.'

     b. Marie *lui*   donne   un livre.
        Marie 3.SG.REC give.PRS.3.SG a   book
        'Marie gives her a book.'

(169) a. Marie connaît   la fin du   film.
        Marie know.PRS.3.SG DEF end of.DEF movie
        'Marie knows the end of the movie.'

     b. Marie *en*   connaît   la fin.
        Marie OBL know.PRS.3.SG DEF end
        'Marie knows the end of it.'

(170) Marie *ne* connaît   pas la fin du   film.
      Marie NEG know.PRS.3.SG NEG DEF end of.DEF movie
      'Marie doesn't know the end of the movie.'

In the second stage of top-down clausal ordering to be discussed in the next section we will come back to this aspect of morphosyntactic alignment.

4.4.4 Ordering of non-hierarchically related units

4.4.4.1 Introduction

As we argued in 4.4.2, the ordering of Clause constituents starts out with the top-down placement of hierarchically related units, and after that places non-hierarchically related units. The two resulting configurations may partly interlock. In determining the position of non-hierarchically related units several factors may play a role, as we illustrated above in our discussion of alignment:

(i) interpersonal factors: pragmatic functions, reference;
(ii) representational factors: semantic functions, designation;
(iii) morphosyntactic factors: syntactic functions, complexity.

All these factors may play a role simultaneously within one language, but in order to single out the effects of each group, we will discuss them here separately, which in each case, given the role of other factors, will lead to partial orderings of constituents.

4.4.4.2 Interpersonal factors

In 2.7.2.6 we gave examples of a Topic-oriented language, Tidore, and a Focus-oriented language, Kisi. The examples from Tidore are repeated here (van Staden 2000: 273):

(171) Turus una=ge,   mina mo-sango   una.
       then 3.SG.M=there 3.SG.F 3.SG.F.A-answer 3.SG.M
       'Then she answered him.'
       "Then he, she answered him."

(172) Tagi nde,   fangato koliho rea.
       go   3.NH.here 1.SG.M.A go.back not.anymore
       'I go and I don't come back anymore.'
       "Given this going, I won't come back anymore."

Apart from the segmental marking, the Topics in these examples are marked through their occurrence in P^{pre}. As one would expect in a system that is strongly driven by pragmatic functions, referential (171), and ascriptive (172) Subacts may occur in this position, and both are resumed within the Clause. It is their Topic status that is crucial for their placement. Thus we get the following partial orderings:

	P^{pre}		P^I
(173)	una=ge^{TOP}		(=171)
(174)	tagi_nde^{TOP}		(=172)

The examples from Kisi (Childs 1995: 270–1) are repeated in (175)–(176):

(175)   Màalóŋ   ó   có   cùùcúúwó   ní.
        rice   he AUX sow   FOC
        'It's rice he is sowing.'

(176)   Pùéŋndáŋ   yá   púéŋ   ní.
        forgetting I   forget FOC
        'It's forgetting that I did.'

Focus is marked in two ways in Kisi: (i) the Focused constituent occurs in intitial position, and (ii) a Focus particle occurs in Clause-final position. This operation can again be applied to both referential (175) and ascriptive (176) Subacts, leading to the following partial orderings:

$$P^I \qquad \ldots \qquad P^F$$

(177)   Màalóŋ^{FOC} ...   ní^{FOC} (=175)

(178)   Pùéŋndáŋ^{FOC} ...   ní^{FOC} (=176)

In Tzotzil (Aissen 1992), if a Topic and a Focus constituent are present, the Topic occurs in the initial position and the Focus in the post-initial position. The language is otherwise predicate-initial, so that the verb now ends up in the third position:

(179)   A   ti   prove tzeb-e   sovra   ch'ak'bat.
        TOP DEF poor   girl-TOP   leftovers was.given
        'It was leftovers that the poor girl was given.'

Thus, if there is only a Topic or a Focus, the predicate is in post-initial position, and if there is neither a Topic nor a Focus, it is in initial position. In our top-down and centripetal approach, this suggests that, if in a language the placement of constituents is driven by pragmatic functions, the placement of these constituents should precede the placement of other constituents, and we predict that the former have a preference for placement at the Clause margins. This ties in neatly with what we saw earlier with respect to the morphological expression of interpersonal alignment, which often masks the expression of semantic functions. Thus, (179) may be shown as:

$$P^I \qquad\qquad\qquad P^{I+1}$$

(180)   A_ti_prove_tzebe^{TOP} sovra^{FOC}

4.4.4.3 Representational factors

As we mentioned above, the semantic functions and designation of semantic categories at the Representational Level may also play a role in the placement of units. These factors relate primarily to the placement of arguments, and to a much lesser extent to predicates, as these, being the nucleus, do not carry semantic functions. There are reasons, however, why in this type of system we would want to start out with the placement of the predicate. Firstly, in many languages a Clause may consist of just a predicate, often containing referential markers which make the lexical expression of arguments potentially superfluous, as in the following example from Abkhaz (Hewitt 1979: 50) (see also 4.2.3 on nucleus-marking languages):

(181)   Yə-sə́-l-te-yt'.
        3.NH-1.SG.DAT-3.F.ERG-give-FIN
        'She gave it to me.'

Secondly, the placement of certain types of argument is often relative to the position of the predicate. In Movima (Haude 2006), which has a hierarchical alignment system, the order in which the arguments are placed after the Clause-initial predicate depends on their place on the animacy hierarchy. The one higher on that hierarchy follows the predicate immediately, while the one lower on the hierarchy follows afterwards, as illustrated in (182)–(183) (Haude 2006: 277):

(182)   Tikoy-na=sne   os   mimi:di.
        kill-DRCT=F.ABS ART.N.PST snake
        'She killed the/a snake.'

(183)   Tikoy-kay-a=sne os   mimi:di.
        kill-INV-V=F.ABS ART.N.PST snake
        'The/a snake killed her.'

We illustrate the phenomenon with contrastive examples in which one of the arguments is realized by a clitic pronoun. However, the same placement rules apply in constructions in which both arguments are realized by noun phrases (Haude 2006: 278). The human participant here outranks the non-human participant and thus immediately follows the verb. The direct/inverse marking indicates the semantic roles of the participants. The main point here is that the constituents of the Clause can arrive at their place effectively if we start out with the predicate in P^I and then put the highest-ranking participant in P^{I+1}, and the next one in P^{I+2}:

$$P^I \qquad\qquad P^{I+1} \qquad P^{I+2}$$
(184)   Tikoy-na^PRED   sne^HUM   os_mimi:di^ANIM

Thus it is useful in representational-based placement systems to start out with the placement of predicates (and, more generally, nuclei) before dealing with the placement of arguments (and, more generally, dependents). Note that we deliberately use the term 'predicate' and not 'verb' here, since there are languages without a proper class of verbs, and since in languages with a class of verbs there are of course predicates other than verbal ones. These considerations lead Hengeveld *et al.* (2004) to classify languages as predicate-initial, predicate-medial, or predicate-final, rather than as VSO, SVO, SOV, etc.

Placement of constituents with respect to their semantic functions is illustrated for Turkish in (185) (Kornfilt 1997: 90):

(185) Hasan-Ø   kitab-ı   Ali-ye   ver-di-Ø.
       Hasan-NOM book-ACC Ali-DAT give-PST-3.SG
       'Hasan gave the book to Ali.'

Turkish has a syntactic function Subject but not a syntactic function Object. The placement of the U and R arguments in (185) is therefore not attributable to syntactic factors. The order represented in (185) may be changed as a result of pragmatic function assignment, but in neutral contexts the Recipient precedes the predicate and is itself preceded by the Undergoer. Again these are relative positions, since in the absence of a Recipient the Undergoer would occupy the position before the predicate, as illustrated in (186) (Kornfilt 1997: 89):

(186) Hasan-Ø   kitab-ı   oku-du-Ø.
       Hasan-NOM book-ACC read-PST-3.SG
       'Hasan read the book.'

Thus the relative ordering of U and R can be shown as follows:

$$P^{F-2} \quad P^{F-1} \quad P^{F}$$

(187) kitab-ı^{U} Ali-ye^{R} ver-di-Ø^{PRED} (=185)

(188)   kitab-ı^{U} oku-du-Ø^{PRED} (=186)

4.4.4.4 Morphosyntactic factors

The morphosyntactic factors involved in the ordering of Clause constituents concern the syntactic functions of constituents and the morphosyntactic nature of those constituents, in particular their level of complexity and weight. Word-order typology traditionally defines basic word order in terms of S, O, and V, thus suggesting that these are the relevant categories across languages, but as we have tried to show, these categories are not universal, and in languages in which they do play a role they may not be decisive for the ordering of constituents. But there are of course many languages where they are highly relevant for ordering. Consider the following Dutch examples:

(189) Ik zag   hem.
       I   see.PST.SG him
       'I saw him.'

(190) Ik heb   hem gezien.
       I   have.PRS.1.SG him see.PTCP
       'I have seen him.'

(191) De   boek-en werden   door Jan gelezen.
       DEF.ART book-PL PASS.AUX.PST.PL by   Jan read.PTCP
       'The books were read by John.'

In Dutch Declarative Clauses, with one exception to be discussed below, the P^I position is reserved for the Subject, a syntactic function, and the absolute P^2 position for the finite verb, a morphosyntactic category. If there is just a lexical main verb, it takes the second position, but if there is an inflected auxiliary verb, this verb takes the second position and the lexical verb takes the final position. The latter is actually a position for non-inflected lexical predicates in general, since non-verbal predicates take that position too:

(192) Hij is   al   heel lang ziek.
       he   COP.PRS.3.SG already very long ill.
       'He has been ill for a long time already.'

Thus, the morphosyntactic encoder has to know whether during the hierarchical part of the placement procedure a finite auxiliary verb has been inserted, before it can put the lexical predicate into the appropriate slot, which is a purely morphosyntactic condition on ordering. Starting out with verb placement is therefore appropriate at the Morphosyntactic Level, just as starting out with predicate placement is appropriate at the Representational Level.

The rigid morphosyntactic character of the ordering of the Clause-initial constituents is also evident from the fact that, in circumstances in which there are no lexical fillers for P^I, a dummy pronoun is inserted, as illustrated in (193) for a zero-place construction and in (194) for a construction with an extraposed subject:

(193) Het regen-t.
       it   rain-PRS.3.SG
       'It's raining.'

(194) Het is   waar dat   het regent.
       it   COP.PRS.3.SG true CONJ it   rain-PRS.3.SG
       'It is true that it rains.'

The only circumstance in which this pattern is interrupted is when a non-subject constituent with Contrast function is placed in initial position. In this case the Subject goes to the immediately postverbal position (P^{2+1}) and does not allow any intervening material. Compare the following examples with (189):

(195)　Hem zag　　ik.
　　　　him　see.PST.SG　I
　　　　'Him I saw.'

(196)　Gisteren　zag　　　ik hem.
　　　　yesterday see.PST.SG　I　him
　　　　'Yesterday I saw him.'

The fact that the pragmatic function of a constituent here overrules syntactic factors is consistent with what we said earlier about the relative application of rules, where those that are based on interpersonal factors have to precede those that are morphosyntactically based. This is shown in the following partial representations:

	P^I	P^2	P^{2+1}	... P^F	
(197)	Ik^{SUBJ}	zag^{VFIN}			(=189)
(198)	ik^{SUBJ}	heb^{VFIN}		gezien^{PRED}	(=190)
(199)	hem^{FOC}	zag^{VFIN}	ik^{SUBJ}		(=195)
(200)	gisteren^{FOC}	zag^{VFIN}	ik^{SUBJ}		(=196)

Now consider the situation in three-place predications. For Dutch the Object function is relevant, as shown in the following examples:

(201)　Ik gaf　　　het　boek aan het　meisje.
　　　　I　give.PST.SG DEF book to　DEF girl.
　　　　'I gave the book to the girl.'

(202)　Ik gaf　　　het　meisje het　boek.
　　　　I　give.PST.SG DEF girl　DEF book.
　　　　'I gave the girl the book.'

The Object is in P^M or in a relative position to the right of P^M, as shown by the fact that the Object moves to the right if a hierarchically higher modifier is occupying P^M:

(203)　Ik gaf　　　gisteren　het boek aan het　meisje.
　　　　I　give.PST.SG yesterday DEF book to　DEF girl
　　　　'I gave the book to the girl yesterday.'

(204) Ik gaf gisteren het meisje het boek.
  I give.PST.SG yesterday DEF girl DEF book
  'I gave the girl the book yesterday.'

These examples may thus be represented as in (205)–(208):

	P^1	P^2	P^M		P^{M+1}	P^F	
(205)	ik^{subj}	gaf^{Vfin}	het_boek^{Obj}			aan_het_meisje^R	(=201)
(206)	ik^{subj}	gaf^{Vfin}	het_meisje^{Obj}			het_boek^U	(=202)
(207)	ik^{subj}	gaf^{Vfin}	gisteren		het_boek^{Obj}	aan_het_meisje^R	(=203)
(208)	ik^{subj}	gaf^{Vfin}	gisteren		het_meisje^{Obj}	het_boek^U	(=204)

The relevance of the Object function is also evident from the occurrence of dummy Objects in the case of extraposition with certain verbs:

(209) Ik betreur *het* niet dat je gekomen bent.
  I regret.PRS.1.SG DUM not CONJ you come.PTCP AUX.PRS.2.SG
  'I do not regret it that you have come.'

(210) Ik wist het niet dat je Engels kon praten.
  I know.PST DUM not CONJ you English can.PST speak.INF
  'I didn't know you could speak English.'

Turning now to the non-Subject/non-Object arguments in (201)–(202), we observe that they are at the right edge of the Clause. That these arguments are actually in a (relative) Clause-final position is evident from the fact that, when there is a verb in Clause-final position, this argument cannot normally be separated from that verb, while other splits are allowed:

(211) Ik heb (gisteren) het boek (gisteren) aan het meisje
  I have (yesterday) DEF book (yesterday) to DEF girl
  (*gisteren) gegeven.
  (yesterday) given
  'I gave the book to the girl (yesterday).'

(212) Ik heb (gisteren) het meisje (gisteren) het boek
  I have (yesterday) DEF girl (yesterday) DEF book
  (*gisteren) gegeven.
  (yesterday) given
  'I gave the girl the book (yesterday).'

We may now give the following placements for Dutch verbs, Subjects, Objects, and non-Subjects/non-Objects, which show the placement of Subjects in P^1, of finite verbs in P^2, of Objects in (a position relative to) P^M, and of predicates (including non-finite verbs) and the non-Subject/non-Object in (a position relative to) P^F.

P^I	P^2	P^M	P^{F-1}	P^F	
(213)	ik^{Subj} heb^{Vfin}	het_boek^{obj}	$aan\_het\_meisje^{Rec}$	$gegeven^{pred}$	(=211)
(214)	ik^{Subj} heb^{Vfin}	het_meisje^{obj} het_boek^{U}		$gegeven^{pred}$	(=212)

Deviations from this pattern again have to do with pragmatic function assignment:

(215) Ik heb   aan het meisje het boek gegeven.
       I   have.PRS.1.SG to DEF girl   DEF book give.PTCP
       'I have given the book to the girl.'

The occurrence of the Object to the right of the recipient in (215) is allowed when the Object is used contrastively (Geerts *et al.* 1984: 990). Thus again we see that the ordering in terms of semantic and syntactic functions may be overruled by pragmatic considerations.

The second position also plays a significant role in the morphosyntactic organization of various languages when it comes to clitic placement. P^2, often referred to as the Wackernagel position in deference to Wackernagel (1892), is in several languages associated with clitics, which may cluster by expanding this position to the right, as in the Czech example (216):

(216) Ne-chtěli=jsme=vám=ho   dát.
       NEG-want.PST.1.PL=1.PL= 2.SG.DAT=3.SG.N give.INF
       'We didn't want to give it to you.'

The existence of a special clitic position has already been mentioned above as an example of morphosyntactic alignment based on the complexity of the constituent rather than on its function. A clitic position may not only be defined with respect to the Clause margins, but also relative to another position, that of the predicate. In European Portuguese, there is considerable evidence to suggest that the clitic (cluster) in that language is located in the above-mentioned Wackernagel position, while the position of the predicate may vary (Mackenzie fc.a). In French, however, the position of the clitic cluster is best defined in terms of the (verbal) predicate, which (except in the imperative mood) it always precedes. Compare the following translational equivalents in Portuguese (217) and French (218):

(217) a. Dei=lh=o.
           give.PST.1.SG=3.SG.DAT=3.SG.M.ACC
           'I gave him/her it.'

       b. Não=lh=o   dei.
           NEG=3.SG.DAT=3.SG.M.ACC give.PST.1.SG
           'I did not give him/her it.'

(218) a. Je=le=lui=ai   donn-é.
           1.SG.NOM=3.SG.M.ACC=3.SG.DAT=AUX.PRS.1SG give-PTCP
           'I gave him/her it.'

       b. Je=ne=le=lui=ai   pas donn-é.
           1.SG.NOM=NEG=3.SG.ACC=3.SG.DAT=AUX.PRS.1SG NEG give-PTCP
           'I did not give him/her it.'

In European Portuguese, the clitic cluster remains in Post-Initial Position, whether the Initial position is occupied by the verb (as in 217a) or a negative (as in 217b)—note that the negative *não* is not a clitic. In French, by contrast, the position of the clitic cluster (*je=le=lui* and *je=ne=le=lui* respectively) is determined as immediately preceding the verb, in this case the auxiliary *ai*.

4.4.5 Templates

In 4.4.2 we discussed the hierarchical aspects of clausal order, and in the preceding sections the configurational aspects. In many cases various of the factors discussed contribute to clausal orders which can be interpreted as the result of the interlocking of various partial orders. In this section we bring the various factors together in the form of templates governing clausal order.

Before moving to the actual templates, recall that so far we have been working with four absolute positions: P^I, P^2, P^M, and P^F, and relative positions deriving from these, without claiming these four to be relevant for all languages. In the examples we have given it was clear that languages make use of the initial position and its expansions to the right, the second position and its expansions to the right, the final position and its expansions to the left, and of the medial position with expansions to the left, to the right, or in both directions. Most languages actually make use of a combination of absolute starting points, but some are logically excluded: P^M can only exist if either P^I or P^F exists as well, and P^2 can only exist if P^I exists as well. Furthermore, in languages that use P^M but not P^I, P^M can only branch to the left, since otherwise it would be P^I. The other way round, in languages that use P^M but not P^F, P^M can only branch to the right, since otherwise it would be P^F. Finally, P^{I+1} does not exist if P^2 exists. Theoretically, we then have the following possibilities:

(219) one absolute position

a.	P^I P^{I+N} $\emptyset$	$\emptyset$		$\emptyset$
b.	$\emptyset$ $\emptyset$	$\emptyset$		P^{F-N} P^F

two absolute positions

c.	P^I	P^2 P^{2+N} $\emptyset$		$\emptyset$
d.	P^I P^{I+N} $\emptyset$	P^M P^{M+N}		$\emptyset$
e.	P^I P^{I+N} $\emptyset$	$\emptyset$		P^{F-N} P^F
f.	$\emptyset$ $\emptyset$	P^{M-N} P^M		P^{F-N} P^F

three absolute positions

g.	p^I	p^2 p^{2+N}	p^M	p^{M+N}	Ø
h.	p^I	p^2 p^{2+N}	Ø		p^{F-N} p^F
i.	p^I p^{I+N} Ø		p^M	p^{M+N}	p^{F-N} p^F
j.	p^I p^{I+N} Ø		p^{M-N} p^M		p^{F-N} p^F
k.	p p^{I+N} Ø		p^{M-N} p^M	p^{M+N}	p^{F-N} p^F

four absolute positions

l.	p^I	p^2 p^{2+N}	p^M	p^{M+N}	p^{F-N} p^F
m.	p^I	p^2 p^{2+N}	p^{M-N} p^M		p^{F-N} p^F
n.	p^I	p^2 p^{2+N}	p^{M-N} p^M	p^{M+N}	p^{F-N} p^F

Leti (van Engelenhoven 2004) is a good example of a language with three absolute positions, as in (219k). It also strictly separates hierarchical ordering and configurational ordering: hierarchical ordering is from the left and the right, while configurational ordering starts from the middle. From the left, discourse particles, modal adverbs, and temporal/locative modifiers are placed. If there is more than one temporal/locative modifier an adverbial one precedes a prepositional one. The ordering that starts from the left thus reflects the hierarchical order of modifiers, while at the same time taking into account the syntactic weight of constituents. From the right, the indicative enclitic, if present, occurs in final position, and is preceded by a maximum of three aspectual and modal adverbs of like rank that may be placed in varying orders, thus again reflecting the hierarchical ordering. The following examples illustrate some possibilities (van Engelenhoven 2004: 239, 208):

(220) Rèkna   side   la=Agustus tujublas ra-sèka=e=lo
       let's_say usually DIR=August 17   3.PL-dance=EXCT=LOC
       Servaru.
       Serwaru.EXCT
       'Let's say they usually do a specific war dance in Serwaru on 17 August.'

(221) Apo püata-samtua=de n-vava   upu   Pui=o.
       SEQ woman-adult=DEM 3.SG-carry.name grandparent Pui=IND
       'And the old lady was called Lady Pui.'

P^M is occupied by the predicate, which may be expanded to the left with a Subject and to the right with an Object. Further expansion with Locative arguments through the use of Preposition Phrases is to the right of the Object, as shown in the following example (van Engelenhoven 2004: 231):

(222) Püata=e   n-vèvla=e   tani=la   ròna=e.
       woman=EXCT 3.SG-forge=EXCT earth.EXCT=DIR vessel=EXCT
       'The woman makes the vessel out of clay.'
       "The woman forges the clay into a vessel."

Thus we may define the following general template for Declarative verbal Clauses in Leti, now adding information about the nature of constituents to the absolute and relative positions:

(223) P^I P^{I+1} P^{I+2} P^{I+3} P^{M-1} P^M P^{M+1}
       $(Cl_1:[$ (Gw_1) $(Advp_1)$ $(Advp_2)$ (Adp_1) $(Np_1)_{Sbj}$ (Vp_1) $(Np_2)_{Obj}$
       P^{M+2} P^{F-3} P^{F-2} P^{F-1} P^F
       (Adp_1) $(Advp_5)$ $(Advp_4)$ $(Advp_3)$ $(Gw_2)]$ $(Cl_1))$

From this template many simpler ones may be derived. Thus, (220)–(222) would require the following templates:

           P^I P^{I+1} P^{I+2} P^M P^F
(224) $(Cl_i:[$ $(Advp_i)$ $(Advp_j)$ (Adp_i) (Vp_i) (Adp_i) $](Cl_i))$ (=220)

           P^I P^{M-1} P^M P^{M+1} P^F
(225) $(Cl_i:[$ (Gw_i) (Np_i) (Vp_i) (Np_j) (Gw_j) $]$ $(Cl_i))$ (=221)

           P^{M-1} P^M P^{M+1} P^{M+2}
(226) $(Cl_i:[$ (Np_i) (Vp_i) (Np_j) (Adp_i) $]$ $(Cl_i))$ (=222)

Note that there is no fixed relation between a position and a constituent type. Thus, P^I is filled with an Adverb Phrase in (224) and with a Grammatical Word in (225); P^F is filled with an Adposition Phrase in (224) and with a Grammatical Word in (225). This is a result of the fact that certain items, when present, have priority over others in hierarchical placement, while, when absent, they leave a slot available for items lower in the hierarchy. Similarly, the templates given here contain information relating to morphosyntactic aspects of ordering only. We indicate the categories of constituents, and thus their weight and complexity, and we indicate the syntactic functions of constituents. Positions are not characterized functionally (e.g. P^I as the position for modal adverbs), since this is representational information not available at the Morphosyntactic Level. Rather, modal adverbs, when available, are sent to that position by the morphosyntactic encoder, thus forcing the next lower modifier to go to the postinitial position P^{I+1}, rather than to the initial position P^I.

Leti provides a nice example of a strict separation of hierarchical ordering and configurational ordering: hierarchical ordering is centripetal, starting from the Clause margins, while configurational ordering is centrifugal, starting from the predicate. This may be represented graphically as follows:

(227)   Hierarchical   Hierarchical

    ——————————▶   ◀——————————

    P^I P^{I+1} P^{I+2} P^{M-2} P^{M-1} P^M P^{M+1} P^{M+2} P^{F-2} P^{F-1} P^F

         ◀———————— ————————▶

                      Configurational

Other clean splits between hierarchical and configurational ordering may be found in certain predicate-initial and predicate-final languages. Consider the Tagalog example (228) that we discussed earlier (Nagaya 2006):

(228)   Sa=kasamaang-palad bhumiagsak si=Gaga   sa=pagsusulit.
       Unfortunately   AV.failed   NOM=Gaga DAT=examination
       'Unfortunately Gaga failed the examination.'

Here the configurational ordering is a continuation of the hierarchical ordering:

(229)   Hierarchical   Configurational

    ——————————▶ ———————————————————————▶

    Sa=kasamaang-palad   bhumiagsak   si=Gaga   sa=pagsusulit.

And in the Hidatsa example (230) (Matthews 1965) the same happens starting from the right edge:

(230)   Wíra i apaari ki   stao   ski.
       tree it grow   INCH   REM.PST CERT
       'The tree must have begun to grow a long time ago.'

(231)   Configurational   Hierarchical

    ◀———————— ———————— ◀——————————————

    Wíra i   apaari ki   stao   ski.

Combinations of hierarchical and configurational ordering are not always as clear-cut as in the examples just presented from Leti, Tagalog, and Hidatsa. More complex interlockings are particularly common among so-called SVO languages. We prefer to call these 'predicate-medial languages', since neither are the functions Subject and Object universal nor is the category of verb available in all languages. Adapting the argument to our terminology, it has been observed that predicate-medial languages subdivide into two types, those that share syntactic characteristics with predicate-initial languages and those whose syntax is closer to predicate-final languages (Comrie 1989: 96; Dik 1997a: 409–11). The division is partly due to the fact that predicate-medial languages may develop out of predicate-initial languages or out of predicate-final languages. Examples of predicate-medial languages with a predicate-initial origin are Breton and Colloquial Arabic; the Romance languages developed a predicate-medial order from predominantly predicate-final Latin.

Given a superficial string of constituents in which the predicate is neither in initial nor in final position, the predicate may be in any of the following positions:

(232) P^{I+1} P^2 P^M P^{F-1}
    a.   pred
    b.   pred
    c.   pred
    d.   pred

In many predicate-initial and predicate-final languages the predicate may appear in P^{I+1} and P^{F-1}, but then only when it is pushed away from its position at the Clause margin, for instance by a pragmatically salient constituent or a higher-layer modifier. These are the situations represented in (232a) and (232d). In predicate-medial languages the predicate may be either in P^2 position (232b) or in P^M position (232c). Type (232c), with the predicate in medial position, was illustrated for Leti. Type (232b), with the predicate in second position is one of the patterns relevant for Dutch, as illustrated earlier. This latter language will be used here to illustrate a complex interlocking of hierarchical and configurational ordering, using all four absolute positions recognized so far.

We argued in 4.4.4.4 that in Dutch the finite verb is in an absolute second position P^2. If P^I is available, i.e. not occupied by a modifier or a pragmatically marked non-Subject, the Subject will go to that position; if it is not, the Subject attaches directly to the right of P^2, and is thus in P^{2+1}:

(233)   a.   Ze   kwam   gisteren.
             she   came   yesterday
        b.   Gisteren   kwam   ze.
             yesterday   came   she

We also argued that Objects are in (a position relative to) P^M, and that the placement of the (non-finite) predicate and the non-Subject/non-Object argument starts out at the right margin of the Clause. The latter claim is reflected in the fact that, when there is a verb in Clause-final position, the non-Subject/non-Object argument has to immediately precede it. What we have not discussed so far is how Clause-internal modifiers are placed. Consider again the following example:

(234)   Ik heb   het boek gisteren aan het meisje gegeven.
        I   have.PRS.1.SG DEF book gisteren to   DEF girl   give.PTCP
        'I gave the book to the girl yesterday.'

In our hierarchical approach to placement, the auxiliary verb *heb-* 'have' and the constituent *gisteren* 'yesterday' have to be placed before all other constituents. The auxiliary verb can go directly to the absolute P^2 position. The adverbial constituent *gisteren* cannot be placed relative to P^I, P^F or P^2, since in (234) it is separated from these positions by other constituents that are still awaiting placement in the process of configurational ordering. The constituent *yesterday* can therefore only be in the Clause-medial absolute position P^M. If this is true, then the Object constituent also has to be in the middle field, given that it may occur on both sides of the adverbial. Compare (234) with (235):

(235) Ik heb   gisteren het boek aan het meisje gegeven.
      I   have.PRS.1.SG gisteren DEF book to   DEF girl   give.PTCP
      'I have given the book to the girl yesterday.'

In (234) *het boek* 'the book' is thus in P^{M-1}, and in (235) it is in P^{M+1}. In the absence of a modifier it is in P^M itself.

Combining these observations, we conclude that the following positions are relevant for Dutch Declarative Clauses, thus illustrating the maximally complex system (219n):

(236) P^I P^2 P^{2+N} P^{M-N} P^M P^{M+N} P^{F-N} P^F

Hierarchical ordering in Dutch makes use of P^I, P^M, and P^F for modifiers, and P^2 for operators. Configurational ordering makes use of all these positions as well, as long as they have not been occupied already. In the latter case, it makes use of relative positions. Thus predicates go to P^2 when available, but otherwise to P^For the last position available relative to this position. Subjects go to P^I when available, and otherwise to P^{2+1}. Objects go to P^M when available, otherwise to a position relative to P^M. Non-Subject/Non-Object arguments go to P^F when available, otherwise to a position relative to P^F.

Further factors playing a role in configurational placement concern the pragmatic functions of constituents and the complexity of constituents. The pragmatic function Focus is connected with P^I, the pragmatic function Contrast with P^F or the last position available relative to this position. Complexity plays a role in the placement of finite embedded Clauses, which prefer the P^F position, thus pushing any other constituent that might want to go there to a position relative to P^F. Thus, the general template for Dutch Declarative main Clauses is used in a highly dynamic way, the only constant element being the presence of a finite (f) verb (Vw) in P^2, as indicated in (237), in which the position that is obligatorily filled as well as its obligatory filler are printed in boldface.

(237) P^I **P^2** P^{2+N} P^{M-N} P^M P^{M+N} P^{F-N} P^F
         (^{f}Vw$_1$)

The placement of constituents other than the finite verb is dynamically calculated in the morphosyntactic encoder, taking into account their hierarchical status, their pragmatic functions, their semantic role, their syntactic function, and their morphosyntactic complexity.

4.4.6 Dummies and support

In some languages dummy elements occur in situations in which no interpersonal or representational material is inserted in an obligatory clausal slot. The reason for this may be that this material is not available at all, or that for some reason it has gone to another position. A dummy may replace an argument or a predicate.

Dummies that do not correspond to any material at the Interpersonal Level or the Representational Level are illustrated in (238)–(239):

(238)   It is raining.

(239)   There is beer without alcohol.

In (238), which is based on a zero-place predication frame, there is no argument at all that can occupy the preverbal subject slot, which has to be obligatorily filled. The dummy pronoun *it* serves here as a default Subject. In (239) a predicate is missing. As argued in 3.6.2.1, non-lexical existentials are characterized by being the expression of a single Referential Subact at the Interpersonal Level. In the case of (239) this Referential Subact corresponds to the constituent *beer withour alcohol*. In the absence of an Ascriptive Subact, the dummy *there* is inserted, which, being non-verbal in nature, subsequently needs the verbal support of a copula.

Dummies also occur when a certain slot remains unfilled because the constituent that would normally go there has gone elsewhere, for instance for information-structural reasons or due to morphosyntactic complexity. Consider the following examples from English and Dutch respectively:

(240)   It is a pity that you have to go.

(241)   Viss-en doen   we hier niet.
        fish-INF do.PRS.PL we here not
        'We do not fish here.'

In (240) the embedded Subject Clause is placed in Clause-final position due to its complexity. As a result, the preverbal Subject position remains unfilled with interpersonal and/or representational material, and is filled by the placeholder *it*. In (241) the predicate *vissen* is focused and for that reason placed in initial position. Since there has to be a finite verb in P^2, the dummy verb *doen* acts as a placeholder for the lexical predicate. Other languages use a copy of the lexical predicate as a dummy in these circumstances, as in the following Spanish example:

(242)   Llov-er   no   llueve.
        rain-INF   not rain.IND.PRS.3.SG
        'It doesn't rain here.'

In Hungarian dummies are used to facilitate the expression of pragmatic functions. Consider the following example (de Groot 1981: 51):

(243)   János azt   mond-t-a,   hogy a   taxi öt-re   jöjjön.
        János DEM   say-PST-OBJP   CONJ DEF taxi five-SUBL come
        'János said that the taxi would come at five.'

Hungarian has special positions for Topical and Focal elements. Topical elements are in Clause-initial position, Focal elements in preverbal position. In cases of complementation, a demonstrative element refers cataphorically to an appositional complement Clause that follows the main Clause. The fact that the demonstrative occupies the Focus position of the main Clause signals that the complement Clause is Focal.

The occurrence of dummy Objects in the absence of a corresponding argument at the Representational Level, i.e. with one-place predicates, seems less common than the occurrence of dummy Subjects in the absence of a corresponding argument, i.e. with zero-place predicates. Yet in some circumstances languages do actually use them. In Dutch there is a restricted use of the following construction:

(244)   Eet/wandel/werk   ze.
        eat/walk/werk.IMP them
        'Have a nice meal/walk/day of work.'
        "Eat/walk/work them."

With certain intransitive verbs in Dutch a third plural dummy object is used, with the effect of turning what would otherwise be an order into a wish.

Dummy placement can only take place after all constituents corresponding to units at the Interpersonal Level and the Representational Level have been assigned a place in the clausal template. Only at that point will it be clear whether all obligatory slots in a template have been filled. It also means we have to indicate which positions in a template are obligatory. Here again we may find interesting crosslinguistic differences. Consider the following examples from Dutch:

(245)   Het is duidelijk dat ze   niet zal komen.
        it is clear   that she not will come
        'It is clear that she will not come.'

(246)   Gisteren was het duidelijk dat ze niet zou   komen.
        yesterday was it   clear   that she not would come
        'Yesterday it was clear that she would not come.'

As we illustrated earlier, in Dutch declarative main clauses the Subject goes to P^I, unless this is occupied by a modifier or pragmatically marked non-Subject, in which case it goes to P^{2+1}. This means we need the following templates for (245)–(246):

(247) P^I P^2 P^{2+1} P^{M-N} P^M P^{M+N} P^{F-N} P^F (=245)
       $(Np_1)_{Subj}$ $(^fVw_1)$ ...

(248) P^I P^2 P^{2+1} P^{M-N} P^M P^{M+N} P^{F-N} P^F (=246)
       (Xp_1) $(^fVw_1)$ $(Np_1)_{Subj}$ ...

Obligatory positions are indicated in bold, and obligatory instantiations of positions are indicated in bold. Thus these representations indicate that in Dutch (i) P^I and P^2 always have to be filled; (ii) the finite verb goes to P^2; (iii) a Subject of the category Np goes to P^I; (iv) unless this position is already occupied, in which case it goes to P^{2+1}. We may now also describe the following construction with two dummies:

(249)   Regen-en doet   het hier niet.
        rain-INF   do.PRS.3.SG het here not.
        'It doesn't rain here.'

In (249) the lexical zero-place predicate *regenen* is placed in initial position for pragmatic reasons. It leaves the P^2 position empty, thus triggering the insertion of the dummy verb *doen*. Since the (dummy) Subject *het* cannot go to P^I it has to go to P^{2+1}, following template (248), in which the two obligatory positions are now both filled with dummies.

   Compare now (245) and (246) with their counterparts in English:

(250)   It is clear that she will not come.

(251)   Yesterday it was clear that she would not come.

In English the Subject position can be defined as the preverbal one. The (finite) verb is in P^M, so the Subject is in P^{M-1}. As we illustrated earlier, modifier placement in English makes use of P^I and P^F and positions relative to these, but, as (251) illustrates, this does not affect the position of the (dummy) Subject. Thus we need only one template to account for the placement of dummy Subjects in English:

(252) P^I P^{M-N} P^M P^{M+N} P^F (=250)
       ... $(Np_1)_{Subj}$ $(^f Vw_1)$ ...

(253)   P^I P^{M-N} P^M P^{M+N} P^F (=251)
        (Xp$_1$) (Np$_1$)$_{Subj}$ (^{f}Vw$_1$) ...

4.4.7 Agreement

Once all slots in a clausal template have been filled, either by material from the Interpersonal Level and the Representational Level or by dummies, rules of agreement are applied, where relevant. Agreement is a mechanism by which information properly pertaining to a single element of the Clause is copied to one or more other elements. We will distinguish here between argument agreement and operator agreement. An example of the former is Subject agreement on verbs, an example of the latter is negative harmony.

Argument agreement should be distinguished from cross-reference. The latter obtains when person marking on the verb is sufficient by itself and may optionally be expanded by a lexically realized argument. The following example is from Kabardian (Colarusso 1992: 77):

(254)   Ø-w-a-s-ʔ^{w}a-ta-aɣ-ś.
        3.ABS-2-DAT-1-say-prolonged-PST-DECL
        'I told it to you.'

The prefixes on the verb are capable of referring by themselves, and we therefore treat them as the bound expression of Referential Subacts. This analysis does not change when the arguments are expressed overtly, as in (255) (Colarusso 1992: 75):

(255)   wa   sa   a-r   Ø-q'ə-s-žə-w-ʔa-aɣ-ś.
        you me   3-ABS   3.ABS-AFF-1-again-2-say-PST-DECL
        'You said it to me.'

In (255) there are in each case two Referential Subacts referring to a single participant. These are thus cases of apposition, and the referential elements on the verb cannot be considered cases of agreement.

True non-referential syntactic agreement is very uncommon (Siewierska 2004: 268). We do find agreement in languages such as French, as in the following example:

(256)   Nous   chant-ons.
        we   sing-1.PL
        'We are singing.'

in which the subject pronoun may not be dropped, unlike the situation in Kabardian. In situations like these we apply a mechanism which copies the relevant features of the Subject Noun Phrase to the verb. The morphosyntactic representation of (256) without copying would be as follows:

(257) $(Cl_i: [(Np_i: (Nw_i: /nu/ (Nw_i)) (Np_i))_{Subj} (Vp_i: (Vw_i: /\int\!\!\bar{a}t/-pres (Vw_i))$
$(Vp_i)] (Cl_i))$

in which the pronoun and verb stem are given in their phonological form, and a secondary operator acts as a placeholder for the expression of present tense on the verb. With copying the situation is as follows:

(258) $(Cl_i: [(Np_i: (Nw_i: /nu/ (Nw_i)) (Np_i))_{Subj} (Vp_i: (Vw_i: /\int\!\!\bar{a}t/-pres<1.Pl>$
$(Vw_i)) (Vp_i)] (Cl_i))$

in which the copied feature is attached to the placeholder for Tense, with which it will fuse in the morphological expression. The copied feature is presented between angled brackets, following the convention introduced in Dik (1997a). The copying rules have to apply after dummy insertion, to ensure that sources and/or targets for the agreement feature are available.

Operator agreement obtains when the expression of an operator goes hand in hand with adaptations in form of elements within its scope. An example that we will come across when discussing subordination in 4.4.8.4 is *consecutio temporum*. Another example, occurring less frequently, is the phenomenon of negative concord, a remarkable feature of Nunggubuyu (Heath 1984). Negation in this language is expressed through one of a number of negative Words. Most of these affect the form of all Phrases within its scope, in the sense that verbs take different subject prefixes and tense markers and nouns obligatorily occur with their noun class marker, which in positive contexts is sensitive to the semantic and pragmatic functions of the Noun Phrase. Consider the following example from Nunggubuyu (Heath 1984: 527):

(259) Yagi *ana:-'-ji* $n^g a$-bura-$n^g i$.
       not   CL-'-here   1.SG-sit-IRR
       'I will not stay here.'

The presence of the noun class marker *ana* on the adverbial noun *ji* shows that the Noun Phrase is in the scope of the negator *yagi*. The subject prefix $n^g a$ on the verb takes a form that is different from its counterpart in positive sentences, and the same goes for the irrealis marker $n^g i$. We may account for this by copying the negative feature to the heads of the various Phrases within the scope of negation. Consider first the representation of (259) without applying the rule of negative harmony:

(260) $(Cl_i: [(Gw_i: /yagi/ (Gw_i)) (Np_i: (Nw_i: [(Aff_i: cl (Aff_i)) (Ns_i: /ji/ (Ns_i))]$
$(Nw_i)) (Np_i)) (Vp_i: (Vw_i: (Aff_j: 1sgsubj (Aff_j)) (Vs_i: /bura/ (Vs_i))$
$(Aff_k: irr (Aff_k))] (Vw_i)) (Vp_i)] (Cl_i))$

Since the forms of the classifier, the subject prefix, and the tense suffix are all sensitive to the presence or absence of a negative particle, they are introduced in the form of the secondary operators Cl, 1SgSubj and Irr in (260). When a negative particle is present, the negative feature is copied to these secondary operators, as in (261):

(261)   (Cl$_i$: [(Gw$_i$: /yagi/ (Gw$_i$)) (Np$_i$: (Nw$_i$: [(Aff$_i$: cl<neg> (Aff$_i$)) (Ns$_i$: /ji/ (Ns$_i$))] (Nw$_i$)) (Np$_i$)) (Vp$_i$: (Vw$_i$: (Aff$_j$: 1sgsubj<neg> (Aff$_j$)) (Vs$_i$: /bura/ (Vs$_i$)) (Aff$_k$: irr<neg> (Aff$_k$))] (Vw$_i$)) (Vp$_i$)] (Cl$_i$))

The phonological encoder then selects the appropriate form of the morphemes in producing the phonological representation of the Clause.

4.4.8 Subordination

4.4.8.1 Introduction

Clauses may occur as constituents of other Clauses as adverbial, complement, or predicate Clauses. Their form, and in some cases also their templates, may be radically different from main Clauses. We first look at these various forms in 4.4.8.2. An important question from an FDG point of view is which interpersonal, representational, and morphosyntactic factors are responsible for the choice of a certain type of subordinate Clause. This is the topic of 4.4.8.3. The expression of operators within subordinate Clauses may be dependent upon the presence of certain operators within the main Clause, as in the case of sequence of tenses, to be discussed in 4.4.8.4. Finally, in some cases semantic constituents of a subordinate Clause may behave as pragmatic or syntactic constituents of the main Clause, as in the case of displacement and raising, to be discussed in 4.4.8.5. We will mainly focus on complement clauses in this section.

4.4.8.2 The form of subordinate Clauses

Not all languages have subordinate Clauses, and some make less use of them than others, using paratactic constructions instead. The latter situation would be the only option in a language without subordination. Pirahã has been claimed to be an example of such a language (Everett 2005: 629):

(262)   Ti kobai-baí 'áoói,   hi 'íkao-ap-áp-iig-á.
        I   see-INTENS foreigner he mouth-pull-up-CONT-DECL
        'I really watch(ed) the foreigner fishing (with line and hook).'
        "I watched the foreigner intensively. He was pulling (fish) out by (their) mouths."

In other languages we find certain types of subordinate Clauses that are exactly like main Clauses, as in the following examples from English and Cofán (Fischer 2007: 393):

(263)   Sheila thinks [Peter is ill].

(264) [Chandia na'en-ni-ngae   qquen su-'fa]=ni=nda=gi   ja-ya.
       clear   river-LOC-MANN   SO   say-PL-LOC-NEWTOP=1   go-IRR
       'If they say (go) to Chandia Na'en, I'll go.'

In (263) the subordinate Clause itself is identical to a main Clause, and we need very little additional machinery to account for it. In the Cofán example (264) a regular verb-final Clause now ends with the case marker =ni and the New Topic marker =nda, both clitics attaching to clausal constituents. This subordinate Clause being the first constituent of the main Clause, the Clause layer subject clitic =gi attaches to it. Despite these markings, the subordinate Clause is internally fully identical to a main Clause. The further marking it receives is external to it, and identical to the kind of marking a regular Noun Phrase would receive. So again, to account for this type of subordinate Clause, we need little additional machinery.

Many languages, however, have subordinate Clauses that are formally distinct from main Clauses, and in several cases they have more than one type of subordinate Clause. Ignoring relative Clauses here, which will be dealt with in 4.5.8, subordinate Clauses may be broadly distinguished from one another by (i) the presence or absence of a conjunction; (ii) the presence or absence of special verb forms; and (iii) the presence of absence of special marking of arguments. In (263) and (264) neither a conjunction nor a special verb form is present, and the arguments are expressed as they would be in a main Clause. We will now discuss some examples of the presence of the elements (i)–(iii).

The use of conjunctions is illustrated for Spanish in (265)–(267):

(265) Juan no   sab-e   [que   Pedro est-á
       Juan NEG know-3.SG.IND.PRS CONJ.FACT Pedro COP-3.SG.IND.PRS
       enfermo.]
       ill.
       'Juan doesn't know that Pedro is ill.'

(266) Juan no   sab-e   [si   Pedro
       Juan NEG know-3.SG.IND.PRS CONJ.NFACT Pedro
       est-á   enfermo.]
       COP-3.SG.IND.PRS ill.
       'Juan doesn't know whether Pedro is ill.'

(267) Juan no   viene   [porque Pedro est-á
       Juan NEG come.3.SG.IND.PRS because Pedro COP-3.SG.IND.PRS
       enfermo.]
       ill.
       'Juan is not coming because Pedro is ill.'

The subordinate Clauses in Spanish differ from main Clauses in the presence of a conjunction in P^I. There are two different conjunctions for complement Clauses, a factual (265) and a non-factual (266) one, which shows that a conjunction may, apart from conjoining two Clauses, participate in the expression of meaning. This is certainly the case for adverbial conjunctions, as in (267), which simultaneously serve the purpose of expressing the semantic function of the adverbial Clause within the main Clause. In all cases the conjunction can be said to be in the P^I position of the subordinate Clause, pushing other material to the right, but not affecting the relative order of those elements. The opposite situation obtains in Nama (Hagman 1973: 257), a language in which the conjunction is in P^F, as shown in (268):

(268) //'īip ke   'aḿ'a-se   kèrè   =/oḿ [/'aé//amsà xuú-kxḿ/xií
       he   DECL true-ADVR REM.PST believe Windhoek from-1.DU
       hāā   !xáis-à].
       come.PFV CONJ-ACC
       'He really believed that we had come from Windhoek.'

Conjunctions may also be in P^2, as in the case of the Czech conditional conjunction =li 'if' in (269). This conjunction cliticizes in second position, where it is followed by an object clitic in the clitic string (de Bray 1969: 505):

(269) [Chceš=li=ho   vidět],...
       want.PRS.2.SG=COND=3.SG.M.ACC see
       'If you want to see him,...'

In our approach to clausal constituent order, these placements can be accounted for in terms of the same principles that were applied for main Clause ordering. Since hierarchical ordering precedes configurational ordering, the placement of the conjunction precedes the placement of configurational units. Therefore the conjunction is necessarily placed in an absolute position, and other constituents have to shift away from that position: to the right of P^I in (265)–(267), to the left of P^F in (268), and to the right of P^2 in (269).

Specific templates are needed in those cases in which the constituent order in subordinate Clauses is different from the one in main Clauses. This is crosslinguistically quite exceptional, an example being Dutch, the main Clause orderings of which we discussed earlier in this chapter. Consider again the following example and the representation of its constituent order:

(270) Ik heb   gisteren het boek aan het meisje gegeven.
       I   have.PRS.1.SG gisteren DEF book to   DEF girl   give.PTCP
       'I gave the book to the girl yesterday.'

(271)

P^I	P^2	P^M	P^{M+1}	P^{F-1}	P^F	
$(Cl_i: [$ $(Np_i)_{Subj}$	${}^f(Vw_i)$	$(Advp_i)$	(Np_j)	(Adp_i)	(Vp_i) $] (Cl_i))$	
Ik	heb	gisteren	het_boek	aan_het_meisje	gegeven	

The subordinate counterpart of (270) is (272):

(272) dat ik gisteren het boek aan het meisje heb
CONJ I.NOM yesterday DEF book to DEF girl have.PRS.1.SG

gegeven
give.PTCP

'that I gave the book to the girl yesterday'

In contrast with main Clauses, in which the finite verb obligatorily goes to P^2, in subordinate Clauses it is the Subject that obligatorily goes there, and the finite verb is placed in Clause-final position to form an single constituent with the main verb, as illustrated by the following examples:

(273) *dat gisteren ik het boek aan het meisje heb gegeven
that yesterday I the book to the girl have given

(274) *dat ik gisteren het boek heb aan het meisje gegeven
that I yesterday the book have to the girl given

The remaining constituents keep the same possibilities as to their placement, so that (272) may be represented as follows:

(275)

P^I	P^2	P^M	P^{M+1}	P^{F-1}	P^F
(Gw_i)	$(Np_i)_{Subj}$	$(Advp_i)$	(Np_j)	(Adp_i)	(Vp_i)
dat	ik	gisteren	het_boek	aan_het_meisje	heb_gegeven

The differences as regards the clausal templates of Declarative main Clauses and subordinate Clauses may thus be summarized as follows:

(276)

	P^I	P^2	P^{2+N}	P^{M-N}	P^M	P^{M+N}	P^{F-N}	P^F	
$({}^{decl}cl_1: [$		$({}^f Vw_1)$							$] (Cl_1))$

(277)

	P^I	P^2	P^{2+N}	P^{M-N}	P^M	P^{M+N}	P^{F-N}	P^F	
$({}^{sub}cl_1: [$	(Gw_1)	$(Np_1)_{Subj}$						$(Vp_1)]$	$(Cl_1))$

Following conventions introduced earlier, obligatory positions and fillers are represented in bold face, and the subtype of the Clause is indicated in superscript preceding the opening variable. It is noteworthy that the number of obligatory positions and fillers is larger in subordinate Clauses, a phenomenon that may be observed frequently crosslinguistically.

Lezgian has a wide range of non-finite verb forms used in subordination, some illustrative examples of which are given in (278)–(280) (Haspelmath 1993: 362, 369, 384):

(278)   Dağustan.di-n fol'kolor.di-n ilim.d-a   q'il.i-n
         Daghestan-GEN folklore-GEN   sciend-INESS head-GEN
         mesʔela-jr.i-kaj   sad [fol'klo.di-n proza.di-n žanr-ijar
         problem-PL-SUBESS one folklore-GEN prose-GEN genre-PL
         klassificirovat' awu-n] ja.
         classifying   do-ANR COP.
         'On of the main tasks in Daghestanian folklore studies is [classifying
         the genres of folklore prose].'

(279)   Nabisat.a-z [ktab k'el-iz]   k'an-zawa.
         Nabisat-DAT book read-INF want-IMPF
         'Nabisat wants to read a book.'

(280)   Dide   Anni.di [ğül.ü-z   fi-daldi]   muallimwil-e
         mother Anni.ERG husband-DAT go-CVB.POST teachership-INESS
         k'walax-na.
         work ᴧOR
         'My mother Anni worked as a teacher until she got married.'

The nominalized predicate in (278) is used in a predicate Clause, the infinitive in (279) in a complement Clause, and the posterior converb in (280) in an adverbial Clause. Instead of speaking of non-finiteness, we prefer to use the term deranking (Stassen 1985, Cristofaro 2003). A deranked verb form is one that cannot be used in a main Clause, and is the counterpart of a balanced verb form, which can be used in a main Clause. These functional definitions can be applied crosslinguistically, while no crosslinguistically valid definition of finiteness can be given.

The form of the deranked verb as such is something that has to be accounted for at the Word layer, and will be discussed in 4.6. The question here is whether special clausal templates are needed to handle Clauses containing balancing or deranking verb forms. In the case of Lezgian, for the ordering of constituents within the subordinate Clause no special templates are needed. The positions it makes use of in subordinate Clauses are the same, though the rules that assign constituents to these positions are different, in the sense that the language is more strictly verb-final in subordinate Clauses, the ordering of main Clause constituents being more sensitive to information-structural considerations. It is, however, necessary to make a distinction between finite and non-finite subordinate Clauses in Lezgian with respect to their behaviour in higher Clauses: deranked Clauses go to canonical positions, or to P^I if they are heavy, while balanced subordinate Clauses go to P^F. Consider the following examples (Haspelmath 1993: 302, 371):

(281) [Abur muq'uf.da-ldi k'el-un   wa ezber-un]   za
       they skill-SRDIR   read-ACTNR and cram-ACTNR I.ERG
       kwe-z   k'ewelaj meslät qalur-zawa.
       you.all-DAT strongly advice show-IMPF
       'I advise you strongly to read and study them carefully.'

(282) Selim.a   dide.di-z   laha-na [x̌i, wič šeher.di-z fe-na].
       Selim.ERG mother-DAT say-AOR CONJ self town-DAT go-AOR
       'Selim told his mother that he was going to town.'

While the deranked complement Clause in (279) is in preverbal position, in (281) it is in P^I due to its heaviness. The balanced subordinate Clause in (282), on the other hand, can only go to P^F. Thus, we need to distinguish between (^{bal}cl$_1$) and (^{der}cl$_1$) in Lezgian, not so much because their internal structure is different, but because they behave differently with respect to their placement in higher Clauses.

A final issue concerning deranked subordinate Clauses concerns the realization of arguments within the subordinate Clause. Here we may distinguish two different cases: (i) an argument cannot be realized within the subordinate Clause, (ii) an argument is realized in a way that is different from its main Clause marking. We will illustrate both cases with examples from Turkish. The first case is illustrated in (283)–(284), which show deranked constructions in which the Subject argument cannot be expressed, while all others can (Kornfilt 1997: 51, 55):

(283) Ben [öl-mek-ten] kork-uyor-du-m.
       I   die-INF-ABL fear-PROG-PST-1.SG
       'I was afraid to die.'

(284) Ahmet [çok çalış-arak]   hedef-in-e   ulaş-tı-Ø.
       Ahmet very work-CVB.MANN aim-3.SG.POSS-DAT reach-PST-3.SG
       'Ahmet attained his goal by working hard.'

The absence of an argument is obligatory, as illustrated in (285)–(286) (Kornfilt 1997: 56; Geoffrey Haig, p.c.):

(285)   *Ben [Ahmet öl-mek-ten] kork-uyor-du-m.
        I   Ahmet die-INF-ABL fear-PROG-PST-1.SG
        'I was afraid for Ahmet to die.'

(286)   *[Ahmet çok çalış-arak]   Zeynep hedef-in-e
        Ahmet   very work-CVB.MANN Zeynep aim-3.SG.POSS-DAT
        ulaş-tı-Ø.
        reach-PST-3.SG
        'Zeynep attained her goal by Ahmet working hard/because Ahmet
        worked hard.'

In constructions such as (283)–(284), there is obligatory coreference between
an argument of the main Clause and an argument of the subordinate Clause.
Since in FDG coreferentiality is dealt with at the Representational Level, this
property does not have to be accounted for at the Morphosyntactic Level.
Yet in the morphosyntactic representation of these Clauses, we cannot simply
leave out the position for the missing Noun Phrase. It is not just any argument
that can be left out in these subordinate constructions, it has to be the Subject
(Kornfilt 1997: 55). Consider the following examples (Bozşahin fc.; Geoffrey
Haig, p.c.) and their underlying representations:

(287)   Çocuk [köpeğ-i sev-mek] ist-iyor-Ø.
        child dog-ACC pet.INF   want-PROG-3.SG
        'The child wants to pet the dog.'

        $(e_i: (f_i: [(f_j: ist (f_j)) (x_i: -çocuk- (x_i))_A (e_j: (f_k: [(f_l: sev (f_l)) (x_i)_A (x_j: -köpek- (x_j))_U] (f_k)) (e_j))_U] (f_i)) (e_i))$

(288)   Köpek [çocuk tarafından sev-il-mek] ist-iyor-Ø.
        dog   child by   pet-PASS-INF want-PROG-3.SG
        'The dog wants to be petted by the child.'

        $(e_i: (f_i: [(f_j: ist (f_j)) (x_j: -köpek- (x_i))_A (e_j: (f_k: [(f_l: sev (f_l)) (x_i: -çocuk- (x_i))_A (x_j)_U] (f_k)) (e_j))_U] (f_i)) (e_i))$

In (287) the Actor slot of the subordinate Clause is coreferential with the Actor
slot of the main Clause, while in (288) the Undergoer slot of the subordinate
Clause is coreferential with the Actor slot of the main Clause. The fact that
in the latter case passive formation is triggered shows that the empty slot in
the subordinate Clause carries the Subject function, which is taken care of at
the Morphosyntactic, not at the Representational Level. The morphosyntactic
templates underlying (287) and (288) show this as follows:

(289)

$$P^I \quad P^{F-1} \quad [\, \emptyset \qquad P^{F-1} \quad P^F \qquad] \qquad P^F \quad (=287)$$

$$(^{main}cl_i: [\, (Np_i) \quad (^{nonfin}cl_j: [\, (Np_i)_{Subj} \, (Np_j) \quad (Vp_i) \qquad]\,(Cl_j))\,(Vp_j)\,]\,(Cl_i))$$

Çocuk   köpeğ-i sev-mek   ist-iyor-Ø.

(290)

$$P^I \quad P^{F-1} \quad [\, \emptyset \qquad P^{F-1} \qquad\quad P^F \qquad\quad] \qquad P^F \quad (=288)$$

$$(^{main}cl_i: [\, (Np_i) \quad (^{nonfin}cl_j: [\, (Np_j)_{Subj} \, (Adp_i) \qquad (Vp_i) \qquad]\,(Cl_j))\,(Vp_j)\,]\,(Cl_i))$$

Köpek   çocuk_tarafından sev-il-mek   ist-iyor-Ø.

Note that the Subject Noun Phrase is present in the template, but not assigned to a position, to indicate that it is the subject properties of the Noun Phrase that are at stake here, not its positional instantiation. Mapping of the coreferential argument to this Np slot during the alignment process then triggers the active voice in the case of (287) and the passive voice in the case of (288).

The realization of arguments in Turkish deranked Clauses can also differ from that in main Clauses in the sense that they are expressed in a different form. Consider the following examples (Kornfilt 1997: 56, 57):

(291) a. Ahmet-Ø   ev-e   dön-dü-Ø.
           Ahmet-NOM house-DAT return-PST-3.SG
           'Ahmet returned to the house.'

       b. [Ahmet-Ø   ev-e   dön-ünce]   Zeynep okul-a
           Ahmet-NOM house-DAT return-CVB.SIM Zeynep school-DAT
           gid-ebil-di-Ø.
           go-ABIL-PST-3.SG
           'When Ahmet returned home Zeynep was able to go to school.'

(292) a. Ahmet-Ø   bütün iş-ler-in-i   yavaşça
           Ahmet-NOM all   task-PL-3.SG.POSS-ACC slowly
           yap-ar-Ø.
           do-AOR-3.SG
           'Ahmet does all his work slowly.'

       b. [Ahmed-in bütün iş-ler-in-i   yavaşça
           Ahmet-GEN all   task-PL-3.SG.POSS-ACC slowly
           yap-tığ-ın]-ı   duy-du-m.
           do-RLS.NMLZ-3.SG.POSS-ACC hear-PST-1.SG
           'I heard that Ahmet does all his work slowly.'

In (291b) the marking of the arguments of the subordinate Clause is realized in the same manner as with the arguments of the main Clause in (291a). This is not the case in (292b), where the Subject argument has the genitive case marker rather than the nominative case marker in (292a). Furthermore, the genitive argument is cross-referenced on the deranked predicate through the third singular possessive marker. In this respect, the overall structure of the Clause resembles that used for Noun Phrases with a possessor, as in (293):

(293)   Ahmed-in   kitab-ı
         Ahmet-GEN   book-3.SG.POSS
         'Ahmet's book.'

Yet the deranked Clause cannot be directly compared to a Noun Phrase, since in many respects it behaves like a main Clause: the Undergoer argument is marked with the accusative suffix, and the modifier *yavaşça* 'slowly' is adverbial, not adjectival.

Given this mixture of features, we have to decide whether to treat nominalizations like that in (292b) as a syntactic nominalization or a lexical nominalization. In the former case, the nominalization has to be treated as a Clause, in the second case, as a Noun Phrase. This problem is well known from the literature (e.g. Mackenzie 1987a, 1996; Koptjevskaja-Tamm 1993; Haspelmath 1996, Malchukov 2004). The position we take here is the one defended in Mackenzie (1996). A nominalization is clausal if the expression of operators and modifiers follows the clausal rather than the phrasal pattern. The nominalization in (292b) accordingly counts as a clausal nominalization, which differs from lexical nominalization in Turkish in that modifiers of the latter are expressed as adjectives (Kornfilt 1997: 450), as can be seen contrastively in the following examples (Geoffrey Haig, p.c.):

(294)   [Asker-ler-in   hemen   yarın
         soldier-PL-GEN   immediately   tomorrow
         dön-me-si]-ni   isti-yor-Ø.
         return-NMLZ-3.SG.POSS-ACC   want-PROG-3.SG
         'The soldiers want to return tomorrow without delay.'

(295)   yarın-ki   önemli   çık-ış   için
         tomorrow-ADJR   important   go.out-NMLZ   because
         'because of tomorrow's important excursion'

Example (294) contains a clausal nominalization, in which the temporal modifier *yarın* 'tomorrow' appear in its adverbial form. In the lexical nominalization in (295), on the other hand, this adverbial is adjectivalized before it can combine with the nominalized verb. The latter type of nominalization will be further dealt with in 4.5.3.

The expression of arguments is not conclusive for classification of a nom-inalization as lexical or clausal, since this can be handled by the alignment system as a case of differential argument marking, adapted to the condi-tions for specific types of subordinate Clauses. Thus, the genitive in (292b) can be seen as the expression of the Subject in the context of this type of clausal nominalizations. The following examples of another type of lexical nominalization in Turkish confirm this analysis (Comrie and Thompson 1985: 364–5):

(296)   a.   Hasan-Ø   mektub-u yaz-dı-Ø.
              Hasan-NOM letter-ACC write-PST-3.SG
              'Hasan wrote the letter.'

        b.   Hasan-ın   mektub-u yaz-ma-sı
              Hasan-GEN letter-ACC write-ACTNR-3.SG.POSS
              'Hasan's writing of the letter'

(297)   a.   Mektub-Ø Hasan tarafından yaz-ıl-dı-Ø.
              letter-NOM Hasan by   write-PASS-PST-3.SG
              'The letter was written by Hasan.'

        b.   mektub-un Hasan tarafından yaz-ıl-ma-sı
              letter-GEN   Hasan by   write-PASS-ACTNR-3.SG.POSS
              'the letter's being written by Hasan'

Note that many languages exhibit alignment shifts in nominalization, e.g. from nominative-accusative alignment to absolutive-ergative alignment, as in Russian (Koptjevskaja-Tamm 1993).

In order to trigger the appropriate expression of arguments in different types of Clauses, these again have to be classified into subtypes, such that the encoder knows which rules to invoke to express the arguments properly.

4.4.8.3 Interpersonal and representational triggers

An important question is now how languages, if they have more than one morphosyntactic template available for the expression of subordinate Clauses, choose between those templates. We will show here that this choice is to a large extent determined by interpersonal and representational factors. In order to show this, we have to return briefly to the various interpersonal and representational units that may underlie subordinate Clauses.

We noted at several places in Chapter 3 that the Representational Level is recursive in nature. As a result, a representational frame may contain units of any level of complexity. Consider the following examples containing a predicate clause, a complement clause, and an adverbial clause respectively:

(298) $(e_i: [(f_i: [(e_j: [(f_j: [(f_k: lose (f_k))$
$\qquad\qquad\qquad\qquad (x_i)_U]$
$\qquad\qquad\qquad (f_j)) (e_j)_U])$
$\qquad\qquad (e_k: [(f_l: [(f_m: hesitate (f_m))$
$\qquad\qquad\qquad\qquad (x_i)_U]$
$\qquad\qquad\qquad (f_l)) (e_k)_U])_U]$
$\qquad (f_i)) (e_i)_U])$
'To hesitate is to lose.'

(299) $(e_i: [(f_i: [(f_j: saw (f_j))$
$\qquad\qquad (x_i: [(f_k: man (f_k)) (x_i)_U])_A$
$\qquad\qquad (e_j: [(f_l: [(f_m: depart (f_m))$
$\qquad\qquad\qquad\qquad (x_j: [(f_n: woman (f_n)) (x_j)_U])_A$
$\qquad\qquad\qquad\qquad (l_i: [(f_o: building (f_o)) (l_i)_U])_{So}]$
$\qquad\qquad\qquad (f_l)) (e_j)_U])_U]$
$\qquad (f_i)) (e_i)_U])$
'The man saw the woman depart from the building.'

(300)

$(e_i: [(f_i: [(f_j: leave (f_j))$
$\qquad\qquad (x_i: [(f_k: man (f_k)) (x_i)_U])_A] (f_i)) (e_i)_U]:$
$\qquad (t_i: [(e_j: [(f_l: [(f_m: return \qquad\qquad (f_m))$
$\qquad\qquad\qquad (x_j: \quad [(f_n: woman (f_n)) \quad (x_j)_U])_A] (f_l)) (e_j)_U]: [(t_i) (e_j)_U])$
$(e_i)_U])$
'The man left when the woman returned.'

In (298) (e_i) occupies the predicate position, in (299) an argument position, and in (300) a modifier position. Its internal complexity in the form of a predication frame is reflected in clausal structures at the Morphosyntactic Level.

Argument and modifier positions may be occupied by any of the representational layers distinguished in Chapter 3. But interpersonal layers, too, may enter the Representational Level when communicative units are referred to, as we argued in 3.14 when discussing reflexive language. As a result, we may classify subordinate constructions in terms of the interpersonal or representational layer that underlies them. In the case of complementation the semantics of the matrix predicate determines what kind of interpersonal or representational unit it can take as a dependent; in the case of adverbial subordination it is the semantic function or lexical conjunction that restricts the layers with which it may combine.

The layers distinguished at the Interpersonal Level and the Representational Level that may potentially underlie a subordinate Clause are listed in (301) and (302):

(301)

Interpersonal layers underlying subordinate Clauses

a. $(\pi M_1: (\pi A_1:[\ldots (\pi C_1: [(T_1)(R_1)] \quad (C_1):\Sigma(C_1))](A_1):\Sigma(A_1))(M_1):\Sigma(M_1))$

b. $(\pi A_1:[\ldots (\pi C_1: [(T_1)(R_1)] \quad (C_1): \Sigma (C_1))] (A_1): \Sigma (A_1))$

c. $(\pi C_1: [(T_1)(R_1)] \quad (C_1): \Sigma (C_1))$

(302)

Representational layers underlying subordinate Clauses

a. $(\pi p_1: (\pi ep_1: (\pi e_1: (\pi f_1: [(f_2) (x_1)] (f_1): \sigma (f_1)) (e_1): \sigma (e_1)) (ep_1): \sigma (ep_1)) (p_1): \sigma (p_1))$

b. $(\pi ep_1: (\pi e_1: (\pi f_1: [(f_2) (x_1)] (f_1): \sigma (f_1)) (e_1): \sigma (e_1)) (ep_1): \sigma (ep_1))$

c. $(\pi e_1: (\pi f_1: [(f_2) (x_1)] (f_1): \sigma (f_1)) (e_1): \sigma (e_1))$

d. $(\pi f_1: [(f_2) (x_1)] (f_1): \sigma (f_1))$

A higher layer generally contains all lower layers. As a result, subordinate constructions can be classified in terms of the highest layer they contain. Furthermore, since every layer brings along its own set of operators and modifiers, we can predict that operators and modifiers pertaining to the highest layer a subordinate Clause contains, as well as all lower ones, can be expressed in that subordinate Clause. Modifiers and operators pertaining to layers higher than the highest layer the subordinate Clause contains are barred from expression in that subordinate Clause.

Let us illustrate this for complement Clauses and the occurrence of modifiers within them (for earlier relevant work on Irish, see Genee 1998). Complement-taking predicates (CTPs) express similar interpersonal and representational functions and meanings to modifiers, which helps us to classify them as taking an argument of a certain type. The classification of complement Clauses in Table 7 therefore takes the function or meaning of the CTP as its point of departure in providing examples of relevant types of complementation.

The following examples, the grammatical alternatives of which were found on the internet, illustrate the use of (combinations of) subordinate Clauses (between square brackets) of the types listed above, and show that the highest

TABLE 7. Classification of complement Clauses

Type of Clause	Function/Meaning of CTP
M	Situating a Move in the wider discourse (e.g. *conclude*, *summarize*)
A	Relating Discourse Acts to one another (e.g. *add*, *go_without_saying*, '*be_firstly*')
C	Transmission and reception of Communicated Content (e.g. *say*, *hear*)
ep	Situating Episodes with respect to each other (e.g. *end_with*, *happen*)
p	Propositional attitude (e.g. *believe*), Inference (e.g. *seem*)
e	Direct Perception (e.g. *perceive*), Volition (e.g. *want*)
f	Aspect (e.g. *start*), Participant-oriented modality (e.g. *able*)

modifier available for the layer concerned, given in italics, can indeed occur in these complement Clause, while higher ones cannot. The ungrammaticality judgements here relate to the use of the modifier with scope over the subordinate Clause only. The predication frames needed for the various types of complementation are also given.

(303)   M-complement: $(f_1: [(f_2: conclude_V (f_2)) (x_1)_A (M_1: [(A_1), (A_2)...] (M_1)\Sigma (M_1))_U] (f_1))$

While it is difficult to make generalizations about such a diverse public, it is easy to conclude [that, *in sum* these actions have led to a net loss of vegetative cover relative to pre-settlement conditions, as well as a substantial change in the type of vegetation present. At the same time, public consciousness regarding the importance of urban vegetation has certainly risen in the last ten years, although how much of that awareness has translated into changed behavior *vis a vis* urban plants in Quito is an open question.] (Internet)

(304)   A-complement $(f_1: [(f_2: go\_without\_saying_V (f_2)) (A_1: [...(C_1)] (A_1): \Sigma (A_1))_U] (f_1))$

It goes without saying [that, *in addition* (*in sum*), issues such as quality and a customer-oriented approach will be kept in mind.] (Internet)

(305)   C-complement $(f_1: [(f_2: say_V (f_2)) (x_1)_A (C_1: [(T_1) (R_1)] (C_1): \Sigma (C_1))_U] (f_1))$

He said [that *reportedly* (*in addition*) there was some history of threats of domestic abuse in the family.] (Internet)

(306)   ep-complement $(f_1: [(f_2: happen_V (f_1)) (ep_1: (e_1:...(e_1)) (ep_1): \sigma (ep_1))_U] (f_1))$

It happened [that *after two years of us being there*, (*reportedly*) we found ourself [sic] in the right time at the right place, but we were not picked up by Taliban and said, come on, now, we are going to cover the war with us.] (Internet)

(307)   p-complement $(f_1: [(f_2: believe_V (f_2)) (x_1)_A (p_1: (e_1:...(e_1)) (p_1): \sigma (p_1))_U] (f_1))$

We believe [that *possibly* (*reportedly*) as much as 60 percent (or more) of the population already believe that the government is hiding what they know about worldly visitors.] (Internet)

(308)   e-complement $(f_1: [(f_2: want_V (f_2)) (x_1)_A (e_1: (f_3:...(f_3)) (e_1): \sigma (e_1))_U] (f_1))$

Lili wanted me [to come over *after lunch* (*possibly*)]. (Internet)

(309) f-complement (f$_1$: [(f$_2$: continue$_V$ (f$_2$)) (x$_1$)$_A$ (f$_3$: [(f$_4$) (x$_1$)$_A$] (f$_3$): σ (f$_3$))$_U$] (f$_1$))

The police continued [to shoot *indiscriminately* into the crowd (*after lunch*)]. (Internet)

This approach not only accounts for the fact that the modifiers and operators that can be expressed in a complement Clause are determined by the type of that Clause, but also provides the means to account for differences in the form and behaviour of complements. As argued in Hengeveld (1989, 1998), many differences in the form of subordinate Clauses can be accounted for in terms of their underlying interpersonal and representational differences. Consider the following examples from Nama. In Nama subordinate constructions may take three different forms. Direct quotation, in which the complement Clause has the status of a Discourse Act (A), is achieved by repeating the original sentence and providing it with the quote particle *tí* (Hagman 1973: 255):

(310) ʼOo-s   ke   //ʼĩsà //xaápá kè   mĩĩ [/ʼúú-ta
       then-3.SG DECL she   again REM.PST say not.know-1.SG
       ʼa   tí].
       PRS   QUOT
       'She said again: "I don't know"'

Where the complement Clause is a Communicated Content (C) or Propositional Content (p), it takes the case-marked complementizer *!xáis-*. Complement Clauses of this type may not take the optional Declarative marker *ke*, which, as illustrated in (310), is allowed in direct quotation. The following examples illustrate a C-complement (311) and a p-complement (312) (Hagman 1973: 257):

(311) Tsĩĩ //ʼĩp-à-kxm̀   ke   kè   mĩĩpa [!úū-kxm
       and 3.SG.M-ACC-1.DU.M   DECL REM.PST tell   go-1.DU
       ta   !xáis-à].
       IMPF CONJ-ACC
       'And we told him that we were going.'

(312) //ʼĩip ke   ʼamʼa-se kèrè   =/om [/ʼaé//amsà xuú-kxm
       he   DECL true-ADV REM.PST believe Windhoek from-1.DU
       /xií   hàa !xáis-à].
       come   PFV CONJ-ACC
       'He really believed that we had come from Windhoek.'

When the complement Clause is the expression of a State-of-Affairs (e) or a Configurational Property (f), it is deranked, taking the form of a nominalization, as in (313)–(314) (Rust 1965: 64, Olpp 1977: 112):

(313) [!Gû-s]   ke   káíse a   !gomba te.
       go-NMLZ   DECL very   PRS   difficult to.me
       'It's very difficult for me to go.'

(314) llîb ge   [xoas-a]   a   ǂan.
       he   DECL write-ACC   PRS   can
       'He can write.'

Thus, the selection of complement Clause types in Nama is triggered by the nature of the interpersonal or representational layers underlying them.

From a crosslinguistic perspective, a strong generalization that can be made is that a subordinate Clause is more likely to be of the deranked type the lower the layer on which it is based (see Hengeveld 1989, 1998). Deranking is the formal counterpart of the diminishing number of primary operators to be expressed morphosyntactically, as visualized in (301)–(302), and may therefore come in different degrees. Thus, the Nama complement Clauses are deranked in the sense that the Declarative marker cannot be expressed within them and that their subordinate status is marked by a conjunction, but they are less deranked than nominalizations in that tense and aspect can be expressed within them, something that is not possible with the nominalizations in (313)–(314).

In view of the generalization given above concerning the degree of deranking and the hierarchical status of the layer underlying a complement Clause, the following examples can be seen as typological extremes. Example (315) is from Evenki (Nedjalkov 1997: 1):

(315) Bejetken gun-e-n   min-tyki [amin-in
       boy   say-RLS-3.SG I-ALL   father-3.SG.POSS
       eme-d'eri-ve-n].
       come-SIM.PTCP-ACC-3.SG.POSS
       'The boy told me that his father was coming.'

This language uses a deranked complement clause for indirect speech, which is the expression of an underlying Communicated Content, and thus one of the highest layers that can be embedded. Our generalization predicts that complement clauses expressing lower layers (ep/p, e, f) in Evenki will all be of the deranked type, and this is indeed the case. The opposite situation holds in Modern Greek (Evangelos Karagiannis p.c.):

(316) Sinéxyise   [na   katevéni].
       continue.PFV.3.SG   CONJ go.down.IMPF.3.SG
       'He continued going down.'

This language uses a balancing complement clause for the lowest type of embedding, the one concerning Configurational Properties. Our generalization says that in this language complement clauses expressing higher layers (e, ep/p, C, A, M) will also be expressed by balancing clauses, and this turns out to be the case too.

There are a number of other properties of subordinate Clauses that influence their expression. Hengeveld (1998) shows that time dependency, presupposedness, and factuality also play a role in some languages in the selection of a Clause template. These factors are reflected in underlying representations in the presence of certain primary operators, which serve as additional triggers for certain templates. We will not go into these issues here, and refer to Hengeveld (1998) for further details.

4.4.8.4 The expression of operators in subordinate Clauses

There may be differences in the expression of operators between main Clauses and subordinate Clauses. We refer here not so much to the possibility of expressing operators, which depends on the nature of the interpersonal and representational layers underlying the subordinate Clause, but to differences in the form in which available operators are expressed. One such difference has already shown up in examples (265)–(266) from Spanish, where the choice of the conjunction for complement Clauses is affected by modal operators. For another illustration of this phenomenon consider the following examples from Jacaltec (Craig 1977):

(317) a. Xal naj [*tato* chuluj   naj presidente].
           said he CONJ will.come DEF president
           'He said that the president would come.'

       b. Xal naj [*chubil* chuluj   naj presidente].
           said he CONJ   will.come DEF president
           'He said that the president would come.'

The complementizer *tato* in (317a) indicates that the current Speaker considers the original speaker unreliable, whereas the complementizer *chubil* in (317b) indicates that the current Speaker considers the original speaker reliable. This distinction pertains to the field of reportativity, an operator category of the Communicated Content underlying indirect speech complements.

Another possible difference between main and subordinate Clauses as regards the expression of operators, namely sequence of tenses (*consecutio temporum*), is an instantiation of what we have earlier identified as operator agreement, now obtaining across the boundary of a main and subordinate Clause. Consider the following example from Amele (Roberts 1987: 48):

(318)   Naus uqa ege [qila bele-q-an   fo=ec]   sisil-t-en.
        Naus he I   today go-1.PL-FUT Q=NMLZ ask-1.SG/3.SG-REM.PST
        'Naus asked me whether we would go today.'
        "Naus asked me whether we will go today."

The main Clause in (318) is in the remote past tense, but the subordinate
Clause is in the future tense, which shows that this is a relative tense, in which
a State-of-Affairs is presented as posterior to the reference point established
by the remote past marker of the main Clause. In such circumstances English
in most cases applies a rule of sequence of tenses, through which the absolute
tense marking of the main Clause is superimposed on the relative tense marking of the subordinate Clause. This means that in English a rule is required that
copies the past feature of the main verb to the future feature of the subordinate
verb, which will then be expressed as a future in the past. In Nama such a
copying rule does not apply, leading to an identical expression of the future
operator in both main and subordinate Clauses.

4.4.8.5 Raising

In some cases a constituent semantically belonging to a subordinate Clause
appears as a constituent of a superordinate Clause (see for early discussion in
FG, Dik 1979 and Bolkestein 1981). As with alignment in general, the triggers
for this dislocation may be interpersonal, representational, or morphosyntactic in nature. Potential interpersonal triggers are pragmatic functions and def-
initeness/specificity; potential representational triggers are semantic functions
and animacy; and potential morphosyntactic triggers are syntactic functions
and degree of complexity. Note that, though we use the traditional terms
'raising' here, we do not want to suggest that the phenomenon involves the
transformation of one basic configuration into another derived one, as will
become clear from our analysis below.

   Interpersonal triggering of raising is illustrated by the following examples
from Hungarian (de Groot 1981: 51):

(319)   a. János azt   mond-t-a,   [hogy a   taxi öt-re   jöjjön].
            János DEM say-PST-OBJP CONJ DEF taxi five-SUBL come
            'János said that the taxi would come at five.'

        b. János öt-re   mond-t-a,   [hogy a   taxi jöjjön].
            János five-SUBL say-PST-OBJP CONJ DEF taxi come
            'János said that the taxi would come at five.'

Two features of Hungarian are relevant for the interpretation of this example.
As illustrated in 4.4.6, Hungarian has special positions for Topical and Focal
elements. Topical elements are in Clause-initial position, Focal elements in

preverbal position. Secondly, in cases of complementation such as the one illustrated in (319a) a demonstrative element refers cataphorically to an appositional complement Clause that follows the main Clause. These two facts taken together show that in (319a) the demonstrative *azt* occupies the Focus position of the main Clause, signalling that the complement Clause is Focal, while the temporal expression *ötre* 'at five' occupies the Focus position of the complement Clause itself. Under these circumstances placement of the Focal constituent of the complement Clause in the Focus position of the main Clause is allowed, in which case the demonstrative does not occur, as illustrated in (319b).

Similarly, placement of the Topic of a complement Clause in the Topic position of the main Clause is possible, as illustrated in (320) (Kenesei, Vago, and Fenyvesi 1998: 178):

(320)　A　könyv-et　Anna　mond-t-a　[hogy　fel-olvas-s-a
　　　　DEF　book-ACC　Anna　say-PST-OBJ　CONJ　PFV-read.PRS-OBJ
　　　　Péter-nek].
　　　　Péter-DAT
　　　　'Anna said she would read the book to Peter.'

Representational triggering of raising can be illustrated with examples from Tuvaluan. The phenomenon itself is illustrated in (321) (Besnier 2000: 110):

(321)　a.　E　　　　see　mafai loa　[o　puli　　ana　　　fo'oliga
　　　　　　NONPST　NEG　can　　indeed CONJ　forgotten 3.SG.POSS features
　　　　　　i　au].
　　　　　　to　1.SG
　　　　b.　E　　　　see　mafai loa　　ana　　　foʻoliga　[o　puli
　　　　　　NONPST　NEG　can　　indeed 3.SG.POSS features CONJ　forgotten
　　　　　　i　au].
　　　　　　to　1.SG
　　　　　　'I will never forget what he looked like.'

In (321a) the absolutive argument *ana foʻoliga* 'his features' of the subordinate clause appears in a main clause position, preceding the conjunction *o*. In Tuvaluan the raised Noun Phrase can have any semantic function, except for Possessive and Standard of Comparison. This restriction may be a result of the fact that these are semantic functions of Noun Phrases embedded within other Phrases. An illustration of semantic functions otherwise allowing raising is given in (322) for Actor (322b), Undergoer (322c), and Location (322d) (Besnier 2000: 114)

(322) a. E maasani [o ave nee Sina te tamaliki ki te
   NONPST used-to CONJ send ERG Sina ART child to ART
   loomatua].
   old.woman

  b. E maasani Sina [o ave te tamaliki ki te
   NONPST used-to Sina CONJ send ART child to ART
   loomatua].
   old.woman

  c. E maasani te tamaliki [o ave nee Sina ki te
   NONPST used-to ART child CONJ send ERG Sina to ART
   loomatua].
   old.woman

  d. E maasani te loomatua [o ave nee Sina te
   NONPST used-to ART old.woman CONJ send ERG Sina ART
   tamaliki ki ei].
   child to ANA
   'Sina often sends the child to the old woman.'

Besnier (1988: 773) states that 'a noun phrase can be raised out of a subordinate clause only if it denotes an entity that is actively involved in bringing about the situation denoted by the entire sentence' or that is 'responsible for the performance of the action denoted by entire sentence, or for the inception of the state denoted by the sentence' (Besnier 1988: 762). This explains why the second of the following two sentences is ill-formed (Besnier 1988: 763):

(323) a. E kkafi nee ia [o see fakatavale nee au].
   NONPST capable ERG he CONJ NEG CAUS.defeated ERG 1.SG
   'He is capable of not getting defeated by me.'

  b. ??E kkafi nee ia [o fakatavale nee au].
   NONPST capable ERG he CONJ CAUS.defeated ERG 1.SG
   'He is capable of getting defeated by me.'

Every Noun Phrase that complies with this general semantic restriction is the potential target of raising in Tuvaluan, which may thus be said to apply representational triggers in the raising process.

 Raising triggered by morphosyntactic factors can be illustrated by means of the following Spanish sentences:

(324) a. Parece   [que Juan escribió   ese   libro].
            seem.IND.PRS.3.SG CONJ Juan write.IND.PST.PFV.3.SG DEM book
            'It seems that Juan wrote that book.'

       b. Juan parece   [hab-er   escrito   ese   libro].
           Juan seem.IND.PRS.3.SG have-INF write.PFV.PTCP DEM book
           'Juan seems to have written that book.'

       c. Ese   libro parece   [hab-er   sido
           DEM book seem.IND.PRS.3.SG have-INF be.PFV.PTCP

           escrito   por Juan].
           write.PFV.PTCP by Juan
           'That book seems to have been written by Juan.'

Raising is restricted in Spanish. Only the Subject of the subordinate clause can
raise, and it can raise only to the Subject position of the superordinate clause.
The Undergoer argument of the subordinate clause can therefore raise only
after passivization. As with Subject assignment in general, there may be all
kinds of contextual and therefore extragrammatical factors that trigger the
choice for a raised or a non-raised construction type. This does not affect
the basically morphosyntactic analysis of the phenomenon in languages like
Spanish.

Raising has several consequences for the proper placement of constituents
in morphosyntactic templates. Following our top-down approach, the template for a subordinate Clause is selected before the placement of the constituents pertaining to that Clause. The latter is only possible if the raised
constituent can be placed in an absolute position or in a position relative to an
already instantiated position. Let us apply this idea to the Spanish examples
in (324). Subjects usually occur before the verb in categorical statements in P^I
or a position relative to P^I, unless they are heavy, in which case they go to the
absolute Clause-final position P^F, which is what has happened in (324a), to be
represented as follows:

(325)
$$P^I \quad P^M \quad\quad P^F \hspace{4cm} (=324a)$$
$$ P^I \quad\quad P^{I+1} \quad\quad P^M \quad\quad P^{M+1}$$
$$(Cl_i\!: [\quad (Vp_i) \quad (Cl_j\!: [\; (Gw_i) \; (Np_i)_{Subj} \; (Vp_j) \quad (Np_j) \quad] \; (Cl_j))_{Subj}] \; (Cl_i))$$
$$ parece \quad\quad que \quad Juan \quad escribió \; ese\_libro$$

The subordinate Clause in P^F has Subject function, triggering third person
singular agreement on the main verb. The predicate is in P^M in (324a), leaving
P^I vacant, since Spanish does not require a dummy Subject constituent. In
the raised variants (324a–b) this position is occupied by the raised Subject,

which now behaves as the Subject of the main Clause, as in the following representation of (324b):

(326)

$$P^I \qquad P^M \qquad P^F \qquad\qquad\qquad\qquad (=324b)$$
$$\varnothing \qquad P^M \qquad\qquad P^{M+1}$$

(Cl$_i$: [(Np$_i$)$_{Subj}$ (Vp$_i$) (Cl$_j$: [(Np$_i$)$_{Subj}$ (Vp$_j$)   (Np$_j$)] (Cl$_j$))] (Cl$_i$))
      Juan   parece   haber_escrito ese_libro

As in other cases of unexpressed Subjects discussed above, we still need to know what the Subject of the subordinate Clause is in order to trigger active or passive encoding, which is why there is a non-realized subordinate Subject in (324b). Subject assignment is different in (324c), which may be represented as follows:

(327)

$$P^I \qquad P^M \qquad P^F \qquad\qquad\qquad\qquad (=324c)$$
$$\varnothing \qquad P^M \qquad\qquad P^{M+1}$$

(Cl$_i$: [(Np$_i$)$_{Subj}$ (Vp$_i$) (Cl$_j$: [(Np$_i$)$_{Subj}$ (Vp$_j$)   (Adp$_i$)] (Cl$_j$))] (Cl$_i$))
      ese_libro parece   haber_sido_escrito por_Juan

In cases in which P^I has already been occupied during the process of hierarchical ordering by e.g. one or more modifiers and or a conjunction, then the raised Subject will go to the first position available to the right of these, i.e. it will go to P^{I+N}. This is illustrated in (328):

(328) Según   esta revista   Juan parece   hab-er
      According.to DEM magazine   Juan seem.IND.PRS.3.SG have-INF
      escrito   ese   libro.
      write.PFV.PTCP   DEM   book
      'According to this magazine Juan seems to have written that book.'

Thus, our approach to placement allows us to find either an absolute or a relative position for raised arguments outside their proper domain.

4.4.9 Coreference

A final issue concerning clausal organization that we will look at relates to coreferentiality and its consequences for the form of clausal constituents, particularly the choice of reflexive pronouns, the possible controllers for these pronouns, and the domain within which coreference exerts its influence. We will again make a distinction between three potential triggers of reflexivity: interpersonal, representational, and morphosyntactic triggers.

In cases in which reflexivity is triggered interpersonally, we predict that the antecedent may be defined in terms of its pragmatic function, while the domain of application is an interpersonal unit, such as a Discourse Act (A) or a Move (M). Lezgian seems to be a good example of such a language. Consider the following example (Haspelmath 1993: 414):

(329) Č'exi buba laha-na x̂i,   wiči-z   k'wal-e   wa?,
       big   father say-AOR CONJ self-DAT house-INESS not
       balxun.di-z ksu-z   k'an-zawa. Balxun.di-k   hawa serin
       balcony-DAT sleep-INF want-IMPF balcony-SUBESS air fresh
       ja, anal wiči-z   dağ.d-a   awa-j   x̂iz že-da.
       COP there self-DAT mountain-INESS be.in-PTCP like be-FUT
       'Grandfather_i said that he_i wanted to sleep on the balcony, not in the
       house. On the balcony the air is fresh, there he_i will feel like he is in the
       mountains.'

Note that the reflexive *wiči* can be used across Clause-boundaries, the antecedent *č'exi_buba* 'grandfather' being in the first Clause, and the reflexive occurring in both the first and the second Clause. Haspelmath (1993: 411) furthermore notes 'that it is not possible to put any syntactic limits on the positions that the antecedent may occupy', giving examples of attributive genitives controlling the reflexive:

(330) Ix̂tin šadwal wiči-z-ni   x̂u-n.i-kdi   Rahman.a-n
       such pleasure self-DAT-also become-NMLZ-SUBDIR Rahman-GEN
       čin-a-ni   šad qʰwer hat-na.
       face-INESS-also glad smile appear-AOR
       'Since such a pleasure had also happened to him_i, a happy smile also
       appeared on Rahman_i's face.'

The main restriction on reflexivization is that the controller must be pragmatically salient (Haspelmath 1993: 411), which within FDG we would deal with in terms of pragmatic functions. The example in (329) furthermore suggests that the domain of application of reflexivization is the Move, since (329) consists of two Discourse Acts, the second serving as an explanation for the first.

In cases in which reflexivity is triggered representationally, we predict that the antecedent may be defined in terms of its semantic function, while the domain of application is a representational unit, such as a Propositional Content (p) or an Episode (ep). Chechen seems to have such a system, given the existence of examples like the following (Nichols 1994: 67; stretch of direct speech omitted):

(331) As '...' šiega a:lčaĥ, cunax cca do:š ʔa dina,
       I.ERG   REFL.ALL said.TEMP this.LOC one word and say.CVB
       daʔajtin-ču de:ke ʔa ca ĥožuš, šie^n vežeraš-ci^n
       SBJ.send-OBL part.ALL and NEG look-CVB REFL.GEN brothers-INS
       dow ʔa dina, šü:ge jo:llu^n huma je:ka^n
       quarrel and make.CVB you.ALL SBJ.be.PRS.PTCP thing divide.INF
       qajkina sa^n ma:ra.
       called my husband.NOM
       'When I said "..." to him$_j$, my husband$_i$ took that as sufficient rea-
       son and, without even looking at the portion that had been sent (to
       him), started a quarrel with his$_i$ brothers and called you to divide their
       possessions.'

Nichols (1994: 68–9) notes that 'control is basically semantically determined:
the most animate or agentive NP is the favored controller'. This coincides with
the fact that (331) describes an Episode, a semantic unit, which seems to serve
as the domain of application of reflexivization. Note furthermore that clause
boundaries do not restrict reflexivization, and that the controller follows the
reflexives in (331).

In cases in which reflexivity is triggered morphosyntactically, we predict
that the antecedent may be defined in terms of its syntactic function, while the
domain of application is a morphosyntactic unit, such as a Clause. Koromfe
illustrates this type of trigger, as in this language only Subjects can be the
antecedent of a reflexive (Rennison 1997: 108):

(332) Də   pa də   gɪllɛ a sallɛ kebre.
       3.SG.HUM give 3.SG.HUM self ART plate.SG big.SG
       'He gave himself the big plate.'

(333) Də   pa a sallɛ kebre də   gɪllɛ bi.
       3.SG.HUM give ART plate.SG big.SG 3.SG.HUM self child.SG
       'He gave the big plate to his own son.'

The morphosyntactic nature of reflexivization is furthermore reflected in the
fact that the domain of application is a single simple Clause, i.e. it does not
apply across any clause border. This includes the border introduced by non-
finite subordinate Clauses.

Coreferential marking restricted to subordinate Clauses is often referred
to as logophoricity. A language employing logophors is Babungo, and its
logophors are different from reflexives. In the absence of true reflexive pronouns, Babungo uses a periphrastic strategy involving the noun ŋwáa 'body'
within Clauses to indicate coreference (Schaub 1985: 110):

(334) Mə̀ sɔ̀   ŋwáa ŋwāa.
      I   wash.PFV body my
      'I_i washed myself_i.'

(335) ŋwɔ́ kàw   shè' ŋwáa wī.
      he love.PFV only body his
      'He_i only loves himself_i.'

This strategy seems to be restricted to Subject controllers. In the case of coreferentiality across the border of a subordinate clause Babungo (Schaub 1985: 111) uses logophoric pronouns, which, too, are controlled by the main clause Subject:

(336) ŋwɔ́ gì   lāa yì   táa jwî.
      he say.PFV CONJ 3.LOG FUT come
      'He_i said that he_i would come.'

(337) ŋwɔ́ yé   lāa yì   gígū.
      he see.PFV CONJ 3.LOG fall.PROG
      'He_i saw that he_i was falling.'

(338) ŋwɔ́ nyìŋ   lāa kɨ́   vǝ̌ŋ sáŋ yí   mē.
      he run.PFV CONJ NEG.IMP they beat 3.LOG NEG
      'He_i ran away so that they should not beat him_i.'

The examples above have shown that the various levels of organization in Functional Discourse Grammar help to account both for the varying nature of the controller (defined in terms of pragmatic, semantic, or syntactic functions), as well as for the various domains of application of reflexivization strategies (interpersonal, representational, or morphosyntactic units). These features help us to generate the correct form of a pronoun. Recall that pronouns in FDG are represented in terms of abstract features, which are introduced at either the Interpersonal or the Representational Level for deictic and anaphoric uses respectively. The expression of these feature sets can now be made sensitive to (i) the presence of a certain type of controller, within (ii) the appropriate domain of application. In languages with interpersonal and representational triggers this means that the appropriate forms can be generated directly by the morphosyntactic encoder, while in the case of morphosyntactic triggers the choice of the correct form can only be made after the morphosyntactic template has been filled.

4.5 Phrases

4.5.1 Introduction

If we ignore the specific order in which constituents occur, a Phrase in a configurational language like English has the following maximum formula, in which every constituent may occur more than once:

(339) $(Xp_1: [(Xw) (Xp)(Cl)] (Xp_1))$

In other words, a Phrase in such a language potentially consists of a sequenced configuration of Words (Xw), other Phrases (Xp), and embedded Clauses (Cl). As regards Words, we have argued earlier that lexical elements are always the heads of Phrases at the Morphosyntactic Level. The reverse is not true: there are Phrases without a lexical head. When Phrases occur within Phrases the structure in (339) is applied recursively, to the extent that languages allow recursion. And the occurrence of Clauses within Phrases allows us to account for various types of subordinate Clauses.

Among the subtypes of (Xp)s we distinguish Verb Phrase (Vp), Noun Phrase (Np), Adjective Phrase (Adjp), adverb Phrase (Advp), and Adposition Phrase (Adp). By a Verb Phrase we understand a Phrase with a Verbal Word as its head, and not the combination of verb and object, as the term is traditionally used. We do not assume that these Phrase types are universally present, neither do we assume, as argued in 3.7.2.3, that there is a one-to-one relation between Phrase types and lexeme types.

In discussing the various properties of Phrases we will illustrate these properties by referring to the various subtypes of Phrases, but we do not aim at an exhaustive treatment of all of them. We will treat Phrases (and similarly Words, in 4.6) by applying the same principles as we applied in our treatment of Clauses. That is, we will build up the morphosyntactic templates of Phrases in a top-down and centripetal manner, until we touch upon configurational units, which are integrated into morphosyntactic templates in view of their alignment properties. The latter are much less relevant at the Phrase layer than they are at the Clause-layer, since most Phrases are based on underlying representations with a single argument, which is furthermore not expressed independently. The exception to this are cases of complex Phrases based on lexically derived heads, such as lexical nominalizations.

Given the parallelism in our approach to Clauses and Phrases, the organization of this section runs parallel to that of 4.4. In 4.5.2 we start with the morphosyntactic expression at Phrase layer of the hierarchically organized corresponding parts of the Interpersonal Level and the Representational Level, starting with the highest layers and working down to the lowest ones.

In 4.5.3 we discuss the alignment properties of the configurational frames underlying Phrases. The ordering of the elements pertaining to these frames is discussed in 4.5.4. The morphosyntactic templates resulting from these steps are discussed in 4.5.5. Obligatory positions in phrasal templates for which no material is available from the Interpersonal and Representational Levels are filled with dummies, such as copular verbs or dummy nominal heads, which will be treated in 4.5.6. We are then ready to treat agreement relations in 4.5.7. Finally, we will pay attention to the form and structure of subordinate Clauses within Phrases in 4.5.8.

4.5.2 Ordering of hierarchically related units

If we restrict ourselves to Phrases with a lexical head, the parts of the Interpersonal Level and the Representational Level to be expressed in a hierarchical manner in a dynamic implementation of the grammar may be summarized as follows:

(340) $\Phi^R/\Sigma^R/\Pi^R \quad \to \quad \phi^v/\sigma^v/\pi^v \quad \to \quad \phi^f/\sigma^f/\pi^f$

(341) $\Phi^T/\Sigma^T/\Pi^T \quad \to \quad (\phi^v/\sigma^v/\pi^v \quad \to \;) \quad \phi^f/\sigma^f/\pi^f$

Referential Subacts (340) evoke a semantic category (v) which contains a (lexical) Property (f), as in (342), where (x) is the more specific instantiation of (v):

(342) R_I
    $(x_i: [(f_i: man (f_i)) (x_i)_U])$
    '(I saw) a man.'

Ascriptive Subacts (341) often map directly onto a Lexical Property (f), as in (343):

(343) T_I
    $(f_i: see (f_i))$
    '(I) saw (a man).'

But Ascriptive Subacts may also evoke other semantic categories (v) which are in turn restricted by a Lexical Property (f), as in (344), where (x) is the more specific instantiation of (v):

(344) T_I
    $(x_i: [(f_i: man (f_i)) (x_i)_U])$
    '(He is) a man.'

Cases like these were discussed in 3.6.2.2.7 and 3.6.2.2.6 on classifying and relational predication frames respectively.

The two strings in (340)–(341) are not completely independent of each other. Referential Subacts, especially, generally contain Ascriptive Subacts. For instance, Adposition Phrases which correspond to a Referential Subact may have a lexical adposition as their head, which corresponds to an Ascriptive Subact and takes an argument that corresponds to a Referential Subact again, as in (345):

(345) R_I T_I R_J
        $(l_i: [(f_i: [(f_i: outside (f_i)) (l_j: [-city\_centre- (l_j)_U])_{Ref}] (l_i)_U])$
        '(He lives) outside the city centre.'

Similarly, Noun Phrases corresponding to a Referential Subact generally contain one or more Ascriptive Subacts, as shown in the following more elaborated version of (342):

(346) R_I T_I T_J
        $(x_i: [(f_i: man (f_i)) (x_i)_U]: [(f_j: big (f_j)) (x_i)_U])$
        '(I saw) a big man.'

Given this added complexity of Referential Subacts, the majority of our examples will illustrate this type of Subact.

Note that in both cases mentioned here the Sub-Subacts are in a configurational relationship within the Referential Subact, so that a choice will have to be made as regards which Sub-Subact has to be developed first in morphosyntax. This point can be illustrated by means of the following constructed and somewhat overloaded, yet grammatical example and its interpersonal and representational counterparts:

(347)   the allegedly defamatory so-called articles

(348) $(+id R_I: [(T_I: [ ] (T_I): so-called (T_I)) (T_J: [ ] (T_J): allegedly (T_J))] (R_I))$
        $(m x_i: [(f_i: article (f_i))   (x_i)_U]: [(f_j: defamatory (f_j))   (x_i)_U])$

In (347) two Properties are ascribed to the Individual (x_i): 'article' and 'defamatory'. Each of these Properties at the Representational Level is evaluated at the Interpersonal Level (see 2.8.2.3), with the modifiers *so-called* and *allegedly* assessing the appropriateness of the two ascriptions. These ascriptions are in an equipollent relationship at the Interpersonal Level. The question which of these has to be developed first is answered at the Representational Level. In order to respect (340), the Ascriptive Subact (T_J) (*allegedly defamatory*) has to be assigned a position first, since (f_j) is a modifier (σ) of (x_i), the instantiation in (348) of the variable (v) in (340). And in view of (341), the modifier *allegedly* has to be assigned a position before the modifier *defamatory* is sent down to morphosyntax.

This joint application of (340) and (341) explains the orderings found in the following series of examples:

(349) a. the allegedly defamatory so-called articles
       b. the defamatory so-called articles
       c. the so-called articles
       d. the articles
       e. articles

These orderings are the only ones possible for the given combination of elements in the intended readings. We may explain this ordering restriction, as shown most fully in (349a), as follows. The article, if present, expresses an interpersonal operator of type π^R and has to be located first according to (340), going to the initial position. Then, as we just argued, (T_J) has to be developed first. (T_J) as a whole forms an Adjective Phrase, which goes to the first relative position available counting from the initial position. Within the Adjective Phrase the interpersonal modifier *allegedly*, being of type Σ^T, is the first item to be assigned a position according to (341). It goes to the first position within the embedded Phrase. The second part of (T_J), the adjective *defamatory*, is placed next, and again takes the next available position to the right within the embedded Phrase. The modifier within (T_I) has to be expressed next, according to (341). It forms an Adjective Phrase that goes to the next position available. Finally, the head of (T_I) is also the head of the Phrase as a whole and is put in the next position available. In the absence of any of the elements just discussed, the remaining items move to the left, as illustrated by (349b–e) or any other possible combination.

Note that by applying this procedure the only absolute position we need for the examples in (349) is P^I, introduced in the previous section. The only other position needed for English Noun Phrases is P^F, which is used for heavy constituents and another class of modifiers to be discussed below. While we used notions such as P^I and P^F in the previous section to indicate the position of Words, Phrases, and Clauses within Clauses, we use them here for the position of Words, Phrases, and Clauses within Phrases. (349a–e) may thus be represented as follows:

(350)

a. P^I P^{I+1} (=349a)

P^I

$(Np_i: [(Gw_i: the (Gw_i)) (Ap_i: [(Advp_i: (advw_i:allegedly(advw_i)) (Advp_i))$

P^{I+2}

P^{I+1}

$(Aw_i:defamatory (Aw_i))](Ap_i))$ $(Ap_j: (Aw_j: so-called (Aw_j)) (Ap_j))$

P^{I+3}

$(Nw_i: articles (Nw_i))] (Np_i))$

b. P^I P^{I+1} (=349b)

$(Np_i: [(Gw_i: the (Gw_i)) (Ap_i: (Aw_i: defamatory (Aw_i)) (Ap_i))$

   P^{I+2} P^{I+3}

   $(Ap_j: (Aw_j: so-called (Aw_j)) (Ap_j)) (Nw_i: articles (Nw_i))] (Np_i))$

c. P^I P^{I+1} (=349c)

$(Np_i: [(Gw_i: the (Gw_i)) (Ap_i: (Aw_i: so-called (Aw_i))(Ap_i))$

   P^{I+2}

   $(Nw_i: articles (Nw_i))] (Np_i))$

d. P^I P^{I+1} (=349d)

$(Np_i: [(Gw_i: the (Gw_i)) (Nw_i: articles (Nw_i))] (Np_i))$

e. P^I (=349e)

$(Np_i: [(Nw_i: articles (Nw_i))] (Np_i))$

English thus illustrates what Rijkhoff (2002) calls the Principle of Scope, which predicts the iconic reflection of hierarchical relations at the Morphosyntactic Level. One of the typological correlates of this when applied to the Noun Phrase is that in the overwhelming majority of languages determiners take a position at one of the Phrase margins.

For a further illustration, and one involving more positional complexity, let us consider the order in Noun Phrases in Basque. Consider the following example (Aitor Arana, p.c.):

(351)   herri   hon=eta=ko   hiru   biztanle   zaharr=ak
        land   DEM=INAN.LOC=ATTR   three   inhabitant   old=DEF.PL
        'the three old inhabitants of this country'

In Basque Noun Phrases lexical modifiers follow the head noun, and non-lexical modifiers occur in initial position. The class of non-lexical modifiers includes phrasal and clausal ones. Most numerals can only occur in the position immediately preceding the head noun. The definiteness marker occurs on the last element of the Noun Phrase, and not necessarily on the head noun, as (351) shows: if there is lexical modifier it will appear on that modifier, and if there is a series of modifiers it will appear on the last one. And in the exceptional case in which a numeral occurs as the last item (which is obligatory with the numeral *bat* 'one' and an option with the numeral *bi* 'two') it will appear on the numeral, as in the following example (Aitor Arana, p.c.):

(352) herri hon=eta=ko   biztanle   zahar bi=ak
       land DEM-LOC.INAN=ATTR inhabitant old   two-DEF.PL
       'the two old inhabitants of this country'

The phrasal nature of the definiteness marker is also a property of case markers and the like. As Trask (2003: 113) puts it, '...nouns cannot in fact be directly inflected at all: in Basque, it is noun phrases, and only noun phrases, which can be inflected'. We therefore prefer to analyse these markers as Phrase-layer (as opposed to Clause-layer) clitics: particles that cliticize to the last element of the Phrase, irrespective of the nature of that element. There are two more such clitics in (353)–(354): the locative particle *eta* acts as a postposition, and the attributive particle *ko* enables a Postposition or Adverb Phrase to act as a nominal modifier.

The interpersonal and representational structure of (351) is given in (353):

(353) $(+id\ R_I:\ [\ \ (T_I)$ (T_J)
       $(3\ x_i:$ $[(f_i:\ biztanle\ (f_i))\ (x_i)_U]:\ \ [(f_j:\ zahar\ (f_j))\ (x_i)_U]:$
       $(T_K:\ (R_J)$ $(T_K))]\ (R_I))$
       $[(f_k:\ (prox\ x_j:\ [-herri-\ (x_j)_U])_L\ (f_k))\ (x_i)_U])$

In the hierarchical placement of the various elements of this structure the expression of the identifiability operator on the Referential Subact (R_I) comes first: it goes to the last position within the phrasal template, P^F. In the next step there are three candidates for placement: the numeral operator and the two modifiers all operate at the same layer. The order of placement is determined by alignment considerations to be discussed in the next section. In this case the two modifiers could be placed in any order, but whatever this order would be, the complex modifier goes to P^I, while the lexical one goes to P^{F-1}. The numeral can then be placed relative to the complex modifier in P^{I+1}. The final element to be placed is the nominal head. One could argue that in (351) it is in P^{I+2}, in P^{F-2}, or in P^M. In the absence of further evidence, we will assume a medial position in cases like these.

We thus may propose the following template for (351):

(354) P^I (=351)
       $(Np_i:\ [\ \ (Adp_i:\ [-herri\_hon=eta=ko]\ (Adp_i))$
       P^{I+1} P^M
       $(Gw_i:\ hiru\ (Gw_i))\ \ (Nw_i:\ biztanle\ (Nw_i))$
       P^{F-1} P^F
       $(Ap_i:\ (Aw_i:\ zahar\ (Aw_i))\ (Ap_i))\ \ (Gw_j:\ ak\ (Gw_j))\ ]\ (Np_i))$

Of course the Adposition Phrase (Adp$_i$) has to be developed further, again using a phrasal template. The result would be as follows:

(355) p^{F-1} (=351)

(Adp$_i$: [(Adp$_j$: [–herri_hon=eta] (Adp$_j$))
p^F

(Gw$_k$: ko (Gw$_k$))] (Adp$_i$))

This contains another Adposition Phrase, to be developed as:

(356) p^{F-1} (=351)

(Adp$_j$: [(Np$_j$: [(Nw$_j$: herri (Nw$_j$)) (Gw$_l$: hon (Gw$_l$)) (Np$_j$))
p^F

(Gw$_m$: eta (Gw$_m$))] (Adp$_i$))

And then the Noun Phrase (Np$_j$) is developed again as:

(357) p^M p^F (=351)

(Np$_j$: [(Nw$_j$: herri (Nw$_j$)) (Gw$_n$: hon (Gw$_n$))] (Np$_j$))

with the cumulative abbreviated result being:

(358) [P^I p^{I+1} p^M p^{F-1} P^F] (=351)

[p^{F-1} p^F]

[p^{F-1} p^F]

[p^M p^F]

[[[[herri hon]= eta]= ko] hiru biztanle zaharr= ak]

When adding a further interpersonal modifier of the Referential Subact, the result is as predicted, given the principles of hierarchical ordering: since it is in the same category as the definiteness marker, it has to be placed immediately after or before the placement of the definiteness marker and relative to it. Consider the following example (Aitor Arana, p.c.), in which the intended reading of the modifier *gaixo* 'poor' is the interpersonal one (cf. 2.8.3.3):

(359)   herri   hon=eta=ko   biztanle   zahar gaixo-ak
        land   DEM=LOC.INAN=ATTR   inhabitant old   poor-DEF.PL
        'poor old inhabitants of this country'

The interpersonal adjective *gaixo* is placed here relative to and immediately preceding the definiteness marker -*ak*, pushing the representational adjective *zahar* to the left, as we would predict on the basis of the principles of hierarchical ordering.

Now let us turn to an example of the order of Words within Verb Phrases. The following example is from Hidatsa (Matthews 1965), and has a Verb Phrase containing the analytic expression of three different operators from the Representational Level:

(360) Wíra i apaari ki   stao   ski.
       tree it grow INCH REM.PST CERT
       'The tree must have begun to grow a long time ago.'

As in many languages (see Foley and Van Valin 1984; Bybee 1985), the semantic scope of the operators (π^f INCH, π^{ep} REM.PST, π^p CERT) is reflected in their surface order. It will be clear from this example that in a top-down approach the auxiliaries in Hidatsa are placed from right to left, as shown below:

(361) p^{F-3} p^{F-2} (=360)
       $(Vp_i: [\ (Vp_j: (Vw_m: apaari \ (Vw_m)) \ (Vp_j)) \ (Gw_j: ki \ (Gw_j))$
       p^{F-1} p^F
       $(Gw_k: stao \ (Gw_k)) \ (Gw_l: ski \ (Gw_l))] \ (Vp_i))$

4.5.3 Alignment

Units making up a Phrase may be equipollent, i.e. not hierarchically related to one another, (i) because they are modifiers and operators of like rank; (ii) because they are part of the same predication frame.

The former case was illustrated for Basque in the preceding section, especially in (351) and its underlying representation in (353), the Representational Layer of which is repeated here for convenience:

(362) $(3 \ x_i: \ [(f_i: biztanle \ (f_i)) \ (x_i)_U]: \ [(f_j: zahar \ (f_j)) \ (x_i)_U]: \ [(f_k: (prox \ x_j: [-herri- \ (x_j)_U])_L \ (f_k)) \ (x_i)_U])$

In terms of the hierarchies in (340)–(341), the π^x operator '3', the σ^x modifier (f_j), and the σ^x modifier (f_k) are all of the same rank. Their coding properties may be sensitive to various interpersonal, representational, and morphosyntactic considerations. For instance, in the case of Basque the major factor determining the placement of modifiers within the Noun Phrase is the morphosyntactic complexity of the modifier.

Units may also be equipollent because they are part of the same predication frame, as illustrated in examples like the following, discussed in 3.6.1:

(363) the brother of the king
       $(x_i: \ [(f_i: \ [(f_j: brother \ (f_j)) \ (x_j: \ [(f_k: king \ (f_k)) \ (x_j)_U])_{Ref}] \ (f_i)) \ (x_i)_U])$

(364) before the meeting
       $(t_i: \ [(f_i: \ [(f_j: before \ (f_j)) \ (e_i: \ [(f_k: meeting \ (f_k)) \ (e_i)_{Ref}]) \ (f_i)_U]) \ (t_i)_U])$

(365) the idea that the world is round
       $(p_i: \ [(f_i: \ [(f_j: idea \ (f_j)) \ (p_j: [-the \ world \ is \ round-] \ (p_j))_U] \ (f_i)) \ (p_i)_U])$

The equipollent units in (363) within (f_i) are (f_j) and (x_j), in (364) (f_j) and (e_i), and in (365) (f_j) and (p_j). Again, the coding properties of these units may be motivated by interpersonal, representational, or morphosyntactic factors. Note that there are other pairs of equipollent units in these examples, such as (f_i) and (x_i) in (363), but since in cases like these one unit remains unexpressed they are less interesting from the point of view of alignment.

Some cases of equipollence thus reflect the relation between a modifier and its head, while others have to do with the relation between a dependent and its nucleus. It is precisely this distinction that languages may or may not mark explicitly in the alignment of units within Phrases. Consider the following examples from Tariana (Aikhenvald 2003: 128, 123):

(366)   waha panisaru
       we   abandoned.village
      'our abandoned village'

(367)   a.   nu-pitana
           1.SG-name
           'my name'

      b.   kuphe i-pitana
           fish   INDF-name
           'the name of a fish'

(366) illustrates inalienable possession, which is expressed through mere juxtaposition, while (367) contains examples of inalienable possession, expressed through pronominal prefixes. In (367a) the inalienably possessed noun has the first person prefix. In the presence of a nominal possessor, the inalienably possessed noun takes the indefinite prefix (367b).

Recall that in 3.6 we analysed alienable possession as in (368), while inalienable possession would be represented as in (369):

(368)   the king's book
      $(x_i: [(f_i: book (f_i)) (x_i)_U]: [(f_j: (x_j: [(f_k: king (f_k)) (x_j)_U])_{Ass} (f_j)) (x_i)_U])$

(369)   the king's brother
      $(x_i: [(f_i: [(f_j: brother (f_j)) (x_j: [(f_k: king (f_k)) (x_j)_U])_{Ref}] (f_i)) (x_i)_U])$

The embedded Noun Phrase *the king* is a modifier of the head *book* in (368), while it is a dependent of the nucleus *brother* in (369).

The pronominal prefixes in the Tariana examples (367) thus mark the argument of a nucleus, not the modifier of a head. Interestingly, it uses the same prefixes as in other cases in which arguments have to be marker on their nuclei. Compare the following examples (Aikhenvald 2003: 123, 67, 229):

(370)   nu-pitana
      1.SG-name
      'my name'

(371) nu-dalipa
       1.SG-near
       'near me'

(372) Nu-ñha-ka.
       1.SG.A-eat-RECPST.VIS
       'I have eaten.'

These examples show that the same pronominal marker is used in relational Noun Phrases (370), Adposition Phrases (371), and Clauses (372). In each case this marker expresses the (first) argument of the nominal, adpositional, and verbal nuclei respectively.

It comes as no surprise that nominalizations pattern in the same way, as in the following examples (Aikhenvald 2003: 467):

(373) nu-dokola-ri
       1.SG-bend-NMLZ.NONPST
       'my joint (of human body)'

(374) nu-mheta-ri
       1.SG-think-NMLZ.NONPST
       'my thought/opinion'

(375) nu-peya-ri
       1.SG-be.in.front-NMLZ.NONPST
       'what or who is in front of me'

The alignment of arguments is thus fully symmetric across Phrase and Clause types in Tariana. Modifiers of heads are never treated in this way.

A quite different system is found in Lango. In this language modifiers are treated in one way, arguments within Phrases in another, and arguments within Clauses in yet another. Alienable possessors are treated in the same way as lexical modifiers, in that they all take the attributive particle à, as illustrated in the following examples (Noonan 1992: 154, 181):

(376) gwôkk à   lócə̀
       dog   ATTR man
       'the man's dog'

(377) dyàŋŋ à   dwôŋ
       cow   ATTR big
       'the big cow'

(378) àjwâtέ   à   têk
       1.SG.hit.PFV-3.SG ATTR hard
       'I hit him hard.'

Inalienable possessors, by contrast, do not take the attributive particle (Noonan 1992: 157):

(379)   bàd dàktàl
        arm doctor
        'the doctor's arm'

Inalienable possessors, the arguments of prepositions, and the subjects of nominalizations are all treated in the same way in that they are expressed through the same set of associative person markers (Noonan 1992: 81, 107, 213):

(380)   ŋut-ɔ́
        neck-1.SG.ASS
        'my neck'

(381)   bɔ̀t-ɔ́
        to-1.SG.ASS
        'to me'

(382)   dákô   kwânnɛ́-rɛ̂
        woman read.INF-3.SG.ASS
        'the woman's reading'

Alienable possessors are expressed through a different set of suffixes (Noonan 1992: 79):

(383)   bɔ̀ŋɔ̀-ná
        dress-1.SG.POSS
        'my dress'

Arguments within Clauses do not share any of the properties mentioned above. They are expressed through their own set of suffixes on the verb, as illustrated above in (378).

English exhibits a third type of system, one in which arguments and modifiers within Phrases are treated in the same way, as in (368)–(369) above, while a different strategy is used for arguments within Clauses.

A fourth type of system is one in which no distinction is made between the three types of constituent. This is the case in Berbice Dutch Creole. Consider the following examples (Kouwenberg 1994: 177, 159, 208, 525):

(384)   eni   brantɛ
        they burn.PFV
        'they burnt'

(385)   eni   bangki
        they bench
        'their bench'

	Lango	Tariana	English	BD Creole
modifier (Phrase)	A	A	A	A
argument (Phrase)	B	B		
argument (Clause)	C		B	

FIGURE 20. Alignment within Phrases

(386) di jɛrma papa
       DEF woman father
       'the woman's father'

(387) a. di minggi angga
           DEF water in
           'in the water'

       b. mɛɛ di bicycle
           with DEF bicycle
           'with the bicycle'

These examples show that simple juxtaposition can be used in all the relevant contexts. The only exception in Berbice Dutch is a specialized possessive pronoun in the third person singular, which has the same distribution as its English counterpart.

The four types of system may now be compared with each other as in Figure 20.

We have not come across one other logical possibility: languages in which modifiers within Phrases and arguments within Clauses are treated the same way, while arguments within Phrases are treated differently.

4.5.4 Ordering of non-hierarchically related units

We already encountered the issue of the ordering of non-hierarchically related units in our discussion of the Basque example in (351) above, repeated as (388) here:

(388) herri hon=eta=ko   hiru biztanle   zaharr=ak
       land DEM=INAN.LOC=ATTR three inhabitant old=DEF.PL
       'the three old inhabitants of this country'

What this example illustrates is that morphosyntactic factors may influence ordering at the Phrase layer. Complex modifiers go to Phrase-initial position, while simple modifiers go to a position relative to P^F. Apart from adnominal Phrases, participial and relative Clauses count as complex modifiers for this rule (Trask 2003: 146, 149):

(389) atzo   ni=k   erosi-ta=ko   liburu=a
       yesterday 1.SG-ERG buy-PTCP-ATTR book-DEF.SG
       'the book I bought yesterday'

(390) lore-ak   eman di-zki-o-da=n   neska
       flowers-DEF.PL give 3.ABS-PL-3.SG.DAT-AUX=COMP girl
       'the girl I have given the flowers to'

We may represent these orderings schematically as:

(391) P^I P^M (=389)
       atzo_ni=k_erosi-ta=ko^{CL} liburu=a

(392) P^I P^M (=390)
       lore-ak_eman_di-zki-o-da=n^{CL} neska

Interpersonal factors may also play a role in the ordering of equipollent units. Thus, as Dryer (2005: 371) notes, in Asmat (Voorhoeve 1965: 140) contrastively used adjectives precede the head noun, while non-contrastively used adjectives follow:

(393) akát   ów
       good   people
       'good people (in contrast to bad people)'

(394) ów   akát
       people good
       'good people'

These examples show that the head is not in a position relative to one of the Phrase margins, but in the medial position, as in:

(395) P^I P^M (=393)
       akát^{+CONTR} ów

(396) P^M P^F (=394)
       ów akát^{-CONTR}

In French some adjectives that normally follow the head, precede it when emphasized, as in the following examples:

(397) une voiture rouge superbe
       a   car   red   magnificent

(398) une SUPERBE   voiture rouge
       a   magnificent car   red

as represented in:

(399) P^I P^M P^{F-1} P^F (=397)
    une voiture rouge superbe

(400) P^I P^{I+1} P^M P^F (=398)
    une SUPERBE voiture rouge

Semantic factors, too, may play an important role in the ordering of modifiers. In English evaluative adjectives precede objective ones. If both are present, age adjectives go in the middle. Thus, (401) is correct but (402) is not:

(401)   a nice old black car

(402)   *a black nice old car

These orderings can be explained in terms of the designation of the adjective, as indicated in:

(403) P^I P^{I+1} P^{I+2} P^{I+3} P^{I+4} (=401)
    a   nice^{EVAL} old^{AGE} black^{OBJV} car

Within the physical class, further meaning distinctions can be made, as illustrated in the following examples:

(404)   a.   the navigable deep rivers
      b.   the deep rivers navigable

In (304a) the adjective *navigable* precedes the head and designates a permanent Property. In (304b) it occurs in the final position also used for complex modifiers, and designates a contingent Property.

    Examples like these may be represented informally as:

(405)   a. P^I P^{I+1} P^{I+2} P^{I+3} (=404a)
        the navigable$^{OBJ/PERM}$ deep$^{OBJ/PERM}$ rivers
      b. P^I P^{I+1} P^{I+2} P^F (=404b)
        the deep$^{OBJ/PERM}$ rivers navigable$^{OBJ/CONTG}$

It thus seems that to a large extent English is semantically organized as regards the positioning of modifiers within the Noun Phrase.

    In all, we have shown in this section that in the ordering of units of like ranks within Phrases may be sensitive to interpersonal, representational, and morphosyntactic factors.

4.5.5 Templates

In defining overall templates at the Clause layer we made use of four absolute positions: P^I, P^2, P^M, and P^F. So far we have given illustrations at the Phrase layer of all of these but P^2. There are certain languages in which this position is relevant at the Phrase layer as well. In languages such as Serbian (Milićević 2004) sentences such as the following occur:

(406)   Mo=me=je   prijatelj Marko posetio juče.
        my=me=COP friend   Marko visited   yesterday
        'My friend Marko visited me yesterday.'

Under certain conditions Serbian clitics that logically belong at the Clause layer are attached to the first Word (rather than the first constituent) of the sentence in a clitic string that may contain a variety of items. If the first Word of the sentence is not a constituent by itself but forms part of a larger Phrase, the clitics may under certain conditions interrupt that Phrase and can then be said to occupy the second position within the Phrase. Thus, in (406) the Phrase *moj...prijatelj* 'my friend' is interrupted by the first person pronominal clitic *me* 'me' and the copula/auxiliary clitic *je*. This becomes clearer when (406) is compared with (407), in which the word order is adapted:

(407)   Juče=me=je   posetio moj prijatelj Marko.
        yesterday=me=COP visited   my   friend   Marko.
        'My friend Marko visited me yesterday.'

In a sense, then, (406) exhibits the opposite process to raising: Clause-layer elements are lowered into the Phrase. We may translate this into our formalism by assuming that Clause-initial Phrases in Serbian have a P^2 position available into which Clause-layer elements may be lowered.

The interesting thing here is that elements are involved that are assigned a position in both the hierarchical and the non-hierarchical processes. Consider the following examples (Schütze 1994: 11):

(408)   Ja=mu=ga   ni-sam   dala.
        I=3.SG.M.DAT=3.SG.ACC NEG-AUX.PST.1.SG given
        'I did not give it to him.'

(409)   Ni-sam=li=mu=ga   dala?
        NEG-AUX.PST.1.SG=Q=3.SG.M.DAT=3.SG.ACC given
        'Did I not give it to him?'

In (408) there is a subject pronoun *ja* in first position, which hosts the clitic string =*mu*=*ga* and is followed by the Verb Phrase *ni-sam dala*. In (409) the subject is dropped, and another phonologically prominent element has to go to the first position of the Clause, the negative auxiliary *nisam*. The clitic string now ends up in the second position within the Vp. The clitic *li* is a hierarchically high operator, being the expression of the Illocution at the Interpersonal Level. It has to be placed before all other elements in (409). In our approach this means that the second position is an absolute position, since there is no other element relative to which the interrogative clitic can be placed. The next element to be assigned a position is then the negative auxiliary that goes to the first position of the Verb Phrase. Only after that can the remaining elements be assigned a location. They are in an equipollent relationship to one another, and their placement depends on alignment considerations. The internal ordering within the clitic string seems semantically motivated (Recipient before Undergoer). The main verb probably goes to the Phrase-final position. The overall analysis of (409) would then be:

(410) P^I (=409)

$\qquad P^I \qquad\qquad\qquad P^2 \qquad\qquad P^{2+1}$

$(Cl_i: [(Vp_i: (^{fin}Vw_i: nisam\ (Vw_i))\ (Gw_i: li\ (Gw_i))\ (Nw_i: mu$

$\qquad P^{2+2} \qquad\qquad P^F$

$(Nw_i))\ (Nw_j: ga\ (Nw_j))\ (^{nonfin}Vw_i: dala\ (Vw_i))]\ (Cl_i))$

Note that it is crucial in this representation that the Verb Phrase involved is in the clausal P^I position. A similar analysis would apply to interrupted Noun Phrases such as the one illustrated in (406).

4.5.6 Dummies and support

Dummies at the phrasal layer remedy the absence of certain interpersonal or representational elements that are necessary for the formation of an appropriate phrase structure, or supply grammatical material that is necessary for an interpersonal or representational unit to occur in a certain slot. There are at least four contexts in which languages require dummies: (i) the absence of a verbal element at the Interpersonal Level or the Representational Level in the realization of an Ascriptive Subact; (ii) the absence of a nominal element at the Interpersonal Level or the Representational Level in the realization of a Referential Subact; (iii) the absence of an interpersonal or representational operator in the realization of an Ascriptive Subact; (iv) the absence of an interpersonal or representational operator in the realization of a Referential Subact.

The first situation can be illustrated by means of the following Spanish examples and their underlying representations:

(411)   Este hombre es   un   carpintero.
        DEM man   COP.PRS.IND.3.SG INDF carpenter
        'This man is a carpenter'

T   R
$(e_i: [(f_i: [(x_i: (f_j: carpintero_N (f_j)) (x_i)_U) (x_j: (f_k: hombre_N (f_k)) (x_j)_U)] (f_i)) (e_i)_U])$

(412)   Este armario   es   de madera.
        DEM cupboard   COP.PRS.IND.3.SG of wood
        'This cupboard is made of wood.'
        "This cupboard is of wood."

T   R
$(e_i: [(f_i: [(f_i: (x_j: madera_N (x_j)))_{So} (f_i)) (x_j: (f_k: armario_N (f_k)) (x_j)_U)_U] (f_i)) (e_i)_U])$

In the underlying representation of both (411) and (412) the main Ascriptive
Subact does not map onto a representational unit containing a verbal lexeme.
In cases like these Spanish requires the support of a verbal copula, which then
serves as the carrier of TMA distinctions. Such a copula is inserted into the
morphosyntactic structure by the morphosyntactic encoder. The driving force
here is the fact that Spanish does not have templates for (main) Clauses that
do not contain a Verb Phrase. Once a clausal template is selected and there is
no lexical verb that can go into the head slot of the Vp, the encoder inserts
the dummy verb which has the actual lexical predicate as its complement. The
Vps in (411) and (412) would then look as follows:

(413) P^I P^{I+1} (=411)
        $(Vp_i: [(Vw_i: \textbf{ser-prs.ind.3.sg} (Vw_i)) (Np_i: [(Gw_i: un-m.sg (Gw_i)) (Nw_i:$
        $carpintero-sg (Nw_i))] (Np_i))] (Vp_i))$
        'es un carpintero'

(414) P^I P^{I+1} (=412)
        $(Vp_i: [(Vw_i: \textbf{ser-prs.ind.3.sg} (Vw_i)) (Adp_i: [(Gw_i: de (Gw_i)) (Np_i:$
        $(Nw_i: madera-sg (Nw_i)) (Np_i))](Adp_i))(Vp_i))$
        'es de madera'

Many languages do not need verbal copula support, or do not need it in certain
circumstances. See Hengeveld (1992) for extensive discussion.
    The second situation can be illustrated by means of the following English
example and its underlying representation:

(415)   a red car and a blue one
        $(x_i: (f_i: car_N (f_i)) (x_i)_U: (f_j: red_A (f_j)) (x_i)_U) \& (x_j: (f_i) (x_j)_U: (f_k: blue_A$
        $(f_k)) (x_j)_U)$

There is a coreferential relation between the heads (f_i) of the descriptions the
two Individuals (x_i) and (x_j), as a result of which the lexical filler of the head
position of the second one may remain empty. In morphosyntax, however, the
corresponding Noun Phrase without a nominal head is not allowed in English.
As a result, the dummy *one* has to be inserted to fill the gap, and subsequently

carries the number distinction. The two conjuncts in (415) thus obey the same morphosyntactic template:

(416) (Np$_i$: [(Gw$_i$: a (Gw$_i$)) (adjp$_i$: (adjw$_i$: red$_A$ (adjw$_i$)) (adjp$_i$)) (Nw$_i$: **car-sg** (Nw$_i$))] (Np$_i$))
'a red car'
(Np$_j$: [(Gw$_j$: a (Gw$_j$)) (adjp$_j$: (adjw$_j$: blue$_A$ (adjw$_j$)) (adjp$_j$)) (Nw$_j$: **one-sg** (Nw$_j$))] (Np$_i$))
'a blue one'

Again, many languages do not require this type of dummy.

The third type of situation obtains, for example, in Samoan (Mosel and Hovdhaugen 1992: 365). This language has a semantically empty tense particle *e*, of which it is claimed that '...in independent Clauses it does not indicate any particular aspectual or temporal relationship...but expresses that the State-of-Affairs generally exists without referring to its inception, duration, or completion, or its location in time.' Samoan has a flexible parts-of-speech system but a rigid morphosyntax, which helps to tell the functions of lexical items apart. The absence of a tense particle would lead to ambiguity, which is resolved by inserting a dummy particle. The following examples illustrate the use of the particle (Mosel and Hovdhaugen 1992: 365, 364):

(417) E   'ai=na   Ø   le   gata.
      GENR eat=ERGR ABS SPEC snake
      'Snakes are edible.'

(418) E   ono o=na   Ø   tausaga.
      GENR six POSS=3.SG SPEC.PL year
      'He is/was six six years old.'
      "Six are/were his years."

(419) E   alu Ø   le   pasi i   Apia.
      GENR go ABS SPEC bus DIR Apia
      'The bus goes to Apia.'

Thus, in the absence of a semantically motivated TMA particle, the Samoan morphosyntactic encoder inserts the dummy particle into the relevant slot in the Vp-template.

The fourth situation can be illustrated by means of some examples from Muna. Consider the following examples (van den Berg 1989: 103):

(420) Ne-gholi   o   pae, o   kenta, o   kambulu bhe kalei.
      3.SG.RLS-buy ART rice ART fish   ART vegetables with banana
      'She bought rice, fish, vegetables and bananas.'

(421)   Inodi o   moghane.
        I   ART man
        'I am a man.'

(422)   O   dahu no-kotou.
        ART dog 3.SG.RLS-bark
        'A dog barks.'

(423)   O   kapoluka no-bisara-mo
        ART tortoise 3.SG.RLS-PFV
        'The tortoise said...'

In many circumstances (roughly, when not following a particle or a verb, or when not otherwise identifiable as a Noun Phrase) Muna Noun Phrases are introduced by the semantically empty article *o*. Rijkhoff (2002: 92f), following Greenberg (1978), identifies the element *o* and similar elements in a wide range of languages as Noun (Phrase) markers, which have no other function but to indicate that the constituent involved is a Noun Phrase. The situation here is somewhat more complex, in the sense that the Noun Phrase marker is not a substitute for other markers that are semantically motivated, but is sensitive to the wider clausal context in which the Noun Phrase occurs.

4.5.7 Agreement

We described agreement in 4.4.7 above as a mechanism by which information pertaining semantically to a single element of the construction under consideration is copied to one or more other elements. We also mentioned there that a distinction has to be made between agreement on the one hand and cross-reference on the other. This distinction is relevant at the Phrase layer as well. In many languages optional (pro)nominal possessors are cross-referenced on the possessum, as in the following Turkish example:

(424)   (Hasan-ın) kitab-ı
        Hasan-GEN book-POSS.3.SG
        'Hasan's book'

In this example the third person singular possessor *Hasan* is cross-referenced on the possessum *kitab-*. The fact that the lexical possessor can be left unexpressed shows that the possessive suffix has referential force of its own, which will be reflected in the presence of a Referential Subact at the Interpersonal Level.

   The situation is different in Maasai. In this language nominal possessors follow the possessum and are preceded by a morpheme that shows agreement in gender with the preceding possessum and agreement in number with the following possessor. This is illustrated in the following examples (Storto 2003: 5–6):

(425) a. òl-díà   lɔ́ɔ́-ìn-kìtúàk
           DET.SG.M-dog POSS.PL.M-DET.PL.F-women.ACC
           'the women's dog'

       b. òl-díà   lɔ́ɔ́-ìl-léwà
           DET.SG.M-dog POSS.PL.M-DET.PL.M-men.ACC
           'the men's dog'

       c. ìl-díà-ín   lɔ́ɔ́-ìn-kìtúàk
           DET.PL.M-dog-PL POSS.PL.M-DET.PL.F-women.ACC
           'the women's dogs'

       d. ìl-díà-ín   lɔ́ɔ́-ìl-léwà
           DET.PL.M-dog-PL POSS.PL.M-DET.PL.M-men.ACC
           'the men's dogs'

As these examples show, the form of the possessive marker *lɔ́ɔ́* marks the masculine gender of the possessum and the plurality of the possessor, and is insensitive to the number of the possessum and the gender of the possessor. In this case the possessor cannot be left unexpressed. It can be replaced by a pronominal possessor, which is different in that it shows agreement in both gender and number with the possessum. Maasai thus qualifies as a language marking (two-way) agreement between possessor and possessum.

A similar distinction applies with respect to agreement in gender and class: in some cases the gender or class markers actually reflect the natural gender or natural class of the semantic category designated by the noun; in other cases the agreement marker reflects the grammatical gender or class of the noun. For the first case, consider the following example from Swahili, cited in Aikhenvald (2000: 38):

(426) ki-faru   m-kubwa
       CL7-rhinoceros CL1-big
       'a big rhinoceros'

The word *faru* in Swahili belongs to class 7, which covers basically inanimates (Ashton 1944: 14), yet the class marker on the adjective is a class 1 marker, which covers animates. Agreement is thus with the natural class of the referent, and not with the grammatical class of the noun.

Agreement with the grammatical class of a noun is illustrated by the following Spanish examples:

(427) un-a   persona   buen-a
       INDF-F person(F) good-F
       'a good person'

(428) un-Ø   edificio alt-o
       INDF-M building high-M
       'a high building'

The fact that the *persona* belongs to the feminine noun class and the noun *edificio* to the masculine noun class cannot be predicted on the basis of their meanings. The agreement is automatic and triggered by inherent features of the head noun.

The procedure accounting for grammatical agreement within Phrases is identical to the one we proposed for agreement at the Clause layer. For a proposal as to how FDG could deal with semantic agreement, see Dikker (2004) and Dikker and van Lier (2005).

4.5.8 Subordination

Phrases may contain other Phrases or Clauses, which within the higher Phrase may act as arguments or modifiers:

(429) the *president's* suite   (Phrase—modifier)

(430) the *president's* son   (Phrase—argument)

(431) the assertion *that he made yesterday* (Clause—modifier)

(432) the assertion *that the world is flat* (Clause—argument)

Various grammatical phenomena are sensitive to the modifier–argument distinction. To mention just two: in English the embedded Phrase in (429) may appear in adjectival form, while the one in (430) may not:

(433) the presidential suite

(434) *the presidential son

The embedded Clause in (431) may alternatively be realized as a non-restrictive relative Clause, but the one in (432) may not:

(435) the assertion, which he made yesterday

(436) *the assertion, which the world is flat

These differences reflect the basic distinction between arguments and modifiers that we applied in Chapter 3 to constructions like these.

Some languages use basically the same templates for subordinate Phrases and Clauses as they do for independent Phrases and Clauses, and we need very few additional rules to account for these. In other languages subordinate Phrases and Clauses may differ in form from independent ones. Let us once more return to the Basque examples we discussed earlier:

(437) herri hon=eta=ko   hiru   biztanle   zaharr=ak
       land   DEM=INAN.LOC=ATTR three inhabitant old=DEF.PL
       'the three old inhabitants of this country'

(438) atzo   ni=k   erosi-ta=ko   liburu=a
       yesterday 1.SG-ERG buy-PTCP-ATTR book-DEF.SG
       'the book I bought yesterday'

(439) lore-ak   eman di-zki-o-da=n   neska
       flowers-DEF.PL give   3.ABS-PL-3.SG.DAT-AUX=COMP girl
       'the girl I have given the flowers to'

Subordinate Phrases in Basque are accompanied by the attributive particle =ko, showing its dependent status, as in (437). Clauses may occur in participial form, as in (438), in which case they have to be accompanied by the attributive particle again. Clauses may also occur in finite form, as in (439), in which case they are accompanied by a complementizer =n. In all cases the embedded Phrase or Clause has to appear in the initial position of the Phrase that it forms part of.

The templates for Phrases and Clauses in Basque to a large extent serve to accommodate subordinate Phrases and Clauses as well: the attributive particle and complementizer simply go to the final position of the template, and push all other elements to the left. Yet the templates have to be identifiable as being of the subordinate type, in order to account for their initial placement in the higher phrasal template. More subtle subdistinctions will have to be made in English, where phrasal and clausal modifiers go to Phrase-final position, except for bare participial modifiers, which participate in the ordering relative to Phrase-initial position just as lexical modifiers do:

(440) the old man / *the man old

(441) the singing man / *the man singing

(442) *the in the garden man / the man in the garden

(443) *the singing a song man / the man singing a song

(444) *the who sings a song man / the man who sings a song

The English morphosyntactic encoder will thus have to be sensitive not only to the non-finite status of the participial modifier, but also to the question whether arguments of the participial form are expressed.

Some languages do not allow the modifying use of certain relational Phrases. Consider the following example from Hungarian (de Groot 1989: 191):

(445) a   kert-ben   levő   fiú / *a   kert-ben   fiú
       ART garden-INESS COP.PTCP.SIM boy / ART garden-INESS boy
       'the boy in the garden'   'the boy in the garden'
       "the in the garden being boy"

Languages such as Hungarian thus require a rule of copula support in these circumstances as well.

Just as at the Clause layer, we find raising phenomena at the Phrase layer, particularly raising of inalienably possessed arguments from the Phrase layer to the Clause layer. Particularly telling are the following examples from Dinka (Andersen 2007: 110):

(446) Mòc à-ɰèr   léc
       man DECL-be.white tooth.PL.OBJRESP
       'The teeth of the man are white.'
       "The man is white with respect to his teeth."

(447) Mòc à-cé   ɰòt   mèer   ìc.
       man DECL-AUX.PRF house illuminate stomach
       'The man has illuminated the room.'
       "The man has illuminated the house with respect to its stomach."

In Andersen's terminology, Dinka has a so-called 'object of respect', which designates the body part with respect to which the predication holds. Under certain circumstances this object is marked tonally, as in (446). Positionally the object of respect is characterized by the fact that it occurs in the position immediately preceding or following the lexical verb. When the preverbal position is occupied by a regular object, it will go to the postverbal position, otherwise it will go to the preverbal position.

For the morphosyntactic analysis of examples like these, the Dinka clausal template should be considered first. In Dinka all clausal absolute positions identified earlier (P^I, P^2, P^M, and P^F) are relevant: P^I for the placement of conjunctions and Topics; P^2 for the placement of finite verbs and the placement of the Subject, if not Topic, relative to it; P^M for the placement of non-finite verbs; and P^F for the placement of adverbial modifiers. The general maximal template would be as follows:

(448) P^I P^{I+1} P^2 P^{2+1} P^{M-1} P^M

(Cl$_i$: [(Gw$_i$) (Np$_i$)^{Top} ^{fin}(Vw) (Np$_j$)$_{Sbj}$ (Np$_k$)$_{Obj}$ ^{nonf}(Vp$_i$)

P^{M+1} P^F

^{InalP}(Np$_l$) (Xp$_1$)] (Cl$_i$))

The underlying semantic and pragmatic representation of (447) would be as in (449):

(449)   (T)   (R)$_{Top}$ (R)   (T)

(e$_i$: (Perf f$_i$: [(f$_j$: mèer (f$_j$)) (x$_i$: –mòc– (x$_i$)$_U$)$_A$ (x$_j$: (f$_k$: [(f$_l$: ἰc (f$_l$))

                'illuminate'   'man'   'stomach'

(R)

(x$_j$: –ɯòt– (x$_j$))$_{Ref}$] (f$_k$)) (x$_j$)$_U$)$_U$] (f$_i$)) (e$_i$))

'house'

In the hierarchical part of the placement procedure the Perfect operator will trigger the insertion of an auxiliary in P^2. This means the lexical predicate will be expressed in a non-finite form and goes to P^M. The A-argument is Topic and therefore goes to P^1, leaving the Subject position in the overall template unoccupied. The Undergoer argument now has to be distributed across two positions: the possessor is treated as an Object and therefore goes to the position immediately preceding the lexical verb, leaving the postverbal position available for the possessed. The result is as in:

(450) P^I P^2 P^{M-1} P^M P^{M+1} (=447)

(Cl$_i$: [(Np$_i$)^{Top} (^{fin}Vw) (Np$_k$)$_{Obj}$ (^{nonf}Vp$_i$) (Np$_l$)^{InalP}] (Cl$_i$))

            Mòc   àcé   ɯòt   mèer   ἰc.

While the treatment of body parts as clausal constituents seems to be obligatory in Dinka under all circumstances, in Tariana it is obligatory if the possessive phrase logically belongs to an argument that is not the subject. The result is then a double object construction, as illustrated in the following example (Aikhenvald 2003: 157):

(451)   Diha-pasi-nuku   di-whida-nuku   du-pisa-taka

        3.SG-AUG-TOP.NON.A/S   3.SG.NF-head-TOP.NON.A/S   3.SG.F-cut-off

        du-pe

        3.SG.F-leave

        'She cut off the head of him—the big one ...'

4.6 Words

4.6.1 Introduction

The following maximally elaborated formula may be used for the template of a (Morphosyntactic) Word, ignoring the specific order in which elements occur, and assuming that every element may occur more than once:

(452) $(Xw_1: [(Xm)(Xw) (Xp) (Cl)] (Xw_1))$

A Word maximally consists of a sequenced configuration of Morphemes (Xm), other Words (Xw), Phrases (Xp), and Clauses (Cl). The latter three categories may come as something of a surprise, but, as we will show below, are needed to account for polysynthetic languages, which play an important role in this section.

In 3.7.2.3 we made a distinction between Lexemes and Words: Lexemes are operative at the Representational Level, Words at the Morphosyntactic Level. There are various reasons to make this distinction.

The first is that a single Word at the Morphosyntactic Level may correspond to various Lexemes at the Representational Level. Recall our semantic analysis of the Word *sword-swallower* in 3.7.2.3:

(453) $(x_i: [(f_i: [(f_j: swallow_V (f_j)) (x_i)_A (x_j: [-sword_N- (x_j)_U])_U])_U] (f_i)) (x_i)_U])$

In this case there are two Lexemes at the Representational Level, each with its own Lexeme class assigned, which yield a single Word at the Morphosyntactic Level.

A second reason to make a distinction between Lexemes and Words is that the opposite may also hold: a single Lexeme at the Representational Level may correspond to various Words at the Morphosyntactic Level. This is true of, for instance, idioms like *kick_the_bucket* 'die', which at the Representational Level forms a single meaning unit of the f-category, while at the Morphosyntactic Level it corresponds to three different Words.

A third reason to distinguish between Lexemes and Words is that, even in languages which make no distinctions at all between Lexeme classes, there are a variety of Word classes. Recall the following Mundari examples (Evans and Osada 2005: 354–5):

(454)   buru=ko   bai-ke-d-a
        mountain=3.PL   make-COMPL-TR-PRED
        'They made the mountain.'

(455)   saan=ko   buru-ke-d-a
        firewood=3.PL   mountain-COMPL-TR-PRED
        'They heaped up the firewood.'

TABLE 8. Correspondences between Lexical and Grammatical Word classes

Lexical Word class	Example	Grammatical Word class	Example
Verb	*exterminate*	Auxiliary Verb	*must, should, be*
Noun	*horseshoe*	Pronoun	*I, it, that*
Adjective	*terrific*	Proadjective	*such*
Adverb	*aloft*	Proadverb	*there, then*
Adposition	*under*	Grammatical Adposition	*of, at*
Conjunction	*while*	Grammatical Conjunction	*that, because*
Particle	*hey, wow*	Grammatical Particle	*just, even*

In (454) the flexible Lexeme *buru* is used referentially and occurs without any inflection. In (455) it occurs with a series of suffixes which are specific to the predicative function in which it is used in this sentence. These examples show that, although there is no reason to distinguish Lexeme classes in Mundari, there is reason to distinguish Word classes, each with its own Morphosyntactic Template.

A fourth reason to distinguish between Lexemes and Words is that there are many Words that have no corresponding Lexeme. This is the case of all grammatical Words, which either correspond to an operator or a function at the Interpersonal or Representational Level or are introduced as dummies or support elements. These often behave in the same way as Words that do correspond to a Lexeme. These Words will be introduced at the Morphosyntactic Level and will be classified according to the analogy between their syntactic distribution and that of Words with lexical content. Pronouns, for instance, display much the same distribution as the Lexeme class Noun but correspond to abstract features at the Interpersonal Level and/or the Representational Level. The correspondences may be represented in Table 8.

The examples of Grammatical Word classes given in Table 8 all correspond to functions, operators or units with an abstract head at the Interpersonal or Representational Level, or to nothing at all in the case of the copula *be*, which, as shown in the previous section, is introduced at the Morphosyntactic Level in response to particular configurations of the Interpersonal and Representational Levels. Table 9 offers, by way of example, some correspondences between Grammatical Words introduced at the Morphosyntactic Level and elements of the Interpersonal and Representational Levels.

As is already clear from Table 9, the correspondence may be with:

(i) an entire semantic unit, as in the case of *you* and *there*; in such cases the morphosyntactic form will be termed a proform;

TABLE 9. Examples of correspondences between Grammatical Words
and elements of the Interpersonal Level and the Representational Level

Form	Interpersonal Level	Representational Level
must	–	Inferential operator
you	$(R_1: [-S, +A] (R_1))$	(x_1)
such	–	Operator prox on (f_1)
there	(R_1)	$(dist\ l_1)$
at	–	L function on (l_1) or (t_1)
because	–	Cause function on (e_1) or (p_1)

(ii) an operator, as in the case of *must* and *such* (for this analysis of
such, see Mackenzie 1997); in such cases the form will be termed an
auxiliary;

(iii) a function, as in the case of *at* and *because*; here the form will be termed
a relator.

Note that the term 'auxiliary' is not restricted to Grammatical Verbs. In
Hebrew, the optional copula in such examples as the following may be
assigned to the class of Pronouns (Grammatical Nouns), being identical to
Pronouns in other, more prototypical uses, and agreeing in number and
gender, although not person, with the argument (cf. Hengeveld 1992: 190–1;
Junger 1981: 117, 122, 130):

(456) Dan (hu)   gadol.
       Dan 3.SG.M big
       'Dan is big.'

(457) Sara (hi)   mora.
       Sara 3.SG.F teacher
       'Sara is a teacher.'

(458) Yossi ve   Dan (hem) xaver-im.
       Yossi and Dan 3.PL.M friend-PL.M
       'Yossi and Dan are friends.'

(459) Ata   (hu)   hexašud.
       2.SG.M 3.SG.M DEF.suspect
       'You are the suspect.'

Auxiliary Adjectives are found in Turkish, as in examples like the following
(Hengeveld 1992: 189; Lewis 1967: 143):

(460) a. Ev-in   bahçe-si   var-dı.
           house-GEN garden-POSS.3.SG COP.POS-PST.3.SG
           'The house had a garden.'
           "lit. There was the house's garden."

       b. Ev-in   bahçe-si   yok-tu.
           house-GEN garden-POSS.3.SG COP.NEG-PST.3.SG
           'The house did not have a garden.'
           "lit. There wasn't the house's garden."

The copulas *var* and *yok* are classified as adjectives, since they have the same inflectional possibilities as lexical adjectives, for example in being incapable of carrying inflection for future tense. If the Representational Level indicates a future tense, the verbal copula *ol-* must be used, which is negated regularly by the verbal suffix *–mı*:

(461) a. Ev-in   bahçe-si   ol-acak-Ø.
           house-GEN garden-POSS.3.SG COP-FUT-3.SG
           'The house will have a garden.'
           "lit. There will be the house's garden."

       b. Ev-in   bahçe-si   ol-mı-yacak-Ø.
           house-GEN garden-POSS.3.SG COP-NEG-FUT-3.SG
           'The house will not have a garden.'
           "lit. There won't be the house's garden."

On this basis *var* and *yok* will be regarded as Auxiliary Adjectives.

Once a systematic and principled distinction is made between Lexemes and Words, productive derivational processes may be interpreted as a way of fitting Lexemes into syntactic slots for which they are not designed. Consider the following pairs of examples from English and Turkish (Kornfilt 1997: 328) respectively:

(462) a. John closed the door.
       b. The door closed.

(463) a. Hasan kapı-yı   kapa-dı.
           Hasan door-ACC close-PST
           'Hasan closed the door.'

       b. Kapı kapa-n-dı.
           door close-INTR-PST
           'The door closed.'

In English the Verb *close* can be used both transitively and intransitively. In Turkish, the intrinsically transitive Verb *kapa* has to be detransitivized before it

TABLE 10. Morpheme classes

Morpheme	Lexical	Dependent
Stem	+	−
Root	+	+
Affix	−	+

can be used in an intransitive context. In FDG the latter (productive) process is seen as obtaining within the grammar, as a morphosyntactic coercion effected by the introduction of a two-place Lexeme into a one-place Predication Frame, leading to an intransitive Verbal Word. This issue will be pursued further in 4.6.6 below.

To the extent that Words are made up of Morphemes, these too can be categorized into different classes. We will distinguish the following basic units in strictly morphosyntactic terms. A stem (Xs) is a Morpheme with lexical content that may occur as the sole lexical component of a Word; a root (Xr) likewise is a Morpheme with lexical content, but one that may only occur in conjunction with another Root or Stem, i.e. is dependent on another Root or Stem. An affix (Aff) is a Morpheme with grammatical content, and may only occur in conjunction with a Stem. Together these three types of morpheme may be defined as in Table 10.

Note that Roots are defined in different ways in different traditions. We use the most restrictive definition here. Depending on the language involved, Lexemes may map onto Roots or Stems, the latter distinction being morphosyntactically rather than semantically motivated. Roots (Xr) and Stems (Xs) may be subdivided into verbal Roots (Vr) and Stems (Vs), nominal Roots (Nr) and Stems (Ns), etc. Affixes of course can be subdivided into Prefixes, Suffixes, Infixes, and Circumfixes, but this will be reflected in our representations by their position rather than by their categorization.

Our treatment of Words below will follow the pattern that we used for Clauses and Phrases above. The ordering of Morphemes within the Word is first considered from a hierarchical perspective in 4.6.2. Then we consider the alignment properties of equipollent units in 4.6.3. Since we are considering the Word layer here, this means that we are entering the domain of incorporating languages, which are the only ones that manifest lexically realized equipollent units at this layer. This type of language will also be the focus of our attention in 4.6.4, where we consider the order of equipollent units. In 4.6.5 we summarize the ordering rules proposed at the Word layer in the form of Templates. 4.6.6 further explores the idea presented above that much of derivational morphology can be interpreted as the formal reflection of coercion effects. It also considers a number of cases in which Morphemes appear to be expletive, in the sense that a Morpheme position has to be obligatorily filled with a dummy Morpheme in the absence of semantic material. In 4.6.7 we consider the limited possibility of having agreement within Words, while in 4.6.8 we go into the embedding of Words and higher units into the Word layer. The last two issues are again relevant to incorporating languages only.

4.6.2 Ordering of hierarchically related units

The ordering of Morphemes within Words is most transparent in aggluti-nating languages. Consider the following example from Tsafiki (Barbacoan; Dickinson 2002: 103) and its underlying representation:

(464)   Manuel ano fi-nu-ti-e.
        Manuel food eat-PERC-REP-DECL
        'It is said Manuel must have eaten.'

(465) $(A_I: [(F_I: DECL (F_I)) (P_I)_S (P_J)_A$ (rep C_I) $] (A_I))$
                                $(perc\ e_i: [-Manuel\ ano\ fi-]\ (e_i))$

Three abstract elements have to be expressed in this situation: the Declarative Illocution, the Reportative operator on the Communicated Content C_I, and the Perception operator on the State-of-Affairs e_i. If we apply our hierarchical approach the Illocution has to be expressed first, then the Reportative operator, and then the Perception operator. This can be achieved straightforwardly by using a Word template for the Verb in (464) with a final position P^F and a number of positions relative to it:

(466) P^{F-3} P^{F-2} P^{F-1} P^F (=464)
        $(Vw_i: [$ (Vs_i) $(Aff_i)^{\pi e}$ $(Aff_j)^{\pi C}$ $(Aff_k)^{ILL}$ $] (Vw_i))$
                    fi   -nu   -ti   -e

For an example of the formation of a Nominal Word consider the following Nivkh example (Savel'eva and Taksami 1970: 203, cited in Mattissen 2003: 240) and its underlying representation:

(467)   hə-ula-bal-doχ
        DEM-high-mountain-ALL
        'to that high mountain'

(468) $(dem\ l_i: (f_i: bal\ (f_i)) (l_i)_U: (f_j: ula\ (f_j)) (l_i)_U (l_i)_U)_{Dir}$

According to our basic rules of hierarchical placement the Semantic Function, being external, has to be expressed first and goes to P^F. The demonstrative comes next and goes to P^I, followed by the modifier, which occupies a position relative to P^I, and is followed by the head which takes the next relative position available. This leads to the following template:

(469) $\quad\quad\quad P^I \quad P^{I+1} \quad P^{I+2} \quad P^F$ $\quad\quad\quad\quad\quad\quad$ (=467)

$\quad\quad\quad (Nw_i: [\ (Aff_i) \ (As_i) \ (Ns_i) \ (Aff_j) \ ] \ (Nw_i))$

$\quad\quad\quad\quad\quad\quad$ hə $\quad$ -ula $\quad$ -bal $\quad$ -doχ

In fusional languages the situation is less transparent, since a single Morpheme may express various categories at the same time. From our hierarchical approach to morphosyntactic expression it follows that the categories fused in a single Morpheme should always be hierarchically contiguous. Thus, we would not expect a single morpheme to express π^f and π^p, while another expressed π^e, for the simple reason that the iconic reflection of hierarchical scope differences would become impossible in such a situation. Boland (2006: 232–4) checked this prediction for a large sample of languages and found that it was indeed confirmed without exceptions.

4.6.3 Alignment

The issue of alignment at the Word layer is relevant for incorporating languages, since only in these languages may equipollent units occur within a single Word. Alignment conditions then determine what kind of arguments and modifiers may be incorporated. These conditions are sensitive to the same type of factors as we found to be relevant for alignment at the Clause layer: (i) interpersonal factors such as pragmatic function and definiteness; (ii) representational factors such as semantic function and animacy; (iii) morphosyntactic factors such as syntactic function and heaviness. We will give a few examples to illustrate how these factors may influence alignment within Words, without aiming at completeness.

Interpersonal factors can be shown to be active in Nivkh. In this language, certain types of argument (see below for details) may be incorporated when they have the same focus value as the verb, but not if they have a different informational value. Consider the following examples (Savel'eva 1966: 125, cited in Mattissen 2003: 107):

(470) T'a ku-ñivɣ-əz-ja.

PROH DEM-person-call-IMP.SG

'Don't call that person.'

(471) ku-ñivx t'a j-əz-ja.

DEM-person PROH 3.SG.U-call-IMP.SG

'That person, don't call him/her.'

In (471) *ku-ñivx* 'that person' is (re)introduced as a Topic and occupies the initial position in the Clause rather than the position of the incorporated argument position within the verb, which is now occupied by an undergoer prefix.

Representational factors can be shown to be especially active in Southern Tiwa (Allen *et al.* 1984). The most significant representational factor is animacy. The presence or absence of a modifier in some circumstances has an influence on the possibility of incorporation, but if we exclude modified Noun Phrases the generalization is that incorporation is obligatory with inanimate and non-human animate Objects (472)–(473) and with inanimate intransitive Subjects (474), optional with human Objects (475), and excluded with all Animate Subjects (476) and with Objects headed by a proper name (477) (Allen *et al.* 1984: 293–301):

(472) a. Ti-shut-pe-ban.
           1.SG.SBJ>SG.OBJ-shirt-make-PST
           'I made the/a shirt.'

       b. *Shut ti-pe-ban.
           shirt 1.SG.SBJ>SG.OBJ-make-PST

(473) a. Ibi-musa-tuwi-ban.
           3.PL.SBJ>PL.OBJ-cat-buy-PST
           'They bought cats.'

       b. *Musan ibi-tuwi-ban.
           cats   3.PL.SBJ>PL.OBJ-buy-PST

(474) a. I-k'uru-k'euwe-m.
           3.SG.SBJ-dipper-old-PRS
           'The dipper is old.'

       b. *K'uru i-k'euwe-m.
           dipper 3.SG.SBJ-old-PRS

(475) a. Ti-seuan-mū-ban.
           1.SG.SBJ>SG.OBJ-man-see-PST
           'I saw the/a man.'

       b. Seuanide ti-mū-ban.
           man   1.SG.SBJ>SG.OBJ-see-PST
           'I saw the/a man.'

(476) a. *I-musa-k'euwe-m.
           3.SG.SBJ-cat-old-PRS

       b. Musan i-k'euwe-m.
           cats   3.SG.SBJ-old-PRS
           'The cats are old.'

(477) a. *Ti-Jesse-mū-ban.
           1.SG.SBJ>SG.OBJ-Jesse-see-PST

       b. Jesse ti-mū-ban.
           Jesse 1.SG.SBJ>SG.OBJ-see-PST
           'I saw Jesse.'

These examples clearly show the working of an animacy hierarchy interacting with the opposition between Subjects and Objects.

The above examples thus also serve to illustrate a morphosyntactic factor that is operative within the process of incorporation in Southern Tiwa. Since this language allows the incorporation of transitive Undergoers as well as intransitive Subjects, it can be said to exhibit absolutive-ergative alignment in its system of incorporation. Another language showing this type of alignment in its incorporation processes is Bininj Gun-Wok, as illustrated by the following examples (Evans 2003: 451):

(478) Al-ekge al-gohbanj   ba-gurlah-bimbu-ni.
       F-DEM   CL-old.person PST.3>3-skin-paint-PST.IMPF
       'That old lady used to paint buffalo hides.'

(479) Ga-wardde-djabdi.
       3-rock-stand.up.straight.NONPST
       'There is a rock standing up straight.'

Nivkh, on the other hand, allows the incorporation of Undergoers but not of intransitive Subjects, and thus shows nominative-accusative alignment in its system of incorporation, as illustrated in the following examples (Otaina 1978: 32, 34, cited in Mattissen 2003: 134, 137):

(480) Təf   tiv-ḍ.
       house cold-IND
       'The house is cold.'

(481) Atak   k'e-seu-ḍ.
       grandfather net-dry-IND
       'Grandfather dried the net.'

The languages can be further compared with respect to their systems of ditransitive alignment. Southern Tiwa has directive-indirective alignment, i.e. the Undergoers of transitive and ditransitive constructions are treated in the same way. Nivkh has primative-secundative alignment, i.e. the Undergoer argument of a transitive construction and the Location argument of a ditransitive construction are treated in the same way. Consider first the following examples from Southern Tiwa (Allen *et al.* 1984: 303):

(482)   Ti-seuan-mū-ban.
         1.SG.SBJ>SG.OBJ-man-see-PST
         'I saw the/a man.'

(483)   Ti-'u'u-wia-ban   ī-'ay.
         1.SG.SBJ>SG.OBJ-baby-give-PST 2.SG-ALL
         'I gave the baby to you.'

In (482) the Undergoer of the transitive construction is incorporated; in the ditransitive construction in (483) it is likewise the Undergoer that is incorporated.

Now consider the following examples from Nivkh (Otaina 1978: 34, cited in Mattissen 2003: 137, 142):

(484)   Atak   k'e-seu-ḍ.
         grandfather   net-dry-IND
         'Grandfather dried the net.'

(485)   Objezḍtik   k'e atak-asqam-ḍ.
         bay_watcher   net grandfather-take_away-IND
         'The bay watcher took the net away from grandfather.'

In (484) the Undergoer of the transitive construction is incorporated, while in (485) the Location argument of the ditransitive construction is incorporated. Note that Nivkh allows the incorporation of a wide range of Location arguments, including Source, Recipient, and Direction.

Parallel to clausal systems of alignment (see 4.4.3), the alignment of arguments with respect to incorporation in Southern Tiwa and Nivkh may now be represented as in Figures 21 and 22.

We may thus conclude that the alignment principles outlined in 4.4.3.4 with respect to the organization of the Clause can also be fruitfully applied to the organization of the Word.

4.6.4 The ordering of non-hierarchically related units

Generally there is only one argument that is incorporated into a Verbal or Nominal Word. The ordering of this argument with respect to the verbal stem

	1-place	2-place	3-place
U	Incorporated		
A		Not incorporated	
R			

FIGURE 21. Alignment of arguments with respect to incorporation in Southern Tiwa

	1-place	2-place	3-place
A	Not incorporated		
R		Incorporated	
U			Not incorporated

FIGURE 22. Alignment of arguments with respect to incorporation in Nivkh

is then a matter of non-hierarchical ordering. There is a strong tendency for incorporated dependents to precede the nucleus, as in the Nivkh and Southern Tiwa examples given earlier. A further Nivkh example is the following (Krejnovič 1937: 30, cited in Mattissen 2003: 240):

(486)   ñ-ətk-ruvŋ-eʁlŋ-gun
        1.SG.POSS-father-sibling-child-PL
        'my father's brother's children'

The semantic representation of (491) would be as in (492):

(487)   (m x_i: [(f$_i$: gun$_N$ (f$_i$)) (1x_j: [(f$_k$: eʁlŋ$_N$ (f$_k$)) (1x_k: [(f$_l$: ruvŋ$_N$ (f$_l$)) (x$_l$)$_{Ref}$] (x$_k$)$_U$)$_{Ref}$] (x$_j$)$_U$)$_{Ref}$] (x$_i$)$_U$)

In the process of hierarchical ordering the plural operator is expressed first and occurs in rightmost position. In the process of ordering non-hierarchically related units, the highest nucleus (*gun*) occurs in the rightmost position available, with its dependent (*ñ-ətk-ruvŋ*) occurring to its left. Within this dependent the nucleus *ruvŋ* again occupies the rightmost position, with its own dependent *ñ-ətk* occurring to its left again. And this process is repeated for the nucleus *ətk* and its dependent *ñ*. The resulting syntactic template at the highest level is:

(488)   p^{F-2} p^{F-1} p^F (=491)
        (Nw$_i$: [(Nw$_j$: −ñətkruvŋ− (Nw$_j$))   (Ns$_i$: eʁlŋ$_N$ (Ns$_i$)) (Aff$_i$: gun
        (Aff$_i$))] (Nw$_i$))

and this template is applied recursively, but without the suffix position, in subsequent steps.

Cross-referencing pronominal argument affixes can also be considered to be the expression of non-hierarchically related units. Consider the following example from Yimas (Foley 1991: 228):

(489)   Wa-mpu-ŋa-r-akn.
        3.SG.ABS-3.PL.ERG-give-PFV-3.SG.DAT
        'They gave it to them.'

Yimas cross-references the A, U, and L arguments on the verb, and the ordering of the affixes is sensitive, among other things, to the person hierarchy: first and second person dative arguments are expressed through prefixes, while third person dative arguments appear as suffixes. The morphosyntactic encoder thus has to apply alignment rules that are sensitive to person features.

Kiowa also expresses up to three arguments on the verb, but in contrast to Yimas, the combination of arguments is expressed by a portmanteau morpheme occupying a fixed position. Consider the following example (Harbour 2003: 546):

(490) á-ǫǫ.
       3.PL.A>3.SG.U>3.PL.LOC-give
       'They gave it to them.'

In Kiowa the ordering of pronominal elements of like rank thus is not an issue.

4.6.5 Templates

The cumulative effects of hierarchical and non-hierarchical ordering are reflected in the Word templates that are available as morphosyntactic primitives in the grammar of a language. Consider the following Chukchee example (Skorik 1961: 103, cited in Mattissen 2006: 292):

(491) Tə-tor-taŋ-pəlwəntə-pojgə-pela-rkən.
       1.SG.A-new-good-metal-spear-leave-PRS.1.SG>3.SG
       'I am leaving a good new metal spear.'

(492) (pres e_i: (f_i: [(f_j: pela (f_j)) (x_i)$_A$ (x_j: (f_k: pojgə (f_k)) (x_j)$_U$: (f_k: pəlwəntə (f_k)) (x_j)$_U$: (f_k: taŋ (f_k)) (x_j)$_U$: (f_k: tor (f_k)) (x_j)$_U$)$_U$

The Undergoer argument *tor-taŋ-pəlwəntə-pojgə* 'a good new metal spear' is itself a complex Word, which acts as a Phrase (see 4.6.8 below) incorporated into the Verbal Word. Its internal organization may be represented as in (493), which starts out with the placement of the head in P^F and then succesively places modifiers in a leftward direction:

(493) P^{F-3} P^{F-2} P^{F-1} (=491)
       (Np$_i$: (Nw$_i$: [(As$_i$: tor (As$_i$)) (As$_j$: taŋ (As$_j$)) (As$_k$: pəlwəntə
              P^F
       (As$_k$))(Ns$_i$: −pojgə (Ns$_i$))] (Nw$_i$)) (Np$_i$))

At the level of the Verbal Word both P^I and P^F are relevant positions, as is evident, among other things, from the existence of verbal circumfixes in Chukchee. In the hierarchical placement of elements the Pres operator has to be expressed first. It goes to the final position in the template for Verbal Words, but as a placeholder, as its form is sensitive to agreement with the Actor and Undergoer arguments. With respect to the placement of non-hierarchically related units, the verbal stem is placed in the position immediately preceding the tense marker. The complex Nominal Word expressing the Undergoer in (491) precedes this verb, while the Actor goes to P^I:

(494) P^I P^{F-2} (=491)

$(Vw_i: [\ (Aff_i: tə\ (Aff_i))\ (Np_i: -tortaŋpəlwəntəpojgə- (Np_i))$

P^{F-1} P^F

$(Vs_i: pela\ (Vs_i))\ (Aff_j: \text{PRES}\ (Aff_j))]\ (Vw_i))$

4.6.6 Dummies and support

There is reason to assume that at the Word layer, too, there may be slots that have to be filled obligatorily and which in the absence of interpersonal or representational material are filled with dummy morphemes. Tariana provides a straightforward example of this phenomenon. Consider the following examples (Aikhenvald 2003: 123):

(495)   a.   nu-pitana
             1.SG-name
             'my name'

        b.   kuphe i-pitana
             fish   INDEF-name
             'the name of a fish'

As discussed in 4.5.3, pronominal inalienably possessed arguments are expressed in Tariana through prefixes on the noun expressing the possessor, as illustrated in (495a). When the argument is itself expressed by a Noun Phrase, there is no cross-referencing on the noun expressing the possessor, but the slot for the pronominal prefix is filled with an indefinite prefix. as shown in (495b). This can be accounted for by having a rule of dummy insertion apply when, after the insertion of the interpersonal and representational material that has to be expressed, an obligatory morpheme slot in the Word template remains unfilled.

An example of dummy subject and object marking comes from Kiowa. Compare the following examples (Harbour 2003: 563, 564):

(496)   Áá   gya-sól.
        poles 3.PL-set_up
        'Poles are set up.'

(497)   Gya-sál.
        3.PL-be.hot
        'It's hot.'

(498)   Áá   gyat-bǫ́ǫ́.
        poles 1.SG>3.PL-see
        'I saw the poles.'

(499)   Gyat-hóú-ai.
        1.SG>3.PL-travel-go.off
        'I ran off.'

Example (496) illustrates the regular expression of a plural subject in a Clause based on a one-place predication frame. The same prefix is used in (497), which is based on a zero-place predication frame. This example illustrates the use of the plural as the unmarked number in Kiowa (see Harbour 2003). In (498) a portmanteau morpheme is used which expresses the two arguments in a two-place predication frame: in this case a first singular A acts on a third plural U. Certain verbs which are used in a one-place predication frame nevertheless require a transitive portmanteau morpheme, as illustrated in (499). This is the morphological parallel to the Dutch Clause-layer object dummies discussed in 4.4.6.

Alongside dummies, which fill the gap left open by the absence of material from the Interpersonal and Representational Levels, there are support morphemes that help Lexemes that by themselves are not suitable for use in certain underlying functions to acquire the wordform required for that function. In the introduction to this section we gave the example of productive intransitivization in Turkish, but many other examples can be given. Consider the following example, discussed in Sadock (1985: 389):

(500)   They american-ize-d Belgium.

in which the adjective *American* is causativized as a result of being introduced into a two-place predication frame. Coercion effects like these allow speakers to creatively adapt the expressive potential of their lexicon to new contexts.

In Krongo, when a noun (Phrase) is used predicatively, it has to be verbalized, as illustrated in the following example (Reh 1985: 242):

(501)   Àakù   m-àa-nímyà.
        3.SG.F F-IMPF-woman
        'She is a woman.'

This can be dealt with in the morphosyntactic encoder as a process that applies when a semantic category headed by a nominal lexeme is inserted into the Verb Phrase slot in a morphosyntactic template.

4.6.7 Agreement

In cases in which an argument is incorporated and the language shows agreement with the kind of argument that is incorporated, then the result is that agreement on the verb is with the argument that is incorporated into that verb. This phenomenon is illustrated in the following example from Southern Tiwa (Allen *et al.* 1984: 293):

(502)   Te-shut-pe-ban.
        1.SG.SBJ>PL.OBJ-shirt-make-PST
        'I made (the) shirts.'

Southern Tiwa has portmanteau morphemes which express the person of the Actor and number of the Undergoer in a single form. The fact that the portmanteau morpheme *te-* is used in (502) shows that the incorporated Undergoer is treated as a regular argument, triggering agreement on the incorporating verb.

4.6.8 Subordination

Subordination at the Word layer occurs when a Word incorporates another Word, a Phrase, or a Clause. An example of Word incorporation was given above in 4.6.5. West Greenlandic provides another example of this process. It is different from the other polysynthetic languages that we have discussed in this section in that the verbal element of the incorporating polysynthetic complex cannot itself be used as a free-standing verb, but belongs to a large set of verbalizing suffixes, which are generally considered to be derivational in nature, but which could also be considered to be lexical roots in our use of that term. The result of polysynthesis is, however, a Verbal Word, just as it is in the cases discussed above. Consider the following examples, taken from Kristoffersen (1992: 153, 154) (square brackets indicate the morphosyntactic unit (part of) which is incorporated):

(503)   (*Utuqqarmik) [palasi]-rpalup-puq.
        old.one.SG.INS   priest-be.like-DECL.3.SG
        'He is like a(n old) priest.'

(504)   [Illu-mut   angisuu-mu]-kar-puq.
        house-SG.ALL   big.one-SG.ALL-go-DECL.3.SG
        'She went to the big house.'

In (503) a bare nominal Stem occurs as part of a Verbal Word. It is uninflected, and cannot take external modifiers. The example contrasts with the one in (504): here an inflected Nominal Word *angisuu-mu* is incorporated, which furthermore can take an external modifier. This is thus a case of a Word embedded in another Word.

Phrase incorporation into a Verbal Word was illustrated in 4.6.5 with the following example from Chukchee (Skorik 1961: 103, discussed in Mattissen 2006: 290):

(505)   Tə-[tor-taŋ-pəlwəntə-pojgə]-pela-rkən.
        1.SG.ABS-new-good-metal-spear-leave-PRES.1.SG>3.SG
        'I am leaving a good, new, metal spear.'

In this case a noun with its modifiers is incorporated within the Verbal Word. It is also cross-referenced on the Verbal Word itself. Together these facts point to the phrasal status of the incorporated noun and its modifiers.

Phrase incorporation into a Nominal Word is illustrated in the Ainu example (506) (Shibatani 1990: 74):

(506)   e-pon-no-poro-setaha
        2.SG.POSS-slight-ADVR-big-dog
        'your slightly big dog'

Given the facts that the stem *poro* is modified by the derived degree expression *ponno*, and that the resulting combination as a whole modifies the nominal stem *setaha*, it follows that the Nominal Word in this example incorporates an Adjective Phrase. The analytical counterpart of (506) would be as in (507) (Shibatani 1990: 74) which confirms the phrasal status of the adjectival modifier:

(507)   pon-no   poro e-esetaha
        slight-ADVR big   2.SG.POSS-dog
        'your slightly big dog'

Clause incorporation is a possibility too, as illustrated in the Bininj Gun-Wok example (508) (Evans 2003: 536):

(508)   Ga-[ganj-ngu-nihmi]-re.
        3-meat-eat-GER-go.PST.PFV
        'He goes along eating meat.'

In (508) the nominal *ganj* 'meat' is clearly an argument of the incorporated verb, not of the incorporating verb. The embedded clausal nature of the incorporated unit is furthermore reflected in the gerundial ending with which the incorporated verb is provided.

Chukchee (Skorik 1948: 83, in Spencer 1995: 459) allows Clause incorporation as well:

(509)   ənko mət-mec-[qora-gərke]-plətko-mək.
 then 1.PL.SBJ-almost-deer-hunt-finish-AOR.1.PL
 'Then we almost finished hunting reindeer.'

4.7 Building up the Morphosyntactic Level

In building up the Morphosyntactic Level, use is made of Morphosyntactic Templates, free and bound Grammatical Morphemes, and Morphosyntactic Operators. Morphosyntactic Templates capture the ordering patterns within a language at the layers of the Linguistic Expression, the Clause, the Phrase, and the Word. Grammatical Morphemes are inserted at the Morphosyntactic Level since they occupy slots in the various morphosyntactic configurations. When a grammatical morpheme is to undergo further phonological adaptation, it is inserted in the form of a Morphosyntactic Operator, which serves as a placeholder that will be replaced by the appropriate phonemic form at the Phonological Level.

The Morphosyntactic Level, as all other levels, is built up in a top-down, hierarchical fashion. The highest layers of analysis are constructed first, and filled in successively by lower morphosyntactic layers. The highest layer we identified in this chapter is the Linguistic Expression. As we argued in 4.3 above, a Linguistic Expression is any set of at least one unit that can be used independently; where there is more than one unit within a Linguistic Expression, they will demonstrably belong together morphosyntactically, while, crucially, one is not part of the other. Only in the latter case does a Linguistic Expression differ superficially from a Clause, so we will take this situation as our point of departure by using an example given earlier in 4.3:

(510)   As for the students, they have heard the news already.

This example has the following Interpersonal and Representational configurations:

(511) $(M_I: [(A_I: [(F_I: DECL (F_I)) (P_I)_S (P_J)_A (C_I: (+id R_I) (C_I))] (A_I))_{Orient}$
$(m x_i: [(f_i: student (f_i)) (x_i)_U])$
$(A_J: [(F_J: DECL (F_J)) (P_J)_S (P_J)_A(C_J: [(T_I) (+id R_J)$
$(+id R_K)] (C_I))] (A_J)) \quad] (M_I))$
$(pres\ ep_i: (ant\ ^{Neg}Pos\ e_i: [(f_j: [(f_k: hear (f_k)) (x_i)_A$
$(p_i: [-news- (p_i)_U])_U] (f_j)) (e_i)_U]) (ep_i))$

A few remarks are in order with respect to these representations: *as for the students* is a Subsidiary Act with the function of Orientation, and has its own Illocution; there is anaphoric reference in the main Clause to the participant in the Orientational Act, as indicated by coindexation; the particle *already* is the expression of the operator ^{Neg}Pos introduced in 3.5.4; and the auxiliary verb *have* is the expression of the operator Ant(erior) in the presence of a higher episodical tense operator Pres(ent). The mappings between the units at the Interpersonal and Representational Levels are as in (512):

(512) [(R_I)]
       (m x_i: [(f_i: student (f_i)) (x_i)$_U$])

[(T_I) (R_J) (R_K)]
($pres$ ep_i: (ant ^{Neg}Pos e_i: [(f_j: [(f_k: hear (f_k)) (x_i)$_A$ (p_i: –news– (p_i))$_U$] (f_j)) (e_i)$_U$]) (ep_i))

The two discourse acts A_I and A_J form a single Linguistic Expression, since the adpositional phrase *as for the students* depends on the main Clause without being part of it. The basic Morphosyntactic Template that we have to select for this particular configuration is given in (513), as explained in 4.3:

(513)   P^{pre} | P^{centre}
       (Le$_i$: [(Adp$_1$) | (Cl$_1$)   ] (Le$_i$))

The index for the Linguistic Expression is given an alphabetic value here, since it is now instantiated. It contains positions for an Adposition Phrase and for a Clause. Since it is the highest in order, we will elaborate the clausal layer first.

   The instantiated Clause makes use of the following Morphosyntactic Template, in line with the observations in 4.4 concerning the relevance of the initial, medial, and final positions for English clausal templates:

(514)   P^I P^M P^{M+1} P^{M+2} P^F
       (Cl$_i$: [(Np$_1$) (^{fin}Vw$_1$) (Vp$_1$) (Np$_2$) (Advp$_1$)] (Cl$_i$))

There is a separate position for the Grammatical Morpheme *have* in this template, which is treated as a Verbal Word, not as a Phrase, as it occupies a position in the template independently of the main verb, i.e. it need not occur contiguously with it, as illustrated in (515):

(515)   The students have already heard the news.

On the basis of information from the Contextual Component, the Morphosyntactic Encoder decides on Subject and Object assignment. The overall result is then as in (516):

(516)
          P^{pre} | P^{centre} |
              | P^I P^M P^{M+1} P^{M+2} P^F |
       (Le$_i$: [(Adp$_1$) | (Cl$_i$: [(Np$_1$)$_{Sbj}$ (^{fin}Vw$_1$) (Vp$_1$) (Np$_2$)$_{Obj}$ (Gw$_1$)](Cl$_i$)) |] (Le$_i$))

The clausal constituents can now be assigned a position in this template following the rules of hierarchical and non-hierarchical ordering explained in 4.4. In the process of hierarchical ordering the auxiliary *have* goes to P^M and next the particle *already* goes to P^F. In the process of non-hierarchical ordering the main verb is placed relative to the medial position, the Object immediately follows, and the Subject goes to P^I. Note that (520) shows that *already* could alternatively have gone to P^{M+1}, immediately following the auxiliary verb, as allowed by the principles of hierarchical ordering.

Each of the Phrases has to be elaborated now. Let us concentrate on the adpositional phrase in P^{pre}. The template for the Adposition Phrase is as in (517):

(517) P^I P^{I+1}
        $(Adp_1: [(Gw_1) (Np_1)] (Adp_1))$

The adposition used is the direct expression of the Orientation function of A_I. Since its form is not sensitive to further processes, it can be inserted directly into the (Gw_1) slot in (517) when the adpositional phrase is instantiated:

(518) $(Adp_i: [(Gw_i:/\text{'æzfə}/ (Gw_i) (Np_1)] (Adp_i))$

There is now a further slot for a Noun Phrase, which uses the template in (519):

(519) P^I P^{I+1}
        $(Np_1: [(Gw_1) (Nw_1)] (Np_1))$

and the Nominal Word that occurs within this template makes itself use of the template in (520):

(520) P^{F-1} P^F
        $(Nw_1: [(Ns_1) (Aff_1)] (Nw_1))$

In accordance with the principles of hierarchical ordering, the expression of the +id Operator of R_I in (511) goes to the (Gw_1) slot in (519); a Morphosyntactic Operator pl representing the expression of the plural operator of the first instance of (x_i) in (511) goes to the (Aff_1) slot in (520); and finally the head noun of (x_i) in (511) goes to the (Ns_1) slot in (520). Since the first and last of these three elements are not sensitive to further phonological adaptation, they can be inserted in their final phonemic form into the Morphosyntactic Templates. The result of these insertions is given in (521):

(521) $[P^I$ P^{I+1}

                                $[P^I$ P^{I+1}
        $(Adp_i: [(Gw_i: /\text{'æzfə}/(Gw_i) (Np_i: [(Gw_j: /\text{ðə}/ (Gw_j)) (Nw_i:$
        $[P^{F-1}$ P^F
        $[(Ns_i: /\text{'stju:dınt}/(Ns_i))$ $(Aff_1: Pl (Aff_i))] (Nw_i))] (Np_i))] (Adp_i))$

Other phrases are elaborated in a similar manner, as illustrated in 4.5.

The insertion and elaboration of the auxiliary verb *have* requires some further steps. First, since this is an irregular verb, it is not inserted in its phonemic form, but in the form of a Morphosyntactic Operator that is itself a translation of the primary operators Pres(ent) and Ant(erior) in (511). This Morphosyntactic Operator is inserted into the slot for the finite verb within the clausal template where it acts as a placeholder for the form that will ultimately be selected at the Phonological Level. Second, the agreement features have to be copied from the Subject Np to this placeholder, as explained in 4.4.7. The result is as in (522):

(522) $(^{\text{fin}}Vw_i: \text{have} < Pl > (Vw_i))$

On the basis of the instruction 'have$<Pl>$' the Phonological Encoder then selects the appropriate ready-made form from the set of phonological primitives.

The full morphosyntactic representation of (510) is then as in (523) shown on page 420:

(523)   As for the students, they have heard the news already.

P^{pre}

   P^I

(Adp$_i$: [(Gw$_i$:/'æzfə/ (Gw$_i$))

   P^{I+1}

      P^I

(Np$_i$: [(Gw$_j$: /ðə/ (Gw$_j$))

   P^{I+1}

         P^{F-1}

(Nw$_i$: [(Ns$_i$: /'stju:dɪnt/(Ns$_i$))

   P^F

(Aff$_1$: /s/ (Aff$_i$))

] (Nw$_i$))

] (Np$_i$))

] (Adp$_i$))

P^{centre}

   P^I

(Cl$_i$: [(Np$_j$: (Nw$_j$: /ðeɪ/ (Nw$_j$)) (Np$_j$))$_{Sbj}$

   P^M

(^{fin}Vw$_i$: have<PL> (Vw$_i$))

P^{M+1}

(Vp$_i$: (Vw$_i$: hear<PSTPTCP> (Vw$_i$)) (Vp$_i$))

P^{M+2}

      P^I

(Np$_k$: [(Gw$_k$: /ðə/ (Gw$_k$))

   P^{I+1}

(Nw$_k$: (Ns$_j$: /nju:z/ (Ns$_j$)) (Nw$_k$))

] (Np$_k$))

P^F

(Gw$_l$: /ɔːl'redɪ/(Gw$_l$))

] (Cl$_i$))

5

The Phonological Level

5.1 Introduction

For each Discourse Act the Phonological Level provides a representation that serves as input to the Output Component. The Phonological Level will be presented here as a partner of the Morphosyntactic Level in being one of the two manifestations of encoding.

Whereas the Output Component, the 'articulator', ultimately deals with such 'analogue' matters as formant frequency, intensity, duration, and spectral characteristics (reflecting individual voice quality, momentary mood swings, etc.), the Phonological Level is 'digital' in parallel with the levels discussed in earlier chapters, containing representations in phonemes that are ultimately based in binary phonological oppositions. This applies most clearly to individual phonological segments (with reference to minimal pairs) but will also be taken to apply to prosodic contrasts (e.g. rising vs falling Intonational Phrases, low vs high Phonological Phrases, etc.). The relationship between the abstract, 'digital', categories of phonological and actual acoustic features is, as Hirst and Di Cristo emphasize, 'far from simple' (1998: 5) and will not be pursued here. Suffice it to say that a number of processes that apply quite generally, irrespective of the structure of the unit under analysis, such as Utterance-final phenomena as creaky voice in Japanese or breathy voice in Finnish, will not be represented phonologically but assigned to the articulator, which clearly has language-specific properties too.

Just as with the other levels, we will take the position that phonological representations are hierarchical in nature, following Nespor and Vogel (1986): for details see 5.2 below. As will become apparent there, we will assume that there are certain default correlations between the layers we postulate for phonology and the layers recognized at other levels. The assumption that not all layers are necessarily relevant to every Utterance, an assumption also made for the other levels, will apply here too. Going further, we will also contend that certain languages lack some of the layers that are required for other languages. We will also allow for the possibility of recursion of the type proposed for the Morphosyntactic Level (cf. Chapter 4), for example permitting, where necessary, the occurrence of Phonological Words within other Phonological

Words. We here follow Schiering *et al.* (fc.) in their proposal that the Prosodic Hierarchy of Nespor and Vogel (1986), which had been assumed to apply to all languages, should be loosened to allow for both the omission and the recursion of layers of analysis; Anderson (2005: 48) similarly reinterprets the prosodic hierarchy as a set of violable constraints.

The Phonological Level receives input from all three other levels and is entirely dependent for its operation upon these levels, to the output of which it applies its own primitives. These primitives encompass (i) the prosodic patterns that apply at each layer of analysis (for example the language-specific division of Intonational Phrases into Phonological Phrases with particular pitch characteristics); (ii) an inventory of segmental sequences (the 'grammatical lexicon') expressing particular configurations of morphemes or placeholders introduced at other levels (for example stressed /o/ in Spanish as an expression, for a particular verb class, of the configuration IndPastPf3Sg, as discussed in 4.2.3); and (iii) a set of tertiary operators (for example those indicating a rising or falling Phonological Phrase), which will have their ultimate effect in the Output Component, just as secondary operators at the Morphosyntactic Level have their effect at the Phonological Level.

Let us now consider the nature of the input from each of the other levels. The input from the Interpersonal Level will consist partly of items already assigned their phonological form at that level. It was argued in Chapter 2, for example, that proper names, having reference but no semantic meaning, are introduced as segmental sequences at the Interpersonal Level: it will be the task of the Phonological Level to integrate these into an Utterance, possibly incorporating morphemes reflecting the rhetorical, pragmatic, or semantic function of the proper name. In addition, certain Expressives (*Wow!*) and Interactives (*Thank you*) will arrive directly from the Interpersonal Level as ready-made sequences of segments (/waʊ/ and /ˈθæŋkjuː/ respectively).

The input will also, for many languages, include an abstract illocutionary predicate, to which the Phonological Level will often react by assigning a particular contour to the corresponding Intonational Phrase into which the components of that Phrase will be inserted (cf. 5.4 below). For many languages, again, the distinctions between Focus and Background, between Topic and Comment, and between Contrast and Overlap are reflected at the layer of the Phonological Phrase (cf. 5.5 below), typically in the presence or absence of extra pitch prominence on a Syllable within that Phrase. The task of the Phonological Level in such languages is to ensure the correct association of the Focus, Topic, or Contrast element(s) with that Syllable. This association then has knock-on effects for the realization of the remainder of the unit in the Output Component.

Another Interpersonal-Level distinction that may be captured phonologically is that between specific and non-specific reference: Torrence (2005: 71) shows that the ambiguity of (1) in Wolof is 'resolved' by the assignment of distinct intonation contours according as *b-enn xaj* is intended as specific or not:

(1) B-enn   xaj, gis-u-më-kó.
    CL-one dog   see-NEG-1.SG-3.SG
    'Not a single dog did I see.' or 'A particular dog I didn't see.'

And in Tongan, as shown by Anderson and Otsuka (2006), definiteness is expressed as reduplication of the final vowel of the Np to which it applies, which in turn affects the stress, which always applies to the penultimate Syllable in a Tongan word (Anderson and Otsuka 2006: 27), the reduplicated vowel constituting a Syllable of its own:

(2) a. Na'e holo   'a   e   fale.
         TNS collapse ABS REFR house
         'A house collapsed.'
         /'na.ʔe 'ho.lo 'ʔa.e 'fa.le/

     b. Na'e holo   'a   e   falé.
         TNS collapse ABS REFR house
         'The house collapsed.'
         /'na.ʔe 'ho.lo 'ʔa.e fa.'le.e/

Let us now consider the input from the Representational Level. Where there are meaning oppositions that are not discriminated at the Morphosyntactic Level (cf. Nespor and Vogel 1986: 249–71 for discussion of various examples in the framework of Prosodic Phonology), the Phonological Level must have means to bring out such distinctions. To use a familiar example, where the Morphosyntactic Level delivers (3a) as (3b), there are two possible analyses at the Representational Level, namely (4a) and (4b):

(3) a. old men and women
     b. /'əʊld 'mæn-PL ænd 'wʊmən-PL/

(4) a. $(mx_i: (f_i: man_N (f_i)) (x_i): (f_j: old_A (f_j)) (x_i)) \& ((mx_j: (f_k: woman_N (f_k)) (x_j))$

     b. $(mx_i: (f_i: man_N (f_i)) (x_i): (f_j: old_A (f_j)) (x_i)) \& ((mx_j: (f_k: woman_N (f_k)) (x_j): (f_j) (x_i)))$

In certain languages, this distinction may be reflected morphosyntactically, cf. Portuguese, in which the adjective follows the noun or series of nouns to which it applies, and in which further disambiguation is achieved through concord:

(5) a. homen-s velh-o-s   e   mulher-es (= (4a))
         man-PL old-M-PL and woman-PL

b. homen-s e   mulher-es velh-o-s (= (4b))
    man-PL   and woman-PL old-M-PL

c. homen-s e   mulher-es velh-a-s ('men and old women')
    man-PL   and woman-PL old-F-PL

In English, however, the combination of a preposed adjective and no agreement makes (3a) ambiguous. In ways that will become more explicit below, English will distinguish one Phonological Phrase (PP) for the meaning in (4a) and two such Phrases for the meaning in (4b), both occurring within a single intonational phrase (IP), as in (6a) and (6b) respectively:

(6) a. (IP_i: (PP_i: /'əʊld 'men ænd 'wɪmɪn/ (PP_i)) (IP_i))
     b. (IP_i: [(PP_i: /'əʊld 'men/ (PP_i)) (PP_j: /ænd 'wɪmɪn / (PP_j))] (IP_i))

Another example is lenition (generally speaking, the replacement of a consonant by a less sonorous one) in Scottish Gaelic, which is very often indicative of a close relation at the Representational Level. Consider the following example:

(7) a. Tha   an   nighean math air bruidhinn.
         COP.PRS DEF girl   good at talking
         'The girl is good at talking.'

     b. Tha   an   nighean mhath air bruidhinn.
         COP.PRS DEF girl   good ASP talking
         'The good girl has been talking.'

In (7a), *math* 'good' does not belong to the representational unit headed by *nighean* 'girl' and does not lenite, retaining its lexical form /ma/, introduced at the Representational Level; in (7b), however, it functions as modifier of *nighean* and therefore does lenite, yielding /ṽa/ at the Phonological Level.

The input from the Morphosyntactic Level already contains a considerable amount of phonological specification. The lexical items introduced into the formulating levels and carried over to the Morphosyntactic Level take the form of phonemic sequences which, depending upon the type of language, may already be marked for one or more of the following:

   (i)   characteristic stress position (cf. Dik 1997a: 453ff.)
   (ii) characteristic tone patterns
   (iii) characteristic quantity indications

In so-called 'free stress languages' (cf. Hirst and Di Cristo 1998: 12), one Syllable in a lexical item will bear the stress in citation form, sometimes distinguishing between forms that would otherwise be homophones, cf. English compact$_V$ /kɒm'pækt/ and compact$_{N/A}$ /'kɒmpækt/. The stress is known as characteristic because it can, in such words as *sixteen* /sɪks'tiːn/, change position within a Phonological Phrase as shown in (8):

(8)   sixteen years
       (PPᵢ: /'sɪkstiːn'jɪəz/ (PPᵢ))

In 'fixed stress languages', where the stress is always assigned to a positionally defined Syllable of the Phonological Word, as in Finnish (first Syllable) or Polish (penultimate Syllable), the lexical form will contain no explicit marking of stress.

In a tone language, such as Thai or Rawang, each Syllable is characteristically associated with a tone, which can serve to distinguish lexical items in the same way as stress does in English. Thus in Rawang (LaPolla 2006: 8), we find that the relationship between a particular verb and its nominalization is indicated by a change of tone: compare *dvshī* 'a spirit who can make you die' and *dvshî* 'cause to die'. The tone is known as characteristic because tones in certain languages can change in particular configurations, a phenomenon often referred to as 'tone sandhi'. Mortensen (2002: 5) gives the following example from Jingpho (with tones represented here as superscripted numbers):

(9)   Lexical representations: pʒaʔ⁵⁵ 'caterpillar'
                                       mut³¹ 'grey'
       Phonological representation: (PPᵢ: /pʒaʔ³¹mut³¹/(PPᵢ)) 'grey caterpillar'

In 'fixed tone languages', such as Vietnamese, no such processes are observed. The lexical tones will survive into phonological representations without change.

Note that there are also languages like Mandarin Chinese, which have both lexical tone and lexical stress (Kratochvil 1998); like Swedish, with tonal accent (where the initial stress of a disyllabic word bears either high or low tone; Gårding 1998); and like Japanese, with accentual tone (where disyllabic words may bear tone or not, and if they do, can attribute accent to the first or second Syllable; Haraguchi 1977). These distinctions are all lexically distinctive, and will be marked as characteristic of the lexical words in those languages, as shown in 5.7 below.

Finally, various languages use oppositions of characteristic quantity (the length of vowels and consonants) to distinguish lexical items. Minimal pairs from Finnish, for example, include /tili/ 'account' vs /tiːli/ 'brick'; or /korpi/ 'wilderness' vs /korpːi/ 'raven' (Sulkala and Karjalainen 1992: 380). These oppositions apply to the (nominative case) citation forms: the application of distinctions at the Morphosyntactic Level can lead to changes at the Phonological Level, cf. *tyttö* /tytːø/ 'girl, nom.' vs *tytön* /tytøn/ 'girl, gen.'; *vapaa*

/vapaː/ 'free', *vapa-in* /vapain/ 'free-SUP' (Sulkala and Karjalainen 1992: 392, 394). In 'fixed quantity languages', such as German, the quantity of vowels and consonants survives into phonological representation without change.

Particular languages can display combinations of the above distinctions and others, too: a remarkable example is Dinka (Andersen 2007: 110), in which derivation and inflection are 'manifested as changes in the quality, the length, the voice quality and the tone of the root vowel and as changes in the final consonant of the root', all within one Syllable.

Much of the terminology of the Phonological Level suggests a very close relationship between it and the Morphosyntactic Level, with the use of such terms as Intonational and Phonological Phrases and Phonological Words. Nevertheless, the relationship between the two encoding levels is not straightforward. Where there is a disparity, the division of an Utterance into Intonational Phrases tends to reflect the analysis at the Interpersonal Level, just as the division into Clauses at the Morphosyntactic Level tends to reflect the analysis at the Representational Level. The attribution of an exclamative operator to every Subact (reflecting a very forceful, possibly angry delivery) may, for example, be reflected in the division of an Utterance into several intonation contours:

(10)   I hate that man!!!

IL: $(\ldots(C_I: [(\text{Emph } T_I) (\text{Excl } R_I: [+S, -A] (R_I)) (\text{Emph } +id R_J)] (C_I))\ldots)$

RL: $(p_i: (e_i: [(f_i: [(f_j: \text{hate}_V (f_j)) (1x_i)_A (\text{rem } 1x_j: (f_j: \text{man}_N (f_j))_U)] (f_i)) (e_i)) (p_i))$

ML: $(Cl_i: [(Np_i: (Nw_i: /aɪ/ (Nw_i)) (Np_i))_{Subj} (Vp_i: (Vw_i: /heɪt/ (Vw_i)) (Vp_i)) (Np_j: [(Gw_i: /ðæt/ (Gw_i)) (Nw_j: /mæn/ (Nw_j))] (Np_j))] (Cl_i))$

PL: $(U_i: [(IP_i: (PP_i: /aɪ/ (PP_i)) (IP_i)) (IP_i: (PP_i: /heɪt/ (PP_i)) (IP_i)) (IP_i: (PP_i: /ðæt/ (PP_i)) (IP_i)) (IP_i: (PP_i: /mæn/ (PP_i)) (IP_i))] (U_i))$

Note that the emphatic operators do not influence the morphosyntactic structure but only the prosodic structure. Other differences will be presented in the relevant sections below.

What emerges from a comparison of languages is that they frequently differ in whether a particular distinction in formulation is expressed morphosyntactically or phonologically. In general there would appear to be a certain trade-off between the two encoding levels, such that a distinction that is encoded morphosyntactically need not also be encoded phonologically and vice versa. Where an illocutionary distinction such as the presence of an Interrogative Illocution is marked morphosyntactically, for example by a particle or a verb form, there may be no need for phonological indication. In Garo (Burling 2004: 67), for example, the 'intonation of questions formed with a question word is not much different from the normal statement intonation'. If the final particle -*ma* or -*ni* is omitted, however, then a rising intonation is required to distinguish the intended Illocution. In tone languages, which use pitch to distinguish lexical items, we may accordingly expect more use to be made of morphosyntactic means for illocutionary distinctions. In the tone language Khoekhoe, for example, the attribution of Focus to a Subact has an effect only on the morphosyntactic structure, the expression of the Subact in question being placed in Clause-initial position; there is no effect upon the intonation (cf. Haacke 2006).

Of particular interest in this context is the non-tone language Wolof, which Rialland and Robert (2001) have shown not to have any intonational marking of Focus. In this language, a Contrast element is placed in Clause-initial position, followed by a marker that is inflected in agreement with the Subject of the Vp which follows this marker. Here is an example (Rialland and Robert 2001: 897):

(11) Lekkuma   mburu mi, ceeb bi   laa   lekk.
      eat.NEG.1.SG bread   DEF rice   DEF CONTR.1.SG eat
      'I didn't eat the bread, it was the rice I ate.'

In the non-tone language English, in a reading out of the translation of (11), even with the morphosyntactic indication of Contrast by means of the cleft construction, the status of *the rice* is also brought out intonationally. But in Wolof, Rialland and Robert find that 'focus', as they call it, 'has no effect on the melodic contour of the sentences' and that versions with and without Contrast are 'equally flat'; they remark that '[t]he complete absence of intonational marking of focus ... is ... remarkable in a non-tone language and seems quite rare from a typological point of view' (2001: 899).

The relation between the two encoding levels is one of partial parallelism. Shattuck-Hufnagel and Turk (1996: 194) come to the following conclusions, which fully apply to our view of the interaction between the Morphosyntactic Level and the Phonological Level of FDG: 'The morphosyntactic hierarchy influences the signal indirectly, via the constraints it imposes on the choices that the Speaker makes among the prosodic possibilities for a given utterance; [t]hese prosodic choices are also influenced by many other factors; [f]or this reason, the prosody of a particular utterance of a sentence cannot be predicted reliably from the text alone; thus, it is necessary to determine the prosodic structure that the Speaker actually used for each particular spoken utterance.'

5.2 The organization of the Phonological Level

As mentioned above, FDG assumes a hierarchical view of phonological structure. This is in keeping with the tradition of Prosodic Phonology, in which 'each constituent of the prosodic hierarchy draws on different types of phonological and nonphonological information' and 'the resulting prosodic constituents are not necessarily isomorphic to any constituents found elsewhere in the grammar' (Nespor and Vogel 1986: 2). The hierarchy proposed by Nespor and Vogel (1986: 11) recognizes 'seven units, from large to small': the Utterance, the Intonational Phrase, the Phonological Phrase, the Clitic Group, the Phonological Word, the Foot, and the Syllable. Syllables in turn consist at least of segments, but syllables are not regarded as a hierarchical unit, since they 'do not serve as the domain of application of phonological rules' (1986: 12), as all the others do; alternatively, syllables may be divided into morae, a mora being a unit such that light syllables have one mora and heavy syllables two.

While accepting the principle of a hierarchical phonology, other authors have questioned the universality of Nespor and Vogel's seven units, frequently referred to as 'domains'. Schiering *et al.* (fc.) have adduced examples of one language (Vietnamese) that does not require all the domains in the proposed hierarchy and of another (Limbu) in which there is necessarily recursion of domains. In Auer's (1993) proposals for a phonological typology, he finds evidence for a maximum of eight domains (intonational phrase, prosodic phrase, phonological phrase, clitic group, phonological word, phonological stem, syllable, and mora), but remarks that in some languages higher domains may be necessary, that intervening categories between syllable and phonological word may be called for, and that mora is not relevant to all languages. Given the consensus on the necessity of hierarchical structure and the continuing debate on the number of layers required, FDG will operate with a fluid view of the hierarchy within the Phonological Level, proposing a basic hierarchy but admitting the possibility of (i) non-instantiation of any of the layers, (ii) recursion of any of the layers, or (iii) addition of further layers in any one language.

Layering at the Phonological Level may thus be shown as follows; note that small capitals are used at the Phonological Level to indicate analytical categories, and that every unit may occur more than once:

(12) $(\pi \text{ U}_1: [$ Utterance
    $(\pi \text{ IP}_1: [$ Intonational Phrase
        $(\pi \text{ PP}_1: [$ Phonological Phrase
            $(\pi \text{ PW}_1: [$ Phonological Word
                $(\pi \text{ F}_1: [$ Foot
                    $(\pi \text{ s})^N$ Syllable
                  $] (\text{F}_1))$ Foot
              $] (\text{PW}_1))$ Phonological Word
          $] (\text{PP}_1))$ Phonological Phrase
      $] (\text{IP}_1)$ Intonational Phrase
   $] (\text{U}_1))$ Utterance

In other words, an Utterance (u_1) consists of one or more intonational Phrases (IP_1), which themselves are composed of one or more Phonological Phrases (PP_1); each PP contains one or more Phonological Words (PW_1), and these are composed of one of more Feet (F_1), which in turn are made of at least one syllable (s_1).

Each layer not only covers a potentially longer stretch of speech than the layer below it but is also characterized by phonological phenomena that are typical for that layer alone. These distinctions will be detailed in the following sections, in which each layer will be dealt with in turn. The Utterance (5.3) names the full stretch of speech under examination and thus is in a default relation with the Move at the Interpersonal Level; Utterances are typically separated by longer pauses than items lower in the hierarchy and it has been suggested that Utterances may display paratones (at least in certain forms of discourse). The Intonational Phrase (5.4) is the domain of a single into-nation contour, i.e. a systematically recognizable pattern of falling or rising overall pitch, often correlating with a particular configuration at the Inter-personal Level, and—where the Morphosyntactic Level provides an ambigu-ous output—indicating the intended relations between Discourse Acts within a Move or between States-of-Affairs within an Episode. The Phonological Phrase (5.5) is a grouping intermediate between the Intonational Phrase and the Phonological Word and is the domain of various phonological operations that apply to a grouping of Phonological Words without extending to the entire Intonational Phrase. The Phonological Word (5.6) is also the domain for a number of more local phonological processes, such as final devoicing in various Germanic and Slavic languages; generalizations that apply to the Phonological Word may mean that more than one morphosyntactic Word is in correspondence with a single Phonological Word or conversely that a single morphosyntactic Word corresponds to more than one Phonological Word. The Phonological Word will consist of one or more Feet, each of which in turn represents a grouping of Syllables (5.7); it is the grouping of Syllables within Feet that gives a language its characteristic rhythmic features.

What emerges from Auer's (1993) typological work on the prosodic phonol-ogy of some thirty-four languages is that languages vary on a complex scale between two prototypes: word-based languages and syllable-based languages. Because the lower end of the phonological hierarchy appears to be the one with the greater degree of language-specific variation, we will in the following sections devote most attention to the higher layers, which are also those that generally most strongly reflect major distinctions made at the Interpersonal Level and the Representational Level. Since we will be progressing from higher to lower layers, the amount of detail given about lower layers will be added gradually, with no more detail being given per layer than is necessary for the understanding of that layer.

5.3 Utterances

The Utterance (u_1) is the largest stretch of speech covered by the Phonological Level. The decision whether to label a stretch of speech as an Utterance is an analytical choice which is impossible to operationalize precisely. Nevertheless, we may venture the relative observation that an Utterance will tend to be separated from surrounding Utterances by a more substantial pause than the Speaker uses to separate intonational Phrases from one another. In Hayes's view (1989: 219), it is characteristic of Utterance boundaries that the pause between them will never be interpreted by the Addressee as a hesitation. An Utterance may in addition typically display pitch distinctions which help to mark it off as a self-contained group of Intonational Phrases. These have been identified as 'paratones' (Brown and Yule 1983: 101), a word derived from 'paragraph'. Paratones are defined for English by Thompson (1994: 65–6) as 'topic-related structural units of spoken discourse which are characterized phonologically by relatively high pitch on the first prominent syllable and by extra low pitch on the final tonic syllable, commonly followed by a significant pause'. Good examples of paratones in monologic speech are news items in radio or television news broadcasts. Brown and Yule (1983: 106) warn, however, that '[f]ailure to mark out explicitly the structural organisation of what a Speaker wishes to communicate may make the Addressee's task of interpretation more difficult, perhaps, but, by itself, would not necessarily constitute a failure to communicate'; in our terms, not every Move will be explicitly marked in speech as an Utterance by means of a paratone.

The relatively prominent pitches observed for English by Thompson at the beginning and end of Utterances appear to have some crosslinguistic validity: thus Venditti (2005: 191) recognizes for Japanese a comparable notion of 'finality', marking the last of a series of Intonational Phrases, commenting that this notion 'is subjective by nature, and will depend on several acoustic and stylistic factors which, in combination, signal that a given Phrase is final. These factors include, but are not limited to: final Fo [fundamental frequency, KH & JLM] lowering, segmental lengthening, creaky voice, amplitude lowering, long pauses, stylized 'finality' contours, etc. For Bininj Gun-Wok, Bishop and Fletcher (2005: 342–3) find that Utterances are characterized by their 'potential for final lowering and substantial pause ... the final two syllables of the Utterance generally undergo phonetic lengthening as a correlate of the boundary.' Although it is noticeable that the descriptions of the phonological and phonetic effects of Utterance demarcation across the three languages English, Japanese, and Bininj Gun-Wok show clear similarities, there are differences in the devices adopted. Thus in Mandarin, a tone language, Jun (2005: 433) reports that 'an utterance is not always marked by a boundary tone', just as 'there is no tonal event marking a prosodic unit within an utterance', i.e. an Intonational Phrase.

A paratone, or its equivalents in other languages, will be represented in FDG as an operator on the (u)-variable. An Utterance with an f-operator (where f stands for falling) will be realized with the 'relatively high pitch on the first prominent syllable' and the 'extra low pitch on the final tonic syllable' which Thompson (1994) sees as being characteristic of paratones in English. If the Intonational Phrase containing the final tonic Syllable also has an f-operator (for instance because it expresses a Declarative Discourse Act), the effect will be cumulative, leading to that 'extra low pitch', as in the following representation:

(13) $(f u_1:[(IP_1:[(h PP_1)...(PP_n)](IP_1))...(f IP_n:[(PP_1)...(PP_n)](IP_n))](u_1))$

where the tonic Syllable in the final (PP) of the final (IP) (here indicated for clarity in italics) will display a deeply falling pitch because of the double effect of the two f-operators.

Note that our approach to Utterance boundaries is distinct from that of Nespor and Vogel, who given their commitment to generative grammar (1986: 19–21), basically take (invented) morphosyntactic sentences as their point of departure in determining the extent of a 'phonological utterance'. They (1986: 238) for instance discuss example (14) as involving a special rule of 'utterance restructuring' whereby the two adjacent Utterances *That's a nice cat* and *Is it yours?* are joined into a single Utterance with a flapped [ɾ] as the realization of the phoneme /t/ (the transcription is ours, not theirs, KH & JLM):

(14)   a.   That's a nice cat. Is it yours?

       b.   /ˈðætsəˈnaɪsˈkæ[ɾ]ɪzɪtˈjɔːz/

This example might be analyzed profitably in FDG as the unified prosodic expression of a single Move with two Discourse Acts, each with its own Illocution (DECL and INTER respectively), so that (14b) would constitute a single Utterance at the Phonological Level, composed of two intonational Phrases.

The pattern for the Utterance will be as follows, where π may be f(alling), but potentially also rising or neutral; in particular languages but also in particular Utterances in languages that do permit an operator in this position, the operator may be absent:

(15) $(\pi u_1: (IP_1^{n \geq 1}) (u_1))$

5.4 Intonational Phrases

Utterances are composed of one or more Intonational Phrases (IP_1). An Intonational Phrase is characterized by internal and external properties: internally, it contains a nucleus, i.e. a pitch movement localized on one or more Syllables which is essential to the characterization of the Intonational Phrase as a whole; externally, the Intonational Phrase is separated from other Intonational Phrases by a pause, typically less long than the pause used to separate Utterances from each other. This pause may also be associated with (or possibly replaced by) a terminal pitch movement, and various other rhythmic or durational indications.

Just as the Utterance will often, but not always, coincide with the Move, so the Intonational Phrase will typically, but not necessarily, coincide with the Discourse Act. As mentioned above with respect to example (10), this default correlation may be overridden by the desire to reflect emphatic operators intonationally or alternatively by a very fast speed of delivery that condenses more than one Discourse Act into one intonation contour (cf. Bolinger's 1989: 97 example *I didn't make you lose it what are you talking about!*, which he describes as a 'macro-constituent answering to a mood or passion'). To return to the type of examples from English given in 2.3.2, (16) will be represented with two Intonational Phrases and (17) with one:

(16)   Celtic won. And Rangers lost.
    $((U_i: [(IP_i: /'seltɪk'wʌn/ (IP_i)) (IP_j: /ənd'reɪndʒəz'lɒst/ (IP_j))] (U_i))$

(17)   Celtic won and Rangers lost.
    $((U_i: (IP_i: /seltɪk'wʌnəndreɪndʒəz'lɒst/ (IP_i)) (U_i))$

Modifiers of Discourse Acts (cf. Section 2.3.3), such as *however* in (18), are typically assigned to their own intonational Phrase:

(18)   Celtic won. However, Rangers lost.
    $((U_i: [(IP_i: /'seltɪk'wʌn/ (IP_i)) (IP_j: /haʊ'evə/ (IP_j)) (IP_k: /'reɪndʒəz'lɒst/ (IP_k))] (U_i))$

Where the modifier interrupts the expression of the Discourse Act, the parts before and after the modifier will normally each be treated as an Intonational Phrase, although there is also the option of integrating the modifier into the Intonational Phrase of the head (cf. Section 2.4.3 on integrated modifiers)—as is reflected in alternative punctuation options in English:

(19)   a.   Celtic won. Rangers, however, lost.
            $(U_i: [(IP_i: /'seltɪk'wʌn/ (IP_i)) (IP_j: /'reɪndʒəz/ (IP_j)) (IP_k: /haʊ'evə/ (IP_k)) (IP_l: /'lɒst/ (IP_l))] (U_i))$

b. Celtic won. Rangers however lost.

(υ_i: [(IP_i: /ˈseltɪkˈwʌn/ (IP_i)) (IP_j: /ˈreɪndʒəzhɑʊevəˈlɒst/ (IP_j))] (υ_i))

Integration also appears to be relevant to the relations among Discourse Acts within a Move. Thus the sequence of an Orientation Discourse Act and Nuclear Discourse Act, or of a Nuclear Discourse Act and Corrective Discourse Act may be subject to a similar process. Di Cristo (1998: 211) considers the following example from French in which he distinguishes (in our terms) two possible divisions of the Move into Discourse Acts, as reflected in two possible divisions of the Utterance into Intonational Phrases:

(20) a. Mon   voisin   il   est   toujours malade.
          1SG.POSS neighbour 3.SG.M be.PRS.3SG always   ill
          'My neighbour, he's always ill; or: My neighbour is always ill.'

      b. ((υ_i: [(IP_i: /mɔ̃vwazɛ̃/ (IP_i)) (IP_j: /ilɛtuʒuʀmalad/ (IP_j)] (υ_i))

      c. ((υ_i: (IP_i: /mɔ̃vwazɛ̃ilɛtuʒuʀmalad/ (IP_i)) (υ_i))

Here (20b) is the phonological realization of the combination of an Orientation Discourse Act and Nuclear Discourse Act, while (20c) corresponds to a single Nuclear Discourse Act. It has been noted (cf. Dik 1997b: 403–4) that the increasing prevalence of the second option (20c) in French is leading to a situation whereby the verb may be reinterpreted at the Morphosyntactic Level as being subject to head-marking (as discussed in Section 4.2.3). For remarks on the integration of elements following the Nuclear Discourse Act, see Dik (1997b: 405). As Cruz-Ferreira (1998: 175) points out with regard to European Portuguese, integration will be resisted if the result causes semantic ambiguity; in other words, its operation is constrained by the need to respect the analysis at the Representational Level:

(21) a. Ela   comeu   a   galinha.
          3.SG.F eat.PST.3.SG DEF.F chicken

      b. ((υ_i: (IP_i: /ˈɛlɐkuˈmeweɡɐˈliɲɐ/ (IP_i)) (υ_i))
          'She ate the chicken.'

      c. ((υ_i: [(IP_i: /ˈɛlɐkuˈmew/ (IP_i)) (IP_j: /ɐˈɡɐliɲɐ/ (IP_j)] (υ_i))
          'It ate, the chicken.'

Similarly, the distinction between direct and indirect speech, where that is not signalled morphosyntactically, will be reflected in the choice between a single Intonational Phrase (with integration of the indirect speech) or separate Intonational Phrases for the quotative element and the quotation, cf. Dascălu-Jinga (1998: 243) on the following Romanian data:

(22) a. Mama   spune   cît   e   de bun.
          Mother say.PRS.3.SG how be.PRS.3.SG of good

      b. ((U$_i$: (IP$_i$: /'mama'spune'kɨtjede'bun/ (IP$_i$)) (U$_i$))
          'Mother says how good it is.'

      c. ((U$_i$: [(IP$_i$: /'mama'spune/ (IP$_i$)) (IP$_j$: /'kɨtjede'bun/ (IP$_j$)] (U$_i$))
          'Mother says, "How good it is!"'

Each Intonational Phrase will contain a global pitch movement, generally upwards or downwards (or neither); these will be represented as operators upon the (IP) variable. In addition, there will be various local pitch movements (often confined to stressed Syllables in stress languages), with particular importance typically being attached to the final pitch movement; these local pitch movements will be represented as operators on the relevant Phonological Phrase, cf. Section 5.5, not as operators on the Intonational Phrase. Global pitch movement correlates in many languages with the Illocution chosen at the Interpersonal Level, while local pitch movement is in correspondence with the assignment of pragmatic functions. In tone languages, as Abe (1998: 362) points out, '[t]ones by their nature resist being perturbed by intonation'— after all, they serve to distinguish lexical meaning. Nevertheless, although tone languages very often resort to morphosyntactic means of indicating illocutionary distinctions and pragmatic functions, they seem generally also to use global and local pitch movements to indicate these interpersonal matters, but without contaminating the system of lexical oppositions borne by the tone system.

It would appear that the majority of languages associate a globally falling pitch movement with DECL and IMP Illocutions and a globally rising movement with INTER Illocution. Where this is not the case, authors explicitly indicate that the language in question is unusual: thus Gordon (2005: 305–6) remarks that '[c]ontrary to the dominant cross-linguistic pattern, Chickasaw speakers usually end a statement with a final rise in fundamental frequency' and that 'both wh- and yes/no-questions in Chickasaw end in a pitch fall commencing immediately after the nuclear pitch accent'. However, it should be noted that the interpersonal nature of a Discourse Act may be reflected in a combination of morphosyntactic and phonological properties. Thus, in English, a question designed to check the validity of a Propositional Content may take the morphosyntactic form of a statement but the phonological form of an Interrogative Illocution (i.e. a globally rising movement):

(23) a. You like that book?
      b. ((U$_i$: (rIP$_i$: /jʊ'laɪkðæt'bʊk/ (IP$_i$)) (U$_i$))

Note that a globally rising movement is indicated by the tertiary operator r, and a globally falling movement by the tertiary operator f.

Since the status of a wh-question is indicated in English by a distinctive wh-word, its status as a question need not be additionally signalled by a rise, hence the preference for the (unmarked) falling intonation in wh-questions. Where such content interrogatives are not signalled morphosyntactically (as for example in languages in which their form is identical to that of an indefinite pronoun, cf. 2.5.2.3), they are likely to have a rising intonation; cf. Haspelmath (1997: 171) on Mandarin Chinese, for which only intonation disambiguates the two readings of the following sentence:

(24) Tā bǎ shénme   shū diū le.
      3.SG ACC what/something book throw PFV
      'What books did she throw away?' (rIP_i)
      'She threw away a certain book.' (fIP_i)

In other languages with such ignorative forms (cf. 2.8.3.4) we may similarly expect the Interrogative Illocution to be signalled intonationally.

Let us now consider the structure of Intonational Phrases in a polysynthetic language like West Greenlandic. In such languages the majority of morphosyntactic Phrases consist of one, relatively complex Word; correspondingly, the Phonological Phrases that compose the Intonational Phrase also tend to coincide with Phonological Words. According to Nagano-Madsen and Bredvad-Jansen (1995: 129), '[i]ntonation in West Greenlandic Eskimo is characterized as terminal tonal contour which appears on each word', where word, then, may be safely reinterpreted as Phonological Phrase. It becomes apparent from Fortescue (1984: 340–3) that each non-final Phrase has its own continuative tonal contour (and that this is the only use of pitch variation in the language), with the illocutionary status of the entire Discourse Act being indicated by the contour of the final Phonological Phrase, which is invariably placed on the antepenultimate mora of that Phrase.

The patterns for the intonational Phrase will appear as follows:

(25) $(\pi\ IP_1: (PP_1^{n \geq 1})\ (IP_1))$

where π may be f(alling) or r(ising). Further operators may prove necessary for the description of particular languages.

Before continuing, let us say a few words about the representation of intonation by means of operators. The Phonological Level will not show the 'melody' of the Intonational Phrase, but rather provide a number of indications at each layer which the articulator, the Output Component of the overall model, will convert into a smoothly flowing result. There is considerable variation between how individual speakers within one language, or in general speakers of one language rather than another, will realize an Intonational Phrase with a rising or a falling tone. What is important is that the overall direction of the Phrase is distinctive and this is determined above all by the orientation of the final movement. Many of the complexities in reaching that end point can be understood as resulting from operators applying at lower layers. It is to these that we now turn, beginning with Phonological Phrases.

5.5 Phonological Phrases

The Intonational Phrase consists of a number of Phonological Phrases (PP_i). Just as the Intonational Phrase typically corresponds with the Discourse Act at the Interpersonal Level, so there is a default relation between a Phonological Phrase and a Subact within the Communicated Content.

A pattern frequently encountered in stress languages (such as English) is that each Phonological Phrase, no matter what the degree of its own internal layering, will contain one Syllable that is more strongly stressed than the surrounding Syllables, including any other stressed ones. One of the Phonological Phrases within an Intonational Phrase, often the last in sequence, will then display local pitch movement on that most stressed Syllable. This pitch movement is systematically used to indicate additional interpersonal distinctions to those marked at the layer of the Intonational Phrase. The Syllable in question is generally known as the nuclear Syllable and is the primary location for the global fall or rise within the Intonational Phrase discussed in the preceding section. In tone languages, in which pitch movement is used for lexical distinctions, Phonological Phrases tend to have a different *raison d'être*, namely as the domain of tone sandhi (cf. 5.1 above); cf. Hoo Ling Soh (2001), who claims that the division of intonational Phrases into Phonological Phrases in Shanghai and Hokkien Chinese (tone languages) is additionally sensitive to definiteness, a feature from the Interpersonal Level in FDG.

Let us consider the Phonological Phrase in the stress language English. Whereas both DECL and IMP Illocutions in English are characterized by a globally falling pitch at the layer of the Intonational Phrase (fIP_i), the fall on the nuclear Syllable tends to be much more marked with the IMP Illocution. This will be indicated by assigning an additional falling tertiary operator to the Phonological Phrase containing the nuclear Syllable. The articulator will interpret such an indication as pertaining to the nuclear Syllable, such that the double indication of fall leads to a more marked result. Consider the following example from English, which may be understood either as a Declarative (probably in the past tense) or as an Imperative with an explicit subject:

(26)   a. You hit the ball.

      b. DECL: (U_i: (fIP_i: [(PP_i: /juː/ (PP_i)) (PP_j: /hɪt/ (PP_j)) (PP_k: /ðəˈbɒl/ (PP_k))] (IP_i)) (U_i))

      c. IMP: (U_i: (fIP_i: [(PP_i: /juː/ (PP_i)) (PP_j: /hɪt/ (PP_j)) (fPP_k: /ðəˈbɒl/ (PP_k))] (IP_i)) (U_i))

The operator on an Intonational Phrase will manifest itself in the nuclear Syllable, i.e. the Syllable /bɒl/ in the final Phonological Phrase (PP_k) in (26b): (PP_k) in (26b) therefore does not need to be marked as falling by means of an operator of its own. In (26c), however, the IMP Illocution is signalled by a combination of an f-operator on the Intonational Phrase as a whole plus an additional f-operator on (PP_k). The result is an instruction to the articulator to reinforce the effect of the fall on /bɒl/. These distinctions serve to distinguish between the two Illocutions.

    The relationship between falls and rises at the two layers need not be reinforcing, however. Tertiary operators at higher layers are reflected in the outermost direction of pitch movements, just as the formal reflections of higher secondary operators are located outside those of lower secondary operators. The operator at the (IP) layer therefore determines the ultimate direction of movement. Consider now Utterance (27a), which has been analysed as containing two Intonational Phrases. The first is marked by the tertiary operator r as globally rising—as is appropriate for the expression of a dependent Discourse Act—but its final Phonological Phrase has been shown as falling:

(27)   a. If you're unsure, call me.

      b. (U_i: [(rIP_i: [(PP_i: /ɪf/ (PP_i)) (fPP_j: /jərʌnˈʃuə/ (PP_j))] (IP_i)) (fIP_j: (fPP_k: /ˈkɔːlmɪ/ (PP_k)) (IP_j))] (U_i))

Given that higher operators determine the outermost direction of pitch movements, the effect of this combination will be for the nuclear Syllable /ʃuə/ to fall and then rise; in the actual realization by the articulator, the falling-and-then-rising pitch movement may be concentrated on the nuclear Syllable or divided over more than one Syllable within the Phonological Phrase. The Imperative Illocution of the second Discourse Act is again reflected in f-operators at the (IP) and (PP) layers, just as in (26c).

    Whereas pitch movement typically reflects illocutionary contrasts, pitch height in a Phonological Phrase is in very many languages associated with the expression of pragmatic functions. Certain languages, as we saw in 2.7.2.2, assign Topic, Focus, or Contrast constituents to particular positions in the morphosyntactic order or employ special syntactic constructions to highlight elements bearing Focus or Contrast. These strategies may have repercussions for the process of phonological encoding, since it applies to the output of the Morphosyntactic Level. Whereas the use of a special syntactic strategy for pragmatic functions may be an unequivocal marking of pragmatic status, we find that such a strategy is very frequently backed up at the Phonological Level. Thus the English cleft construction mentioned in 2.7.2.5 as expressing the combination of Focus and Contrast is normally associated with an Intonational Phrase in which the Phonological Phrase containing the expression of the Focus-Contrast element is marked as high. Thus one possible representation of an Utterance of example (28a), taken from 2.7.2.5, is as in (28b):

(28) a. It was the zoo that they went to, not the museum.
      b. $(U_i: [(IP_i: [(PP_i: /'ɪtwəz/ (PP_i)) (hPP_j: /ðə'zuː/ (PP_j)) (PP_k: /ðətðeɪ'wentːʊ/ (PP_k))] (IP_i)) (fIP_j: [(hPP_l: /'nɒt/ (PP_l)) (PP_m: /ðəmjuː'ziːəm/ (PP_m))] (IP_j))] (U_i))$

The effect of (28b) is for the first Intonational Phrase to have a rising pitch in its final Phonological Phrase (cf. Hirst and Di Cristo 1998: 27 on 'unfinished utterances or continuatives'), but with a preceding high pitch on /zuː/; the articulator will react by letting the pitch fall again after this Syllable so that it can rise again on the Syllables /'wentːʊ/. In the second Intonational Phrase, there will be high pitch on /'nɒt/ and a falling pitch, induced by the f-operator on (IP_j), on /'ziːəm/. Contrast may also be combined with Topic: Lee (1999) indicates that the combination of Contrast and Topic in Korean and Japanese is associated with high tone on the element expressing that combination.

As we have seen, then, in addition to the pitch movement indicated by the operators f and r, Syllables may be characterized by relative pitch with respect to the overall contour of the Intonational Phrase, namely as high or low, shown by the operators h and l respectively, cf. (28b). Consider example (29a):

(29) a. That I deny.
      b. $(fIP_i: [(hPP_i: /'ðæt/ (PP_i)) (PP_j: /aɪdɪn'aɪ/ (PP_j))] (IP_i))$

in which, let us assume, Contrast is assigned at the Interpersonal Level to the Subact *that* and Focus to the Subact *deny*. Where the Focus falls in the final Phonological Phrase, as here, its presence is not indicated separately from the pitch movement induced by the operator on the Intonational Phrase. In (29b), accordingly, it is the falling (nuclear) tone paralleling the DECL Illocution that also indicates the Focus status of *deny*. The Contrast is reflected in the high and relatively steady pitch of the expression of *that*. Now consider (30a), discussed in 2.7.2.3 as indicating Contrast on *that* and Focus on *never*:

(30) a. That I never said.
      b. $(fIP_i: [(hPP_i: /'ðæt/ (PP_i)) (PP_j: /aɪ'nevə/ (PP_j)) (lPP_k: /'sed/ (PP_k))] (IP_i))$

Again, the Contrast-bearing *that* receives high tone. The Focus on *never* leads to the fall induced by the f-operator on (IP$_i$) being located in the second-last Phonological Phrase; the l-operator on the final Phonological Phrase has the effect of keeping the pitch low after the fall in the preceding Phrase. We now see that Focus is indicated by realizing the overall contour (i.e. falling or rising) of the Intonational Phrase on the last Phonological Phrase not marked as high or low. In (30b) that is (PP$_j$).

In English, the syntax of the Clause usually is geared to ensuring Clause-final placement for the element associated with Focus assignment; the default effect on the Phonological Level is thus for the final Phonological Phrase to indicate both the Illocution and the placement of the Focus, as in (31):

(31) a. I saw [a heron]$_{Foc}$.

  b. (fIP$_i$: [(PP$_i$: /aɪ'sɔː/ (PP$_i$)) (PP$_j$: /ə'herən/ (PP$_j$))] (IP$_i$))

Where more than one Focus applies within a Communicated Content, this may still be expressed as a single Intonational Phrase (here we follow Brown and Yule 1983: 165). Since English typically does not rearrange the syntax to accommodate such cases, it is at the Phonological Level that the non-final Focuses will be marked, as in the following phonological representations of examples (176) and (177) from 2.7.2.2, repeated here for convenience as (32) and (33) respectively:

(32) a. [Peter]$_{Foc}$ had bought [a book]$_{Foc}$.

  b. (fIP$_i$: [(fPP$_i$: /'piːtə/ (PP$_i$)) (PP$_j$: /həd'bɔːt/ (PP$_j$)) (PP$_j$: /ə'bʊk/ (PP$_j$))] (IP$_i$))

(33) a. [A train arrived]$_{Foc}$.

  b. (fIP$_i$: [(fPP$_i$: /ə'treɪn/ (PP$_i$)) (PP$_j$: /ə'raɪvd/ (PP$_j$))] (IP$_i$))

In (32b), the effect is to produce falling pitch on /piː/ (typically extended to the following Syllable /tə/) and again, because of the f-operator on (IP$_i$), on /bʊk/, in the final Phonological Phrase. In (33b), similarly, we will hear two falling Syllables within the same (IP$_i$).

Of particular interest in this context is an Utterance such as (34a), in which the entire Communicated Content is in Focus. (34a) differs from (33a) in having a Topic, namely *the train*. English signals this particular configuration as follows, i.e. with the Comment marked with a steady low pitch:

(34) a. [[The train]$_{Top}$ arrived]$_{Foc}$

  b. (fIP$_i$: [(fPP$_i$: /ðə'treɪn/ (PP$_i$)) (lPP$_j$: /ə'raɪvd/ (PP$_j$))] (IP$_i$))

The f-operator on (IP$_i$) would normally induce a falling intonation on the Syllable /raɪvd/; however, this is rendered impossible by the presence of the l-operator on (PP$_j$), cf. (30b) above. The articulator will interpret this as an instruction to keep the fundamental frequency low after the fall on the Syllable /treɪn/. Such examples have been much discussed in the literature (for ample references and the statement that the processes concerned are 'still not fully understood', see Hirst 1998: 60) and are often said to involve de-accentuation of the post-nuclear material; here we interpret the effect on the final Phonological Phrase as a lack of pitch movement rather than of accentuation.

Whereas, as we have seen, English tends to prefer phonological to morphosyntactic means for signalling pragmatic functions, other languages with more flexible syntax can arrange the constituents in such a way that the final (or some other) position comes to house the element with the pragmatic function. Thus European Portuguese (cf. Cruz-Ferreira 1998: 173–4) in (35) signals Focus function with a word order that permits the Focus to correspond with the final Phonological Phrase, as in English; in (36), however, the Contrast-bearing Subject *ela* is placed finally, signalling its interpersonal function, and now attracts the falling tone of the final Phonological Phrase:

(35) a. Eu prefir-o que ela [venha]$_{Foc}$.
         1.SG prefer-1.SG COMP 3SG.F come.3.SG.PRS.SBJV
         'I would prefer her to come.'

     b. (fIP$_i$: [(PP$_i$: /ew'prfiru/ (PP$_i$)) (PP$_j$: /'kjɛlɐ/ (PP$_j$)) (PP$_k$: /'veɲɐ/ (PP$_k$))] (IP$_i$))

(36) a. Eu prefir-o que venha [ela]$_{Contr}$.
         1.SG prefer-1.SG COMP come.3.SG.PRS.SBJV 3SG.F
         'I would prefer that she should be the one to come.'

     b. (fIP$_i$: [(PP$_i$: /ew'prfiru/ (PP$_i$)) (PP$_j$: /'kveɲɐ / (PP$_j$)) (PP$_k$: /'ɛlɐ/ (PP$_k$))] (IP$_i$))

In other languages, the syntactic position for Focus is not final, yet is associated with falling intonation. In Hungarian, for example, it is the immediately preverbal position that is occupied by the Focus (unless the verb itself is in Focus). Here the Phonological Level will mark the post-Focus Phonological Phrases as low, so that the falling tone of the Intonational Phrase is appropriately assigned to the last Phonological Phrase not so marked, i.e. (PP$_j$) in the following example, already cited in 2.7.2.2 as (185) (Kenesei *et al.* 1998: 166):

(37) a. A vendégek tegnap érkeztek a szállodá-ba
         the guests yesterday arrived the hotel-LOC
         'It was yesterday that the guests arrived at the hotel.'

     b. (fIP$_i$: [(PP$_i$: /ɒ'vɛndeːgɛk/ (PP$_i$)) (PP$_j$: /'tɛgnɒp/ (PP$_j$)) (lPP$_k$: /'eːrkɛstɛk/ (PP$_k$)) (lPP$_l$: /ɒ'saːlːodaːbɒ/ (PP$_l$))] (IP$_i$))

Downing (2006) has shown that in Chitumbuka, the Focus element does not display specific phonological features: rather it is the non-Focus elements, in our terms the Background, that are marked. Syntactically, a Focus or Contrast element can appear Clause-initially in Chitumbuka:

(38) ma-búuku [β]a-ka-pása [β]áana
6-book 2-TAM-give 2-child
'They gave the children books.' (answering 'What did they give the children?')

In this language, every Word lexically contains a Syllable with high tone. The phonological effect of Focus assignment, as Downing describes it (2006: 61), is not to heighten the pitch of the Focus element, but to lower the high tone of the (following) non-Focus elements (a process known as downstep). This can be shown by indicating all the Phonological Phrases following the Focus elements as follows:

(39) $(\text{lPP}_1: [\ldots(\text{PW}_1: [\ldots(\text{hs}_n)\ldots] (\text{PW}_1))\ldots] (\text{PP}_1))$

such that the low pitch at the PP layer will lower the tone of the high Syllable inside each post-Focus PW. The effect of the higher-placed operator l is in this language to lower the high tone of the Syllable (s_n).

In 2.4.4 it was mentioned that one way to signal an ironic intention can be through intonation, for example in an ironic rendering of (40a). Given a non-ironic intention, we might expect a representation at the Phonological Level such as that given in (40b). A Speaker may signal that an ironic interpretation is intended by promoting the communicatively insignificant word *is* to the status of a Phonological Phrase and locating the nuclear Syllable there, as in (40c):

(40) a. That is interesting.
 b. $(\text{fIP}_i: [(\text{PP}_i: /'ð\text{ætiz}/ (\text{PP}_i)) (\text{PP}_j: /'\text{intristiŋ}/ (\text{PP}_j))] (\text{IP}_i))$
 c. $(\text{fIP}_i: [(\text{PP}_i: /'ð\text{æt}/ (\text{PP}_i)) (\text{rPP}_j: /'iz/ (\text{PP}_j)) (\text{lPP}_k: /'\text{intristiŋ}/ (\text{PP}_k))]$
 $(\text{IP}_i))$

(40c) will lead the articulator to produce a rise-fall on the second Phonological Phrase (cf. the fall-rise in (27b) above), with the l-operator on the final Phonological Phrase keeping its pitch from rising again.

In Chapter 2, mention was made of the Emphatic operator, which applies to Discourse Acts, Communicated Contents, or Ascriptive Subacts. In many languages, emphasis can be expressed (rather iconically) by extra intonational prominence. The prominence may be cumulative, as in English (41) or (42), where the falling and rising operators on the Intonational Phrase are reinforced by parallel operators on the Phonological Phrase:

(41) a. Horrible!

  b. (fIP$_i$: (fPP$_i$: /'hɒrıbl/ (PP$_i$)) (IP$_i$))

(42) a. Really??

  b. (rIP$_i$: (rPP$_i$: /'rɪəlı/ (PP$_i$)) (IP$_i$))

Alternatively, the effect of emphasis may be to shift the stress to an earlier unstressed Syllable within the same Phonological Phrase, as in French (43):

(43) a. Formidable!

  b. (fIP$_i$: (PP$_i$: (PW$_i$: [(ss$_i$: /fɔR/ (s$_i$)) (s$_j$: /mi/ (s$_j$)) (s$_k$: /dabl/ (s$_k$))] (PW$_i$)) (PP$_i$)) (IP$_i$))

In French, the unmarked position for the stressed Syllable (ss$_1$) in a Phonological Phrase is the final Syllable; emphasis is indicated by assigning stress to a non-final Syllable. See Hirst and Di Cristo (1998: 33) for an overview of the strategies for the phonological expression of emphasis found in a range of languages.

Not all languages use the Phonological Phrase for the expression of information from the Interpersonal Level. Let us close this section by looking briefly at Acehnese (Durie 1985: 30), in which the Phonological Phrase is characterized by nothing else than that it must contain a stressed Syllable, which is always the final Syllable in that Phrase, the only exceptions being a few enclitics that are 'extrametrical', i.e. their Syllables are not integrated into a Phonological Phrase but simply occur as part of the complex head of the Intonational Phrase. It will be clear, then, that Acehnese has no need of a Phonological Word layer. Here is an example from Durie (1985: 61), where | is the symbol he uses to indicate extrametricality of the following material, in this case Syllable (s$_p$):

(44) a. teungöh=geu=peu-jak aneuk=miet|=geuh
        middle=3=CAUS-go   child=small=3
        'He is walking his child.'

  b. (fIP$_i$: [(PP$_i$: [(s$_i$: /teun/ (s$_i$)) (s$_j$: /göh/ (s$_j$)) (s$_k$: /peu/ (s$_k$)) (ss$_l$: /jak/ (s$_l$))] (PP$_i$)) (PP$_j$: [(s$_m$: /a/ (s$_m$)) (s$_n$: /neuk/ (s$_n$)) (ss$_o$: /miet/ (s$_o$))] (PP$_j$)) (s$_p$: /geuh/ (s$_p$))] (IP$_i$))

However, even in Acehnese there is some interaction with the Interpersonal Level. Undergoers in that language are cross-referenced by enclitic pronouns (Durie 1985: 201). These pronouns are usually attached to the verb but may be attached to a following modifier if the latter is part of the Comment, cf. the enclitic *geuh* in (45):

(45) keu=lôn   hana=galak lê|=geuh
      DAT=1.SG NEG.be=like anymore=3
      'He doesn't like me any more.'

We may conclude from the preceding discussion that the pattern for the Phonological Phrase will appear as follows, where π is drawn from the set $\{f, r, h, l, n\}$:

(46) $(\pi\ \text{PP}_1: (\text{PW}_1{}^{n\geq1})\ (\text{PP}_1))$ or $(\pi\ \text{PP}_1: (\text{S}_1{}^{n\geq1})\ (\text{PP}_1))$

5.6 Phonological Words

The Phonological Word (PW_1), for those languages in which such a category needs to be recognized, is a segment of phonological structure which displays at least one phonological characteristic that is criterial for its status as a Phonological Word and which (possibly together with other Phonological Words) forms a Phonological Phrase. The characteristics that distinguish Phonological Words differ immensely from language to language, as shown by Dixon and Aikhenvald (2002: 14–18), who distinguish segmental features (such as the requirement in some languages that a Phonological Word contain at least two Syllables), prosodic features (for example, the word as the domain of nasalization in certain languages), and restrictions on the domain of phonological rules (such as palatalization). Unsurprisingly, given the diversity of criteria for wordhood at this level, it has also been claimed that languages exist without any need for a Phonological Word layer, i.e. where there is no evidence for a criterial phonological characteristic; in 5.5, we saw that this applies to Acehnese. Schiering *et al.* (fc.) find that no layers are necessary in the analysis of Vietnamese between the Syllable and the Phonological Phrase, and this may apply more generally to tone languages. On the other hand, they argue, more than one word layer may be needed for certain languages: they report Peperkamp's (1997) finding that the stress placement rule in Neapolitan Italian is straightforward if the word is analysed as a recursive domain (i.e. with a structure that recognizes words within words at the Phonological Level) and themselves contend that in Limbu, 'multiple nonisomorphic word domains can be motivated'.

   The Phonological Word is so called, of course, because of its rough correspondence to the morphosyntactic Word. In Chapter 4 it was shown how languages have been typologized into four classes according to their morphological characteristics. Generally speaking, the correlation between morphosyntactic Words and Phonological Words is best in isolating, agglutinating and fusional languages. For example, with regard to our example in 4.2.3 of an isolating language, Fijian, Dixon (1988: 21) observes, using stress as the criterial property of Phonological Words, that '[o]ften the two units do coincide', though one morphosyntactic Word may correspond to two Phonological Words (as in (47a)), and two morphosyntactic Words may correspond to one Phonological Word (as in (47b)):

(47)   a.   réi.-ta'ína
            rejoice.at-TR
       b.   í+na
            at+ART

As a contrasting example, consider now the agglutinating language Turkish—again to use stress as criterial—which has a good correlation between morphosyntactic and Phonological Word, with primary stress being placed on the final Syllable of the morphosyntactic Word, no matter how complex, so that in (48) it falls on the Syllable /dan/ (Kabak and Vogel 2001: 316):

(48)   kitap-lık-lar-ım-ız-dan
       book-case-PL-1-PL-ABL
       'from our bookcases'

However, personal and place names and various other classes of Word may form exceptions to this rule, cf. *İstanbul*, stressed on the second Syllable and *Ankara*, stressed on the first. In addition there is a closed classes of affixes (listed by Kabak and Vogel 2001: 328), which cause word stress to be moved to the Syllable immediately preceding them. Kabak and Vogel (2001: 329) show, however, that these exceptions can be dealt with such that the Phonological Word survives as the domain of stress assignment.

In polysynthetic languages, by contrast, it is not unusual for a single morphosyntactic Word to correspond to several Phonological Words. In Yimas (Foley 1991: 80), Phonological Words are characterized by a number of properties, notably the presence of primary stress. Although with nouns and adjectives there is a high coincidence between morphosyntactic and Phonological Words, this does not apply to verbs. Thus the verb in (49)—proved to be a single morphosyntactic Word by the presence of the negative *ta*—divides into three Phonological Words, as shown by the number of primary stresses:

(49)   Mamparŋkat ta-mpu-'park-mpi-'kapik-mpi-'wark-ra.
       branch-5-PL NEG-3.PL.A-split-SEQ-break-SEQ-tie-V.PL.O
       'They didn't split the branches, break them and tie them.'

In languages without polysynthesis, too, instances are readily found of morphosyntactic Words that correspond to more than one Phonological Word. An example is given by Booij (2005: 163) of the Dutch morphosyntactic Word in (50), which corresponds to two Words at the Phonological Level:

(50)   rood-achtig (spelled *roodachtig*)
       red-APPROX
       (PP$_i$: [(PW$_i$: /'ro:t/ (PW$_i$)) (PW$_j$: /'ɑxtəɣ/ (PW$_j$))] (PP$_i$))
       'reddish'

Evidence for the (pw)-status of /ˈɑxtəɣ/ can be drawn from the fact that /ˈroːt/ displays Final Devoicing (the lexical form of the adjective being /ˈroːd/, as is proved *inter alia* by the inflected forms /ˈroːdə/ *rode* 'red, attr. (unless indef. neut. sing.)', and /ˈroːdər/ *roder* 'redder'). As Booij points out, there is an alternative to the form in (50), namely *rodig* 'reddish', in which the suffix /əɣ/ -*ig* does not form a Phonological Word of its own, and which is correspondingly pronounced /ˈroːdəɣ/.

Phonological Words can be subject to 'gapping', as in the following example from Dutch, in which the Word *rozeachtig* 'pinkish' was interestingly misspelled as two separate orthographic words:

(51) Dit is   een   mooi-e   ketting van rood-Ø
      this be.3PS.PRS INDF beautiful-ATTR necklace of   red-NONATTR
      en   roze achtig-e   tint-en.
      and   pink APPROX-ATTR   colour-PL
      'This is a beautiful necklace with reddish and pinkish colours.'
      (Internet)

That there is 'gapping' here is apparent from the non-attributive form of the adjective *rood*, realizing with final devoicing as /ˈroːt/. This phenomenon must accordingly be seen as involving the absence of a Phonological Word boundary (cf. Vigário 2003 for corresponding phenomena in European Portuguese). At the Morphosyntactic Level the Word *roodachtige* will be analysed as in (52a), i.e. as one Word containing the suffixes /ˈɑxtəɣ/ and /ə/; at the Phonological Level, however, /ˈroːt/ *rood*, /ˈrɔzə/ *roze* and /ˈɑxtəɣə/ *achtige* will all appear as Phonological Words, as shown in (52b):

(52) a. (adjw$_i$: [(adjm$_i$: /roːt/ (m$_i$)) (m$_j$: /ˈɑxtəɣ/ (m$_j$)) (m$_k$: /ə/ (m$_k$))]
          (adjw$_i$))
      b. (pp$_i$: [(pw$_i$: /roːt/ (pw$_i$)) ...(pw$_j$: /ˈrɔzə/ (pw$_j$)) (pw$_k$: /ˈɑxtəɣə/
          (pw$_k$))...] (pp$_i$))

Similar phenomena apply to certain (but not all) prefixes, cf. (53), for English:

(53) a. (pp$_i$: [(pw$_i$: /ˈeks/ (pw$_i$)) (pw$_j$: /ˈæktə/ (pw$_j$))] (pp$_i$)) *ex-actor*
      b. (pp$_i$: (pw$_i$: /ɪgzˈæktə/ (pw$_i$)) (pp$_i$)) *exacter*

where (53a) consists of two Phonological Words, cf. also *an ex and current friend*, but (53b) of one—with corresponding effects on the segments corresponding to orthographic *ex* (i.e. /ˈeks/ vs /ɪgz/. And the same phenomena are found with compounds in English (cf. Booij 2005: 176), each constituent of which corresponds with one Phonological Word, cf. (54):

(54) (pp$_i$: [(pw$_i$: /ˈset/ (pw$_i$)) (pw$_j$: /ˈθɪərɪ/ (pw$_j$))] (pp$_i$))
      'set theory'

In Modern Greek, however, as Nespor and Vogel (1986: 112–13) point out, compounds are single Phonological Words.

The relationship between morphosyntactic and Phonological Words becomes more complex when clitics are taken into account. Clitics, which cannot be dealt with here as fully as they deserve (but cf. Anderson 2005), are forms which are treated as Words at the Morphosyntactic Level and are ordered as such by the templates applying to that level; at the Phonological Level a clitic is treated as part of the Phonological Word formed by its integration. Phonologically (although not morphosyntactically) they are thus like affixes. Consider the following example from French:

(55)   Donne-m-en (spelled Donne-m'en)
        /dɔn'mɑ̃/
        give.IMP-1.SG.REC-INDF
        'Give me some.'

The clitics *me* and *en* are positioned with respect to each other and the verb at the Morphosyntactic Level, as indicated in (56a). The whole Phonological Phrase consists of one Phonological Word, which is, in keeping with a general rule for Phonological Phrases in French, stressed on the final Syllable, as indicated in (56b):

(56)   a. $(Cl_i: [(Vp_i: (Vw_i: /dɔn/ (Vw_i)) (Vp_i)) (Np_i: (Nw_i: me (Nw_i))$
              $(Np_i)) (Np_j: (Nw_j: /ɑ̃/ (Nw_j)))] (Cl_i))$
        b. $(U_i: (fIP_i: (PP_i: (PW_i: [(S_i: /dɔn/ (S_i)) (S_j: /mɑ̃/ (S_j))] (PW_i)) (PP_i))$
              $IP_i)) U_i))$

The integration of a clitic may or may not have segmental effects upon either itself or the element to which it attaches: thus the form of the genitive clitic in English, as /s/, /z/, or /ɪz/, is dependent upon the nature of the immediately preceding phoneme; and in rapid speech attachment of the clitic /mɪ/ to /'gɪv/ 'give' can affect the form of the latter, yielding /'gɪmɪ/ 'gimme' (for further details of the possible phonological effects of cliticization, see Schiering 2005). Kabak and Vogel (2001) consider clitics in Turkish, for example as in (57), in which the copula appears in its clitic form:

(57)   Kaba-y-dı-nız.
        rude-COP-PST-2.PL
        'You were rude'

The stress here falls on the second Syllable /ba/, suggesting—given the conclusion reported above, that Turkish Phonological Words are stressed on their final Syllable—that example (57) indeed consists of more than a Phonological Word. They analyse the whole as a 'Clitic Group' (a layer they take to lie between the Phonological Word and the Phonological Phrase, and already argued for by Nespor and Vogel 1986). For many languages, however, it appears adequate to regard the clitic as being integrated into the Phonological Word, as is argued for Dutch by Booij (1996).

A distinction is drawn between proclisis and enclisis, according to the direction of attachment (rightward and leftward respectively). Booij (1996) shows that while proclisis is possible in Dutch, there is a preference for enclisis in that language; only the latter involves actual integration into the Phonological Word. Other examples of enclisis are such phenomena as the cliticization of articles to the preposition rather than the following noun in such instances from German as (58):

(58) Zu-m   Wohl!
      to-DEF.N.DAT.SG well-being
      'To well-being, i.e. Cheers!'

or the preposition to the preceding verb in such Leti instances as (59), from van Engelenhoven (2004: 202):

(59) Aumtïètnalo   kevïake.
      a=u-mtïètna=lo kevïaka=e
      s=1.SG.sit=LOC   suitcase=INDEXER
      'I sit on the suitcase.'

and of the attachment of the demonstrative to the preceding word, 'regardless of that word's syntactic affiliation' (Anderson 2005: 16–17), in Kʷakʷ'ala:

(60) Yəlkʷəmas=ida   bəgʷanəma=x̣=a   'watsi=s=a   gʷax̣ƛux̣ʷ.
      cause.hurt=DEM man=OBJ=DEM   dog=INS=DEM stick
      'The man hurt the dog with a stick.'

Mackenzie (fc.a) argues that clitics in European Portuguese, although apparently sometimes proclitic and sometimes enclitic, are in fact always enclitic to the occupant of the morphosyntactic P^I position. Alleged instances of mesoclisis (where the clitic is situated between two suffixes of the verb in the future or conditional tense) are also re-analysed as instances of endoclisis. Even in a strongly prefixing language like Acehnese (Durie 1985: 29), the only true clitics are enclitic: apparent proclitics are simply unstressed because they are non-final in their Phonological Phrase—cf. the discussion of Acehnese in 5.5 above.

As we saw in Chapter 4, the input to the Phonological Level from the Morphosyntactic Level consists of an ordered sequence of elements, some of which already have a phonological form shown as a sequence of phonemes, and some of which have an abstract form (termed 'morphosyntactic operators'). One of the tasks of the Phonological Level is to convert all placeholders into phonological form and to integrate them into a Phonological Word. To achieve this, the Phonological Level has a store of primitives at its disposal which provide phonemic material with which to replace the placeholders in the input. This store of primitives constitutes the 'grammatical lexicon' of the language under analysis. As the reader will recall, placeholders are included in the Morphosyntactic Level only where the intended expression is not definitively established at that level.

Let us now consider this process, focusing as a simple example on the phonological realization of the placeholding morpheme Past in English, which involves both lexical and phonological conditioning. The formation of the past form of a verb will be dependent upon a distinction indicated in the lexicon between regular and irregular verbs. In the lexicon, a regular verb has only one phonological form; an irregular verb has several. Thus the lexical verb *sing* is in effect shorthand for the options {/sɪŋ/, /sæŋ/, /sʌŋ/} plus a statement of the conditions for the use of each. A configuration such as (61a) at the Morphosyntactic Level accordingly entails the choice at the Phonological Level of (61b):

(61)   a.   (Vw$_i$: sing-Past (Vw$_i$))
        b.   (pw$_i$: /'sæŋ/ (pw$_i$))

In the case of a regular verb such as *loot*, there is only one form provided by the lexicon, namely /luːt/. In creating the past tense of this form, the Phonological Level adds a suffix, the choice of which is sensitive to the nature of the final phoneme of the lexical item. In (62b), representing *looted*, the suffix /ɪd/ is attached after the alveolar plosive /t/:

(62)   a.   (Vw$_i$: /'luːt/-Past (Vw$_i$))
        b.   (pw$_i$: /'luːtɪd/ (pw$_i$))

The application of a placeholder at the Morphosyntactic Level indicates that no definitive form can be added at that level. In Spanish, for example, the definite article with singular feminine nouns is displayed as a placeholder because its form is dependent upon the first phoneme of the word following it: *el* if a stressed /a/ follows, *la* elsewhere:

(63)   a.   el   alma (/'alma/)
             DEF.SG.F soul
             'the soul'

        b.   la   mujer
             DEF.SG.F. woman
             'the woman'

Mutatis mutandis, similar remarks apply to the English singular indefinite article *a/an*, the French singular masculine demonstrative determiner *ce/cet*, and generally to all cases of suppletion.

Let us consider (64) from French, already discussed in 4.4.7 as (256):

(64)   Nous chant-ons.
        we   sing-1.PL
        'We are singing.'

We saw there that examples like this presuppose a mechanism at the Morphosyntactic Level which copies the relevant features of the Subject Noun Phrase to the verb, yielding (65):

(65) $(Cl_i: [(Np_i: (Nw_i: /nu/ (Nw_i)) (Np_i))_{Subj} (Vp_i: (Vw_i: /\int \tilde{a}t/-pres<1.Pl>$
        $(Vw_i)) (Vp_i)] (Cl_i))$

The representation at the Phonological Level shows how the two placeholders Pres and <1.Pl> are fused:

(66) $(U_i: (fIP_i: (PP_i: [(PW_i: /nu/ (PW_i)) (PW_j: /\int \tilde{a}t\tilde{o}/ (PW_j))] (PP_i)) IP_i)) U_i))$

The pattern for the Phonological Word differs from those of higher layers in not requiring any tertiary operators in the languages we have considered; in 5.7 below, however, we will see that operators are required for accentual tone languages such as Japanese. The Phonological Word will therefore appear as follows:

(67) $(\pi w_1: (F_1^{n \geq 1}) (PW_1))$

where it is shown as consisting of a number of Feet. It is to Feet, and the Syllables that compose them, that the following section turns.

5.7 Phonemes, Syllables, and Feet

In preceding examples, we have shown phonological representations rather informally, namely in the form of sequences of phonemes, and where appropriate indicating which Syllable bears primary stress, as in example (41b), which—with the addition of the Phonological Word layer—may be shown as (68):

(68) $(fIP_i: (fPP_i: (PW_i: /\text{'}h\text{ɒ}rɪbl/ (PW_i)) (PP_i)) (IP_i))$

The purpose of this section is to explore the layers that may apply at lower layers than that of the Phonological Word. In a stress language such as English, phonemes group into Syllables, and Syllables into Feet, and these call for the application of corresponding layers of analysis. Let us work from the phoneme back up to the Foot, as the layer immediately under that of the Phonological Word.

Phonemes group into Syllables. A Syllable consists maximally of three parts, ordered incrementally as follows: an onset, a head, and a coda, whereby the head and the coda together form the rhyme. Certain languages require an onset, others permit Words without one. With respect to codas the opposite holds, in the sense that while many languages permit Words without one, there are also a few that do not allow one. The head is obligatory and is necessarily a sonorant, i.e. either a vowel or a sonorant consonant, as in the case of the /l/ in the last Syllable of (68). The Syllable may be classified as either heavy or light, the criteria for this distinction varying from language to language. In some, the distinction is a matter of the moraic structure of the rhyme, where a mora is a unit of duration: bimoraic rhymes yield a heavy and monomoraic rhymes a light Syllable.

Certain languages, however, including many from the Salishan group, may display Phonological Words that lack any sonorants: in Bella Coola (now preferably known as Nuxálk), '[m]any words consist solely of obstruents, cf. *p'xwlht* "bunchberry" ' (Nater 1984: 5); *lh* indicates a lateral fricative [λ]). Consider the following 'somewhat contrived' example, with the lateral fricatives indicated as /λ/ (Nater 1984: 5):

(69)   Cλ-p'xwλt-λp-λλs+kw-ts'.
        have-bunchberry-tree-PLUP-POSS+REP-then
        'Then he had in his possession a bunchberry plant.'

Such examples have been analysed in different ways. One possibility is to regard the Syllable layer as simply not being relevant for them (see the discussion in Bagemihl 1991); so again we countenance the possibility of a layer not being instantiated in a particular language (type).

A problem for the division of Phonological Words into Syllables is the existence in many languages, English included, of ambisyllabicity: this arises where the coda of (s_n) also functions as the onset of (s_{n+1}). In a possible pronunciation of a Word such as *horrible*, for example, one way of indicating Syllable divisions is as follows:

(70) $(\text{pw}_i: (\text{F}_i: [(\text{ss}_i: /h\text{Dr}/ (s_i)) (s_j: /r\text{Ib}/ (s_j)) (s_k: /bl/ (s_k)] (\text{F}_i)) (\text{pw}_i))$

As Maddieson (2005a: 54) points out, speakers are more certain about the number of Syllables in a Phonological Word than the exact placement of the divisions between them. In our approach, we will permit adjacent Syllables to share phonemes in the way shown in (70); it is the articulator (Output Component) that will reduce such sequences to single phonemes (through a process of degemination). However, it will have to be sensitive to the presence of morphosyntactic structure too, to avoid degeminating in such cases as *soulless* in (71), which involves a morphologically complex Word, a situation that blocks degemination:

(71)   ML: (adjw$_i$: [(nm$_i$: /səʊl/ (m$_i$)) (m$_j$: /lɪs/ (m$_j$))] (adjw$_i$))
       PL: (pw$_i$: (F$_i$: [(ss$_i$: /səʊl// (s$_i$)) (s$_j$: /lɪs/ (s$_j$))] (F$_i$)) (pw$_i$))

In stress languages, Syllables will differ in the relative stress assigned to each (which, as we will see, forms the basis for Foot structure), where stress may be realized by the articulator as a difference in loudness, pitch, duration, or intensity or some combination of these. A fundamental difference is made between stress languages with derivable and non-derivable stress, the 'free stress' and 'fixed stress' languages of 5.1 above. In the former, the assignment of stress is derivable from the position of the Syllable in the Phonological Word; in the description of such languages, FDG will not mark the Syllable in question but will leave it to the articulator to assign the appropriate stress. In the latter, where assignment of stress is not so derivable, FDG will mark stress by means of the stress operator s, as shown in (68) above.

In an examination of a database of 500 non-tone languages, Goedemans and van der Hulst (2005a) established that the majority of those languages (281/500; 56.2 per cent) have stress distributions that are derivable from the position of the Syllable within the Word; there are strong preferences for stressing penultimate (110/281; 39.1 per cent) and initial (92/281; 32.7 per cent) syllables. Even in languages with variable stress, a dominant pattern may be discerned, such as a preference in Spanish for penultimate stress (Goedemans and van der Hulst 2005a: 63).

Goedemans and van der Hulst (2005b) find that for the remaining 219 languages of their sample, all but 26 have stress that is predictable given the relative weight of the Syllables. Heavy Syllables, as defined above, tend to attract stress. Where a heavy and a light Syllable co-occur, the heavy one will attract the stress; where two heavy or two light Syllables co-occur, so-called right-edge languages have a preference for stressing the second of two heavy and the first of two light Syllables, while left-edge languages prefer to stress the first of two equally weighted Syllables, whether these are light or heavy (Goedemans and van der Hulst 2005b: 66); unbounded languages differ in not considering edges when calculating the placement of stress. In addition to this classification of languages, there are right-oriented and left-oriented languages, which place the stress anywhere in the last or first three Syllables of the Word respectively. On this basis, some familiar languages emerge as follows: English as right-oriented, French as right-edge, Russian as unbounded, Basque as left-edge, and Mandarin Chinese as unpredictable. Although the study of weight-sensitive stress systems has revealed the extent to which stress is derivable from Syllable weight, FDG will maintain the option of indicating the location of stress in such languages by means of the s-operator, since, as shown by Goedemans and van der Hulst (2005c), the factors they have shown to determine 'weight' are highly variable, also including non-phonological matters such as the lexical vs. non-lexical status of the Syllable. As discussed in 5.1 above, FDG lexical entries in free-stress languages will contain an indication of characteristic stress position, which can be adapted under the influence of rhythmic factors.

Languages differ in the extent to which the divisions between Words and between morphemes at the Morphosyntactic Level are retained in the division of Phonological Words into Syllables. In Acehnese, in which there is no layer of the Phonological Word (cf. 5.5 above), Syllable boundaries will correspond well with the division into meaning units at the Morphosyntactic Level. In French, by comparison, the division of the Phonological Phrase into units is strongly influenced by the language's preference for Syllables with CV structure. Consider the following example, in which we abstract from possible layers intermediate between Phonological Phrase and Syllable (the presence of the Foot layer in French is currently a matter of controversy: Jun and Fougeron's 2000 model makes no such assumption, but this is contested by Montreuil 2002):

(72)   le-s   ancien-s   élève-s
        DEF-PL former-PL pupil-PL
        'the former pupils'
        $(PP_i: [(s_i: /le// (s_i)) (s_j: /z\tilde{a}/ (s_j)) (s_k: /sj\tilde{\varepsilon}/ (s_k)) (s_l: /ze/ (s_l)) (s_m: /l\varepsilon v/ (s_m))] (PP_i))$

Only the final Syllable of this example has a coda, and the result is that units are created (with the exception of (s_i)) which have no correspondence to morphosyntactic units.

In stress languages, Syllables group into Feet, where the Foot is a layer intermediate between the Syllable and the Phonological Word, such that each Foot has one strong Syllable and a number of weaker Syllables. The recurrence of strong Syllables tends to show enough isochronicity in speech to create a sense of rhythm, and it is this that is represented by the Foot layer. A fundamental distinction is drawn between trochaic Feet, in which the first Syllable in the Foot is strong, and iambic Feet, in which the last Syllable is strong. Goedemans and van der Hulst (2005d) find that of the 184 languages in their sample that have a clear Foot type, 153 (83.2 per cent) have trochaic Feet, and they consider the theoretical option that all iambic systems can be reanalysed as trochaic ones. Languages without rhythm, 98 in their sample, may be regarded as lacking a Foot layer—although Goedemans and van der Hulst (2005d: 74) are prepared to admit Feet to such languages if they 'silently' condition other aspects of the phonology.

Feet differ in their strength with respect to each other within a Phonological Word. Consider the following Phonological Phrase from English:

(73)   agricultural entrepreneurs
   $(\text{PP}_i: [(\text{PW}_i: [(\text{F}_i: [(\text{ss}_i: /\text{æg}/ (\text{s}_i)) (\text{s}_j: /\text{rɪ}/ (\text{s}_j))] (\text{F}_i)) (\text{sF}_j: [(\text{ss}_k: /\text{kʌl}/ (\text{s}_k))$
   $(\text{s}_l: /\text{tʃə}/ (\text{s}_l)) (\text{s}_m: /\text{rl}/ (\text{s}_m))] (\text{F}_j))] (\text{PW}_i)) (\text{PW}_j: [(\text{F}_k: [(\text{ss}_n: /\text{ɒn}/ (\text{s}_n)) (\text{s}_o:$
   $/\text{trɪ}/ (\text{s}_o)) (\text{s}_p: /\text{prɪ}/ (\text{s}_p))] (\text{F}_k)) (\text{sF}_l: (\text{ss}_r: /\text{nɜːz}/ (\text{s}_r)) (\text{F}_l))] (\text{PW}_j))] (\text{PP}_i))$

We see that the Phrase breaks into two Phonological Words; these in turn each divide into two Feet. All the Feet are trochaic, as is apparent from the fact that their first Syllable bears the s-operator. In each case the Feet themselves differ in strength: in the first Word, the Foot /kʌltʃərl/ contains the Word's primary stress and the Foot /ægrɪ/ contains its secondary stress; in the second Word, the Foot /nɜːz/ bears the primary stress and the Foot /entrɪprɪ/ contains the secondary stress. Thus primary stress results from the coincidence of a strong Foot and a strong Syllable within it, and secondary stress from the occurrence of a strong Syllable in a Foot not marked as strong.

In tone languages, it is the Syllable that is the basic location of tonal distinctions. Tertiary operators such as {h, n, l, r, f}, all but one of which, namely m(iddle), have already been introduced for the characterization of Intonational and Phonological Phrases, apply again at this layer. Consider the following examples from Thai (Maddieson 2005b: 58):

(74)   a.   kʰáá 'tradeᵥ' $(\text{h s}_i: /\text{kʰaː}/ (\text{s}_i))$
       b.   kʰāā 'get stuck' $(\text{n s}_i: /\text{kʰaː}/ (\text{s}_i))$
       c.   kʰàà 'galangal' $(\text{l s}_i: /\text{kʰaː}/ (\text{s}_i))$
       d.   kʰǎá 'leg' $(\text{r s}_i: /\text{kʰaː}/ (\text{s}_i))$
       e.   kʰáà 'declarative politeness particle for female speakers'
                                                           $(\text{f s}_i: /\text{kʰaː}/ (\text{s}_i))$

In a tonal accent language like Swedish (cf. 5.1) above, it will be necessary to combine operators, such that a stressed Syllable (ss_1) will additionally be marked for high or low tone (examples from Gårding 1998: 114):

(75)   a.   tank-en
            tank-DEF
            'the tank'
            $(\text{F}_i: [(\text{hss}_i: /\text{tʰaŋk}/ (\text{s}_i)) (\text{s}_j: /\text{ɛn}/ (\text{s}_j))] (\text{F}_i))$

b. tank-en
    thought-DEF
    'the thought'
    (F_i: [(lss$_i$: /t^{h}aŋk/ (s$_i$)) (s$_j$: /ɛn/ (s$_j$))] (F_i))

In an accentual tone system like Japanese, by contrast, we find that tone applies (from the lexicon) to the Phonological Word and that the s-operator can then apply within Words with a high tone (the only tone in Japanese) to either the first or last Syllable. The following example is developed from Hirst and Di Cristo (1998: 10):

(76)   a. káki 'oyster'
            (hpw$_i$: [(ss$_i$: /ka/ (s$_i$)) (s$_j$: /ki/ (s$_j$))] (pw$_i$))

        b. kakí 'fence'
            (hpw$_i$: [(s$_i$: /ka/ (s$_i$)) (ss$_j$: /ki/ (s$_j$))] (pw$_i$))

        c. kaki 'persimmon'
            (pw$_i$: [(s$_i$: /ka/ (s$_i$)) (s$_j$: /ki/ (s$_j$))] (pw$_i$))

It may seem that the layers lower than that of the Phonological Word are of purely formal interest with little significance for a functional analysis of language, but in fact these layers of the Phonological Level interact with the other levels in the same way as higher layers. Let us consider the formation of comparative forms of adjectives in English and the relevance of the phonological category 'Syllable' to their formation. There is an alternation between two ways of expressing the comparative form of a gradable adjective (abstracting from individual cases of suppletion as in *good* > *better*, etc.): one involves an Adjective Phrase of the form *more* /mɔː/ Adj, while the other calls for the morphological option of appending the suffix *-er* /-ə/. Which form is chosen is dependent upon the phonological characteristics of the adjective: the suffix is preferred where the stem is monosyllabic or disyllabic with an unstressed second Syllable, cf. /ˈəʊld/ 'old' /ˈəʊldə/ 'older; /ˈlaɪvlɪ/ 'lively' /ˈlaɪvlɪə/ 'livelier'. Where the stem has three or more Syllables, the syntactic option is taken: /pəˈsɪstənt/ 'persistent' /ˈmɔː pəˈsɪstənt/ 'more persistent'. Where a disyllabic stem has a stressed second Syllable, both forms may be found for several adjectives. The choice seems to be lexically determined and arbitrary: we find /pəˈlaɪtə/ 'politer' /əʊˈbiːsə/ 'obeser' /əˈlɜːtə/ 'alerter' /pəˈtiːtə/ 'petiter', alongside corresponding forms with *more*; however, /əˈfreɪdə/ '?afraider' and /ʌpˈsetə/ '?upsetter' seem ill-formed.

Since the choice is largely determined by the phonological neighbourhood, it is at the Phonological Level that the phenomenon has to be dealt with. Let us consider the following examples:

(77)   a.   John is bigger than his brother.
       b.   *John is more big than his brother.

(78)   a.   John is more intelligent than his brother.
       b.   *John is intelligenter than his brother.

We hold that *more* in (78a) is lexical, since it can be modified by adverbs as in (79):

(79)   a.   John is much more intelligent than his brother.
       b.   John is markedly more intelligent than his brother.

and because *more* takes the *than* clause as an obligatory complement, as demonstrated by the ungrammaticality of (80):

(80)   *John is intelligent than his brother.

The predication frame underlying (78a) and (79a–b) will therefore appear as follows:

(81) $(f_1: [(f_2: [(f_3: Adj (f_3): [(f_4: more (f_4): [(f_5: Adv (f_5)) (f_4)_U]) (f_3)_U])$
       $(x_1)_{Standard})] (f_2)) (x_2)_U] (f_1))$

Our hypothesis is now that frame (81) also underlies (77a); note that in (82), *much* and *markedly* do not modify *big* but rather indicate the degree of difference in exactly the same way as *more* is modified in (79a–b):

(82)   John is markedly bigger than his brother.

On this basis, we assume that the same frame applies to (77a) as to (78a). This means that at the Morphosyntactic Level (77) will appear as though it were (the ill-formed) *John is more big than his brother*. It is the Phonological Level which, having access to the phonological structure of the Utterance, applies the appropriate form, as a suffix, in the same way as it applies rules of lexical priority.
    The patterns that apply to Feet and Syllables may now be shown as follows:

(83) $(\pi F_1: [\pi s_1^{n \geq 1}: / ... / (s_1))] (F_1)$
       where $\pi = \{s, \emptyset\}$
             $\pi = \{h, m, l, f, r; s, \emptyset\}$

5.8 Building up the Phonological Level

In the construction of the Phonological Level, use is made of prosodic patterns, an inventory of segmental sequences, and tertiary operators. Prosodic patterns come in various types, corresponding to the layers that characterize the ultimate phonological representation; which patterns are required for a particular language is an empirical question. In a language in which all the layers discussed in the preceding sections are instantiated, the Utterance pattern captures the configuration of Intonational Phrases (IP) within the Utterance, the IP pattern captures the configuration of Phonological Phrases (PP) within Intonational Phrases, the PP pattern captures the configuration of Phonological Words (PW) within Phonological Phrases, the PW pattern captures the configuration of Feet (F) within Phonological Words, the F pattern captures the configuration of Syllables (s) within the Foot, and the s pattern captures the configuration of phonemes within the Syllable. The inventory of segmental sequences applies to replace non-phonological material inherited from the Morphosyntactic Level at the PP and PW layers, as has been argued in 5.6 and will again be demonstrated below. Tertiary operators apply to variables at the various layers. Which operators are required per layer is again an empirical question to be determined from language to language, but in preceding sections we have found evidence for operators at all U, IP, PP, PW, F, and s layers.

In keeping with the general architecture of FDG, the process of building up the structure of the Phonological Level advances in a top-down fashion, starting with the largest units and then filling these with smaller ones. We start with the Utterance, analysing example (84), which one must imagine being produced in a situation in which the Speaker knows that the referent of *he* is under pressure to leave his work. In other words, the question is asking for justification of the compulsion to resign, as expressed by the Word *forced*.

(84)   If he doesn't want to go, why should he be forced to submit his resignation?

Since the number of IPs in an Utterance is unlimited, we can use the pattern in (85), but now with the subscripts on the variable (U) alphabetic rather than numerical, to show instantiation:

(85) $(U_i: (IP_1^{n \geq 1}) (U_i))$

If there is no paratone, as we may expect here, the operator on U will not be instantiated.

We may now fill the Intonational Phrase positions which constitute the Utterance with appropriate IP patterns, developing the general pattern for IPs:

(86) $(\pi IP_1: (PP_1^{n \geq 1}) (IP_1))$

Utterance (84), let us assume, consists of two Intonational Phrases (although other analyses would be possible with either very rapid speech or very emphatic speech). The result is the following structure:

(87) $(U_i: [(r \ IP_i: (PP_1^{n\geq1}) (IP_i)) (f \ IP_j: (PP_1^{n\geq1}) (IP_j))] (U_i))$

Note that the first IP has a rising contour, reflecting its status as a dependent Discourse Act within the Move at the Interpersonal Level, and that the second IP has a falling contour, reflecting its status as a wh-question. Notice again that the instantiation of the U and IP variables is shown in the use of alphabetic rather than numerical subscripts.

The next step is to develop the Phonological Phrase layer within each Intonational Phrase, using the pattern in (88):

(88) $(\pi \ PP_1: (PW_1^{n\geq1}) (PP_1))$

Probably as a partial reflection of the presupposed nature of the information in the *if*-Clause, the Speaker—let us assume—divides the first IP into two PPs, but partitions the second IP, which represents the Nuclear Discourse Act, into four PPs. The result is as follows:

(89) $(U_i: [(r \ IP_i: [(PP_i: (PW_1^{n\geq1}) (PP_i)) (f \ PP_j: (PW_1^{n\geq1}) (PP_j))] (IP_i))$
     $(f \ IP_j: [(h \ PP_k: (PW_1^{n\geq1}) (PP_k)) (PP_l: (PW_1^{n\geq1}) (PP_l)) (PP_m: (PW_1^{n\geq1})$
     $(PP_m)) (l \ PP_n: (PW_1^{n\geq1}) (PP_n)) (l \ PP_o: (PW_1^{n\geq1}) (PP_o))] (IP_j))] (U_i))$

Notice that (PP_j) bears the operator f: this will ensure that the articulator produces a fall-rise contour, as explained in 5.5. The fall may be limited to the final PW of the PP, namely /ˈgoʊ/, or spread out over the entire PP. In IP_j, the first PP carries an operator 'high', as frequently applies to the wh-word in wh-questions. And the presence of the operator 'low' on (PP_n) and (PP_o) indicates that the fall of Intonational Phrase (IP_j) comes in the preceding PP not marked for height, i.e. (PP_m). The desired effect, then, is for the pitch in IP_j to start high and then to fall in PP_m, staying low in PP_n and PP_o. No prediction is made for the pitch in PP_l, which could remain at the same height as PP_k, with the voice falling in PP_m; alternatively it could also fall but with a rise at the end to prepare for the fall in PP_m. Both options can be taken by speakers (i.e. by the Output Component in our overall model) without communicative difference and the representation allows for them both.

The next step is for the PWs within the PPs to be instantiated, using the pattern shown in (90):

(90) $(\pi \ w_1: (F_1^{n\geq1}) (PW_1))$

In this particular example all the PPs correspond to one PW except for PP_j, which consists of three Words. We will therefore only develop that one here, to clarify how that applies. (Notice that in English PWs do not have operators.) The following representation may be given for PP_j:

(91) $(f \ PP_j: [(PW_j: (F_1^{n\geq1}) (PW_j)) (PW_l: (F_1^{n\geq1}) (PW_l)) (PW_m: (F_1^{n\geq1}) (PW_m))]$
     $(PP_j))$

The Phonological Words are only partially in correspondence with the morphosyntactic Words. This is because of the occurrence of clitics in the Utterance, namely both occurrences of *he* and both occurrences of *to*, as well as the occurrence of *n't*, and of *be*. The sequence of Phonological Words in the example (let us assume, because non-clitic pronunciations of all these clitics—with *n't* being replaced by *not*—are in principle possible) will thus be as follows:

(92)　/'ɪfhɪ/ /'dʌznt/ /'wɒnttʊ/ /'gəʊ/ /'waɪ/ /'ʃʊdhɪbɪ/ /'fɔːsttʊ/ /sʌb'mɪthɪz/
　　　/ˌrezɪg'neɪʃn/

What the Phonological Level 'inherits' from the Morphosyntactic Level, however, is a mixture of phonemic and morphosyntactic information: the former where the definitive form is already available at that level, the latter where the definitive form has to be supplied from the inventory. The information received from the Morphosyntactic Level will be as follows, paring it back to the sequence of morphosyntactic Words:

(93)　(Cl_i: [(/'ɪf/) (he)$_{Subj}$ (do-3.sg.pres) (not) (/'wɒnt/) (to) (/'gəʊ/)] (Cl_i))
　　　(Cl_j: [(/'waɪ/) (/'ʃʊd/) (he)$_{Subj}$ (be) (/'fɔːs/-Part) (to) (/sʌb'mɪt/) (/hɪz/)
　　　(/ˌrezɪg'neɪʃn/] (Cl_i))

Notice that (he)$_{Subj}$, as explained in 4.1.3, is a placeholder for the forms {/hiː, hɪ/} from which the Phonological Level must make a choice; similarly (to) is a placeholder for {/tuː, tʊ/}, (not) for {/nɒt/, /nt/}, and (be) for {/biː, bɪ/ and others not relevant here}. The choice is in the case of (he) determined by the input from the Interpersonal Level: where (he)$_{Subj}$ corresponds to a Referential Subact that is in Focus or Contrast or is subject to emphasis, the form /hiː/ will be selected, as in (95):

(94)　It is he$_{Foc}$ /hiː, *hɪ/ who has been chosen.

Similar remarks apply to (to) and (be). None of the occurrences of (he), (to), or (be) in (85) is subject to any of these pragmatic functions: for that reason the analysis will display the forms /hɪ, tʊ/, and /bɪ/ respectively and none of them will be analysed as forming a Phonological Word.

　　The auxiliary verb (do) is introduced at the Morphosyntactic Level, where it also takes the agreement affix 3.sg.pres. As shown in example (61) above with regard to the verb *sing*, *do* cannot be represented as a sequence of phonemes at the Morphosyntactic Level because its form is not definitive. The presence of this placeholding representation in the input stimulates the Phonological Level to supply from its inventory of unpredictable forms the form that corresponds to the combination with the suffix 3.sg.pres, namely /dʌz/. To this form is appended, within the same Phonological Word, the clitic /=nt/, which is already in its definitive phonological form.

Finally, the morphosyntactic operator Part (participle; cf. (16) in 4.1.3) is converted to the phonological form /t/ by selection of the phonologically conditioned appropriate form from the set {/d, t, ɪd/} (after a check that /ˈfɔːs/ is not subject to the principle of 'lexical priority').

The representation shown here, it should be stressed, shows a pronunciation that reflects an average tempo of speech, given the proposed division into Phonological Words. The consequence is that the Phonological Level is not called upon to permit any deletion, in keeping with the principles of FDG. Thus, for example, as expressions of (be-3.sg.pres), /z/ is regarded as an alternative version of /ɪz/ rather than as resulting from deletion of /ɪ/. We assume, however, that in allegro speech, the Output Component does have the option of deleting phonemes, assimilating neighbouring phonemes to each other, or reducing vowels to /ə/. Thus we assume that possible deletions in the pronunciation of example (84), e.g. as in (95), which retains the division into Phonological Words, will be handled by the articulator:

(95) /ˈɪfi/ /ˈdʌzn/ /ˈwɒnə/ /ˈɡəʊ/ /ˈwaɪ/ /ˈʃʊdɪbɪ/ /ˈfɔːstə/ /sʌbˈmɪtɪz/
      /ˌrezɪɡˈneɪʃn/

It will be apparent from (95) that each of the PWs in example (84) corresponds to one Foot, except for the last in the Utterance (PW_q), which contains two stressed Syllables, /ˌre/ with secondary stress and /ˈneɪʃ/ with primary stress. Based on the structure of Feet repeated in (96):

(96) $(\pi \, F_1: [(\pi \, s_1{}^{n \geq 1}: / \ldots / (s_1))] \, (F_1))$

we arrive at the representation in (97):

(97) $((PW_q: [(F_q: [(s \, s_y: /re/ \, (s_y)) \, (s_z: /zɪɡ/ \, (s_z))] \, (F_q)) \, (s \, F_r: [(s \, s_{aa}: /neɪʃ/ \, (s_{aa})) \, (s_{bb}: /n/ \, (s_{bb}))] \, (F_r))] \, (PW_j))$

We are now ready to give the full analysis of example (84), following steps in a top-down manner; stepwise additions are shown in bold:

1. $(U_i: (IP_1{}^{n \geq 1}) \, (U_i))$
2. $(U_i: [(\mathbf{r} \, IP_i: (PP_1{}^{n \geq 1}) \, (IP_i)) \, (\mathbf{f} \, IP_j: (PP_1{}^{n \geq 1}) \, (IP_j))] \, (U_i))$
3. $(U_i: [(\mathbf{r} \, IP_i: [(PP_i: (PW_1{}^{n \geq 1}) \, (PP_i)) \, (\mathbf{f} \, PP_j: (PW_1{}^{n \geq 1}) \, (PP_j))] \, (IP_i))$
    $(\mathbf{f} \, IP_j: [(\mathbf{h} \, PP_k: (PW_1{}^{n \geq 1}) \, (PP_k)) \, (PP_l: (PW_1{}^{n \geq 1}) \, (PP_l)) \, (PP_m: (PW_1{}^{n \geq 1})$
    $(PP_m)) \, (lPP_n: (PW_1{}^{n \geq 1}) \, (PP_n)) \, (l \, PP_o: (PW_1{}^{n \geq 1}) \, (PP_o))] \, (IP_j))] \, (U_i))$
4. $(U_i: [(\mathbf{r} \, IP_i: [(PP_i: (PW_i: (F_1{}^{n \geq 1}) \, (PW_i)) \, (PP_i)) \, ((\mathbf{f} \, PP_j: [\, (PW_j: (F_1{}^{n \geq 1}) \, (PW_j))$
    $(PW_k: (F_1{}^{n \geq 1}) \, (PW_k)) \, (PW_l: (F_1{}^{n \geq 1}) \, (PW_l))] \, (PP_j)))] \, (IP_i)) \, (\mathbf{f} \, IP_j: [(\mathbf{h} \, PP_k:$
    $(PW_m: (F_1{}^{n \geq 1}) \, (PW_m)) \, (PP_k)) \, (PP_l: (PW_n: (F_1{}^{n \geq 1}) \, (PW_n)) \, (PP_l)) \, (PP_m:$

$(PW_o: (F_1{}^{n\geq1}) (PW_o)) (PP_m)) (l PP_n: (PW_p: (F_1{}^{n\geq1}) (PW_p)) (PP_n)) (l PP_o:$
$(PW_q: (F_1{}^{n\geq1}) (PW_q)) (PP_o))] (IP_j))] (U_i))$

5. $(U_i: [(r IP_i: [(PP_i: (PW_i: (\pi F_i: [(\pi s_1{}^{n\geq1}: / ... / (s_1))] (F_i)) (PW_i)) (PP_i)) ((f$
$PP_j: [(PW_j: (\pi F_j: [(\pi s_1{}^{n\geq1}: / ... / (s_1))] (F_j)) (PW_j)) (PW_k: (\pi F_k: [(\pi s_1{}^{n\geq1}:$
$/ ... / (s_1))] (F_k)) (PW_k)) (PW_l: (\pi F_1: (\pi s_1{}^{n\geq1}: / ... / (s_1)) (F_1)) (PW_l))]$
$(PP_j)))] (IP_i)) (f IP_j: [(h PP_k: (PW_m: (\pi F_m: (\pi s_1{}^{n\geq1}: / ... / (s_1)) (F_m))$
$(PW_m)) (PP_k)) (PP_l: (PW_n: (\pi F_n: (\pi s_1{}^{n\geq1}: / ... / (s_1)) (F_n)) (PW_n)) (PP_l))$
$(PP_m: (PW_o: (\pi F_o: (\pi s_1{}^{n\geq1}: / ... / (s_1)) (F_o)) (PW_o)) (PP_m)) (l PP_n: (PW_p:$
$(\pi F_p: (\pi s_1{}^{n\geq1}: / ... / (s_1)) (F_p)) (PW_p)) (PP_n)) (l PP_o: (PW_q: [(\pi F_q: (\pi s_1{}^{n\geq1}:$
$/ ... / (s_1)) (F_q)) (\pi F_r: (\pi s_1{}^{n\geq1}: / ... / (s_1)) (F_r))] (PW_q)) (PP_o))] (IP_j))]$
$(U_i))$

6. $(U_i: [(r IP_i: [(PP_i: (PW_i: (F_i: [(s s_i: /ıf/ (s_i)) (s_j: /hı/ (s_j))] (F_i)) (PW_i)) (PP_i))$
$((f PP_j: [(PW_j: (F_j: [(s s_k: /dʌz/ (s_k)) (s_l: /nt/ (s_l))] (F_j)) (PW_j)) (PW_k: (F_k:$
$[(s s_m: /wɒnt/ (s_m)) (s_n: /tʊ/ (s_n))] (F_k)) (PW_k)) (PW_l: (F_1: (s s_o: /gəʊ/$
$(s_o)) (F_1)) (PW_l)) (PP_j))] (IP_i)) (f IP_j: [(h PP_k: (PW_m: (F_m: (s s_p: /waı/$
$(s_p)) (F_m)) (PW_m)) (PP_k)) (PP_l: (PW_n: (F_n: [(s s_q: /ʃʊd/ (s_q)) (s_r: /hı/ (s_r))$
$(s_s: /bı/ (s_s))] (F_n)) (PW_n)) (PP_l)) (PP_m: (PW_o: (F_o: [(s s_t: /fɔːst/ (s_t)) (s_u:$
$/tʊ/ (s_u))] (F_o)) (PW_o)) (PP_m)) (l PP_n: (PW_p: (F_p: [(s s_v: /sʌb/ (s_v)) (s_w:$
$/mıt/ (s_w)) (s_x: /hız/ (s_x))] (F_p)) (PW_p)) (PP_n)) (l PP_o: (PW_q: [(F_q: [(s s_y:$
$/re/ (s_y)) (s_z: /zıg/ (s_z))] (F_q)) (s F_r: [(s s_{aa}: /neıʃ/ (s_{aa})) (s_{bb}: /n/ (s_{bb}))]$
$(F_r))] (PW_q)) (PP_o))] (IP_j))] (U_i))$

The complete phonological representation may be more easily surveyed in the
following form:
$(U_i: [$

$\quad(r IP_i: [$

$\quad\quad\quad(PP_i:\quad(PW_i:$

$\quad\quad\quad\quad\quad\quad\quad(F_i: [$

$\quad\quad\quad\quad\quad\quad\quad\quad\quad\quad(s s_i: /ıf/ (s_i))$

$\quad\quad\quad\quad\quad\quad\quad\quad\quad\quad(s_j: /hı/ (s_j))$

$\quad\quad\quad\quad\quad\quad\quad] (F_i))$

$\quad\quad\quad\quad\quad\quad(PW_i))$

$\quad\quad\quad(PP_i))$

$\quad\quad\quad(f PP_j:\quad[(PW_j:$

$\quad\quad\quad\quad\quad\quad\quad(F_j: [$

$\quad\quad\quad\quad\quad\quad\quad\quad\quad\quad(s s_k: /dʌz/ (s_k))$

$\quad\quad\quad\quad\quad\quad\quad\quad\quad\quad(s_l: /nt/ (s_l))$

$\quad\quad\quad\quad\quad\quad\quad] (F_j))$

$\quad\quad\quad\quad\quad\quad(PW_j))$

$\quad\quad\quad\quad\quad\quad(PW_k:$

$\quad\quad\quad\quad\quad\quad\quad(F_k: [$

$\quad\quad\quad\quad\quad\quad\quad\quad\quad\quad(s s_m: /wɒnt/ (s_m))$

$(s_n: /tʊ/ (s_n))$

$] (F_k))$

$(PW_k))$

$(PW_l:$

$\quad (F_l:$

$\quad\quad (s\ s_o: /gəʊ/ (s_o))$

$\quad (F_l))$

$(PW_l))$

$(PP_j))$

$] (IP_i))$

$(f\ IP_j: [$

$\quad (h\ PP_k:$

$\quad\quad (PW_m:$

$\quad\quad\quad (F_m:$

$\quad\quad\quad\quad (s\ s_p: /waɪ/ (s_p))$

$\quad\quad\quad (F_m))$

$\quad\quad (PW_m))$

$\quad (PP_k))$

$\quad (PP_l:$

$\quad\quad (PW_n:$

$\quad\quad\quad (F_n: [$

$\quad\quad\quad\quad (s\ s_q: /ʃʊd/ (s_q))$

$\quad\quad\quad\quad (s_r: /hɪ/ (s_r))$

$\quad\quad\quad\quad (s_s: /bɪ/ (s_s))$

$\quad\quad\quad] (F_n))$

$\quad\quad (PW_n))$

$\quad (PP_l))$

$\quad (PP_m:$

$\quad\quad (PW_o:$

$\quad\quad\quad (F_o: [$

$\quad\quad\quad\quad (s\ s_t: /fɔːst/ (s_t))$

$\quad\quad\quad\quad (s_u: /tʊ/ (s_u))$

$\quad\quad\quad] (F_o))$

$\quad\quad (PW_o))$

$\quad (PP_m))$

$\quad (l\ PP_n:$

$\quad\quad (PW_p:$

$\quad\quad\quad (F_p: [$

$\quad\quad\quad\quad (s\ s_v: /sʌb/ (s_v))$

$\quad\quad\quad\quad (s_w: /mɪt/ (s_w))$

$\quad\quad\quad\quad (s_x: /hɪz/ (s_x))$

$$] \; (F_p))$$
$$(PW_p))$$
$$(PP_n))$$
$$(l \; PP_o:$$
$$(PW_q: [$$
$$(F_q: [$$
$$(s \; s_y: /re/ \; (s_y))$$
$$(s_z: /zIg/ \; (s_z))]$$
$$(F_q))$$
$$(s \; F_r: [$$
$$(s \; s_{aa}: /neI\int/ \; (s_{aa}))$$
$$(s_{bb}: /n/ \; (s_{bb}))$$
$$] \; (F_r))$$
$$] \; (PW_q))$$
$$(PP_o))]$$
$$(IP_j))]$$
$$(U_i))$$

References

Aarts, Bas (2007), *Syntactic Gradience: The Nature of Grammatical Indeterminacy.* Oxford: Oxford University Press.

Abe, Isamu (1998), 'Intonation in Japanese', in Daniel Hirst and Albert Di Cristo (eds.), *Intonation Systems: A Survey of Twenty Languages.* Cambridge: Cambridge University Press, 360–75.

Aboh, Enoch (2005), 'The category P: The Kwa paradox', *Linguistic Analysis* 32: 615–46.

Adelaar, Willem F. H. (1977), *Tarma Quechua: Grammar, Texts, Dictionary.* Lisse: Peter de Ridder.

Adger, David and Ramchand, Gillian (2003), 'Predication and equation', *Linguistic Inquiry* 34.1: 591–656.

Aikhenvald, Alexandra Y. (2000), *Classifiers: A Typology of Noun Categorization Devices.* Oxford: Oxford University Press.

—— (2003), *A Grammar of Tariana, from Northwest Amazonia* (Cambridge Grammatical Descriptions). Cambridge: Cambridge University Press.

—— (2004), *Evidentiality.* Oxford: Oxford University Press.

Aissen, Judith (1983), 'Indirect Object advancement in Tzotzil', in David Perlmutter (ed.), *Studies in Relational Grammar I.* Chicago, IL: University of Chicago Press, 272–302.

—— (1992), 'Topic and Focus in Mayan', *Language* 51: 43–80.

—— (2003), 'Differential object marking: Iconicity vs. economy', *Natural Language and Linguistic Theory* 21.3: 435–83.

Allen, Barbara J., Gardiner, Donna B., and Frantz, Donald G. (1984), 'Noun incorporation in Southern Tiwa', *IJAL* 50, 292–311.

Allwood, Jens, Andersson, Lars-Gunnar, and Dahl, Östen (1977), *Logic in Linguistics.* Cambridge: Cambridge University Press.

Andersen, Torben (2007), 'Auxiliary verbs in Dinka', *Studies in Language* 31.1: 89–116.

Anderson, Stephen (2005), *Aspects of the Theory of Clitics.* Oxford: Oxford University Press.

Anderson, Victoria and Otsuka, Yuko (2006), 'The phonetics and phonology of definitive accent in Tongan', *Oceanic Linguistics* 45.1: 21–42.

Anstey, Matthew P. (2004), 'Functional Grammar from its inception', in J. Lachlan Mackenzie and María de los Ángeles Gómez-González (eds.), *A New Architecture for Functional Grammar.* Berlin and New York, NY: Mouton de Gruyter, 23–71.

—— (2006), 'Towards a Functional Discourse Grammar analysis of Tiberian Hebrew', Ph.D. dissertation, Vrije Universiteit Amsterdam.

Anstey, Matthew P. and Mackenzie, J. Lachlan (eds.) (2005), *Crucial Readings in Functional Grammar.* Berlin and New York, NY: Mouton de Gruyter.

Antunes de Araujo, Gabriel (2004), 'A grammar of Sabanê, a Nambikwaran language'. Ph.D. dissertation, Vrije Universiteit Amsterdam. Utrecht: LOT.

Asher, Ronald E. and Kumari, T. C. (1997), *Malayalam* (Descriptive Grammars). London and New York, NY: Routledge.

Ashton, Ethel O. (1944), *Swahili Grammar (Including Intonation)*. London: Longman.

Auer, Peter (1993), 'Is a rhythm-based typology possible? A study on the role of prosody in phonological typology'. *KontRi Arbeitspapiere* 21. University of Konstanz: FG Sprachwissenschaft.

Awbery, Gwenllian M. (1976), *The Syntax of Welsh: A Transformational Study of the Passive*. Cambridge: Cambridge University Press.

Baar, Tim van (1997), 'Continuation and change in FG', in Christopher S. Butler, John H. Connolly, Richard A. Gatward, and Roel M. Vismans (eds.), *A Fund of Ideas: Recent Developments in Functional Grammar*. Amsterdam: IFOTT, 42–59.

Bagemihl, Bruce (1991), 'Syllable structure in Bella Coola', *Linguistic Inquiry* 22: 589–646.

Bakker, Dik (1999), 'FG expression rules: From templates to constituent structure', *Working Papers in Functional Grammar* 67. Amsterdam: University of Amsterdam.

—— (2001), 'The FG expression rules: A dynamic model', *Revista Canaria de Estudios Ingleses* 42: 15–54.

—— (2005), 'Expression and agreement: Some more arguments for the dynamic expression model', in Kees Hengeveld and Casper de Groot (eds.), *Morphosyntactic Expression in Functional Grammar*. Berlin and New York, NY. Mouton de Gruyter, 1–40.

—— and Siewierska, Anna (2004), 'Towards a speaker model of Functional Grammar', in J. Lachlan Mackenzie and María A. Gómez-González (eds.), *A New Architecture for Functional Grammar*. Berlin and New York, NY: Mouton de Gruyter, 325–64.

—— —— (2007), 'Another take on the notion Subject', in Mike Hannay and Gerard J. Steen (eds.), *Structural-functional Studies in English Grammar* (Studies in Language Companion Series 83). Amsterdam: Benjamins, 141–58.

Barðdal, Jóhanna (2001), 'Case in Icelandic: A synchronic, diachronic and comparative approach' (Lundastudier i Nordisk språkvetenskap A 57). Ph.D. dissertation, Department of Scandinavian Languages, University of Lund.

Barnes, Janet (1994), 'Tuyuca', in Peter Kahrel and René van den Berg (eds.), *Typological Studies in Negation* (Typological Studies in Language 29). Amsterdam and Philadelphia, PA: Benjamins, 325–42.

Bendor-Samuel, David (1972), *Hierarchical structures in Guajajara* (Summer Institute of Linguistics Publications in Linguistics and Related Fields, 37). Norman: Summer Institute of Linguistics of the University of Oklahoma.

Berg, Marinus E. van den (1989), *Modern Standaard Chinees: Een Functionele Inleiding*. Bussum: Coutinho.

Berg, René van den (1989), *A Grammar of the Muna Language* (Verhandelingen van het Koninklijk Instituut voor Taal-, Land- en Volkenkunde 139). Dordrecht: Foris.

Berlin, Brent and Kay, Paul (1969), *Basic Color Terms: Their Universality and Evolution*. Berkeley, CA: University of California Press.

Besnier, Niko (1988), 'Semantic and pragmatic constraints on Tuvaluan raising', *Linguistics* 26: 747–78.

—— (2000), *Tuvuluan: A Polynesian Language of the Central Pacific* (Descriptive Grammars). London: Routledge.

Bhatia, Tej K. (1993), *Punjabi: A Cognitive-Descriptive Grammar* (Descriptive Grammars). London: Routledge.

Bickel, Balthasar (fc.), 'Grammatical relations typology', in Jae-Jung Song (ed.), *The Oxford Handbook of Typology*. Oxford: Oxford University Press.

—— (in prep.), 'On the typological variables of relativization'. Available as <http://www.uni-leipzig.de/~bickel/research/presentations/rc@mpi-eva_june 2004bb.pdf>.

Bishop, Judith and Fletcher, Janet (2005), 'Intonation in six dialects of Bininj Gun-wok', in Sun-Ah Jun (ed.), *Prosodic Typology: The Phonology of Intonation and Phrasing*. Oxford: Oxford University Press, 331–61.

Blake, Barry J. (1983), 'Structure and word order in Kalkatungu: The anatomy of a flat language', *Australian Journal of Linguistics* 3.2: 143–75.

Boas, Franz (1888), 'Myths and legends of the Çatloltq II', *The American Antiquarian and Oriental Journal* 10: 366–73.

Boër, Steven E. and Lycan, William G. (1980), 'A performadox in truth-conditional semantics'. *Linguistics and Philosophy* 4.1: 71–100.

Bógoras, Waldemar (1917), *Koryak texts* (Publications of the American Ethnological Society 5). Leiden: Brill.

Boland, Annerieke (2006), *Aspect, Tense and Modality: Theory, Typology, Acquisition*. Utrecht: LOT.

Bolinger, Dwight (1967), 'Adjectives in English: Attribution and predication', *Lingua* 18.1: 1–34.

—— (1989), *Intonation and its Uses*. London: Arnold.

Bolkestein, A. Machtelt (1981), 'Embedded predications, displacement and pseudo-argument formation in Latin', in A. Machtelt Bolkestein, Henk A. Combé, Simon C. Dik, Casper de Groot, Jadranka Gvozdanović, Albert Rijksbaron, and Co Vet, *Predication and Expression in Functional Grammar*. London: Academic Press, 63–112.

—— (1985), 'Discourse and case-marking: Three-place predicates in Latin', in Christian Touratier (ed.), *Syntaxe et latin*. Aix-en-Provence: Université de Provence, 191–225.

—— and Risselada, Rodie (1987), 'The pragmatic motivation of syntactic and semantic perspective', in Jef Verschueren and Marcella Bertuccelli-Papi (eds.), *The Pragmatic Perspective*. Amsterdam and Philadelphia, PA: Benjamins, 497–512.

Booij, Geert E. (1996), 'Cliticization as prosodic integration: The case of Dutch', *The Linguistic Review* 13: 219–42.

—— (2002), *The Morphology of Dutch*. Oxford: Oxford University Press.

—— (2005), *The Grammar of Words: An Introduction to Linguistic Morphology*. Oxford: Oxford University Press.

Bozşahin, Cem (fc.), 'On the Turkish controllee'. *ICTL 2004 Proceedings*.

Bradshaw, Joel (1993), 'Subject relationships within serial verb constructions in Numbani and Jabêm', *Oceanic Linguistics* 32.1: 133–62.

Bray, R. G. A de (1969), *Guide to the Slavonic Languages*. 2nd revised edition. London: Dent & Sons.

Bresnan, Joan (1995), 'Lexicality and argument structure', Unpublished manuscript. Available as <http://www.stanford.edu/~bresnan/paris.pdf>.

Bril, Isabelle (2004), 'Complex nuclei in Oceanic languages: contribution to an areal typology', in Isabelle Bril and Françoise Ozanne-Rivierre (eds.), *Complex Predicates in Oceanic Languages: Studies in the Dynamics of Binding and Boundedness*. Berlin: Mouton de Gruyter, 1–46.

Brown, Gillian and Yule, George (1983), *Discourse Analysis* (Cambridge Textbooks in Linguistics). Cambridge: Cambridge University Press.

Brown, Richard (1985), 'Term operators', in A. Machtelt Bolkestein, Casper de Groot, and J. Lachlan Mackenzie (eds.), *Predicates and Terms in Functional Grammar* (Functional Grammar Series 2). Dordrecht: Foris, 127–45.

Bryant, Greg A. and Fox Tree, Jean E. (2002), 'Recognizing verbal irony in spontaneous speech', *Metaphor and Symbol* 17.2: 99–117.

Bühler, Karl (1934), *Sprachtheorie: Die Darstellungsfunktion der Sprache*. Jena: Fischer.

Burling, Robbins (1961), *A Garo Grammar* (Deccan College Monograph Series, 25). Poona: Deccan College Postgraduate and Research Institute.

—— (2004), *The Language of the Modhupur Mandi (Garo)*. Vol I: *Grammar*. New Delhi: Bibliophile South Asia and Morganville, NJ: Promilla.

Butler, Christopher S. (2003), *Structure and Function: A Guide to Three Major Structural-Functional Theories* (Studies in Language Companion Series 63 and 64). Amsterdam and Philadelphia, PA: Benjamins.

—— (2004), 'Corpus studies and functional linguistic theories', *Functions of Language* 11.2: 147–86.

—— (2008a), 'Interpersonal meaning in the noun phrase', in Jan Rijkhoff and Daniel García Velasco (eds.), *The Noun Phrase in Functional Discourse Grammar*. Berlin and New York, NY: Mouton de Gruyter.

—— (2008b), 'Cognitive adequacy in structural-functional theories of language'. *Language Sciences* 30.1: 1–30.

Bybee, Joan L. (1985), *Morphology: A Study of the Relation between Meaning and Form*. Amsterdam and Philadelphia, PA: Benjamins.

—— Perkins, Revere D., and Pagliuca, William (1994), *The Evolution of Grammar: Tense, Aspect and Modality in the Languages of the World*. Chicago: University of Chicago Press.

Caffarel, Alice J. R. and Matthiessen, Christian M. I. M. (eds.) (2004), *Language Typology: A Functional Perspective*. Amsterdam and Philadelphia, PA: Benjamins.

Carlson, Robert (1994), *A Grammar of Supyire* (Mouton Grammar Library 14). Berlin and New York, NY: Mouton de Gruyter.

Castrén, M. Alexander (1858), *Versuch einer jenissei-ostjakischen und kottischen Sprachlehre, nebst Wörterverzeichnissen aus den genannten Sprachen* (Nordische Reisen und Forschungen 12). St. Petersburg: Buchdruckerei der Kaiserlichen Akademie der Wissenschaften.

Chao, Y. R. (1968), *A Grammar of Spoken Chinese*. Berkeley and Los Angeles, CA: University of California Press.

Cheng, Lisa L.-S. (1991), *On the Typology of Wh-Questions*. New York, NY: Garland.

Childs, G. Tucker (1995), *A Grammar of Kisi: A Southern Atlantic Language* (Mouton Grammar Library 16). Berlin and New York, NY: Mouton de Gruyter.

Cinque, Guglielmo (1999), *Adverbs and Functional Heads: A Cross-Linguistic Perspective*. Oxford: Oxford University Press.

Clark, Eve and Clark, Herbert H. (1979), 'When nouns surface as verbs', *Language* 55.4: 767–811.

Coates, Jennifer (1983), *The Semantics of the Modal Auxiliaries*. London: Croom Helm.

Colarusso, John (1992), *A Grammar of the Kabardian Language*. Calgary: University of Calgary Press.

Cole, Peter (1982), *Imbabura Quechua* (Lingua Descriptive Studies 5). Amsterdam: North-Holland.

——and Son, Min-Jeong (2004), 'The argument structure of verbs with the suffix *–kan* in Indonesian', *Oceanic Linguistics* 43.2: 339–64.

Comrie, Bernard (1976), *Aspect*. Cambridge: Cambridge University Press.

——(1985), *Tense* (Cambridge Textbooks in Linguistics). Cambridge: Cambridge University Press.

——(1989), *Language Universals and Linguistic Typology*. 2nd revised edition. Oxford and Cambridge, MA: Blackwell.

——and Thompson, Sandra A. (1985), 'Lexical nominalization', in Timothy Shopen (ed.), *Language Typology and Syntactic Description. Vol 3: Grammatical Categories and the Lexicon*. Cambridge: Cambridge University Press, 349–98.

Connolly, John (1991), *Constituent Order in Functional Grammar: Synchronic and Diachronic Perspectives* (Functional Grammar Series 14). Berlin and New York, NY: Foris.

——(2004), 'The question of discourse representation in Functional Discourse Grammar', in J. Lachlan Mackenzie and María de los Ángeles Gómez-González (eds.), *A New Architecture for Functional Grammar*. Berlin and New York, NY: Mouton de Gruyter, 89–116.

Cornish, Francis (2002), 'Anaphora: lexico-textual structure, or means for utterance integration within a discourse? A critique of the Functional Grammar account'. *Linguistics* 40.3, 469–93.

——(2004), 'Absence of (ascriptive) predication, Topic and Focus: The case of "thetic" clauses', in Henk Aertsen, Mike Hannay, and Rod Lyall (eds.), *Words in their Places: A Festschrift for J. Lachlan Mackenzie*. Amsterdam: Vrije Universiteit Amsterdam, 211–27.

Craig, Colette Grinevald (1977), *The Structure of Jacaltec*. Austin: University of Texas Press.

Crevels, Mily (2000), 'Concession: A typological study'. Ph.D. dissertation, University of Amsterdam. Utrecht: LOT.

Cristofaro, Sonia (2003), *Subordination* (Oxford Studies in Typology and Linguistic Theory). Oxford: Oxford University Press.

Crowley, Terry (1985), 'Common noun phrase marking in Proto-Oceanic'. *Oceanic Linguistics* 24.1–2: 135–93.

Cruz-Ferreira, Madalena (1998), 'Intonation in European Portuguese', in Daniel Hirst and Albert Di Cristo (eds.), *Intonation Systems: A Survey of Twenty Languages.* Cambridge: Cambridge University Press, 167–78.

Cunha, Celso and Cintra, Luís F. Lindsey (2001), *Nova Gramática do Português Contemporâneo*, 8th impression. Rio de Janeiro: Nova Fronteira.

Curnow, Timothy Jowan (2002), 'Evidentiality and me: The interaction of evidentials and first person', in Cynthia Allen (ed.), *Proceedings of the 2001 Conference of the Australian Linguistic Society*, <http://www.als.asn.au>.

Cuvalay-Haak, Martine (1997), *The Verb in Literary and Colloquial Arabic.* Berlin and New York, NY: Mouton de Gruyter.

Dahl, Östen (1985), *Tense and Aspect Systems.* Oxford: Blackwell.

Dascălu-Jinga, Laurenţia (1998), 'Intonation in Romanian', in Daniel Hirst and Albert Di Cristo (eds.), *Intonation Systems: A Survey of Twenty Languages.* Cambridge: Cambridge University Press, 239–60.

Declerck, Renaat (1996), 'A functional typology of *when*-clauses', *Functions of Language* 3.2: 185–234.

Derbyshire, Desmond C. (1979), *Hixkaryana* (Lingua Descriptive Series). Amsterdam: North-Holland.

Di Cristo, Albert (1998), 'Intonation in French', in Daniel Hirst and Albert Di Cristo (eds.), *Intonation Systems: A Survey of Twenty Languages.* Cambridge: Cambridge University Press, 195–218.

Dickinson, Connie (2002), 'Complex predicates in Tsafiki'. Doctoral dissertation, University of Oregon.

Dik, Simon C. (1975), 'The semantic representation of manner adverbials', in Albert Kraak (ed.), *Linguistics in the Netherlands 1972–1973.* Assen: Van Gorcum, 96–121.

—— (1978), *Functional Grammar.* Amsterdam: North-Holland.

—— (1979), 'Raising in a Functional Grammar'. *Lingua* 47: 119–40.

—— (1980), *Studies in Functional Grammar.* London: Academic Press.

—— (1986), 'On the notion "Functional Explanation" ', *Belgian Journal of Linguistics* 1: 11–52.

—— (1992), *Functional Grammar in Prolog: An Integrated Implementation for English, French, and Dutch.* Berlin and New York, NY: Mouton de Gruyter.

—— (1997a), *The Theory of Functional Grammar. Part I: The Structure of the Clause* (Functional Grammar Series 20). 2nd revised edition. Edited by Kees Hengeveld. Berlin and New York, NY: Mouton de Gruyter.

—— (1997b), *The Theory of Functional Grammar. Part II: Complex and Derived Constructions* (Functional Grammar Series 21). Edited by Kees Hengeveld. Berlin and New York, NY: Mouton de Gruyter.

—— and Hengeveld, Kees (1991), 'The hierarchical structure of the clause and the typology of perception verb complements', *Linguistics* 29.2: 231–59.

—— —— Vester, Elselien, and Vet, Co (1990), 'The hierarchical structure of the clause and the typology of adverbial satellites', in Jan Nuyts, A. Machtelt Bolkestein, and

Co Vet (eds.), *Layers and Levels of Representation in Language Theory*. Amsterdam and Philadelphia, PA: Benjamins, 25–70.

Dikker, Suzanne (2004), 'On the whereabouts of gender and number agreement: location and accessibility', in Kees Hengeveld (ed.), *Morphology in Functional Discourse Grammar. Working Papers in Functional Grammar* 79, 41–57.

—— and Lier, Eva van (2005), 'The interplay between syntactic and conceptual information: agreement domains in FDG', in J. Lachlan Mackenzie and María de los Ángeles Gómez-González (eds.), *Studies in Functional Discourse Grammar*. Bern: Peter Lang, 83–108.

Dixon, R. M. W. (1988), *A Grammar of Boumaa Fijian*. Chicago, IL and London: University of Chicago Press.

—— (1997), *The Rise and Fall of Languages*. Cambridge: Cambridge University Press.

—— (2000), 'Categories of the noun phrase in Jarawara', *Journal of Linguistics* 36: 487–510.

—— (2004), *The Jarawara Language of Southern Amazonia*. Oxford: Oxford University Press.

—— and Aikhenvald, Alexandra (2002), 'Word: A typological framework', in R. M. W. Dixon and Alexandra Aikhenvald, *Word: A Cross-Linguistic Typology*. Cambridge: Cambridge University Press, 1–41.

Donaldson, Tamsin (1980), *Ngiyambaa*. Cambridge: Cambridge University Press.

Downing, Laura J. (2006), 'The prosody and syntax of focus in Chitumbuka'. *ZAS Papers in Linguistics* 43: 55–79.

Dryer, Matthew S. (1986), 'Primary Objects, Secondary Objects, and Antidative', *Language* 62: 808–45.

—— (2005), 'Determining dominant word order', in Martin Haspelmath, Matthew S. Dryer, David Gil, and Bernard Comrie (eds.), *The World Atlas of Language Structures*. Oxford: Oxford University Press, 371.

—— (2006), 'Descriptive theories, explanatory theories, and basic linguistic theory', in Felix Ameka, Alan Dench, and Nicholas Evans, *Catching Language: The Standard Challenge of Grammar Writing*. Berlin and New York, NY: Mouton de Gruyter, 207–34.

Durie, Mark (1985), *A Grammar of Acehnese: On the Basis of a Dialect of North Aceh* (Verhandelingen van het Koninklijk Instituut voor Taal-, Land- en Volkenkunde 112). Dordrecht and Cinnaminson, NJ: Foris.

Eijk, Jan van (1997), *The Lillooet Language*. Vancouver: UBC Press.

Ekman, Paul, Friesen, Wallace V., and Ellsworth, Phoebe (1972), *Emotion in the Human Face: Guidelines for Research and an Integration of Findings*. New York, NY: Pergamon.

Engelenhoven, Aone van (2004), *Leti, A Language of Soutwest Maluku* (Verhandelingen van het Koninklijk Instituut voor Taal-, Land- en Volkenkunde 211). Leiden: KITLV Press.

Ersen-Rasch, Margarete I. (1980), *Türkisch für Sie: Grammatik*. Munich: Hueber.

Evans, Nicholas D. (1995), *A Grammar of Kayardild: With Historical-Comparative Notes on Tangkic* (Mouton Grammar Library 15). Berlin and New York, NY: Mouton de Gruyter.

Evans, Nicholas D. (2000), 'Kinship verbs', in Petra M. Vogel and Bernard Comrie (eds.), *Approaches to the Typology of Word Classes*. Berlin: Mouton de Gruyter, 103–72.

——(2003), *Bininj Gun-Wok: A Pan-Dialectal Grammar of Mayali, Kunwinjku and Kune*. 2 vols. Canberra: Australian National University.

——and Osada, Toshiki (2005), 'Mundari: The myth of a language without word classes', *Linguistic Typology* 9.3: 351–90.

Everett, Daniel (2005), 'Cultural constraints on grammar and cognition in Pirahã: Another look at the design features of human language', *Current Anthropology* 46.4: 621–46.

——and Kern, Barbara (1997), *Wari': The Pacaas Novos Language of Western Brazil* (Descriptive Grammars). London and New York, NY: Routledge.

Fähnrich, Heinz (1986), *Kurze Grammatik der georgischen Sprache*. Leipzig: Langenscheidt & Verlag Enzyklopädie.

Falk, Yehuda N. (2006), *Subjects and Universal Grammar: An Explanatory Theory* (Cambridge Studies in Linguistics 113). Cambridge: Cambridge University Press.

Falster Jakobsen, Lisbeth (2005), 'Pronominal expression rule ordering in Danish and the question of a discourse grammar', in Casper de Groot and Kees Hengeveld (eds.), *Morphosyntactic Expression in Functional Grammar*. Berlin and New York, NY: Mouton de Gruyter, 503–24.

Faust, Norma (1973), *Lecciones para el aprendizaje del idioma Shipibo-Conibo*. Lima, Peru: Summer Institute of Linguistics and Yarinacocha: Instituto Lingüístico de Verano.

Fawcett, Robin (2000), *A Theory of Syntax for Systemic Functional Linguistics* (Current Issues in Linguistic Theory 206). Amsterdam and Philadelphia, PA: Benjamins.

——(2007), *Alternative Architectures for Systemic Functional Linguistics. How do we Choose?* London: Equinox.

Fischer, Rafael (2007), 'Clause linkage in Cofán (A'ingae)', in W. Leo Wetzels (ed.), *Language Endangerment and Endangered Languages: Linguistic and Anthropological Studies with Special Emphasis on the Languages and Cultures of the Andean-Amazonian Border Area*. Leiden: CNWS, 381–99.

Foley, William A. (1986), *The Papuan Languages of New Guinea*. Cambridge: Cambridge University Press.

——(1991), *The Yimas Language of New Guinea*. Stanford, CA: Stanford University Press.

——(2005), 'Semantic parameters and the unaccusative split in the Austronesian language family', *Studies in Language* 29.2: 385–430.

——and Olson, Mike (1985), 'Clausehood and verb serialization', in Johanna Nichols and Anthony Woodbury (eds.), *Grammar Inside and Outside the Clause*. Cambridge: Cambridge University Press, 17–60.

——and Van Valin Jr, Robert D. (1984), *Functional Syntax and Universal Grammar*. Cambridge: Cambridge University Press.

Fortescue, Michael (1984), *West Greenlandic* (Croom Helm Descriptive Grammars). London, Sydney, and Dover, NH: Croom Helm.

—— (2004), 'The complementarity of the process and pattern interpretations of Functional Grammar', in J. Lachlan Mackenzie and María de los Ángeles Gómez-González (eds.), *A New Architecture for Functional Grammar* (Functional Grammar Series 24). Berlin and New York, NY: Mouton de Gruyter, 151–78.

—— (2007), 'The non-linearity of speech production', in Mike Hannay and Gerard J. Steen (eds.), *Structural-Functional Studies in English Grammar*. Amsterdam and Philadelphia, PA: Benjamins, 337–51.

García Velasco, Daniel (2003), *Funcionalismo y Lingüística: La Gramática Funcional de S. C. Dik*. Oviedo: Universidad de Oviedo.

—— (fc.), 'Conversion in English and its implications for Functional Discourse Grammar'.

—— and Hengeveld, Kees (2002), 'Do we need predicate frames?', in Ricardo Mairal Usón and María Jesús Pérez Quintero (eds.), *New Perspectives on Argument Structure in Functional Grammar* (Functional Grammar Series 25). Berlin: Mouton de Gruyter, 95–123.

García Velasco, Daniel and Rijkhoff, Jan N. M. (eds.) (2008), *The Noun Phrase in Functional Discoverse Grammar* (Trends in Linguistics 195). Berlin: Mouton de Gruyter.

Gårding, Eva (1998), 'Intonation in Swedish', in Daniel Hirst and Albert Di Cristo (eds.), *Intonation Systems: A Survey of Twenty Languages*. Cambridge: Cambridge University Press, 112–30.

Geerts, Guido, Haeseryn, Walter, Rooij, Jaap de, and Toorn, M. C. van der (1984), *Algemene Nederlandse Spraakkunst*. Groningen: Wolters-Noordhoff.

Geluykens, Roland (1987), 'Tails (right-dislocation) as a repair mechanism in English conversation', in Jan Nuyts and Georges de Schutter (eds.), *Getting One's Words into Line*. Dordrecht: Foris, 119–29.

Genee, Inge (1998), *Sentential Complementation in a Functional Grammar of Irish*. Utrecht: LOT.

Gernsbacher, Morton Ann (1990), *Language Comprehension as Structure-Building*. Hillsdale, NJ: Erlbaum.

Geuder, Wilhelm (2000), 'Oriented adverbs: Issues in the lexical semantics of event adverbs'. Ph.D. thesis, Universität Tübingen. Available as <http://w210.ub.uni-tuebingen.de/dbt/volltexte/2002/546/pdf/geuder-oriadverbs.pdf>.

Givón, Talmy (1984), *Syntax: A Functional-Typological Introduction*. Amsterdam and Philadelphia, PA: Benjamins.

—— (1995), *Functionalism and Grammar*. Amsterdam and Philadelphia, PA: Benjamins.

—— (2002), *Biolinguistics: The Santa Barbara Lectures*. Amsterdam and Philadelphia, PA: Benjamins.

Goedemans, Rob and Hulst, Harry van der (2005a), 'Fixed stress locations', in Martin Haspelmath, Matthew S. Dryer, David Gil, and Bernard Comrie (eds.), *The World Atlas of Language Structures*. Oxford: Oxford University Press, 62–5.

—— —— (2005b), 'Weight factors in weight-sensitive stress systems', in Martin Haspelmath, Matthew S. Dryer, David Gil, and Bernard Comrie (eds.), *The World Atlas of Language Structures*. Oxford: Oxford University Press, 70–3.

Goedemans, Rob and Hulst, Harry van der (2005c), 'Weight-sensitive stress', in Martin Haspelmath, Matthew S. Dryer, David Gil, and Bernard Comrie (eds.), *The World Atlas of Language Structures*. Oxford: Oxford University Press, 66–9.

———— (2005d), 'Rhythm types', in Martin Haspelmath, Matthew S. Dryer, David Gil, and Bernard Comrie (eds.), *The World Atlas of Language Structures*. Oxford: Oxford University Press, 74–7.

Golla, Victor (1985), *A Short Practical Grammar of Hupa*. Hoopa Valley: Hupa Language Program.

Golumbia, David (2004), 'The interpretation of nonconfigurationality', *Language and Communication* 24: 1–22.

Gómez Soliño, José S. (1995), 'Texto e contexto en la teoría de la Gramática Funcional', *Revista de Lenguas para Fines Específicos* 2: 199–216.

Gonçalves, Sebastião Carlos Leite (2003), 'Gramaticalização, modalidade epistémica e evidencialidade: Um estudo de caso no português do Brasil'. Ph.D. dissertation, Universidade Estadual de Campinas, SP, Brazil.

Gonzálvez García, Francisco and Butler, Christopher S. (2006), 'Mapping functional-cognitive space', *Annual Review of Cognitive Linguistics* 4: 39–96.

Goossens, Louis (1987), 'The auxiliarisation of the English modals', in Martin Harris and Paolo Ramat (eds.), *Historical Development of the Auxiliaries*. Berlin: Mouton de Gruyter, 111–43.

Gordon, Lynn (1986), 'The development of evidentials in Maricopa', in Wallace L. Chafe and Johanna Nichols (eds.), *Evidentiality: The Linguistic Encoding of Epis temology*. Norwood, NJ: Ablex, 75–88.

Gordon, Matthew K. (2005), 'Intonational phonology of Chickasaw', in Sun-Ah Jun (ed.), *Prosodic Typology: The Phonology of Intonation and Phrasing*. Oxford: Oxford University Press, 301–30.

Greenberg, Joseph H. (1978), 'How does a language acquire gender markers?', in Joseph H. Greenberg, Charles A. Ferguson, and Edith A. Moravcsik (eds.), *Universals of Human Language. Vol. 3: Word Structure*. Stanford: Stanford University Press, 48–82.

Gronemeyer, Claire (1997), 'Evidentiality in Lithuanian', *Working Papers* 46, Lund: Institutionen för Lingvistik, Lunds Universitet, Sweden, 93–112.

Groot, Casper de (1981), 'Sentence-intertwining in Hungarian', in A. Machtelt Bolkestein, Henk A. Combé, Simon C. Dik, Casper de Groot, Jadranka Gvozdanović, Albert Rijksbaron, and Co Vet, *Predication and Expression in Functional Grammar*. London: Academic Press, 41–62.

———— (1989), *Predicate Structure in a Functional Grammar of Hungarian* (Functional Grammar Series 11). Dordrecht: Foris.

———— (2000), 'The absentive', in Östen Dahl (ed.), *Tense and Aspect in the Languages of Europe*. Berlin: Mouton de Gruyter, 641–67.

Groot, Casper de and Hengeveld, Kees (eds.) (2005), *Morphosyntactic Expression in Functional Grammar* (Functional Grammar Series 27). Berlin and New York, NY: Mouton de Gruyter.

Groot, Casper de and Limburg, Machiel (1986), 'Pronominal elements: Diachrony, typology, and formalization in Functional Grammar'. *Working Papers in Functional Grammar* 12.

Haacke, Wilfrid H. G. (2006), 'Syntactic focus marking in Khoekhoe ("Nama/Damara")', *ZAS Papers in Linguistics* 46: 105–27.

Hagman, Roy Stephen (1973), 'Nama Hottentot Grammar'. Ph.D. dissertation, Columbia University.

Hale, Kenneth L. (1983), 'Warlpiri and the grammar of non-configurational languages', *Natural Language and Linguistic Theory* 1: 5–47.

Halliday, Michael A. K. (1970), 'Functional diversity in language, as seen from a consideration of modality and mood in English', *Foundations of Language* 6: 322–61.

—— (1985), *An Introduction to Functional Grammar*, London, Victoria, and Baltimore, MD: Edward Arnold.

—— (1994), 'Systemic theory', in Ronald E. Asher and J. M. Y. Simpson (eds.), *The Encyclopedia of Language and Linguistics*. Oxford: Pergamon Press, 4505–8.

—— and Matthiessen, Christian M. I. M. (2004), *An Introduction to Functional Grammar* (3rd revised edition of Halliday 1985). London: Hodder Arnold.

Hannay, Mike (1985), *English Existentials in Functional Grammar* (Functional Grammar Series 3). Dordrecht: Foris.

—— (1991), 'Pragmatic function assignment and word order variation in a Functional Grammar of English', *Journal of Pragmatics* 16: 131–55.

—— and Kroon, Caroline (2005), 'Acts and the relationship between grammar and discourse', *Functions of Language* 12.1: 87–124.

—— and Martínez-Caro, Elena (2008), 'Last things first? A FDG approach to clause-final Focus constituents in English and Spanish', in María A. Gómez-González, J. Lachlan Mackenzie, and Elsa González-Álvarez (eds.), *Languages and Cultures in Contrast and Comparison*. Amsterdam and Philadelphia, PA: Benjamins, 33–68.

—— and Vester, Elseline (1987), 'Non-restrictive relatives and the representation of complex sentences', in Johan van der Auwera and Louis Goossens (eds.), *Ins and Outs of the Predication* (Functional Grammar Series 6). Dordrecht and Providence, RI: Foris, 39–52.

Haraguchi, Shosuke (1977), *The Tone Pattern of Japanese: An Autosegmental Theory of Tonology*. Tokyo: Kaitakusha.

Harbour, Daniel (2003), 'The Kiowa case for feature insertion'. *Natural Language and Linguistic Theory* 21: 543–78.

Harder, Peter (1996), *Functional Semantics: A Theory of Meaning, Structure and Tense in English* (Trends in Linguistics Studies and Monographs 87). Berlin and New York, NY: Mouton de Gruyter.

—— (2004), 'Comment clauses, Functional Discourse Grammar and the grammar–discourse interface', in J. Lachlan Mackenzie and María de los Ángeles Gómez-González (eds.), *A New Architecture for Functional Grammar*. Berlin and New York, NY: Mouton de Gruyter: 197–210.

—— (2007), 'Grammar, flow and procedural knowledge: Structure and function at the interface between grammar and discourse', in Mike Hannay and Gerard J. Steen (eds.), *Structural-Functional Studies in English Grammar*. Amsterdam and Philadelphia, PA: Benjamins, 309–35.

Harris, Alice Carmichael (1981), *Georgian Syntax: A Study in Relational Grammar* (Cambridge Studies in Linguistics 33). Cambridge: Cambridge University Press.

Harrison, Sheldon P. (1976), *Mokilese Reference Grammar*. With the assistance of Salich Y. Albert. Honolulu, HI: The University Press of Hawaii.

Haspelmath, Martin (1993), *A grammar of Lezgian* (Mouton Grammar Library 9). Berlin: Mouton de Gruyter.

—— (1996), 'Word-class-changing inflection and morphological theory', in Geert Booij and Jaap van Marle (eds.), *Yearbook of Morphology 1995*. Dordrecht: Kluwer, 43–66.

—— (1997), *Indefinite Pronouns* (Oxford Studies in Typology and Linguistic Theory). Oxford: Oxford University Press.

—— (2002), *Understanding Morphology* (Understanding Language Series). London: Arnold.

—— (2007), 'Ditransitive alignment splits and inverse alignment', *Functions of Language* 14.1: 79–102.

Hattnher, Marize M. D. and Hengeveld, Kees (eds.) (2007), *Advances in Functional Discourse Grammar. Alfa—Revista de Lingüística* 51.2.

Haude, Katharina (2006), 'A Grammar of Movima'. Ph.D. dissertation, Radboud University Nijmegen.

Hausa Online Grammar. Available at <http://www.humnet.ucla.edu/humnet/aflang/Hausa/Hausa_online_grammar/grammar_frame.html>.

Hayes, Bruce (1989), 'The prosodic hierarchy in meter', in Paul Kiparsky and Gilbert Youmans (eds.), *Rhythm and Meter*. Orlando, FL: Academic Press, 201–60.

Heath, Jeffrey (1984), *Functional Grammar of Nunggubuyu*. Canberra: Australian Institute of Aboriginal Studies.

—— (1986), 'Syntactic and lexical aspects of nonconfigurationality in Nunggubuyu (Australia)', *Natural Language and Linguistic Theory* 4: 375–408.

Hengeveld, Kees (1989), 'Layers and operators in Functional Grammar', *Journal of Linguistics* 25.1: 127–57.

—— (1992), *Non-Verbal Predication: Theory, Typology, Diachrony* (Functional Grammar Series 15). Berlin and New York, NY: Mouton de Gruyter.

—— (1997), 'Cohesion in Functional Grammar', in Christopher S. Butler, John H. Connolly, Richard A. Gatward, and Roel M. Vismans (eds.), *Discourse and Pragmatics in Functional Grammar* (Functional Grammar Series 18). Berlin: Mouton de Gruyter, 1–16.

—— (1998), 'Adverbial clauses in the languages of Europe', in Johan van der Auwera (ed.), *Adverbial Constructions in the Languages of Europe* (Empirical Approaches to Language Typology/Eurotyp 20–3). Berlin: Mouton de Gruyter, 335–419.

—— (2000), 'The architecture of a Functional Discourse Grammar'. Paper presented at the Ninth International Conference on Functional Grammar, Madrid.

—— (2004a), 'The architecture of a Functional Discourse Grammar', in J. Lachlan Mackenzie and María A. Gómez-González (eds.), *A New Architecture for Functional Grammar* (Functional Grammar Series 24). Berlin: Mouton de Gruyter, 1–21.

——(2004b), 'Epilogue', in J. Lachlan Mackenzie and María A. Gómez-González (eds.), *A New Architecture for Functional Grammar* (Functional Grammar Series 24). Berlin: Mouton de Gruyter, 365–78.

——(2004c), 'Mood and modality', in Geert Booij, Christian Lehmann, and Joachim Mugdan (eds.), *Morphology: A Handbook on Inflection and Word Formation*, Vol. 2. Berlin: Mouton de Gruyter, 1190–202.

——(2004d), 'State-of-Affairs concepts', in Geert Booij, Christian Lehmann, and Joachim Mugdan (eds.), *Morphology: A Handbook on Inflection and Word Formation*, Vol. 2. Berlin: Mouton de Gruyter, 1104–11.

——(2008), 'The noun phrase in Functional Discourse Grammar', in Daniel García Velasco and Jan Rijkhoff (eds.), *The Noun Phrase in Functional Discourse Grammar* (Trends in Linguistics). Berlin: Mouton de Gruyter.

——and Heesakkers, Tanna (n.d.), 'Valency in Functional Discourse Grammar'. Unpublished paper, University of Amsterdam.

——and Lier, Eva van (2008), 'Parts of speech and dependent clauses in Functional Discourse Grammar'. *Studies in Language* 32.3: 753–85.

——and Mackenzie, J. Lachlan (2005), 'Interpersonal functions, representational categories, and syntactic templates in Functional Discourse Grammar', in María A. Gómez-González and J. Lachlan Mackenzie (eds.), *Studies in Functional Discourse Grammar* (Linguistic Insights 26). Bern: Peter Lang, 9–27.

————(2006), 'Functional Discourse Grammar', in Keith Brown (ed.), *Encyclopedia of Language and Linguistics*. 2nd edition, vol. 4. Oxford: Elsevier, 668–76.

————(fc.), 'Functional Discourse Grammar', in Bernd Heine and Heiko Narrog (eds.), *The Oxford Handbook of Linguistic Analysis*. Oxford: Oxford University Press.

——Nazareth Bechara, Eli, Gomes Camacho, Roberto, Regina Guerra, Alessandra, Peres de Oliveira, Taísa, Penhavel, Eduardo, Goreti Pezatti, Erotilde, Santana, Liliane, Rosa Francisco de Souza, Edson, and de Sousa Teixeira, Maria Luiza (2007), 'Basic illocutions in the native languages of Brazil', in Marize Hattnher and Kees Hengeveld (eds.), *Advances in Functional Discourse Grammar. Alfa—Revista de Lingüística* 51.2: 73–90.

——Rijkhoff, Jan, and Siewierska, Anna (2004), 'Parts-of-speech systems and word order', *Journal of Linguistics* 40.3: 527–70.

——and Wanders, Gerry (2007), 'Adverbial conjunctions in Functional Discourse Grammar', in Mike Hannay and Gerard J. Steen (eds.), *Structural-Functional Studies in English Grammar: In Honour of Lachlan Mackenzie* (Studies in Language Companion Series 83). Amsterdam and Philadelphia, PA: Benjamins, 209–26.

——and Wanders, Gerry (eds.) (fc.), *Semantic representation in Functional Discourse Grammar*. Special issue of *Lingua*.

Hewitt, Brian G. (1979), *Abkhaz* (Lingua Descriptive Studies 2). Amsterdam: North-Holland.

Himmelmann, Nikolaus P. (2004), 'Tagalog', in Geert Booij, Christian Lehmann, Joachim Mugdan, and Stavros Skopeteas (eds.), *Morphology: A Handbook on Inflection and Word Formation*, Vol. 2. Berlin: Mouton de Gruyter, 1473–90.

Himmelmann, Nikolaus P. (2005), 'Tagalog', in Karl Alexander Adelaar and Nikolaus P. Himmelmann (eds.), *The Austronesian Languages of Asia and Madagascar*. London: Routledge, 350–76.

—— (fc.), 'Lexical categories and voice in Tagalog', in Simon Musgrave and Peter K. Austin (eds.), *Voice and Grammatical Functions in Austronesian Languages*. CSLI Publications, Center for the Study of Language and Information, Stanford University, California.

—— and Schulze-Berndt, Eva (2006), 'Issues in the syntax and semantics of participant-oriented adjuncts' in Nikolaus Himmelmann and Eva Schulze-Berndt (eds.), *Secondary Predication and Adverbial Modification: The Typology of Depictives*. Oxford: Oxford University Press, 1–27.

Hinds, John (1986), *Japanese* (Croom Helm Descriptive Grammars). London, Sydney, and Dover, NH: Croom Helm.

Hirst, Daniel (1998), 'Intonation in British English', in Daniel Hirst and Albert Di Cristo (eds.), *Intonation Systems: A Survey of Twenty Languages*. Cambridge: Cambridge University Press, 56–77.

—— and Di Cristo, Albert (1998), 'A survey of intonation systems', in Daniel Hirst and Albert Di Cristo (eds.), *Intonation Systems: A Survey of Twenty Languages*. Cambridge: Cambridge University Press, 1–44.

Hoo Ling Soh (2001), 'The syntax and semantics of phonological phrasing in Shanghai and Hokkien', *Journal of East Asian Linguistics* 10: 37–80.

Hopper, Paul (1987), 'Emergent grammar', *Berkeley Linguistics Society* 13: 139–57

Hsieh, Fuhui and Huang, Shuanfan (2006), 'The pragmatics of case marking in Saisiyat', *Oceanic Linguistics* 45.1: 91–109.

Hualde, José Ignacio and Urbina, Jon Ortiz de (eds.) (2003), *A Grammar of Basque* (Mouton Grammar Library 26). Berlin and New York, NY: Mouton de Gruyter.

Hundius, Harald and Kölver, Ulrike (1983), 'Syntax and semantics of numeral classifiers in Thai', *Studies in Language* 7.2: 97–132.

Huttar, George L. and Huttar, Mary L. (1994), *Ndyuka* (Descriptive Grammars). London and New York, NY: Routledge.

Jackendoff, Ray (2002), *Foundations of Language: Brain, Meaning, Grammar, Evolution*. Oxford: Oxford University Press.

Jadir, Mohamed (2005), 'Marqueurs de discours et cohérence de discours: les cas de *car, parce que* et *puisque*', *Hermès* 34: 169–97.

Jakobson, Roman (1971), 'Shifters, verbal categories, and the Russian verb', in *Selected Writings*, Vol. 2. The Hague: Mouton, 130–47.

Jansen, Bert, Koopman, Hilda, and Muysken, Pieter (1978), 'Serial verbs in Creole languages', *Amsterdam Creole Studies* 2: 125–59.

Jun, Sun-Ah (2005), 'Prosodic typology' in Sun-Ah Jun (ed.), *Prosodic Typology: The Phonology of Intonation and Phrasing*. Oxford: Oxford University Press, 430–58.

—— and Fougeron, Cécile (2000), 'A phonological model of French intonation', in Antonis Botinis (ed.), *Intonation: Analysis, Modeling and Technology*. Dordrecht: Kluwer Academic, 209–42.

Junger, Judith (1981), 'Copula constructions in Modern Hebrew', in Teun Hoekstra, Harry van der Hulst, and Michael Moortgat (eds.), *Perspectives on Functional Grammar*. Dordrecht: Foris, 117–34.

Kabak, Barış and Vogel, Irene (2001), 'The phonological word and stress assignment in Turkish', *Phonology* 18: 315–60.

Kahr, Joan Casper (1975), 'Adpositions and locationals: Typology and diachronic development', *Working Papers in Language Universals* 19: 21–54.

Kahrel, Peter (1987), 'On zero terms and negative polarity', in Johan van der Auwera and Louis Goossens (eds.), *Ins and Outs of the Predication* (Functional Grammar Series 6). Dordrecht: Foris, 67–76.

Kay, Paul, Berlin, Brent, Maffi, Luisa, and Merrifield, William (1997), 'Color naming across languages', in C. L. Hardin and Luisa Maffi (eds.), *Color Categories in Thought and Language*. Cambridge: Cambridge University Press, 21–58.

Keenan, Edward (1976), 'Towards a universal definition of "subject" ', in Charles N. Li (ed.), *Subject and Topic*. New York, NY: Academic Press.

Keijzer, Merel (2007), *Last In First Out? An Investigation of the Regression Hypothesis in Dutch Emigrants in Anglophone Canada*. Utrecht: LOT.

Keizer, M. Evelien (1992), 'Predicates as referring expressions', in Michael Fortescue, Peter Harder, and Lars Kristoffersen (eds.), *Layered Structure and Reference in a Functional Perspective* (Pragmatics & Beyond New Series 23). Amsterdam: Benjamins, 1–28.

—— (2007), *The English Noun Phrase: The Nature of Linguistic Classification* (Studies in English Language). Cambridge: Cambridge University Press.

Kenesei, István, Vago, Robert M., and Fenyvesi, Anna (1998), *Hungarian* (Descriptive Grammars). London and New York, NY: Routledge.

Koptjevskaja-Tamm, Maria (1993), *Nominalizations*. London: Routledge.

Kornfilt, Jaklin (1997), *Turkish* (Descriptive Grammars). London: Routledge.

Kouwenberg, Silvia (1994), *A Grammar of Berbice Dutch Creole* (Mouton Grammar Library 12). Berlin: Mouton de Gruyter.

Kracht, Marcus (2004), 'Language and space', Unpublished paper, Department of Linguistics, UCLA.

Kratochvil, Paul (1998), 'Intonation in Beijing Chinese', in Daniel Hirst and Albert Di Cristo (eds.), *Intonation Systems: A Survey of Twenty Languages*. Cambridge: Cambridge University Press, 417–31.

Krejnovič, E. A. (1937), *Fonetika nivxskogo (giljackogo) jazyka* [Nivkh phonetics]. Moscow and Leningrad: Institut Narodov Severa.

Kristoffersen, Lars (1992), 'Derivation and inflection in a functional grammar of West Greenlandic', in Michael Fortescue, Peter Harder, and Lars Kristoffersen (eds.), *Layered Structure and Reference in a Functional Perspective* (Pragmatics and Beyond New Series 23). Amsterdam: Benjamins, 143–71.

Kroon, Caroline (1995), *Discourse Particles in Latin* (Amsterdam Studies in Classical Philology 4). Amsterdam: Gieben.

LaPolla, Randy (2006), 'Nominalization in Rawang'. Unpublished paper. Available at <http://victoria.linguistlist.org/~lapolla/nw/RawangNominalization.pdf>.

Lee, Chungmin (1999), 'Topic, contrastive topic and focus: What's on our minds'. Available at <http://www.mind.sccs.chukyo-u.ac.jp/jcss/ICCS/99/olp/pt1/pt1.htm>.

Lee, Sun-Hee (2001), 'Argument Composition and Linearization: Korean Complex Predicates and Scrambling', *Ohio State University Working Papers in Linguistics* 56: 53–78.

Lefebvre, Claire and Brousseau, Anne-Marie (2002), *A Grammar of Fongbe* (Mouton Grammar Library 25). Berlin and New York, NY: Mouton de Gruyter.

Legate, Julie Anne (2003), 'The configurational structure of a nonconfigurational language', in Pierre Pica (ed.), *Linguistic Variation Yearbook, Vol. 1 (2001)*. Amsterdam and Philadelphia, PA: Benjamins, 61–104.

Levelt, Willem J. M. (1989), *Speaking*. Cambridge, MA: MIT Press.

Levinson, Stephen C. (1983), *Pragmatics*. Cambridge: Cambridge University Press.

——(1997), 'From outer to inner space: Linguistic categories and non-linguistic thinking', in Jan Nuyts and Eric Pederson (eds.), *Language and Conceptualization*. Cambridge: Cambridge University Press: 13–45.

Lewis, G. L. (1967), *Turkish Grammar*. Oxford: Clarendon.

Li, Charles N. and Thompson, Sandra A. (1981), *Mandarin Chinese: A Functional Reference Grammar*. Berkeley, CA, Los Angeles, CA, and London: University of California Press.

Lier, Eva van (2005), 'The explanatory power of typological hierarchies: Developmental perspectives on non-verbal predication', in Casper de Groot and Kees Hengeveld (eds.), *Morphosyntactic Expression in Functional Grammar*. Berlin and New York, NY: Mouton de Gruyter, 249–80.

Lucy, John A. (1992), *Grammatical Categories and Cognition: A Case Study of the Linguistic Relativity Hypothesis* (Studies in the Social and Cultural Foundations of Language 13). Cambridge: Cambridge University Press.

Lucy, John A. (ed.) (1993), *Reflexive Language: Reported Speech and Metapragmatics*. Cambridge: Cambridge University Press.

Lyons, John (1977), *Semantics*. 2 vols. Cambridge: Cambridge University Press.

——(1989), 'Semantic ascent: A neglected aspect of syntactic typology', in Doug Arnold, Martin Atkinson, Jacques Durand, Claire Grover, and Louise Sadler (eds.), *Essays on Grammatical Theory and Universal Grammar*. Oxford: Clarendon Press, 153–86.

MacDonald, Lorna (1990), *A Grammar of Tauya* (Mouton Grammar Library 6). Berlin and New York, NY: Mouton de Gruyter.

Mackenzie, J. Lachlan (1983), 'Nominal predicates in a Functional Grammar of English', in Simon C. Dik (ed.), *Advances in Functional Grammar* (Publications in Linguistic Science 11). Dordrecht: Foris, 31–51.

——(1987a), 'Nominalization and basic constituent ordering', in Johan van der Auwera and Louis Goossens (eds.), *Ins and Outs of the Predication*. Dordrecht: Foris, 93–105.

——(1987b), 'The representation of nominal predicates in the fund', *Working Papers in Functional Grammar* 25.

—— (1992), 'Places and things', in Michael Fortescue, Peter Harder, and Lars Kristoffersen (eds.), *Layered Structure and Reference in a Functional Perspective*. Amsterdam: Benjamins, 253–76.

—— (1996), 'English nominalizations in the layered model of the sentence', in Betty Devriendt, Louis Goossens, and Johan van der Auwera (eds.), *Complex Structures: A Functionalist Perspective*. Berlin: Mouton de Gruyter, 325–55.

—— (1997), 'Grammar, discourse and knowledge: The use of *such* in written English', in Jan Aarts, Inge de Mönnick, and Herman Wekker (eds.), *Studies in English Language and Teaching: In Honour of Flor Aarts*. Amsterdam: Rodopi, 85–105.

—— (1998a), 'On referring to manners', in Johan van der Auwera, Frank Durieux, and Ludo Lejeune (eds.), *English as a Human Language*. Munich: Lincom, 241–51.

—— (1998b), 'The basis of syntax in the holophrase', in Mike Hannay and A. Machtelt Bolkestein (eds.), *Functional Grammar and Verbal Interaction*. Amsterdam and Philadelphia, PA: Benjamins, 267–95.

—— (2000), 'First things first: Towards an Incremental Functional Grammar', *Acta Linguistica Hafniensia* 32: 23–44.

—— (2001), 'Adverbs and adpositions: The Cinderella categories of Functional Grammar', *Revista Canaria de Estudios Ingleses* 42: 119–35.

—— (2004a), 'Incremental Functional Grammar and the language of football commentary', *British and American Studies* 10: 237–48.

—— (2004b), 'Functional Discourse Grammar and language production', in J. Lachlan Mackenzie and María A. Gómez-González (eds.), *A New Architecture for Functional Grammar*, Berlin and New York, NY: Mouton de Gruyter, 179–95.

—— (2004c), 'Entity concepts', in Geert Booij, Christian Lehmann, Joachim Mugdan, and Stavros Skopeteas (eds.), *Morphology: A Handbook on Inflection and Word Formation*, Vol. 2. Berlin: Mouton de Gruyter, 973–82.

—— (fc.a), 'The contrast between pronoun position in European Portuguese and Castilian Spanish: An application of Functional Grammar', in María A. Gómez-González, J. Lachlan Mackenzie, and Elsa González-Álvarez (eds.), *Current Trends in Contrastive Linguistics: Functional and Cognitive Perspectives*. Amsterdam and Philadelphia, PA: Benjamins.

—— (fc.b), 'Investigating the inventory of semantic categories in Functional Discourse Grammar: Content interrogatives in a sample of 50 languages'.

Mackenzie, J. Lachlan and Gómez-González, María de los Ángeles (eds.) (2004), *A New Architecture for Functional Grammar* (Functional Grammar Series 24). Berlin: Mouton de Gruyter.

—— —— (eds.) (2005), *Studies in Functional Discourse Grammar* (Linguistic Insights 26). Berne, Berlin, Brussels, Frankfurt a. M., New York, Oxford, and Vienna: Peter Lang.

Mackenzie, J. Lachlan and Hannay, Mike (1982), 'Predicational predicates and focus constructions in a Functional Grammar of English', *Lingua*, 56: 43–57.

—— and Keizer, M. Evelien (1991), 'On assigning pragmatic functions in English', *Pragmatics* 1: 169–215.

Maddieson, Ian (2005a), 'Syllable structure', in Martin Haspelmath, Matthew S. Dryer, David Gil, and Bernard Comrie (eds.), *The World Atlas of Language Structures*. Oxford: Oxford University Press, 54–7.

—— (2005b), 'Tone', in Martin Haspelmath, Matthew S. Dryer, David Gil, and Bernard Comrie (eds.), *The World Atlas of Language Structures*. Oxford: Oxford University Press, 58–61.

Mahootian, Shahrzad (1997), *Persian* (Descriptive Grammars). With the assistance of Lewis Gebhardt. London: Routledge.

Malchukov, Andrej (2004), *Nominalization/Verbalization. Constraining a Typology of Transcategorial Operations*. Munich: LINCOM Europa.

Maslova, Elena (2003), *A Grammar of Kolyma Yukaghir* (Mouton Grammar Library 27), Berlin and New York, NY: Mouton de Gruyter.

Matsumoto, Yo (2003), 'Typologies of lexicalization patterns and event integration: Clarifications and reformulations', in Shui Chiba *et al.* (eds.), *Empirical and Theoretical Investigations into Language: A Festschrift for Majaru Kajita*, Tokyo: Kaitakusha, 403–18.

Matthews, George Hubert (1965), *Hidatsa Syntax*. The Hague: Mouton.

Mattissen, Johanna (2003), *Dependent-Head Synthesis in Nivkh: A Contribution to a Typology of Polysynthesis* (Typological Studies in Language 57). Amsterdam: Benjamins.

—— (2004), 'Structural types of complex noun forms', in Waldfried Premper (ed.), *Dimensionen und Kontinua: Beiträge zu Hansjakob Seilers Universalienforschung*. Berlin: Akademie Verlag, 35–56.

—— (2006), 'The ontology and diachrony of polysynthesis', in Dieter Wunderlich (ed.), *Advances in the Theory of the Lexicon*. Berlin: Mouton de Gruyter, 287–353.

McLendon, Sally (2003), 'Evidentials in Eastern Pomo with a comparative survey of the category in other Pomoan languages', in Alexandra Y. Aikhenvald and R. M. W. Dixon (eds.), *Studies in Evidentiality* (Typological Studies in Language 54). Amsterdam and Philadelphia, PA: Benjamins, 101–29.

Meyer, Roland and Mleinek, Ina (2006), 'How prosody signals force and focus: A study of pitch accents in Russian yes-no questions', *Journal of Pragmatics* 38: 1615–35.

Milićević, Jasmina (2004), 'Linear placement of clitics and syntactic dependencies (Serbian Second-Position Clitics)'. *Dialog-21* <http://www.dialog-21.ru/Archive/2004/Milicevich.htm>.

Miller, Amy (2001), *A Grammar of Jamul Tiipay*. Berlin and New York, NY: Mouton de Gruyter.

Miller, Jim and Weinert, Regina (1998), *Spontaneous Spoken Language: Syntax and Discourse*. Oxford: Clarendon.

Miller, Marion (1999), *Desano Grammar* (Studies in the Languages of Colombia 6). Arlington: Summer Institute of Linguistics.

Miller, Philip H. and Sag, Ivan A. (1997), 'French Clitic Movement without Clitics or Movement', *Natural Language and Linguistic Theory* 15: 573–639.

Milner, G. B. (1972), *Fijian Grammar*. 3rd edition. Suva, Fiji: Government Press.

Mithun-Williams, Marianne (1984), 'The evolution of noun incorporation', *Language* 60.4: 847–94.

Montreuil, Jean-Pierre (2002), 'Vestigial feet in French', Unpublished paper, University of Texas at Austin, Austin TX. Available at <http://uts.cc.utexas.edu/~tls/2002tls/Jean-Pierre_Montreuil.pdf>.

Mortensen, David (2002), '*Semper Infidelis*: Anti-identity in A-Hmao and Jingpho tone sandhi chains'. Available at <http://socrates.berkeley.edu/~dmort/semper_infidelis.pdf>.

Mosel, Ulrike and Hovdhaugen, Even (1992), *Samoan Reference Grammar* (Instituttet for Sammenlignende Kulturforskning B85). Oslo: Scandinavian University Press.

Moutaouakil, Ahmed (1989), *Pragmatic Functions in a Functional Grammar of Arabic* (Functional Grammar Series, 8). Dordrecht: Foris.

—— (2004), 'Function-independent morpho-syntax', in Henk Aertsen, Mike Hannay, and Rod Lyall (eds.), *Words in their Places: A Festschrift for J. Lachlan Mackenzie*, Amsterdam: Vrije Universiteit Amsterdam, 143–51.

—— (2005), 'Exclamation: sentence type, illocution or modality', in Casper de Groot and Kees Hengeveld (eds.), *Morphosyntactic Expression in Functional Grammar*. Berlin and New York, NY: Mouton de Gruyter, 351–79.

Munro, Pamela and Gordon, Lynn (1982), 'Syntactic relations in Western Muskogean', *Language* 58: 81–115.

Nagano-Madsen, Yasuko and Bredvad-Jensen, Anne-Christine (1995), 'Analysis of intonational phrasing in West Greenlandic Eskimo reading text'. *Working Papers* 44: 129–44. Department of Linguistics and Phonetics, Lund University.

Nagaya, Naonori (2006), 'Information structure and constituent structure in Tagalog', *Language and Linguistics* 8: 343–72.

Nater, Hank F. (1984), *The Bella Coola Language* (Mercury series; Canadian Ethnology Service 92). Ottawa: National Museums of Canada.

Nedergaard Thomsen, Ole (2005), 'Direction diathesis and obviation in Functional Grammar: The case of the inverse in Mapudungun, an indigenous language of south central Chile', in Casper de Groot and Kees Hengeveld (eds.), *Morphosyntactic Expression in Functional Grammar*. Berlin and New York, NY: Mouton de Gruyter, 447–82.

Nedjalkov, Igor (1997), *Evenki* (Descriptive Grammars). London and New York, NY: Routledge.

Nespor, Marina and Vogel, Irene (1986), *Prosodic Phonology*. Dordrecht and Riverton, NJ: Foris.

Newmeyer, Frederick J. (2003), 'Grammar is grammar and usage is usage', *Language* 79: 682–707.

Nichols, Johanna (1986), 'Head-marking and dependent-marking grammar', *Language* 62: 56–119.

—— (1994), 'Chechen', in Rieks Smeets (ed.), *The Indigenous Languages of the Caucasus. Volume 4: North East Caucasian Languages*. Delmar, NY: Caravan Books, 1–77.

Noonan, Michael (1992), *A Grammar of Lango* (Mouton Grammar Library 7). Berlin: Mouton de Gruyter.

Olbertz, Hella (1998), *Verbal Periphrases in a Functional Grammar of Spanish*. Berlin and New York, NY: Mouton de Gruyter.

Olpp, J. (1977), *Nama-grammatika*. Soos verwerk deur H. J. Krüger. Windhoek: Inboorling-Taalburo van die Departement van Bantoe-Onderwijs.

Olson, Michael L. (1981), 'Barai Clause Junctures: Toward a Functional Theory of Inter-Clausal Relations'. Ph.D. dissertation, Australian National University.

Otaina, G. A. (1978), *Kačestvennye glagoly v nivxskom jazyke* [Nivkh verbs denoting quality and property]. Moscow: Nauka.

Palmer, Frank R. (1986), *Mood and Modality*. Cambridge: Cambridge University Press.

Pandharipande, Rajeshwari V. (1997), *Marathi* (Descriptive Grammars). London and New York, NY: Routledge.

Pantcheva, Marina (2006), 'Persian preposition classes', Unpublished paper, University of Tromsø, <http://www.hum.uit.no/mra/HOs/V2006/4PersianPs.pdf>.

Parks, Douglas R. (1976), *A Grammar of Pawnee*. New York, NY: Garland.

Payne, Doris L. (1990), *The Pragmatics of Word Order: Typological Dimensions of Verb-Initial Languages*. Berlin: Mouton de Gruyter.

Pederson, Eric and Nuyts, Jan (1997), 'On the relationship between language and conceptualization', in Jan Nuyts and Eric Pederson (eds.), *Language and Conceptualization*. Cambridge: Cambridge University Press: 1–12.

Peperkamp, Sharon (1997), *Prosodic Words*. The Hague: Holland Academic Graphics.

Pérez Quintero, María Jesús (2002), *Adverbial Subordination in English: A Functional Approach*. Amsterdam and New York, NY: Rodopi.

Pinkster, Harm (2004), 'Attitudinal and illocutionary satellites in Latin', in Henk Aertsen, Mike Hannay, and Rod Lyall (eds.), *Words in their Places: A Festschrift for J. Lachlan Mackenzie*. Amsterdam: Vrije Universiteit Amsterdam, 191–8.

Polanyi, Livia and Scha, Remko (1983), 'On the recursive structure of discourse', in Konrad Ehlich and Henk Van Riemsdijk (eds.), *Connectedness in Sentence, Discourse and Text*, Tilburg: Tilburg University, 141–78.

Pultr, Alois (1960), *Lehrbuch der Koreanischen Sprache*. Halle (Saale): VEB Max Niemeyer.

Pym, Noreen with Bonnie Larrimore (1979), *Papers on Iwaidja Phonology and Grammar* (Working Papers of SIL-AAB A2). Darwin: Summer Institute of Linguistics.

Ramirez, Henri (1997), *A fala Tukano dos ye'pa-masa, tome 1: Gramática*. Manaus: CEDEM.

Rau, D. Victoria (2002), 'Nominalization in Yami', *Language and Linguistics* 3.2: 165–95.

Redeker, Gisela (2006), 'Discourse markers as attentional cues at discourse transitions', in Kerstin Fischer (ed.), *Approaches to Discourse Particles* (Studies in Pragmatics 1). Amsterdam: Elsevier, 339–58.

Reesink, Ger P. (1987), *Structures and their Functions in Usan, a Papuan Language of Papua New Guinea*. Amsterdam: Benjamins.

Reh, Mechthild (1985), *Die Krongo-Sprache (nìino mó-dì). Beschreibung, Texte, Wörterverzeichnis* (Kölner Beitrâge zur Afrikanistik 12). Berlin: Reimer.

Reichenbach, Hans (1947), *Elements of Symbolic Logic*. New York, NY: Macmillan.

Renck, Gunther L. (1975), *A Grammar of Yagaria* (Pacific Linguistics, B-40). Canberra: Australian National University.

Rennison, John R. (1997), *Koromfe* (Descriptive Grammars). London and New York, NY: Routledge.

Rialland, Annie and Robert, Stéphane (2001), 'The intonational system of Wolof', *Linguistics* 39.5: 893–939.

Rijkhoff, Jan N. M. (1995), 'Bystander and social deixis: some programmatic remarks on the grammar/pragmatics interface'. *Working Papers in Functional Grammar* 58.

—— (2002), *The Noun Phrase*. Oxford: Oxford University Press.

—— (2003), 'When can a language have nouns and verbs?', *Acta Linguistica Hafniensia* 35: 7–38.

—— (2008) 'Layers, levels and contexts', in Jan Rijkhoff and Daniel García Velasco (eds.), *The Noun Phrase in Functional Discourse Grammar*. Berlin and New York, NY: Mouton de Gruyter.

—— Bakker, Dik, Hengeveld, Kees, and Kahrel, Peter (1993), 'A method of language sampling', *Studies in Language* 17.1: 169–203.

Risselada, Rodie (1993), *Imperatives and Other Directive Expressions in Latin* (Amsterdam Studies in Classical Philology 2). Amsterdam: Gieben.

Roberts, John R. (1987), *Amele* (Croom Helm Descriptive Grammars Series). London: Croom Helm.

Robins, Robert H. (1959), 'Nominal and verbal derivation in Sundanese', *Lingua* 8: 337–69.

Romero-Figeroa, Andrés (1997), *A Reference Grammar of Warao* (LINCOM Studies in Native American Linguistics 06). Munich and Newcastle: Lincom Europa.

Rust, F. (1965), *Praktische Namagrammatik*, (Communications from The School of African Studies University of Cape Town, 31). Cape Town/Amsterdam: A. A. Balkema.

Sadock, Jerrold M. (1985), 'Autolexical syntax: A proposal for the treatment of noun incorporation and similar phenomena', *Natural Language and Linguistic Theory* 3: 379–439.

—— (1991), *Autolexical Syntax: A Theory of Parallel Grammatical Representations*. Chicago: University of Chicago Press.

—— and Zwicky, Arnold M. (1985), 'Speech act distinctions in syntax', in Timothy Shopen (ed.), *Language Typology and Syntactic Description Vol. I: Clause Structure*. Cambridge: Cambridge University Press, 155–96.

Saltarelli, Mario (1988), *Basque* (Croom Helm Descriptive Grammars). London, New York, NY, and Sydney: Croom Helm.

Sasse, Hans-Jürgen (1987), 'The thetic/categorial distinction revisited', *Linguistics* 25: 511–80.

Saul, Janice E. and Freiberger Wilson, Nancy (1980), *Nung Grammar* (Summer Institute of Linguistics Publications in Linguistics 62). Dallas: Summer Institute of Linguistics.

Saunders, Barbara A. C. and Brakel, Jaap van (1997), 'Are there non-trivial constraints on color categorization?' *Brain and Behavioral Sciences* 20: 167–79.

Savel'eva, V. N. (1966), Review of *Grammatika nivxskogo jazyka* [Nivkh grammar], 2 vols. Moscow and Leningrad: Nauka.

——and Taksami, Č. M. (1970), *Nivxsko-Russkij Slovar'* [Nivkh-Russian dictionary]. Moscow: Sovetskaja Enciklopedija.

Schaaik, Gerjan van (1985), 'Verb based terms and modality in Turkish'. Unpublished paper, University of Amsterdam.

——(1992), 'The treatment of Turkish nominal compounds in FG', in Michael Fortescue, Peter Harder, and Lars Kristoffersen (eds.), *Layered Structure and Reference in a Functional Perspective* (Pragmatics and Beyond New Series 23). Amsterdam: Benjamins, 231–52.

Schachter, Paul and Otanes, Fe T. (1972), *Tagalog Reference Grammar*. Berkeley, CA: University of California Press.

Schaub, Willi (1985), *Babungo* (Croom Helm Descriptive Grammars). London, Sydney, and Dover, NH: Croom Helm.

Schiering, René (2005), 'Segmental effects of cliticization: towards a typology', Talk to New Reflections on Grammaticalization Conference, Santiago de Compostela, Galicia, Spain. Available at <http://www.uni-leipzig.de/~schier/>.

——Hildebrandt, Kristine A., and Bickel, Balthasar (fc.), 'Cross-linguistic challenges for the prosodic hierarchy: Evidence from word domains'. Available at <http://www.uni-leipzig.de/~schier/>.

Schütz, Albert J. (1985), *The Fijian Language*. Honolulu, HI: University of Hawaii Press.

Schütze, Carson T. (1994), 'Serbo-Croatian second position clitic placement and the phonology-syntax interface', in Andrew Carnie, Heidi Harley, and Tony Bures (eds.), *Papers on Phonology and Morphology. MIT Working Papers in Linguistics* 21: 373–473.

Searle, John (1969), *Speech Acts*. Cambridge: Cambridge University Press.

Seki, Lucy (2000), *Gramática do Kamaiurá: Língua Tupi-Guarani do Alto Xingu*. Campinas: Universidade Estadual de Campinas.

Shattuck-Hufnagel, Stefanie and Turk, Alice E. (1996), 'A prosody tutorial for investigators of auditory sentence processing', *Journal of Psycholinguistic Research* 25.2: 193–247.

Shibatani, Masayoshi (1990), *The Languages of Japan*. Cambridge: Cambridge University Press.

Siewierska, Anna (1991), *Functional Grammar* (Linguistic Theory Guides). London: Routledge.

——(2004), *Person*. Cambridge: Cambridge University Press.

——and Bakker, Dik (2002), 'Adpositions, the lexicon and expression rules', in Ricardo Mairal Usón and María Jesús Pérez Quintero (eds.), *New Perspectives on Argument Structure in Functional Grammar*. Berlin and New York, NY: Mouton de Gruyter, 125–77.

Sinclair, John M. and Coulthard, Richard M. (1975), *Towards an Analysis of Discourse: The English Used by Teachers and Pupils*. London: Oxford University Press.

Skorik, Pjotr J. (1948), *Očerk po syntaksisu čukotskogo jazyka: Inkorporatsija* [Outline of Chukchee Syntax: Incorporation]. Leningrad: Učpedgiz.

—— (1961/1977), *Grammatika čukotskogo jazyka* [Grammar of Chukchee], 2 vols. Moscow: Izdatel'stvo Akademii Nauk.

Slobin, Dan I. (1996), 'From "thought and language" to "thinking for speaking"', in John J. Gumperz and Stephen C. Levinson (eds.), *Rethinking Linguistic Relativity.* Cambridge: Cambridge University Press: 70–96.

Smeets, Ineke (1989), 'A Mapuche Grammar'. Ph.D. dissertation, University of Leiden.

Smit, Niels (2005), 'Noun incorporation in Functional Discourse Grammar', in Casper de Groot and Kees Hengeveld (eds.), *Morphosyntactic Expression in Functional Grammar.* Berlin and New York, NY: Mouton de Gruyter, 87–134.

—— (fc.), 'Informational frames in Functional Discourse Grammar', Manuscript, University of Amsterdam.

—— and Staden, Miriam van (2007), 'Representational layering in FDG', in Marize Hattnher and Kees Hengeveld (eds.), *Advances in Functional Discourse Grammar.* *Alfa—Revista de Lingüística* 51.2: 143–64.

Spencer, Andrew (1995), 'Incorporation in Chukchi', *Language* 71.3: 439–89.

Spruit, Arie (1986), 'Abkhaz Studies'. Ph.D. dissertation, University of Leiden.

Staden, Miriam van (2000), 'Tidore: A Linguistic Description of a Language of the North Moluccas'. Dissertation, University of Leiden.

Staden, Miriam van and Keizer, M. Evelien (eds.) (fc.), *Interpersonal Grammar: A Cross-Linguistic Perspective.* Special issue of *Linguistics.*

Stanchev, Svilen B. (1997), 'Pragmatic functions and special sentence position in Bulgarian', in John H. Connolly, Roel M. Vismans, Christopher S. Butler, and Richard A. Gatward (eds.), *Discourse and Pragmatics in Functional Grammar.* Berlin and New York, NY: Mouton de Gruyter, 121–35.

Stassen, Leon (1985), *Comparison and Universal Grammar.* Oxford: Blackwell.

Steedman, Mark J. (1977), 'Verbs, time and modality', *Cognitive Science* 1: 216–34.

Storto, Gianluca (2003), 'Agreement in Maasai and the Syntax of Possessive DPs (II)', in William E. Griffin (ed.), *The Role of Agreement in Natural Language: TLS 5 Proceedings,* (Texas Linguistic Forum 53). Austin, TX: Texas Linguistic Society, 193–206.

Stroomer, Harry (1987), *A Comparative Study of Three Southern Oromo Dialects in Kenya: Phonology, Morphology and Vocabulary* (Cushitic Language Studies 6). Hamburg: Buske.

Sulkala, Helena and Karjalainen, Merja (1992), *Finnish* (Descriptive Grammars). London and New York, NY: Routledge.

Suttles, Wayne (2004), *Musqueam Reference Grammar.* Vancouver: UBC Press.

Sweetser, Eve E. (1990), *From Etymology to Pragmatics: Metaphorical and Cultural Aspects of Semantic Structure* (Cambridge Studies in Linguistics 54). Cambridge: Cambridge University Press.

Talmy, Leonard (1991), 'Path to realization: A typology of event conflation', in Laurel A. Sutton *et al.* (eds.), *Proceedings of BLS 17.* Berkeley, CA: Berkeley Linguistics Society, 480–519.

Thompson, Susan (1994), 'Aspects of cohesion in monologue', *Applied Linguistics* 15: 58–75.

Torner, Sergi (2005), 'On the morphological nature of Spanish adverbs ending in *-mente*', *Probus* 17: 115–44.

Torrence, William Harold (2005), 'On the Distribution of Complementizers in Wolof'. Ph.D. dissertation, University of California Los Angeles.

Trask, R. L. (2003), 'The Noun phrase: Nouns, determiners and modifiers; pronouns and names', in José Ignacio Hualde and Jon Ortiz de Urbina (eds.), *A Grammar of Basque* (Mouton Grammar Library 26). Berlin: Mouton de Gruyter, 113–70.

Uyechi, Linda Ann N. (1996), *The Geometry of Visual Phonology*. Cambridge: Cambridge University Press.

van de Velde, Freek (2007), 'Interpersonal modification in the English noun phrase', *Functions of Language* 14: 203–30.

van der Auwera, Johan (1981), Tagalog *Ang*: An exercise in universal grammar', in Saskia Daalder and Marinel Gerritsen (eds.), *Linguistics in the Netherlands 1981*. Amsterdam: North-Holland, 127–39.

——— (1990), 'De structuur van de term'. Aggregation dissertation, Antwerp: Universiteit Antwerpen, UIA.

——— (1997), 'Cosubordination', *Working Papers in Functional Grammar* 63.

Van Valin, Jr, Robert D. (1999), 'A typology of the interaction of focus structure and syntax', in E. V. Rakhilina and Y. G. Testelets (eds.), *Typology and Linguistic Theory: From Description to Explanation. For the 60th Birthday of Aleksandr E. Kibrik*. Moscow: Languages of Russian Culture, 511–24.

——— (2001), *An Introduction to Syntax*. Cambridge: Cambridge University Press.

——— (2004), 'Semantic macroroles in Role and Reference Grammar', in Rolf Kailuweit and Martin Hummel (eds.), *Semantische Rollen*. Tübingen: Narr, 62–82.

——— (2005), *Exploring the Syntax-Semantics Interface*. Cambridge: Cambridge University Press.

——— and LaPolla, Randy (1997), *Syntax: Structure, Meaning and Function*. Cambridge: Cambridge University Press.

Venditti, Jennifer J. (2005), 'The J_ToBI model of Japanese intonation', in Sun-Ah Jun (ed.), *Prosodic Typology: The Phonology of Intonation and Phrasing*. Oxford: Oxford University Press, 172–200.

Vet, Co (1986), 'A pragmatic approach to tense in Functional Grammar', *Working Papers in Functional Grammar* 16.

——— (1990), 'Aktionsart, aspect and duration adverbials', in Harm Pinkster and Inge Genee (eds.), *Unity in Diversity: Papers Presented to Simon C. Dik on his 50th Birthday*. Dordrecht: Foris, 279–89.

Vigário, Marina (2003), 'Quando meia palavra basta: Apagamento de palavras fonológicas em estruturas coordenadas', in Ivo Castro and Inês Duarte (eds.), *Razões e Emoção: Miscelânea e estudos em homenagem a Maria Helena Mira Mateus*, Vol. II. Lisbon: Imprensa Nacional-Casa da Moeda, 415–35.

Vismans, Roel (1994), 'Modal Particles in Dutch Directives: A Study in Functional Grammar'. Ph.D. dissertation, Vrije Universiteit Amsterdam. Amsterdam: IFOTT.

Voegelin, Charles L. (1935), *Tübatulabal Grammar* (University of California Publications in American Archaeology and Ethnology 34.2: 55–190). Berkeley, CA: University of California Press.

Voorhoeve, C. L. (1965), *The Flamingo Bay Dialect of the Asmat Language* (Verhandelingen van het Koninklijk Instituut voor Taal-, Land- en Volkenkunde 46). The Hague: Martinus Nijhoff.

Voort, Hein van der (2004), *A Grammar of Kwaza* (Mouton Grammar Library 29). Berlin and New York, NY: Mouton de Gruyter.

Vossen, Piek (1995). *Grammatical and Conceptual Individuation in the Lexicon.* Amsterdam: IFOTT.

Vries, Lourens de (1985), 'Topic and Focus in Wambon discourse', in A. Machtelt Bolkestein, Casper de Groot, and J. Lachlan Mackenzie (eds.), *Syntax and Pragmatics in Functional Grammar*. Dordrecht: Foris, 155–80.

—— (1989), 'Studies in Wambon and Kombai'. Dissertation, University of Amsterdam.

Vries, Mark de (2002), 'The Syntax of Relativization'. Ph.D. dissertation, University of Amsterdam. Utrecht: LOT.

Wackernagel, Jakob (1892), 'Über ein Gesetz der indogermanischen Wortstellung', *Indogermanische Forschungen* 1: 333–436.

Wali, Kashi and Koul, Omkar N. (1997), *Kashmiri: A Cognitive-Descriptive Grammar* (Descriptive Grammars). London and New York, NY: Routledge.

Wanders, Gerry (in prep.), *Typology and Diachrony: On the Use of the Subjunctive in Adverbial Clauses in the Ibero-Romance Languages.*

Watanabe, Honoré (2003), *A Morphological Description of Sliammon, Mainland Comox Salish, with a Sketch of Syntax*. Kyoto: Nakanishi.

Watters, David E. (2002), *A Grammar of Kham* (Cambridge Grammatical Descriptions). Cambridge: Cambridge University Press.

Watters, John R. (1979), 'Focus in Aghem: A study of its formal correlates and typology', in Larry Hyman (ed.), *Aghem Grammatical Structure*. Los Angeles, CA: University of Southern California, 137–97.

Whorf, Benjamin Lee (1945), 'Grammatical categories', *Language* 21: 1–11.

Wiese, Heike (fc.), 'Numeral-Klassifikatoren und die Distribution von Nomen: Konzeptuelle, semantische und syntaktische Aspekte', to appear in Norbert Fries and Wilfried Kürschner (eds.), *Akten des III. Ost-West-Kolloquiums für Sprachwissenschaft*. Tübingen: Narr. Available as <http://www2.hu-berlin.de/linguistik/institut/wiese/publications/HWOstWest.pdf>.

Willett, Thomas (1988), 'A cross-linguistic survey of the grammaticization of evidentiality', *Studies in Language* 12.1: 51–97.

Wolvengrey, Arok (2005), 'Inversion and the absence of grammatical relations in Plains Cree', in Casper de Groot and Kees Hengeveld (eds.), *Morphosyntactic Expression in Functional Grammar* (Functional Grammar Series 27). Berlin and New York, NY: Mouton de Gruyter, 419–45.

Language Index

Name Index

Subject Index

Bold type indicates the page where a technical term is explained most extensively if this is different from its first occurrence.

Printed in Poland
by Amazon Fulfillment
Poland Sp. z o.o., Wrocław

67659824R00298